Web Multimedia Development

David Miller

New Riders Publishing, Indianapolis, Indiana

Development Editors
Ami Frank, Naomi Goldman, Suzanne Snyder

Acquisitions Editor
Julie Fairweather

Software Specialist
Steve Flatt

Senior Editor
Sarah Kearns

Project Editors
Gina Brown
Becky Tapley

Copy Editors
Cliff Shubs, Molly Warnes, Paul Worthington, Phil Worthington

Technical Editor
Chris Stone

Associate Marketing Manager
Tamara Apple

Acquisitions Coordinator
Tracy Turgeson

Administrative Coordinator
Karen Opal

Cover Designer
Sandra Schroeder

Cover Illustrator
Jean Fowley

Cover Production
Aren Howell

Book Designer
Sandra Schroeder

Production Manager
Kelly Dobbs

Production Team Supervisor
Laurie Casey

Graphics Image Specialists
Steve Adams, Debbie Bolnuis, Kevin Cliburn, Tammy Graham, Dan Harris

Production Analysts
Jason Hand, Erich J. Richter

Production Team
Daniel Caparo, Cindy Fields, Diana Groth, Janelle Herber, William Huys Jr., Malinda Kuhn, Lori Price, Beth Rago, Megan Wade

Indexers
Cheryl Dietsch, Jennifer Eberhardt

Web Multimedia Development

By David Miller

Published by:

New Riders Publishing

201 West 103rd Street

Indianapolis, IN 46290 USA

Printed in the United States of America 1 2 3 4 5 6 7 8 9 0

Library of Congress Cataloging-in-Publication Data

`***CIP data available upon request***`

Warning and Disclaimer

This book is designed to provide information about Web multimedia techniques and products. Every effort has been made to make this book as complete and as accurate as possible, but no warranty or fitness is implied.

The information is provided on an "as is" basis. The author and New Riders Publishing shall have neither liability nor responsibility to any person or entity with respect to any loss or damages arising from the information contained in this book or from the use of the disks or programs that may accompany it.

Publisher *Don Fowley*

Publishing Manager *Julie Fairweather*

Marketing Manager *Mary Foote*

Managing Editor *Carla Hall*

About the Author

David Miller is a Multimedia Application Developer and Instructional Technology Specialist for the School of Education and New Media Center at Stanford University. He is a Web site administrator, designer, and programmer in the San Francisco Bay area and teaches classes in Instructional Technology and Web multimedia. Dave is completing his Ph.D. at Stanford. His home page is `http://www-leland.stanford.edu/~dmiller/`

Trademark Acknowledgments

Dedication

To my sister, the best designer I know.
—Dave Miller

Acknowledgments

I'd like to thank my family for their love and support. I'd also like to thank the great crew at New Riders, Suzanne Snyder (editor extraordinaire), Tracy Turgeson, Becky Tapley, Chris Stone, Naomi Goldman, Sarah Kearns, Julie Fairweather, Don Fowley, David Dwyer, and everyone else who has played a part in getting this book together.

I'd also like to thank the many friends who have helped out on the long and winding road to this book including Lois Brooks, Gary Ernst, Alan Garber, Mary Goldstein, Decker Walker, Elizabeth Miller, Phil Farrell, Bob Coleman, Ros HaLevi, Chip Haven, Terry Kato, Don Garlick, Gary Andolina, and anyone else I might have missed.

Contents at a Glance

Table of Contents

Introduction

Multimedia on the Web has exploded in the last year with the integration of multimedia playback features in Netscape Navigator 3.0 and Microsoft Internet Explorer 3.0. Standard multimedia formats such as QuickTime, Director, and MIDI have been adapted to the Web, and new technology such as streaming audio and video, VRML, Java, and client-side scripting are enabling a whole new class of Web applications and rich, multimedia content. This book is designed to show what is possible on the Web today, with its diverse browsers and platforms, and how to optimize multimedia content for quality user experience and high-performance Web playback.

Who Should Read this Book

This book is designed to be a real-world, no-nonsense, practical guide to creating multimedia Web sites. The emphasis is on using inexpensive or readily available cross-platform tools to create high-quality, low bandwidth media that downloads fast, plays back on the most number of systems and browsers, and makes users want to come back for more. A basic knowledge of the Web and HTML is assumed and a familiarity with popular multimedia and graphics programs is helpful but not required.

This book is for both Macintosh and Windows users and content developers. Although many studies indicate that a majority of Web multimedia is created on Macintosh systems, a majority of Web users actually use Windows. Many of the tools and technologies discussed in this book, such as QuickTime, Director, FreeHand, Photoshop, Premiere, and others are available on Macintosh, Windows, and, in some cases, Unix systems. When shareware and freeware programs are discussed, examples for both Macintosh and Windows platforms are provided if possible. The tutorials and procedures for creating Web multimedia are designed to be applicable across applications and platforms.

This book is for you if you want to spice up your home page with some neat graphics, create a Web page for your indie band, build Web-based, multimedia-rich learning environments for your school, repurpose CD-ROM-based training materials for the corporate intranet, or create globally accessible multimedia mega-sites for advertising and promotion.

What this Book Contains

This book is divided into two parts. Chapters 1 through 5 discuss design issues involved with providing multimedia content on the Web and building high-impact multimedia Web sites. Chapters 6 through 15 discuss how to create multimedia content that is optimized in both quality and download time for the Web.

- **Chapter 1: Multimedia on the Web.** Chapter 1 provides a brief history and perspective of multimedia on the Web, as well as background on the mechanisms that currently deliver multimedia on the Web.

- **Chapter 2: Planning Multimedia Web Sites.** Chapter 2 covers the first steps in the beginning of any multimedia Web site design process—define your goals, define your audience, and determine the technical limitations and needs of your users. It presents a design methodology you can use that will save you a lot of headaches later.
- **Chapter 3: The Web and HyperMedia Design.** Chapter 3 discusses the unique aspects of the Web as publishing and communications medium and provides general guidelines on information design, presentation design, page design, and user interface principles for the Web with an emphasis on multimedia Web pages.
- **Chapter 4: Designing the Layout of Your Web Pages.** Chapter 4 gets into the nitty-gritty of implementing user interfaces for multimedia Web pages, page layout, typography, page prototyping, backgrounds, and how to create grid-based layouts with tables and frames.
- **Chapter 5: Designing Multimedia Web Pages.** This chapter shows you how to do the following:
    - Design multimedia pages that maximize the user experience
    - Use HTML tags to maximize performance
    - Use HTML for graphics, helper apps, multimedia plug-ins, ActiveX controls, and Java
    - Use multimedia extensions for HTML
    - Design pages that will look good on the maximum number of browsers
    - Provide alternate content for non-multimedia viewers
- **Chapter 6: Using Graphics to Add Dynamic Content.** Graphics are the most common and widely supported multimedia element on the Web. Among other things, this chapter covers:
    - The features of the two most popular image formats for inline graphics, GIF and JPEG
    - Tips on how to make graphics look great and load fast
    - Cross-platform color management

- How to create high-quality vector graphics for the Web using FreeHand
- How to use graphics in page backgrounds
- How to create pages with dynamic graphics

- **Chapter 7: Animation.** When people talk about Web multimedia, they often mean animated graphics. This chapter covers how to:
  - Create GIF animations
  - Create animations for Netscape Plug-Ins and ActiveX controls using free or inexpensive authoring tools
  - Create Server-Push animations
  - Create animations using JavaScript
  - Create animations that look professional using tried-and-true animation techniques

- **Chapter 8: Animating with Shockwave for Director.** Perhaps the most popular animation format on the Web, Shockwave for Macromedia Director can do a lot more than create animated bullets and spinning logos. In this chapter, besides learning the ins and outs of Shockwave technology, you learn how to:
  - Animate in Director
  - Create low-bandwidth animations for the Web
  - Create low-bandwidth, high-quality audio using Shockwave for Audio
  - Use Internet extensions to Lingo
  - Save user data across sessions
  - Optimize the user experience of "shocked" pages
  - Author Web pages that use the Shockwave ActiveX Control
  - Generate dynamic HTML documents on-the-fly with new Shockwave features and JavaScript

- **Chapter 9: Video.** Video is the most bandwidth-hungry media type on the Web. Besides learning about the latest advances in streaming video, video formats, and compression, you learn how to:

    - Shoot video that digitizes and compresses well for the Web
    - Optimize digitizing from video tape or other sources
    - Compress video for the Web
    - Create video clips with non-linear video editing applications
    - Use desktop video-conferencing applications
    - Integrate video-conferencing with Web pages

- **Chapter 10: Animating with QuickTime Digital Video.** QuickTime has become the closest thing to a standard, cross-platform multimedia container format, and QuickTime playback capabilities are built into the major browsers. But QuickTime is more than just digital video. This chapter covers video and animation with QuickTime. In this chapter, learn how to:
    - Digitize and compress video for QuickTime
    - Create QuickTime video clips with non-linear video editing applications
    - Optimize QuickTime for the Web
    - Compress video for optimal quality and small file size
    - Use MoviePlayer and Premiere for authoring Web-ready QuickTime movies and animations
    - Optimize user experience with HTML extensions to the QuickTime Plug-In

- **Chapter 11: Audio.** Audio is an often neglected and underused part of multimedia. But it can be more powerful than visuals in setting a mood and tone. Besides learning about cross-platform MIDI, digital audio formats, and telephony, learn how to:
    - Use MIDI and QuickTime Music Tracks on the Web for low-bandwidth music
    - Convert and edit MIDI files and QuickTime Music Tracks with MoviePlayer
    - Embed background music in a Web page
    - Make your pages talk

Note

Chapter 11 covers QuickTime Audio, and Chapter 12 covers QuickTime VR.

    - Create and capture digital audio
    - Optimize the quality of low-bandwidth audio for the Web
    - Create seamless low-bandwidth audio loops
    - Perform EQ and normalization tricks for the Web
    - Downsample while maintaining quality
    - Embed digital audio in a Web page
    - Use LiveConnect and LiveAudio
    - Use Shockwave for Audio
    - Use RealAudio
    - Synch sound with other media

- **Chapter 12: 3D and Virtual Reality.** Use 3D graphics to build your own corner of cyberspace. In this chapter, learn how to:
    - Use 2D programs to create 3D graphics for the Web
    - Use 3D programs to create 3D graphics for the Web
    - Create QuickTime VR for the Web
- **Chapter 13: VRML.** With VRML, an ASCII text-based language, you can describe 3D scenes to create interactive, navigable 3D worlds. This chapter shows you how to:
    - Create VRML worlds in any text editor
    - Embed links and update content dynamically in VRML worlds
    - Use popular VRML world creators to create 3D Web sites
    - Convert 3D models to VRML
- **Chapter 14: Scripting Multimedia Web Pages.** Client-side scripting is an exciting new tool for Web authors with many applications for multimedia Web pages. Besides providing a whirlwind tour of JavaScript and VBScript, this chapter teaches you how to:
    - Use JavaScript to create dynamic HTML documents on-the-fly
    - Use JavaScript to create and assemble animations on-the-fly

    - Use JavaScript to enhance the user interface and interactivity
    - Use LiveConnect to communicate with Plug-Ins

- **Chapter 15: Java.** The Java programming language is the most talked about phenomena on the Web. In this chapter, learn how to:
    - Convert QuickTime movies to Java applets with sound and streaming playback
    - Create Java animations and richly interactive interfaces in Java without coding a single line
- **Chapter 16: Keeping an Eye on the Horizon.** This chapter informs you of advances in multimedia on the Web, and provides you with URLs of places to go to find the latest developments.

Software and Hardware Needs

Many of the programs used in examples in this book are freeware and shareware. Some are provided on this CD. If you decide to keep a shareware program, please pay the shareware fee so the programmer can continue making useful tools.

Other tools used in this book are inexpensive commercial products or products that are very common in most multimedia toolkits. The tutorials and procedures outlined here are designed in such a way that you should be able to apply the same principles and procedures to other programs.

On the hardware side, multimedia authoring demands a lot of your system. Typically, multimedia developers have the fastest CPU available, tons of RAM and hard drive space, and 24-bit accelerated video. But because most Web multimedia files have to be small, short, and with low color-depth and low bandwidth, you may be able to get by with much less in the way of hardware. Hardware and software requirements for media, such as video and audio, are discussed in each chapter. Today, with any Macintosh system or multimedia PC, you can create a lot of multimedia for the Web.

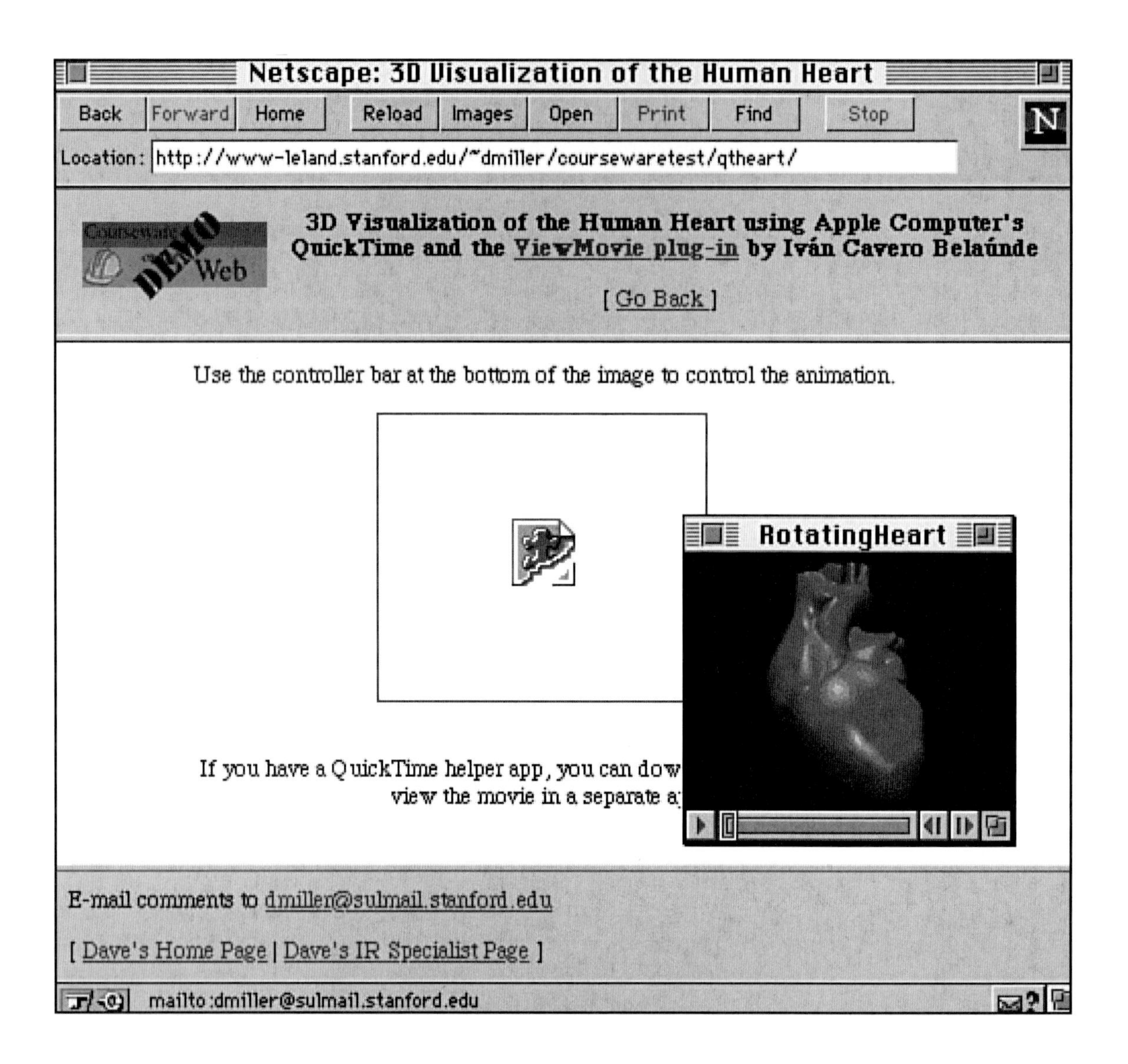

In the last year, interactive multimedia has gone from being a peripheral component of Web pages that is implemented with external helper apps to being an integral part of Web pages and Web browsers. The Web was not originally designed for integrated multimedia. This chapter discusses some of the history and current delivery mechanisms for multimedia on the Web.

chapter

1

Multimedia on the Web

Multimedia on the Web has only been possible within the last year or two, with the advent of faster processors, cross-platform media formats such as QuickTime, and most recently, the addition of multimedia features to Web browsers. Right now, the major bottleneck to delivering rich, multimedia content is the slow connection speed of most users' computers. This bandwidth problem is somewhat mitigated on corporate and university intranets, where multimedia on the Web can be an effective way for workgroups to share digital assets and as a powerful training and educational tool.

This chapter discusses:

- A brief history of the Internet and multimedia on the Web
- The mechanisms used to deliver Web-based multimedia

Brief History

To understand the limitations of delivering Internet multimedia, which is characterized by extremely large file sizes and the necessity for synchronized, continuous playback, it is helpful to understand how the Internet was built and how it was originally used.

It is generally well known that the Internet was originally created for U.S. defense purposes by the Advanced Research Projects Agency or ARPA (`http://www.arpa.mil`) of the United States Department of Defense, in the late 1960s and early 1970s. The original purpose of ARPAnet was to link defense contractors, military installations, and research labs to facilitate research and information exchange. In the 1980s, the National Science Foundation expanded ARPAnet and created a network connecting supercomputing centers, universities, and research centers. During this time many universities, research centers, and other organizations all over the world connected to the NSFnet and the Internet, as we know it today, began to take shape. In this phase of the Internet, commercial use was discouraged and the Internet was used mainly for information exchange, education, and research. Information was exchanged using communications protocols, such as telnet, ftp, and nntp, which were optimized for text or binary file transfer and command-line input.

The NSFnet originally used 56 Kbps dedicated (56 Kbps per second or about 7 KB/s) telephone lines. In 1988, the NSF contracted with Merit Network Inc. to upgrade the backbone or main trunk lines of the network to T1 lines (190 Kbps or 1.5 Mbps). In 1992 the network was upgraded to T3 lines (45 Mbps). It is important to understand that multimedia on networks require high-capacity lines. In fact, it wasn't until the NSF upgraded the Internet backbones that multimedia became possible over the Internet.

Birth of the Web

The foundations of the World Wide Web were developed in the early 1990s by Tim Berners-Lee and associates at CERN, the European Laboratory for Particle Physics in Geneva, Switzerland. Initially, it was created as a way to serve hypertext documents and share research on **TCP/IP**-based, client-server networks. Documents were initially viewed by a text-based, command-line browser. HTML was the page description language used to display information and create hypertext links and HTTP was the communications protocol used to connect machines to the World Wide Web.

In February, 1993, The U.S. National Center for Supercomputing Applications (NCSA) released a free graphical browser for Unix systems called Mosaic. Mosaic was the first Web browser to incorporate some of the standard elements of graphical user interface (GUI), such as the interface of Macintosh computers and X-Windows, into a Web browser. In addition, Mosaic provided the capability to view graphics directly in the Web page, and supported other media types, such as digital audio files and animation, through applications on the client machine called helper apps. When Mosaic was released, there were about 50 Web servers and you could browse the entire World Wide Web in a few hours.

Author Note

Webmasters at various sites in the Bay area report use of Netscape browsers at around 90 percent. Between 95–97 percent of users on the Stanford Intranet, for instance, are browsing with Netscape Navigator.

Later in 1993, Mosaic was ported to Macintosh systems and Windows systems. By the end of that year, there were hundreds of Web servers. The multimedia capabilities of graphical browsers, such as Mosaic, were one of the features that made the Web so popular.

Note

TCP/IP is the language of the Internet. Using TCP/IP, computers connected to the Internet can locate each other, send and receive data, and be reasonably assured that the data sent by one computer arrives at its destination without error.

The Internet Goes Commercial

In 1994, the developers of Mosaic left NCSA, and formed a separate company, which later became the Netscape Communications Corporation. In July of that year, MIT and CERN announced the formation of the W3 Consortium, a non-profit organization to guide the evolution of technical standards for the Web. In April of 1995, the NSF relinquished control of the network to commercial providers, meaning commercial use was now acceptable. It is important to note that commercialization became possible after the Web's explosive growth, when a critical mass of users made the Web cost-effective for businesses.

In 1995, the Netscape Web browser, called Navigator, became the most popular browser on the Web. Usage statistics are difficult to gather, but surveys by independent groups generally indicate Netscape Navigator is used by 75–95 percent of Web users.

Netscape introduced many extensions to HTML, the basic page description language of Web pages. The most recent versions of Netscape Navigator provide tremendous support for multimedia data types, including the following:

Note

Embedded players are small programs external to the browser (for example, Netscape Plug-Ins and ActiveX controls) that enable the viewing and playing of multimedia content directly on the Web page.

- Built-in support for embedded Apple QuickTime movies and digital video.
- Digital audio.
- Three-dimensional, virtual reality environments.

Netscape's extensible Plug-In architecture enables the creation of embedded players for other multimedia data types, such as Macromedia Director files and Adobe Acrobat digital documents. In this book you learn how to create these kinds of digital media using shareware and commercial tools and learn ways to optimize digital media for playback on the Web with Netscape Navigator, Internet Explorer, and other browsers.

Note

Accurate usage statistics for the Internet as a whole are difficult to gather. In the late 1980s and in the early 1990s, Internet growth has been explosive by any measure. For example, between 1988 and 1994 network traffic levels, measured by the amount of data packets that are sent over the original NSFnet backbone, doubled every 18 months or so and have increased by 1000 percent.

In 1996, Microsoft entered the browser market with Internet Explorer, which matched many of Netscape Navigator's features. Microsoft is pushing its own multimedia Plug-In technology called ActiveX, based on their OLE (Object Linking and Embedding) technology. As of this writing, Internet Explorer's market share is around 5–10 percent. This book shows you how to provide multimedia Web content that is compatible with Internet Explorer and the widest possible range of browsers.

Note

Chapter 5, "Designing Multimedia Web Pages", discusses how to embed ActiveX controls in HTML documents that can be viewed by Internet Explorer.

Another major development in 1995 and 1996, was the ability to incorporate Java applets (based on Sun Microsystems' cross-platform Java programming language) in Web browsers and the widespread adoption of the Java programming language. Java applets are small programs written in the Java programming language that you can embed in Web pages, like Netscape Plug-Ins. Java applets are downloaded and run on the user's machine. In Chapter 15, "Java", this book will show you how to embed Java applets in a Web page and use some of the new Java authoring tools that are available. Java has great potential for providing multimedia content on the Web, and will become even more important in the future.

Intranets

Recently, organizations and enterprise departments have started using Web browsers as front-ends to enterprise-wide information systems. Information systems are hosted by Web servers on internal, TCP/IP-based local area networks (LANs). These internal networks are commonly called **intranets**. Bandwidth on intranets is significantly greater than on the global Internet. Application of Web-based multimedia on intranets has great potential.

Multimedia on the Web

Multimedia on computers generally refers to the integration of text, graphics, audio, video, and animation in a single computer document, such as embedding video and sound in a Web page. Computer multimedia often has the added element of interactivity. For example, in a video embedded on a Web page, the user can choose to play or pause the video, rewind it, or change the sound volume.

Web browsers display multimedia content in three basic ways:

- **Native, inline.** Native, inline media can be displayed directly on the Web page without any additional programs or viewers. All graphical browsers natively support GIF graphics. Some natively support JPEG graphics and other media types.
- **Helper applications.** Until recently, this was the standard way to view multimedia content on the Web. Displaying non-native multimedia using helper applications can be done with almost all browsers. Multimedia content is downloaded to the client's hard disk and then it is displayed in a separate player application, such as MoviePlayer, or PLAYER.EXE, in the case of QuickTime video.
- **Inline with external code modules such as Netscape-compatible Plug-Ins or Java applets.** These external "mini-programs" enable you to play back multimedia content directly in the Web page. These features appeared in Web browsers beginning with Netscape Navigator 2.0. Several multimedia Plug-Ins are automatically installed with Netscape Navigator 3.0.

Note

Native means a feature is supported by the Web browser without the need for any additional software. **Inline** means displayed directly in the Web page.

In this section, you learn about the MIME typing system, which is the multimedia file naming and delivery mechanism that underlies multimedia on the Web. You also learn about delivering multimedia with helper apps and inline content with Plug-Ins.

For greater detail on how to embed multimedia in HTML documents, see Chapter 5, "Designing Multimedia Web Pages."

MIME

MIME (Multipurpose Internet Mail Extensions) was originally developed to send multimedia content, such as graphics, audio, and video via e-mail. MIME includes a standardized way to identify and characterize multimedia content. MIME has been integrated into the HTTP protocol, the main communications protocol used by Web servers, as a way to identify and characterize multimedia content on the Web.

MIME Types and SubTypes

Every document, graphic, and multimedia file on the Web can be characterized by a MIME type and sub-type. For example, the MIME type "text" and sub-type "plain" indicates an ASCII text file. MIME types and sub-types are commonly written like so: `"text/plain"`. An HTML document has the MIME type and sub-type of `"text/html"`. A GIF file has the type `"image/gif"`. Browsers and Web servers use the MIME type and sub-type to determine how to process multimedia data.

File Name Extensions

The most common way to distinguish computer files with different MIME types is to use standardized file name extensions. Each Web server contains a large table that associates a particular file name extension to a particular MIME type. For example, all HTML files on a particular server have the `".html"` extension and can be associated with MIME type `"text/html"`. All JPEG files on the server have a file name extension of `".jpg"` or `".jpeg"`and can be associated with the MIME type `"image/jpeg"`.

How Browsers Use MIME Types

When a browser requests a file called `"banner.gif"`, for example, the Web server looks up the file name extension in its MIME type table, determines the file is a GIF file, then sends the MIME type information back to the browser. The browser then determines the appropriate action, such as display the GIF inline or to launch a helper app or Plug-In.

All Web browsers can display content of MIME type "`text/plain`" and "`text/html`". In addition, most graphical browsers can display inline images of type "`image/gif`", images in GIF format, and sometimes "`image/jpeg`", images in JPEG format.

Server Setup

Each Web server must be set up to handle different MIME types. Multiple file name extensions can be associated with the same MIME type. For example, files with a file name extensions of "`.qt`" and "`.mov`" are commonly associated with the MIME type "`video/quicktime`".

If you are serving multimedia content from a Web site, you have to make sure that:

- Your multimedia files have the correct file name extensions.
- The server has been set up to associate these extensions with a particular MIME type.

Most Web authoring tools come with information about file name extensions and MIME types for their particular media type. For example, Shockwave for Director files can have file name extensions of "`.dcr,.dxr,.dir`" and are associated with the type "`application/x-director`". Consult your Web server documentation or Web server administrator about configuring the Web server for different MIME types.

Helper Apps

Helper applications are a way for Web browsers to display or process MIME types and multimedia content that the browsers cannot display natively. In other words, helper apps provide you with the Web's rich, multimedia content without your browser needing to have the viewing capabilities for myriad multimedia data types built directly into it. For example, to display a QuickTime video, browsers don't need to include special display capabilities for viewing video. Instead they can launch a separate viewing application on the local client machine. This separate application handles display of the video. Helper apps are still used extensively today to provide multimedia content.

Figure 1.1

Helper app used in lieu of an inline Plug-In.

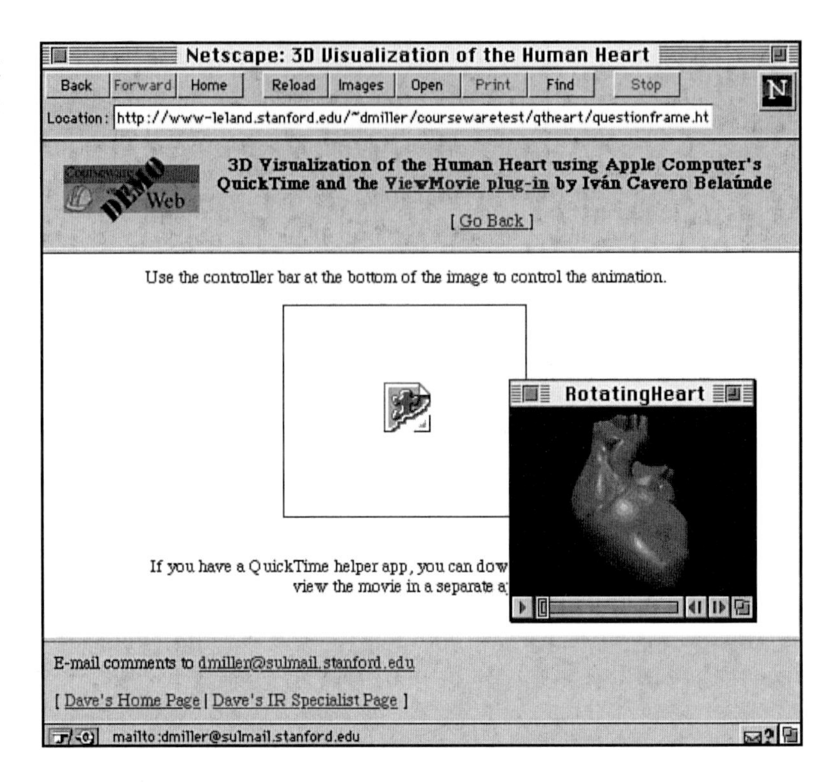

Drawbacks of Helper Apps

A drawback of helper apps is that media displays in a separate, disconnected window. There is no integration between information in the page and the helper app. Also, users must have the appropriate helper app on their machines, must configure their machines properly to use this app, and must have the system resources to support helper apps. See Chapter 5 for a detailed discussion of helper apps.

Browser Setup

Browsers know which helper app to launch by using a MIME type association table. This table is usually configured in a Web browser preference setting. Some settings in this table are preconfigured, but usually the user must manually associate a particular helper application with a particular MIME type. For example, when a Web server tells a Windows browser that data of type `"video/quicktime"` is coming down the wire, the browser knows to launch the program PLAYER.EXE by looking up the MIME type and helper app association in the local type association table.

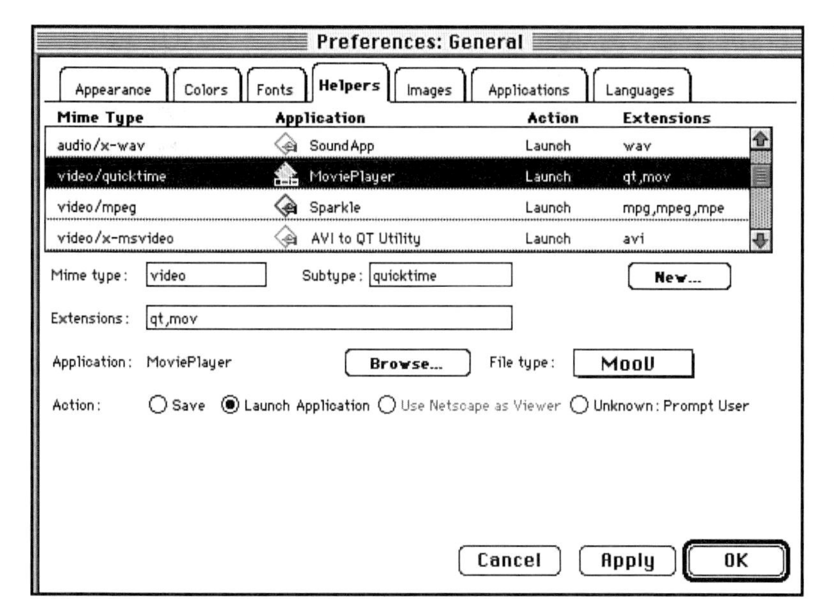

Figure 1.2

Setting up helper apps in Netscape Navigator (CMS).

Inline Multimedia: Web Browsers as Multimedia Authoring Tools

inline multimedia

Netscape Plug-Ins

ActiveX controls

Inline multimedia is multimedia content that is displayed directly in the Web page along with the document text. The ability to display inline graphics as GIF files (discussed in Chapter 6, "Using Graphics Add Dynamic Content,") has been present in graphical Web browsers since 1993. Netscape Navigator and other Web browsers are beginning to provide built-in or native support for other inline graphics and multimedia file types. Much of this additional functionality is provided by external code modules called **Plug-Ins** or **ActiveX controls**. With the release of Netscape Navigator 3.0, the Netscape Web browser provides out-of-the-box support for several multimedia data types and has become a powerful media integration and multimedia authoring tool in its own right.

The first generation of inline multimedia Plug-Ins are used in much the same way as inline GIFs. The multimedia displays inline, in the Web page, and the user often has the option of using standard controllers, such as play and pause buttons, to control playback. The second generation of inline multimedia Plug-Ins are providing more sophisticated media integration. Netscape's LiveConnect and Microsoft's VBScript enable sharing of information and interoperability between various Web page elements such as Netscape Plug-Ins, OLE/ActiveX controls, OpenDoc parts, the HTML document, Java, JavaScript, the Web server, and other resources on the Internet.

Plug-Ins

The Netscape Plug-In architecture, discussed in greater detail in Chapter 5, enables developers to extend the functionality of the Netscape Web browser. Plug-Ins enable the display of interactive animations, VRML (Virtual Reality Modeling Language) worlds, QuickTime media, Macromedia Director files, Authorware files and FreeHand vector graphics, Adobe Acrobat digital documents, and many other data types.

Plug-Ins must be downloaded and installed by users. Future versions of Netscape Navigator will automatically download Plug-Ins as needed. Netscape Navigator 3.0 ships with several integrated Plug-Ins (so the user doesn't have to download or configure anything), providing out-of-the-box support for the following inline components:

- QuickTime media for Macs and Windows
- Video for Windows (AVI) on Windows machines
- AIFF, WAV, AU, digital audio and MIDI sound
- (VRML) Virtual Reality Modeling Language
- Java applets

The latest version of Navigator includes a helper app for real-time audio and data collaboration. Netscape Plug-Ins will purportedly be supported by other major browsers, such as MSIE (Microsoft Internet Explorer) and Apple Computer's CyberDog.

OLE/ActiveX

OLE/ActiveX is Microsoft's Internet component architecture based on their OLE technology. At the time of this writing, it is only available in beta versions on Windows 95/NT, although Microsoft has announced it eventually will be ported to other platforms. It is natively supported in Windows 95 and Windows NT versions of the Microsoft browser Internet Explorer. Netscape Navigator support for OLE/ActiveX is via a Netscape Plug-In.

OLE/ActiveX is an alternative to Netscape Plug-Ins, Java, and JavaScript and might play a larger role on the Web in the future. Chapter 5 discusses embedding OLE/ActiveX controls in greater detail.

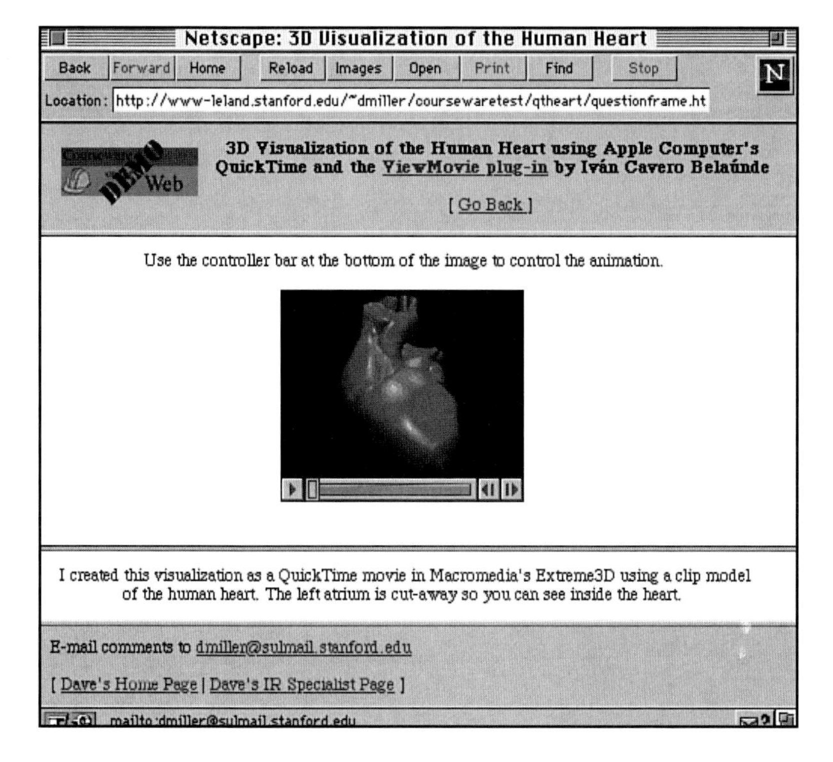

Figure 1.3

Embedded QuickTime video using Plug-Ins.

OpenDoc

OpenDoc is a component software architecture for Macintosh and Windows that is supported by several companies besides Apple Computer and IBM. Netscape has announced plans to turn Netscape Navigator into an OpenDoc part that can be embedded within any OpenDoc-aware application, such as a CyberDog document, word processing document, or graphics program. CyberDog is an OpenDoc-based suite of Internet tools from Apple Computer that supports Netscape Plug-Ins, Java, and Netscape Navigator as the browser component of the suite.

Client-Side Scripting

Client-side scripting is one of the most useful additions to the recent crop of browsers. Client-side scripting enables Web authors to provide features previously restricted to server-side scripts, written in languages such as Perl or C. Features provided by client-side scripting include image maps, dynamic images, forms validation, testing of the user's machines for presence of Plug-Ins, and the ability to share data between Plug-Ins and Java applets.

JavaScript is the scripting language used by Netscape Navigator. Most, but not all, JavaScript features are supported in MSIE. VBScript is Microsoft's scripting language based on Visual Basic. It is only supported by MSIE. See Chapter 15, "Java," for further aspects of scripting with JavaScript and VBScript.

Java Multimedia

Java is an object-oriented platform-independent programming language developed by Sun Microsystems. Java is commonly touted as a way to add multimedia to Web pages. At this time other tools such as QuickTime, Shockwave, and GIF animation, enable easier and faster development, higher quality media, broader client support, and smaller file sizes than Java-based multimedia. This state of affairs might change in the coming year with the addition of sophisticated multimedia features to Java and the maturation of Java development tools. Chapter 15 looks at several of these tools in.

The World-Wide Wait

The hype that surrounds the Web and multimedia contributes to the public's expectation of full-screen, full-motion, TV-quality, interactive multimedia streaming off their Web pages. The reality, of course, falls far short of this ideal.

The biggest roadblock to delivering multimedia on the Web is the time it takes to download rich, multimedia content over slow network lines. Although some multimedia display capabilities, such as JPEG compression or video playback from hard disk, are dependent on the speed and processing power of the local computer, the main limiting factor for multimedia on the Web is the long download times of large multimedia files. In most cases, the multimedia element has to be completely downloaded to the user's disk before it can be viewed. New streaming technologies are starting to address this problem by enabling playback to begin before download is complete.

A top priority for multimedia content providers is keeping file sizes to a minimum to reduce the download time. This restriction usually means a reduction in media quality, such as fewer colors in graphics or a slower frame rate for video. It's up to the multimedia author to balance the tradeoff between file size and quality.

Two Kinds of Web Users

People connect to the Web in different ways. For the purposes of delivering multimedia content, you can look at Web users as falling into two groups:

- Those that connect via modems at 28.8 Kbps or less
- Those that connect at higher speeds, typically 56 Kbps or higher

The first group are typically home users. They are often paying per minute charges for Internet and Web access.

The second group is typical of corporate or university intranets. This group often has Web access subsidized by their company or school. Users in this group usually reside on a shared local area network; thus, moving large multimedia files to individual workstations impacts performance of the network for all users on the local network.

Data Rate and Bandwidth

data transfer rate

Multimedia producers often look at the data transfer rate for a particular system as the major limiting factor in the kinds and quality of multimedia content that they can deliver. **Data transfer rate** or **data rate** is the amount of information transferred to the user's display per unit of time. It is typically measured in kilobytes per second or KB/s. Data rates are usually limited by the user's hardware. Data rates for multimedia playback from 1x and 2x CD-ROM are typically in the range of 100–250 KB/s.

bandwidth

Internet users talk of a similar concept called **bandwidth.** Bandwidth refers to the amount of data that can be transferred down a wire or connection per unit time. It is typically measured in kilobits per second or Kbps. Modems enable a maximum theoretical bandwidth of 28.8 Kbps on phone lines, although in practice it is somewhat less. Most studies indicate the majority of home users are still connecting to the Internet at 14.4 Kbps or less. The bandwidth on a dedicated ISDN connection ranges from about 64–128 Kbps. Users on local area networks typically have bandwidth in the same general range, dependent on network traffic. On shared local area networks, such as TCP/IP-based intranets, this available bandwidth is divided up between multiple users. The actual bandwidth available to an individual user depends on network traffic.

The following table compares the data rate and bandwidth capabilities of typical Web connections with more familiar multimedia delivery systems—CD-ROM and television.

Note

How do KB/s compare to Kbps?

1 Byte equals 8 bits

Table 1.1

Data Rate versus Bandwidth at Popular Connection Speeds

Connection	Data Rate (KB/s)	Bandwidth(Kbps)
14.4 modem	1.6	14.4
Single line ISDN	8.2	65.5
T1	192	1536
CD-ROM	150	1200
TV	27000	216000

These figures have several implications for multimedia on the Web:

- Multimedia is largely a "wait for it to download and then play it" experience.
- To achieve data rates comparable to CD-ROM over current modems, streaming technologies have to achieve compression ratios that are 10–100 times what they are for CD-ROM.
- Internal networks have the bandwidth necessary for the delivery of many types of multimedia, although they still have less bandwidth than a slow CD-ROM.

Another area that impacts delivering multimedia on the global Internet is the saturation of the Internet backbones or main trunk lines and many of the performance and bottleneck issues related to the explosive growth of the Internet. Router-storms, Internet service brown-outs, and the inability to connect to overcrowded sites are becoming increasingly common. Not all of these problems are related to moving large multimedia files around the Net, but multimedia does tax the limits of the current infrastructure as more people log on and start streaming video or downloading 1 MB QuickTime movies.

If you develop a multimedia Web site, be kind to the Net and its bandwidth and leave small footprints. Tips in this book will help you effectively use multimedia on the Web without chasing away your users with long downloads or adding to the general Internet gridlock.

Note

Most of the multimedia on the Web is in compressed format to yield smaller file sizes for downloading. The compression ratio is the ratio of the file size of the source material with its file size after compression and is a measure of the effectiveness of the compressing technique.

Streaming

streaming

Streaming is the continuous delivery of time-based media, such as animation, audio, or video, to a user's machine in real-time. The user doesn't have to wait for the file to be completely downloaded before viewing the content. The rest of the file is downloaded from the server (streamed) in the background while the animation or other time-based media plays on the client.

Streaming can be tricky to implement. The Internet wasn't designed for the delivery of continuous, synchronized, time-based data. Internet data is packet-based, which means it is delivered asynchronously in discontinuous chunks. You don't know when each discrete chunk will arrive at its destination. It will get there whenever it can, bouncing around the Net looking for the best path. Interruptions in the continuous data stream can cause stutters and gaps during playback of animation.

Most streaming technology uses proprietary data formats and buffering systems to implement continuous playback. Audio and video-conferencing on the Web use streaming data formats, as do some animation and QuickTime formats.

Over slow modem connections, streaming audio and streaming video is barely usable. Streaming media is more practical on internal intranets. The latest versions of Web browsers are incorporating audio and video-conferencing features that use streaming technology. Chapter 9, "Video," will discuss some of the options for delivering streaming video and video-conferencing, Chapter 11, "Audio," will discuss audio aspects, and Chapter 7, "Animation," will discuss streaming in animation.

Why Use the Web and Multimedia?

Many organizations and individuals are rushing to publish material on the Web. Web publishing has the following benefits that will be discussed in more detail in Chapters 2, "Planning Multimedia Web Sites," and 3, "The Web and Hypermedia Design":

- 24-hour access
- Global access
- Cross-platform delivery
- Associative linking (hypertext and hypermedia)
- Easy to add interactivity
- Easy to update
- Easy access (if you have a computer on the Net)

The advantages to putting multimedia on the Web include:

- All the advantages of other Web-based media just mentioned.
- Engages multiple senses, provides reinforcement, and feedback.
- Illustrates some concepts better than a text-based description.
- Communicates more effectively in some areas.
- Animated, dynamic content that can be updated in real-time.
- Multimedia cues and information design can help make abstract information spaces concrete and usable.
- Provides a "hook" that makes a site stand out from the babel of the Web and make users want to return.
- Browsers provide a cross-platform interface and multimedia authoring environment.

The disadvantages include:

- Bandwidth limitations.
- Slow networks.
- HTML as a primitive page layout language.
- Interactivity and multimedia support and playback on the Web is still limited compared to other media, such as CD-ROM.
- Copyright and intellectual property issues.

Conclusion

Many of the things you can do on CD-ROM, you can now do on the Web. Unfortunately, Web bandwidth is 10–100 times less than CD-ROM, requiring extreme compression to deliver data to a user's machine. The benefits of Web publishing in general, can out weigh these drawbacks. Companies are furiously working to provide solutions to the "bandwidth problem." Stay tuned.

In the meantime, this book shows you how to add high-quality multimedia to your Web site, today, and how to design multimedia Web sites and multimedia content within the unique technical contraints of the Web.

You just found out that your boss wants to put all your company's CD-ROM-based training materials on the Web. Or maybe, the Chamber of Commerce wants you to produce a multimedia Web site advertising the city's tourist attractions. You have a budget, a delivery date, and a design team.

Now what do you do? This chapter discusses a design strategy you should follow before you code your first line of HTML or shoot your first video.

chapter

2

Planning Multimedia Web Sites

This chapter looks at some of the issues you should consider when you first set out to create a multimedia Web site or add multimedia elements to an existing site. Before you begin, ask yourself these questions:

- What does the Web site do?
- Who is it for?
- What platform will it run on?
- What are the technical limitations of bandwidth and display effecting your users?
- Why do you want to use multimedia?
- What will be the investment in time and money to create multimedia content?

Defining these issues at the outset will save you grief later on. This chapter outlines some of the initial steps you should take in designing a multimedia Web site. It is geared toward large site development, but many of the same suggestions apply to a personal home page.

Determining Your Mission and Audience

The first step in Web site design is the analysis phase. Narrow down your goals and Web site specifications. What exactly do you want the Web site to do? Who is the audience? Web sites can take many forms and no development strategy fits every project. Some are developed by single authors, others by design teams with large budgets. Each project has its unique design requirements and creative solutions. All projects share the goal of using the Web to communicate with rich, multimedia content. The project development strategy and design guidelines presented in this chapter can be adapted to the design goals of your project.

Defining Your Site's Goals

The first step in any design process is to clearly state the project's goals and mission. If your site is a small, personal home page this is easy to do, but if your site is a large, commercial site or has the potential to grow in the future you want to clearly and succinctly think through the reasons you are putting up your Web site. Why do you need this site? Why do your users want to visit it? What is the site trying to accomplish? After the user has visited your Web site is he entertained, educated, or informed?

The first step is to ask yourself, "What is this Web site trying to accomplish? Why does the Web site exist?" Are you trying to sell something; provide access to reference material; reduce the client load on the customer support division? Write down these goals. In many ways, this is the most important part of the design process. At every decision point in your project, you should ask yourself, "Does this help me accomplish my goals?"

Another way to look at goal definition is to specify the message that you want to convey; what story are you trying to tell? Why does the user want to visit this site? What's the hook?

Write a statement of goals and make sure everyone on the development team has a copy. Every element of the project, including graphics, layout, and information design, should reflect these goals.

Defining Your Site's Uses

This section lists some of the possible uses for a Web site. Each use presents its own multimedia design challenges.

Using Your Site to Provide Information

Probably the most common use of the Web is to provide information for people who are actively searching for it. The Web has many advantages for providing information that are discussed in this book. For example, for people who just want to read the technical specifications for a new product, providing a lot of multimedia content may be an unnecessary overhead and may actually drive users away. But if multimedia content adds value, such as an animation that illustrates a key benefit of the technical specifications in this example, or provides animated graphical display of information, then it may be a useful addition to the site and people might want to see it.

Using Your Site to Gather Information

You can also use your Web site to gather information from people who visit the Web site. This information can be as simple as a request for e-mail feedback or as involved as detailed demographics collected with Web-based forms. Either way, determine how you will process the data that you collect and how you will store and analyze it. Often, forms and other data collection methods can be made more understandable by going beyond the simple interface provided by HTML forms and using a multimedia Plug-In, such as Shockwave for Director or Authorware along with server-side scripts.

Using Your Site for Educational Purposes

The Web can be an extremely effective way to publish educational materials. The Web can be used for course hand-outs, homework exercises, help manuals, how-to advice, frequently asked questions, and training for employees.

Multimedia elements can add to the user experience, engaging multiple senses and providing illustrations of the dynamic process that would be impossible or expensive to provide through more traditional methods. Many educational institutions have local area networks that have the bandwidth to support Web multimedia.

Using Your Site for Communication

Communication via the Web has lagged behind the rest of the Internet, and has typically meant sending e-mail via hypertext links, or posting to threaded discussion lists, similar to a newsgroup. New communication features that are beginning to show up on the Web include real-time chat, audio-conferencing and telephony, shared whiteboards, video-conferencing, and collaborative groupware.

Using Your Site for Public Relations

A site devoted to public relations and marketing should look slick. Multimedia can be a great hook. Multimedia at such a site should have high-production values and be entertaining. It should not place inordinate demands on a user's systems. The site might also provide an index of press releases, downloadable interactive press kits, short backgrounders, and anything else that might be useful for the user.

Using Your Site for Customer Support

A Web site can be an effective way to reduce customer support costs by providing technical notes, software updates, online manuals, frequently asked questions, contact numbers, and demos. Be judicious in your use of multimedia at such a site. Users are here to get information quickly.

Using Your Site for Sales

Selling products is the goal of many commercial sites. Unresolved issues surround electronic commerce. Many sites collect information over the Web and then use telephone contacts to transfer sensitive information, such as credit card numbers.

Many companies are starting to put product catalogs on the Web. Multimedia should be used if it adds value to the site. A QuickTime animation of a model showing some new fashion, or an interactive Shockwave piece that enables the user to see a sweater in different colors are both good uses of multimedia in product sales.

Using Your Site for Internal Communications

With the growth of TCP/IP-based intranets, Web servers are being dedicated to internal communication needs of departments, enterprises, and workgroups. Web servers can provide company information, employee policies, reference, and training at the click of a button. Multimedia can be a very effective way to illustrate a process. Bandwidth restrictions are less on internal intranets, enabling more sophisticated multimedia applications. Groupware products, such as Lotus Notes, are becoming more tightly integrated with the Web, enabling Web-based collaboration.

Defining Your Audience

The next step in designing a multimedia Web site is to define your target audience. Who are you trying to reach? Do you want to make your site accessible to the maximum number of users or are you interested in targeting a specific, narrowly defined group? Will the majority of your users connect to your site with a modem, or will they connect to a local server from a corporate intranet?

Corporate and university intranets are good sites for multimedia Web servers. An educator at a university or the publications specialist for a corporation can be assured users have relatively high-speed network connectivity and access to multimedia capable computers. A university class in chemistry could provide VRML models of different molecules or a staff training department could provide QuickTime movies of manufacturing processes for employee training.

If users connect to your site via modem, then possibilities for multimedia are more limiting. You especially don't want to make people wait to download multimedia if they are paying per-minute connect fees. If multimedia is crucial to your site and users will connect via modem, you may be able to target the audience of a site to a specific group, such as students enrolled in a class, employees of a company, or subscribers to a magazine. Consider providing CD-ROMs or other local storage for your large multimedia files and using the Web site for text-based updates, gathering information, and other communication needs.

Demographics

Make a list of the demographics of typical users (education, age, familiarity with Web, and the subject matter of your proposed site). Is your product for twelve-year old gamers or their computer-naïve elders? What do these typical users want from your Web site? What assumptions and attitudes do they bring with them?

For example, computer-naïve users might need more instructions on using interface elements, such as standard multimedia controllers. They may be more comfortable with reading text. In contrast, a twelve-year old gamer might be used to a visually rich environment and may not be phased by multiple media and grunge fonts.

Talk To Your Users

A little informal market research can't hurt, especially if you don't have access to market research data. Ask your users how they use the Web. What do they like about similar Web sites, what don't they like, and what do they wish they could do that they can't do now?

After you define your audience, you may want to change your site's goals. Do it now. Rip up your statement of goals and start over. It is easier to make changes early in the development process.

Specific Audience

Your audience may be a specific group, such as graphic designers, students in a class, or subscribers to a magazine. Evaluate the needs of the group and target multimedia appropriately. Graphic designers, for example, will have 24-bit displays and expect great visuals. Magazine subscribers may be looking for software downloads of products mentioned in the paper version of the magazine. Consider including an online survey asking questions such as "Why do you visit this site?" or "What makes you return?"

> **Note**
>
> There are many Web sites with useful developer information, including:
>
> `http://www.aw.com/devpress`
>
> `http://www.trace.wisc.edu`
>
> `http://www.gsa.gov/coca`
>
> `http://www.webable.com`

Your Audience Is the Global Internet

Publishing on the global Internet brings your Web site to a vast global audience who has a bewildering array of connection types and display capabilities.

Your Web site will be viewed internationally by people from many different cultures. Be aware of the cultural assumptions about visual symbols, colors, and slang terms. For example, in Islamic countries green is often a holy color, and in Japan, white is associated with death.

Is the site accessible to people with hearing loss, sight impairments, or limited motor skills? Designing for maximum accessibility often improves the design for everyone. Multimedia can be a help here. For example, it is relatively easy to add speech synthesis capabilities to Web pages with Talker, a Netscape Plug-In for Macintosh systems (discussed in Chapter 11, "Audio"). With minimal effort on the part of the designer, you can have the text of a Web page read out loud by the computer.

Your Audience Is the Local Intranet

Many organizations are using the Web to publish internal information, such as employee manuals and training materials. Companies are also using Web browsers as front-ends to corporate databases. Another use of internal Webs is as collaborative work environments.

When developing for internal use you can often assume certain levels of platform and browser support. Knowing user hardware and software configurations simplifies development, because you don't have to develop for every possible hardware and software combination.

When delivering multimedia over shared, internal networks, you need to evaluate the impact of moving large multimedia files over the network. One way to do this is to establish a baseline for the time it takes to transfer typical files across the network, and then time the transferring of the same files while there is a high network load, such as when a video-conference is occurring across the network or when several users access the same multimedia-rich Web page on your server.

You need to consider security issues, such as restricting access via domain or password. Most servers enable you to set access restrictions to specific directories on the server, either via domain restrictions, such as only enabling access to users from within a company's local area network, or via password.

Technical Limitations

Now that you've defined the goals for your multimedia Web site and identified your target audience, you must define the hardware and software limitations of your users. These include:

- The speed at which your audience connects to your site (the most important technical limitation!)
- The computers and monitors they use
- The Web browsers they have and which version they are using

Determining Connection Speed

Probably the most important limiting factor in Web multimedia is connection speed or bandwidth. People visiting your Web site never see and hear your whizzy animation, video, and sound if they give up waiting for huge files to download.

Table 2.1 shows some estimated download times at different connection speeds. All times are approximate; your mileage may vary. Download time will be affected by variables outside your control such as server load and network traffic. A good rule of thumb for delivering multimedia to home users on 14.4 modems is that one kilobyte (1 KB) of data can be downloaded in one second. On a local area network you might get rates approaching 4–10 KB per second.

Table 2.1

Sample download times on some selected connections

Connection Speed	Data Rate	Download Time/10 KB
14.4 Kbps	1.6 KB	5–10 seconds
28.8 Kbps	2.5 KB	3–7 seconds
64 Kbps	8.2 KB	2–4 seconds
1.5 Mbps	192 KB	1 second

The file size and download time of multimedia elements is extremely variable. File size depends on several factors, such as the dimensions of the multimedia element, the color-depth, and compression used. Download time is dependent on external factors beyond your control, such as server load and network traffic. This book goes into great detail on ways to make multimedia small and discusses the quality trade-offs involved.

The average graphical Web page with a few inline graphics might be in the 20–40 KB range. A page of this size would take 20–30 seconds to download over a 14.4 modem connection. A simple Shockwave interactive animation with 1-bit graphics can be as little as 3 KB, but 10–100 KB is more typical. A 160×120, 36-frame QuickTime movie with an optimized 8-bit palette can be around 100 KB. Web pages in this size range can take one to two minutes to download over a 14.4 modem connection.

Estimating Server Bandwidth Requirements

Another bottleneck in delivering multimedia is the type of connection on the server end. Of course, faster is better. Determining whether your server is up to the task of serving multimedia files depends on several factors such as:

- **Connection speed.** How big is the pipe connected to your server? Most server hardware and software on the market has enough throughput for a T1 line, so connection speed to the server is not a major bottleneck in these cases. Connection speed comes into play when servers are being used on intranets with higher connection speeds. Slower servers may not be able to utilize the available bandwidth.

- **Dedicated connection versus Shared connection.** A shared connection means the server will have to share available bandwidth with other network traffic.
- **Number of connections per minute.** Each connection will consume server RAM and processing time. Remember, a single Web page with four separate inline graphics requires five separate connections to the server. Thus, two users connecting to this page within a minute opens ten separate connections.
- **Average document size.** When evaluating server requirements, factor in the average Web page size. Some Web pages, such as site indices or table of contents, may be 3 KB, but pages with embedded video could be over 1,000 KB. You can improve perceived performance by making the most frequently accessed pages small in size.
- **Will slow user connections degrade server response time?** Users on slow connections force the server to keep individual connections open for a longer period of time.

For multimedia, a dedicated T1 line or greater is preferred, although you might be able to get by with a dedicated ISDN line if traffic at your site is low and your average document size is low. Tables 2.2 and 2.3 give rough estimates of the average document size and number of connections you can sustain before server performance degrades. Over a shared intranet, bandwidth can be seven to eight times that of a T1 line, but the server will be splitting the available bandwidth with other users.

Table 2.2

Estimated Average HTML Document Size Before Performance Degrades on a Dedicated ISDN Line

Average Document Size	Connections/minute
64 KB	1
6.4 KB	10
1 KB	100

Table 2.3

Estimated Average HTML Document Size Before Performance Degrades on a Dedicated T1 Line

Average Document Size	Connections/minute
1,500 KB	1
150 KB	10
15 KB	100

Assuming your average document is 20 KB in size, requires an average of five separate connections (for inline graphics and embedded multimedia), and that your network traffic is estimated to max out at two connections per minute during local business hours, a dedicated T1 line is more than adequate and leaves you room for expansion. Even the slowest server hardware and software is up to the task of serving multimedia over T1 lines at these rates.

Improving Server Performance

Because multimedia files are so large, they place special demands on a Web server. Some suggestions to increase the performance of a server are the following:

- **Increase the limit on TCP connections.** During heavy usage this improves server response time for individual connections.
- **Get a faster CPU.** A faster CPU processes connection requests faster.
- **Add more memory.** Each connection typically requires about 100 KB of memory on Macintosh servers to 500 KB of memory on high-end Unix servers.
- **Get a faster hard disk.** This is rarely a bottleneck, because most hard disks are fast enough to keep up with demanding Web servers, but this may be an issue with older machines.
- **Put multimedia files on a separate server from your HTML documents.** By dedicating a separate server for multimedia, you free up your main server to process other requests while the multimedia server handles the large multimedia files.

Multimedia Impact on LANs/Intranets

If you are delivering multimedia over a shared local area network or intranet, you have to consider the impact on network traffic. Moving large files over networks can quickly bog down network performance for everyone on the network. Fortunately, you can use network management tools to monitor the performance of your local network and forecast the impact multimedia has on your enterprise. First, establish a baseline performance for your network. Then time the transfer of these same files during increased load, such as when a video-conference is in session. For example, some video-conferencing programs, such as Apple Computer's QuickTime Conferencing, contain built-in flow control mechanisms that automatically reduce video transmission and try to maintain audio continuity over busy networks. Other programs automatically reduce picture quality while trying to maintain frame rates.

Multimedia applications such as desktop video-conferencing sometimes include the ability to adjust their performance based on network traffic so the entire network bandwidth isn't consumed. Dedicated video and audio servers typically have ways to adjust server performance to network traffic.

Platform Differences

One of the benefits of publishing multimedia on the Web is that you can create one version of your multimedia content, place it on a centralized server, and then have it delivered to Windows, Macs, and Unix machines. Because Web browsers exist for these major platforms, content you create once can be delivered simultaneously on multiple platforms.

You need to be aware of some platform differences. For example, many Netscape Plug-Ins, which implement much of the multimedia capabilities on the Web, don't exist for Unix platforms. Chapter 5, "Designing Multimedia Web Pages," contains some suggestions on what you can do as a Web author for users who can't view your media because of hardware and software limitations.

The same browser on different platforms doesn't always display HTML pages the same way. Pages look different on

Windows and Macintosh platforms, even within the same browser. Some cross-platform issues include the following:

- Differences in fonts between platforms means that text wraps and breaks differently and takes up different amounts of space on the screen within an HTML page.
- Monitors on Windows machines tend to be darker.
- Windows reserves certain colors for the interface so possible palettes are smaller than 256 colors on 8-bit displays.

It's always a good idea to define the platforms that you support and to test your Web pages on these platforms early in the design process.

Monitor

What is the typical monitor setup for your users? The size of the monitor and the resolution in pixels limits the amount of screen real estate available to display your Web page. The color-depth places important constraints on the kind of graphics and visuals you can provide. The unfortunate reality for the Web is that most users use 8-bit, 640×480 monitors.

Resolution

Most users probably have 13– to 15–inch monitors with display resolutions of 640×480 pixels. This size places constraints on screen real estate and the amount of material you can place on a single Web page. Test your pages on monitors of this size, especially if you design on 17–inch or larger monitors. Users typically don't like to scroll around, so it's good if you can fit all the content of your Web page within the confines of the typical 640×480 monitor.

Remember that the Web browser interface occupies some of the screen and that some browsers enable users to customize display of the browser interface. For example, Netscape Navigator enables you to customize the toolbar so that there is more vertical screen room to display a Web page. The maximum effective screen dimensions for your Web page are around 600×300 pixels, assuming the browser toolbar takes up its maximum screen space.

Note

If thin clients, Web browsers on personal digital assistants, and intranet appliances, such as Apple Computer's Newton, become more common, there may be additional restrictions on screen size, color-depth, and resolution.

Color-depth

Color-depth or *bit-depth* refers to the number of colors that can be displayed on a monitor at any one time. Color-depths are typically 8-bit, 16-bit, and 24-bit. Most users have 8-bit monitors and are only able to display 256 colors on the screen any time. These 256 colors are stored in a color table called a *palette.*

Sixteen-bit and 24-bit monitors don't use palettes. Monitors of this type are sometimes called *true color* or *high color* monitors. They can display thousands to millions of colors simultaneously. Most designers, videographers, and other graphic artists have 24-bit displays.

Some older monitors have color-depths less than 8-bit and can display even fewer colors. The following table shows the color-depth in bits and the number of colors possible at that depth. Displays at color-depths of 8-bit or less store the colors in a palette.

Table 2.4

Number of Colors Available at Different Bit-Depths

Color-depth	Number of colors
1-bit	2 colors
2-bit	4 colors
4-bit	16 colors
5-bit	32 colors
6-bit	64 colors
7-bit	128 colors
8-bit	256 colors
16-bit	65536 colors
24-bit	16 million colors

Most Web users have 8-bit displays. This color-depth places limitations on graphics and visuals. These limitations are discussed extensively in the section on graphics and maximizing performance (see Chapter 6, "Using Graphics to Add Dynamic Content"). If your audience includes graphics professionals, scientists, or engineers, who have 24-bit color displays, you might be able to design for higher color-depths. Alternately, if your material is delivered to users with 4-bit, 16-color monitors, common on some older PCs, or viewed on personal digital assistants or black-and-white displays, you are limited in the color range of graphics and visuals.

Gamma

Gamma is the measure of contrast in the midtones of a display device or media element. Different monitors have different gamma values. This difference is most apparent across different platforms. Generally, graphics created on a Mac appear darker on a PC. See Chapter 6 on how to adjust the gamma value of a graphic.

Sound

Most Macs have built-in sound. Windows machines typically need a separate sound card and speakers. It is probably best to keep sounds at 8-bit, 11 kHz, mono. If you use MIDI, users have to have a MIDI-capable sound board or computer. These issues are discussed in detail in Chapter 11.

CPU

CPU speed also has an effect on the speed that Web pages are displayed. A Web page is decoded by the local processor, so a fast processor improves the time it takes to format text, background tiles, tables, and frames.

The local processor impacts the performance of multimedia elements, such as the playback of digital video and digital audio, and the decompressing of JPEG graphics, which depends on the CPU for display.

Disk Space

Many types of multimedia, such as Shockwave, perform better with large disk caches, in excess of 10 MB or more. Users must also have enough disk space for browser programs and Plug-Ins.

Memory

The amount of memory or RAM your users have places constraints on the kind of multimedia you can deliver.

Many types of multimedia require large amounts of memory for the browser, helper apps, or Plug-Ins. For example, the first versions of Netscape's Live3D VRML Plug-In for Navigator required 16–24 MB of application RAM. Shockwave animations work best if the browser has been allocated about 10 MB of your PC's memory. The steep RAM requirement places Live3D and Shockwave outside the range of users with 8 MB systems unless virtual memory schemes are used.

Web Browser Limitations

In addition to the limitations of your users' computers, you might be limited by what browser they use. This is further complicated by the fast upgrade schedule of the Netscape and Microsoft browsers, with changes in feature sets occurring every 4–6 months.

Browser development for each platform is not always concurrent. Versions of browsers for different platforms such as Windows 3.1, Windows 95, Windows NT, Macintosh 68K, Macintosh PowerPC, Silicon Graphics, and various flavors of Unix don't all have the same capabilities and feature sets, even within the same version of the same product. One version supports JavaScript, another doesn't support Plug-Ins, one version supports that HTML extension, another browser doesn't support it. This variability has become a real headache for Web developers.

If you are designing pages for an internal corporate or university site, you might have the luxury of designing for a particular browser. If you are designing for a site that will be accessible to the public, Netscape Navigator is typically listed as having 75–95 percent of the global browser market. The second most popular browser is Microsoft's Internet Explorer (MSIE), which typically is listed as having five to ten percent of the browser market as of this writing. Fortunately, MSIE supports nearly all of the features of Netscape Navigator. Table 2.5 shows the hardware requirements for Netscape Navigator 3.0, including the platforms and processors it accommodates, the minimum memory and disk space it requires, the amount of memory recommended for using Live3D, and Netscape's implementation of VRML.

Note

An added complication is that, within the Netscape market share, for example, users use version 1, version 2, version 3, and version 4 (beta) of the Navigator browser. The same holds true for other browsers.

Table 2.5

*Minimum Hardware Requirements for Netscape Navigator 3.0**

Platform	Processor	Memory (Min)	Memory (Recommended)	Memory (Live3D)	Disk Space (Minimum)
Win3.1	386sx	4 MB	8 MB	16 MB	3 MB
Win95	386sx	6 MB	8 MB	16 MB	9 MB
WinNT	386sx	6 MB	8 MB	16 MB	9 MB
Macintosh	68020	7 MB	9 MB	24 MB	6 MB
Unix	N/A	16 MB	32 MB	32 MB	15 MB

The memory requirements for using Live3D are current as of this writing, but may be reduced by the time you read this.

Note

Unix requirements vary by platform. Sound card for Windows machines, audio input, and microphone/speaker are required for CoolTalk. (CoolTalk is the audio-conferencing and shared data/whiteboard application included with Netscape 3.0)

HTML and Multimedia Support

What HTML elements does the browser of your typical user support? For example, HTML tables are very handy for page layout. If the browser does not support tables, the document displays in a single long column. Netscape Navigator, Internet Explorer, and Spyglass Mosaic all support tables.

Because of updates and rapidly changing feature sets, it can be difficult to track the capabilities of the various browsers. For example, a browser may claim to support tables, but doesn't implement all the attributes of tables or it claims JavaScript support, but reading the fine print reveals that many features are incompletely implemented.

This book attempts to track the feature sets of Navigator 2.0, Navigator 3.0, MSIE 2.0, and MSIE 3.0. All graphical browsers in common use support helper apps for the display of multimedia. Table 2.6 lists some of the multimedia features of commonly used browsers.

Table 2.6

Browser Support for Popular Multimedia Formats

	Netscape 2.0	MSIE 2	Netscape 3.0	MSIE 3
Netscape Plug-Ins	Yes	Mac only	Yes	Yes
OLE/ActiveX	Need Plug-In	No	Need Plug-In	Yes
JavaScript	Yes	Most features	Yes	Most features; doesn't support new features in v3
VBScript	No	No	No	Yes
Java	Windows95/NT Only	No	Yes	Windows 95/NT only
VRML	Need Plug-In	Need Plug-In	Yes	Need Plug-In
QuickTime	Need Plug-In	Yes	Yes	Yes
AVI	Need Plug-In	Yes	Yes	Yes
AIFF	Yes	No	Yes	Yes
WAV	Need Plug-In	Yes	Yes	Yes
AU	Yes	No	Yes	Yes
MIDI	Need Plug-In	Yes	Yes	Yes
Progressive JPEG	Yes	No	Yes	No
Tables	Yes	Yes	Yes	Yes
Frames	Yes	No	Yes	Yes
Client-side Image Maps	Yes	No	Yes	No

Costs of Multimedia

Creating a multimedia Web site requires a substantial investment in time and resources. Besides design, set-up, and on-going maintenance of the site, you are required to create original multimedia content that has been optimized and tweaked for the Web. Cost of multimedia includes:

- Software tools for content creation
- Training to use software tools
- Asset management, tracking, version control, and cataloging
- Storage of digital media
- Hardware and software required for digitizing audio and video

Conclusion

Before you begin creating a multimedia Web site, it's important to clearly define your goals, characterize your target audience, and specify the minimum hardware and software platform you support. These specifications and requirements guide every design decision you make. The following chapters show you how to design multimedia Web sites and create high-quality multimedia content that takes into account the technical limitations of your users and the design goals of your Web site.

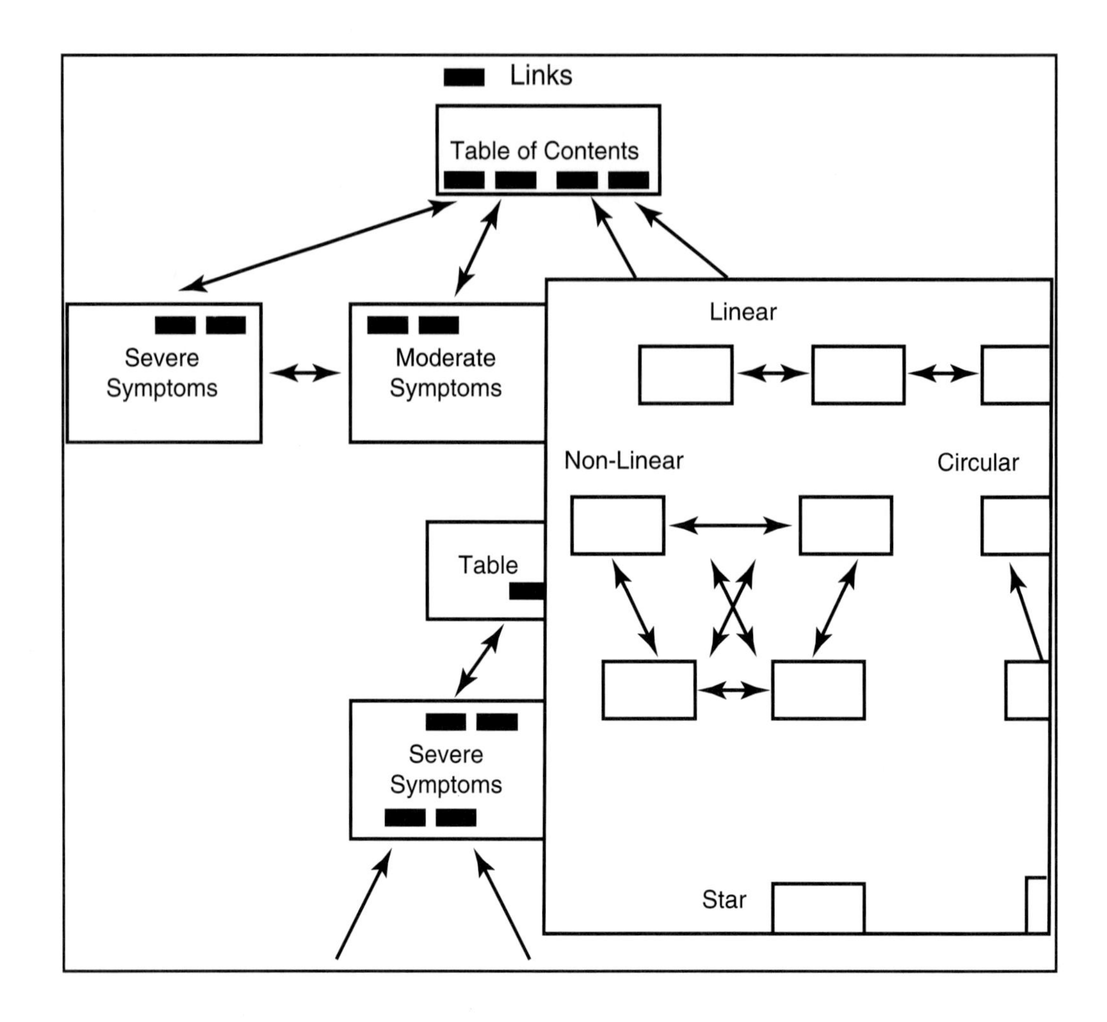

In the headlong rush to publish on the Web, authors and publishers are applying techniques and strategies from other media, such as print and CD-ROM, to Web publishing. This chapter discusses how to take advantage of the unique aspects of the Web to communicate effectively.

chapter

3

The Web and Hypermedia Design

The Web is a unique communication and publishing medium. Nothing quite like it has ever existed. Creating multimedia Web sites involves several new challenges and issues. If you are coming to Web multimedia with a desktop publishing background or a CD-ROM publishing background, you will be able to apply many of your skills to the new medium. But the unique character of the Web requires a different perspective on information design. When designing Web sites you are part interface designer, part usability engineer, part graphic designer, and part programmer.

The technical limitations of hardware and software that are particular to the Web were discussed in Chapter 2, "Planning Multimedia Web Sites." This chapter discusses ways to communicate effectively on the Web and some of the unique issues raised by hypermedia. Although geared toward design of large Web sites, you can apply the same principles to your home page. This chapter looks specifically at:

- Characteristics of the Web and hypermedia as a communication medium
- Designing Web-based information structures
- User-centered design on the Web
- Web-based environmental design and interface design

Note

In 1945, Vannevar Bush, science advisor to President Roosevelt during WWII and director of the U.S. Office of Scientific Research and Development, described a system of linked information similar in concept to the current Web. For more information on this part of the Web's history, see:

`http://www.isg.sfu.ca/~duchier/mise/vbush`

Ted Nelson, software designer, writer, and film-maker, coined the phrase hypermedia in the 1960s to describe a nonlinear system of networked, linked multimedia.

The Web as a Communication and Publishing Medium

The explosive popularity of the Web has been driven in part by how easy it is for anyone to publish material and have it potentially reach millions of people. Corporations, organizations, universities, professional associations, departments, and workgroups are using the Web for both internal publishing and communicating with other interested people all over the world.

There are both economic benefits and detriments to publishing on the Web. Understanding the unique features of Web publishing can help minimize your costs. This section discusses some of the unique qualities of Web-based publishing and communications, and some of the differences between the Web and other communications media.

Benefits of Publishing on the Web

Many people and organizations are in a headlong rush to publish on the World Wide Web without regard to the time, effort, and money involved. By knowing the benefits of Web communication you can target your Web publishing to be used in the most effective way.

- **Anywhere—Global Access.** The Web is a distributed, networked information medium. It can be accessed by anybody anywhere in the world, as long as they have a computer with a TCP/IP connection to the Internet and a Web browser. Also, the Web knows no borders. Your audience can be in Singapore, Sri Lanka, or Sweden. Thus you need to design content with cultural differences in mind.
- **Anything—The Entire Web is the Information Space.** The entire gazillion megabyte content of the Web is accessible to you. Information is not limited to the local server. It is very easy to integrate content from Web sites all over the world into a single document for local users. In one sense, the entire Web is your hard drive. This accessibility places a responsibility on Web authors to honor copyright and usage restrictions.

- **Any Time—24-hour Access.** The Web never sleeps. It never shuts down like ordinary computer networks so it can be accessed 24 hours a day. When it's midnight in North America, it's rush hour in Western Europe.
- **Cross-platform.** Browsers provide a consistent interface and feature set across multiple platforms. Although there are still system-specific peculiarities, which will be discussed in this book, cross-platform development for the Web is generally easier than developing a cross-platform CD or application. You can usually create one version of your multimedia content, place it on a centralized server, and then have it delivered to Windows, Macs, and Unix machines.
- **Web Browsers as Multimedia Application Shells.** Web browsers are becoming multimedia development platforms. Much of the basic interface, navigation, multimedia integration, and system integration required by multimedia application development is provided by the Web browser. You can think of the Web browser as an application shell for your multimedia content. It provides the basic navigation support, interface support, and operating system integration you need for rapid application development. Installation and operating system tasks are shifted to the Web browser so that you can focus on content.
- **Easy-to-use.** The Web is popular because of the easy-to-use, simple graphical user interface provided by Web browsers. The only command users need to know is the mouse click.
- **Integration of TCP/IP-Based Services.** Web browsers provide one-stop access to diverse Internet services such as FTP, Gopher, e-mail, and Usenet. Previously, these services used command-line interfaces or required different applications each with a different interface. Thus, it's easy to integrate Internet resources that reside on FTP sites, Gopher servers, or newsgroups with local content.
- **Easy to Publish.** Web publishing short-circuits many of the barriers to entry in traditional publishing. You can instantly publish to millions of people all over the world. There is no need for publishers and distributors in the traditional sense of the word. Anyone can publish and distribute material on the Web as long as they have access

Tip

Because the veracity of information on the Web can be difficult to judge, Caveat Emptor should be your motto. Another aspect of the distributed nature of the Web is that a remote site you link to today may not exist tomorrow. Maintaining valid links is one of the costs of Web publishing.

to a Web server, FTP site, or Gopher server. The Web is very democratic in this sense.

A drawback to this publishing free-for-all is the lack of editorial judgement and filtering provided by publishers and editors. It can be difficult to track the source of information on the Web or to judge its veracity. Also, distribution and display costs are shifted to Internet service providers and users.

- **The Distribution Media is the Net.** Publishing on the Web doesn't use paper. You don't need expensive presses, inks, and papers to publish color graphics. You don't need to burn a CD-ROM or distribute material on floppies. As mentioned, distribution and display costs are shifted to Internet service providers and users.

- **Modular and Easy to Update.** The Web is inherently modular because a Web site is divided into HTML documents, linked graphics and multimedia elements. When one document, graphic, or piece of your Web site becomes outdated, it is easy to replace it without significantly modifying the entire Web site.

  Web publishing is a continuing process, not a one-time event. Thus, it is relatively easy to provide fresh, just-in-time information that is hot off the presses.

  Contrast this updating capability with a CD-ROM or magazine where the content is frozen at publication time. To update a CD-ROM, you would have to burn an entirely new CD.

  Modularity and ease of updating also makes it easy to expand your site or add new features and content areas.

  On the Web, you can also provide real-time updates of information. For example, you could update a VRML model of the earth with real-time satellite data, or provide the ubiquitous streaming stock ticker tape.

- **Associative Linking and Interactivity.** One of the most powerful features of the Web is the ability to create hyperlinks between associated content. Just about anything can be a button in HTML. Adding interactivity and navigation is just a matter of adding a line of HTML code.

Ease of hyperlinking presents challenges to the information designer. It's tempting to link to everything. Links cost in terms of maintenance, creating a site environment and context, usability, and providing users with a conceptual map of the information space. Carefully consider the benefits of each link.

- **Distributed, Nonhierarchical Structure.** The Web has no top. It isn't run by a central authority. Control of the network is distributed. You can enter the Web at any point.
- **Porous.** The Web is a porous medium, that is, a user can drop into your Web site at any document or file as long as he or she has the URL.
- **Open.** Unless you specifically place access restrictions on your site, anything you publish on the Web can be downloaded and saved by users anywhere in the world. Raw HTML code for any document can be viewed in most browsers with the View Document Source command.
- **Multimedia Content and Rich Media.** The Web began as a text-based information system. The original creators of the Web designed an open extensible system. With the release of Netscape Navigator 3.0 and MSIE 3.0, the Web has become a cross-platform, multimedia development platform with browsers providing built-in support for many multimedia data types.

Limitations

Many of the unique features of Web publishing can be viewed either as benefits or limitations, depending on the goals of your Web site and the kinds of information you are providing. This section discusses some of the special problems that arise when you are putting information on the Web.

- **Lack of Context.** The dynamic, distributed, nonhierarchical nature of the Web along with the capability to link to anything, can make it hard for users to find their way through Web-based information. It is easy to get lost on the Web. Users click around rapidly and then have to ask themselves "Where am I? How did I get here?"

You have little control over how people enter or leave your site. You have more control over pathways within your site, but users can still jump anywhere if they have the URL.

A big part of successful Web site design is providing Web users with a sense of context. Several ways to do this are discussed in this and following chapters.

Note

Because of the limitations of HTML, Web pages tend to look the same, although this is changing with new HTML tags. Graphics and multimedia can be a way to "brand" your site and provide the Web equivalent of signposts and landmarks.

- **Reading on a Computer.** A computer screen is not the best medium on which to read a lot of text. Monitors are bright and sometimes flickering or they can be obscured by glare. Monitors can be tiring on the eyes. Users will be at desks and workstations that may not be set up properly, leading to eye, back, and neck strain. Compare this experience to curling up in a comfy couch with a good book or magazine.
- **Limited Attention Span.** Web users tend to surf the Web, similar to channel surfing on a TV. They click, click, click rapidly through content until something catches their eye. The time they spend on your page can be as little as six or seven seconds, assuming they even wait long enough for the page to download. In that respect, snappy multimedia that loads quickly can be a good hook to capture Web surfers. Otherwise, Web users may never see your page if it takes a long time to download. They'll have moved on.
- **Limitations of HTML.** HTML is a very limited page description language. From its inception and its roots in SGML (Standard Generalized Markup Language, an international standard for text information processing), HTML was designed to define hyperlinks and document structure and not document appearance. Thus, the choices that you have to define the appearance of your documents is limited.
- **User Altered Pages.** Users can customize the display of HTML tags in their browsers, such as fonts and colors. Just the simple act of resizing the browser window can dramatically affect the appearance and layout of a Web page.
- **User Hardware and Software Limitations.** Other limitations you have to consider when designing multimedia Web pages are your users' connection speed, hardware and software limitations, and operating system differences. These considerations are especially important when developing rich multimedia content for the Web. The

previous chapter discussed connection speed and hardware and software limitations in detail. Following chapters show you how to rise above these limitations and create effective multimedia Web sites.

- **Security.** The Web and the Internet were designed for the free flow of information. Servers commonly reside on Unix computers that have an open architecture and many ways to access system resources. Globally accessible Web resources may be vulnerable to vandalism.

Warning

Copyright and intellectual property. Because the Web is so open, protecting copyright and intellectual property is difficult. At the very least, include a copyright notice in the footer of your web pages. The Library of Congress has placed much useful material on copyrights at:

`gopher://marvel.loc.gov/11/copyright`

Designing Web-Based Information Structures: General Guidelines for Web Design

This section discusses how to build an information framework or structure for your multimedia Web site. As you begin to sketch out this framework, consider the following characteristics of Web-based information.

Note

For a complete guide to security issues see:

Actually Useful Internet Security Techniques by Larry J. Hughes Jr. and *Internet Security Professional Reference* from New Riders Publishing.

Readability

You need to make your pages readable on computer screens. Ask yourself the following questions. The answers directly relate to the readability of your Web pages:

- Is the background too busy to read the text or does it distract from the graphics and other visual elements?
- Is the background a bright, saturated color or does it provide low contrast with the text color making the text hard to read?
- Can the user differentiate active links and visited links?
- Is there plenty of white space to help the page breathe?
- Are appropriate HTML codes, such as headings and lists, used to reveal the underlying information structure?

Multimedia may conflict with readability. For example, don't have animations on pages where you want users to read a lot of text (see fig.3.1).

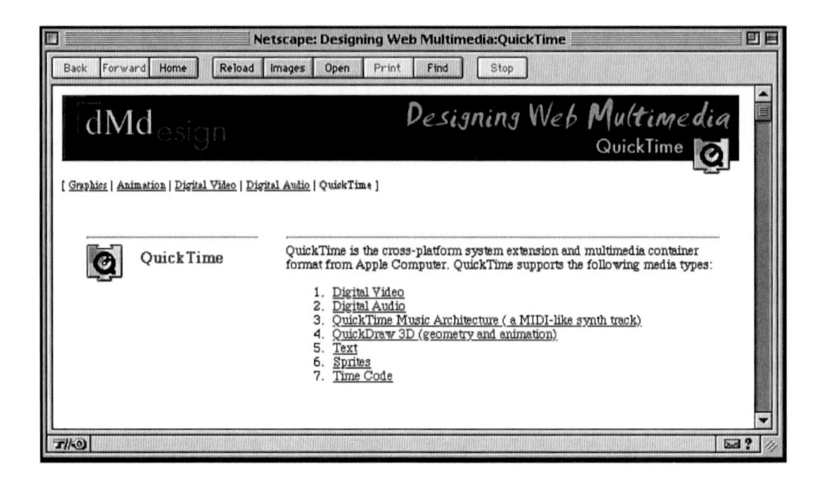

Figure 3.1

Web page designed to use white space, repeated icons, and the less-is-more philosophy.

Make Pages Short

Many Web users do not spend a lot of time reading text. Users tend to scan a Web page for key words or interesting content. They generally don't like to scroll through long documents.

Even if you are publishing a text-heavy document such as an employee benefits manual or technical documentation for a software program, you'll want to break up the document into small bite-size chunks for online reading. A single Web page with large amounts of text takes a long time to download. Scrolling through a large document is awkward to read and to use on the Web.

Each Web page should convey one major idea (or message). If you are reorganizing a document for the Web, look at the internal organization of that document. Decide what sub-heading or subtopic you would like to break the document into.

Another way to look at designing short Web pages is to think of the page as a bullet-point slide for a talk. Present your Web page as a series of main bullet-points. Each main point can contain a link to more detailed supporting information.

Put Your Most Important Information First

Another good technique is to put the most important information first. You can do this in a variety of ways:

- Put a navigation bar with links to the main content sections of your site at the top of the page.
- In lists, put the most important topic first.
- Distill your main point into a single sentence or two and put that sentence at the top of your page.
- Set off this summary or abstract with a different font or text style or indent it with the BLOCKQUOTE tag.

Think of this technique as a sort of executive summary for busy people who don't care about all the details or supporting information, but want the main point.

Less Is More

For each Web page, determine how much information users really need on that page. Do they really need to know all the supporting details? Do they really need to link to every Web page that has anything remotely to do with your topic?

Your screen real estate is limited. Keep it concise and to the point. Precision and conciseness in language and design make it easier for users to get to the information they want.

Tip

The less text and multimedia you have on a page, the faster it loads.

White Space Is Your Friend

Probably the three main rules of thumb for designing Web sites to be read on cramped computer screens are "Use white space. Use white space. Use white space." Let your page breathe. The background doesn't necessarily need to be white, but the color should enhance readability.

Find out more about how to create effective backgrounds in Chapter 6, "Using Graphics to Add Dynamic Content." Learn how to lay out pages with white space in Chapter 4, "Designing the Layout of Your Web Pages."

Usability and Consistency

Keep the page layout and navigation features on your pages consistent in form and function. Don't force your users to relearn the interface or functionality on every Web page.

Much of this chapter provides tips on analyzing your information and implementing a consistent, functional interface. Spending time in analysis and prototype design at the outset pays off in an elegant, extensible, and usable Web site.

Three Clicks To Get Anywhere

Most Web sites are designed in a hierarchy of pages. Keep the hierarchical structure simple. Ask yourself the following questions:

- How deep is the hierarchy?
- Do users have to click multiple times to get to the actual information and content?
- How many indexes or table of contents pages must they wade through to get to the meat of the site?

Design information structures so that the user takes no more than three steps to get anywhere on your site.

Retrieval Time and Browser Support

Note

If you use HTML tags that aren't supported by all browsers, include some indication of this as a courtesy to the user.

Always keep in mind how long it takes the typical user to load a page. Loading time is especially critical for the most frequently accessed pages, such as home pages or entry points to specific content areas.

One of this book's primary focuses is on ways to reduce loading time.

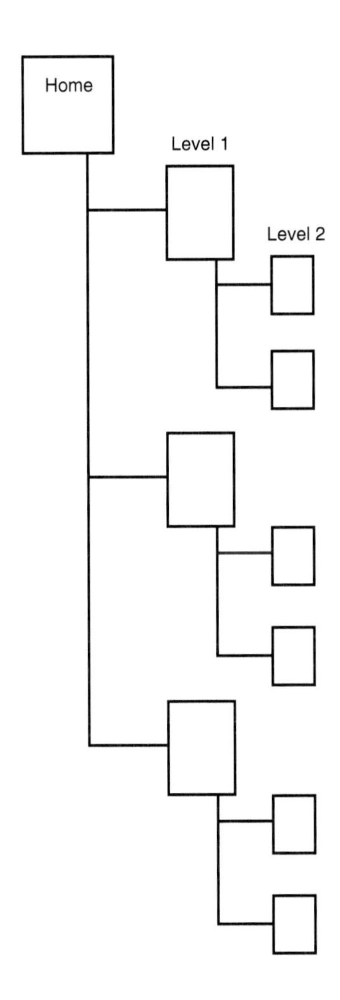

Figure 3.2

Hierarchical Web site structure.

User-Centered Design

User-centered design puts user tasks and needs at the center of your design strategy. What is the user trying to do on each Web page? Try to define a single task or group of tasks that the typical user will try to accomplish. A typical user task might be:

- Typing in the URL for the home page
- Scanning home page for new material
- Downloading software updates

If the latter two tasks are an important part of your Web site's function, consider including a What's New section at the top of the main page, or provide a direct link to an FTP site with the latest software upgrades.

The goal of task-centered design is to make it easy for users to find the information they want. What good is all your information if it can't be found?

A helpful tool in task-centered design is the task-flow diagram. Task-flow diagrams are a way to visualize user pathways through an information space. Each task or group of tasks could be represented by a Web page. The links between Web pages represent the user's path through the information space.

By defining the typical user tasks and pathways through the information, you can focus your development time and resources on the most important, well-worn paths.

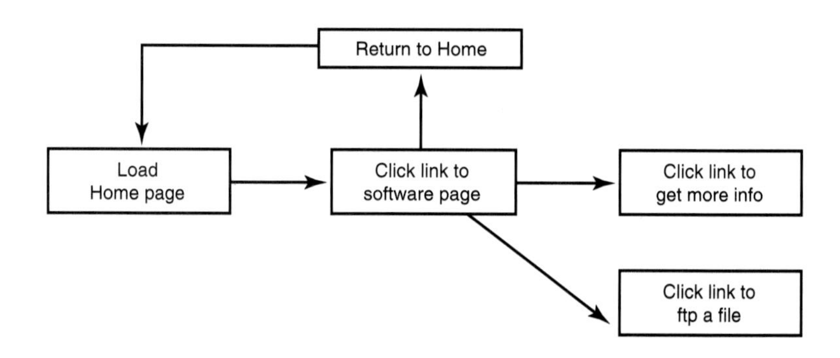

Figure 3.3

Task-flow diagram.

Topics and Sub-Topics

Divide your information into topics and sub-topics based on functional features and typical user tasks. First, write down topic headings and sub-headings without regard to context or hierarchy. What is most important about this information?

Use your statement of goals and your task-flow diagrams to place groups of related topics in context. What is the most important topic in each group? What assumptions are you making by grouping topics this way?

Possible ways to break up information into sections and subsections include:

- **Category.** Categories can be anything appropriate to the content. Be aware of the underlying assumptions in your categories. Are you inadvertently emphasizing one aspect of the information at the expense of another?
- **Scaled quantity.** Cheap to expensive or easy to difficult.
- **Spatially.** A map.
- **Temporally.** A time line.
- **Alphabetically.** If text searching is important.

If you are reorganizing existing material, such as course notes or a training manual, look at the existing information structure of the material and see how it applies to the goals of your project.

Hierarchy

Arrange categories hierarchically and draw links between topics. Use sticky notes or a whiteboard to sketch relationships quickly. What relationships in the information do you want to emphasize? Does the hierarchy support user tasks that were defined visually in your task-flow diagrams?

The hierarchy shouldn't be too deep—maybe three levels. The links you draw between sections and topics become the hypertext links that a user follows to access the information. Generally, links should flow logically between sections without unexpected jumps or leaps.

It should be easy for the user to get to the most important information. Does it take more than three jumps to get to any place in your information structure? At the end of this process, you should have a flow-chart. The flow-chart is the information map for your project. Figure 3.4 shows two possible flowcharts and link structures for the same information.

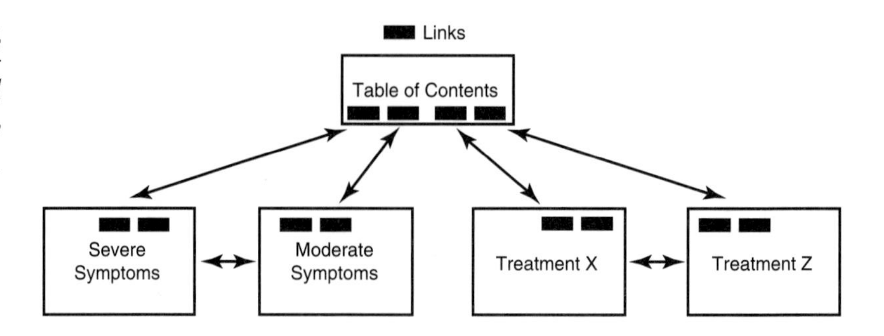

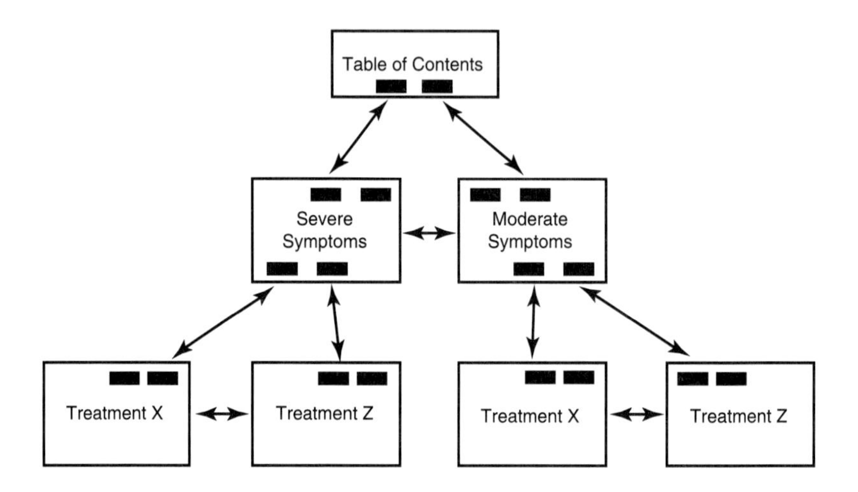

Figure 3.4

Possible hierarchies and flow-charts for the same information.

Flow-chart

A flow-chart merges your information hierarchy with your task-flow diagrams.

For each section and sub-section of your flow-chart ask these questions:

- What tasks is the user going to perform in this section?
- What is the goal of this section?

Write down the tasks and goals for each section. These items form the basis for the navigational design and interface design. If you can't articulate a task and a goal for a section maybe you should rethink your information structure.

Try a simple text-based HTML prototype. Don't worry about content, graphics, or page layout. Just put in the main links between sections. Test your Web site as if you were a naïve user. Better yet, test your user task set on representative users of your site.

Don't worry about how this all fits on a computer screen or how to do this in HTML. That part of the design process comes in the next step.

Finding Your Way in Cyberspace

Many people speak of the Internet and the Web as a place within a larger matrix called cyberspace. Although the Web and the Internet are just a bunch of computers and computer files linked by cables, wires, and software, the spatial metaphor is a useful way to organize the vast amounts of information on the Web.

Humans are visual, spatial creatures that naturally organize information in three dimensions. For example, your home is divided into rooms. Each room serves a specific purpose and is the location of specific behavior.

A feature of cyberspace is that the spatial dimension exists independently of physical space. The sense of place and of space is created by the interface, content, and tasks performed. People have a hard time visualizing abstract information spaces. Multimedia cues and information design can help make information spaces concrete and usable. Graphical user interfaces on Macintosh, Windows 95 and X-Windows systems use a two-dimensional spatial metaphor to organize information space. VRML (Virtual Reality Modeling Language—a text-based language that describes 3D worlds on the Web) brings a 3D spatial metaphor to the Web.

The next section discusses the general principles of user interface design and some of the specific interface requirements of Web information spaces.

Web Interface

Use of the Web exploded when Web browsers provided a graphical user interface to the Web. One advantage or disadvantage, depending on how you look at it, of designing multimedia for the Web is that you can assume a standard interface provided by the browser. Browsers provide navigational controls, such as the Back and Forward buttons, history lists, and support of system tasks such as printing services and the ability to save files to disk.

User Interface Principles

How you design your interface depends on the goals of your Web site. Making your Web site easy to use is usually one of those goals. The easiest interfaces to use are transparent; they get out of the way and let the user get her work done.

The Web browser contains its own interface. Any interface you design for a Web page extends and complements the browser interface.The interface you design is contained within the browser interface and is part of a visually complex computer screen. Even though the Web browser provides many interface functions, you can't always depend on it being visible, because the user can customize it in various ways.

Compared to the interface features common in desktop operating systems, such as three-dimensional buttons with multiple visual states, audio feedback, rollover and highlighting behavior, and context-sensitive help, Web hypertext links are a primitive graphical user interface element.

Shockwave, Java applets, and VRML worlds can be used to provide a richer user interface. Figure 3.5 shows a rich, user interface implemented with Shockwave.

If you use these tools to provide a richer interface remember these tips:

- Users like to feel in control of the computer and to directly manipulate objects on the screen.
- Don't take control away from the user.
- Be consistent in the ways that you indicate which objects can be clicked, dragged, or edited.
- When the user manipulates something, provide visual and aural feedback.
- If a user starts a process that will take more than a few seconds to complete, use Shockwave or Java to show a watch or other busy cursor.
- Design a consistent interface. A particular button or hyperlink navigation bar should always have the same

function and be in the same place. It shouldn't disappear unexpectedly or suddenly do something different.

- Let the user make mistakes and undo actions. Don't be rigid in your design. Consider enabling the user to customize the interface in some way.

Figure 3.5

Using Macromedia Shockwave for Director for a rich user interface.

Interactivity and Navigation

On each screen the user should be able to answer these questions:

- Where am I?
- Where can I go?
- How do I get there?

Navigation should be simple, consistent, and intuitive. Some navigation and interactivity issues to consider include:

- How deep is your information structure? Does it take more than three clicks to get anywhere?
- Web browsers provide a standard set of navigational controls, including a Back button and a history list of

Note

Apple Computer has made their excellent user interface guidelines available for free on the Internet. You can find these guidelines along with a lot of other useful material at the URL:

`http://www.info.apple.com/`

recently visited sites. Don't depend on the browser interface for navigation within your site. Information cues and context can be better provided by custom navigation links within your site.

- Make links descriptive. Within the link text, indicate what happens or where the user goes if they click on the link by using words such as: download, e-mail or home page.
- On every page, provide links to major intersections or overview pages such as the main page, site map, or main second level table of contents and entry points.
- Simple navigational icons such as Back or Up may not contain enough information to orient the user within the Web space. Be more descriptive.
- On long pages, provide a list of internal topics or a mini-table of contents at the top of the page. Within the body of the long document provide internal links back to the top of the page.
- Generally, group together buttons, controls, or hyperlinks that have related functions.
- Keep groups of navigation links in a consistent screen location. If for some reason a button or hyperlink is inactive or unavailable, it is better to show this by dimming, or some other way, than by having the button disappear or move to another location.
- Make sure the function of each button and control is clear. Provide descriptive text for hyperlinks. If you use graphics buttons, don't create similar looking buttons that do different things.

  If the button that takes you to the next screen is a right-pointing arrow, don't use a similar right-pointing arrow for another function, such as playing digital video. If you use an icon for a button in one screen, don't reuse the icon as part of a non-clickable graphic somewhere else in the Web site. If you use drop-shadows, 3D chiseled edges, or HTML table borders to indicate clickable regions, don't incorporate these elements in other graphics. The user will think they are buttons.
- If you use icons or graphics as buttons, be sure to provide alternate navigation for users who have graphics turned off or are using a text-based browser.

You can use the ALT attribute of the IMG tag to provide text alternatives to graphic-based links. You can also provide a text-based hyperlink button bar that duplicates the functionality of your graphic-based button bar.

For graphic-based buttons and icons, consider incorporating text labels into your buttons. Clear, easy-to-understand icons can be hard to design for certain functions. If you use text labels, it's generally best to capitalize the first letter of each word with the rest of the word in lowercase.

- Besides navigational elements, what other screen elements will the user be able to manipulate? Ask yourself the following questions:

  What media controls will you provide?

  Is it necessary for the user to have frame-by-frame control of digital video? Of sound volume?

  How will the user interact with large chunks of related text that won't fit on one screen? with scroll bars? by jumping to a new screen?

Interaction Topologies

Creating hyperlinks between pages and information is very easy to do on the Web. It's tempting to place a lot of links on a Web page. But with hyperlinks, less is more. Presenting too many choices, with dozens of links on a page going off on many different tangents, can be confusing to a user.

It's your job as an information designer to figure out what the main benefit to the user is and to channel the user to these choices. But remember, the Web is porous. A user can enter your site at any page as long as they have the URL for that page. Designing interaction pathways can be a challenge. A Web site has to be like a flatworm—wherever you cut it, it has to be able to grow back the entire site.

How should you link pages within a specific Web? Some interaction topologies to consider (see figure 3.6) include:

- **Linear.** Pages are linked in linear sequence, similar to a slide show. Users can go forward and backward in the sequence.

- **Non-linear.** Within any specific content area, users can link to any page from any other page.
- **Circular.** Pages are linked in linear sequence, with the last page pointing back to the first page.
- **Star.** A main page links to subsidiary pages. Subsidiary pages can only link back to the main page.

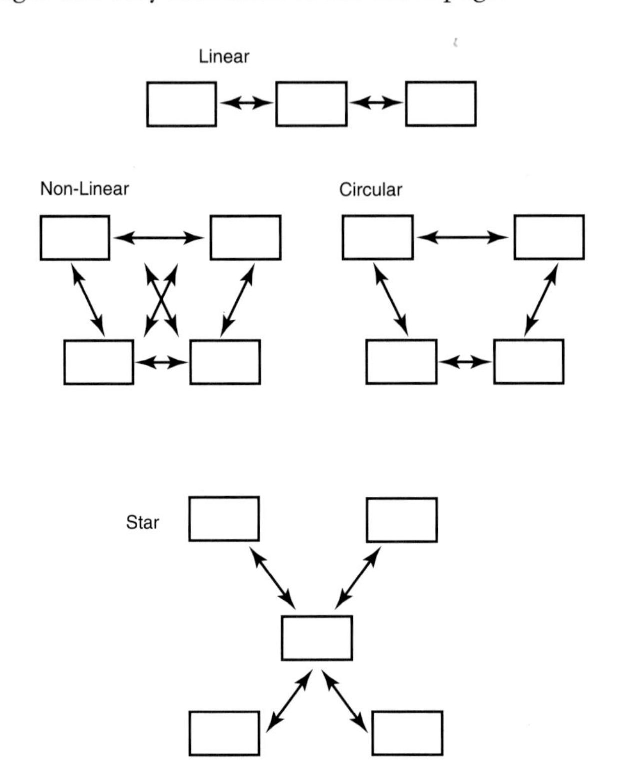

Figure 3.6

Possible interaction topologies.

How will users jump between levels within a Web? Consider providing second- and third-level entry pages or table of contents for specific content areas.

Consider how users will exit your site. Controlling how users exit your site can help reinforce a sense of place and context. Links outside of the Web site can be handled in different ways.

You can provide:

- No external links.
- All external links on a single page.
- External links only from high-level pages such as second-level entry points.
- No restrictions on external links.
- A universal exit page that users will go to whenever they click on a link that exits the site; usually implemented with server-side scripting.

Context, Signposts and Landmarks

One of the most important issues in Web site design is the need to provide context or environment. A key feature of the Web is the ability to link anywhere. This feature can also be very disorienting. Design a consistent visual brand or marking for your site that enables users to quickly identify where they are.

Graphical identity elements can be a way to mark your site. Highlight graphical elements or provide other visual cues that indicate where the user is within the Web site or information space. Repeat these elements consistently through a site. Although repetition of similar elements helps to brand a site, you also need to differentiate various content sections or levels within the information hierarchy. See Chapter 4, "Designing the Layout of Your Web Pages," for more information on using graphical identity elements.

Simple navigational icons such as Back or Up may not contain enough information to orient the user within the Web space. What does Up mean? Where does the Back button go? Be more descriptive.

Tip

On each page, consider providing a link to a global site map or site index.

Information Cues

Information cues can be very simple, and can include such elements as:

- Using descriptive document titles within <TITLE> tags
- Providing organizational and publisher information in headers or footers
- Providing contact and e-mail addresses
- Indicating the freshness of the information with the date modified
- Indicating copyright
- Using appropriate HTML formatting such as headings and lists, that reflect the underlying information structure

Universal Grid

A page layout grid is a good way to ensure a consistent look and feel for Web pages. The grid should reinforce and support the underlying information structure. Consistent size and placement of repeated elements is a good way to provide context. A page layout grid places important requirements on the characteristics of included multimedia, such as their dimensions.

Unfortunately, HTML is a primitive page layout language. Chapter 4 details how to create page layout grids with HTML.

Conclusion

As a communication medium, the Web has unique characteristics that are fundamentally different from print or CD-ROM. These characteristics include:

- The ability to hyperlink to information all over the world.
- The Web is distributed and nonhierarchical.
- Global access unconstrained by space or time.
- Ease of publication for average users.

The suggestions in this chapter should help you design Web sites that take advantage of the Web's characteristics as a communication medium, to communicate effectively with your audience, and to provide easy access to information.

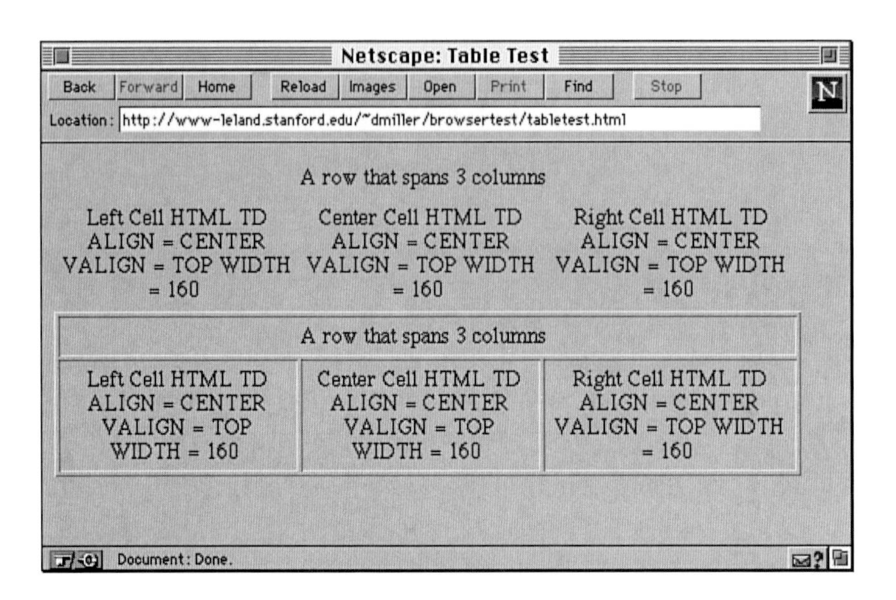

You've completed designing the overall hierarchy and information structure of your site. Now you are ready to start actually coding HTML and creating Web pages. This chapter discusses page and presentation design within the technical contraints of the Web and HTML.

chapter

4

Designing the Layout of Your Web Pages

Designing page layout and page presentation is the next step in the design process.

Remember, HTML provides primitive page layout. If you come from a desktop publishing background you will despair at the limited range of options HTML gives you for page design and layout. Also, after you have a page looking decent on your local machine, it will probably not look the same on different machines or with different browsers. It will even look different on different versions of the same browser, using the same platform. And then the user will resize the browser window and text and graphics will flow haphazardly over the page, or the user will change display fonts and table cells won't wrap the same way. The challenge is to design good-looking, readable Web pages within the technical constraints of your user's systems and the limitations of HTML.

But there is hope. Both Netscape Navigator and Internet Explorer are introducing new HTML tags for page layout and formatting. The next "official" version of the HTML standard will probably support many of these tags. This chapter looks at:

- Strategies and techniques for designing Web pages
- Page layout and presentation issues
- HTML tags you can use to accomplish page layout

Strategies and Techniques for Designing Web Pages

To design an effective and visually compelling Web site, you should follow a logical sequence of events that gradually develops the details of your site. An outline of the design steps might be:

- Create a storyboard
- Sketch out your page types: main page, second- and third-level entry pages, and content pages
- Develop page specifications for each page type
- Create an HTML prototype
- Create HTML templates for each page type

Throughout this section, you receive tips on good design practices.

Storyboard

storyboarding

In film, television, and traditional multimedia design, **storyboarding** is an illustrated scene-by-scene or shot-by-shot description of the narrative sequence of events in a storyline. For the Web, storyboarding usually means sketching out rough screen layouts for individual Web pages and arranging the pages within an information hierarchy and flow-chart.

When designing screen layouts and interfaces, don't worry about the details. Just block out the positions of the main interface elements, such as buttons, text, graphics, and digital video. You can use paper and pen, a draw program, or HTML editors to sketch out the interface. Creating your storyboard in HTML can help you visualize the Web-based structure and screen layout and might help you identify problems in your information design. Your storyboard can serve as the basis for a prototype of your Web site and as a basis for HTML templates for your final Web pages.

Page Types

Different pages on your site have different functions. For example, many Web sites have the following:

- A main entry point or home page
- Several second-level entry points or subsidiary index pages
- A site map
- A page from which to download software
- Content pages of various types

Design a consistent look for each page type. Consistent visual design helps the user tell where he is within a site.

Main Page

The main page is the entry point to the site. As such, it should set up the navigational and context cues and the graphic style for your site. The entry point should give the user a good idea of what she will find at your site. Follow the principle, described in Chapter 3, "The Web and Hypermedia Design," of putting the most important information first.

Tip

The main page is a good place to include a "What's New" paragraph with recent updates.

This will probably be the most frequently accessed page on your site. The main page is a good place to put multimedia hooks to grab the user's attention, but because this will be the most frequently accessed page, make sure multimedia elements load fast and don't bog down your server.

Second- and Third-Level Entry Points

Second- and third-level entry point pages are entry points to specific content areas, categories, or sub-topics. Carry through graphic identity elements from the main page, but make it clear that the user is on another level of the information hierarchy. You can indicate different hierarchy levels by the size, position, or color of identity graphics.

Note

Chapter 5, "Designing Multimedia Web Pages," provides general tips on creating fast-loading content. Chapter 6, "Using Graphics to Add Dynamic Content," provides more details on creating low-bandwidth graphics. Other chapters provide tips on optimizing specific media types, such as QuickTime, Shockwave, and Audio.

Consider providing a consistent way to return to the main home page, main index, or site map. Provide a link that is placed consistently in the same location or a button that is part of your graphic identity element, so users can jump out of the hierarchy if they want.

Content Pages

Content pages contain the most important information on your site. Chapter 5 discusses specific design issues and HTML for multimedia-rich content pages. Here it is important to carry through graphic identity elements, while simultaneously providing clear visual and textual differentiation between different content areas. Again, using backgrounds, modifying identity graphics slightly, or providing a content-specific icon or graphic can visually "brand" the content area. Create page templates for different content areas to ensure consistency.

Tip

One way to visually define different areas on your Web site and provide context cues is to use background colors and background graphics. Backgrounds provide the only layering possibilities in HTML documents. See the section on backgrounds in Chapter 6 for details on implementing backgrounds.

Page Specifications

It's often a good idea to come up with specific requirements for each type of Web page at your site. These page requirements or specifications ensure a consistent implementation and a consistent look across a large site or organization. Page specifications can be a short document that lists the kinds, sizes, and placement of page elements. For example, here is a document titled "Page Specifications for Departmental Pages."

1. Header consisting of:
    - Departmental logo in upper left. Use graphic identity element found in directory `./graphics/logohead.gif`
    - Any other workgroup graphic identity elements not to exceed 320 pixels in width and 120 pixels in height, not to exceed 5K in size, using the departmental palette found in `../graphics/palette/department.plt`

    - Text-based, navigational button bar (see template in directory `../templates/navigation_buttons.html`)
2. Body not to exceed two screens on a 640×480 monitor
3. Footer consisting of:
    - Full URL of page
    - Date modified
    - E-mail contact for page maintainer

After page specs have been finalized, provide HTML templates for Web authors.

Graphic Identity Elements

Page specifications should include graphic identity elements. These are consistent visual elements, such as a logo, that "brand" your site and provide important visual clues on context and location within the Web site. Graphic identity elements are repeated within a site and appear on almost every page. Thus, they should:

- Load fast
- Have minimum file size
- Not distract from other content elements on the page

Graphic identity elements should appear on a Web page in a consistent position, proximity, and alignment relative to other page elements. Graphic identity elements should be designed so that they:

- Are recognizable at a glance
- Are legible
- Convey the appropriate message
- Can be sized to fit in different spaces

Prototyping with HTML

It's easy to set up a prototype in HTML. First, begin with a text-based prototype that contains document titles, other text-based identity elements, and a few hyperlinks. Add graphics and multimedia elements a piece at a time. Use proxy or placeholder graphics to gauge layout and then link in the final graphics later.

Test your prototypes:

- On different platforms
- With different browsers
- Over slow links

Create Page Templates

After you have decided on a prototype, create HTML templates of each page type. A template is an HTML file with all the formatting and layout, but with placeholders for content. Using templates makes it easy to reproduce pages with a consistent look and to add links to specific content.

Page Elements That Users Can Change

Many elements of Web page presentation can be changed by the user. You have no control over these features. Users can alter these aspects of the page and page layout in unpredictable ways:

- **Browser window size**—Resizing the browser window can cause text and graphics to flow unpredictably. You can mitigate this effect somewhat by using grid-based table layouts with fixed table sizes (discussed subsequently) but you then introduce other potential layout problems because of the different ways different browsers and different operating systems format content within tables.
- **Fonts**—Users can set display fonts to whatever they want. You have no control over fonts that have major effects on page layout. You can mitigate this problem somewhat by using the `<FONT FACE = SystemFont></FONT>` tag in Navigator 3.0 and Internet Explorer 3.0 (discussed subsequently), but this is not supported by older browsers and you might be restricted to using the most common installed system fonts such as Times, Courier, Arial, and so on.

- **Text size**—Users can set point sizes to whatever they want. You can mitigate this problem somewhat by using the `<FONT SIZE = absoluteSize_or_relativeSize></FONT>` tag in Navigator 3.0 and Internet Explorer 3.0. For example, `<FONT SIZE = -2>` Text`</FONT>` sets the point size of enclosed text to a point size that is two points less than the setting in the browser's point size preferences.
- **Link colors**—You can specify link colors using the LINK, ALINK, and VLINK attributes of the BODY tag to set the link, active link color, and visited link color respectively. If you use a background image and image loading is turned off, then these colors are ignored.
- **Image loading**—Users, especially on modems, may turn off images. To provide text-based alternate content for images, use the ALT tag (discussed in Chapters 5, "Designing Multimedia Web Pages," and 6, "Using Graphics to Add Dynamic Content"). You can force users to see images using Java applets even if they have images turned off, but they need to have a Java-enabled browser.
- **JavaScript or Java functionality can be turned off by users**—You can provide alternate content using the NOSCRIPT tag and inserting HTML within the APPLET tag as discussed in Chapter 5, Chapter 14, "Scripting Multimedia Web Pages," and Chapter 15, "Java."

Grid-based Page Layout

A page layout grid is a framework or scaffolding that defines rectangular regions on a page into which text and graphics will be placed. Well-designed page layout grids enhance readability and help create a consistent look across pages. Grids are especially useful on the Web, where users typically do not read a lot of body text and just scan pages for interesting information and key words. Grids can draw the readers' eyes to important information. A consistent grid applied across an entire Web site can go a long way toward providing important context cues, making navigation and access to information easier, and letting pages breathe.

Note

Letting pages breathe means using a lot of white space so content elements aren't crowded and packed tightly together.

You can set up page layout grids for Web pages in HTML using HTML tables, frames, the PRE tag, or invisible GIFs to space out page elements. For example, you can use table cells in HTML tables to define rectangular regions of a page layout grid. Each technique has certain benefits and limitations that are discussed in detail in following sections. Again remember that HTML is not a page layout language, so don't expect to be able to do all the things you can do in Quark XPress when laying out pages in HTML.

The following sections discuss:

- Implementing grids using generic HTML tags, such as PRE and BLOCKQUOTE, supported by most browsers
- Using HTML tables for layout
- Using frames for layout
- Browser-specific layout extensions

HTML for Indentation and Layout

One way to implement a page layout grid is to use HTML tags for indentation to move content elements horizontally across the page by specified amounts. This section looks at some HTML tags you can use to provide indentation and alignment on HTML pages. Most of these tags are HTML 2.0-compliant and are supported by most browsers.

PRE

In the dark ages, 1993-1994, using the <PRE></PRE> tag was the only way to format tabular data or specify alignment in an HTML document. Using the <PRE> tag is analogous to using a typewriter without tab stops to set up a table.

The text within PRE tags is in a mono-spaced font. All blank spaces, line breaks, and carriage returns are preserved. You align text within PRE tags by laboriously using the space bar. The advantage of using the PRE tag is that all browsers support it. You can also produce some interesting type effects, such as ASCII-based graphics, which are hard to do any other way.

BLOCKQUOTE

The <BLOCKQUOTE></BLOCKQUOTE> tag shifts enclosed text to the right.

Netscape Navigator and Internet Explorer support nested BLOCKQUOTE tags. For example, the HTML code:

```
<BLOCKQUOTE>
     BLOCKQUOTE used once
</BLOCKQUOTE>

<P>

<BLOCKQUOTE><BLOCKQUOTE><BLOCKQUOTE>
     BLOCKQUOTE used three times
</BLOCKQUOTE></BLOCKQUOTE></BLOCKQUOTE>
```

will look like:

```
BLOCKQUOTE used once

               BLOCKQUOTE used three times
```

Nested Lists

The <DL> tag is used to denote the beginning and ending of definition or glossary lists. It typically takes the form:

```
<DL>
<DT> Definition Term
          <DD> Definition Data
<DT> Definition Term
          <DD> Definition Data

</DL>
```

that in a Web browser would look like:

```
Definition Term
     Definition Data
Definition Term
     Definition Data
```

The definition data is indented five spaces underneath the definition term. You can nest definition lists to provide indentation and alignment. For example, this HTML code:

```
<DL>
<DT> Definition Term
          <DD> Definition Data
```

```
<DT> Definition Term
          <DD> <DL><DT>Definition Data
                                                <DD>More Data
                   </DL>

</DL>
```

will produce this display:

```
Definition Term
     Definition Data
Definition Term
     Definition Data
          More Data
```

Nest more definition lists to move text across the page. For example, the HTML code:

```
<DL>
<DT> Definition Term
          <DD> Definition Data
<DT> Definition Term
          <DD> <DL><DL><DL><DT>Definition Data
                         <DD>More Data
               </DL></DL></DL>

</DL>
```

will produce this display:

```
Definition Term
     Definition Data
Definition Term
               Definition Data
                    More Data
```

The line “More Data” is indented 20 spaces.

This use of the DL tag might not be supported in browsers other than Netscape Navigator 2 and later and MSIE 2 or later. Test HTML code on different browsers to make sure they handle nested definition lists correctly.

IMG ALIGN, HSPACE, and VSPACE

You can also use alignment attributes of the IMG tag to create crude page layouts. See the section on HTML tags for multimedia in Chapter 5 for a detailed discussion of these tags, including Netscape extensions to the alignment attributes.

Spacing GIFs

Another way to create alignment of page elements is to use transparent, solid-color GIFs, or GIFs that are the same color as the background of the Web page. Because these GIFs are invisible you can use them to create white space on your Web page and to flow text and other graphics around them.

You can use the WIDTH and HEIGHT attributes of the IMG tag to resize the GIF to the size you want. But, if the browser window is resized, text and graphics may flow in unpredictable ways. Chapter 5 discusses the IMG tag and its various alignment attributes.

Grid-based Layout with Tables

Tables were introduced in Netscape Navigator 1.1 and have become part of the draft HTML 3.2 standard. Most other major browsers, including Internet Explorer and NCSA Mosaic, support HTML tables to a varying degree. Some browsers, such as text-based browsers do not support tables, in which case, tables appear as long single column of text.

Tables can be used to create a page layout grid. The size of tables and the size of individual cells within tables can be:

- Determined by the browser at display time based on a "best-fit" for content and window size
- Specified in exact pixel dimensions
- Specified as a percentage of the browser window

Figure 4.1 is an example of a three-column layout using tables.

You can specify fixed pixel sizes for table rows, columns, and individual cells. These fixed sizes will not change if the user resizes the browser window. You can specify relative sizes as a percentage of the visible browser window. Although this gives the Web author some control over page layout, availability of fonts, cross-platform display differences, and user preferences can change the appearance and wrapping of content within tables.

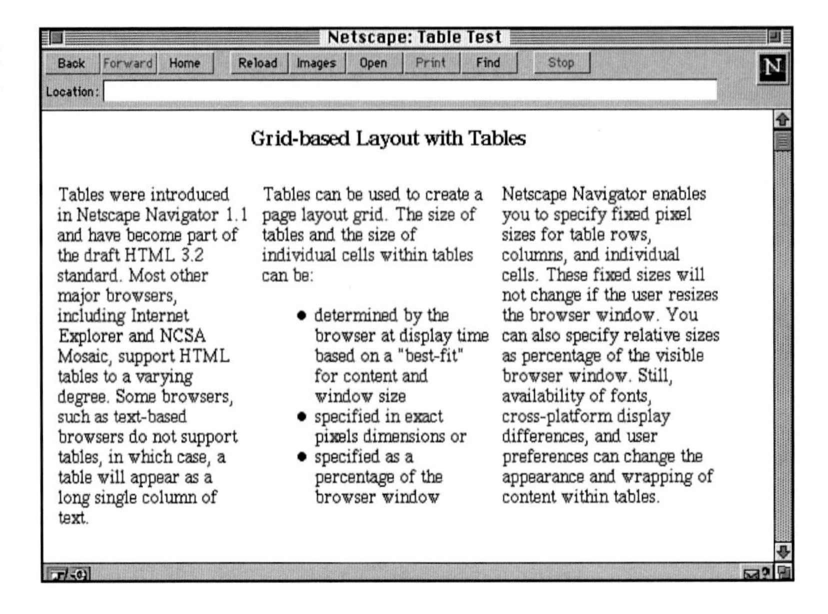

Figure 4.1

Three-column page layout with tables.

Drawbacks of Tables

The drawbacks of tables include:

- On different platforms, differences in font sizes can make text within table cells wrap differently.
- Some multimedia elements, such as Shockwave animations, embedded in table cells may crash the browser.
- Tables are not supported by all browsers (this is becoming less of an issue).
- Inconsistent interpretation of table tags and attributes between browsers, for example, Navigator 2.0 ignores background colors in table cells, although Navigator 3.0 recognizes background colors. Nested tables might be interpreted differently by different browsers.

Creating a Page Layout Grid with Tables

HTML tables are a great way to create page layout grids. The individual cells of the table can be set to specific sizes and can be filled with text, graphic, or other multimedia content.

Tables are enclosed in <TABLE></TABLE> tags. Attributes of the TABLE tag include:

- BORDER, which specifies a chiseled, 3D border to your table in pixels. Specify BORDER = 0 for page layout grids, if you don't want the user to see your layout grid.
- CELLPADDING, which is the gutter or margin inside each cell. This attribute moves the content of the cell away from the cell border.
- WIDTH, which can specify the width of the table in pixels or set it to a percentage of the visible window.

Here is some sample HTML:

```
<TABLE BORDER = 0 CELLPADDING = 4 WIDTH = 480>
</TABLE>
```

Adding Rows to Tables

To add a row to a table use the <TR></TR> tags. Attributes of the TR tag include:

- ALIGN, which specifies horizontal alignment with values of LEFT, CENTER, and RIGHT
- VALIGN, which specifies vertical alignment with values of TOP, MIDDLE, BOTTOM, and BASELINE

For example:

```
<TABLE BORDER = 0 CELLPADDING = 4 WIDTH = 480>

<TR ALIGN = CENTER VALIGN = TOP >
</TR>
</TABLE>
```

creates a table row in which the content is horizontally aligned in the center of each cell and vertically aligned to the top of the cell.

Adding Cells to Tables

You can add individual table cells using the <TD></TD> (Table Data) tags.

Attributes of the TD tag include:

- ALIGN—Horizontal alignment with values of LEFT, CENTER, and RIGHT.

- VALIGN—Vertical alignment with values of TOP, MIDDLE, BOTTOM, and BASELINE.
- ROWSPAN—The number of rows the cell spans.
- COLSPAN—The number of columns the cell spans.
- NOWRAP—Turns off automatic wrapping of content.
- WIDTH—Fix the width of the column in pixels or set it to a percentage of the visible window.

The following HTML code:

```
<TABLE BORDER = 0 CELLPADDING = 4 WIDTH = 480>

<TR ALIGN = CENTER VALIGN = TOP >

<TD ALIGN = CENTER VALIGN = TOP WIDTH = 160>
Left Cell HTML TD ALIGN = CENTER VALIGN = TOP WIDTH =
➥160
</TD>

<TD ALIGN = CENTER VALIGN = TOP WIDTH = 160>
Center Cell HTML TD ALIGN = CENTER VALIGN = TOP WIDTH =
➥160
</TD>

<TD ALIGN = CENTER VALIGN = TOP WIDTH = 160>
Right Cell HTML TD ALIGN = CENTER VALIGN = TOP WIDTH =
➥160
</TD>

</TR>
</TABLE>
```

creates a table that looks like the top part of figure 4.2. The bottom part of the figure is the same HTML table , but with `BORDER = 1`. Notice the different wrapping of cell contents.

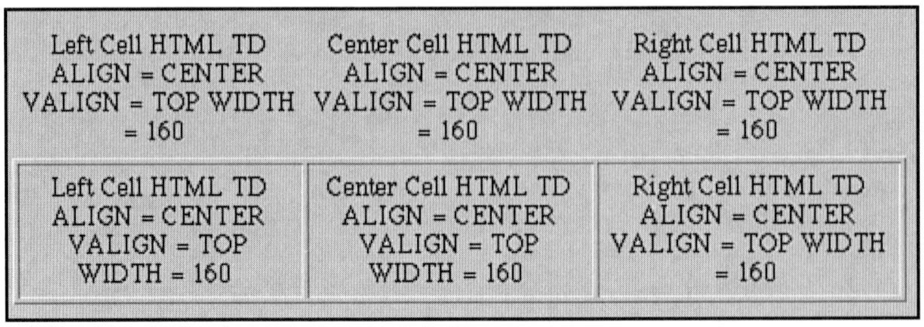

Left Cell HTML TD ALIGN = CENTER VALIGN = TOP WIDTH = 160	Center Cell HTML TD ALIGN = CENTER VALIGN = TOP WIDTH = 160	Right Cell HTML TD ALIGN = CENTER VALIGN = TOP WIDTH = 160
Left Cell HTML TD ALIGN = CENTER VALIGN = TOP WIDTH = 160	Center Cell HTML TD ALIGN = CENTER VALIGN = TOP WIDTH = 160	Right Cell HTML TD ALIGN = CENTER VALIGN = TOP WIDTH = 160

Figure 4.2

HTML table with and without a border.

Using the COLSPAN Attribute

The COLSPAN attribute enables you to create a table column that spans several table rows. For example, the following HTML creates a row that spans the entire table.

```
<TABLE BORDER = 0 CELLPADDING = 4 WIDTH = 480>

<TR ALIGN = CENTER VALIGN = TOP >

<TD ALIGN = CENTER VALIGN = TOP COLSPAN = 3>
A row that spans 3 columns
</TD>

</TR>

<TR ALIGN = CENTER VALIGN = TOP >

<TD ALIGN = CENTER VALIGN = TOP WIDTH = 160>
Left Cell HTML TD ALIGN = CENTER VALIGN = TOP WIDTH =
➥160
</TD>

<TD ALIGN = CENTER VALIGN = TOP WIDTH = 160>
Center Cell HTML TD ALIGN = CENTER VALIGN = TOP WIDTH =
➥160
</TD>

<TD ALIGN = CENTER VALIGN = TOP WIDTH = 160>
Right Cell HTML TD ALIGN = CENTER VALIGN = TOP WIDTH =
➥160
</TD>

</TR>
</TABLE>
```

This table will look like figure 4.3.

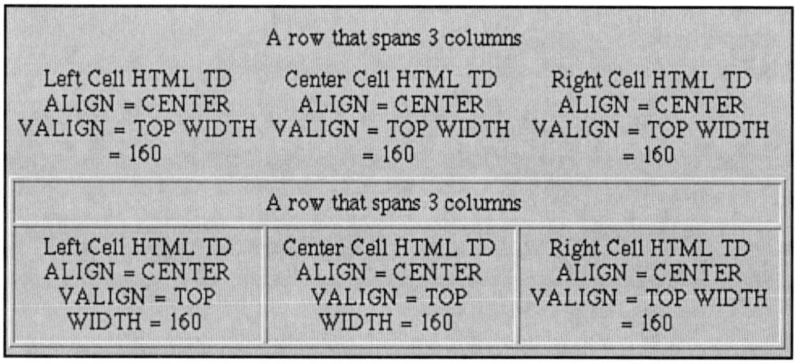

A row that spans 3 columns		
Left Cell HTML TD ALIGN = CENTER VALIGN = TOP WIDTH = 160	Center Cell HTML TD ALIGN = CENTER VALIGN = TOP WIDTH = 160	Right Cell HTML TD ALIGN = CENTER VALIGN = TOP WIDTH = 160

A row that spans 3 columns		
Left Cell HTML TD ALIGN = CENTER VALIGN = TOP WIDTH = 160	Center Cell HTML TD ALIGN = CENTER VALIGN = TOP WIDTH = 160	Right Cell HTML TD ALIGN = CENTER VALIGN = TOP WIDTH = 160

Figure 4.3

HTML table using COLSPAN.

Note

Learn more about tables at:

http://www.ncsa.uiuc.edu/General/Internet/WWW/HTMLPrimer.html#TA

The size of this table is fixed using the WIDTH attribute. The table won't change size if the user resizes the browser window. The appearance of the text within the cell depends on the fonts set in the user preferences, fonts available on the local system, and font display differences between operating systems.

Creating Navigation Bars with Tables

You can create navigational button bars with tables by putting hypertext links in your table cells. Add borders to give buttons that chiseled 3D look.

But that's not all! You can also place inline GIFs in table cells. By making GIFs links, each cell graphic becomes a button. Surround the IMG tag with an `<A HREF = "myLink"></A>` tag to create a link for the GIF. See Chapters 5, "Designing Multimedia Web Pages," and 6, "Using Graphics to Add Dynamic Content," for details. Sometimes a table with a few small graphics loads faster than an image map.

Netscape Navigator 3.0 Enhancements for Tables

The BGCOLOR attribute enables you to specify a background color for your table. You can use it with the TABLE, TR, TH, and TD tags to specify the background color for the entire table, an entire row, the table header, or individual cells. This attribute is supported by MSIE 3 as well as Netscape.

Here's some sample HTML:

```
<TABLE >
<TR>
<TD BGCOLOR=#000000>
Colored cell
</TD>
</TR>

<TR>
<TD BGCOLOR=#FFFFFF>
Another Colored cell
</TD>
</TR>
</TABLE>
```

This code creates a table with two cells. The first cell is black and the second cell is white.

Frames

Frames are a way to divide up the browser window into multiple rectangular regions or windows. Each frame displays a separate HTML document and can be updated independently of other frames (see fig. 4.4). You can also target specific frames from hyperlinks and events in another frame; for example providing a hyperlinked table of contents in one frame that displays the actual content in a separate frame.

Frames enable you to preserve context, such as a graphic identity banner or table of contents, while the user drills down through the information space displayed in a separate frame.

Frames can be made so that they have:

- Resizable borders
- Invisible borders
- Fixed, inflexible size
- Scroll bars or no scroll bars

Frames are supported in Netscape Navigator 2.0 and later, and in MSIE 3 and later.

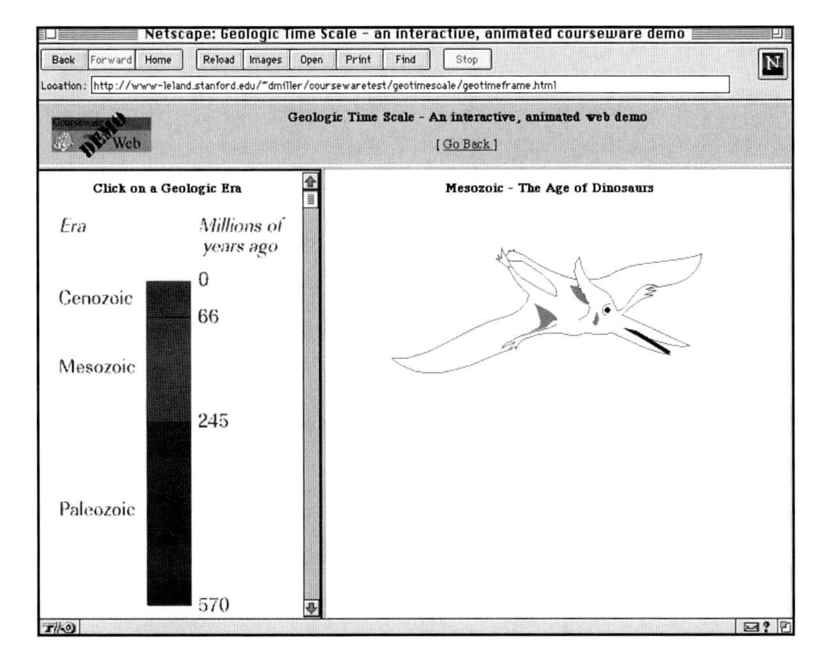

Figure 4.4

Using a client-side image map in one frame to display Shockwave animations in another frame.

Drawbacks of Frames

Frames have drawbacks, such as:

- They can use a lot of memory.
- They can take a long time to load.
- Navigation with frames can be counter-intuitive because pressing the Back button jumps out of the framed document entirely. (This issue has been addressed in version 3.0 of Navigator and MSIE.)
- Not all browsers support frames (although Navigator 2.0 and later and MSIE 3 and later support them, as mentioned above.)
- Browsers that do support frames don't support all the same features, such as the Netscape enhancements described in the following section.

Creating Frames

You divide the browser window into frames using the <FRAMESET></FRAMESET> tags. The FRAMESET tag can take the following attributes:

- ROWS—Creates rows of frames.
- COLS—Creates columns of frames.

These attributes take as values a fixed pixel size, a percentage size of the browser window, or an asterisk "*", which indicates the frame should take up all remaining space.

You define the frames within a FRAMESET tag using, you guessed it, the FRAME tag.

The FRAME tag can take the following attributes:

- SRC—The URL to the HTML document to be displayed in the frame.
- NAME—The name of the frame, useful when targeting the frame with a URL.
- MARGINWIDTH—The space on either side of a document in a frame.
- MARGINHEIGHT—The space above and below a document in a frame.

- SCROLLING—Enables or disables scroll bars for the frame. Possible values are YES, NO, and AUTO.
- NORESIZE—Prevents the user from resizing the frames.

The frame document in figure 4.4 was created with this HTML:

```
<FRAMESET ROWS="62, *">
<FRAME SRC="geotimetitle.html " NAME="title"
SCROLLING="no" NORESIZE>

      <FRAMESET COLS="270, 320">
      <FRAME SRC="geotime.html" NAME="imapframe"
➥MARGINWIDTH="10"
      MARGINHEIGHT="10"  NORESIZE>
      <FRAME SRC="shock.html" NAME="shockframe"
➥MARGINWIDTH=0
      MARGINHEIGHT="10" NORESIZE>
      </FRAMESET>

</FRAMESET>
<NOFRAME>
This demo requires Netscape 2.0.  Please <A HREF="ftp:/
➥/ftp.netscape.com">
download</A> Netscape 2.0 to view this demo.
To view the interactive, animations you will need
the <A HREF="http://www.macromedia.com/">Macromedia
➥Director Shockwave plug-in</A>.<P>
<NOFRAME>
```

The <NOFRAME><NOFRAME> tag enables you to provide alternate content to browsers that don't support the FRAMESET or FRAME tag.

> **Note**
>
> Find out more about using frames at:
>
> Frames Basics
>
> **http://home.netscape.com/comprod/products/navigator/version_2.0/frames/index.html**
>
> Frames Syntax
>
> **http://home.netscape.com/assist/net_sites/frame_syntax.html**
>
> Frames Implementation
>
> **http://home.netscape.com/assist/net_sites/frame_implement.html**

Netscape 3.0 Enhancements for Frames

The FRAMEBORDER, BORDER, and BORDERCOLOR attributes to the FRAME and FRAMESET tags enable you to control the following:

- Whether frames have borders
- Border thickness in pixels
- Color of frame borders

At this time, MSIE 3.0 supports the FRAMEBORDER attribute, but not the other attributes.

The FRAMEBORDER attribute can be set in the FRAMESET tag or in the FRAME tag. The possible values of FRAMEBORDER are YES and NO. The default value is YES.

When used in the FRAMESET tag, FRAMEBORDER sets the default value for all frames in that frameset. When used in the FRAME tag, FRAMEBORDER sets the presence of borders for a specific frame. A border is turned off only if all the frames sharing it have their FRAMEBORDER attribute set to NO.

Netscape Navigator 3.0 HTML Extensions for Layout and Typography

Note

For more information on the new frame enhancements visit:

`http://home.netscape.com/comprod/products/navigator/version_3.0/new_features.html`

Netscape 3 introduced several tags that enable you to control page layout and alignment. As of this writing they are not recognized by other browsers, except for the FACE attribute of the FONT tag which is recognized by MSIE 3.0.

MULTICOL

The `<MULTICOL></MULTICOL>` tag displays text that is contained within the tag in multiple columns. For versions of Navigator before version 3, and other browsers that don't recognize this tag, the text is displayed in a single column.

The MULTICOL tag takes three attributes:

- COLS—Controls the number of columns. This attribute is required.
- GUTTER—Controls the space between the columns.
- WIDTH—Controls the total width of all columns together, although Netscape documentation indicates that this controls the width of the individual columns. The columns all have the same width and are divided equally within the width specified in the WIDTH attribute. The WIDTH attribute can be in absolute pixels or percentage of the browser window. If the WIDTH attribute is not set, column width is adjusted to fill the browser window.

Here's some sample HTML:

```
<MULTICOL COLS=2 GUTTER=8 WIDTH=100%>

Some text some more text. This will be displayed in two
columns that take up the entire width of the browser
window. Text flows from the first column into the
second.
</MULTICOL>
```

SPACER

The SPACER tag, introduced by Navigator 3.0, enables you to set up rectangular areas of white space, indent text lines, and increase the space between lines. The SPACER tag is ignored by Navigator 2.0 and other browsers that don't recognize this tag.

The new SPACER tag has these attributes:

- TYPE—Can take three values: HORIZONTAL, VERTICAL, and BLOCK
- SIZE
- WIDTH
- HEIGHT
- ALIGN

Use the SPACER tag to do these tasks:

- This HTML code indents the text line in which it occurs by 50 pixels:

  ```
  <SPACER TYPE=HORIZONTAL SIZE=50>
  ```

- This HTML code creates vertical white space of 50 pixels:

  ```
  <SPACER TYPE=VERTICAL SIZE=50>
  ```

- This HTML code creates a block of white space 50×50 pixels:

  <SPACER TYPE=BLOCK WIDTH=50 HEIGHT=50>

  Text flows around this block as if it were an invisible GIF placed in the HTML document using the IMG tag.

FONT FACE

The FACE attribute of the FONT tag enables you to specify a particular font for a range of text. The font must be present on the user's system. You can specify multiple fonts. When the page is displayed the browser goes through the list of fonts until it finds one that is present on the user's system. If none of the fonts are present, it displays the text with the default font.

This tag is supported by MSIE 3.0 and Navigator 3.0. In browsers that do not support this tag, such as MSIE 2.0 and Navigator 2.0, it is ignored.

<FONT FACE="HELVETICA, ARIAL"><B>This text will display in Arial bold or Helvetica bold, depending on whether you have a PC or a Macintosh.</B></FONT>

MSIE 3.0 Extensions for Layout and Typography

MSIE 3.0 is the first browser to support Cascading Style Sheets (CSS), which is a proposed part of the HTML 3.2 standard. It also supports many other enhancements in typography and layout that are not yet supported by other browsers. Visit `http://microsoft.com/ie/ie3/` for all the latest news.

Note

Netscape 3 has also introduced other enhancements to improve HTML layout and typography, including HTML 3.2 extensions to the paragraph tag. To find out about the latest supported tags visit:

`http://home.netscape.com/comprod/products/navigator/version_3.0/`

or

`http://help.netscape.com/docs.html`

Getting Ready for HTML 3.2

Here are a few tips to help you get your HTML documents ready for the new HTML 3.2 standard. The HTML 3.2 standard is still in draft stage and hasn't been finalized. Backward compatibility with previous HTML standards is a top priority. If you incorporate the following suggestions into your current HTML documents it will make upgrading and migrating to the new standard easier, and ensure a measure of compatibility with future browsers.

- Make sure your entire document is enclosed by <HTML></HTML> tags.
- Use the <HEAD></HEAD> tags.

- Make sure the body of your document is enclosed in <BODY></BODY> tags.
- Put the <P> tag at the beginning of paragraphs. It wouldn't hurt to enclose paragraphs in <P></P> tags. Eventually, browsers conforming to the new standards may not support a less rigorous application of the <P> tag.

Multimedia Web pages push the limits of Web systems and HTML. This chapter discusses page and presentation design for multimedia on the Web with a special emphasis on optimizing the user experience.

chapter

5

Designing Multimedia Web Pages

Since the advent of Netscape Plug-Ins and OLE/ActiveX controls, multimedia objects can be embedded directly into the Web page. From a layout and presentation perspective, this is a big improvement over the disconnected floating windows provided by helper apps. But it does present its own issues, such as how to integrate the multimedia element with the rest of the page and how to give the user control of the media and provide a user-friendly experience.

This chapter discusses some of the issues of page design and Web-based multimedia. It provides tips on how to:

- Design pages that integrate multimedia with the rest of the Web page
- Improve the user's experience by creating user-friendly Web multimedia
- Improve download time and maximize performance
- Use HTML extensions to embed multimedia in HTML documents
- Display multimedia consistently in different browsers and platforms

Integrating Multimedia in Web Pages

Plan how you will integrate multimedia elements into the Web page. As you create your Web-based multimedia, ask yourself these questions:

- Will the background of your multimedia element match the background of your page?
- Does the size of the multimedia element fit within the page layout grids you have set up? (See Chapter 4 "Designing the Layout of Your Web pages,"for more information on grid-based page layout.)
- Will other elements on the page, such as text, graphic identity elements, and navigational controls, also fit on the page?
- Is the multimedia element rendered in the 216-color, cross-platform browser palette? If the multimedia element asserts a custom palette on 8-bit or 256-color displays, colors in the rest of the Web page and in the rest of the user's display may change unpredictably or contain dithering artifacts. These and other palette issues are discussed in detail in Chapter 6 "Using Graphics to Add Dynamic Content."
- Will your graphics and multimedia palettes conflict? This is a common problem when multiple graphic elements are concerned. You may have created adaptive or custom palettes to maximize the appearance of individual graphic elements. When all the elements are included on the same page the total number of colors used will exceed 256, the limit of 8-bit displays. Again, color management strategies are discussed in Chapter 6.
- Do you have competing multimedia elements, such as two looping animations that distract the user and diffuse the focus of your page?
- Do you have multiple sounds playing? Are the sounds loud, looping, or annoying in some way?
- Do you enable the user to control time-based media?

Warning

If you embed your multimedia element within a table cell or frame, be sure to test it on multiple platforms and browsers. Some first generation Plug-Ins crash when embedded in tables or frames.

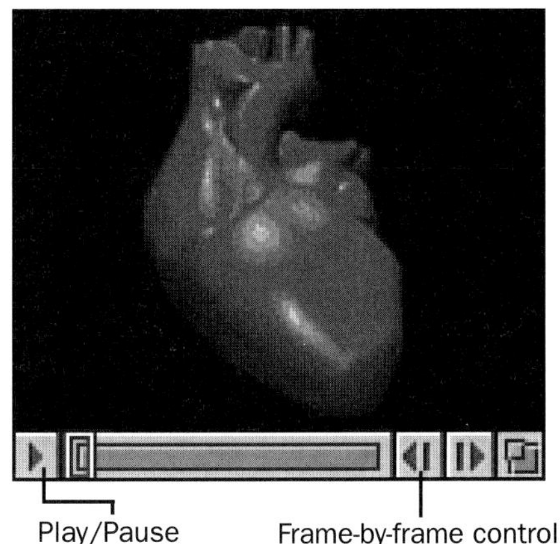

Figure 5.1

Standard QuickTime controller for embedded multimedia.

- Does your multimedia element, such as a Shockwave animation or Java applet, take over the processor on the local machine so that all interactivity or other processor activity on the computer grinds to a halt? Test your pages under low memory and slow processor speeds to see if they are usable on minimum systems.
- If you have many multimedia elements on a page, are they competing for system resources? For example, are they trying to play back two sounds at the same time on a Windows machine?
- Does the multimedia element fit within the visual context of the page, or is it obtrusive and distracting? Are palettes and graphic styles similar between page elements and multimedia elements? Consider integrating graphic elements from the page into the multimedia element to reinforce stylistic unity and context.

Warning

Using multiple media elements in general, such as two sounds, three GIF animations and a VRML world, can overload processors and the user's ability to view your site.

Interactivity and User Control

Users like to feel in control of the computer. They don't like the feeling of losing control of their system. When you add multimedia to your Web page you may want to:

- Provide ways for users to stop or pause looping animations and looping sounds
- Control sound volume
- Control playback and media manipulation with the standard controllers provided by such media as QuickTime and Shockwave for Freehand
- Provide sophisticated interactivity with Shockwave for Director/Authorware, Toolbook, IconAuthor, CelAnimator, WebPainter, Java Applets, or OLE/ActiveX controls

Show Sizes and Download Times

A hyperlink to a multimedia-rich page should give users some indication of what to expect if they click on that link. Will clicking a link initiate a potentially long download that will tie up the computer for many minutes? Warn users before they commit to a large download. Give your users some idea about the download time before they click on a link or go to a page that is media intensive. One way to do this is to indicate the size in kilobytes and the estimated download time next to each link. Include the media size in KB and the estimated download time over 14.4 modems (about one second per kilobyte). You can include this information in a smaller relative type size using the SIZE attribute of the FONT tag; for example:

```
<FONT SIZE = -2> 107 KB (about 1.5 minutes on a 14.4
➥modem)</FONT>
```

Thumbnails

Another way to provide a teaser or hint of what a long media download will provide is to create a small, low-bandwidth *thumbnail* graphic of a larger file such as a large 24-bit graphic or long QuickTime movie.

You can also create short clips of video or animation. For example, before downloading a 500 KB QuickTime movie, you could provide a small three or four frame GIF animation. This animation will play on Netscape 2.0 or later and MSIE 3.0 or later and give the users a taste of the full-blown movie.

Provide Low-Bandwidth Alternate Content

It's usually a good idea to provide alternate content for browsers that don't support multimedia features or for users who don't want to download the multimedia. A good way to do this is to provide a single frame from a QuickTime movie as a gif, or a text description of the media element.

If you choose to do so, use the NOEMBED tag to provide alternate content. See the section "Alternate Content" for more information.

You could provide alternate pages or provide for information on two versions of a media element; for example, a very short 8-bit video clip and longer 16-bit clip.

Provide Helper App Support

If you embed a multimedia element directly in a Web page, and the multimedia element also has helper app support, then you can also provide a link to the media element. This way, users who don't have the necessary Plug-In or browser, but have helper app functionality, can still view the media if they have their helper apps set up correctly.

Provide External Links to Helper Apps and Plug-Ins

Your multimedia Web page may require helper applications or Plug-Ins that users do not have. Provide links to places on the Web where they can find the necessary programs. The upcoming section on HTML shows how to use the PLUGINSPAGE attribute with the EMBED tag to point users' browsers to appropriate download sites.

Provide Low-Bandwidth Entry Points

One way to shield users from large downloads is to provide an entry-point page or a table of contents page before going to a media-rich part of your site. You can display thumbnails, indicate download times, and provide links to Plug-Ins and helper apps from this single low-bandwidth page.

HTML for Multimedia

Note

An HTML tag is part of an HTML file surrounded with greater-than and less-than symbols (an example of which is <EMBED>), and interpreted by a Web browser that controls various attributes of the text, image, or other elements.

This section provides an overview of the HTML tags that you will need to embed multimedia objects in your Web page. Specifically, this section shows you how to:

- Provide rich content such as sound and digital video with the HREF tag
- Use the IMG tag to provide inline graphics
- Use the EMBED tag to embed inline multimedia in Netscape Navigator 2.0 or later
- Use Internet Explorer tags to embed inline multimedia
- Use these HTML tags so that your multimedia Web pages load fast and can be viewed by both Netscape Navigator and MSIE

Browser Support of Tags

The EMBED tag is used by Netscape to embed multimedia elements that require Netscape Plug-Ins to display. Beginning with Netscape 3.0, many multimedia Plug-Ins are automatically installed with Navigator, so you don't have to worry about users having the appropriate Plug-Ins. As of this writing, Netscape 3.0 will automatically support the following media types:

- QuickTime for Mac and Windows
- Video for Windows
- AIFF audio
- WAV audio
- AU audio
- GIF animation
- VRML worlds

MSIE supports a different set of multimedia tags that are only supported in MSIE. MSIE also has introduced a different Plug-In technology called ActiveX that is based on OLE (Object Linking and Embedding) technology. At this time, OLE/ActiveX is only supported in MSIE 3.0 for Windows 95 and Windows NT. MSIE 3.0 will purportedly support Netscape Plug-Ins. Tags that MSIE supports are discussed later in this chapter.

The following table lists browser support for multimedia tags at the time of this writing:

Table 5.1

Multimedia Tag Support

Feature	Netscape 2.0	MSIE 2.0	Netscape 3.0	MSIE 3.0
Plug-Ins	Yes	Mac only	Yes	n/a
ActiveX	No	No	No	Windows 95 and NT only
EMBED tag	Yes	Mac only	Yes	n/a
MSIE tags	No	Yes	No	Yes
OBJECT tag	No	No	No	Windows 95 and NT only

Note

The draft HTML 3.2 standard contains a new tag called the OBJECT tag. The OBJECT tag, as proposed, provides a standardized way to embed multimedia elements in the Web page. The OBJECT tag specs, as of this writing, can be found at the site presented below. At this time the final HTML 3.2 specs have not been determined.

Find out the latest about the OBJECT tag at:

`http://www.w3.org/pub/WWW/TR/WD-object#object`

and the evolving HTML 3.2 specs in general at:

`http://www.w3.org/`

There are seven different ways you can use HTML in multimedia:

1. Helper Apps (HREF tag)
2. Graphics
3. Netscape Plug-Ins
4. Multimedia extensions for MSIE
5. OLE/Active X controls
6. Java applets
7. The new Object tag

These are covered in more detail in the following sections.

HREF and Helper Apps

The simplest way to provide multimedia content on your site is to link to the content files using the HREF tag. This way is compatible with most browsers, but requires users to:

- Have an appropriate helper application
- Configure their browsers to use the helper application correctly

Clicking on the link initiates download of the media file. After the file has been completely downloaded, the browser automatically launches a helper application to display the media. Your browser knows which helper application to launch based on the file name extension of the data. For example, if your browser is asked to display a file with the `.mov` extension, it realizes it is a QuickTime movie and then automatically opens the file with SimpleText or PLAYER.EXE. See Table 5.2 for a list of file extensions.

Here is an example of some HTML code that creates a link to a QuickTime movie:

```
<A HREF="MyQTMovie.mov"> QuickTime movie </A>
```

`"MyQTMovie.mov"` is the path name to the QuickTime movie file on the Web server. In this case, the QuickTime movie file is in the same directory as the HTML document. Note the `.mov` extension on the file name. The file name of your media must have the appropriate extension to launch the helper app.

Table 5.2

Some Common File Types and File Name Extensions

File Type	Extension
Plain text	.txt
HTML document	.html
GIF image	.gif
TIFF image	.tiff
X Bitmap image	.xbm
JPEG image	.jpg or .jpeg
PostScript file	.ps
AIFF audio file	.aiff
AU audio file	.au
WAV audio file	.wav
MIDI sound file	.mid
QuickTime movie	.mov
MPEG movie	.mpeg or .mpg
VfW movie	.avi
VRML	.wrl

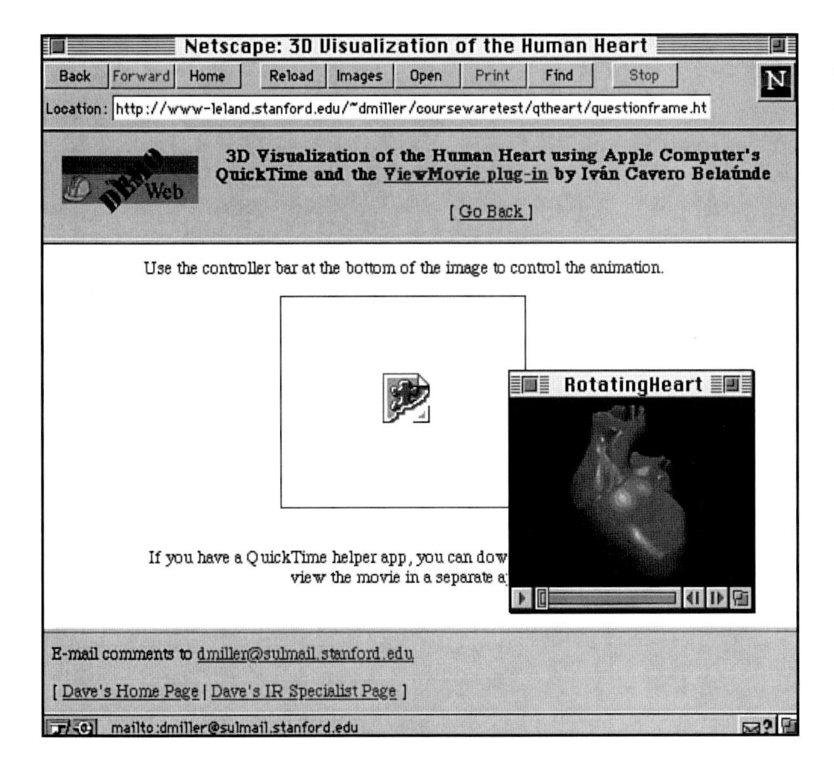

Figure 5.2

A QuickTime animation displayed by a helper app.

Configuring Helper Apps

To provide multimedia using helper apps, users must correctly set up their browsers. To configure a helper app for QuickTime, for example, you need to tell your browser that files ending in `.mov` and `.qt` have the MIME type video/quicktime and should be launched by an appropriate QuickTime player application such as SimpleText, MoviePlayer, or PLAYER.EXE, depending upon which system you have.

If you have Netscape Navigator, it should come already configured for playing many types of multimedia content. Netscape Navigator 3.0 comes with several multimedia Plug-Ins. Netscape Navigator 2.0 comes configured for many common helper apps. Different browsers will have different procedures to configure helper apps. The following directions show how to setup a helper application for QuickTime content in Netscape Navigator 2.0. The process is similar in other browsers and for other multimedia types.

1. From the Netscape Options menu, choose General Preferences/Helpers.
2. Type in the Mime type "video."

3. Type in the Mime sub-type "quicktime."
4. Type in the extension ".qt,mov."
5. Set the Action to "Launch Application."
6. Click on "Browse," and select the application you want to use to display and play back QuickTime content, such as MoviePlayer or SimpleText on a Macintosh or PLAYER.EXE on Windows.
7. Close the preferences panel of Netscape, and close Netscape. Then, restart Netscape.

Obtaining Helper Apps

- You can find general information about helper applications at:

  http://home.netscape.com/assist/helper_apps/index.html

- Helper apps for Macintosh systems can be found at:

  Info-Mac HyperArchive

  http://hyperarchive.lcs.mit.edu/HyperArchive.html

  University of Michigan Archives

  http://www-personal.umich.edu/~sdamask/umich-mirrors/

  University of Texas Mac Archive

  http://wwwhost.ots.utexas.edu/mac/

  Netscape

  http://home.netscape.com/assist/helper_apps/
  ➥mac_helpers.html

- Helper apps for Unix systems can be found at:

  NCSA

  ftp://ftp.ncsa.uiuc.edu/Mosaic/Unix/viewers/

  Netscape

  http://home.netscape.com/assist/helper_apps/

```
➥unix_helpers.html
```

Helper apps for Windows systems can be found at:

Stroud's Consummate Winsock List

```
http://www.frontiernet.net/cwsapps/inx2.html
```

Netscape

```
http://home.netscape.com/assist/helper_apps/
➥windows_helpers.html
```

IMG

Inline graphics are embedded in HTML documents using the IMG tag. The IMG tag requires an SRC attribute. This attribute is an URL to the source graphic in quotes. The source graphic should have a file name with the appropriate extension such as `.gif`. The graphic will be displayed inline or directly in thc Web page. The IMG tag is supported by all graphical browsers. The IMG tag also has other attributes, such as ALIGN and ALT, to control the appearance of the graphic. These attributes are discussed in the following sections.

The IMG tag is also used by MSIE to embed multimedia content. This use of the IMG tag is only recognized by MSIE. MSIE's use of the IMG tag to embed other types of multimedia is discussed later in this chapter.

ALIGN

The ALIGN attribute of the IMG tag has three values:

- TOP
- MIDDLE
- BOTTOM

and is written in this form:

```
<IMG SRC="myGreatGraphic.gif" ALIGN = TOP>
```

This attribute will align the current line of text to the top, middle, or bottom of the image. The default behavior is aligned to the bottom of the image.

ALT

The ALT attribute enables you to display alternate text that will be displayed:

- In text-only browsers
- If images have been turned off
- If images cannot load for some other reason

ALT is written in the form:

```
<IMG SRC="myGreatGraphic.gif" ALT= "You're missing my
➥fabulous graphic!">
```

Include an ALT attribute with all your IMG tags so users get an idea of what they are missing. The alternate text will act as a link if the image is also a link.

Netscape Navigator Extensions to the IMG Tag

This section describes Netscape extensions to the IMG tag that are supported in Netscape Navigator 2.0 or later. Many of these are so useful that they have been supported by other browsers and might be adopted in the next HTML standard.

LOWSRC

The LOWSRC attribute enables you to specify another graphic file that will download first and display before the graphic file that is specified in the SRC attribute. You can use this to download a low-resolution, low-color-depth version of your SRC file that will download and display quickly. As the main SRC graphic downloads it is displayed over the LOWSRC graphic. LOWSRC is commonly used to display a 1-bit, black-and-white version of a larger color graphic.

The 1-bit graphic downloads quickly and then the color graphic is displayed. The overall impression is of a snappy download with the color graphic being poured into the black-and-white version. You can also use the LOWSRC attribute to perform simple two-frame animation. The LOWSRC graphic will not be displayed if the SRC graphic referenced by the SRC attribute is in the disk or memory cache. So, if a user visits your site twice in a session, the LOWSRC graphic will probably not be displayed the second time.

HTML for the LOWSRC attribute looks like this:

```
<IMG LOWSRC = "myTeenyGraphic.gif"
➥SRC="myGreatGraphic.gif" ALT= "Logo Graphic">
```

WIDTH and HEIGHT

The WIDTH and HEIGHT attributes specify the dimensions of your graphic or embedded multimedia element. They are used by Netscape 2.0 and MSIE 3.0 or later to layout text around an image before the image is downloaded and are written:

```
<IMG SRC="myGreatGraphic.gif" ALT= "Logo Graphic"
➥WIDTH = 160 HEIGHT = 120>
```

You can use the WIDTH and HEIGHT attributes to scale an image, but you can get better results scaling images in a graphics program. You can also give the HEIGHT and WIDTH as percentage values of the browser window, but browsers other than Netscape Navigator, such as MSIE, will interpret these as pixel values.

Tip

Use the WIDTH and HEIGHT attributes to speed up the download of the text on your Web page and help give the impression of snappy response time. In addition, some early versions of Netscape Plug-Ins required these attributes in all graphics and multimedia elements for the Plug-In to work properly.

BORDER

The BORDER attribute enables you to put a simple black border or frame around a graphic. If you use a graphic in conjunction with the HREF tag, you can turn the border off by setting the BORDER = 0. For example:

```
<A HREF = "anotherWebPage.html"><IMG SRC="myLink.gif"
➥ALT= "A link somewhere else" BORDER = 0></A>
```

will turn the border off around your link graphic.

Alignment Extensions

Netscape has introduced several alignment extensions for in-line graphics. Probably the most useful of these are:

- ALIGN=LEFT
- ALIGN=RIGHT values for the ALIGN attribute
- HSPACE
- VSPACE attributes

The ALIGN=LEFT and ALIGN=RIGHT values align a graphic to the left or right margins of the page, respectively. You can use the HSPACE and VSPACE attributes to control the white space around a graphic. For example:

```
<IMG SRC="myGreat.gif" ALT= "A really great graphic"
➥ALIGN = RIGHT HSPACE = 16>
```

aligns the graphic to the right edge of the Web page and gives 16 pixels of horizontal space around the graphic before text is displayed.

Netscape has also introduced these new values for the ALIGN attribute:

- ALIGN = ABSBOTTOM aligns the bottom of the graphic with the bottom of the line.
- ALIGN = ABSMIDDLE aligns the middle of the graphic with the middle of the line.
- ALIGN = TEXTTOP aligns the the graphic with the top of the text.

Netscape Plug-Ins

Netscape Plug-Ins are external code modules that extend the functionality of the Netscape Web browser. Much of the inline multimedia content on the Web is implemented with Netscape Plug-Ins. One of the down sides of using Plug-Ins is that users must download the appropriate Plug-In and place it in Navigator's Plug-Ins folder before they can view multimedia content. Fortunately, several Plug-Ins are automatically installed with Netscape Navigator 3.0. These automatically installed Plug-Ins enable out-of-the-box playback of:

- QuickTime for Mac and Windows
- Video for Windows for Windows 95 and Windows NT
- AIFF,WAV, and AU digital audio
- MIDI sound
- VRML worlds

QuickTime Virtual Reality (QTVR) playback is enabled by the addition of a component from Apple Computer. CoolTalk, Netscape's Internet audio conferencing and data sharing extension, is implemented as a helper app.

Support for Netscape Plug-Ins are supposed to be included in MSIE 3.0. Netscape Plug-Ins are also supported by CyberDog, Apple Computers Open Doc-based suite of Internet tools.

LiveConnect is Netscape's term for the integration of Plug-Ins, Java applets, JavaScript functions, and your Web page. LiveConnect enables the creation of more dynamic, interactive Web pages. For example, you could use a JavaScript function to set the start frame of an embedded video based on user input at run-time. Netscape Plug-Ins need to be rewritten to support the LiveConnect features. Several Plug-Ins included with Netscape Navigator 3.0 are LiveConnect enabled. These Plug-Ins and their new capabilties are discussed in subsequent chapters on creating multimedia content.

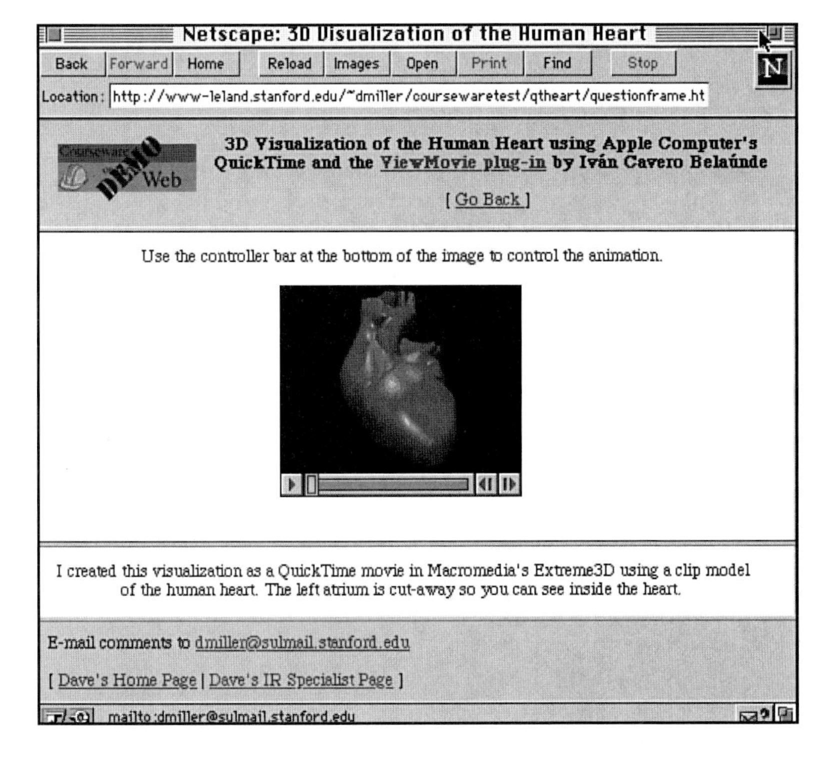

Figure 5.3

Embedded multimedia with a Netscape Plug-In.

EMBED

To embed Plug-In media in a Web page use the EMBED tag. Netscape Navigator 2.0 or later recognizes this tag. Here is sample HTML:

```
<EMBED SRC="mymovie.dcr" WIDTH=175 HEIGHT=135 >
```

The value of the SRC attribute is the URL to the media element, similar to the SRC tag for IMG (graphic) elements. Be sure the file name in your SRC tag has the appropriate file name extension for the media type. In this example, the extension ".dcr" indicates a Shockwave animation.

Unfortunately, the ALT attribute doesn't work with the EMBED tag as of this writing. To provide alternate content in browsers that do not recognize the EMBED tag, such as MSIE 2.0 on Windows, use the NOEMBED tag.

PLUGINSPAGE

Note

MSIE 2.0 for Windows doesn't support the EMBED tag or Netscape Plug-Ins. When MSIE 2.0 encounters a Web page with an EMBED tag, it displays a gray rectangle in place of the multimedia element referenced by the EMBED tag.

MSIE 3.0 will purportedly support the EMBED tag and Netscape Plug-In. As of this writing, MSIE 3.0 will not load the necessary Netscape Plug-In but instead prompt the user to download an alternate ActiveX control.

MSIE 2.0 for Macintosh does support the EMBED tag and will display most Netscape Plug-Ins, although some features may not be supported, such as network extensions to Shockwave.

Include the PLUGINSPAGE parameter for users who may not have the necessary Plug-In installed. The PLUGINSPAGE parameter directs Web browsers without the necessary Plug-In to a Web page where they can download the appropriate Plug-In. The value of the PLUGINSPAGE parameter is a fully-qualified URL, in quotes, where the user can download the appropriate Plug-In. Here is some sample HTML code:

```
<EMBED SRC="myQT.mov" HEIGHT=144 WIDTH=160 PLUGINSPAGE
➥= "http://quicktime.apple.com/qt/sw/sw.html" >
```

Alternate Content

This section discusses aspects of the following topics:

- Alternate content for browsers that don't support the EMBED tag
- Alternate content for Microsoft browsers

NOEMBED

Even though many multimedia playback capabilities are standard equipment with Netscape and Microsoft browsers, many users will not be using these browsers or will not have multimedia Plug-Ins installed on their machines.

To provide multimedia content for these users, follow these guidelines:

- For browsers that don't support the EMBED tag, use the NOEMBED tag to provide alternate content.

- Always use the PLUGINSPAGE parameter (described in the previous section) of the EMBED tag to point users to an URL where they can download the appropriate Plug-In.
- For users that have helper apps correctly configured, provide a link to your movie with the HREF tag.

The following is sample HTML that implements all these suggestions. This example uses QuickTime multimedia content, but this technique will work for other multimedia data types that use Netscape Plug-Ins.

```
<EMBED SRC="MyQT.mov" HEIGHT=144 WIDTH=160 PLUGINSPAGE
➥= "http://quicktime.apple.com/qt/sw/sw.html">
```

```
<NOEMBED>
```

```
<IMG SRC="MyQTFrame.gif" HEIGHT=120 WIDTH=160>
```

If you don't have the QuickTime Plug-In, but have a QuickTime helper app, click on the link below to view the QuickTime movie.

```
</NOEMBED>
```

View the <A HREF="MyQT.mov"> QuickTime movie </A> if you have your browser set up with the right helper application.

Browsers that don't support the EMBED tag will display the file MyQTFrame.gif and also enable users to view the original QuickTime file if they have helper apps. In the instance where browsers support the EMBED tag but the users lack Plug-Ins to play QuickTime, the users can still see the content using a helper app.

Providing Alternate Content for Microsoft Browsers

MSIE 2.0 or later uses the DYNSRC attribute with the IMG tag to embed AVI movies and VRML worlds in a Web page. Following is sample HTML that implements alternate content for MSIE 2.0 for Windows. This example uses QuickTime multimedia content, but this technique will work for other multimedia data types that use Netscape Plug-Ins:

```
<EMBED SRC="MyQT.mov" HEIGHT=144 WIDTH=160 PLUGINSPAGE
➥= "http://quicktime.apple.com/qt/sw/sw.html">
```

```
<NOEMBED>
```

```
<IMG SRC="MyQTFrame.gif"  DYNSRC = "MyQT.avi"
➥HEIGHT=120 WIDTH=160>
If you don't have the QuickTime Plug-In, but have a
QuickTime helper app, click on the link below to view
the movie.
</NOEMBED>
```

You can also view the original <A HREF="MyQT.mov"> QuickTime movie </A> if you have your browser set up with the right helper application.

On Windows versions of MSIE 2.0, this HTML will play an alternate AVI movie and enable users to view the original QuickTime file, if they have helper apps. Other browsers that don't support the EMBED and don't support the Microsoft DYNSRC tag will display the file "MyQTFrame.gif" and also enable the user to view the original QuickTime file if they have helper apps.

On Macintosh versions of MSIE 2.0, the browser will attempt to load the appropriate Netscape Plug-In if present, otherwise it will show an error message. The user can click on the link <A HREF= "MyQT.mov"> QuickTime movie </A> and MSIE 2.0 or later will download the QuickTime file and play it in a separate, floating window without the need of a helper app. Other media types will be played or viewed by helper apps if the browser has been configured correctly.

Netscape's Use of OLE

On Windows 95 and Windows NT systems, if a Plug-In is not present to handle the media type encountered in the EMBED tag, Netscape Navigator 2.0 and later will play multimedia as an embedded OLE object within the browser page. Navigator will use OLE associations set up in the Windows 95 file type association registry. To edit the file associations:

1. Launch Windows Internet Explorer.
2. Choose Options under the View menu.
3. Click on File Types.
4. To add a new type, click the New Type button; to edit an existing type, select a registered file type and click the Edit button.

The OLE object will be displayed within the dimensions specified in the WIDTH and HEIGHT attributes of the EMBED tag. If the application used to display the object has a controller, such as MPLAYER.EXE for AVI files, the media will be scaled to make room for the controller. If playback of media as an OLE object is a possibility, test your page to see if there are unpredictable interactions or behavior. This is mainly an issue with Netscape Navigator 2.0, since Netscape Navigator 3.0 has built-in support for the most popular multimedia types.

Using OLE/ActiveX Controls in Netscape

ActiveX controls

ActiveX is Microsoft's component software architecture for the Web based on OLE (Object Linking and Embedding). It is similar in spirit to Netscape Plug-Ins. The external OLE/ActiveX modules are called *controls*. **OLE/ActiveX control** are a new element on the Web, and are an alternate way to embed multimedia content in Web pages. At this time, the only browsers that support OLE/ActiveX controls natively are MSIE 3.0 for Windows 95 and Windows NT. Other platforms and browsers may be supported by the time you read this.

Although Netscape Navigator doesn't natively support OLE/ActiveX controls, you can add OLE/ActiveX capabilities to Navigator 2.0 or later using a Netscape Plug-In with the EMBED tag.

As of this writing, two Plug-Ins, NCompass from NCompass Labs and OpenScape from OneWave Inc., enable you to embed OLE/ActiveX controls. Find out the latest about these Plug-Ins at:

`http://www.ncompasslabs.com/`

`http://www.busWeb.com/"`

Multimedia Extensions for MSIE

MSIE for Windows 2.0 or later uses the IMG tag and BGSOUND tag to embed multimedia elements in an HTML document. The Microsoft extensions to the IMG and BGSOUND tags are only recognized by Microsoft browsers.

In MSIE 3.0 for Windows 95 and Windows NT, OLE/ActiveX controls are embedded in HTML documents using the OBJECT tag, discussed later in this section.

As of this writing, the feature set of MSIE 3.0 had not been finalized. Multimedia support in MSIE 3.0 will probably be through external OLE/ActiveX controls with backward compatibility for tags used in MSIE 2.0.

Embedding Multimedia Elements for MSIE Browsers

To embed Video for Windows (AVI) files or VRML worlds in an HTML document for the MSIE browsers, use the DYNSRC attribute on Windows systems.

The DYNSRC attribute is used like so:

```
<IMG SRC="MyMovieFrame.gif"  DYNSRC = "MyMovie.avi"
➥HEIGHT=120 WIDTH=160>
```

The BGSOUND tag can be used to embed WAV and MIDI files in an HTML page that will played back on Microsoft browsers. The syntax is:

```
<BGSOUND SRC="MyTune.mid"  >
```

New OBJECT Tag

The OBJECT tag is a new HTML tag proposed by the World Wide Web Consortium (W3 Consortium), a non-profit group formed to establish standards for the Web. The OBJECT tag is proposed as a way to standardize the embedding of multimedia content in Web pages. At the time of this writing, the OBJECT tag is only supported in MSIE 3.0 for Windows 95 and Windows NT for the embedding of OLE/ActiveX controls.

Note

MSIE 2.0 for Windows doesn't recognize the EMBED tag or Netscape Plug-Ins. MSIE 2.0 for Macintosh will recognize the EMBED tag and will display most Netscape Plug-Ins, although some features of individual Plug-Ins may not be supported, such as network extensions to Shockwave.

MSIE 3.0 will supposedly support Netscape Plug-Ins and recognize the EMBED tag.

Following is an example of the proposed OBJECT tag syntax for embedding a Shockwave movie:

```
    <OBJECT DATA=myShockwave.dcr
            TYPE="application/x-director"
            WIDTH=288 HEIGHT=200>

           <IMG SRC=myShockwave.gif ALT="A cool
➥Shockwave movie">

    </OBJECT>
```

The IMG tag provides alternate content for use in case the user doesn't have Shockwave display capabilities.

Embedding OLE/ActiveX Controls in HTML Pages

MSIE 3.0 for Windows 95 and Windows NT supports Microsoft's component software architecture based on OLE called ActiveX. OLE/ActiveX is a new technology, whereas Netscape Plug-Ins have been around for about a year as of this writing. Many features of OLE/ActiveX may change by the time you read this.

Note

Find out the latest about the OBJECT tag at:

http://www.w3.org/pub/WWW/TR/WD-object#object

and the evolving HTML 3.2 specs in general at:

http://www.w3.org/

Several ActiveX controls are included in MSIE 3.0 for Windows 95. They are:

- Chart
- Label
- New Item
- Preloader
- Timer

The CLASSID attribute uses the clsid:URL scheme to specify the ActiveX class identifier. See the documentation for your ActiveX control and learn how to implement this attribute. The IMG tag provides alternate content in case the user doesn't have ActiveX display capabilities. You can also use the EMBED tag within the OBJECT tag to provide content for Netscape Plug-Ins and ActiveX controls:

```
<OBJECT
ID=clock1
CLASSID="clsid:663C8FEF-1EF9-11CF-A3DB-080036F12502"
DATA="http://www.company.com/ole/activex/clock.stm">

<EMBED SRC="MyClockQT.mov" HEIGHT=144 WIDTH=160
➥PLUGINSPAGE = "http://quicktime.apple.com/qt/sw/
➥sw.html">

</OBJECT>
```

Test this HTML in your target browsers to make sure both EMBED and OBJECT tags are displayed correctly.

Note

For all the latest information on authoring for Microsoft browsers visit:

http://www.microsoft.com/workshop/

Embedding Java Applets in HTML Pages

Java programs are called applets. Embed Java applets in an HTML page using the <APPLET></APPLET> tag. See figure 5.4 for a sample applet.

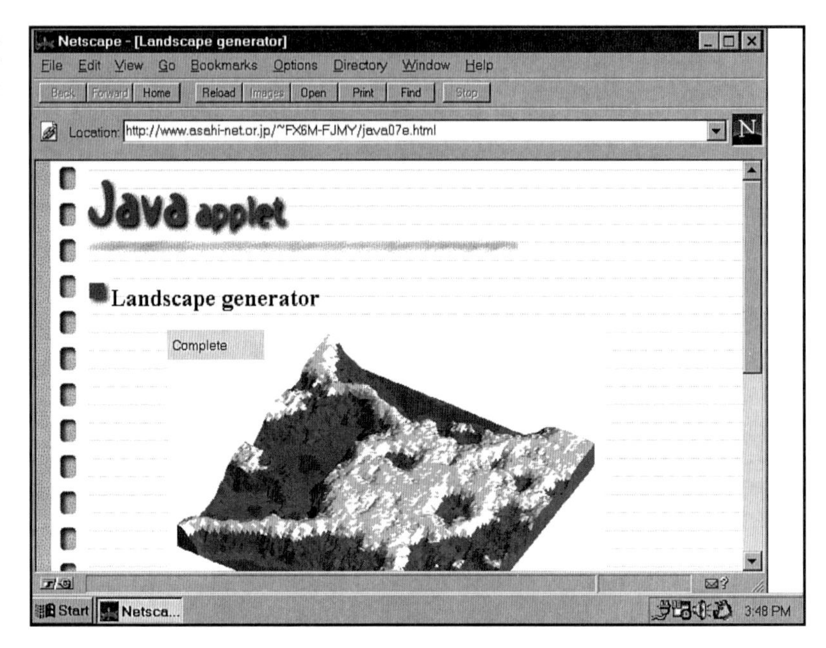

Figure 5.4

An embedded Java applet sample.

An APPLET tag takes the following required attributes:

- CODE is the file name of the applet.
- WIDTH and HEIGHT are the dimensions of the applet in pixels.

Sample HTML would look like:

```
<APPLET CODE  = myJavaApplet.class WIDTH = 160
➥HEIGHT=120></APPLET>
```

These attributes are optional:

- CODEBASE is the path name to the applet that is specified in the CODE attribute.
- ALIGN takes values of TOP, MIDDLE, and BOTTOM and aligns text similar to the IMG tag.

- ALT enables you to provide alternate text if the user doesn't have a Java-enabled browser or has disabled Java.

The <PARAM> tag is used to pass applet-specific parameters to the Java applet:

```
<APPLET CODE  = myJavaAnimationApplet.class WIDTH = 160
➥HEIGHT=120>
<PARAM NAME=frame VALUE = "animationFrame1.gif">
</APPLET>
```

To provide alternate content for users who do not have a Java-enabled browser or have disabled Java, you can use the ALT attribute and put alternate HTML code within the APPLET tag:

```
<APPLET CODE  = myJavaAnimationApplet.class CODEBASE =
➥WIDTH = 160 HEIGHT=120>
<PARAM NAME=frame VALUE = "animationFrame1.gif">

<H3>This page contains a Java-based animation.</H3>
You will need a <A HREF http://www.javasoft.com>Java</
➥A>-enabled browser to view this animation.
</APPLET>
```

Note

Find out the latest about Java at:

`http://www.javasoft.com/`

Creating Dynamic Pages with Client-Side Scripting

script

One of the most exciting new features incorporated in Netscape Navigator 3.0 and MSIE 3.0 is the addition of client-side scripting capabilities. Client-side scripting means that a **script** or mini-program executes or runs on the local client machine or Web browser rather than on a Web server.

Client-side scripting is implemented with two different programming languages: JavaScript on Netscape Navigator 2.0, Netscape Navigator 3.0, and MSIE 3.0 and VBScript (Visual Basic Script) on MSIE 3.0. Client-side scripting enables you to create dynamic documents, enhance interactivity, perform forms validation, share information between Plug-Ins, applets, and other page elements, and generally perform operations that had previously been restricted to scripts and programs written in programming languages such as Perl and C that resided on servers.

Table 5.3

Client-Side Scripting Support

	Navigator 2.0	Navigator 3.0	MSIE2.0	MSIE 3.0
JavaScript	Yes	Yes	No	Yes
VBScript	No	No	No	Yes

Embed scripts directly in an HTML document using the <SCRIPT></SCRIPT> tag like so:

```
<SCRIPT LANGUAGE = "JavaScript"

<!--  Your script goes here-->
</SCRIPT>
```

Note

For more information on JavaScript see:

http://home.netscape.com/eng/mozilla/2.0/handbook/javascript/index.html

http://home.netscape.com/eng/mozilla/3.0/handbook/javascript/index.html

http://home.netscape.com/comprod/products/navigator/version_2.0/script/script_info/index.html

http://www.gamelan.com/

For more information on VBScript see:

http://www.microsoft.com/workshop/

See Chapter 14, "VRML"for examples of scripts you can use to enhance your multimedia Web pages.

Image Maps

Image maps are often used as navigation tools. They provide a method of combining hyperlinks with a visual interface upon which you can point and click.

Image maps come in:

- Server-side image maps
- Client-side image maps

Server-side image maps require a special program on the server while *client-side* image maps can be created entirely within an HTML document and are processed on the client. Client-side image maps were introduced in Netscape 2.0 and will probably be supported in MSIE 3.0. They may be added to the evolving HTML standard.

Add client-side image maps using the USEMAP attribute and <MAP></MAP> tag. Server-side image maps use the ISMAP attribute. See Chapter 6, "Using Graphics to Add Dynamic Content," for a complete description.

Implementing Server-Side Image Maps

Server-side image maps use a program on the server to convert mouse-clicks to URLs. To implement a server-side image map you need three parts:

1. A program on the server that translates the location of the mouse click into a URL and loads it into the browser. This program is typically called "imagemap" and is found in the cgi-bin directory.
2. An image map graphic.
3. A text-based map definition file that contains:
   - Pixel coordinates of clickable regions on the graphic.
   - The URLs that correspond to each clickable region.

The HTML for embedding a server-side image map typically looks something like:

```
<A HREF = "http://www.server.com/cgi-bin/imagemap/
➥myImageMap.map"><IMG SRC= "myImageMap.gif" BORDER=0
➥ISMAP></A>
```

where:

- `myImageMap.gif` is the name of the image map graphic.
- `http://www.server.com/cgi-bin/imagemap` is the location of the image map program.
- `myImageMap.map` is the name of the text-based map definition file that contains coordinates of clickable regions and associated URLs.
- The `ISMAP` attribute tells the server the graphic is an image map.

Image maps are implemented differently on different servers. Typically, the differences are in the path to the image map program, `http://www.server.com/cgi-bin/imagemap` in this case, and the way to specify the location of the text-based map file. Check with your server documentation to see how it is implemented on your system.

Implementing Client-Side Image Maps

Client-side image maps, in many ways, are easier to set up and implement. You don't need special access to the server or a special server-based image map program. The processing of mouse clicks is performed by the browser. Another benefit of client-side image maps is that you can target frames with URLs in client-side image maps. This way, you can have an image map in one frame that can change the content of another frame. At this time only Netscape 2.0 or later supports client-side image maps, but new versions of MSIE should support it, and client-side image maps may be added to the emerging HTML 3.2 standard.

You can define the clickable regions, or hotspots, for the image map in an HTML document within the <MAP></MAP> tag. Usually, Web authors embed this tag within the HTML document that contains the map, but it can be in any HTML document that can be referenced with a URL. Here is a sample HTML for the MAP tag that defines hotspots for a navigation image map:

```
<MAP NAME="navigation_map">
<AREA SHAPE="RECT" COORDS="0,0,30,76" HREF =
➥"index.html">
<AREA SHAPE="RECT" COORDS="0,77,30,149" HREF =
➥"dmdesign1.html">
<AREA SHAPE="RECT" COORDS="0,150,30,221" HREF =
➥"webmedia1.html">
<AREA SHAPE="RECT" COORDS="0,222,30,294" HREF =
➥"sciedu1.html">
<AREA SHAPE="RECT" COORDS="0,295,30,370" HREF =
➥"mus1.html">
</MAP>
```

If your hotspots are all rectangular you can omit the SHAPE="RECT" attribute. You can also have circular hotspots using the CIRCLE attributes. Circles are defined by three numbers that specify the horizontal and vertical coordinates of the center of the circle and its radius in pixels. You can also specify arbitrary polygonal hotspots using the POLY attribute, where coordinates are vertices of the polygon.

Turning Images into Client-Side Image Maps

You can turn an image into a client-side image map by adding the USEMAP attribute to an IMG tag. The value of the

USEMAP is a URL or anchor to the HTML document that contains a map hotspot definition within the <MAP></MAP> tags. You can reference the map definition with the value of the NAME attribute that you specified in the MAP tag. In the previous example, the name is navigation_map. To reference a map definition in the same file as the image map, append the name with a #. For example, this HTML:

```
<IMG SRC="../images/maps/map1.gif"
➥USEMAP="#navigation_map">
```

references the map definition named `#navigation_map` that is contained within <MAP></MAP> tags within the same HTML file as the image map. Figure 8.23 shows a client-side image map on the left that loads different Shockwave animations.

You can mix tags for client-side and server-side image maps like so:

```
<A HREF = "/cgi-bin/imagemap/
➥myMapDefinitionFile.map"><IMG SRC= "myImageMap.gif"
➥USEMAP = "#navigation_map" ISMAP></A>
```

If a browser supports client-side image maps, the client-side map will run. If a browser doesn't support client-side image maps, the browser will ignore those tags and the server-side version will run.

Note

Visit:

http://home.netscape.com/assist/net_sites/html_extensions_3.html

for Netscape's documentation on client-side image maps and other Navigator HTML extensions.

Drawbacks

Clickable image maps tend to be overused on the Web. Image maps are useful for real maps, such as the map of a city showing the locations of different tourist attractions that are clickable links to pages about the attractions. Another use for image maps might be for complex, two-dimensional information distributions like an organization chart. Clickable image maps have many drawbacks such as:

- Large image maps can take a long time to download.
- No feedback of visited and active links exists as does for hypertext.
- Users may have images turned off. Be sure and provide alternate text-based navigation in case they do, or they won't be able to navigate anywhere!

- The performance of server-side image maps is dependent on the server load and how fast the server can run the map script. On busy or slow servers, map processing can be time-consuming. Also, different implementations of image maps mean server-side image maps aren't portable to different servers. In contrast, client-side image maps that are processed by the browser, don't require server intervention and are portable.

Faking Image Maps with TABLE Tags

You can fake an image map by embedding graphics in HTML table cells and making them clickable by adding an HREF tag. In some cases, a few small graphics may load faster than one large graphic. Here is some sample HTML:

```
<TABLE BORDER = 0 CELLPADDING = 0 CELLSPACING = 0>

<TR>
<TD><A HREF = "home.html"><IMG WIDTH=150 HEIGHT=67
➥BORDER = 0 SRC = "home.gif" ALT = ""><</TD>
<TD><A HREF = "section.html"><IMG WIDTH=150 HEIGHT=67
BORDER = 0 SRC = "section.gif" ALT = ""></A></TD>
<TD><A HREF = "where.html"><IMG WIDTH=150 HEIGHT=67
➥BORDER = 0 SRC = "location.gif" ALT = ""></A>
</TD>
<TD><A HREF = "whatsnew.html"><IMG WIDTH=150 HEIGHT=67
➥BORDER = 0 SRC = "new.gif" ALT = ""></A>
</TD>
</TR>
</table>
```

This HTML creates a table in which the table cells are completely filled with a clickable graphic. Make sure that the following attributes BORDER, CELLPADDING , and CELLSPACING are all set to zero so that no spaces show between your graphics.

Maximizing Performance

This section provides a quick checklist of ways to maximize the performance of your multimedia Web pages. See subsequent chapters for details.

Whether you follow the advice given here depends on the goals of your Web site, your audience, and their connection speed. If your main audience is made up of modem users connecting at 14.4 kbs, you will design pages differently than if your audience is entirely on a campus intranet connecting at Ethernet speeds. There will be many factors outside your control, such as network traffic and server load, that will also affect performance.

- Less is fast.

  The first step in decreasing download time is to reduce the total size of each Web page. Every byte counts. Never pass up the opportunity to shave a byte off a graphic or text. Be precise and concise in your text copy. Add graphics only if they add value. Typical users may only wait 6-10 seconds for a page to download.

  - Reduce the total amount of text on a page. Provide text in small, screen-size chunks that will download quickly. Most users don't want to scroll through a lot of text and probably won't read a lot of text on a Web page anyway; they will instead scan text quickly for key words and interesting links.
  - Reduce the total number of inline graphics and multimedia elements.
  - Reduce the file size of inline graphics and multimedia elements.

- Make your most frequently accessed pages small.

  What is the usage pattern for your site? Examine the usage statistics or task-flow diagrams for your site and determine the most frequently accessed pages. Make these pages the smallest pages on your site.

  Your main, top-level page will probably be accessed most frequently. Entry points to second-level content areas will also be accessed frequently. The main, top-level pages and entry point pages should be the most compact pages on your site, under 30 KB would be a good rule of thumb.

- Minimize the number of different graphics and media.

  When you are serving multimedia content, it is important to remember that each file, inline graphic, and multimedia element embedded in your HTML document will require a separate, independent connection to the server. An HTML document with ten separate inline graphics will require ten separate connections to the HTTP server to retrieve each file.

If you want to include multiple graphics, consider referencing the same graphic several times. The browser will be able to retrieve the file from the disk or memory cache without having to open another connection to the server.

- Add multimedia only if it adds value.

  Web multimedia is an exciting new area in Web content, but don't use multimedia just to say you use it. When GIF animation support was added to the major browsers, animated GIFs danced on every Web page, taking over the browser status bar and distracting users from reading text.

  Ask yourself, what value does this multimedia element add to my Web page? Does it add to the visual impact? What is the effect on download time? What is the multimedia element trying to communicate? Can this be more effectively communicated another way?

- Provide low-bandwidth alternate content and thumbnails.

  Many users are connecting from home where they are paying per-minute connect charges. Provide low-bandwidth versions and thumbnails of multimedia content so users on slow connections can get a taste of the content. Provide text-only pages for text-based browsers.

  Users may have image loading turned off to improve response time. Use the ALT parameter of the IMG tag to provide text describing a graphic's purpose or content. This text will also provide an alternate text-based link if the graphic is a button or link.

  It's a not good idea to rely on these elements to provide all the essential information or navigation for your site. The most important information on your page should be included in the page's text. Also, include text-based navigation links if you use an image map for navigation.

- Use LOWSRC with the IMG tag.

  A common use of this tag is to download a one bit, black-and-white image and then download the full-color graphic over it.

- Use local storage (CD-ROM, Hard Disk, or Cache).

  Another way to improve performance is to place bandwidth-hungry media, such as video and large graphics, on a local storage medium such as CD-ROM or hard disk. This requires an installation procedure or that the user download the media and place it in a predetermined cache or directory.

  By using the same graphics repeatedly at a site media will need only to be downloaded once, as it will be loaded from the users' disk or memory cache.

- Use HEIGHT and WIDTH parameters on all IMG and EMBED tags.
- Reduce the dimensions of large media files.

  The dimensions of multimedia elements should be the smallest possible.

- Reduce palette to the 216-color cross-platform browser palette.

  See Chapter 6 for using palettes with graphics.

- Reduce palette to as few colors as possible.
- Use GIFs for solid color graphics, for example, logos and illustrations.
- Interlace GIFs.
- Use JPEG for continuous-tone photographic imagery.

  This is a general rule of thumb for JPEG usage. Your mileage may vary depending upon the kind of image you have and its size.

- Use progressive JPEG.

  Although not all browsers support progressive JPEG.

- Edit video and animation.

  Examine each frame in your video and animation. What are the essential elements you want to communicate? Pare down the video or animation to the scenes with the most impact. Think of it like a movie trailer or a six-second reel for a client. Only show your best stuff. Do you really have to fade from black at the beginning and fade to black at the end? Put video credits and video text within the text of the Web page.

- Compress video.

  Use a high-quality video source with minimal visual noise. It will compress better. Compression trade-offs can be easily compared using expert tools such as Terran Interactive's Movie Cleaner Pro and Web Motion Plug-In.

- Use a maximum mono, 8-bit 11kHz, digital audio.
- Use MIDI.

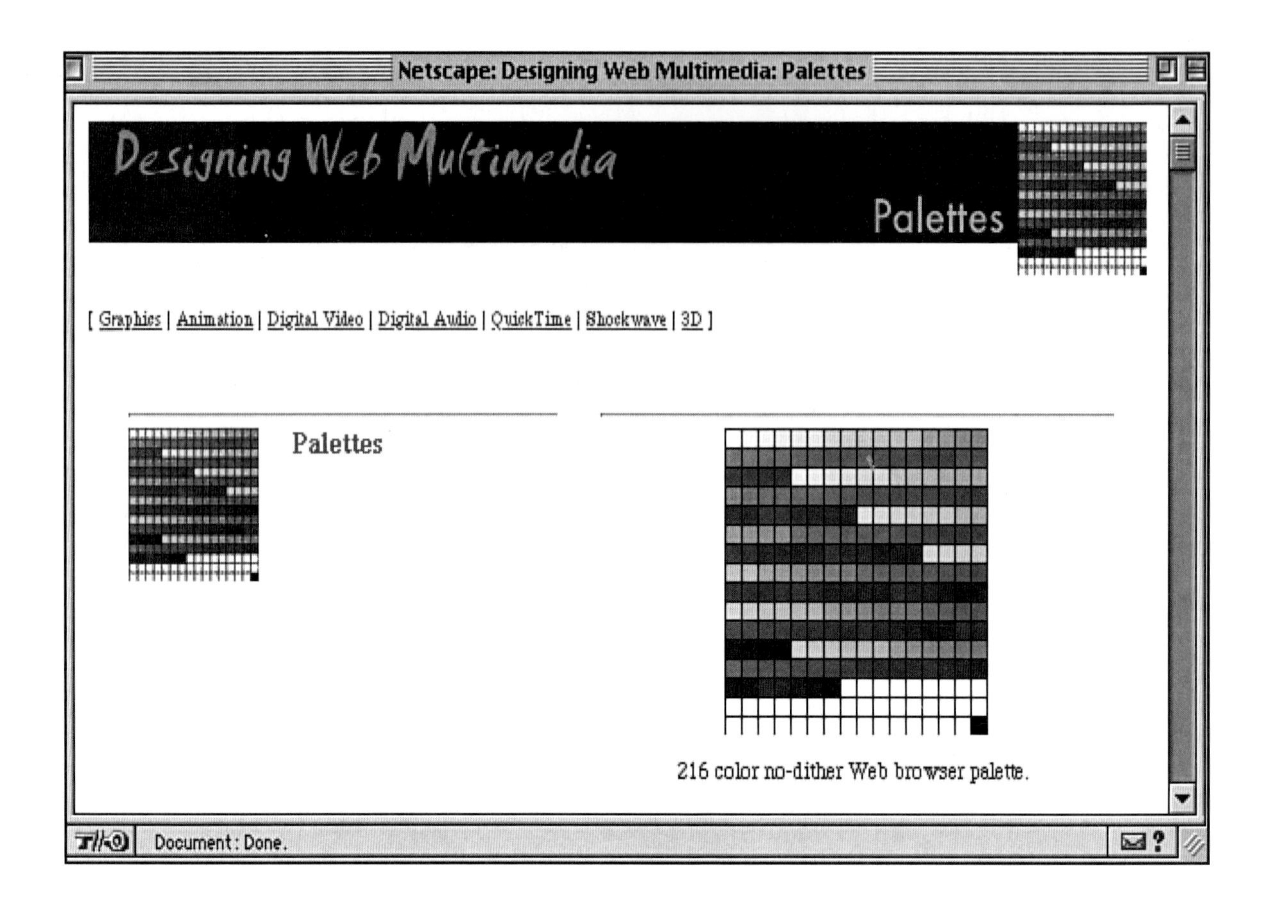

Graphics were the first inline multimedia supported by Web browsers. Graphical Web pages, when designed right, provide enhanced ease-of-use.

chapter

6

Using Graphics to Add Dynamic Content

Graphics are the easiest and most widely supported way to add rich content to your Web site. This chapter discusses some ways you can use graphics in your Web pages:

- Describes the features of the two most popular image formats for inline graphics, GIF and JPEG, and lists some of the tools you can use for creating and editing these types of graphics.
- Shows you ways to make your graphics look great on as many systems as possible and how to make graphics load fast, so users aren't waiting forever to see them.
- Provides tutorials on the following topics:
  A. How to create fast-loading, great-looking graphics
  B. How to create high-quality vector graphics for the Web using FreeHand
  C. How to use graphics in page backgrounds
  D. How to create pages with dynamic graphics

Image Formats

GIF and JPEG are today's most commonly used image formats for inline graphics. GIF stands for Graphics Interchange Format and was developed specifically for online graphics. JPEG stands for the Joint Photographic Experts Group, and was developed as a way to compress digital photographs. This section describes features of GIF and JPEG, as well as other file formats.

GIF

LZW compression

GIF uses a compression algorithm called Lempel-Ziv and Welch or **LZW compression.** This compression algorithm works best with large areas of flat, solid color. GIF graphics are limited to a maximum 8-bit color palette or a maximum total of 256 colors. Extensions to the GIF format support the following features:

interlacing

- **Interlacing.** Interlaced GIFs are initially displayed at low resolution and then displayed at progressively higher resolution as more file information is downloaded. Most browsers support interlacing. If a browser does not support interlacing it will display the file normally, that is, only display the image after all the image data has been downloaded. This topic will be discussed at greater length in the "Creating Interlaced GIFs" portion of this chapter.

transparency

- **Transparency.** The ability to make a single color transparent or invisible so that the underlying background shows through. This is similar to a one-color mask if you are familiar with masks or a key color transparency such as blue-screening video. Most browsers support transparency. If a browser does not support transparency it will display the file normally, that is the color designated as transparent is visible. This topic will be discussed at greater length in the "Creating a Transparent GIF" section of this chapter.

animation

- **Animation.** The ability to support multiple frames in a single file for animation. GIF animation format is supported by Netscape 2.0 or later and Internet Explorer 3.0 or later.

Table 6.1 shows the GIF features that are supported by today's popular browsers.

Table 6.1

Browser Support for GIF File Extensions

Feature	Netscape 2.0	MSIE 2	Netscape 3.0	MSIE 3.0
Interlacing	Yes	Yes	Yes	Yes
Transparency	Yes	Yes	Yes	Yes
Animation	Yes	No	Yes	Yes

JPEG

JPEG uses a **lossy compression** algorithm. This means that the compression algorithm discards some of the image data when it compresses an image. For this reason, it's a good idea only to compress an image with JPEG compression once. Each time you compress with JPEG compression you are discarding more data.

Tip

For the Web, save GIF files with the `.gif` file name extension.

When you save an image with JPEG compression in a graphics program you are typically given a choice of quality settings (from low to high-quality). As with most compression formats, higher quality settings lead to larger files. For Web graphics, it's a good idea to preserve a copy of your original, high-quality image and then save it as a different file at different quality settings to see which setting is acceptable for your Web site.

lossy compression

For display in a Web browser, JPEG compressed graphics need to be decompressed by the browser after downloading. This decompression can add to the total time it takes to display the image, especially on machines with slower processors. For this reason, JPEG compressed files sometimes take longer to display than GIF files of the same size.

Tip

JPEG generally works best with continuous-tone, 24-bit, photographic quality graphics.

Beginning with Navigator 2.0, Netscape introduced an extension to JPEG called **Progressive JPEG** that partially addresses this problem. A Progressive JPEG file displays in stages, beginning at a low resolution and proceeding to a high resolution, similar to an interlaced GIF. Progressive JPEG is supported by Netscape Navigator 2.0 or later and Internet Explorer 3.0 or later. Table 6.2 shows the JPEG features that are supported by today's popular browsers.

Progressive JPEG

Table 6.2

Browser Support for JPEG

Feature	Netscape 2.0	MSIE 2.0	Netscape 3.0	MSIE 3.0
JPEG	Yes	Yes	Yes	Yes
Progressive JPEG	Yes	No	Yes	Yes

Tip

For the Web, save JPEG files with the **.jpg** or **.jpeg** file name extension. Consult your server documentation for information on the file name extension is supports.

Other Graphic Formats

Other formats, such as XBM, TIFF, PNG, and BMP can be used to display graphics on the Web. There are also Netscape Plug-Ins that facilitate the display of specialized formats.

XBM format

The **XBM format** is a little known, black and white, bitmap graphic format that is native to the X Windows system. It is supported by most browsers. XBM graphics can be used for black and white line art.

TIFF format

You can display other graphic formats, such as **TIFF format** graphics using helper apps. TIFF is a common cross-platform bitmap format supported by many illustration and graphics programs. See Chapter 5, "Designing Multimedia Web Pages," for instructions on how to link to files.

PNG format

lossless compression

alpha channels

The **PNG format** stands for Portable Network Graphics. It is a graphic format developed by Thomas Boutell that provides many features of GIF files and JPEG files, along with support of features such as **lossless compression** and **alpha channels**. At present, browsers don't support it, but it might be included in the next version of the HTML standard. You can find out the latest information about the PNG format at:

```
http://www.boutell.com/boutell/png/
```

Many other graphic formats are supported by Netscape Plug-Ins. These formats provide useful features, such as high-resolution, zoom, and support for vector-based graphics.

For example, the Lightning Strike Plug-Ins is a cross-platform viewer for high-quality, highly compressed images saved in a proprietary image format that uses wavelet compression technology. Find out more about this format at:

```
http://www.infinop.com/html/infinop.html
```

The Shockwave for FreeHand Plug-Ins enable you to view high-resolution, high-quality postscript vector graphics created in FreeHand. FreeHand graphics are scalable and resolution independent, unlike bitmaps, providing several levels of magnification and panning. How to incorporate FreeHand graphics in your Web pages is discussed later in this chapter.

Internet Explorer supports **BMP format** graphics. BMP is the native bitmap graphic format for Windows systems. BMP graphics only display in Internet Explorer.

BMP format

Browsers and Palettes

Palettes, are also called color tables or Color Look-Up Tables (CLUT). A palette contains the range of colors that are displayed in its corresponding graphic. By definition, palettes contain 256 colors (the maximum amount on 8-bit systems) or less. On computer monitors that have 8-bit color-depth or less, the color palette contains the limited range of colors that can be displayed on that monitor at any one time. Palettes can also be attached to a graphic or to a QuickTime movie.

Dithering

Most users have 8-bit displays. On 8-bit displays, when a browser encounters a 24-bit image, it dithers the 24-bit image to an 8-bit palette. **Dithering** is the process by which a computer, display, or graphics program simulates a broad range of colors with a more limited range of colors. Dithering uses patterns of individual pixels that are colored with the limited range of colors. Your eyes merge the dithered pattern of pixels and hopefully create the perception of a new color that is not actually present in the image.

dithering

Tip

For more information about Web palettes, visit Bob Cunningham's site at:

http://www.connect.hawaii.com/hc/webmasters/Netscape.colors.html

On Macintosh systems, Netscape Navigator dithers graphics to the Macintosh system palette. On Windows systems, it dithers to a 216-color palette. GIF files generally compress to a smaller file size if colors are not dithered. Figure 6.1 shows the effect of converting a digital photograph to a GIF that is dithered to the 216-color Web palette.

Figure 6.1

Upper graphic is a non-dithered GIF. Lower graphic is dithered.

There are some instances where you can assert a custom palette that overrides the browser palette, as with Shockwave Plug-Ins. Generally, you are limited to the fixed palette of the Web browser.

If color fidelity and non-dithering colors are important to your design, test your page on multiple systems and monitors to see how graphics are displayed. The following sections go into detail on palette issues with Web graphics and provide tips on ways to manage color in Web graphics.

No Dither Cross-Platform Palette

There are 216 colors that display without dithering on 8-bit systems, within most browsers on Macintosh and Windows systems. The 216 colors are contained in a special palette that can be found on the CD. This palette is available in the versions mentioned in Table 6.3.

Use these colors to ensure consistent color display on 8-bit monitors on different systems. How to use this special palette in Web graphics is discussed later in this chapter.

Table 6.3

Files Containing the 216 Color Web Palette on the CD

File type	File name
Macintosh PICT	216 color Web palette
Photoshop palette	216color
Windows BMP	216color.bmp
Windows palette	216Web.pal

Creating Web Graphics

You can employ some techniques and methods to make sure your graphics display properly on the Web. This section addresses the following issues:

- When to use GIFs and when to use JPEGs
- What the tools are for, creating and editing GIFs and JPEGs

- How to create JPEGs and Progressive JPEGs
- How to make your Web graphics look great on as many systems as possible
- How to make your Web graphics load faster

When To Use GIFs versus JPEGs

As with most multimedia on the Web, there are trade-offs between compression (file size) and quality. The goal is to compress your graphics to as small a size as possible, but still maintain acceptable quality. What works best for you depends on the characteristics of your source graphic, such as the number of colors, their distribution, the purpose of the graphic, and the display features of your users.

GIFs work best with the following:

- Line art
- Illustration graphics
- Cartoon art
- Graphics with areas of flat and solid color

JPEGs work best with the following:

- Continuous-tone art
- Digital photographs
- Scans

Note

JPEGs can be saved as 8-bit or 24-bit graphics. JPEGs saved as 8-bit or 24-bit graphics are dithered by browsers to the browser's fixed palette on 8-bit 256 color displays. Use JPEGs if your users have 24-bit displays.

The format you choose depends on the particular characteristics of the graphic, the technical limitations of your audience, and the purpose of the graphic. If you are creating an online portfolio of art work to help you get a job at a graphic design firm, you probably want to use the JPEG format. If you are designing a logo that will appear on every page in a site, that will need to be downloaded quickly and be viewable on the maximum number of systems, you want to use a flat-color GIF.

If you are creating a large, flat-color graphic, such as a logo, that will be viewed by users on slow connections, you want to use GIF. It's a good idea to view the graphic on Windows, Mac, and Unix platforms at 256 colors to see how the graphic is converted to 8-bit color on each system.

Figure 6.2 shows three flat color graphics. The top graphic is the original file, the middle graphic is the file saved as GIF, and the bottom graphic is the file saved as JPEG. Note the blotchy appearance of the JPEG. Figure 6.3 shows three digital photographs. The top graphic is the original file, the middle graphic is the file saved as GIF, and the bottom graphic is the file saved as JPEG.

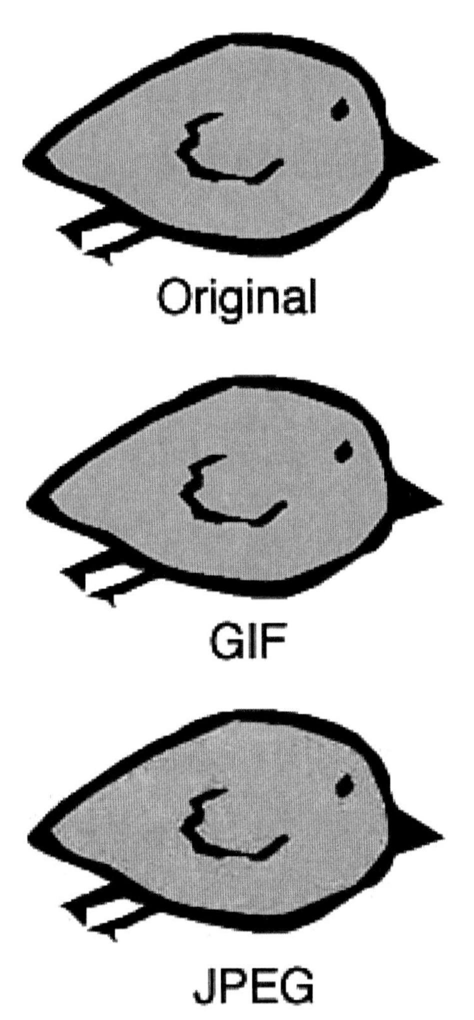

Figure 6.2

Flat color graphic saved as GIF and JPEG.

Figure 6.3

Digital photograph saved as GIF and as JPEG.

Original

GIF

JPEG

Graphics Tools

There are many good tools you can use for creating and editing GIF and JPEG graphics. These include commercial products, shareware, and freeware. This section highlights a few programs.

Many graphics programs support the GIF file format. Support for GIF format extensions, such as interlacing, transparency, and animation is less widespread. To have features such as interlacing and transparency in Photoshop you need the free GIF89a Export Photoshop Plug-Ins. You can download this Plug-Ins program from:

```
http://www.adobe.com/prodindex/photoshop/main.html
```

Most graphics programs save files with JPEG compression. Many graphics programs enable you to set the quality settings for JPEG compression, with low-quality providing the most compression, but lowest image quality and high-quality providing the least compression. Because JPEG is a lossy compression scheme (original image data is lost during compression) only compress your original graphic once to avoid image degradation.

Tip

See Chapter 8, "Animating with Shockwave for Director," for a discussion of GIF animation tools.

Tools for creation of Progressive JPEG, the new progressive display format available in Netscape 2.0 or later, are limited. On the Mac, you can use the excellent ProJPEG Photoshop Plug-Ins from BoxTop software that enables you to save in Progressive JPEG format from inside Photoshop. These Plug-Ins can be found on the Web at:

```
http://www.aris.com/boxtop/ProJPEG/
```

Web graphics can be created with any graphics program that saves files in GIF or JPEG format. Web graphics need to have a resolution of 72 dpi and commonly are restricted to an 8-bit palette. Thus, you don't need an expensive graphics program that is designed for professional level print or photographic quality work. You might be able to use shareware or freeware programs to create all the Web graphics you need. If you have professional level programs, great! They contain many sophisticated tools that make your job easier. Many of the tips presented in this Chapter use Adobe Photoshop, which is probably a tool used by most graphic artists and designers on Mac, Windows, and Unix systems. Another useful professional level tool available for Mac and Windows is Fractal Design Painter. For more information about Fractal Design Painter go to this Web site:

```
http://www.fractal.com
```

A very useful tool is Equilibrium Technology's Debabelizer, available on the CD that comes with this book. It performs sophisticated palette manipulations, batch processing, and file conversions. You can download special scripts or macros that automate much of the process of optimizing graphics for the Web. At this time, Debabelizer is only available for the Mac. Programs on Windows that provide some of Debabelizer's functionality include Brenda, HiJaak Pro, and Collage Complete or some of the general graphics programs such as PaintShop Pro, GIF Construction Kit, and LView Pro.

Useful shareware programs for Web graphics on the Mac include GraphicConverter, GIFConverter, Clip2Gif, GifBuilder, JPEGView, and Transparency.

Creating JPEGs

In general JPEG compression works best with 24-bit continuous-tone imagery such as digital photography.

To save a file as JPEG in Photoshop:

1. Choose Mode, RGB Color.
2. Choose File, Save As.
3. Choose JPEG in the file format pop-up menu.
4. Try a medium or low-quality setting that produces smaller file sizes to see if the quality is acceptable.
5. Click OK.

Debabelizer enables you to save JPEGs as 8-bit or 24-bit images. Choose Save As in the File menu and select JPEG from the file type pop-up menu.

Creating Progressive JPEGs

Progressive JPEG is a new JPEG format that enables the rapid display of a low-resolution version of a JPEG graphic and then the progressive display of higher resolution versions as more data is downloaded. At this time it is only supported by Netscape Navigator 2.0 or later.

You can create Progressive JPEGs in Photoshop using the ProJPEG Photoshop Plug-Ins from BoxTop Software. To install ProJPEG place it inside the file formats folder in your Photoshop Plug-Ins folder. The next time you launch Photoshop, ProJPEG will be an available file format in the Save, Save As, and Save Copy As commands in Photoshop's File menu.

ProJPEG does not open CMYK JPEG files. If the file has an alpha channel, save CMYK files as JPEGs or save a file in JPEG format.

To create a Progressive JPEG file with ProJPEG in Photoshop:

1. Choose File, Save As.
2. Choose ProJPEG from the file format pop-up menu.
3. Set compression quality with a slider control.
4. Check the option for Progressive JPEG.
5. Click OK.

Note

Equilibrium Technology has made batch processing scripts, designed specifically for creating JPEG Web graphics, available free at:

`http://www.equil.com/SoftwareScripts.html`

Maximizing Graphic Quality for the Web

The following list and editing tips provide some helpful hints on ways you can maximize the appearance of your images within the limitations and idiosyncracies of the Web.

- **Work Big then Reduce Size For the Web.** Web graphics tend to be small in size. Small graphics download faster and fit comfortably within a browser window. If you create a graphic from scratch, it's sometimes easier to work at a larger scale and then reduce the size of the graphic for the Web.

  If you work at a resolution other than 72 dpi—for example, if you are working on a graphic that was scanned in at 100 dpi—be sure to convert the graphic to 72 dpi when you are ready to put it on the Web.

- **Work at 24-bits.** By working at a higher color-depth, all editing and transformation operations that you perform have more image information to work with and the results of such operations usually look better.

Reduce color-depth to 8-bit or compress to GIF or JPEG as the very last step in the graphic creation process. Save a 24-bit original of the graphic so that you can work on it later if necessary.

- **Reduce Size, Resolution, and Color-Depth as the Last Step.** Save any editing that reduces the actual amount of data, such as color correction, color-depth reduction, and scaling to the end of the editing process. In particular, only perform color-depth reduction as the very last step, right before you convert the graphic to GIF or JPEG for the Web.
- **Make Multiple Copies at Different Settings and Compare On-Screen Appearance.** The result of reducing color-depths and downsampling graphics depends on the various settings you use for downsampling and the characteristics of the source graphic. It's often a good idea to work on multiple copies of a source graphic and try different downsampling settings on each one. Then, you can compare each downsampled version side-by-side on-screen to see which one looks the best.
- **Keep 24-Bit Master.** Keep a high-quality master version of your original graphic. This way, if you need to go back and edit or change the original, you are working with a high-quality original. If you use Photoshop or Fractal Design Painter, save the graphic in its native format to keep Photoshop layers or Painter floaters intact.
- **Scanning.** If you are scanning images for use on the Web, try to use original photographic prints rather than printed images. Scanned printed images might contain artifacts called moiré patterns.

  Scan at the highest color-depth you can, such as 24-bits. It's a good idea to scan at higher resolution, such as 100 dpi or above, so you can capture as much image information as you can. Then, reduce the resolution to 72 dpi when you convert the graphic for the Web.

There are ways that you can edit your images to enhance the way they look on the Web. The following section explores this topic. You learn some special techniques you can use to modify your images' appearance, such as the following:

- How to create transparent GIFs
- How to remove anti-aliased edges in Photoshop and Debabelizer images
- How to create drop shadows

Image Editing Tips

Whether you are working with scanned images or original graphics you might need to adjust the color cast or contrast of the image for online display. Differences in display across monitors and platforms means an image looks slightly different on different systems. For instance, monitors for Wintel PCs tend to be darker than other monitors.

Computer monitors can make some images appear washed out. To ensure color fidelity perform the following steps:

1. View the graphic on different systems and displays.
2. Use various image processing tools to adjust your image so that it looks good on most systems.

This section provides some basic image processing tips to help you do this.

You can use the brightness and contrast controls to adjust an image, but these controls tend to reduce the range of values in your graphic image. For example, you get better results in Photoshop if you use the nonlinear image adjustment controls, such as Adjust, Levels or Adjust, Curves under the Image menu. These controls enable you to adjust the brightness of the image, that is the relative lightness or darkness of an individual color or gray value. Other graphics programs have similar image adjustment commands.

Tip

A common image processing task is to adjust the value and contrast of an image to give it visual punch. If you need to adjust colors and contrast, try to do it all in one step. Each time you adjust the image you are losing some of the original data. Performing multiple color corrections can degrade the image over time.

This section examines how to make the following image adjustments:

- Adjust your tonal range with Photoshop's Levels command
- Adjust gamma with PaintShop Pro
- Adjust contrast with Photoshop's Curves command
- Adjust individual color channels

Adjusting Tonal Range with Photoshop's Levels Command

The Levels command in Photoshop enables you to adjust the tonal range in your image. With the Levels command you can adjust the following:

- The brightness levels of the entire image
- A selection within an image
- Color channels independently

The Levels dialog box contains a histogram with three sliders to adjust input tonal range and two sliders to adjust output tonal range. Figure 6.4 shows the Levels dialog box in Photoshop.

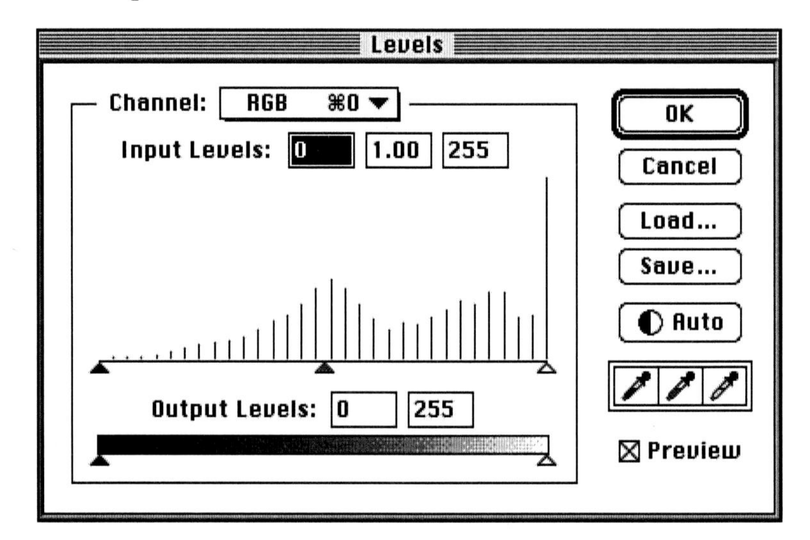

Figure 6.4

The Levels dialog box in Photoshop.

To darken the image move the black input slider to the right. To lighten the image move the white input slider to the left.

Tip

Macintosh users: Images created on Macs often need to be lightened so that they don't appear too dark on Windows systems.

The middle gray slider adjusts the image's gamma value, which is the brightness level of the medium gray in the image. You need to adjust the gamma value of images for the Web to accommodate cross-platform differences in the gamma value of displays.The gamma slider enables you to do this without changing the brightness values of the shadows and highlights in an image. Move the gamma slider to the left to lighten the medium values in the image.

Adjusting Gamma in PaintShop Pro

You might need to darken images created on a Windows system so that they don't appear too light on other systems. To adjust gamma in PaintShop Pro:

1. Choose Colors, Adjust, Gamma Correct.
2. In the Gamma Correct dialog box, shown in figure 6.5, reduce the value in the Correction box. Try reducing it to a value between 1.70 and 2.0 for cross-platform optimization.
3. Click OK.

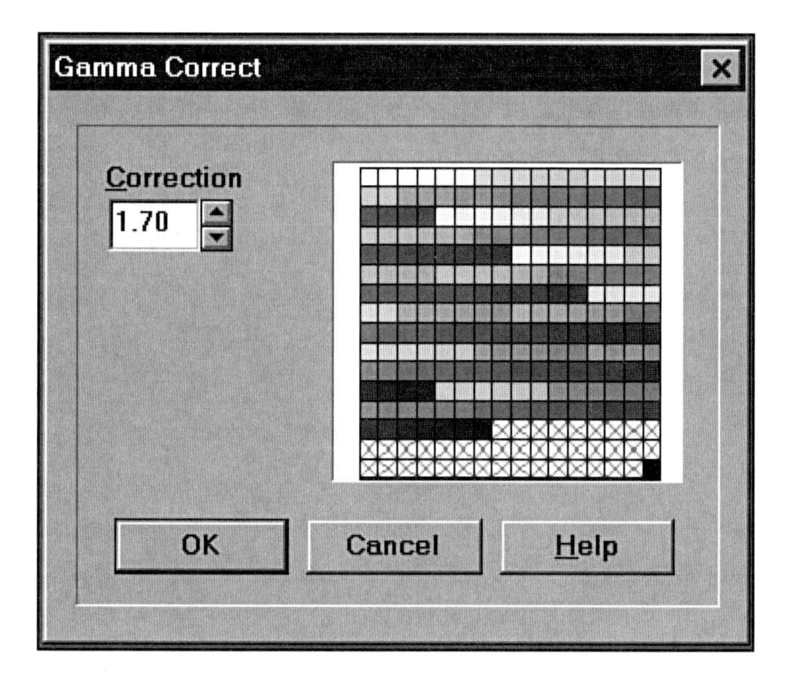

Figure 6.5

Gamma Correct dialog box in PaintShop Pro.

Adjusting Contrast with the Curves Command in Photoshop

The Curves command in Photoshop is a more powerful way to change the brightness values of an image. The Curves command contains a brightness graph, in which the vertical axis represents output brightness levels and the horizontal axis represents the original brightness levels. The brightness curve represents a mapping of input brightness values to output brightness values. Figure 6.6 shows the Curves dialog box in Photoshop.

Figure 6.6

The Curves dialog box in Photoshop.

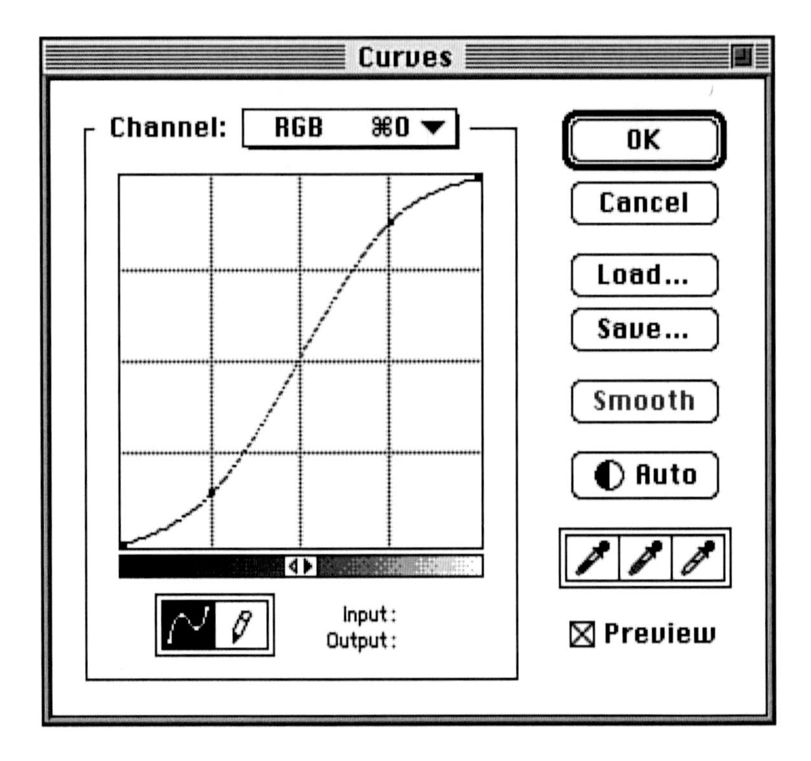

Here are two tips on how to use the Curves command to adjust your image's contrast:

- An S-shaped curve increases the contrast in an image. The more you increase the slope of the center part of the S and decrease the slope at the tails of the S, the more you increase the contrast. Figure 6.7 shows a digital photograph before and after image adjustment.
- A backward S-shaped curve decreases the contrast in an image.

Making Color Corrections

You can use the Levels dialog box and the Curves dialog box in Photoshop to adjust individual color channels independently. You might want to do this to remove unwanted color casts in an image. For example, if your scans come out with a slight greenish cast, you can use the Levels and Curves commands on the Green channel to adjust the brightness values and reduce the greenish cast.

Figure 6.7

Graphic image before and after image adjustment with the Curves command.

Converting Gray-scale to Color and Duotone Images

The 216-color, cross-platform browser palette has a range of only four grays in it. This limitation can create posterized gray-scale graphics on 8-bit Windows systems. Posterized graphics have noticable discrete color bands and colors do not grade smoothly into each other.

To convert a gray-scale graphic to the 216-color browser palette in Photoshop:

1. Choose Mode, RGB Color to convert the graphic to an RGB graphic.

2. Choose Mode, Indexed Color to convert the graphic to an indexed color graphic.
3. Try selecting the Dither option to see if this improves the appearance of the gray-scale graphic with a reduced palette.
4. In the Indexed Color dialog box, choose the Custom option.
5. Click Load.
6. Find and load the 216-color Web palette.

A **duotone** is traditionally a graphic that is printed with two inks. On the computer, it is a graphic that is displayed within a range of two colors. In some cases, duotones may give better display results on 8-bit systems than gray-scale images, because the 216-color palette has a greater range of blues, greens, and reds than the range of grays.

To create a a duotone from a gray-scale image in Photoshop:

1. Start with a gray-scale graphic.
2. Choose Mode, Duotone.
3. Click Load in the Duotone Options dialog box, shown in figure 6.8.

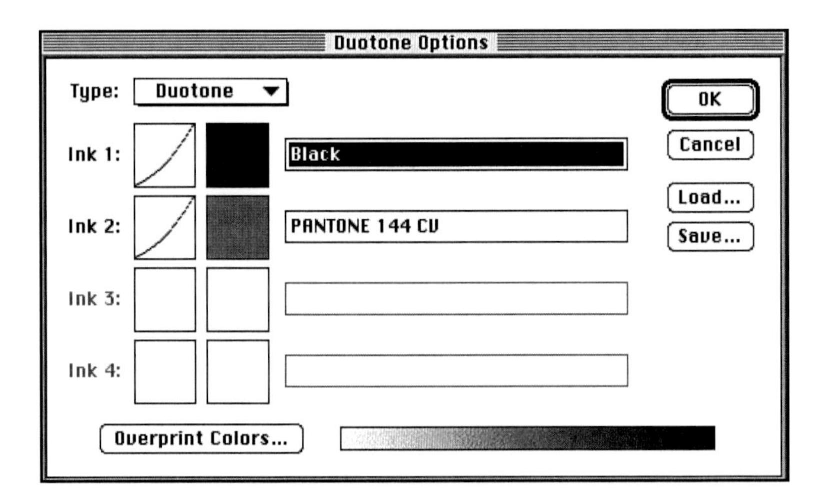

Figure 6.8

Duotone Options dialog box in Photoshop.

4. Open a Duotone preset. Duotone presets are in the Goodies: Duotone Presets folder that is installed with Photoshop. Some of the blue and brown Duotone presets look alright with gray-scale images.

5. Click OK.
6. Convert to the 216-color Web palette, following the instructions presented earlier in this section.
7. See if the quality is acceptable. Otherwise, choose Revert in the File menu and try again.

Creating a Transparent GIF

Transparent GIFs enable you to make one color of your GIF transparent, with the result being similar to a one-color mask or key color transparency. You would use this feature to layer irregularly-shaped artwork over a background and have the background show through. There are several programs that enable you to select one color in your GIF file to be transparent.

To create a transparent GIF in Photoshop, you need the items described in the Tools box.

Tools
Photoshop 3
GIF89a Export Photoshop Plug-Ins

You can download the free GIF89a Export Photoshop Plug-Ins at `http://www.adobe.com/prodindex/photoshop/main.html`.

To create a transparent GIF in Photoshop:

1. Choose Indexed Color in the Mode menu and convert the graphic to the palette you want. (See the section on palettes for Web graphics in this chapter for details.)
2. Choose File, Export: Gif89 Export.
3. In the Export dialog box, click on the eyedropper tool.
4. Choose the color you want to make transparent.

On Windows systems, you can create transparent GIFs with PaintShop Pro, LView, and the GIF Construction Kit.

Note

Transparency is a handy free utility for the Macintosh created by Aaron Giles that enables you to open GIF files and choose a color to be transparent. It can be obtained from most shareware archives such as:

`http://hyperarchive.lcs.mit.edu/HyperArchive/HyperArchive.html`

To create a transparent GIF in PaintShop Pro, you need the following tools:

Tools
PaintShop Pro

1. Determine the palette index number of the color you want to make transparent by selecting Colors, Edit Palette.
2. Choose Save As under the File menu.
3. Choose List Files of Type: GIF—CompuServe.
4. Choose File Sub-Format: Version 89a—Interlaced or Non-Interlaced to create an interlaced or non-interalced GIF respectively. See the section on creating interlaced GIFs for more information.
5. Choose Options.
6. Choose the Set Transparency Value option and enter the palette index number from step 1.
7. Click OK.

You can use other programs to create transparent GIFs, but the procedure is generally the same.

Note

Aliases are the stair-stepped, jagged edges of color fields in computer-generated imagery. Aliasing is a consequence of the pixel-based, discontinuous nature of computer images; rounded edges and color gradients have to be resolved into square pixels.

Anti-aliasing uses different techniques to blend or blur the jagged edges in computer images so that computer imagery looks more like a continuous-tone photograph.

Aliasing

Although transparent GIFs are a way to layer irregularly-shaped artwork on your Web page, you are limited to a one-color mask. If your graphic is anti-aliased against the transparent color, the edges have the dreaded anti-aliased fringe (see fig. 6.9). Many paint tools in programs such as Photoshop create graphics with anti-aliased edges by default. By double-clicking on tools in Photoshop you can usually bring up a dialog box with settings for a tool that enables you to turn anti-aliasing off.

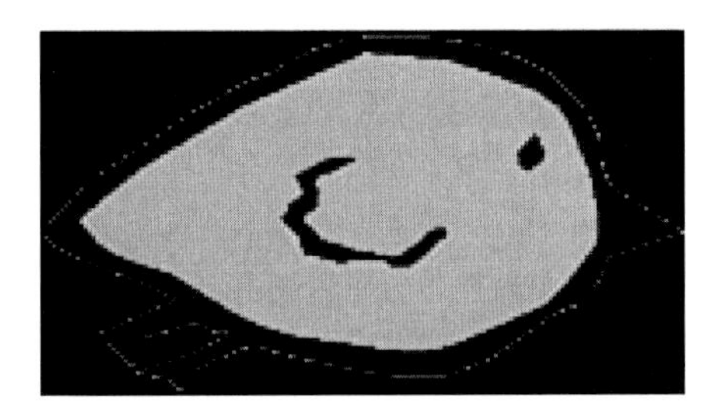

Figure 6.9

Anti-alias fringe.

To create irregularly-shaped artwork with anti-aliased edges that blend into your Web page background, don't use transparent GIFs. Instead, create the anti-aliased graphic against a background that is the same background as your Web page.

Removing Anti-Aliased Edges in Photoshop

Removing anti-aliased edges or fringes on graphics is a common task when creating or repurposing artwork for the Web. In Photoshop, there are several ways to remove anti-aliased edges from graphics. Most involve modifying a selection outline around the anti-aliased object and copying and pasting selections into new files or against new backgrounds. The following discussion assumes a basic knowledge of Photoshop.

Tools
Photoshop 3

If the graphic has an alpha channel that corresponds to the object's edges, you can use the Threshold command to modify the alpha channel and create a selection outline that removes the anti-aliased edges.

1. Choose the alpha channel in the Photoshop Layers palette.
2. Choose Image: Map: Threshold.
3. Adjust the slider so that the white area shrinks.
4. Choose the RGB channel in the Layers palette.
5. Load the alpha channel as a selection.
6. Repeat this process until you have a clean-edged selection outline.

Another technique is:

1. Choose the object by loading the alpha channel, by using the Magic Wand tool or Color Range command, or by painting the selection mask in QuickMask mode. QuickMask creates a temporary mask that you can paint into to create irregular selection outlines. See Photoshop's documentation for details.
2. After you have a selection outline around the anti-aliased object, choose Select: Modify: Contract with a value of 1 pixel. This command should shrink your selection outline by one pixel and remove most of the anti-aliased halo.
3. After you have removed the anti-aliasing to your liking, copy and paste the object into another Photoshop file.

A third technique works with a floating selection, such as after you've pasted an object into a new file. You can use the Select: Matting: Remove White Matte, Select: Matting: Remove Black Matte, or Select: Matting: Defringe command to remove any extraneous pixels if you've rendered against a black, white, or colored background.

The technique that works best for your images depends on the shape and color of the object and its background.

Removing Anti-Aliased Edges in Debabelizer

The following steps remove anti-aliased edges in Equilibrium Technology's Debabelizer.

Tools
Debabelizer

1. Open the image or drag-and-drop it on the Debabelizer icon.
2. Choose Option: Dithering & Background Color from the Palette menu.
3. Choose Color index in the Dither Options & Background Color dialog box (see fig. 6.10).
4. Move the cursor over the image until it turns into an eyedropper and click on the background color.

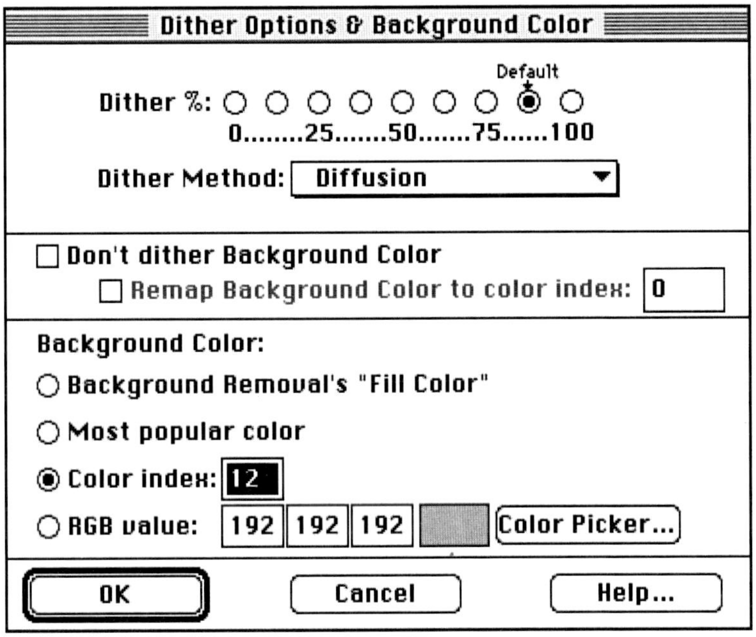

Figure 6.10

Dither Options & Background Color dialog box in Debabelizer.

5. Click OK.
6. Choose Shave—Outline: Shave Edges from the Palette menu.

Drop Shadows

Drop shadows are a common, and some would say overused, way to add dimensionality and visual punch to an otherwise flat Web page. There are many ways to create drop shadows, including special Photoshop Plug-Ins and built-in commands in Fractal Design Painter.

There are several ways to create drop shadows in Photoshop without Plug-Ins. The basic idea is to do the following:

1. Create a selection of the object that you want to cast a drop shadow, such as text or a logo.
2. Send this selection to a separate layer behind the object.
3. Fill it with gray.
4. Blur it a bit.
5. Finally, offset it a little bit behind the object.

The key to making drop shadows for Web pages is to create your drop shadow against a background layer that is the same as the background of your Web page.

Tools
Photoshop 3

Here is one way to create a drop shadow in Photoshop:

1. Open the file that contains the graphic object to which you want to add a drop shadow. Make sure the file is in RGB Color mode.
2. Make sure the background layer is the same background as your Web page. If not, create a layer underneath the graphic object and make it the same background as your Web page.
3. Choose the graphic object that you want to cast a shadow. There are many ways to make selections in Photoshop. For example, you can use the Magic Wand tool or Color Range command. If the object is on a layer in which the surrounding area is transparent, press Command+Option+T to select everything on that layer that is not transparent.
4. After you have the selection outline, float the selection by pressing Command+J. If the edges of the graphic are anti-aliased, you might have to shrink the selection by a pixel to get rid of the anti-alias fringe. See the previous section on removing anti-aliased edges in Photoshop for details.
5. Open the Layers palette.
6. Option double-click on the floating selection to create a separate layer.
7. Make the underlying layer active and select the graphic object that you want to cast a shadow, again. Press Delete.
8. Press D to set the color chips to their default value.
9. Choose Fill from the Edit menu
10. Select Foreground Color and 50 percent to 70 percent Opacity. Click OK.

11. Deselect the filled selection by pressing Command+D.
12. While the layer is still the active layer, select Blur: Gaussian Blur from the Filter menu. Choose a radius of two or three pixels, or whatever value looks good to you. This command blurs the layer, giving the shadow fuzzy borders.
13. Press V to choose the Move tool.
14. Use the arrow keys to offset the shadow where you want it (see fig. 6.11).

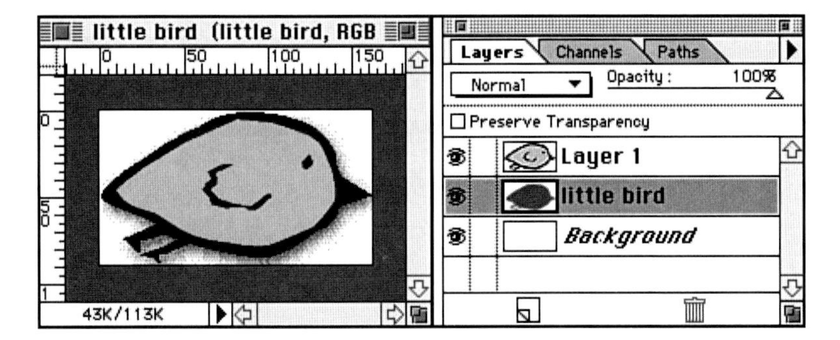

Figure 6.11

Creating drop shadows in Photoshop.

For more Photoshop tips, see *Inside Photoshop* from New Riders Publishing.

Making Graphics Load Fast

This section provides tips on how to create compact, compressed graphics that download fast on the Web. In general, you should cultivate the following habits:

- Minimize the total number of different graphics on your site.
- Include HEIGHT and WIDTH attributes in your IMG and EMBED tags.
- Use interlaced GIFs and Progressive JPEGs.
- Use techniques that minimize the size of your files.
- Use techniques that improve your GIF compression.

Minimize the Total Number of Different Graphics

Each inline graphic or multimedia element requires opening a separate connection to the Web server to retrieve that graphic. If the server is loaded or the network is busy, graphics can take a while to load. Minimize the server connection overhead by reducing the total number of inline graphic elements.

Note

For each graphic, ask yourself, does this graphic add value to the page? Is it really necessary to communicate my message?

If you use the same graphic more than once, most browsers load a copy from the local disk cache instead of opening a new connection to the Web server.

Always Include the HEIGHT and WIDTH Attributes

If you use the HEIGHT and WIDTH attributes in your IMG and EMBED tags (discussed later in the "HTML for Inline Graphics" section of this chapter), Netscape Navigator lays out the Web page, using the HEIGHT and WIDTH attributes to reserve space for graphics while downloading text first around the space reserved for graphics. The graphics then fill in the reserved space in the page layout. Users can read the text of the page before the graphics have been completely downloaded. The overall impression is that of a faster loading page.

Use Interlaced GIFs and Progressive JPEGs

Interlaced GIFs and Progressive JPEGs rapidly display low-resolution versions of graphics first and then progressively display higher resolution versions as more information is downloaded over the Web. Most graphical browsers support interlaced GIFs. At this time, Netscape Navigator 2.0 or later supports Progressive JPEGs.

Creating Interlaced GIFs

Several different commercial and shareware products enable you to create interlaced GIFs. The products we focus on in this section include Photoshop, Debabelizer, GIFConverter—a shareware program—and PaintShop Pro.

Creating Interlaced GIFs in Photoshop

To create an interlaced GIF in Photoshop, you need the tools shown in the Tools box.

Tools
Photoshop 3
GIF89a Export Photoshop Plug-Ins

> **Note**
>
> **Interlaced GIFs** are initially displayed at low resolution and then displayed at progressively higher resolutions as more file information is downloaded. Most browsers support interlacing. If a browser does not support interlacing it displays the file normally, that is, only displays the image after all the image data has been downloaded.

Then you need to follow these steps:

1. Make sure you have the GIF89a Export Photoshop Plug-Ins installed. Again, Plug-Ins is available free at:

   `http://www.adobe.com/prodindex/photoshop/main.html`

2. Choose Export: GIF89a Export under the File menu.
3. Check the Interlace check box in the GIF89a Export dialog box (see fig. 6.12).

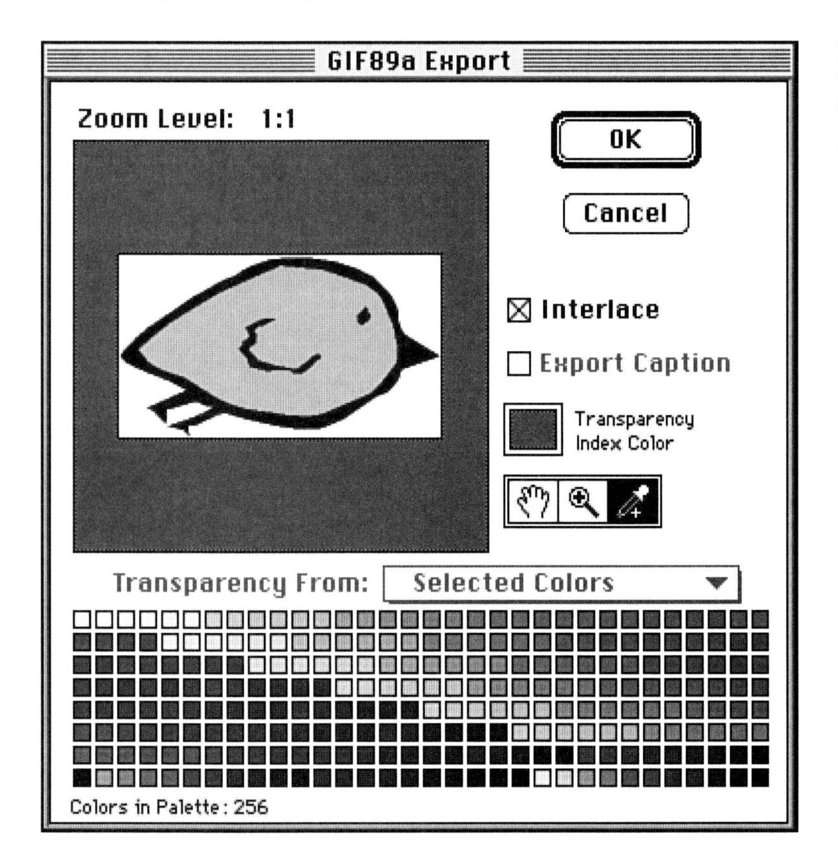

Figure 6.12

GIF89a Export dialog box in Photoshop.

Note

You can perform color-depth reduction in the Save Type dialog box.

Creating Interlaced GIFs in Debabelizer

To create an interlaced GIF in Debabelizer, you need to follow these steps:

1. Choose Save As under the File menu.
2. Choose GIF: Interlaced in the Save Type pop-up menu (see fig. 6.13).

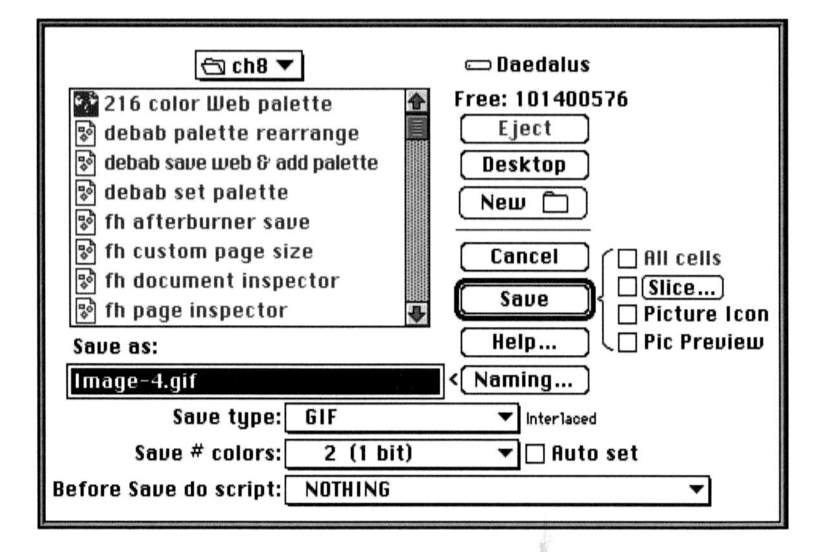

Figure 6.13

Save As dialog box in Debabelizer.

Batch Processing GIF Conversion in Debabelizer

Batch processing enables you to process a whole pile of graphics with the same settings rather than doing each graphic by hand. Debabelizer is a great tool for the job on Macs, although Brenda the Batch Renderer can perform similar functions on Windows. To batch process GIF conversion for a folder full of graphics in Debabelizer:

1. Choose all the graphics that you want to convert in the Finder.
2. Drag-and-drop them on the Debabelizer icon.
3. In Debabelizer, choose Batch: Save under the File menu.
4. Choose GIF: Interlaced in the Save Type pop-up in the Batch Save dialog box, as shown in figure 6.14.
5. You can also set the destination folder for saved images, perform file name conversions, and perform any previously saved scripts on the graphics.

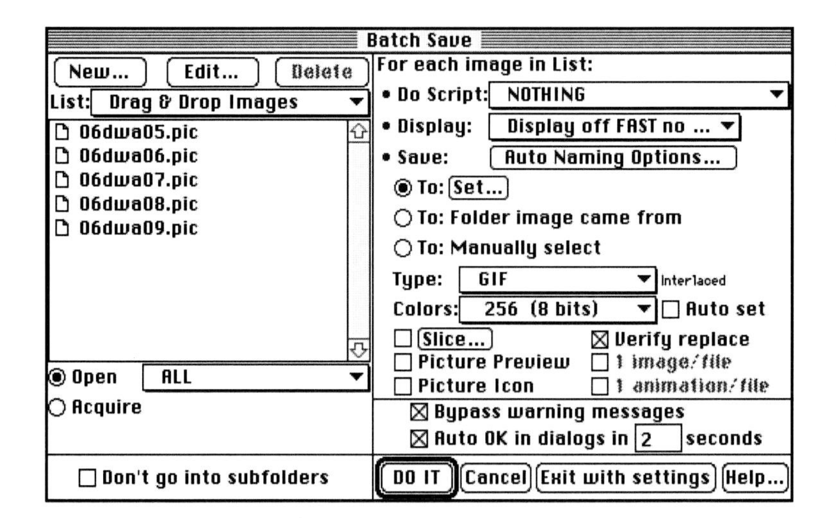

Figure 6.14

Batch Save dialog box in Debabelizer.

Creating Interlaced GIFs with GIFConverter

GIFConverter is an excellent shareware application for Macintosh available to be downloaded from many places on the Net. To create interlaced GIFs with GIFConverter:

1. Choose File, Save As.
2. Choose GIF from the File Type pop-up menu.
3. Click the Options button.
4. Check the Interlaced check box.
5. Click OK.

Note

Equilibrium Technology has made available free batch processing scripts designed specifically for creating GIF Web graphics. You can obtain these scripts at:

`http://www.equil.com/SoftwareScripts.html`

To create an interlaced GIF with PaintShop Pro:

1. Choose Save As under the File menu (see fig. 6.15).
2. Choose List Files of Type: GIF—CompuServe.
3. Choose File Sub-Format: Version 89a—Interlaced.
4. Click OK.

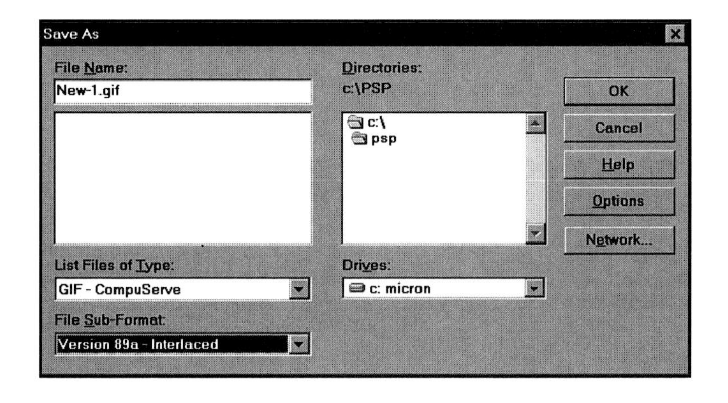

Figure 6.15

Save As an interlaced GIF in PaintShop Pro.

Minimize File Size

Of course, minimizing the file size in kilobytes of each graphic decreases download time. As with most digital media, there is a tradeoff. Large files have more information and are generally higher quality. Small files have less information and are lower quality. The cross-over point between acceptable quality and acceptable download time is up to you. Remember, download times for modem users are on the order of one second for every kilobyte and users might not wait more than 10 or 12 seconds for your page to download.

Getting an accurate idea of file size depends on many things, including the block size of the hard disk that the file resides on.

Note

On a Mac, use the Get Info command to get an accurate reading of the file size. On Windows machines, the most accurate reading of file size is in DOS.

Specific ways to cut down your file size are:

- Minimize the dimensions of your graphics.
- Adopt a color management strategy that:
  - Reduces the number of colors
  - Reduces dithering
  - Makes use of adaptive palettes
  - Converts gray-scale images to color or duotone
- Optimize the compression of your GIF files.

The following sections address specific ways to minimize file sizes.

Minimize Dimensions of Graphics

The larger the graphic, the larger the file size and the longer it takes to download. Does your logo really need to be 640×480 in size? Scale or reduce the dimensions of your graphic down to the smallest possible size that is readable and still serves its visual purpose.

Tip

If the graphic has a background color that is the same as your page, or if you are using transparency, shave off excess pixels around the borders of the graphic.

Two ways to change the dimensions of a graphic are:

1. You can crop the graphic or select a portion of the original graphic and discard the rest.
2. You can scale the graphic, which reduces the dimensions of the graphic and all its graphic elements.

Scaling may introduce artifacts (artifacts are blocky patterns of pixels introduced when computers try to squeeze graphic information into a smaller space) or make graphics hard to read, so be sure and remember to undo your scaling if you don't like the results. It's best to perform scaling operations on 24-bit graphics or graphics with the maximum amount of image information.

In Photoshop, you can crop a graphic with the Crop tool or the Canvas Size command under the Image menu. To scale a graphic, use the Image Size command under the Image menu.

Tip

To create the highest quality scaled-down graphic, perform the scale reduction after you have completed editing the graphic, but before you have reduced the color to 8-bit.

To crop a graphic in Debabelizer use the Trim command under the Edit menu or the Document Size command under the Edit menu. The Trim command can be used to trim the graphic to the smallest rectangle that encloses a specific graphic object. To scale a graphic in Debabelizer, use the Scale command under the Edit menu.

To reduce the dimensions of your graphic in PaintShop Pro, choose Resize under the Image menu and enter the new dimensions in pixels. To crop your graphic, first select the part of the graphic you want to keep, then choose Crop under the Image menu. The graphic will be cropped to the selection rectangle.

Adopting a Color Management Strategy

Because of the limitations of the 8-bit display systems that most users have, the colors that your graphic might display are unpredictable. Intelligent color management can help. The best color management strategy for your particular graphic image depends on:

- The colors, bit depth, and visual characteristics of your source image, such as continuous-tone images or flat-color graphics
- The purpose of the image
- The display capabilities of your target audience (8-bit or 24-bit)

The following sections are tips for reducing file size through color management.

Reduce the Number of Colors

By reducing the number of colors in your graphic image, you can reduce the file size and download time. Reducing colors can reduce file size by 10–50 percent. This chapter discusses many ways to reduce the number of colors in graphics for the Web.

Reduce Dithering

A good cross-platform color management strategy addresses the problem of dithering, described earlier in this chapter. Dithered graphics have more information stored in their files, compared to files of non-dithered, flat-color graphics. In other words, there are color variations in dithered graphics, which means more pixel information, and that adds up to a larger file size.

On Macintosh and most Unix systems, the Netscape browser dithers to a 256-color palette that is similar to the Macintosh system palette. On 8-bit, 256-color Windows systems, the Netscape browser dithers to a 216-color palette that is a subset of this 256-color palette.

Note

To read what Netscape has to say about palettes on 8-bit Windows systems visit:

`http://www.netscape.com/assist/support/client/tn/windows/10117.html`

Because the 216-color Windows browser palette is a subset of the 256-color palette used on other systems, you can use these 216 colors and be reasonably assured the colors won't dither on all systems. Use these colors for flat, solid color areas in Web graphics such as logos, buttons, illustration-style art, bitmap text, line art, or flat-color backgrounds. The following section shows you how to convert to a 216-color palette.

Note

Equilibrium has created a series of scripts for Debabelizer that helps you to create cross-platform, non-dithering GIFs. You can find them at: **`http://www.equil.com/SoftwareScripts.html`**.

Convert to the 216-Color Palette

One cross-platform color management strategy you can employ is to create graphics with areas of flat, solid colors using the 216-color palette. For graphics where higher color fidelity is important, you could use an expanded 256-color palette. Then, your graphic displays with all 256 colors on systems that support it. Test your graphic on the Windows systems to see if the dithering on Windows systems is acceptable.

To convert your graphic to the 216-color Web palette in Photoshop:

1. First convert your graphic to indexed color by choosing Indexed Color under the Mode menu. If the graphic is already an indexed color image, choose Mode, RGB color then Mode, Indexed Color to get the Indexed Color dialog box (see fig. 6.16).

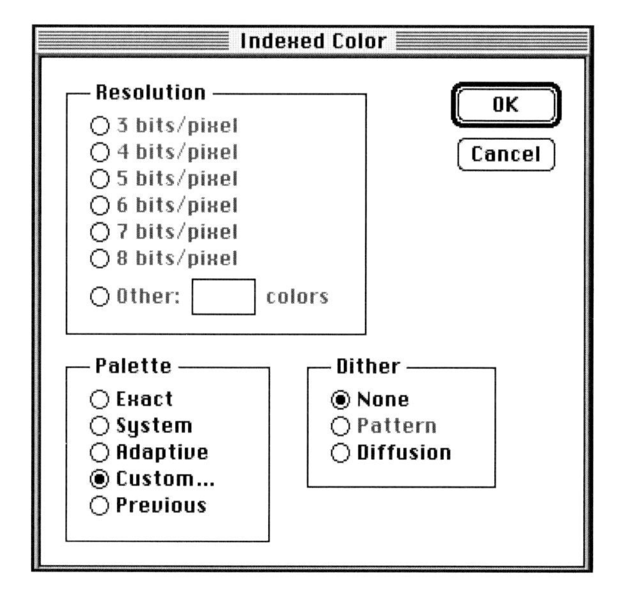

Figure 6.16

Indexed Color dialog box in Photoshop.

2. If the graphic predominantly contains areas of flat color choose the Dither None option.
3. Choose Custom.
4. Click Load.
5. Find and load the 216-color Web palette (see fig. 6.17).

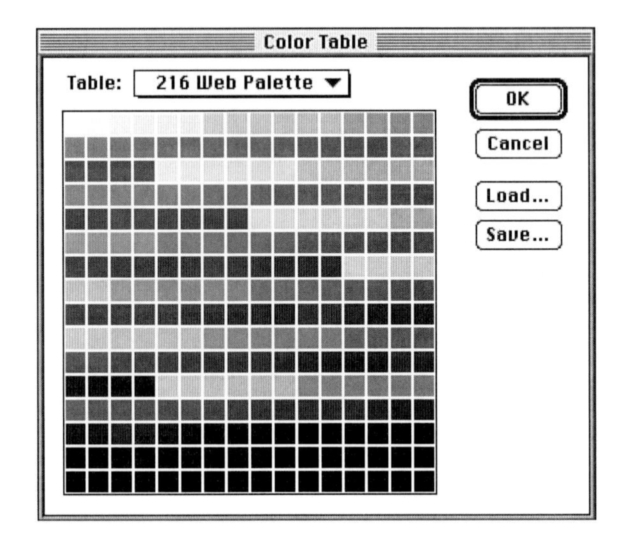

Figure 6.17

Color Table dialog box in Photoshop.

6. Click OK.

To add the 216-color Web palette to Debabelizer's list of saved palettes:

1. Drag the PICT file 216-color Web palette from the CD onto the Debabelizer icon or open it with the Open command.
2. Choose Rearrange from the Palette menu (see fig. 6.18).
3. Drag the black color chip from the 255 slot and drag it to the 215 slot.

Rearrange

This palette is rearranged from the last session. Hit "No arrange" to start over.

Undo
Revert
No Arrange
Rearrange:
pixels
palette
both
Help...
Cancel
OK

0	1	2	3	4	5	6	7	8	9	10	11	12	13	14	15
16	17	18	19	20	21	22	23	24	25	26	27	28	29	30	31
32	33	34	35	36	37	38	39	40	41	42	43	44	45	46	47
48	49	50	51	52	53	54	55	56	57	58	59	60	61	62	63
64	65	66	67	68	69	70	71	72	73	74	75	76	77	78	79
80	81	82	83	84	85	86	87	88	89	90	91	92	93	94	95
96	97	98	99	100	101	102	103	104	105	106	107	108	109	110	111
112	113	114	115	116	117	118	119	120	121	122	123	124	125	126	127
128	129	130	131	132	133	134	135	136	137	138	139	140	141	142	143
144	145	146	147	148	149	150	151	152	153	154	155	156	157	158	159
160	161	162	163	164	165	166	167	168	169	170	171	172	173	174	175
176	177	178	179	180	181	182	183	184	185	186	187	188	189	190	191
192	193	194	195	196	197	198	199	200	201	202	203	204	205	206	207
208	209	210	211	212	213	214	215	216	217	218	219	220	221	222	223
224	225	226	227	228	229	230	231	232	233	234	235	236	237	238	239
240	241	242	243	244	245	246	247	248	249	250	251	252	253	254	255

Figure 6.18

Rearranging palette color chips in Debabelizer.

4. Click OK.
5. Choose Palette: Save from the Palette menu.
6. Give the palette a name.
7. Enter 216 for the number of colors in the palette.
8. Click Add.

To convert your graphic to the 216-color Web palette in Debabelizer:

1. Choose Set Palette & Remap Pixels from the Palette menu.
2. Choose the 216-color Web palette that you just created from the Set Palette pop-up menu (see fig. 6.19).

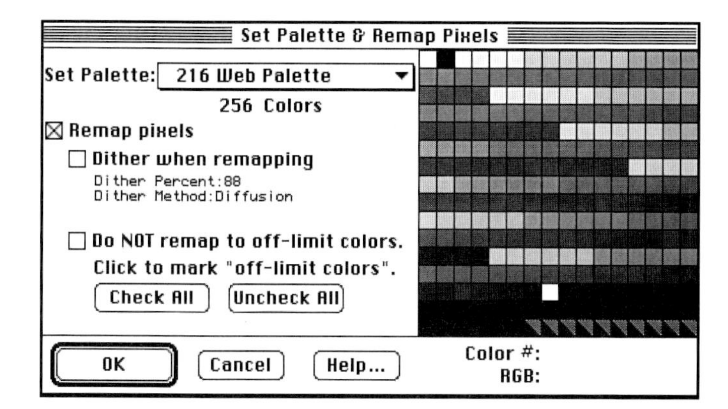

Figure 6.19

Set Palette & Remap Pixels dialog box in Debabelizer.

3. Check Remap pixels.
4. Uncheck Dither when remapping if you have a flat-color graphic.
5. Click OK.

On Windows systems, you must have the 216-color palette saved in the Microsoft palette format or use the file `216Web.pal` on this book's CD. To convert your graphic to the 216-color Web palette in PaintShop Pro:

1. Choose Load Palette under the Colors menu.
2. Find the palette file you want to use (see fig. 6.20), such as the file `216Web.pal` on this book's CD.
3. Choose Nearest Color if you want to map the colors in the graphic to the nearest colors in the new palette. Choose Error Diffusion to perform dithering of colors.
4. Click OK.

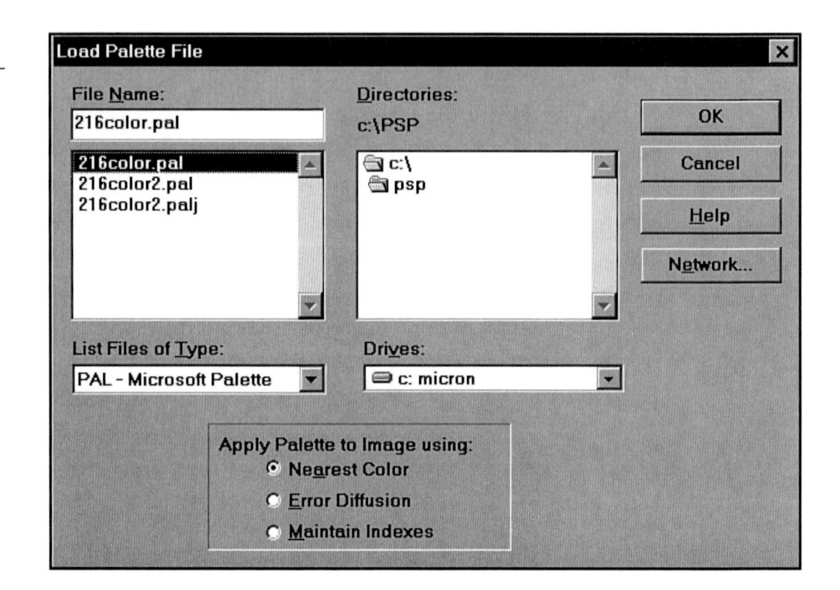

Figure 6.20

The Load Palette File dialog box in PaintShop Pro.

Adaptive Palettes

Many graphics programs enable you to create adaptive palettes, optimized palettes, or super palettes. These programs, such as Photoshop or Debabelizer, create a 256-color "best-fit" palette based on the particular colors found in a specific image. These colors are carefully chosen to maximize the graphic image quality. If color fidelity is important and JPEGs aren't an option, consider creating an adaptive palette GIF. On 16-bit displays or 24-bit displays, the browser shows the GIF with the special optimized (adaptive) palette. On 8-bit displays, the browser dithers the adaptive palette GIF to the current system palette. View the graphic on 8-bit displays on different platforms to see if the dithering is acceptable.

To create an adaptive palette in Photoshop:

1. First, convert your graphic to indexed color by choosing Indexed Color under the Mode menu. If the graphic is already an indexed color image, choose Mode, RGB color then Mode, Indexed Color to get the Indexed Color dialog box.
2. If the graphic predominantly contains areas of flat color choose the Dither None option.
3. Choose Adaptive.

Note

For useful information about Web palettes for graphic designers visit Lynda Weinman's site at:

`http://www.lynda.com/hex.html`

Lynda Weinman's book from New Riders, *Designing Web Graphics*, is an excellent resource for anyone creating graphics on the Web.

Debabelizer has many sophisticated palette optimization features, including creating an optimized super palette based on the colors in several different graphics. You can also create a Super Palette from just one image. To create a Super Palette in Debabelizer:

1. Choose Super Palette: Initialize under the Palette menu to clear out old Super Palettes.
2. Choose Super Palette: Factor in This Picture under the Palette menu to factor in the currently open graphic.
3. Choose Super Palette: Create Super Palette under the Palette menu (see fig. 6.21).

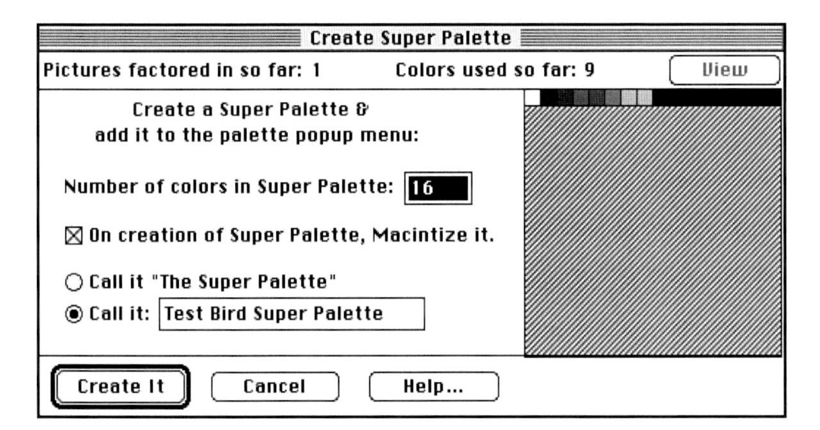

Figure 6.21

Create Super Palette dialog box in Debabelizer.

4. Give the palette a name. It will be added to Debabelizer's list of palettes.
5. Choose Set Palette & Remap Pixels from the Palette menu.

6. Choose the Super Palette you just created from the Set Palette pop-up menu.

To create an optimal palette in PaintShop Pro:

1. Choose the entire image or a portion of the image that contains representative colors.
2. Choose Count Colors Used under the Colors menu. Note the number of colors in your image.
3. Choose X Color under the Colors: Decrease Color Depth menu as shown in figure 6.22.

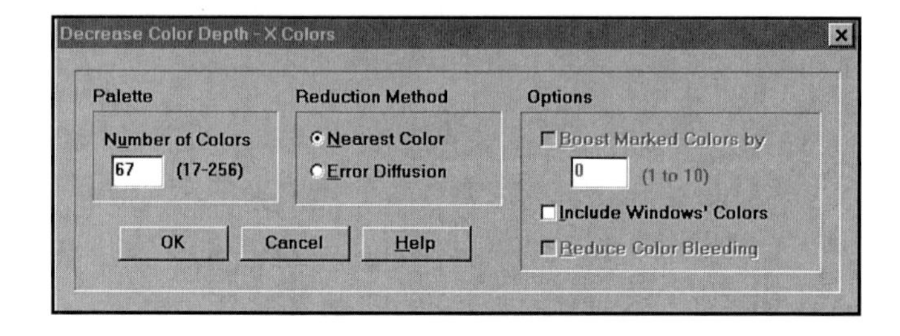

Figure 6.22

Decrease Color Depth-X Colors dialog box in PaintShop Pro.

4. Enter the number of colors; this number should be a minimum of 17 and a maximum of 256 or the number of colors noted in step 2, whichever is less. If you specify a number smaller than the number of colors specified in step 2 your graphic file will be smaller, but you will be changing the color distribution of your graphic.
5. To avoid dithering of colors choose Nearest Color. To perform dithering choose Error Diffusion.
6. Click OK.

Other Palette Reduction Tips

After you have converted your graphic to the 216-color cross-platform Web palette, you might be able to reduce the file size further by using an Exact palette with fewer bits/pixels. An Exact palette is only available as an option in Photoshop if the image uses 256 colors or less. The Exact palette only contains colors that are in the original image and there is no dithering. For example, you might save your image with the 216-color browser palette, but only 27 colors out of that palette are actually used in the graphic. An Exact palette only contains those 27 colors. To reduce the number of bits/pixels with an Exact palette in Photoshop:

1. If your graphic is already an indexed color graphic, choose Mode, RGB Color, then choose Mode, Indexed Color to convert the graphic back to indexed color and show the Indexed Color dialog box.
2. In the Indexed Color dialog box choose Exact. Choose an option less than 8-bits/pixel, such as 7-bits/pixel or 6-bits/pixel.
3. View the image and see if it is acceptable quality.

To reduce palettes in PaintShop Pro:

1. Make sure no portions of the image are selected.
2. Choose Count Colors Used under the Colors menu. Note the number of colors in your image.
3. Choose X Color under the Colors/Decrease Color Depth menu.
4. Enter the number of colors. This number should be less than the number of colors noted in step 2.
5. To avoid dithering of colors choose Nearest Color. To perform dithering choose Error Diffusion.
6. Click OK.

You can reduce the number of colors in a palette in Photoshop from the Indexed Color dialog box. If your image is already an indexed color graphic, choose RGB Color from the Mode menu and then Indexed Color from the Mode menu to get the Indexed Color dialog box. To ensure that you use non-dithering Web colors, you might try converting to the non-dithering Web palette first, then performing a second palette conversion to an Exact palette with fewer bits per pixel.

Tip

Perform palette reduction as the very last step in converting your graphics for the Web.

The following are several ways to perform palette reduction in Debabelizer:

- Reduce the number of bits per pixel when you save the file.
- Choose Change Pixel Depth under the Palette menu.

- Choose Set Palette & Remap Pixels under the Palette menu to set the palette to a saved palette such as the 216-color Web palette. You can also use free scripts for this purpose that you can download from:

  `http://www.equil.com/SoftwareScripts.html`

To reduce the number of colors in a palette in PaintShop Pro:

1. Make sure no portions of the image are selected.
2. Choose Decrease Color Depth under the Colors menu.
3. Choose one of the default number of colors such as 256 Colors or 16 Colors or choose X Colors to enter a custom number of colors.
4. In the Decrease Color Depth dialog box, choose Nearest Color to avoid dithering of colors. To perform dithering choose Error Diffusion or Ordered Dither.
5. Click OK.

Help the Compressor

Because of the way GIF compression works, you can improve compression of GIF graphics and the speed at which your files load, if you:

- **Use flat colors.** Generally, flat, solid colors, without gradients, compress better.
- **Don't dither flat-color GIFs.** Choose the No Dither option in your graphics program if this option is present.
- **Apply gradients from top to bottom.** If you do use gradients, gradients that progress from top to bottom compress better than gradients that progress from right to left.

Creating Backgrounds

Background colors and background graphics are an easy way to provide context cues and visually brand different areas on your Web site. Backgrounds also provide the only layering possibilities in HTML documents. Background colors and background graphics were introduced in Netscape Navigator 2.0 and are supported in recent versions of MSIE. Some older browsers ignore tags that set background colors and background graphics, in which case your Web page appears with the default browser background color.

Here are some tips concerning backgrounds:

- Backgrounds shouldn't make your page hard to read. You want people to read the text on your page. Don't place a busy patterned background behind a lot of text.
- If you have dark-colored text, then choose a light-colored background and vice versa. White is a nice background color with dark-colored text, but can strain the eyes if you are reading a lot of text. Avoid bright vibrant colors for backgrounds.
- For solid background colors, you probably want to stick to the 216 colors that won't dither on 8-bit displays on different platforms.

Background graphics add to download times, so keep your background graphics very small, for example under 10 KB, especially if you have a lot of other graphics.

Tip

Backgrounds should be subdued. Be subtle. Don't create a background that is similar in color or value to the colors of hyperlinks and text. Avoid saturated, high-pitched colors for backgrounds.

Specifying Background Colors

You specify the background color of the Web page in HTML with the BGCOLOR attribute of the BODY tag. The BGCOLOR attribute is supported by Navigator 2.0 or later and MSIE 2.0 or later. It's written as follows:

```
<BODY BGCOLOR = #FFFFFF>
```

This code sets the background color of the page to white.

The BGCOLOR takes on the value of the RGB value of the color in hexadecimal notation. Stick to the 216 colors that won't dither on 8-bit displays on different platforms for solid background colors.

Background Colors in Table Cells

Table cells are the rectangles that make up part of an HTML table.

Note

For hexadecimal versions of the 216-color browser palette colors, visit Lynda Weinman's site at:

http://www.lynda.com/hex.html

The appendix to this book also contains additional information on this topic.

In Navigator 3.0 and MSIE you can set the background color of table cells using the BGCOLOR attribute like so:

```
<TD BGCOLOR = #FFFFFF> a table cell with a background
➥color </TD>
```

Tiled Background Graphics

You can use the BACKGROUND attribute of the BODY tag to tile a graphic in the background. The BACKGROUND attribute looks like:

```
<BODY BACKGROUND = "myBackGround.gif">
```

where `myBackGround.gif` is an URL for the graphic you want to appear in the background.

Use small graphics for tiled backgrounds; under 7–10 KB for example. You can also use a single very large graphic, or a very long graphic that extends beyond the range of the browser window to produce interesting effects. If your graphic has a lot of flat color areas it can be compressed to a very small GIF file.

Warning

If you use interlaced GIFs or Progressive JPEGs for background tiles, the progressive increase in resolution may be distracting. It may also make your pages hard to read while the resolution increases. It may be best to avoid interlaced background tiles, unless you are looking for a particular effect.

There are several ways to create a seamless tiled background in Photoshop depending on the kind of graphic you start with. One way is as follows:

1. Open the graphic you want to use as a tile. Make sure it is in RGB Color mode.
2. Choose Other: Offset under the Filter menu.
3. Choose an appropriate offset value; 50 pixels for example.
4. Use the Rubber Stamp tool to brush out the seams.

Creating a seamless tile in Fractal Design Painter is easy.

1. Choose New under the File menu and give the new document the dimensions of the tile.
2. Choose Patterns: Define Pattern under the Tools menu.
3. Paint away. Your painting will automatically wrap around.

Vector Graphics

Programs that use vector graphics include object-oriented, PostScript drawing programs such as Macromedia FreeHand and Adobe Illustrator. Vector graphics use mathematical formulas to describe graphic elements, and have the following benefits:

- Because graphic elements are mathematical formulas, and not bitmaps as they are in a program like Photoshop, file sizes are much smaller.
- Graphics are scalable, meaning that they can be enlarged without becoming jagged or pixellated.

Because of the small file size and inherent scalability, vector graphics hold much promise for the Web. This section discusses using Macromedia's Shockwave for FreeHand to display FreeHand vector graphics within a Web page.

Shockwave for FreeHand

Shockwave for FreeHand is a Netscape Plug-In that provides the capability to display native FreeHand graphic files within your Netscape Navigator 2.0 or later Web pages. The Plug-Ins and authoring tools are available for both Mac and Windows. An URL for finding these tools is provided later in this chapter.

Shockwave for FreeHand consists of three parts:

- Shockwave for FreeHand Plug-Ins enables users to view inline FreeHand graphics directly in the Web page in Netscape Navigator 2.0 or later. In addition the user can zoom and pan around the image using command keys or an optional controller.
- Afterburner Xtra is a compression utility for the FreeHand graphics program that enables designers to export compressed FreeHand graphic files for the Web or import compressed files for editing.
- URLs Xtra for FreeHand enables designers to add URL hotspots to FreeHand graphic objects. It enables you to create clickable image maps with hotspots.

Shockwave for Freehand displays on the Web nearly everything you can display in FreeHand itself. It does not support:

- EPS files
- Linked TIFF files, although you can use embedded TIFFs
- PostScript lines and fills
- Some text effects and formatting, such as range kerning

To print a FreeHand graphic from Netscape for Macintosh, choose the Print command under the File menu. To print a FreeHand graphic on Windows systems you need to:

1. Save the graphic to your local hard disk.
2. Open the file in Navigator with the Open File command.
3. Choose Print.

Note

For the latest Shockwave or FreeHand Plug-Ins and documentation on their use, visit:

`http://www.macromedia.com/shockwave/freehand/index2.html`

Setting Up Web Servers for Shockwave for FreeHand

To serve FreeHand graphics from your Web site, the Web server needs to be set up to associate MIME type `image`, and subtype `x-freehand` with extensions `fh4`, `fh5`, `fhc`.

When you transfer your FreeHand graphic files to the server, be sure and transfer them in binary mode and as raw data if your FTP software has that option.

Creating Shockwave for FreeHand Graphics

To create graphics with Shockwave for FreeHand you need the tools listed in the Tools box:

Tools
FreeHand
Afterburner Xtra in your FreeHand Xtras folder
URLs Xtra in your FreeHand Xtras folder

Setting Up Your FreeHand Document for Shockwave

First, you must set up your FreeHand document:

1. Choose the Document Setup icon on the Document Inspector palette (see fig. 6.23).
2. In the pop-up menu, set the unit of measure to Points. The dimensions of the graphic in points is approximately equal to the dimension of the graphic in pixels.

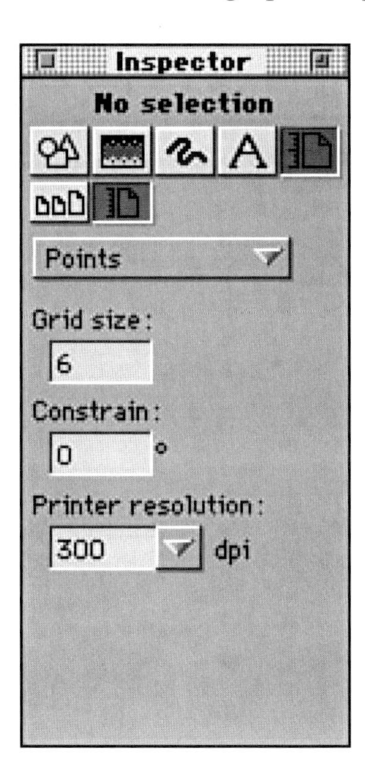

Figure 6.23

Document Inspector palette.

3. Choose the Pages icon on the Document Inspector palette.
4. Drag the little page rectangle to the lower left of the page display area. The Page Inspector palette appears as shown in figure 6.24.

Figure 6.24

Page Inspector palette.

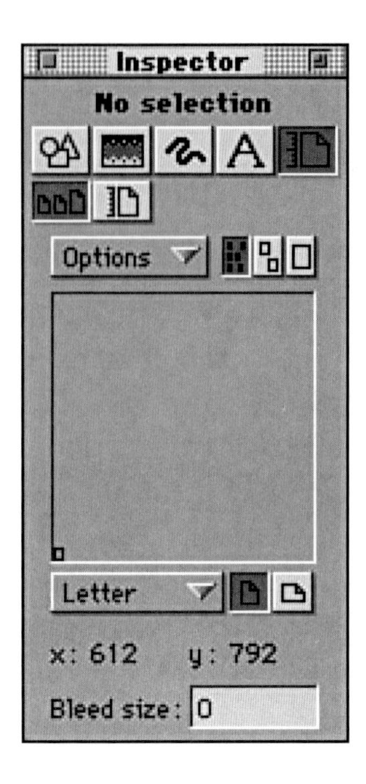

5. If you have embedded TIFF graphics, do the following:
   - Under the File menu, choose Preferences.
   - Choose Import/Output.
   - Check "Embed TIFF/EPS upon import rather than links (increases file size)."

   Because TIFF graphics are bitmaps, they add substantially to total file size.

Following these steps ensures the smoothest conversion to Shockwave graphics for the Web.

Optimizing Your FreeHand Document for the Web

Now create your FreeHand document. You can use more than one page, because the user can see other pages by panning. The last page visible in FreeHand when you create a compressed FreeHand graphic with Afterburner is the first page visible in Netscape. More pages increases file size, so try not to use more than one page.

The following are some file size reduction tips:

- Only use one page.
- Keep dimensions as small as possible.
- Do not use embedded TIFFs.
- Delete unused background graphics or any object that is invisible or covered over by other objects.
- Choose Options, Remove in the Layers palette to remove any selected, invisible layers.
- Choose Delete, Unused Named Colors in the Xtras menu to remove unused colors.
- For complex objects, choose Cleanup, Simplify under the Xtras menu to reduce the number of points.
- Do not use Paste Inside.
- Compress the graphic with the Afterburner utility.
- To avoid dithering, use the 216-color cross-platform Web palette. To ensure you use these colors, place the palette as a PICT graphic in your FreeHand document, then use the FreeHand eyedropper to select individual colors from the palette. Delete the palette before you compress the FreeHand document for the Web.

Tip

Use cross-platform fonts, such as Courier, Times, and Arial. If you use fonts that might not be present on the user's system, you can embed font outlines by selecting the text and choosing Convert to Paths under the Type menu to convert your fonts to path outlines. This increases the size of your FreeHand document.

Creating Image Maps with FreeHand

Shockwave for FreeHand enables you to create sophisticated image maps. All the image map processing is done by the Shockwave for FreeHand Plug-Ins. You can make any FreeHand object a clickable hotspot, by attaching an URL to the FreeHand object. You must have the URLs Xtra in your Xtra folder. To attach an URL to a FreeHand object:

1. Choose Other, URLs under the Window menu.
2. Choose New under the Options menu in the URLs window.
3. Type in the URL. You can use relative URLs, but the URL will be relative to the FreeHand document not the HTML document within which it is embedded.
4. Choose the URL and drag it on to the FreeHand graphic object that you want it to be linked to.

Note

If you want to display the toolbar in the Web page with your FreeHand graphic, the graphic must be at least 149 pixels wide. More details about displaying the Toolbar can be found later in this chapter in "Embedding a FreeHand Document with HTML."

Reduce To Fit

After you've created your FreeHand document, reduce the page size to fit precisely around your graphic objects:

1. Choose all of your graphic objects.
2. Choose Group under the Arrange menu.
3. Drag the group to the lower left corner of the page.
4. While the grouped objects are still selected, choose the Object Inspector.
5. Write down the dimensions of the grouped graphics in the Object Inspector.
6. Choose the Page Inspector (see fig. 6.25).
7. Choose Custom from the page size pop-up menu.

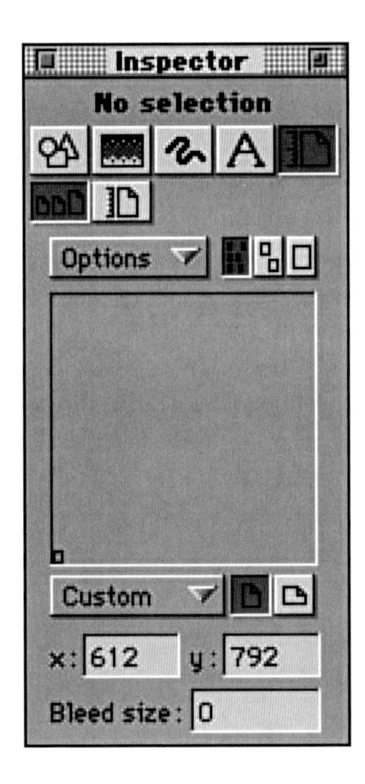

Figure 6.25

Setting Custom page size.

8. Enter the dimensions of the grouped objects as the page size. You use these dimensions when you embed your FreeHand graphic in your HTML document.
9. Ungroup objects if you want.

Compressing with Afterburner

After you have completed creating your FreeHand graphic, use the Afterburner Xtra to compress it for the Web:

1. Open the document in FreeHand. If the document is already open, save the FreeHand document as shown in figure 6.26.
2. Choose Afterburner, Compress Document under the Xtras menu.
3. Enter a file name. Be sure the file name has the `.fhc` extension.
4. To lock a document, check the Locked option. A locked document can be viewed by the Shockwave for FreeHand Plug-Ins but cannot be opened again in FreeHand.

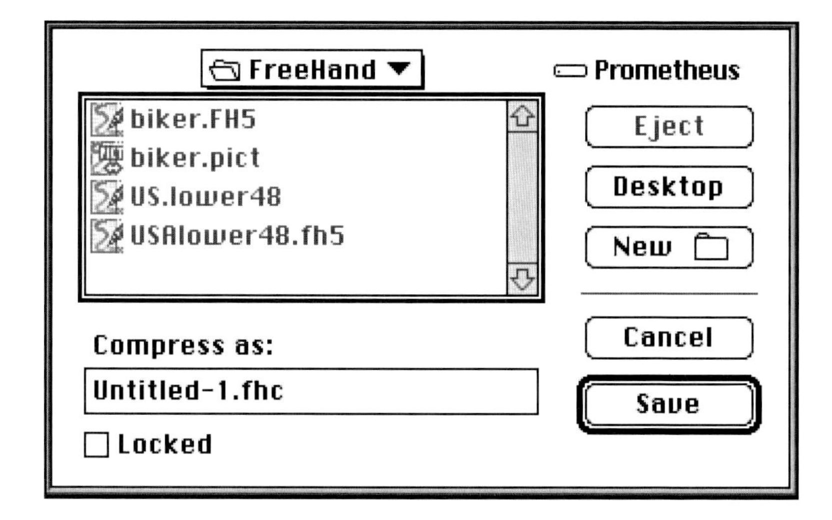

Figure 6.26

Saving a compressed FreeHand file.

Opening Compressed Files

A file compressed with Afterburner can be opened again in FreeHand, if it is not locked. To open a compressed file in FreeHand:

1. Choose Afterburner, Decompress Document under the Xtras menu.
2. Choose the file you wish to open. Only files with the `.fhc` suffix will be available.
3. Click OK.

Embedding a FreeHand Document with HTML

To embed a FreeHand graphic in an HTML document use the following HTML code (see fig. 6.27 and fig. 6.28):

```
<EMBED SRC="myFreeHandGraphic.fhc" WIDTH=480 HEIGHT=340
TOOLBAR = TOP>
```

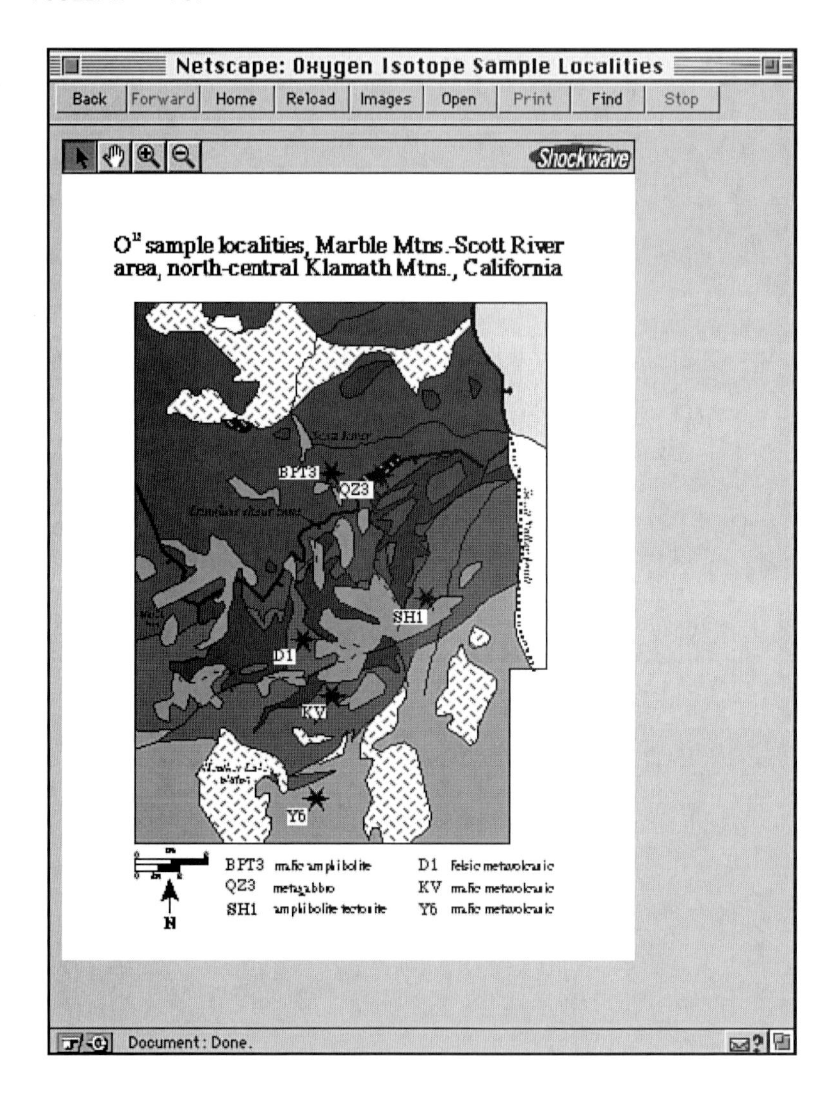

Figure 6.27

Shockwave for FreeHand displaying a map.

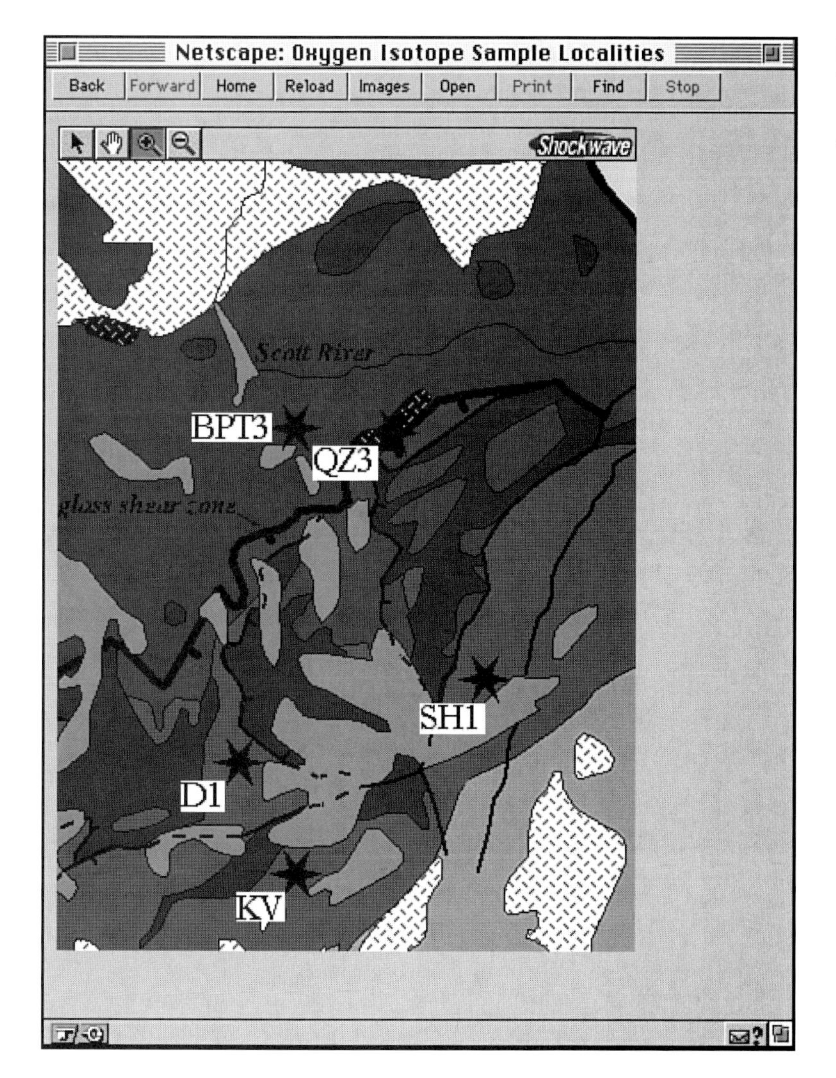

Figure 6.28

Using the zoom tool in Shockwave for FreeHand.

The TOOLBAR attribute places a toolbar at the top of your graphic that enables the user to pan and zoom around the graphic. The toolbar is 20 pixels high, so you must add 20 pixels to the HEIGHT dimension of the graphic to display the toolbar. You can also put the toolbar at the bottom of the graphic by setting `TOOLBAR = BOTTOM`.

Table 6.4 lists keyboard shortcuts for toolbar functions.

Table 6.4

Keyboard Shortcuts for Toolbar Functions in Shockwave for FreeHand

Function	Macintosh	Windows
Zoom-in	Command click	Right-button click, Control left-button click
Zoom-out	Command-option click	Alt right-button click, Control+Alt left-button click
Return to default	Command-Shift click	Shift Right-button magnification click, Shift+Control left-button click
Pan	Control click and drag	Spacebar click and drag

Dynamic Images

Dynamic images are images that change periodically, but are not considered animation. One of the most frequent uses of dynamic images is to load a different splash screen, logo, or billboard, either randomly or based on some criteria such as the time of day, each time a page is uploaded. Another application of dynamic images is to change an image while the user is visiting the page, like an animation with a very slow frame rate. For example, this application is commonly used for dynamic billboards that display rotating ads for 30 second intervals.

LOWSRC Tag

You can create dynamic images by using the LOWSRC attribute of the IMG tag in HTML. This attribute enables you to specify a low-bandwidth graphic that downloads before the graphic file that is specified in the SRC. You can use the LOWSRC attribute to create simple two-frame animations. See the section on the LOWSRC attribute in the section on HTML for inline graphics for more information.

META Tag

You can use the HTTP-EQUIV attribute of the META tag to create dynamic images. This attribute automatically loads a new HTML document after a specific length of time. This technique violates some interface principles because it takes control away from the user, and can disorient the user. But it may have applications in certain situations.

Place the following HTML between the <HEAD></HEAD> tags of your HTML document:

```
<META HTTP-EQUIV=REFRESH CONTENT="20;
➥URL=myNewPage.html">
```

When a user loads this HTML document, the page displays for 20 seconds. Then the document `myNewPage.html` is loaded in the Web browser.

GIF Animations with Long Interframe Delays

GIF animation tools on this book's CD enable you to set a time delay between frames in a GIF animation. If you set this delay to a long period of time, you can create the impression of a dynamically updating image. See Chapter 7, "Animation," for instructions on how to set up GIF animations with long interframe delays using GIFBuilder and the GIF Construction Kit. See Chapter 14, "Scripting Multimedia Web Pages," to find out how to do this with JavaScript.

Random Image Display Using CGI

Several CGI scripts are available on the Web that enable you to display random images in a Web page. You need access to a CGI directory on a Web server to run these scripts.

One of the best sources for CGI scripts on the Web is Matt's Script Archive at `http://worldwidemart.com/scripts/`.

You can check out his dynamic image displayer at `http://worldwidemart.com/scripts/image.shtml`.

This script enables you to display either a random inlined graphic or a random background from a list of images that you specify.

Dynamic Images Using JavaScript and Java

Netscape Navigator 3.0 has new JavaScript functions that enable you to change and update inline images on the fly. See Chapter 14 to learn how to do this.

You can also create dynamic images using Java. See Chapter 15, "Java," for details.

The Dynamic Billboard Java applet enables you to change graphics, the length of time each graphic is displayed, and the type of transition between graphics. The Dynamic Billboard Java Applet has been consistently rated in the Top Ten of all Java applets by the JARS (Java Applet Rating Service) rating service and is free. You can find the Dynamic Billboard Applet at:

`http://www.db.erau.edu/java/billboard/`

Recently released Java tools enable you to create your own types of dynamic images.

Note

Two excellent sources for examples of Java applets are:

`http://www.jars.com/`

`http://www.gamelan.com/`

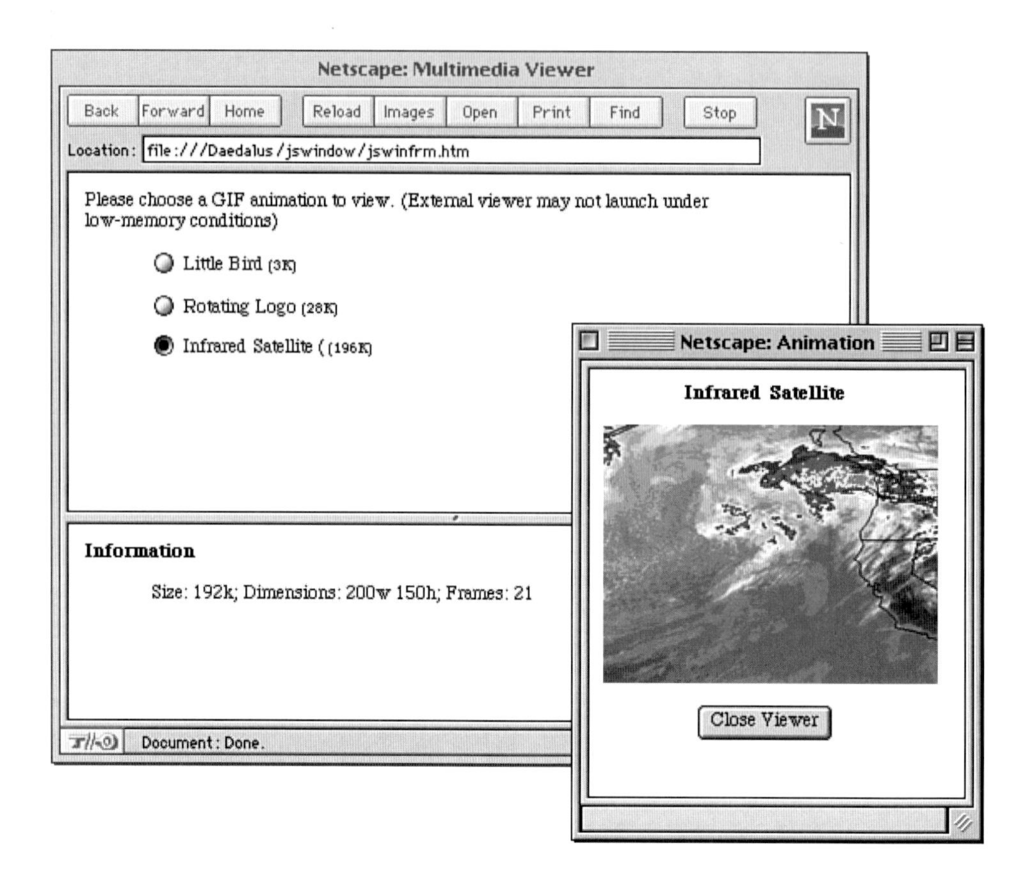

Creating effective animations within the limitations of Web playback can be one of the most demanding tasks for the Web designer. If you use television or film as your measure of high-quality animation, the Web has a long way to go to match these production values. Used judiciously and with awareness of the limited bandwidth of your users, Web animations can add to the enjoyment and information content of your Web site.

chapter

7

Animation

To most people, multimedia on the Web means animated graphics. Animated graphics can be as simple as an animated bullet that loops endlessly or as complex as a full multimedia piece that integrates sound, animation, interactivity, and dynamic data from the Internet or a local computer.

Besides attracting attention, you can use animations to illustrate changes over time, visualize 3D objects, or simulate a dynamic process (see fig. 7.1).

This chapter shows you how to do the following:

- Create animations using tried and true animation techniques
- Create GIF animations
- Create server-push animations
- Create animations for Netscape Plug-Ins and ActiveX controls

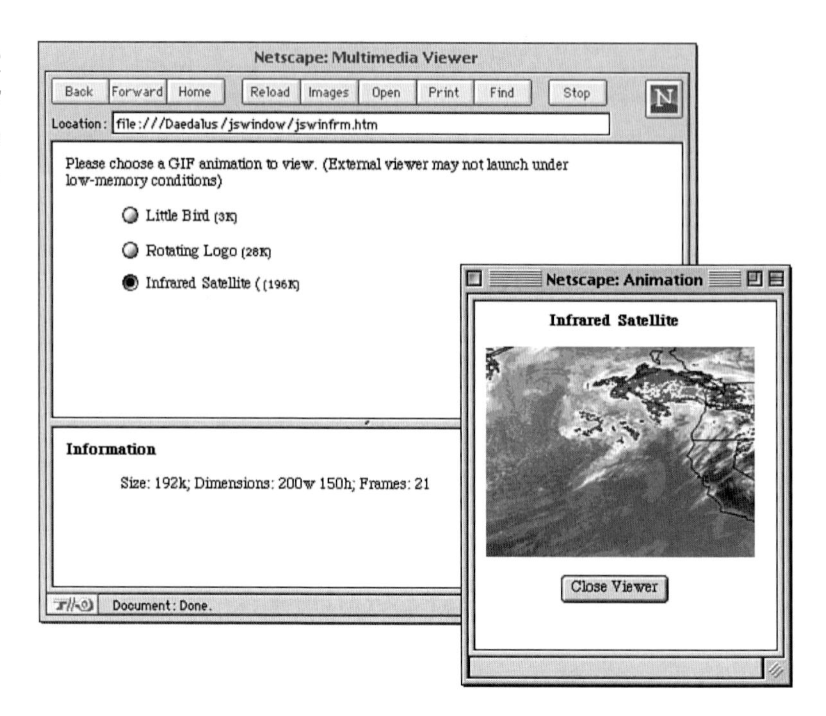

Figure 7.1

Dynamically created GIF animation of real-time satellite data.

Animation on the Web

persistence of vision

Animations are created from a sequence of still images. The images are displayed rapidly in succession so that the eye is fooled into perceiving continuous motion. People perceive the sequence of still images as motion because of a phenomenon called persistence of vision. **Persistence of vision** is the tendency of the eye and brain to continue to perceive an image even after it disappears.

inline animations

There are several ways to add animated graphics to Web pages. You can display animations directly in the Web page in your browser, much like you would image files. These are called **inline animations.** You can display animations by launching client-side, helper applications that will display animations within separate windows. Some animation formats enable you to incorporate sound and interactivity. Many require special viewers for playback.

Overcoming Obstacles

Several factors limit the use of animation on the Web, including the following:

- Bandwidth
- Download time
- The asynchronous nature of the Internet
- Differences in platforms, browser support, and file formats

These obstacles are discussed in more detail in subsequent sections.

Typically, Web animations are computer files that must be completely downloaded to the client machine before playback begins. Even some of the smallest animation files can be quite large and take a long time to download. You can circumvent the aforementioned obstacles to some extent, therefore, by reducing your animations' file size.

Many of the tricks you have learned for reducing file size of graphics, audio, and digital video also apply to animations, only you have to perform your optimizations on every animation frame. To aid you, many authoring tools, such as Director's Afterburner, MovieStar, WebPainter, FutureSplash Animator, and WebAnimator, provide built-in compression and color management specifically for Web animations.

Note

If you get into any serious animation production work, invest in a graphics batch processor, such as Equilibrium Debabelizer on Mac or Brenda the Batch Renderer on Windows:

`http://www.netnet.net/pub/mirrors/truesapce/utils/`

It takes less time than processing each individual frame by hand.

Bandwidth Considerations

Corporate and university LANs or intranets often have bandwidth and network speeds that exceed what is available to the average home user. Typical transfer rates range from 10–50 KB per second, or more under optimal conditions. In these environments, Web animation can be a powerful tool for training, instruction, and sharing of information. The Web enables information providers to serve rich, multimedia, just-in-time content that can communicate more effectively than other delivery methods. Figure 7.2 is from a series of Web-based instructional materials that uses animation to illustrate a process; in this case, installing Netscape Plug-Ins.

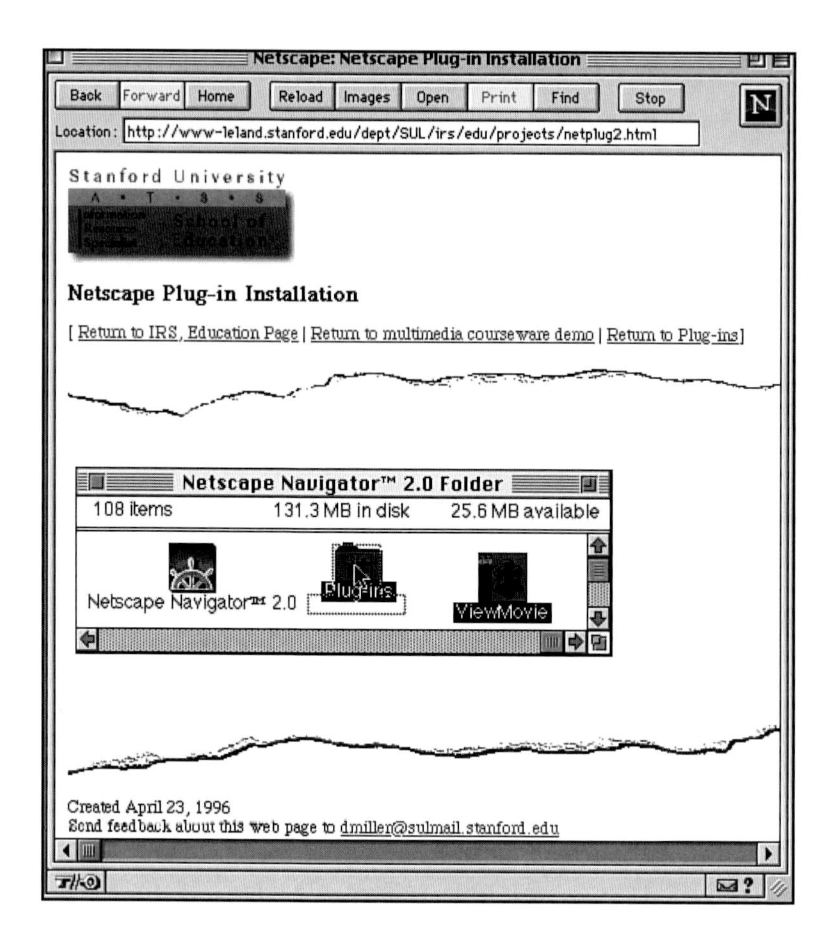

Figure 7.2

GIF animation in a Web page illustrating how to install a Netscape Plug-In.

As bandwidth increases, Web animation becomes more practical. In the meantime, you probably should try to be bandwidth-friendly and use Web animation judiciously.

Estimating Download Time

Most users connect to the Web with 28.8 bps-or-less modems. They can download data at a maximum rate of about 2.5 KB per second. For modem users, it's probably safe to expect about a second of download time for each KB of data or 1–2 minutes of download time for every 100 KB of animation. One to two minutes on the Web can seem like an eternity to users. Modem users don't have the patience to sit through long downloads just to see a spinning logo. They might put up with longer download times if they perceived an added benefit. Animations that provide game play, illustrate a dynamic process, enhance the visualization of complex data, clearly and succinctly explain a task, bring increased interactivity, or have a wow factor (like navigable 3D environments or an interactive character) might be worth the download time for some users.

Streaming

streaming

Many animation programs use proprietary data formats and a technique called streaming as a way around bandwidth limitations. **Streaming** is the capability of specially formatted time-based media, such as animation, to begin playback before the entire file has been completely downloaded. The rest of the file is downloaded from the server, or *streamed*, in the background while the animation or other time-based media plays on the client. Streaming circumvents the problem of having to download the entire file to the local hard disk before playback begins, so playback of animation begins much sooner.

Streaming can be tricky to implement because Internet data is packet-based and wasn't designed for the delivery of continuous, synchronized, time-based data. Interruptions in the continuous data stream can cause stutters and gaps during playback of animation.

Animation Formats

Another problem with Web animation is that after users retrieve animation files, they must have the proper helper applications or Plug-Ins before they can display the animation, or their browsers must natively support the particular animation format. Several animation formats exist today, with varying capabilities and uses.

Note

Animation on the Web certainly seems primitive compared to video and film animation, or even to CD-ROM animation. Web animations are characterized by small viewing areas and herky-jerky motions. You won't see a Web version of *Toy Story* anytime soon.

So why bother with animation? Animation is good way to draw attention to and add interest in an otherwise static Web page. On the other hand, it can distract people from reading the information you're serving them. So, use animated graphics judiciously; putting animations on a Web page whose primary purpose is to serve information you want people to read isn't a good idea.

Principles, Tools, and Techniques of Animation

Computer animation software can perform many of the tedious and repetitive animation tasks that historically, teams of animators have performed by working day and night for weeks or months. Plus, computer animation software provides all the benefits of digital editing. Some artists think computer animation has a certain coldness or sterile style compared to hand-drawn animation. This stylistic gap has narrowed some as tools and methods of animation have evolved.

The following section describes some basic animation principles and terminology, including specific aspects of computer animation, as follows:

- Cel animation
- Flip-book animation
- Sprite, path, and vector animation
- Frame rate
- Key frames and tweening
- Character animation
- Timelines, tracks, and animation sequencers
- Key frame transitions
- 2D versus 3D animation
- Animation special effects
- Processing graphics files

This section also emphasizes tools and techniques that are available on relatively inexpensive desktop computers, as opposed to the expensive hardware and software used by many production houses and film studios.

Cel Animation

cel

The term **cel** (only one "l") comes from ***celluloid***, the material that made up early motion picture film. It refers to the transparent piece of film that is used in traditional hand-drawn animation. Nowadays, this transparent film is usually made from acetate, not celluloid.

Pieces of an animation are drawn on individual pieces of acetate or cels. Animation cels are generally layered to produce a single animation frame. There is a separate cel for the background layer and a separate cel for each object that moves independently over the background.

layering
frames

Layering enables the animator to isolate and redraw the parts of the image that change between successive frames. A **frame** consists of the background and the overlying cels; it is like a snapshot, showing the action of the animation at one instant in time. Drawing on acetate enables the animator to lay successive frames one on top of the other and see at a glance how the animation progresses through time. Many of the processes and terminology of traditional cel-based animation, such as layering, key frames, and tweening, have carried over into computer animation.

Note

By the way, animation frames have nothing to do with Web browser frames.

Flip-Book Animation

Flip-book style animation or frame-based animation is the simplest kind of animation to visualize. As a kid, you probably had one of those flip-books that had a series of drawings in the margins of successive pages. When you thumbed through the book rapidly, the drawings appeared to move.

On a computer, flip-book animation means displaying a sequence of graphic files.

The simplest and slowest form of this is the slide show. Slide shows on the Web typically are used to support a presentation and can be an effective and relatively bandwidth-friendly way to provide multimedia information on the Web. Slide shows can be created with some of the animation software featured in this book. Because slide shows don't need to display a sequence of frames rapidly to simulate smooth motion, they can play back over slow or busy networks.

To produce animation or the illusion of motion, graphic images are displayed in rapid succession. Each image is slightly different from the one before. The graphic images are displayed so fast that the viewer is fooled into perceiving a moving image. In film, this display rate is 24 images, or frames, per second, but on the Web you will probably have to settle for less. For playback on a computer, the entire graphic file has to be "painted" on the computer screen for each animation frame.

Note

On the Web, GIF animation and server-push animation use a form of flip-book animation. GIF animation uses a sequence of GIF files stored in a special GIF animation file format, and server-push animation rapidly displays separate graphic files, usually GIF or JPEG, that are stored on the Web server.

The problem with this form of animation on bandwidth-sensitive mediums such as the Web is that it's hard to update each frame fast enough that the viewer perceives smooth, continuous motion.

Apple Computer's QuickTime, Macromedia's Shockwave, and much of the animation software featured on the CD use various algorithms to compress files, so that instead of having to update the entire screen display for each frame, as you must in flip-book animation, you only update the parts of the screen display that have changed between frames. This compression leads to smaller file sizes and faster playback.

Sprite, Path, and Vector Animation

sprite-based animation
cast-based animation
sprites

Sprite-based animation, sometimes called **cast-based animation,** as in a cast of characters, is very common in computer arcade games and computer animation programs. Sprite-based animation is similar to the traditional animation technique where an object is overlaid and animated on top of a static background graphic. A **sprite** is any part of your animation that moves independently, such as a flying bird, a rotating planet, a bouncing ball, or a spinning logo. The sprite animates and moves as an independent object. In sprite-based animation, a single image or series of images can be attached to a sprite. The sprite can animate in one place, as with a rotating planet, or move along a path, as with a flying bird.

Sprite-based computer animation is different from flip-book style computer animation in that for each successive frame, you only update the part of the computer screen that contains the sprite. You don't have to update the entire screen display for each frame, as you have to do with flip-book style animation.

File sizes and bandwidth requirements for sprite-based animation are typically less than those for flip-book style animation. Sprite-based animation programs typically use an off-screen buffer to composite frames to provide fast, smooth animation.

Motion Paths

path-based animation
motion paths

Sometimes sprite animation is called **path-based animation.** In path-based animation, you attach a sprite to a **motion path,** a curve drawn through the positions of the sprite in successive frames. The sprite moves along this path during the course of the animation. The sprite can be a single, rigid bitmap that doesn't change, or it can be a series of bitmaps that form an animation loop or cycle.

For example, you could create a short, self-contained three- or four-frame animation loop of a bird flapping its wings. Most computer animation software enables you to create animation loops of this sort.

To create an animation of this bird flying across your screen, you would do the following:

1. Place the loop on the left edge of the screen in the first frame.
2. Move the loop progressively farther to the right in successive frames.

The path of the flying bird is its motion path; when animated, you see the bird flapping its wings as its flies across the screen.

Spline-Based Animation

When objects move, they usually don't follow a straight line; as such, motion paths are generally more believable if they are curved. Computer animation programs typically enable you to create spline-based, curved motion paths. **Splines** are mathematical representations of a curve.

splines

To define spline-based curves, you first position a series of anchor points. The curve itself passes through the anchor points. The anchor points define the beginning and end points of different parts of the curve. Each anchor point has control handles that enable you to change the shape of the curve between two anchor points. Figure 7.3 shows a spline-based motion path for an animation of a jet fighter—note the anchor point with control handles.

Note

If you use a 2D drawing program like Macromedia FreeHand or Adobe Illustrator, you are already familiar with spline curves. These programs use a type of spline curve called a *Bézier curve*.

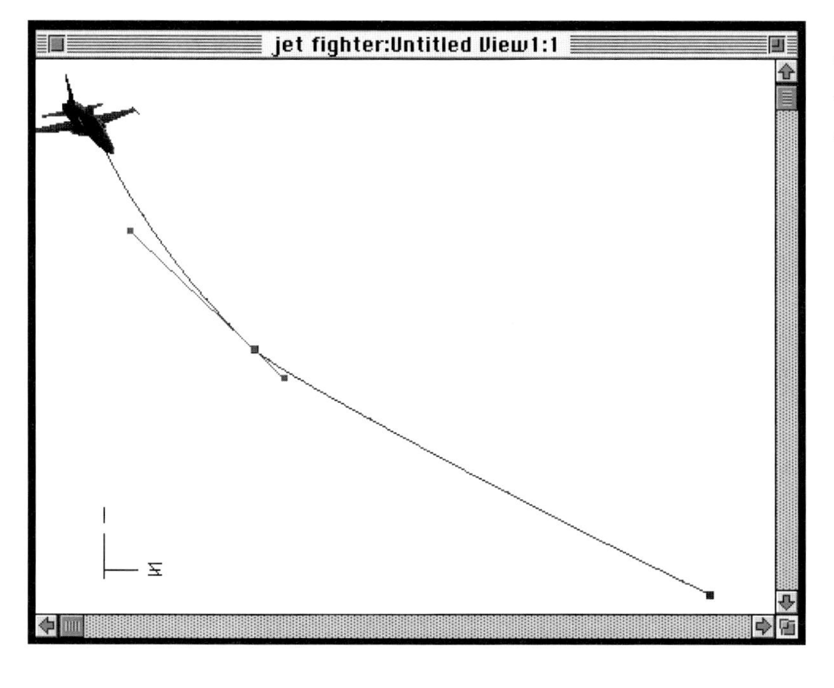

Figure 7.3

A spline-based motion path for a jet fighter.

Most animation programs enable you to vary the rate of motion along a path. If a motion path has a sharp bend, for example, an object slows down as it approaches the bend and then speeds up as it comes around the bend. Some programs provide highly sophisticated control of the velocity of sprites along paths.

Vector-Based Animation

vector based animation

Vector-based animation is similar to bitmap-based sprite animation. Rather than use bitmaps for sprites, vector-based programs use mathematical formulas to describe sprites. These formulas are similar to the formulas that describe spline curves.

Note

If an image is *pixellated*, you can see the individual, square pixels that make it up. Pixellation, or the *jaggies*, is a common problem in computer-generated images, especially along curved and high-contrast edges.

Because objects are mathematical formulas, not bitmaps, file sizes are much smaller. Another benefit of vector-based animation is that graphics are *scalable*; that is, they can be enlarged without becoming jagged or pixellated. Vector-based animation holds promise for Web animation. Several of the Plug-Ins and authoring tools listed in the appendix, such as Sizzler and FutureSplash, use vector-based animation.

Frame Rate

Frame rate is expressed as the number of frames per second (fps) of animation. Frame rates for film are 24 frames per second. Video frame rates are 30 (actually 29.97, but who's counting?) For Web animations, you will want to minimize the frame rate to reduce the total file size as much as possible.

The minimum frame rate before unacceptable jerkiness sets in depends on the particular animation. Frame rates of 10 to 15 frames per second typically yield acceptable results, and you might be able to get away with five to eight frames per second. Web playback can be affected by many variables outside the author's control, so consider Web frame rates to be estimates.

Key Frames and Tweening

key frames

In traditional animation, lead animators draw the most important frames, or **key frames.** These frames establish the main dramatic poses, define the flow of action, and create the animation's graphic style. The hundreds or thousands of intermediate frames that appear between these main key frames are typically drawn by posses of animators sweating away for days and weeks at light tables. This process of creating intermediate frames between key frames is called **tweening.**

tweening

Computers follow this same model. Fortunately, the computer will generate most of the intermediate frames—all you have to worry about is creating the key frames.

Note

Key frames are typically drawn at the most important or extreme poses that define the action, or at places where the action or viewpoint changes or shifts.

On the computer, you place key frames along a time line. The distance between key frames on the timeline determines the amount of time between key frames and in turn, the time between key frames (a.k.a, the *frame rate*) determines the number of intermediate frames that are generated. If the frame rate is ten frames per second, for example, and you have a key frame at second 1.5 and second 3.5, the computer generates 20 intermediate frames.

For complex animations, it's a good idea to rough-out your animation before you commit to rendering key frames. First, sketch the main poses and positions. Then, create a *spacing chart*. A spacing chart (see fig. 7.4) is a sketch map of the action with rough key frames positioned relative to time along a horizontal axis.

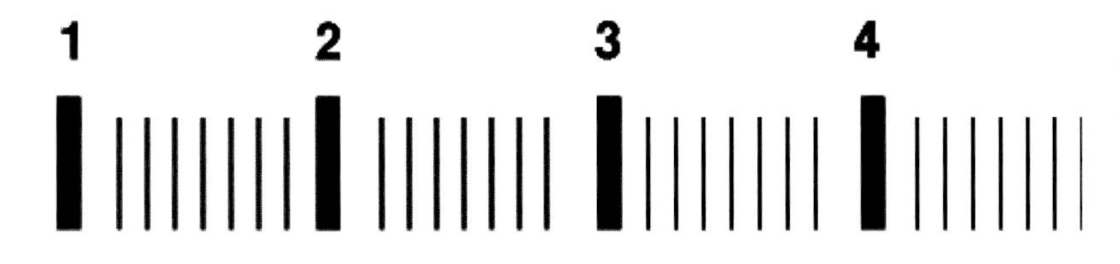

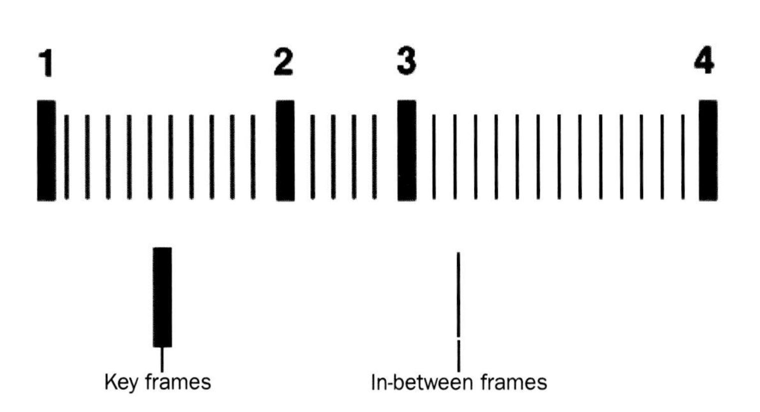

Figure 7.4

A spacing chart.

Character Animation

Character animation is a special branch of animation. It's the kind you typically see when you watch cartoons. It differs from other kinds of animation, such as motion graphics or animated logos, in that it involves complex organic shapes with multiple secondary, hierarchical motions. Just think of a talking animated character. Besides a moving mouth, the character's eyes, face, and hands are all moving at the same time.

Although it is fairly easy to animate a single, rigid bitmap over time, animating a believable living character is quite an art and takes a considerable amount of work. The techniques that make animated characters believable can also be applied to inanimate objects. Many of these techniques are discussed later, in the section on animation techniques.

Timelines, Tracks, and Animation Sequencers

Computer animation software typically mimics the process of traditional cel-based animation. Most programs contain a database of media objects, sprites, or *cast-members*. These objects can be placed on a virtual light table or *stage*. Computer animation software provides multiple layers that you can use to set up your animation. Each animated object is placed on its own layer, much like layers of animation cels in traditional animation. Figure 7.5 illustrates the layering and database user interface of Macromedia Director. Sprites from the database of media objects or cast are placed on the virtual animation stand or stage. Sprites in this animation occupy layer three from frame one to frame ten.

Most computer animation software uses a track-based timeline or sequencer to choreograph animation. Track-based timelines and sequencers provide a visual overview of the animation. Each track represents a property that animates over time. The track contains the key frame and animation information for that property. To inspect a property along the track, you typically position a playback head at a particular time or frame along the track. Each individual object can have several animation tracks associated with it; a single object could have a separate track for each of several time-varying parameters, such as position, size, shape, velocity, or surface properties.

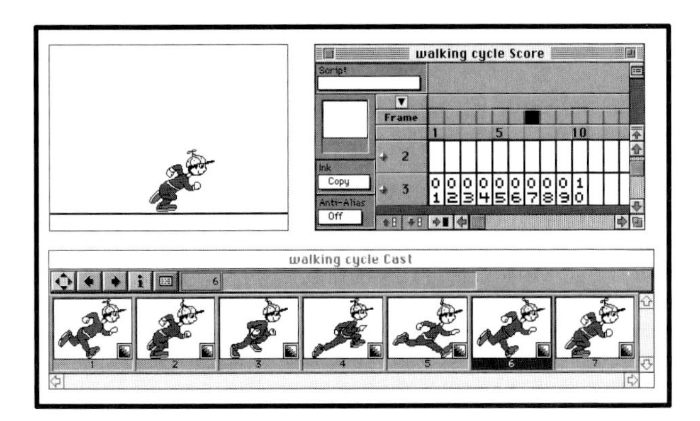

Figure 7.5

Macromedia Director user interface.

You create a key frame by picking a point on the time line and then choosing a value for a time-varying parameter, such as position or color, at this single point in time. The computer generates or tweens intermediate frames between key frames, interpolating the values for the parameters you've specified. Figure 7.6 illustrates an animation sequencer from a 3D animation program. Note the track in the lower window. The jet fighter object has a position track with a key frame near frame five and an orientation track with a key frame near frame three. In this case, to set another key frame, you would:

1. Move the playback head to the frame or time you want to add a new key frame.
2. Choose the property track you want to animate.
3. Enter a new value for the property.

Different animation software handles this differently, but the concept is similar.

Note

Tracks in animation software are similar to tracks in a music recording. Instead of each instrument or vocal having its own track, each object parameter has a track with the animation software acting as the visual mixer.

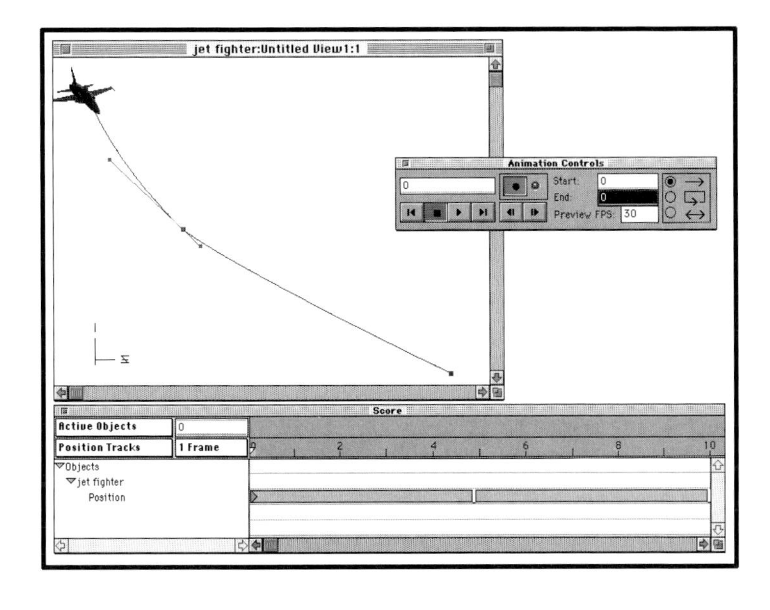

Figure 7.6

An animation sequencer.

Smoothing Key Frame Transitions

Because key frames mark transitions between properties in your animation, making these transitions appear smooth is important. Many computer animation programs provide ways of smoothing out the rough edges in key frame transitions caused by linear motion paths and lack of correct registration.

Linear versus Curved Motion Paths

These rough edges are caused because most computers create linear motion paths between position key frames. Linear motion paths contain sharp angle bends at the key frames. Figure 7.7 shows a linear motion path between three positions of a bouncing ball. Many programs will automatically smooth the sharp corners for you. In some programs, motion paths are fully editable curves.

Figure 7.7

Linear versus curved animation paths.

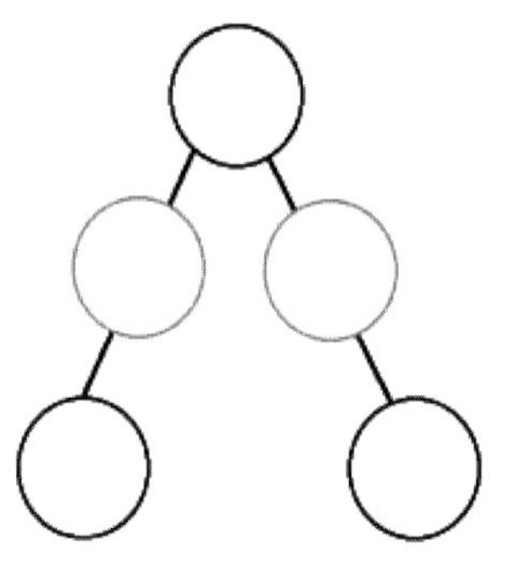

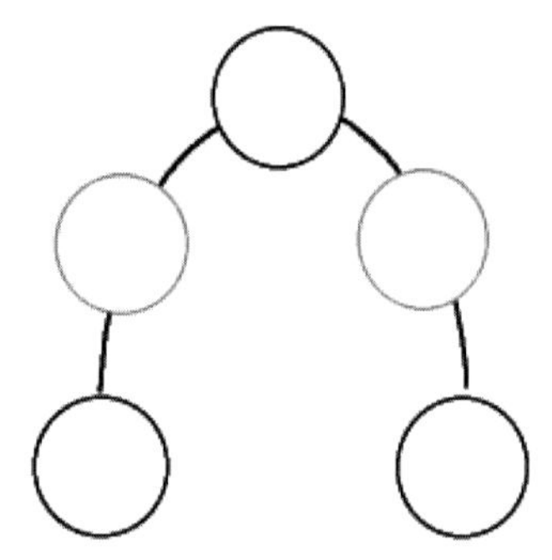

Registration

Note

As you might recall, in the flip-book, the drawings on each page were kept aligned and in register because the book was bound on one side.

To ensure smooth transitions between frames, each frame must be carefully aligned or registered with other frames. Traditional animators typically keep their drawings registered by using a light table with a peg bar and drawing paper or acetate that has punched holes that fit into the peg bar. Another handy tool is a sheet of acetate with a ruled grid that is laid out in the same aspect ratio as the animation frame. The grid can be used to align pieces of the animation consistently from frame to frame. Most computer animation programs provide similar functions for placement and alignment, such as a Snap-to-Grid command.

A **registration point** is a point on a cel or frame that lines up with the same point on every other other cel or frame. Choosing the correct registration point is especially important when you create an animation loop or cycling motion. Usually, the best place to put a registration point in an animation loop is at a point on the object that remains stationary during the loop.

registration point

Computer graphics programs usually have grid and alignment commands that help computer-based animators register their drawings, as illustrated in Figure 7.8. Figure 7.9 illustrates the registration tool in Director. To set a registration point in Director:

1. Choose the registration tool from the tool palette.
2. Click on a point on the bitmap graphic.

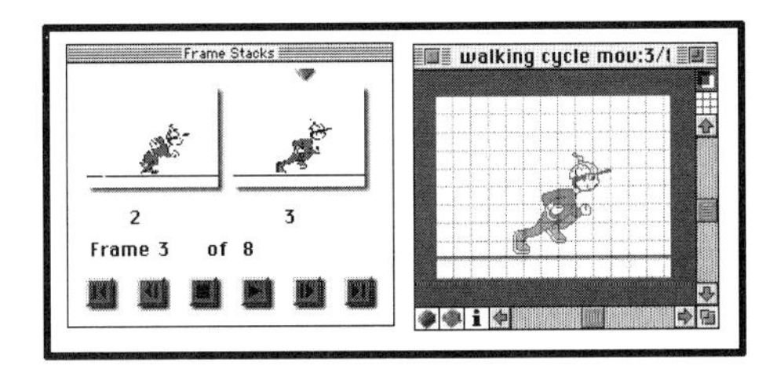

Figure 7.8

Superimposed grid for alignment of frames.

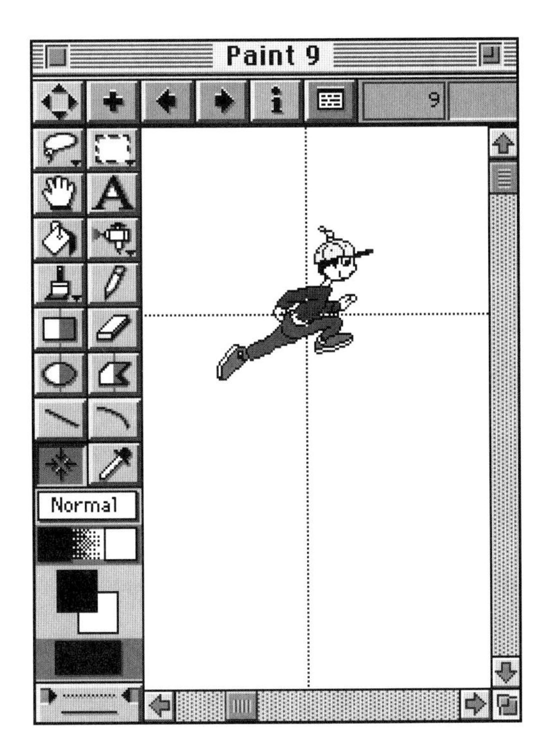

Figure 7.9

Setting a registration point in Director.

Processing Animated Graphics Files

Animation software falls into two broad categories, 2D and 3D. 2D animation programs require the artist to add perspective and shading. 3D programs will do a lot of this work for you, but 3D animations typically require a longer time to set up and create. Many 3D programs have integrated drawing, modeling, animating, and rendering tools that enable you to create your animation entirely within one program. Which type of animation software you use depends on the type of project, budget, development time, and the graphic style you are trying to achieve. In Chapter 12, "3D and Virtual Reality," you learn more about using 2D and 3D programs to add dimensionality to your animations.

Processing Graphics Files

Some programs, such as integrated 3D programs and 2D animation programs like Fractal Design Painter and Macromedia Director, enable you to draw your animation frames and create your animation in one program. You may draw your key frames in one program, export them as separate graphic files, process the files in some way, such as reduce their color-depth or dimensions, import them into an animation program, and then use another program to prepare the animation for the Web.

This section provides some general hints on processing graphic files. These hints include using an image processing program, creating frames of larger dimensions than you will need later, reducing your color-depth, optimizing your palette, and marking your original dimensions and registration points. Having a macro utility or batch file capability is tremendously helpful when processing animation files. You often generate sequences of separate graphic files that you need to resize, crop, or otherwise change globally in some way.

Note

Equilibrium Technology makes batch processing scripts designed specifically for Web graphics available at no cost:

`http://www.equil.com/SoftwareScripts.html`

Using an Image Processing Program

Many of the graphics processing tasks discussed in Chapter 6, "Using Graphic to Add Dynamic Content," can also be applied to animation frames. Equilibrium Technology Debabelizer is an image processing program that contains many useful commands for post-processing animation files.

These commands include palette optimization, file conversion, and sprite optimization. All these processes can be automated and run in batch mode. Debabelizer runs on a Macintosh. The program Brenda is the closest equivalent on Windows.

Think Big

Creating your animation frames with larger horizontal and vertical dimensions than the final dimensions you plan to use for final playback on the Web often turns out to be an invaluable tactic. Web animations will have dimensions typical of multimedia animation, such as 320 × 240 or smaller. But, you might want to repurpose your animations for film or video, or use frames in collateral print material. You might also end up changing the size of your animation to fit into a different Web page layout.

Shrinking a large graphic is better than increasing the size of a small graphic, so you should create your graphics at a larger size than you think you need. After you create your animation frames, use a batch processing program or macro to resize them for the Web. If you create larger graphics, be sure to create them with the same aspect ratio as the Web version. If your Web animation has dimensions of 160 × 120, for example, create larger size graphics at sizes such as 320 × 240, 640 × 480, and so forth.

Color-Depth Reduction

If your graphics are 24-bit and you want to use them in an 8-bit Web animation, you need to reduce their color-depth. Of course, you can create the image at a color-depth of 8 bits, but many 3-D animation programs have high-quality, 24-bit renderers. You're often better off to render at the higher quality and then reduce the bit depth in another program for the Web. The quality of a color-depth reduction depends on the particular palette and the colors used in the graphic.

A common problem with reducing color-depth is that a smooth gradient, such as a smooth, shadowed surface, shows discrete color bands rather than a smoothly varying color change when you reduce it from 24-bit to 8-bit. Before you reduce the color-depth, use Photoshop or other image processing software to add a small amount of noise to smooth gradients and see if this helps reduce banding.

Large areas of flat, solid color in animations can have annoying pixel drift when dithered to 8-bit color. Avoid dithering solid-color areas when you reduce color-depth. It's a good idea to output a test color-depth reduction to see how the 24-bit animation looks at 8-bit. Consider creating an 8-bit super palette in Equilibrium Technology's Debabelizer. A *superpalette* is an optimal palette based on colors you can find in a range of different images, such as frames in an animation.

dithering

Dithering is the process by which an image processing program approximates the original high-bit depth color with a more limited range of colors. It usually involves replacing the original high-bit depth color with a pattern of other colors, which our eyes merge and tend to perceive as continuous color.

pixel drift

Pixel drift occurs in animations because the dithering pattern is not consistent between frames. Colored pixels within a dithered pattern appear to shimmy or move back and forth.

Palette Optimization

Warning

Some animation programs, such as Shockwave, enable you to assert a custom palette—at the price of changing all the colors in the rest of the computer display.

Web playback places special demands on palette optimization. Different systems have different system palettes. Different browsers assert their own palettes while they are running as the foreground application.

There are 216 "safe" colors that browsers on different platforms share. These colors won't dither on different systems and therefore are good to use for flat areas of color. Chapter 6 discusses many of these issues in detail. Lynda Weinman's recent book from New Riders, *Designing Web Graphics*, also discusses palette issues for Web graphics.

Preserve Dimensions and Registration Points

As you post-process separate animation frames, you might want to preserve the original dimensions of each frame to preserve registration points. Outline each frame with a solid line, or paint small, solid-color squares in the upper-left and lower-right corners of the image. When you import these graphics into an animation program, the original size and registration points are preserved. If you want to crop your frames to reduce file size and save disk space, consider doing this as the last step, after the animation has been set up, so that you don't lose your registration points.

Animation Techniques

This section discusses some basic techniques that make your animations more professional, life-like, and believable:

- Onion skinning
- Cut-outs
- Ease-in/ease-out and velocity curves
- Squash and stretch
- Cycling
- Secondary action and overlapping action
- Hierarchical motion
- Anticipation, action, reaction
- Line of action
- Exaggeration

These techniques include ways to draw animations and ways to choreograph and stage your animations. Timing is enormously important in choreographing animations. Watch your favorite cartoon animations to see some of these techniques in action.

There are no hard and fast rules. What technique works best for you depends on your particular animation and design goals. Experiment with a few techniques using rough sketches to see which one works best.

Onion Skinning

Onion skinning is a drawing technique borrowed from traditional cel animation that helps the animator create the illusion of smooth motion. In traditional cel animation, each frame is drawn on layers of transparent acetate or cels. Rather than working on each frame in isolation, animators lay these transparent cels one on top of the other. This enables them to see previous and following frames as they are drawing the current frame.

Onion skinning is an easy way to see a complete sequence of frames at a glance and to see how each frame flows into the frames before and after. Many 2D animation programs, such as Macromedia Director, Fractal Design Painter (see figure 7.10), and FutureWave's CelAnimator support onion skinning. You can even use the layering and transparency features in image processing programs such as Photoshop to simulate onion skinning.

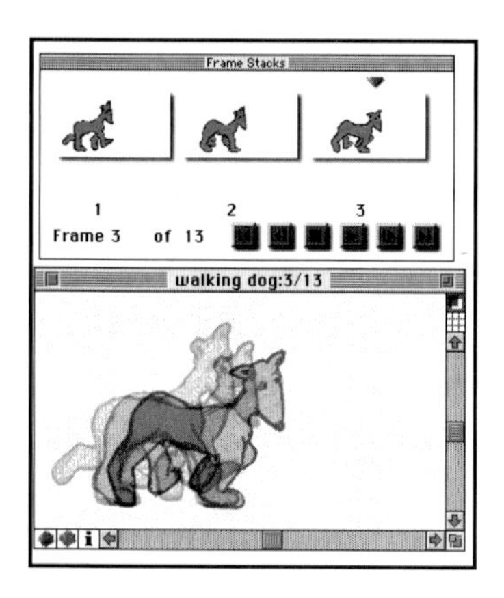

Figure 7.10

An example of onion skinning.

Cut-Outs

Animation *cut-outs* is another technique borrowed from traditional cel animation. When the motion of a character is limited, for example, to a wave of the hand, just redrawing the hand and arm is easier than redrawing the entire character for each frame. The character can be drawn once and used as a background. The separate hand graphics or cut-outs are composited on the background figure to simulate movement. An example of cut-outs for different arm and hand positions is shown in figure 7.11. This technique is useful in animating limited motion, such as mouth movements during dialogue.

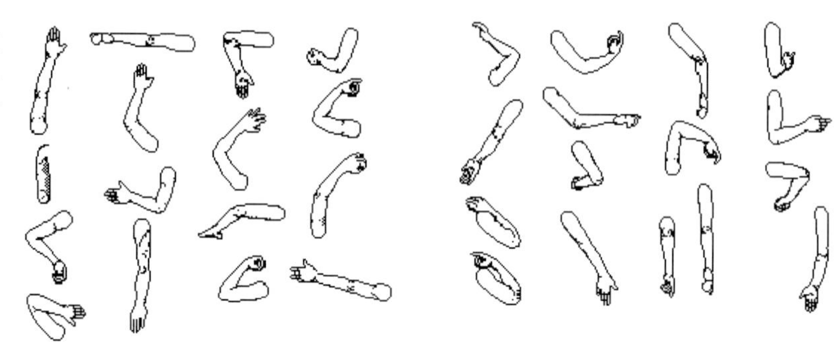

Figure 7.11

An example of cut-outs for different arm and hand positions.

Traditional 2D computer graphics programs—Macromedia FreeHand, for example—have features such as layering and blending of Bézier curves that make generating and experimenting with cut-outs easy.

Tip

You can draw an animated figure in separate pieces or as separate closed curves. Draw a separate piece for each part of the figure that will move independently. In a character animation, for example, make a separate piece for torso, head, limbs, and facial parts. Create a library of possible positions for each piece. You can then mix, match, and composite the pieces in different ways. Cut-outs are easy to create in computer graphics programs.

Ease-in/Ease-out and Velocity Curves

In the real world, objects generally don't move at a constant rate; they are affected by gravity. A race car slows down as it banks into a curve and speeds up as it comes out of a curve. An airplane gradually builds up to cruising speed. A transition from one motion state to another, such as starting, stopping, or turning, is typically rendered as a key frame. The gradual slowing down and speeding up as objects approach and leave key frames is called **ease-in** and **ease-out**.

ease-in/ease-out

You could lay out these velocity changes by hand. Slow movement has small changes between frames. Fast movement has large changes. Transitions between one motion state and another are hard to lay out smoothly. Fortunately, this is one area where computers can help.

Most computer animation programs enable you to control the deceleration and acceleration of objects (ease-in, ease-out) by a specified amount over a certain range of frames. For example, you can take an object from zero to top speed in 60 frames for a gradual acceleration, or in five frames for a fast acceleration. The computer makes sure the animation looks smooth. Some programs have more detailed velocity control and enable you to assign velocity curves to an object. **Velocity curves** are editable spline curves that define the velocity of an object at any given point. Velocity curves are usually depicted in a separate track in animation sequencers with velocity increasing along the Y axis. Figure 7.12 illustrates a velocity curve track in the program After Effects.

velocity curves

Note

A velocity curve for simple deceleration followed by acceleration (ease-in/ease-out) would be U-shaped.

Figure 7.12

An example of a velocity curve for a position track in Adobe After Effects.

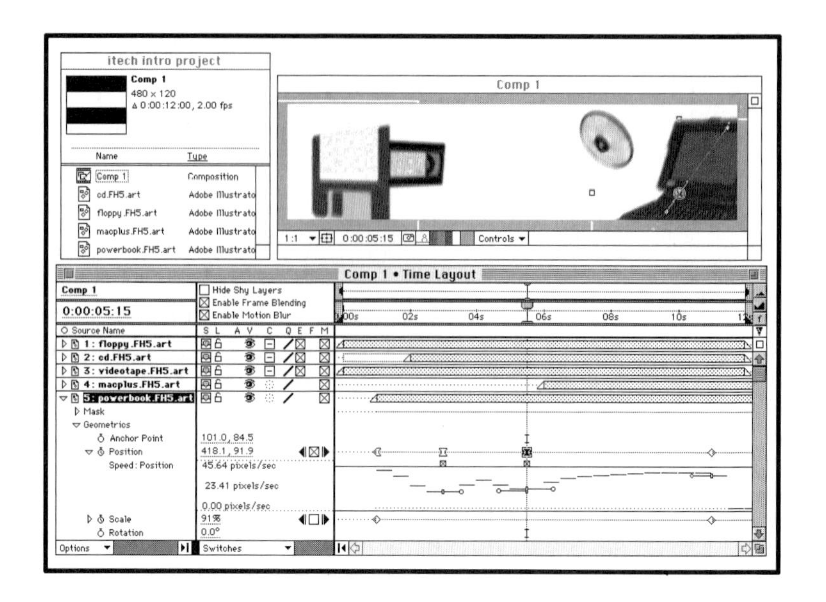

Squash and Stretch

Squash and stretch means your animated object should have "give"; in other words, it should move as if it was made up of something soft and squishy like a sandbag or water balloon. Have your animated object stretch in the direction of movement, as shown in figure 7.13. Then, when the object stops, changes direction, or hits an immovable object, show the object compressing or squashing in the direction of movement. Squash and stretch is a simple way to give the feeling of weight to an object in motion. It is also a good way to show anticipation, recoil, and follow-through—concepts that will be discussed in later sections of this chapter. Figure 7.13, a composite of a bouncing ball animation, illustrates squash and stretch. Note that as the ball flies through the air, it stretches in the direction of movement.

Figure 7.13

Squash and stretch.

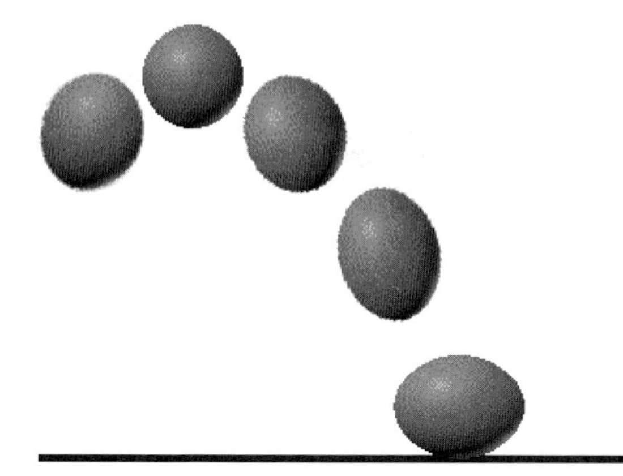

Looping

Many actions are repetitive and can be decomposed into a single cycle or looping action over a few frames. The classic example of animation looping is a walking, two-legged figure. A complete loop for a walking, two-legged figure is two steps. You can animate a two step loop in ten frames. After you create this loop, you can have your walking figure take an infinite number of steps by just repeating the ten-frame loop.

Figure 7.1 at the beginning of this chapter is an illustration of a cycle for a galloping horse. It's important to pick the best registration point to start a loop. Pick a point that remains stationary during the loop. Figure 7.9 illustrates setting a registration point in Director.

Secondary Action and Overlapping Action

It's easy to assign a static bitmap or sprite to a motion path and have it move across thc screen. It's also pretty boring. One way to create interesting animations is to add secondary actions to the main action. Secondary actions can be simple. For example, if you are animating a spaceship moving across the screen, you can add simple secondary actions such as a flickering flame emanating from the exhaust pipes, a rotating turret, or a waving alien in the cockpit. If you are animating a flying superhero, show his cape fluttering. These kinds of secondary actions can be added with a simple two- or three-frame animation loop.

Overlapping action, when two or more actions overlap in time, and **follow-through**, where an action proceeds through it's final ending point, add a dimension of time to secondary actions. Don't have all the parts of your character or object arrive in the same place all at the same time. When your flying superhero stops and lands on the ground, for example, show his cape fluttering into position a second or two after he comes to a complete stop.

overlapping action
follow-through

Loose, flowing parts of an object, such as hair, clothing, and the tails of animals, are commonly used to show follow-through. Figure 7.14 shows one way to animate a loose, flowing part of an object such as a cape or tail. When you animate into a key frame or position, bring the object or character and its loose flowing parts or dangling limbs slightly past the position. Then bring them back into the key frame position.

Figure 7.14

Animating secondary action

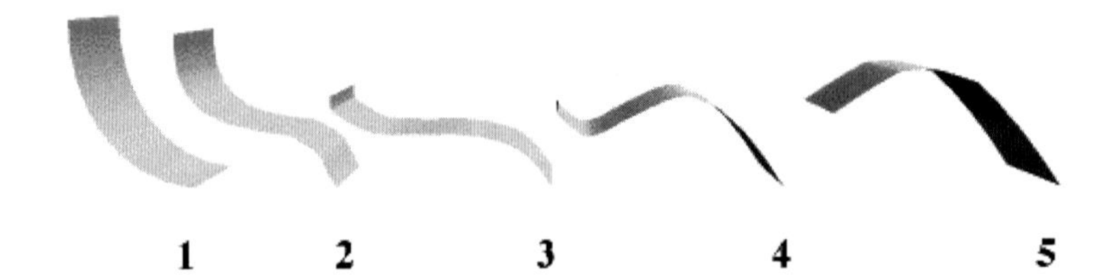

Hierarchical Motion

Hierarchical motion is created by attaching or linking an object or animation loop to another object or loop so that the first loop moves with the second. The flying bird animation discussed previously is an example of hierarchical motion. First, create a short three- or four-frame loop of a bird flapping its wings. Then, attach this loop to a second object—in this case, a motion path—so that the flapping bird flies across the screen.

The Solar System is another example of a hierarchical motion system (see fig. 7.15). Moons revolve around their planets, planet-moon systems revolve around the sun, and the sun revolves around the galactic core. Each subsystem, such as a planet-moon system, is linked to the next system higher up in the hierarchy, in this case the sun. The subsystem follows the higher system wherever it goes.

Figure 7.15

An example of a hierarchical motion system—the Solar System.

Many computer programs enable you to set up hierarchical links between objects and animated subsystems. In the Solar System example, here is the procedure you would follow:

1. Create the rotating planet and rotating moon as separate animation loops.
2. Attach the rotating moon to an elliptical path around the planet, creating a second-level loop.
3. Link the combined planet/moon loop to an elliptical path around the sun for a third-level loop.

If, subsequently, you moved the sun to a different position, the planets and moons would all move with the sun to the new location.

Anticipation, Action, Reaction

Watch your favorite cartoon characters. You'll see that they are masters of the "setup." The mouse holds the flower pot over the open door, waiting for his nemesis, the cat, to come charging through. You know what is going to happen, and it adds to your enjoyment. The main comedic premise of many cartoons is this kind of anticipated action/reaction between two characters. Anticipation extends to inanimate objects, too. The fuse on the bomb gets shorter and shorter; a couch stretches and bends just before it breaks into a thousand pieces. You can add to the anticipation and help setup the viewer by showing some small movement prior to the primary motion, like a baseball pitcher getting ready to throw. Get set, wind up, it's the pitch!

For every action, there is an equal and opposite reaction, also known as **reaction-recovery**. Watch your favorite cartoon and you'll see an ebb and flow of action, reaction, and recovery—like a pendulum—between characters. Often, you really won't see the action taking place. What you see is the anticipation, the setup, the start of the action, and then the reaction. This is called a **fake**.

reaction-recovery

fake

To illustrate a fake in the preceding flower pot example, you might animate a stretched, motion-blurred flower pot falling toward the cat's head. The next frame might be the cat's head squashing under the weight and pieces of the flower pot falling off its forehead. You never actually draw the real contact between the two objects.

Note

A good way to see how animators achieve their effects is to rent a video of your favorite animated feature film, or videotape your favorite cartoon show and go through it frame by frame on a VCR.

You can use this sort of faking in other situations. Your character leans back, preparing to dash off. In the next frame, he takes his first step into the run. The next frame is a motion blur effect. The motion blur effect is animated from point A to point B. Then show the character wobbling to a stop.

Line of Action

The *line of action* is an imaginary line that extends through the main action of your animation. For effective Web-based animations, make the line of action simple and direct.

The line of action is commonly arc-shaped or curved rather than straight. In figure animations, it typically follows the main character's spine and goes through the character's head, arm, or leg. In some cartoons, the line of action is S-shaped or made up of opposing arcs that change in a rhythmic, wave-like motion.

Look at newspaper cartoons or comic books and try to sketch in one or two lines that follow the main action. When you create your own animations, sketch in the line of action first and then draw the rest of your animation around it. Figure 7.16 shows a line of action through a running figure.

Figure 7.16

Line of action.

Exaggeration

Exaggeration is another way to add impact to your animations. This is especially true of Web animations, which are generally small, because of bandwidth considerations. They will play in tiny little rectangles in your Web page, maybe 32 × 32 pixels. Animations may be competing with other page elements or other windows on a computer screen.

If you want your animation to be noticed, exaggerate the colors and motion. Zoom a graphic element from zero to full size in a second or two. Exaggerate the secondary motions so that they're noticed. If you are animating an old jalopy, have it bounce up and down on its worn-out shocks. Or if you are animating a spaceship, bend back the tail fins as the spaceship accelerates to warp speed.

Exaggerated **foreshortening**, in which the parts of an object closest to a viewer loom large, can be especially effective in producing the illusion of depth.

foreshortening

GIF Animation

GIF animation is a special extension to the GIF graphic format that has been around for years. Beginning with Netscape Navigator 2.0, animated GIFs have been increasingly supported in Web browsers. Animated GIFs consist of a sequence of animation frames that are displayed successively in the Web page and can be used in Web pages just like regular GIFs.

This section discusses the following subjects:

- Advantages and disadvantages of GIF animation
- Browser support of GIF animation
- GIF animation design considerations
- Tools used in GIF animations
- Creating GIF animations on your Mac with GIFBuilder
- Creating GIF animations with GIF Construction Set

GIF animations can take advantage of many of the optimizations that you can use on static GIFs. See Chapter 6 for details on creating GIF graphics for the Web.

Advantages and Disadvantages of GIF Animation

For Web animation, advantages of animated GIFs are:

- Easy to create. Authors don't need to know programming languages or have special access to a Web server.

- Easy to integrate in a Web page; used the same way as regular GIFs—by using the IMG tag.
- Faster than server-push animation, described later in this chapter.
- Generally compact with all the compression of GIFs, such as palette assignment and LZW compression.
- Broadly supported on browsers and platforms.

Most of the disadvantages of GIF animations are connected to browser support, as described in the following section. These disadvantages include:

- Not all browsers support animated GIFs, although Netscape Navigator 2.0 or later and Internet Explorer 3.0 or later do.
- The browsers that do support animated GIFs don't consistently support all features of animated GIFs, such as looping and transparency.
- Infinitely looping GIFs are annoying, although users can turn off the animation by clicking on the browser's Stop button.
- GIF animations take over the browser status bar, so users cannot receive feedback via the browser status bar.
- GIF animation repeatedly hits the local hard disk cache, tying up system resources and interfering with other interactivity on a Web page.
- There is no interactivity; that is, no ability to pause or start playback like you can with QuickTime, and no embedded hotspots or buttons like in Shockwave.
- No sound.
- Not all browsers display animation at the same frame rate.

Browser Support

Although Netscape Navigator 2.0 or later and Internet Explorer 3.0 support animated GIFs, they do not support all features of the spec or all features that are supported in popular authoring tools.

Probably the best way to see what features are supported is to follow the suggestions and tips furnished here and test your animations on target browsers.

Although you can specify the number of loops for animated GIFs, not all browsers support this feature. In Netscape Navigator 2.0, for example, you can specify that your animated GIF loop only once or that it loop endlessly without stopping—with no in between. Navigator 3.0 now enables you to set a specific number of loops.

Use long interframe delays to pause loops or break up loops. For example, if you set a long interframe delay at the end of a loop, the animation pauses before going into the next iteration. You can use this feature to get around the number of loop limitations of older browsers.

GIF animations take over the status bar and system resources such as hard disk access. Inform users that they can click on the Stop button of their browsers to stop the animation.

Integrate the background of your animation frames with the background of the Web page. You can specify that a certain color in your animated GIF be transparent so that the background shows through. Transparency reduces file size and enhances page integration. Unfortunately, transparency is not always supported and depends on the presence of background images and colors in the Web page. Test transparent animated GIFs on target machines.

Revert to Background and Revert to Previous are aspects of the GIF animation spec that enable transparency, compact file size, and a limited form of sprite-based animation. Although supported in authoring tools, these are not always supported in browsers. Support in browsers is dependent on the characteristics of other frames in the animation, presence of background images in the Web page, characteristics of the local machine, and so on. If you use these parts of the animated GIF spec, be sure to test your animation on target systems.

Warning

On some Windows systems, animated GIFs may only display at a slow frame rate—three frames per second, for example.

Browsers that do not support animated GIFs usually handle animated GIFs by:

- Displaying the first frame in the animation.
- Displaying the last frame in the animation.
- Displaying the broken graphic icon.

If some of your users do not have animated GIF support, you should make your first and last frames representative of your animation.

Design Considerations

Be judicious in the use of GIF animations. GIF animations can be as annoying such as the BLINK tag, especially on pages with a lot of text that you want users to read. Use GIF animations to:

- Draw attention to the pertinent information on a page, such as the main point.
- Provide entertainment, such as an animated character.
- Illustrate a dynamic process.
- Illustrate multiple views of an object.
- Provide a self-running slideshow with long interframe delays.
- Keep animations small and the number of frames low.
- Use the 216-color cross-platform palette.

Tools

There are excellent shareware tools to create GIF animations. If you use these tools, please support the authors so that they can continue to provide excellent software. Many commercial tools, such as MovieStar, are beginning to add GIF animation export options.

Windows

Gif Construction Set for Windows

`http://www.mindworkshop.com/alchemy/alchemy.html`

Mac

GifBuilder

Smart Dubbing 1.0v6 by Alco Blom and Vincent Verweij

`http://www.xs4all.nl/~polder/`

GIFMation BoxTop Software

`http://www.aris.com/boxtop/GIFmation/`

WebPainter Mac (Windows soon)

`http://www.totallyhip.com/webpaint/2_webpnt.htm`

MovieStar Mac (Windows)

`http://www.beingthere.com/moviestar/plugins/`
`➥getmstar.html`

FutureSplash Animator (Mac Win95/NT)

`http://www.futurewave.com`

Unix

GifMerge

`http://www.iis.ee.ethz.ch/~kiwi/gifmerge.html`

GIFLOOP Perl script

`http://www.homecom.com/gifanim.html`

Creating GIF Animations on Your Mac with GIFBuilder

Tools
GifBuilder
Animation frames as GIF files

GifBuilder by Yves Piguet is a scriptable utility that creates animated GIF files on the Macintosh. It can import PICT, GIF, TIFF, layered Photoshop 3 images, QuickTime movies, FilmStrips, or PICS, via drag-and-drop, menu commands, or AppleScript. It can be used with other scriptable applications like Yves Piguet's great `clip2gif` to automate GIF production and to assemble animated GIFs and other graphics at run-time for Macintosh Web servers or on the client machine.

You can find out more about clip2gif and GifBuilder at:

`http://iawww.epfl.ch/Staff/Yves.Piguet/clip2gif-home/`
`GifBuilder.html`

Before you begin, create your animation frames using some of the programs and techniques described in previous sections. Create your animation as a sequence of PICT, GIF, TIFF, Photoshop files, as Photoshop 3.0 layers, or as a QuickTime movie, Adobe Premiere/Photoshop FilmStrip file, or PICs animation. If you create the animation as a sequence of separate graphic files, give them names such as frame.000, frame.001., frame.002, and the like.

Setting Up a GIF Animation in GIFBuilder

To set up an animation from a sequence of animation frames saved as PICT, GIF, TIFF, or in the Photoshop format:

1. In the Macintosh Finder, choose the icon of the first frame in the animation sequence and drag it onto the GifBuilder icon (see fig. 7.17).
2. GifBuilder will launch.
3. Choose the remaining frames and drag them into the GifBuilder window (see fig. 7.18).

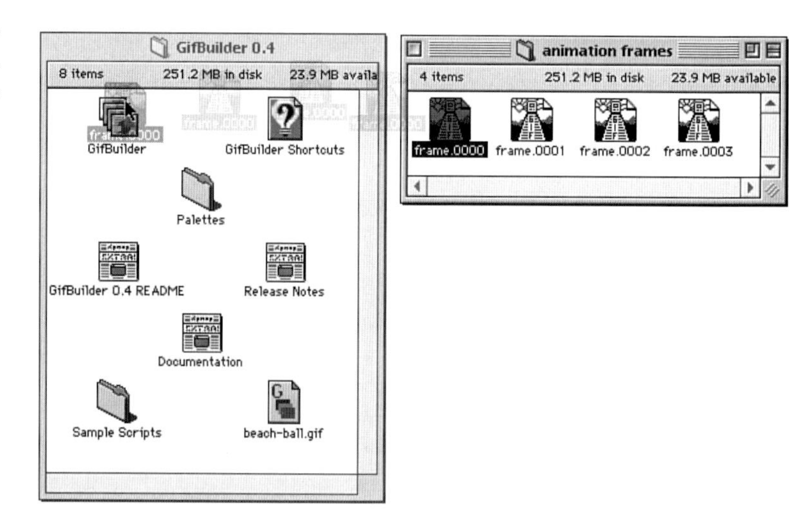

Figure 7.17

Adding the first frame to new GIF animation in GifBuilder.

You can also add animation frames by choosing File, Add Frame.

To import QuickTime movies, FilmStrips, and PICs, choose File, Convert and then select the file you want to convert.

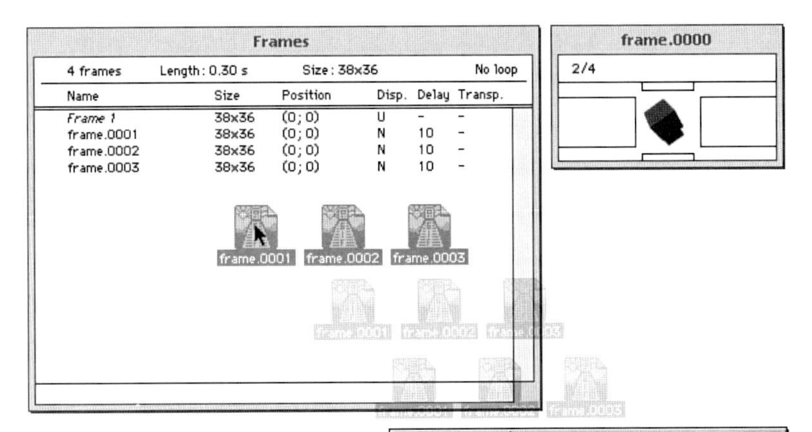

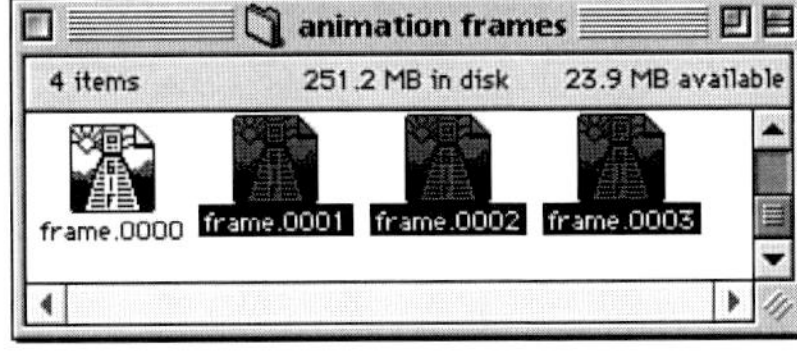

Figure 7.18

Adding remaining frames.

To import layered Photoshop files (where each layer is a separate animation frame), choose File, Open and choose the layered Photoshop file.

Setting Up Palettes

GifBuilder comes with a set of ready-made palettes specifically for the Web. To use GifBuilder with the 216-color cross-platform Web browser palette, choose Colors: 6x6x6 Palette from the Options menu.

Setting Up Loops, Interframe Delays, and Frame Optimization

To set up looping characteristics, choose Loop from the Options menu and enter the number of loops (see fig. 7.19). If you only want the animation to loop once, you don't need to choose this option, or you can select No. Currently, only Netscape Navigator recognizes looping. Navigator 2.0 ignores the number of loops set and loops endlessly regardless of settings other than 1, 0, or No. Navigator 3.0 does recognize the number of loops specified.

Figure 7.19

Creating looping GIF animations.

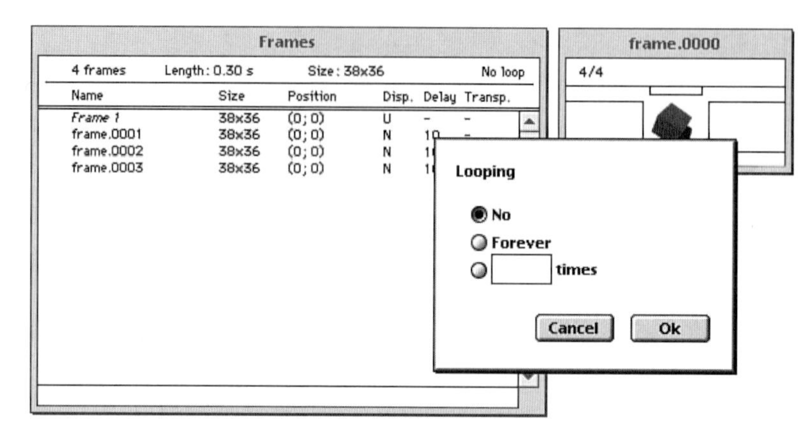

interframe delay

To set **interframe delay**—the amount of time between the display of successive frames—double-click on the number in the delay column that is in the row of the frame you want to delay and enter a new value in the dialog box (see fig. 7.20). You may choose the frame in the GifBuilder window and select Interframe delay from the Options menu.

Figure 7.20

Setting Interframe delay.

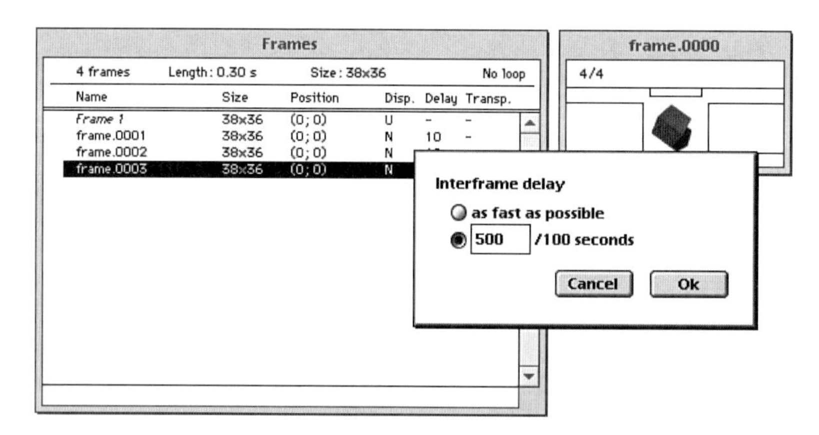

It is a good idea to choose Frame Optimization from the Options menu. This setting can reduce the file size substantially. If you use Frame Optimization, test the animation on your target browsers and machines to make sure it is displayed correctly.

Creating GIF Animations with GIF Construction Set

GIF Construction Set from AlchemyMindworks is a great shareware utility for Windows available at:

```
http://www.mindworkshop.com/alchemy/gifcon.html
```

GIF Construction Set takes a little different approach to creating animated GIFs than GifBuilder does (see fig. 7.21). To understand how GIF Construction Set works, it's helpful to know a little bit about the animated GIF specs.

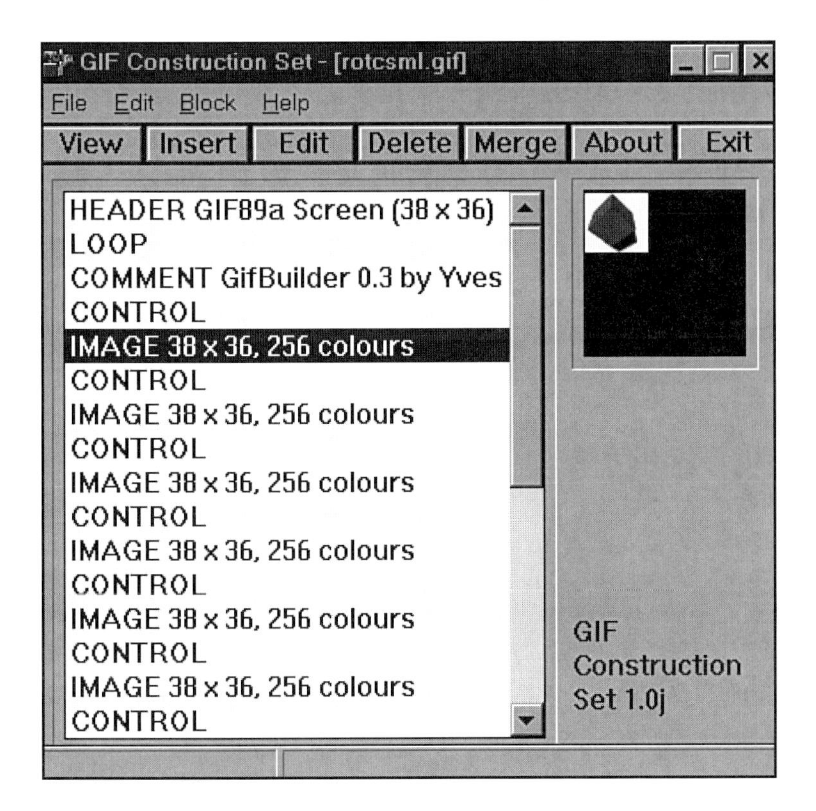

Figure 7.21

Creating an animated GIF with GIF Construction Set.

Animated GIF Format

GIFs contain different data types called **blocks.** Animated GIFs are a type of multiple-block GIF. Each image within an animated GIF constitutes an Image block. Other types of blocks include Header blocks, Loop blocks, Plain Text blocks, Comment blocks, and Control blocks.

blocks

- The Header block in GIF Construction Set contains information about the file, including:
  - GIF version of the file
  - Dimensions of the file
  - Palette of the file
- The Header block is required.
- The Loop block specifies looping characteristics of the animation.

- The Image block contains the animation frame and information about the display characteristics of that frame, such as:
    - Frame dimensions
    - Position of the frame within the area specified in the Header block, with the upper-left corner having coordinates (0,0)
    - Interlacing
    - Palette
- A Control block controls display characteristics of the image that immediately follows it in the GIF Construction Set window. If you use Control blocks, never insert any other block between the Control block and the subsequent Image block.
- Use Control blocks to set such features as:
    - Transparency (not supported by all browsers)
    - Wait for user input (not supported by browsers)
    - Interframe delay
    - Remove frame characteristics (partially supported by browsers)

Not all GIF viewers support all of these block types. GIF Construction Set enables you to insert different block types in a sequence. For example, to create an animated GIF, insert a sequence of GIF animation frames into the GIF Construction Set window.

In GIF Construction Set, you insert blocks by choosing the line in the GIF Construction Set window after which you want to insert a new block, and clicking on the Insert button. To edit a block, choose the block in the GIF Construction Set window and click on the Edit button.

Setting Up a GIF Animation in GIF Construction Set

First, create your animation frames in a separate application. Follow the instructions in Chapter 6 on how to create GIF images for the Web. For best results you may want to create the GIFs using the 216-color cross-platform browser palette.

When you create the animation frames, note the dimensions of the frames in pixels. For best results, the first frame should be the largest, or all the frames should be the same size.

1. Launch GIF Construction Set and choose File, New.
2. The GIF Construction Set window shows a blank file structure, except for a Header block. Choose the Header block line in the GIF Construction Set window and click on the Edit button in the button bar (see fig. 7.22).

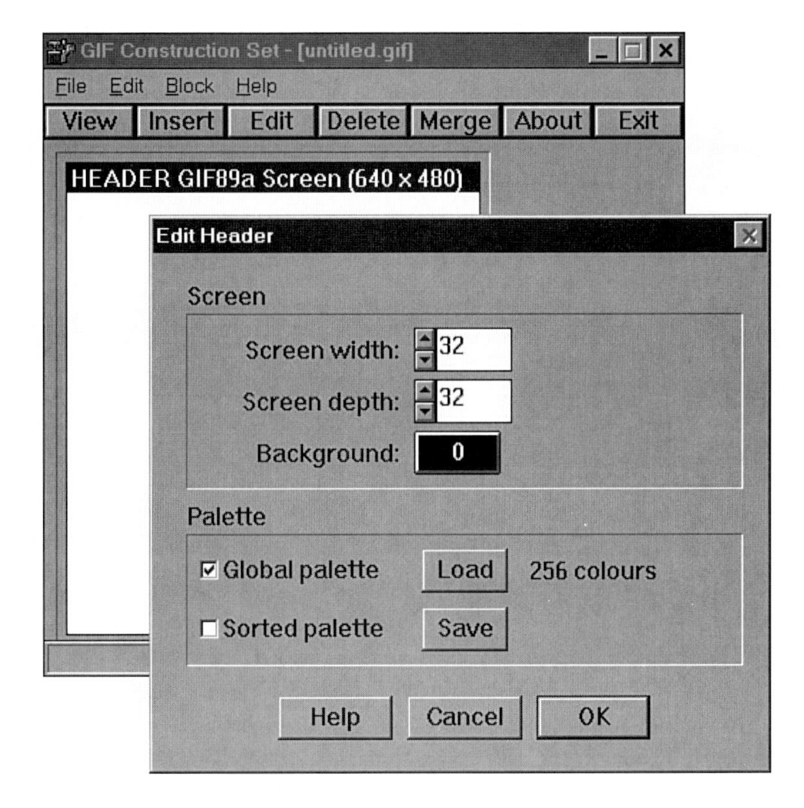

Figure 7.22

Edit Header block.

3. In the Screen box, enter the width and height of the largest frame in your animation. The largest frame should be the first frame.
4. Check the Global palette box.

Insert First GIF and Set Palette

1. Choose the Header line in the GIF Construction Set window.
2. Click on the Insert button (see fig. 7.23).

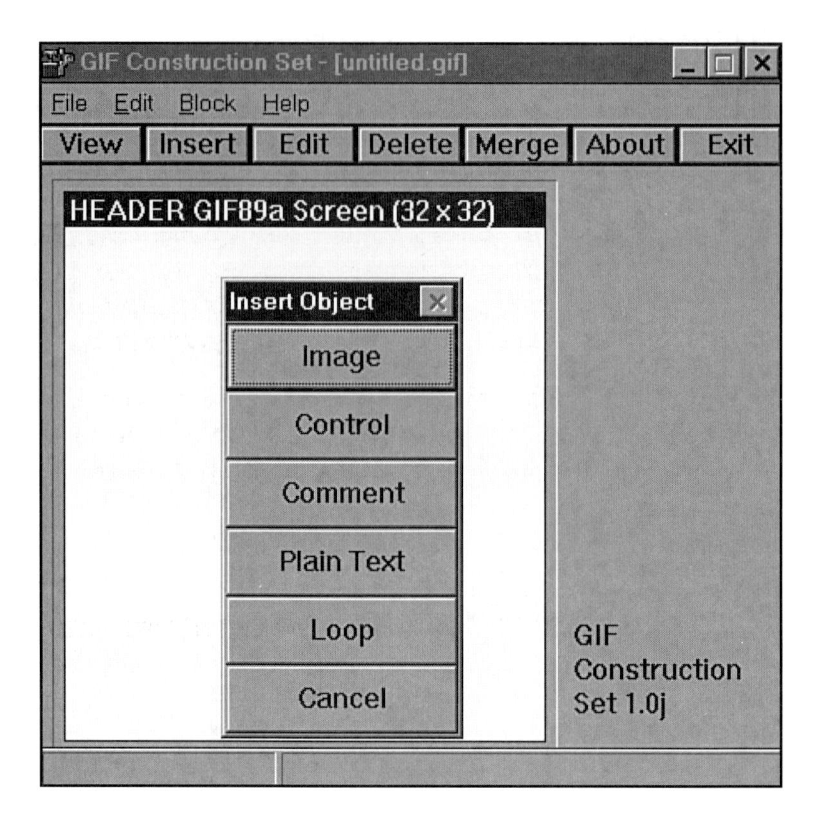

Figure 7.23

Insert blocks.

3. Click on the Image button.
4. In the File dialog box, choose the animation frame you want to insert (see fig. 7.24).

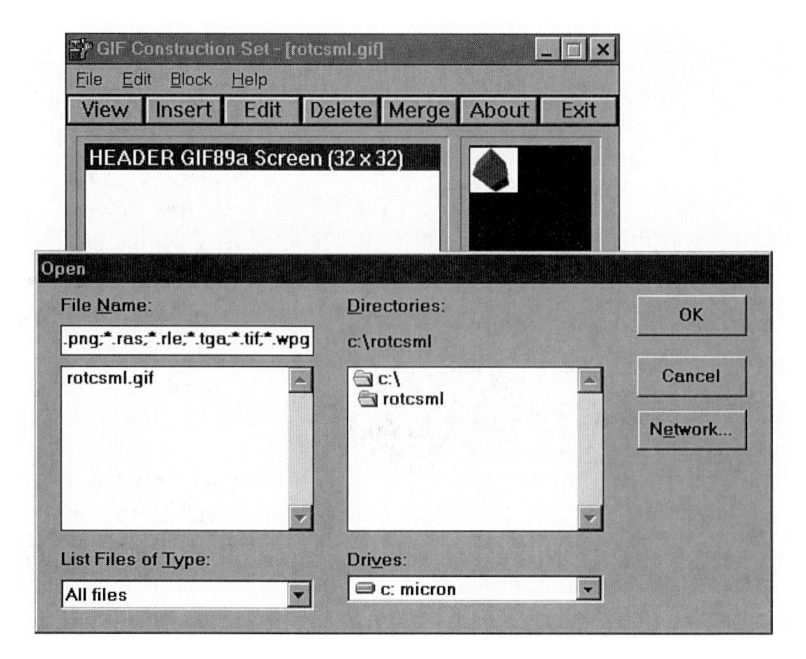

Figure 7.24

Choosing animation frame to insert.

5. If you have created this image with the 216-color cross-platform palette, choose the option "Use this image as the global palette."
6. Click on OK.

Inserting Multiple GIFs

To insert the remaining animation frames:

1. Choose the object line in the GIF Construction Set window after which you want to insert the animation frame.
2. Click on the Insert button.
3. Click on the Image button.
4. In the File dialog box, choose the animation frame you want to insert.

Setting Loops

To make a looping animation you need to insert a Loop block. If you want the animation to loop only once, you don't need to insert a Loop block.

1. Choose the Header line in the GIF Construction Set window.
2. Click on the Insert button.
3. Click on the Loop button.
4. Choose the Loop line in the GIF Construction Set window.
5. Click on the Edit button.
6. Set the number of loops. These settings will be ignored by browsers other than Navigator 3.0.

Warning

Currently, this block is only recognized by Netscape Navigator. Navigator 2.0 ignores the number of loops set in this block and loops forever. Navigator 3.0 does recognize the number of loops specified in this block.

Using Control Blocks To Set Interframe Delays

You can use Control blocks to set interframe delay (the amount of time that the image is displayed, in hundredths of a second). Note that many Windows systems will not accept low values. You can also use interframe delay to pause a looping animation between loops.

Tip

Remember, Control blocks must be inserted before an Image block. There can be no intervening blocks.

To set an interframe delay of 5 seconds:

1. Choose the line in the GIF Construction Set window that is directly above the line of animation frame to which you want to add the Control block (see fig. 7.25). You must do this because the Insert command always inserts a block after the currently selected line in the GIF Construction Set window.
2. Click on the Insert button.
3. Click on the Control button.
4. Choose the line in the GIF Construction Set window that contains the Control block.
5. Click on the Edit button.
6. To set the interframe delay to 5 seconds, enter 500 (hundredths of a second) in the Delay box. Click on OK.

Figure 7.25

Editing Control blocks.

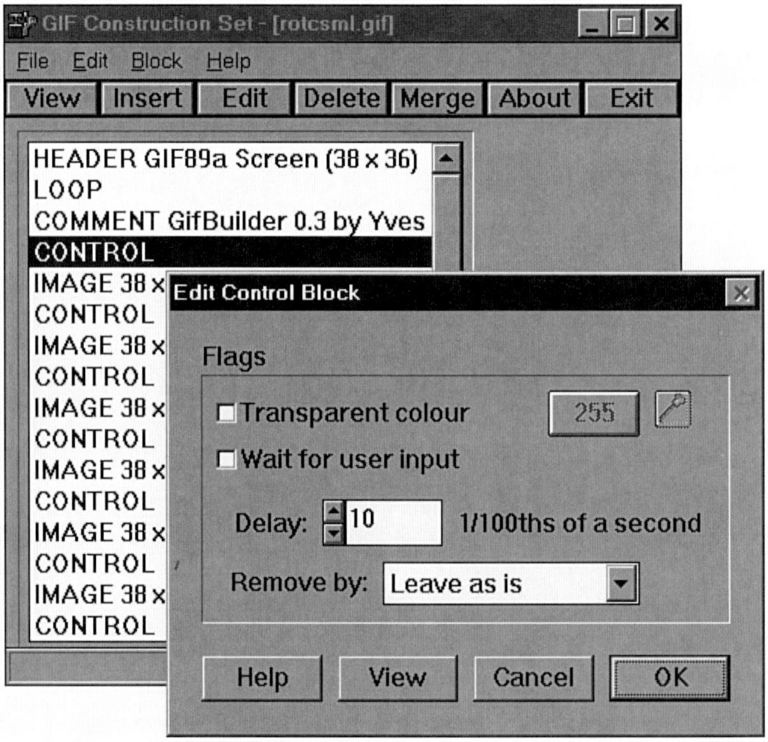

Using Image and Control Blocks to Minimize File Size

Depending on the kind of animation you have, you can use the features of the Image block to optimize file size. One technique you can use is to keep a background image in place throughout the animation while a smaller animation plays in front of the background. This is the same procedure that is performed automatically in GifBuilder with the File Optimization command. In GIF Construction Set, you have to edit animation frames by hand, and set the Image block settings for each frame.

1. Create your background frame for frame one.
2. Create the animation frames that will overlay this background.

It is important to maintain registration points between frames. The easiest way to do this for GIF Construction Set is to create all your frames in such a way that they are registered at the upper-left corner. This may not be possible, depending on your animation.

You should note the pixel coordinates of the overlaid animation frames relative to the background frame with the upper-left corner of the background frame being coordinate 0,0. Then create all your overlaid animation frames with the upper-left corner at the same pixel coordinates.

1. Insert the Images into your animation using the procedures previously described.
2. Insert Control blocks before each Image block, except the first Image (which should be your background) using the procedures previously described.
3. For each Image block (except the first):

    a. Choose the Image block in the GIF Construction Set window.

    b. Click on the Edit button.

    c. Enter the pixel coordinates relative to the upper-left corner of the background image in the Image left and Image top boxes (see fig. 7.26).

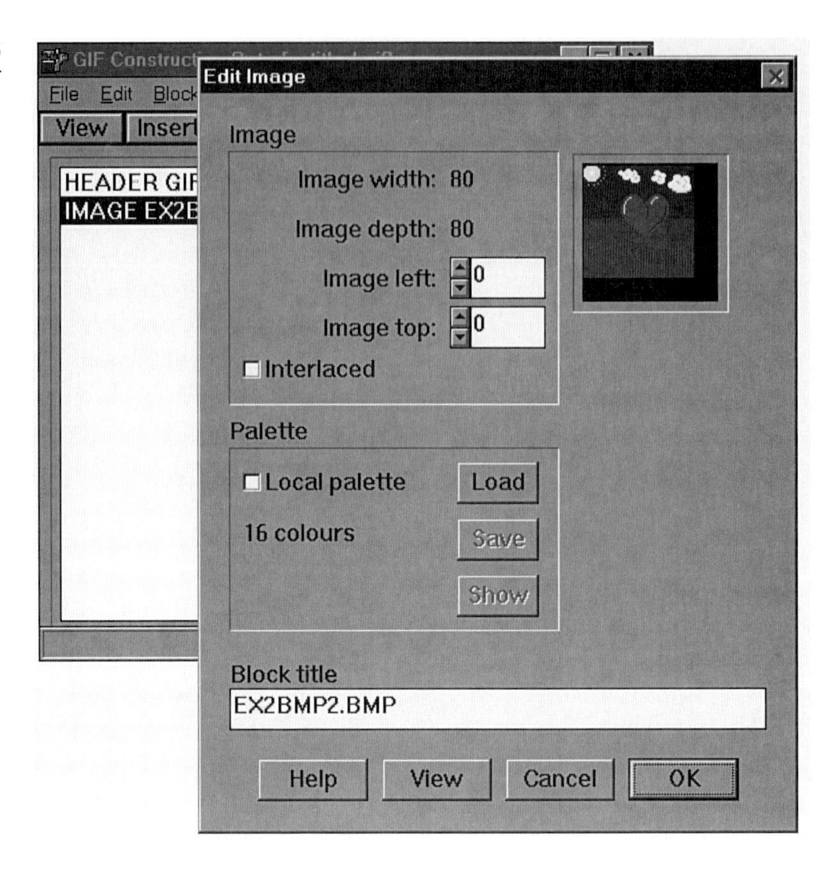

Figure 7.26

Editing Image blocks.

4. After you complete step 3, repeat the following substeps for each Control block:
   a. Choose the Control block in the GIF Construction Set window.
   b. Click on the Edit button.
   c. Choose Previous Image in the Removed by pop-up menu.

Test your animation on target machines and browsers because the aspects of the animated GIF specs used here may not be supported on all browsers.

Server-Push Animation

server-push

One of the first ways devised to add animated inline graphics to a Web page was through a technique called **server-push**. Server-push animation works by "pushing" a sequence of graphics onto the page. The graphics are displayed so rapidly (as long as the network isn't too slow) that they produce the illusion of smooth motion.

Server-push animations require a CGI (Common Gateway Interface) script. A CGI script is written in a programming language such as Perl or C and resides in a special directory on the Web server.

CGI programs that use server-push animation send successive graphics files from the server to the Web browser page. The CGI program is typically specified in the SRC attribute of an IMG tag. When the browser loads the page with the IMG tag, it calls the CGI program which then pushes a sequence of images, inline, onto the page. Here's some sample HTML:

```
<IMG WIDTH = 32 HEIGHT = 32 SRC = "/cgi-bin/
➥server_push.cgi".
```

In this example, `server_push.cgi` is the name of the CGI program that displays the animation inline, in the Web page.

This section discusses the following subjects:

- Advantages and disadvantages of server-push animation
- A ready-made server-push CGI script

Advantages and Disadvantages of Server-Push Animation

Advantages of server-push animation include:

- Works in a wide range of browsers.
- Doesn't require users to have special viewers or Plug-Ins.
- Can use a wide variety of image formats, such as JPEG.
- Can specify the number of loop iterations (although the latest versions of browsers are beginning to support this feature in GIF animations).
- Can change animation frames at runtime with scripting to provide custom animations.

Disadvantages include:

- Requires a knowledge of CGI scripting and a programming language such as Perl and C.
- Requires access to the special cgi-bin directory on a Web server.
- Playback depends on server load and network traffic; each frame has to be sent by the server in its entirety, which can place a load on the server and is not an efficient use of bandwidth.
- Limited interactivity.

The server-push technique is being used less as more browsers (beginning with Netscape Navigator 2.0) support other techniques, such as GIF animation.

A Ready-Made Server-Push CGI Script

You can obtain a server-push CGI script to use for your own animations along with a lot of other scripts at Matt's Script Archive:

`http://worldwidemart.com/scripts/`

The server-push animation script can be found at:

`http://worldwidemart.com/scripts/animation.shtml`

This script is written in Perl, a great cross-platform scripting language. To customize this script for your Web site, change the following lines in the script:

- **`$times = 1.`** Change the number 1 to the number of loops you want the animation to run.
- **`$basefile = /path/to/images/.`** Change `/path/to/images/` to the absolute path of the directory that contains your animation graphics.
- **`@files =(begin.gif,second.gif,third.gif,last.gif).`** Change the file names, `begin.gif`, `second.gif`, and so on, to the file names of your animation frames in the order in which you want the animation sequence to run.

- **`$con_type = gif`.** Change gif to the file format of the animation frames; the format can be one of those listed in the following table. Note that your server must support the image type also.

Table 7.2 provides the file formats for animations using Matt's server-push animation script.

Table 7.2

Animation File Formats for Matt's Animation Script

Format	File name extension
gif	gif
jpeg	jpeg, jpg, jpe
ief	ief
tiff	tiff, tif
x-cmu-raster	ras
x-portable-anymap	pnm
x-portable-bitmap	pbm
x-portable-graymap	pgm
x-portable-pixmap	ppm
x-rgb	rgb
x-xbitmap	xbm
x-xpixmap	xpm
x-xwindowdump	xwd

Creating Animations with JavaScript

The following technique uses JavaScript to create an animation. JavaScript is the client-side scripting language developed by Netscape. Using JavaScript doesn't require any server intervention or knowledge of CGI scripting. For a more detailed description of JavaScript, see Chapter 14, "Scripting Multimedia Web Pages."

As of this writing, the following JavaScript animation requires Netscape Navigator 3.0.

This section covers the following:

- Advantages and disadvantages of JavaScript animation
- How JavaScript animation code works
- Embedding JavaScript animation in HTML

Advantages and Disadvantages of JavaScript

JavaScript animations can use any inline graphic format supported by the browser, such as JPEG or GIF. They don't require server intervention and can be customized easily at runtime, based on a user's input or environment. As of this writing, JavaScript animation runs only in Netscape Navigator 3.0 or greater.

Some JavaScript Animation Code

To create animations in JavaScript, put this script within the HEAD tag of an HTML document:

```
<SCRIPT LANGUAGE = "JavaScript">
var secondsToWait = 1000*0.2  //number of milliseconds
➥between frames
var imageNum = 1    //index number of first frame
var imageMax = 3    //number of frames
// Create an array and load it with images
myImages = new Array()
for(i = 1; i < (imageMax + 1); i++) {
   myImages[i] = new Image()
   myImages[i].src = "image" + i + ".gif"
   }
// Function that changes images
function changeFrame() {
   document.dynamicImage.src = myImages[imageNum].src

   imageNum++
   if(imageNum > imageMax) {
   imageNum = 1

   }
}

</SCRIPT>
```

The function `changeFrame` will change the graphic named `dynamicImage` after the time specified in `secondsToWait` has passed. Here's how to customize the function `changeFrame`:

1. To add your own animation frames, the frames must be named as follows, up to the number specified in imageMax:

   `image1.gif`

   `image2.gif`

   The graphics must be in the same directory as the HTML document that contains this script.

2. In the above code, images are displayed for 1/5 of a second, then changed for a frame rate of five frames per second. To change the frame rate, change the `secondsToWait` variable. For example, to create an animation with a frame rate of ten frames per second, you would write:

   ```
   var secondsToWait = 1000*0.1   //number of
   ➥milliseconds between frames
   ```

3. To change the number of total frames in the animation, change the imageMax variable to the total number of frames.

Note

If you want to create an animation of JPEG files, change this line:

```
myImages[i].src = "image" + i
+ ".gif"
```

to this:

```
myImages[i].src = "image" + i +
".jpg"
```

and name your image files like this:

```
image1.jpg

image2.jpg
```

Embedding JavaScript Animation in HTML

To embed the animation in an HTML document, you set the onLoad event handler of the IMG tag to `"setTimeout('changeFrame()', secondsToWait)."` The function `"setTimeout"` is a built-in JavaScript function. The setTimeout function will call the `"changeFrame"` function after `"secondsToWait"` seconds have passed. This function will be reset every time you load a new image. For example,

```
<IMG NAME="dynamicImage" SRC="image0.gif" WIDTH = 119
➥HEIGHT = 68 ALT="Dynamic Gif"
➥onLoad="setTimeout('changeFrame()', secondsToWait)">
```

Besides being able to animate JPEGs, because this animation is implemented as a client-side JavaScript, the Web author can create a script that dynamically changes the parameters of the animation, such as the images that make up the animation frames, the frame rate, or total number of frames, based on certain conditions at runtime. Web authors can create an animation that configures itself based on the user's browser or the time of day, for example. See the section on dynamic billboards in Chapter 14 for a detailed description of a similar dynamic image JavaScript function and ways to create dynamic documents.

Animation Plug-Ins and ActiveX Controls

There are numerous Netscape-compatible Plug-Ins and ActiveX controls that provide playback of animations in Web pages. Some also provide sound playback and interactivity. QuickTime Plug-In for animation is covered in Chapter 10, "Animating with QuickTime Digital Video." Shockwave Plug-In is covered in Chapter 9, "Video."

Following is a list of some of the available animation Plug-Ins:

- Astound Web Player by Gold Disk

  `http://www.golddisk.com/awp.html`

- Emblaze Plug-In and authoring tool by Interactive Media Group

  `http://Geo.inter.net/Geo/technology/emblaze/downloads.html`

- FutureSplash Plug-In, ActiveX control and authoring tool by FutureWave

  `http://www.futurewave.com`

- mBED Plug-In, ActiveX control and authoring tools by mBED Software (see fig. 7.27)

  `http://www.mbed.com/`

Animations can be created on the Web from authoring tools that run from Web pages.

- MovieStar Plug-In and authoring tool by Intelligence at Large

  `http://www.beingthere.com/`

- SCREAM Plug-In by Saved by Technology

  `http://www.savedbytech.com/sbt/Plug_In.html`

- Sizzler Plug-In, ActiveX control, CyberDog part, and authoring tool by TotallyHip

  `http://www.totallyhip.com/`

- WebAnimator Plug-In and authoring Tool by DeltaPoint

  `http://www.deltapoint.com/`

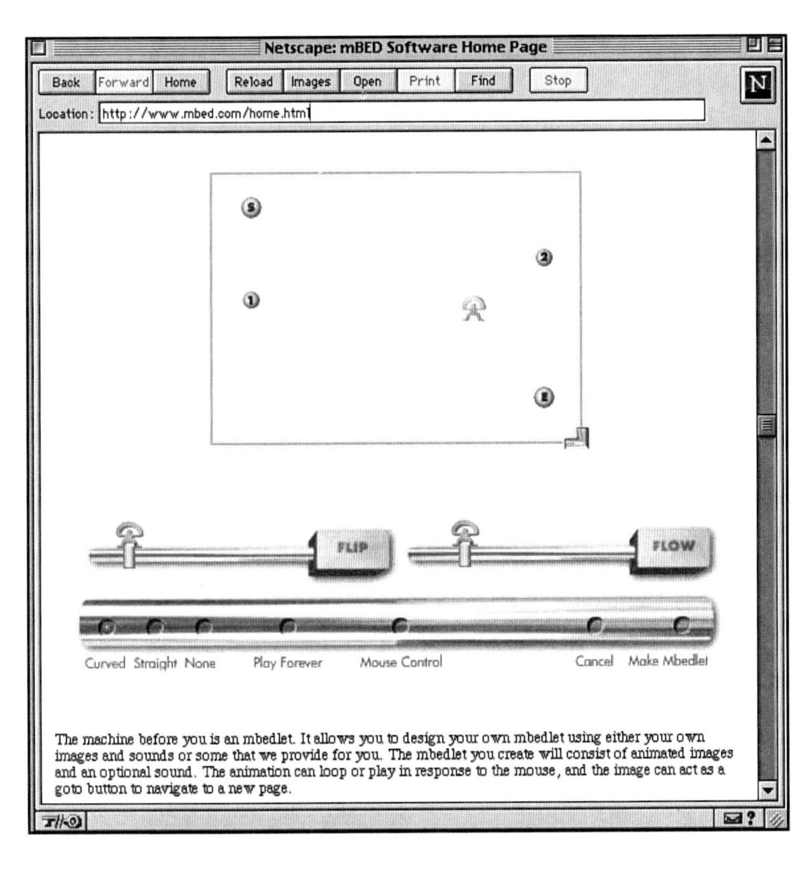

Figure 7.27

mBed authoring, creating animations from a Web page.

This section looks at the following authoring tools in more detail:

- FutureSplash Animator
- WebAnimator
- MovieStar
- Sizzler/WebPainter

FutureSplash Animator

FutureWave's FutureSplash Animator and FutureSplash Player have been built from the ground up for Web animation.

FutureSplash Animator is a relatively inexpensive Web animation authoring tool available for Macintosh, Power Macintosh, Windows 95, and Windows NT. Trial versions of FutureSplash Animator should be available from FutureWave's Web site. You can export animations in FutureWave's proprietary animation format, which requires the FutureWave viewer, or as QuickTime movies on the Mac or AVI movies on Windows. Animations consist of high-quality, compact, interactive vector-graphics. Sound is not supported as of this writing.

FutureSplash Player is required to view animation in FutureSplash format. FutureSplash Player is a Netscape Navigator-compatible Plug-In for Mac, PowerMac, and Windows 95/NT, and an ActiveX control for Microsoft's Internet Explorer 3.0 for Windows 95/NT. Unix and Java versions of the Player are in the works. FutureSplash Player provides streamed playback of animations and adjusts quality of playback to the user's system. It can also be used to provide high-quality, non-animated vector graphics on the Web (see fig. 7.28). The FutureSplash Player is available free at:

`http://www.futurewave.com/`

Figure 7.28

Anti-aliased, vector-based FutureSplash animation.

FutureSplash Features

FutureSplash animations have many features that make them ideal for the Web:

- Animations are vector-based and are made up of resolution-independent Bézier curves similar to vector-based drawing programs, such as FreeHand or Illustrator.

That means they are very compact compared to the bitmap graphics that make up the primary graphic content in animation formats such as Shockwave. Vector-based also means that users can zoom in on FutureSplash graphics and observe fine detail without loss of quality.

- Has many HTML attributes to control display.
- Player can scale quality and color-depth based on capabilities of user's local machine.
- Animations are streamed; high-quality playback begins rapidly.
- Easy to add interactivity; no scripting required.
- LiveConnect enabled. FutureSplash animations can communicate with JavaScript function, Java applets.
- Enables you to author on Mac, PowerMac, or Windows 95/NT.
- Great vector-based drawing tools based on FutureWave's SmartSketch product.
- Outline fonts can be embedded into graphic images.
- Vector graphics and outline fonts are anti-aliased.
- Small Player Size—FutureSplash Player files range between 80 and 150K (uncompressed) depending on the platform.

FutureSplash File Format Support

FutureSplash supports the following file formats:

- Animation formats

    FutureSplash Player

    Animated GIF

    EPS 3.0 Sequence

    Adobe Illustrator Sequence

    DXF Sequence

    JPEG Sequence

    GIF Sequence

  - QuickTime Movie (Macintosh)
  - PICT Sequence (Macintosh)
  - Windows AVI (Windows)
  - EMF Sequence (Windows)
  - WMF Sequence (Windows)
  - Bitmap Sequence (Windows)
- Image formats
  - Adobe Illustrator (88, 3.0, 5.0, 6.0)
  - AutoCad DXF
  - JPEG Image
  - GIF Image
  - PICT Bitmap & Vector-based (Macintosh)
  - Enhanced Metafile EMF (Windows)
  - Windows Metafile WMF (Windows)
  - Bitmap BMP (Windows)
- No sound support
- Export formats
  - FutureSplash Player SPL (see fig 7.29)
  - EPS 3.0
  - QuickTime(Macintosh)
  - Windows AVI (Windows)

Figure 7.29

Compact, fast-loading, animated comic book done with FutureSplash animation by ISYS Idea Systems, Inc.

Adding FutureSplash Animations to Your Web Page

To serve FutureSplash animations from your Web page, set up your Web server to associate the `.spl` file name extension to MIME Type application/futuresplash.

To embed FutureSplash animations in your Web pages for both the Netscape Plug-In and ActiveX control, use the following HTML:

```
<OBJECT
id="movie"
classid="clsid:D27CDB6E-AE6D-11cf-96B8-444553540000"
codebase="http://www.futurewave.com/fsplash.cab"
width=260 height=102 align=right>
<PARAM NAME="Movie" VALUE="newsseal.spl">
<EMBED SRC="newsseal.spl" PLUGINSPAGE="http://
➥www.futurewave.com/downloadfs.htm"
width=260 height=102 align=right>
</OBJECT>
```

Change the value of the VALUE parameter and SRC attribute to the URL of your FutureSplash animation.

The FutureSplash Player recognizes several HTML attributes to the EMBED tags and PARAMs to the OBJECT tags that control display and playback. Visit FutureWave's Web site for documentation on the latest features. Of note are a set of tags that enable you to optimize playback for animation speed or graphics quality based on the user's system. For example:

- **QUALITY=LOW.** Optimizes playback for speed.
- **QUALITY=HIGH.** Optimizes playback for graphic quality rather than animation playback.
- **QUALITY=AUTOLOW.** (default) Starts playback at low-quality and then switches to high-quality on fast systems.
- **QUALITY=AUTOHIGH.** Starts playback at high-quality and then switches to low-quality on slow systems. Use these settings for single frame-movies displaying vector graphics.

WebAnimator

Deltapoint's WebAnimator is an inexpensive but powerful Web animation, Web-based graphic, and presentation tool kit available for Macintosh (see fig. 7.30). A Windows version is in the works. You can export animations in Deltapoint's proprietary animation format, which requires the WebAnimator viewer, or as QuickTime movies. You can download a free 30-day trial version of the WebAnimator authoring tool at:

`http://www.deltapoint.com/`

Figure 7.30

Authoring animated Web pages with WebAnimator.

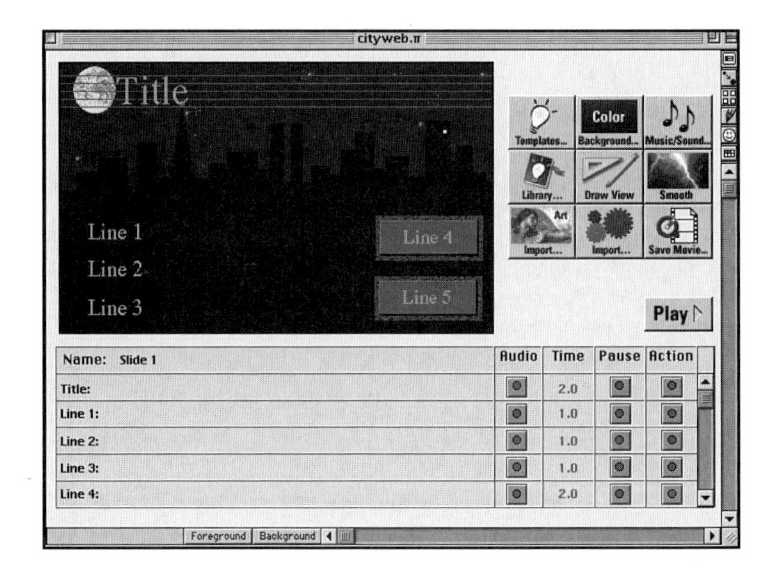

WebAnimator Features

Figure 7.31 shows features of WebAnimator authoring tool. The features include:

- Cel-based and sprite-based animation
- Sound integration
- Integrated drawing tools
- Media integrations and synchronization
- Interactivity added by setting properties in dialog boxes
- Libraries of templates for creating Web graphics and animation, including navigational elements and identity graphics

Note

The WebAnimator viewer is a Netscape Plug-In and is available free for Mac and Windows systems.

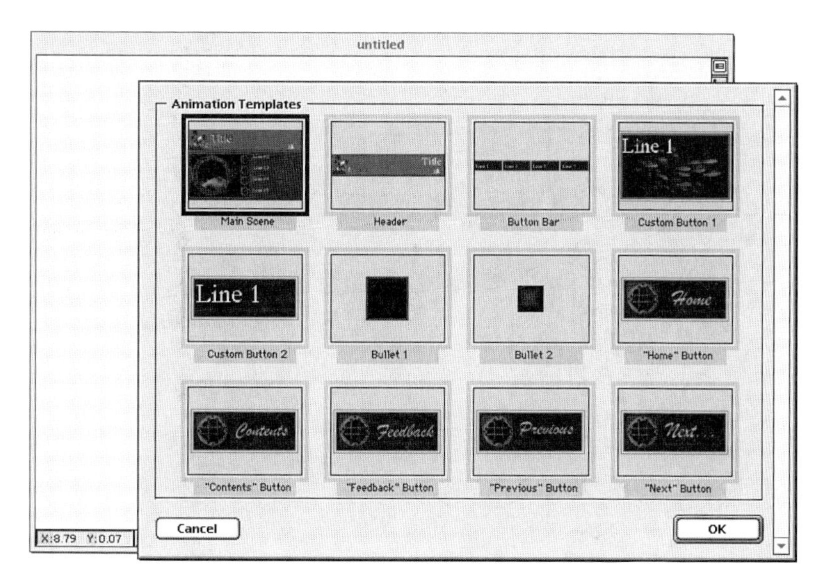

Figure 7.31

Template libraries in WebAnimator.

WebAnimator File Format Support

WebAnimator supports the following file formats:

- Import Formats

  PICT

  BMP

  GIF

  JPG

  PCX

PNG

TGA

TIFF

AIFF

Macintosh 'snd'

SoundEdit

PICS

- Export formats

  WebAnimator files

  QuickTime movies

Figure 7.32 shows how to create animated buttons in WebAnimator.

Figure 7.32

Creating animated buttons.

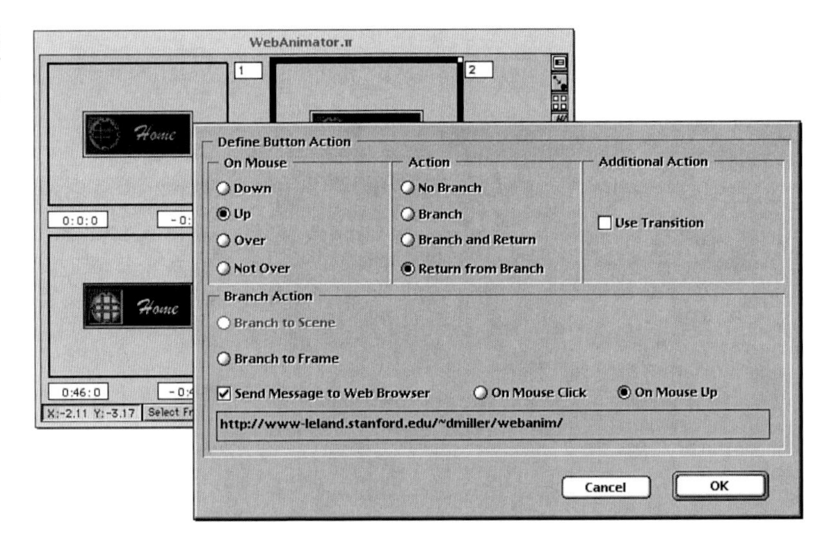

MovieStar

MovieStar from Intelligence At Large is an inexpensive but powerful QuickTime and animation authoring tool with many unique features optimized for creating Web content. It is currently available for Macintosh. You can download a free, fully functional demo that limits the length of the movie and animations you can create at:

`http://www.beingthere.com/`

MovieStar features

MovieStar has powerful QuickTime and animation features that you won't find even in more expensive programs. With MovieStar you can import diverse content, integrate it into a single multimedia presentation, and then export it to Web-optimized QuickTime movies, complete with HTML tags, animated GIFs, and multipart MIME format files for multimedia e-mail attachments.

MovieStar File Format Support

MovieStar imports the following formats:

- QuickTime video
- PICs
- PICT graphics
- QuickTime audio
- AIFF
- CD Audio
- MIDI
- SND
- Live digitized video
- Live digitized audio
- Styled text

MovieStar exports the following formats:

- Web-optimized Fast-Start QuickTime
- QuickTime video
- QuickTime audio
- Animated GIF
- AIFF
- Multipart MIME
- PICT graphics

Each media type within a MovieStar project can have various properties associated with it, including timing and synchronization information, such as when the media object appears, location and scaling, transitions, transparency, and animation.

MovieStar also has the ability to digitize video and audio directly into the project (see fig. 7.33).

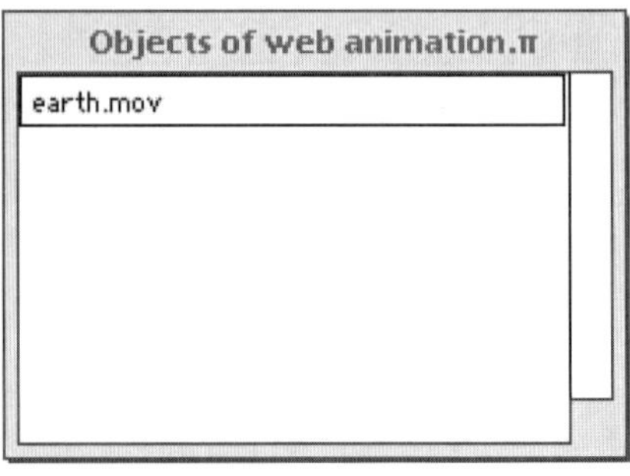

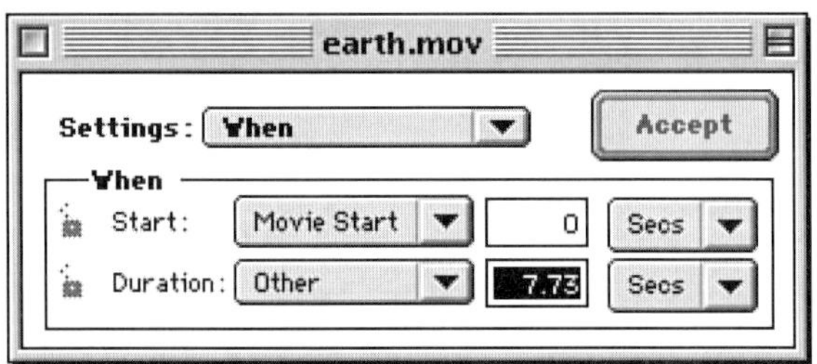

Figure 7.33

MovieStar, QuickTime, and animation authoring tool.

Setting Up a Project in MovieStar

Although MovieStar is primarily a QuickTime authoring tool, you also can use it to create GIF animations. To set up your project (see fig. 7.34):

1. Launch MovieStar. A new untitled project window appears.
2. Choose Project, Project Settings to give animation dimensions that are suitable for Web delivery—namely, 160 × 120 or less.
3. Choose Project, Background Color to set a background color.

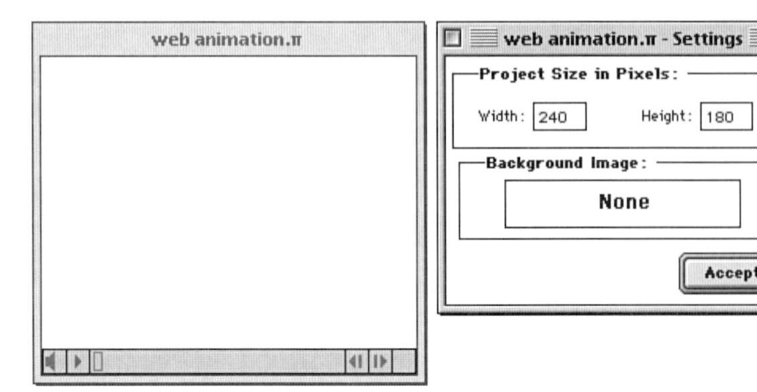

Figure 7.34

Setting up a MovieStar project.

Importing Media in MovieStar

Import different media types into your project by choosing Project, Import. Imported media objects are added to your object list. Media objects in MovieStar can have different properties associated with them, such as locations, start points and end points, transitions, transparency, and so on. You can view a list of the objects in your project by choosing Project, Objects (see fig. 7.35).

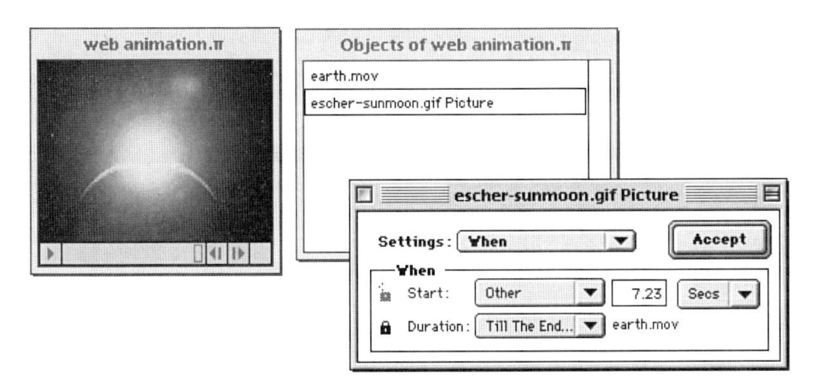

Figure 7.35

Importing media.

Changing Properties in MovieStar

You can change the properties of an object at any time by:

- Double-clicking on the object in the project window to bring up the object's property dialog box.
- Choosing Project, Objects and double-clicking on the object in the list view.

Figure 7.36 shows the Drawing Effects of an object set at Transparent.

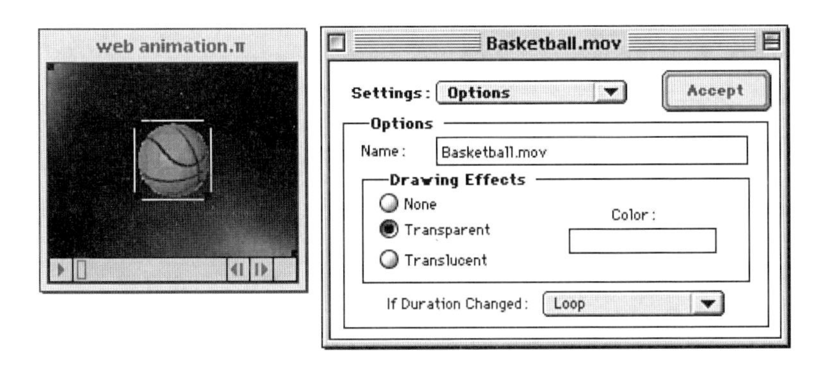

Figure 7.36

Setting transparency.

Add text to your project by choosing Objects, New Text (see fig. 7.37).

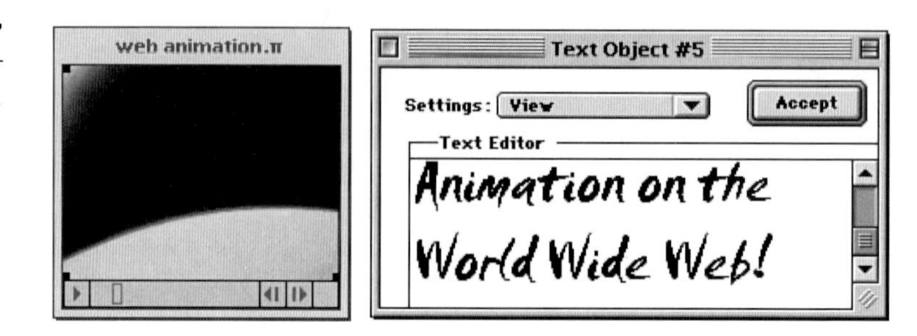

Figure 7.37

Adding text.

Digitize video and audio into your project using the commands from the Audio and Video menu.

Adding Animation

MovieStar provides real-time animation of objects in the MovieStar project window. To animate an object:

1. Move the playback slider to the place in the movie where you want the animation to begin.
2. Choose the object you want to animate.
3. Choose Object, Animate.
4. Now, click on the object with the mouse and drag it around the window. MovieStar records your mouse movements and turns it into an animation. Unfortunately, MovieStar provides limited feedback while dragging.
5. Play back the animation.
6. If you don't like the results, choose Object, Remove Animation.

You also can create simple animated transitions with the Transition properties of an object (see fig. 7.38).

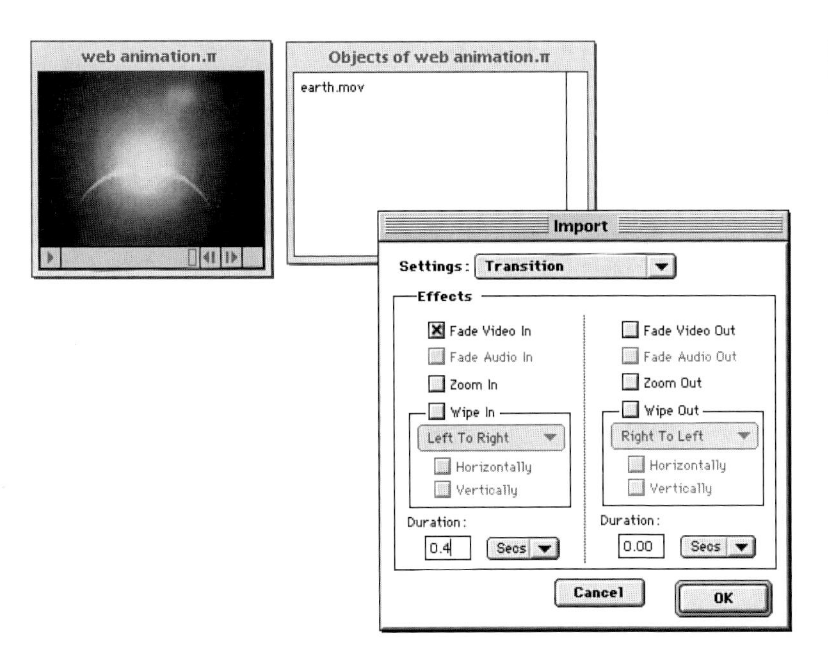

Figure 7.38

Animated transitions.

Exporting Web-based QuickTime, GIF Animations, and Multipart MIME

After you create your project and integrate and synchronize the various media types, you can export the finished product to a Web-optimized Fast-Start QuickTime movie complete with an HTML document, a GIF animation, or as a Multipart MIME format file. You also can export the audio of your project as an AIFF file and the text of your project as a text file.

Sizzler

sprite files

Sizzler is a suite of free cross-platform (Mac and Windows 95/NT) viewers and simple conversion tools that enables you to view and create Web-based animations with short sounds, called **sprite files**. Sizzler includes:

- Netscape Plug-In
- ActiveX control
- OpenDoc viewer for Cyberdog

- Sizzler Java classes
- Sizzler conversion tool

Animations are streamed without special servers. Animations are viewed with the Sizzler Netscape Plug-In, ActivcX control, and OpenDoc viewer for Cyberdog (an OpenDoc component that can play inside an OpenDoc container), or with the Sizzler Java libraries as a Java applet.

Sizzler animations are streamed. A low resolution version of the animation downloads rapidly and then becomes progressively more detailed as more data is downloaded. The effect is somewhat like an interlaced GIF (see fig. 7.39).

Figure 7.39

Sizzler streaming animation.

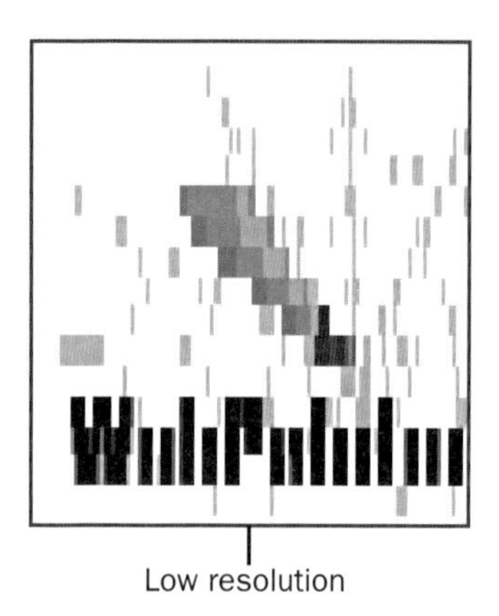

Users will need the free Sizzler Plug-In, Sizzler ActiveX Control, Sizzler Cyberdog part, or a Java-enabled browser to view animations.

The Sizzler application is a free stand-alone conversion utility you can use to create streaming animations with sound or Java applets (see fig. 7.40). With Sizzler you can:

- Import QuickTime movies and PICs format files on a Macintosh and export Sizzler animations that can be played back by Sizzler Netscape Plug-In, ActiveX control, CyberDog part, and also as a Java applet.
- Import AVIs or DIB lists (sequentially numbered bitmaps, such as pict01.bmp, pict02.bmp, etc.) on Windows 95/NT, and export Sizzler animations that can be played back by Sizzler Netscape Plug-In, ActiveX control, and also as a Java applet.

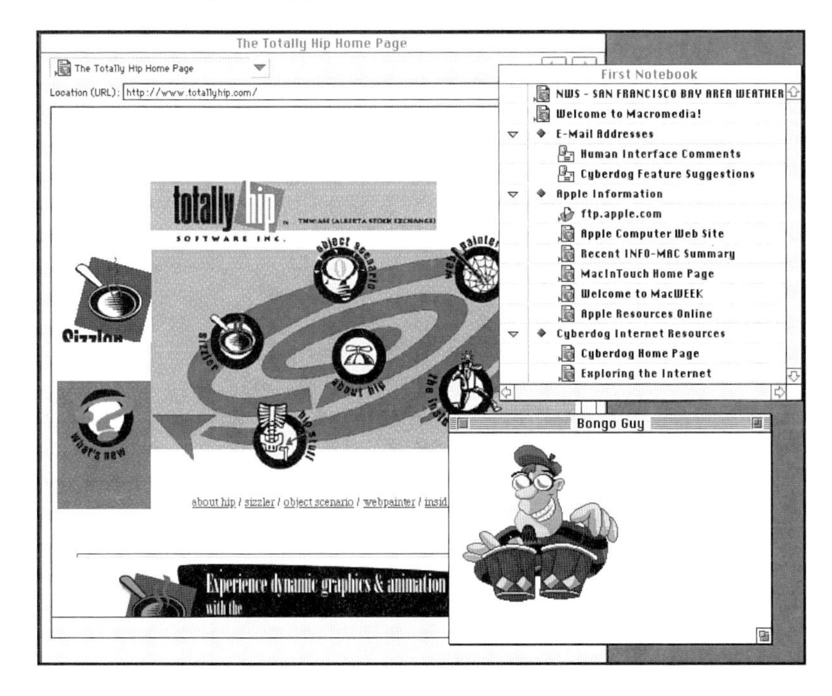

Figure 7.40

Sizzler animations playing as stand-alone OpenDoc parts and as a Netscape Plug-In inside the Cyberdog browser.

To serve Sizzler sprite files, you must configure your Web server to associate the MIME type `application/x-sprite` with the file name extensions `.sprite, .spr`.

WebPainter

WebPainter is a full featured animation program specifically designed to create Web animations, including Sizzler sprite files for Netscape Plug-Ins, ActiveX controls, OpenDoc, GIF animations, QuickTime movies, and Java applets. It is currently available in beta for Macintosh. A Windows version may be available by the time you read this. Check out the following site for more information:

```
http://www.totallyhip.com/
```

WebPainter can import GIF, PICT, PICs, and QuickTime movies. WebPainter projects can be exported as the following:

- Animated GIFs
- Separate GIF animation frames
- PICs files
- Separate PICT animation frames
- QuickTime movies
- QuickTime Sprite Track movies
- Sizzler for ActiveX
- Sizzler for OpenDoc part (Cyberdog)
- Sizzler for Netscape Plug-In
- Sizzler Java applet

Creating Sizzler Animations with Sizzler Converter

On a Macintosh:

1. Drag-and-drop a QuickTime movie or PICs file onto the Sizzler icon or launch Sizzler and choose Open from the File menu (see fig. 7.41).
2. In the dialog box, choose the options you'd like, such as frames per second, and a hyperlink for the animation file.
3. To add sound, click on the Add Sound button and choose a Macintosh SND file. Other sound formats should be supported in the future.
4. Choose either play sound continuously or play sound from a particular frame.
5. Interleave settings specify where you want the sound to begin. For example, From Start will begin playback immediately, whereas From Medium Resolution will start playback when a medium resolution version of the file has been downloaded.
6. Choose the output option either for playback from a Netscape Plug-In, ActiveX control, Cyberdog part, or Java applet.

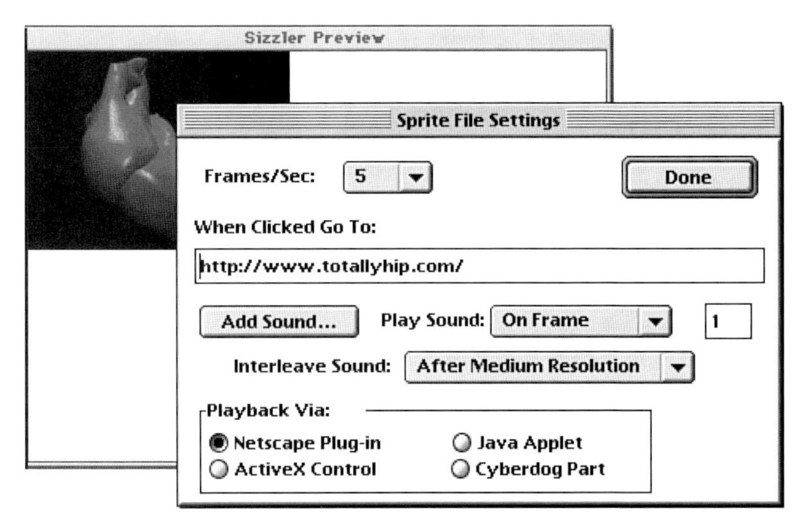

Figure 7.41

Sizzler converter.

On Windows:

1. Launch the Sizzler editor.
2. Choose File, Objects/Insert Image.
3. Choose the files that you want to use.
4. To add sound, choose File, Objects/Add Sound.
5. Choose a WAV file. Future versions of Sizzler should support other sound file formats.
6. Choose the sound in the Editor window.
7. Choose File, Objects/Properties.
8. Choose the Sound options you want to use.

Which Plug-In To Use?

You generally must download and install the special viewer Plug-In for the particular file before you can use most animation Plug-Ins. QuickTime animations and Shockwave animations in MSIE 3.0 and Netscape Navigator 4.0 are special exceptions. If you do decide to use an animation Plug-In, many factors contribute to determining which one you would want to use, including the following:

- Existing source material
- In-house expertise in animation software

- Purpose of the animation
- If the animation requires sound
- If the animation requires user interactivity
- Filesize/download and time/bandwidth considerations

For example, FutureSplash consists of high-quality vector graphics, streaming playback, and extremely small file sizes, provides user interactivity, and requires a relatively inexpensive authoring program, but doesn't support sound, whereas Sizzler supports Java applets, sound, and minimal interactivity.

Conclusion

Used with consideration of your users and with awareness of the limited bandwidth available, Web animations can add to the enjoyment and information content of your Web site. When placed in appropriate places on your Web site, animations can be the hook that brings people back for a second visit. If used improperly, animations can be annoying and get in the way of users viewing the content of your site.

Currently, there is a multitude of ways to add animations to your site. The most popular techniques are described in this book. Which technique works for you depends on your server, your network connectivity, the design goals and purposes of your Web site, the availability of tools, your user profile, and the availability of viewers.

Also, be aware that delivering Web-based animation will be changing in the next year. Faster Internet access will make multimedia content more practical. Probably, the most talked about Web innovation has been the cross-platform, Java programming language. Java multimedia extensions from Sun, Macromedia, and Silicon Graphics, Apple Computer's QuickTime Media Layer and QuickTime extensions to Java, and Adobe System's Bravo imaging engine for Java, had just been announced or promised at the time of this writing.

These extensions to Java promise the capability to embed mini-viewers with downloadable multimedia objects, removing the need for Plug-Ins or explicit browser support to view your content. Similar features will be present in Microsoft's OLE/ActiveX controls. How all this will play out remains to be seen. In the meantime, this book will provide you with a rich tool kit that you can use to add animations to your Web sites today.

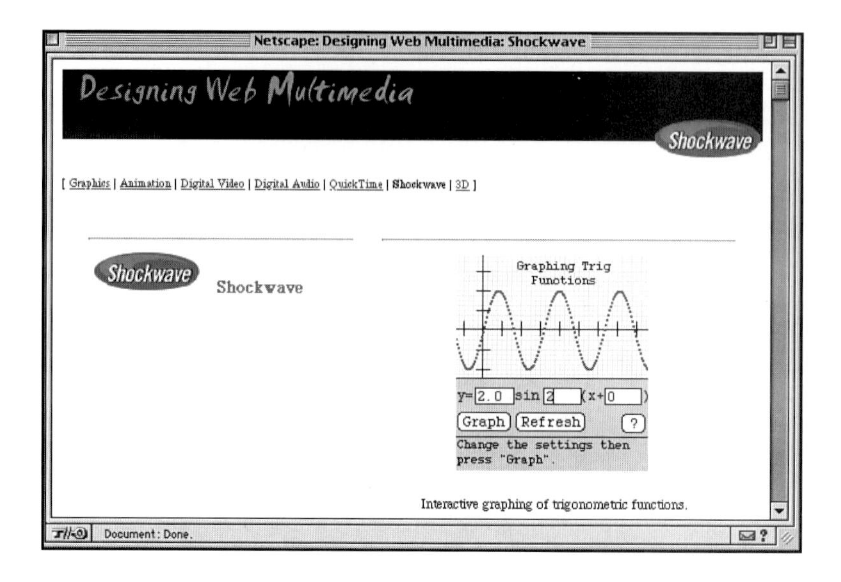

Arguably the most popular animation format on the Web, and rapidly being integrated with major Web browsers, Shockwave for Macromedia Director can do a lot more than create animated bullets.

chapter

8

Animating with Shockwave for Director

Shockwave is the name Macromedia uses for a series of viewers and authoring utilities that enable the following Macromedia products to be viewed on the Web:

- Director, a cross-platform animation and authoring tool for interactive multimedia
- FreeHand, a cross-platform, vector-based post-script drawing package
- Authorware, a cross-platform, interactive multime-dia authoring tool popular in computer-based training applications
- SoundEdit, a digital audio editing tool for the Macintosh

Macromedia's Shockwave Plug-In for Netscape Navigator was one of the first animation Plug-Ins. Shockwave enables Director authors to publish interactive, multimedia content on the Web. You'll need Director—the popular 2D animation and authoring tool—for Macintosh or Windows in order to create Shockwave animations.

The Director authoring tool is used in CD-ROM publishing, broadcast video and film, interactive ads and marketing materials, kiosks, presentations, games, prototypes, courseware, and just about any application that requires interactivity, animation, or the integration of multiple media such as text, graphics, digital audio, and digital video.

Note

You can find a save-disabled version of Director 5, and versions of the Shockwave Plug-In and Afterburner compression utility, on this book's CD.

The Shockwave for Director Plug-In enables the playback of Director files directly in Web pages. Shockwave consists of:

- A Plug-In for Netscape-compatible Web browsers that plays Dircctor files directly in the Web page
- The Afterburner file compression/post-processing tool
- Special Internet extensions to Lingo, Director's object-oriented scripting language

Figure 8.1 illustrates a Shockwave movie playing in a Web page.

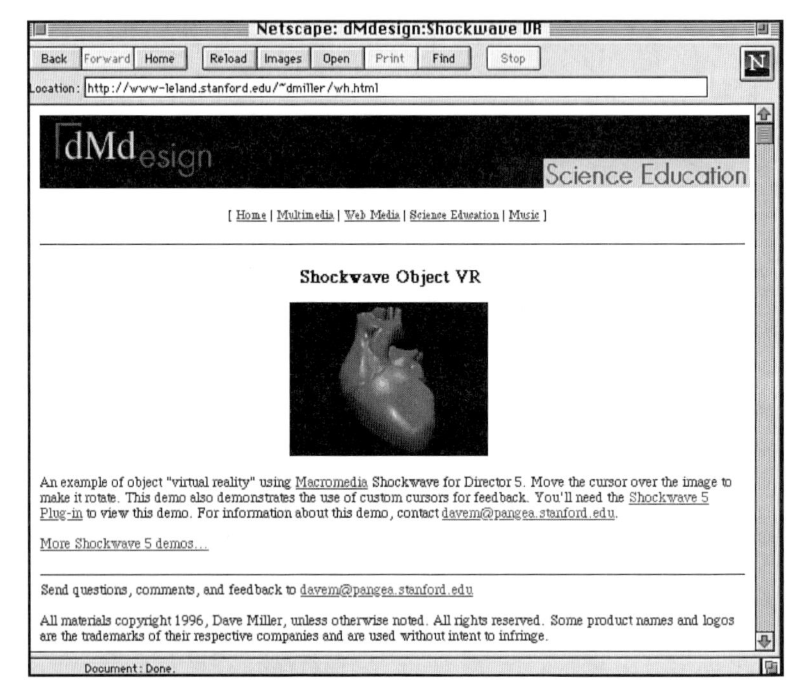

Figure 8.1

An interactive, 3D Shockwave movie playing in a Web page.

Tip

Users must have the Shockwave Plug-In in the Netscape Plug-Ins folder to play back Director files embedded in Web pages.

This chapter focuses on the Shockwave for Director Plug-In for Macintosh and Windows. The examples in this chapter use the following:

- Director 5 authoring tool
- Shockwave for Audio Xtras
- Shockwave for Director 5 Plug-In

Overview of Director and Shockwave

> **Note**
>
> You can obtain the latest version of the Shockwave Plug-In; Shockwave for Audio Xtras; and Afterburner compression utility from:
>
> `http://www.macromedia.com/shockwave/`

To create Shockwave animations for the Web, you will need the Director authoring program for either Macintosh or Windows. Shockwave animations created on either the Macintosh or Windows computers will play back in any browser that supports the Shockwave Plug-In. This section provides you with information about Director's and Shockwave Plug-In's animation and file features.

Director's Animation Features

Director provides several features helpful to animators, including integrated paint tools, layering, onion-skinning, ease-in and ease-out, and frame-based timelines (see Chapter 7, "Animation," for a discussion of these techniques). Director uses sprite-based animation, but also has limited vector-based tools. It also provides several different animation techniques such as in-betweening, real-time recording, and step recording.

Lingo

Director titles can integrate text, graphics, digital video, and digital audio. Interactivity and navigation are provided by **Lingo**, Director's powerful, object-oriented scripting language. You can also animate sprites programmatically with Lingo. Director does not support motion paths or hierarchical linking, but you can simulate these features with film loops and Lingo.

If all you want to do is create short animations and spinning logos for a Web page, Director might be overkill. Competing products, such as WebPainter from TotallyHip, FutureSplashAnimator from FutureSplash, WebAnimator from DeltaPoint, Emblaze from the Interactive Media Group, and mBEDLets from mBED Software are cheaper, provide very good animation tools, have been developed from the ground up for Web animation, and in some cases provide for interactivity. There are demo versions of these programs on the accompanying CD.

movie

projectors

A Director file is called a **movie**. Director enables you to create license-free, run-time players of your Director movies called **projectors**. A projector contains an embedded playback engine so users can view your Director movie without any additional software.

Pros and Cons of Director and Shockwave

One of the best features of Director is that Director files created on one platform can be easily transferred to another platform. A Director movie created on a Macintosh can be easily opened in the Director authoring environment on a Windows computer, and vice versa.

Unfortunately, to create a license-free run-time player for both Macintosh and Windows you will need a copy of the Director programs for both Macintosh and Windows. You can't create a cross-platform Projector on a single platform. A Projector created with the Mac-based tool will only play on a Mac and a Projector created with the Windows-based tool will only play on Windows machines.

Shockwave provides a way around this limitation; a Shockwave movie created on one platform can be viewed in a Web browser on other platforms.

As with most Web-based multimedia, Shockwave is a "wait for it to download and then play it" technology. File size and download time are the biggest limiting factors. Fortunately, to begin with, Director files are inherently compressed and the Afterburner utility compresses Director files even more.

Reducing Download Time

To reduce download time, create Director files that are as small as possible. This chapter provides some tips on how to do that. You can also check out the excellent Shockwave Developer's Guide at:

```
http://www.macromedia.com/shockwave/director5/
contents.html
```

Download time can be affected by many variables outside your control, such as server load and network traffic. Don't expect to put your 20 MB Director Projector on the Web. Shockwave movies should be around 100 KB or less. On a 14.4 modem, a 100 KB Shockwave animation can take 3 or 4 minutes to download. Small 10 KB movies can download in seconds.

This table lists some sample download times on different connections. All times are approximate; your mileage may vary.

	Connection		
Size	**14.4 KB/s(Home)**	**56 KB/s(ISDN)**	**1.5MB/s (xIntranetor LAN)**
10 KB	5-10 seconds	2 seconds	1 sec
100 KB	1-2 minutes	15-20 seconds	2-4 seconds
1000 KB	10-15 minutes	2-4 minutes	10-15 seconds

The following URL has a Shockwave movie that helps you estimate download time based on the file size of your movie:

```
http://www.macromedia.com/shockwave/director5/
moviedocs/download.html
```

Note

Other Web-based animation tools such as WebPainter from TotallyHip or CelAnimator from FutureWave enable the creation of streaming animation. Streaming is the ability to start playback of an animation file or other time-based media before the entire file has been downloaded. The rest of the file is downloaded in the background while the animation is playing. The user doesn't have to wait for the whole file to download to see something. Shockwave for Authorware supports a kind of streaming. As of this writing, Director doesn't support streaming, but may support streaming by the time you read this.

System Requirements for Director Authoring

The minimum system requirements for authoring in Director on Windows systems are:

- Windows 3.1, Windows 95, or Windows NT
- 486/66 processor
- 8 MB RAM
- 2X speed CD-ROM drive

The minimum system requirements for authoring in Director on Macintosh systems are:

- Mac OS 7.1 or later
- 68040 or PowerPC processor
- 8 MB RAM
- 2X speed CD-ROM drive

Note

Macromedia provides a list of supported video cards and sound cards. Visit the following site for the latest information:

`http://www.macromedia.com/`

Browser Support

Currently, Shockwave for Director is supported in Netscape Navigator 2.0 or later for Macintosh, Windows 3.1, Windows 95, and Windows NT, and is partially supported in Microsoft Internet Explorer 2.0 for Macintosh. The Shockwave Plug-In is included with Netscape's PowerPack 2.0 add-ons for the Navigator browser and is also available free from Macromedia's Web site at:

`http://www.macromedia.com/Tools/Shockwave/index.html`

Shockwave for Director is also an ActiveX control for Windows 95 and Windows NT versions of MSIE 3. Furthermore, Macromedia has announced Shockwave bundling deals with Microsoft Internet Explorer 3, America Online, Compuserve, and Apple Computer's CyberDog and Internet Connection Kit.

The following table lists browser support for Shockwave at the time of this writing:

Warning

Shockwave makes large demands on memory and disk space. Recommended setting for Web browser RAM is 10 MB. Recommended cache size is 10 MB.

Table 8.1

Browser Support for Shockwave

Feature	Netscape 2.0	MSIE 2	Netscape 3.0	MSIE 3.0
Shockwave Plug-In	Yes	Mac-only	No NetLingo	Yes
Shockwave 95/ ActiveX	No	No	No	Windows NT only

Getting Started in Director

This section gives a brief overview of Director. If you've never used Director or are just starting out, this section provides an introduction to creating Shockwave animations in Director, but it is not meant to replace reading the manuals. If you've been using Director for a while, you might want to skip this section, which addresses the following subjects:

- Director authoring
- The Lingo scripting language
- Xtras: Shockwave for Audio Xtras, and Afterburner

Director Authoring

Authoring in Director involves the following steps:

- Create the content for your Director movie, either in Director or another program such as Photoshop, After Effects, or Premiere.
- Import the content into a Director movie file.
- Choreograph animations using Director's frame-based timeline.
- Add interactivity with Lingo, the object-oriented scripting language of Director.

The Director authoring environment consists of several parts:

- **Cast** A multimedia database where content is stored.
- **Score** A frame-based timeline where you set key frames, choreograph animation, and script interactivity.
- **Stage** The place your cast performs; the stage is what the user sees when they play your Director movie.
- **Content editors** for different media types.

Figure 8.2 illustrates the Director authoring environment.

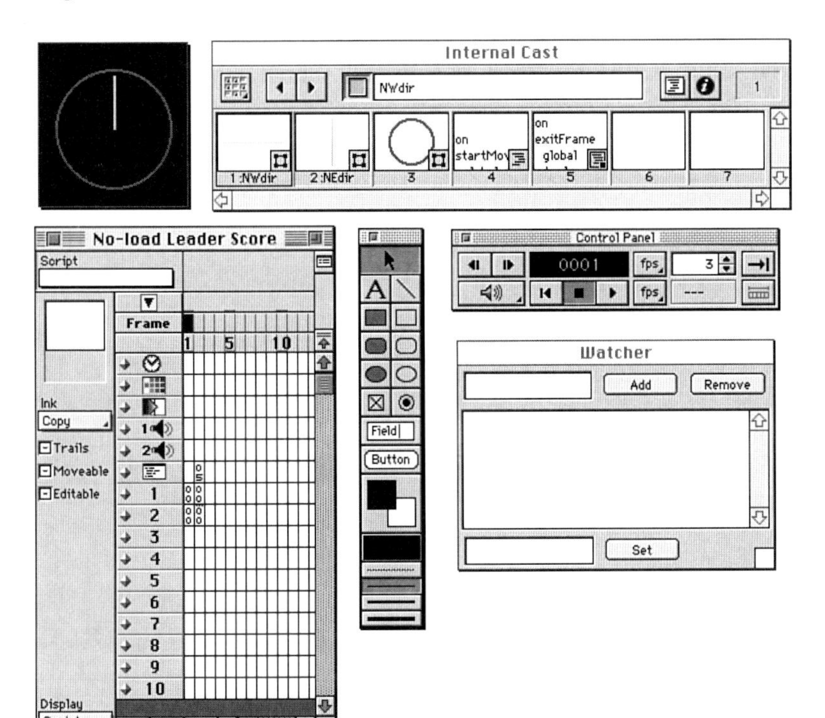

Figure 8.2

Director authoring environment.

cast member

All of the media content (graphics, text, sound, and digital video, and Lingo scripts) for your movie are stored in the Cast. Each media element or script is called a **cast member**. Figure 8.3 shows the Director Cast Window for an active project.

Figure 8.3

The Director Cast Window.

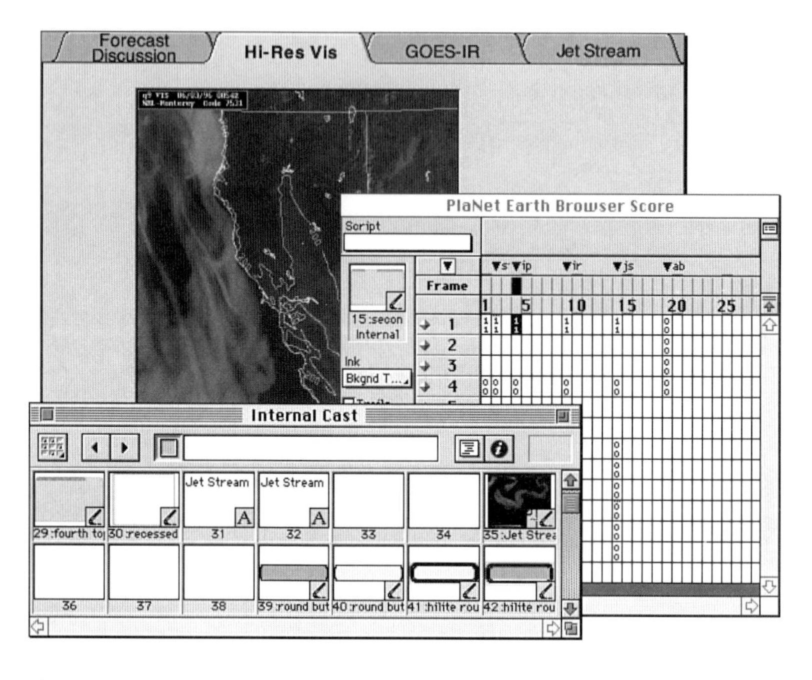

channels

sprite

The Score is a frame-based timeline that contains 48 layers. In Director, layers are called **channels**. Each channel can contain a sprite. A **sprite** is a copy of a cast member that has been placed on the stage. You can place a cast member on the stage by dragging it from the Cast. The cast member will be automatically copied into a channel.

Note

The Director Score resembles a spreadsheet. Channels represent rows and frames represent columns. A single channel at a particular frame is typically called a **cell**—a term that carries over from spreadsheet technology and should not be confused with **cel**, defined in the previous chapter.

The same cast member can be copied into multiple channels, so a single cast member can be used to create multiple sprites. Sprites in higher numbered channels appear above sprites in lower numbered channels. The Director Score Window is illustrated in figure 8.4.

When the movie plays, it generally follows this sequence:

1. The playback head advances to a frame.
2. The sprites in that frame are displayed.
3. Lingo commands are executed.
4. The playback head advances to the next frame.

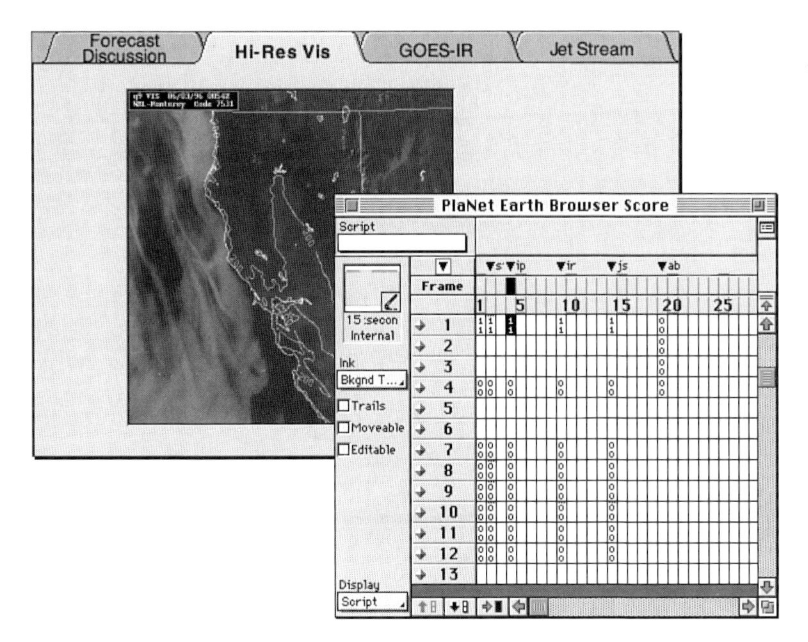

Figure 8.4

The Director Score Window.

You can use the Score and one of Director's animation techniques such as in-betweening, discussed later in the chapter, to animate your sprites across multiple frames.

The Lingo Scripting Language

handlers

Lingo is Director's object-oriented scripting language. Individual scripts are called **handlers.** You can also use Lingo to control the behavior and properties of sprites, such as color or position. You make a sprite respond to Lingo commands with the Lingo puppetsprite commands. For example,

```
puppetsprite 12, TRUE
```

is a Lingo command that turns the sprite in channel 12 into a puppet.

The puppetsprite command tells Director that a particular sprite is now being controlled by Lingo (i.e., is a Lingo "puppet") and is not being controlled by the Score. The Score behavior of that particular sprite is ignored until you turn off the puppeting.

Note

You don't need to know Lingo to create animations in Director, but Lingo animation sometimes results in smaller file sizes.

Shockwave excludes special networking extensions to the Lingo scripting language. Also, some Lingo commands are disabled by Shockwave. These will be discussed in subsequent sections of this chapter.

Note

Afterburner, the file compression utility for Shockwave, is a kind of Xtra called a Tools Xtra. You "burn" Director movies with Afterburner by selecting the Afterburner Xtra in the Xtras menu.

Tip

You'll probably use other tools (Photoshop, an integrated 3D program such as Extreme 3D, or a sound-editing tool such as SoundEdit) to help you create content for your Director project.

To save time, use a graphic batch processing program such as Equilibrium Technology's Debabelizer to script repetitive processing of animation frames.

Xtras

Xtras are small software modules that extend the functionality of Director 5, similar to Plug-Ins in Photoshop. For example, the Shockwave for Audio Xtra for Director, discussed later in the chapter, enables you to compress audio files embedded in your Shockwave Director movie. Xtras replace the functionality of XObjects in previous versions of Director. Most XObjects still work in Director 5.

Xtras can be placed in the Xtras folder in the same folder as the Director application, or in C:\Program Files\Common Files\Macromedia\Xtras folder on Windows 95 and Windows NT, the c:\Windows\Macromed\Xtras directory on Windows 3.1, or the System:Macromedia Xtras Folder on the Macintosh.

You can open Xtras from within Shockwave movies. You should, however, make sure your users have the Xtra and have placed it in the appropriate Shockwave support folder on their hard drive. (See a following section on the Shockwave support folder for a discussion on using Xtras in Shockwave.)

Shockwave for Audio Xtras

Shockwave for Audio Xtras is part of the Shockwave and Afterburner distribution from Macromedia. The Shockwave for Audio Xtras enable you to:

- Compress embedded audio in Director
- Create specially formatted streaming audio files with SoundEdit on a Macintosh
- Play back streaming audio from Shockwave movies

These features will be discussed at greater length later in the section, "Sound with Shockwave."

No special server is required to play back audio. Audio will only playback from a Shockwave movie. Compression ratios for audio are as high as 176:1. Playback rates are as low as 8 Kbps; this enables playback even over slow modem connections.

Shockwave for Audio Xtras consists of several components for authoring and playback. In most cases, playback Xtras will be automatically installed in the correct places on your hard drive when you run the Shockwave installer, and the authoring Xtras will be automatically installed when you run the Afterburner installer. The following tables list Xtras and locations.

- **Shockwave for Audio Xtras for Authoring in Director.** These Xtras must be in your Director 5 Xtras folder.

Table 8.2

Shockwave for Audio Xtras for Authoring

Macintosh	Windows
SWA Compression Xtra	SWACmpr.x32
SWA Settings (DIR) Xtra	SWASttng.x32
SWA Streaming Xtra*	SWA Streaming Xtra*

* A copy of these Xtras must also be in the special Shockwave folder within your Netscape Plug-Ins folder.

- **Shockwave for Audio Xtras for Authoring in SoundEdit 16.** These Xtras must be in SoundEdit 16's Xtras folder.

Table 8.3

Shockwave for Audio Xtras for Authoring in SoundEdit 16

Macintosh	Windows
SWA Export Xtra	Not available
SWA Settings (SE) Xtra	Not available

- **Shockwave for Audio Xtras for playback in Netscape Navigator.** These Xtras must be in a special Shockwave folder within your Netscape Plug-Ins folder.

Table 8.4

Shockwave for Audio Xtras for Playback in Netscape Navigator

Macintosh	Windows
SWA Decompression Xtra	SWADCmpr.x32

Afterburner

Afterburner is a free-file compression utility from Macromedia. Use Afterburner to compress your Director movie for playback over the Internet. Afterburner is a separate application and drag-and-drop utility for Director 4. In Director 5, Afterburner is a Tools Xtra that you place in the Xtras folder in the same folder as the Director application or in C:\Program Files\Common Files\Macromedia\Xtras folder on Windows 95 and Windows NT, the C:\Windows\Macromed\Xtras directory on Windows 3.1, or the System:Macromedia Xtras Folder on the Macintosh. In Director 5, access Afterburner from the Xtras menu.

As of this writing, Afterburner compresses audio based on the settings you make when you choose Shockwave for Audio Settings... from the Xtras menu in Director. According to Macromedia's documentation, the compressor works best with 1-bit and 8-bit graphics, so plan your graphics accordingly.

You can download Afterburner over the Internet from:

```
http://www.macromedia.com/
```

Creating Animations in Director

Director provides several ways to create animations. This section briefly describes the many ways you can create animations, without scripting, using Director's Score.

- In-betweening
- Cast to Time
- Space to Time
- Step Recording
- Real-Time Recording
- Other Animation Techniques
- PowerApplets

You can also create animations with Director's scripting language, Lingo. In some cases, Lingo animation may create smaller Shockwave files.

In-betweening

In betweening, or **tweening,** is an animation technique you are probably familiar with if you've used other animation software. In betweening uses the computer to interpolate intermediate frames between **key frames.** (See Chapter 7 for a discussion of key frames.) Figure 8.5 shows an example of using in-betweening. To create a key frame in Director:

tweening

key frames

1. Move the playback head to the frame where you want to create a key frame.
2. Select a channel in the score.
3. Drag a cast member from the Cast Window and place it on the stage. The cast member is copied into that channel. This copy of the cast member is called a sprite.
4. Set the properties, appearance, and position for the sprite by clicking and dragging on the stage, using the sprite properties dialog box or the Tools Palette. You've now set the first key frame.
5. Repeat this procedure for each key frame.
6. Select the range of cells between key frames.
7. Choose In Between from the Modify menu. Director automatically fills in intervening frames. Director also provides ease-in and ease-out and additional controls with the In-Between Special command.

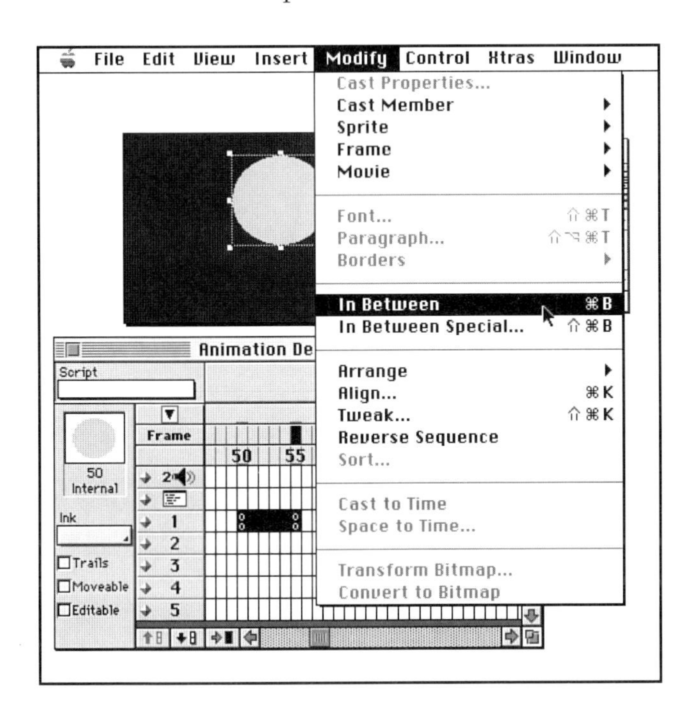

Figure 8.5

In-betweening in the Score.

Cast to Time

Cast to Time

Cast to Time takes a sequence of cast members in the Cast Window and places them in a single channel in the Director Score. The cast members are placed in the Score, one frame after the other, in the same sequence that they appear in the Cast Window. This animation technique is handy if you've created a series of frames or cels in the Director Paint window or have imported a series of animation frames using the Import/File command. Figure 8.6 shows an example of using Cast to Time. To use the Cast to Time feature:

1. Select a channel in the Score where you want the animation to start.
2. Select the sequence of cast members in the Cast Window.
3. Choose Cast to Time from the Modify menu.

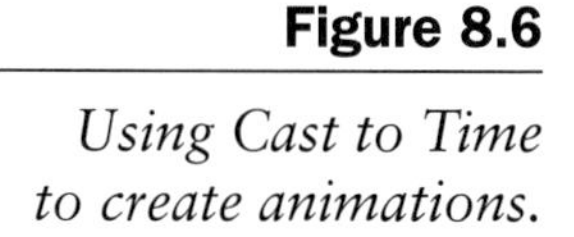

Figure 8.6

Using Cast to Time to create animations.

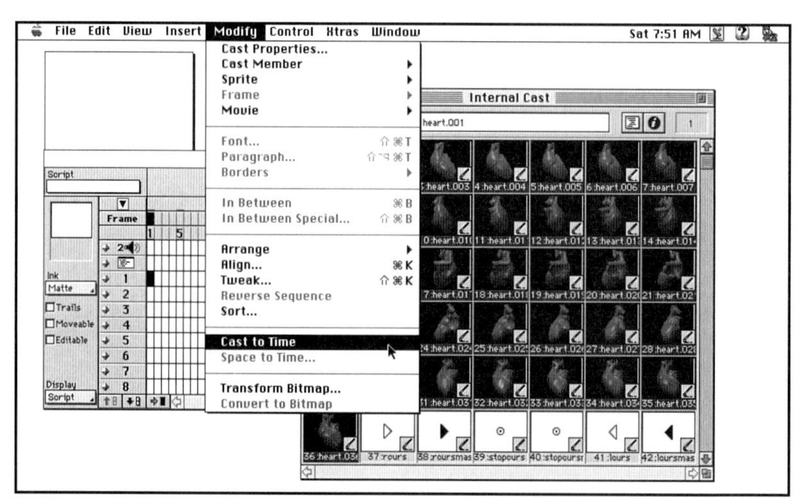

Space to Time

Space to Time enables you to arrange your entire animation on the stage in a single frame. This technique is similar to overlaying a series of transparent animation cels, one on top of another, and is handy if you want to see the entire animation at a glance.

1. Arrange your sprites in layers so that higher layers represent later frames.

2. Once you've arranged the sprites the way you want, select them all.
3. Choose Space to Time from the Modify menu.

Director will take the sequence of layers and turn them into a sequence of frames. Figure 8.7 illustrates using Space to Time.

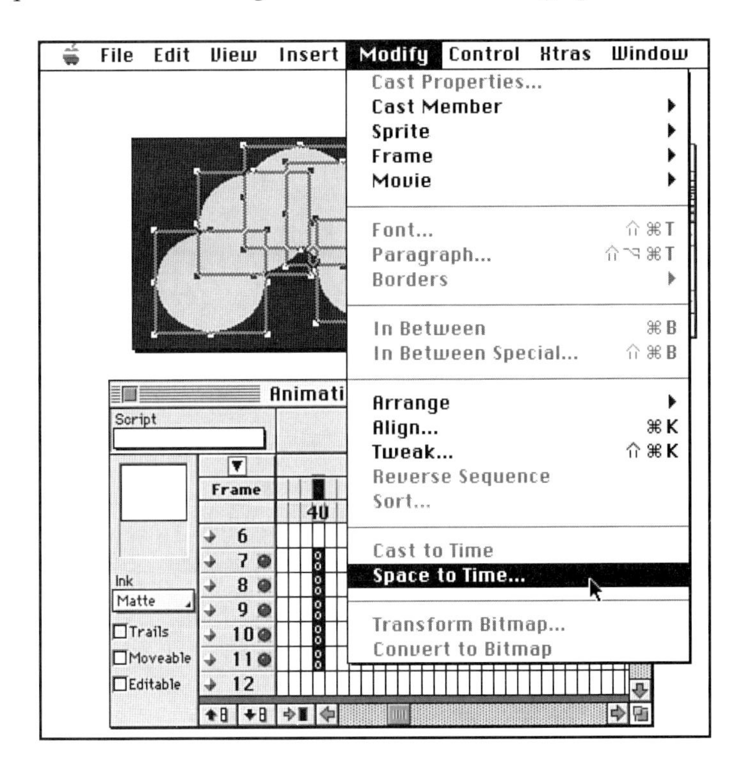

Figure 8.7

Using Space to Time to create animations.

Step Recording

Step recording is a kind of frame-by-frame animation. Step recording is automatically activated whenever you drag a cast member to the stage. A red indicator light will show up in the currently active channel when Step recording is activated for that channel. Figure 8.8 illustrates Step recording. To use Step recording:

step recording

1. Position the sprite in the current frame.
2. Step forward to the next frame using the Control Panel.
3. Position the sprite in that frame.
4. Step forward to the next frame.
5. Position the sprite again, and so on.

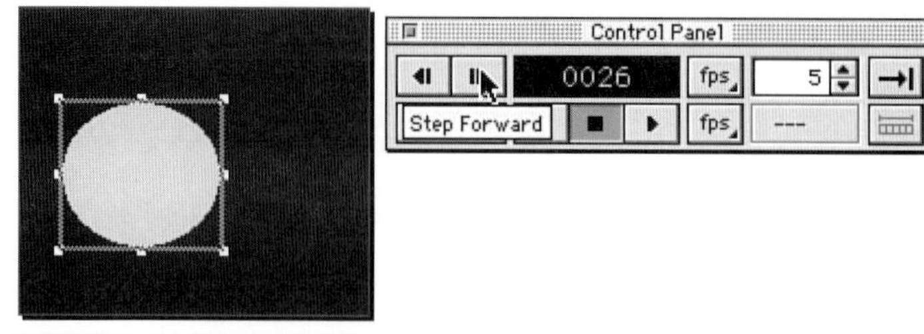

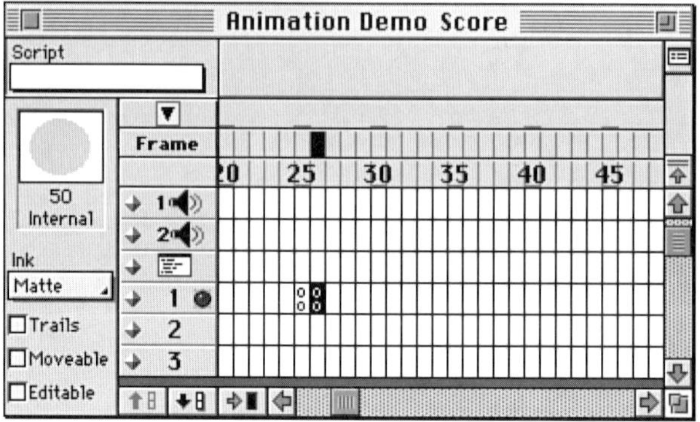

Figure 8.8

Step recording in the Score.

Real-time Recording

real-time recording

Real-time recording records the movement of the sprite as you drag it across the stage in real-time. Figure 8.9 illustrates real-time recording. To record sprites in real-time:

1. Move the playback head to the place in the Score where you want the animation to begin.
2. Select the cast member you want to animate in the Cast Window.
3. Hold down the Control key and the spacebar. A white indicator light appears in the currently active channel when real-time recording is activated.
4. Drag the mouse across the stage.
5. Release the mouse when you are done recording. Director will create a sequence of sprites in the Score, based on your mouse dragging.

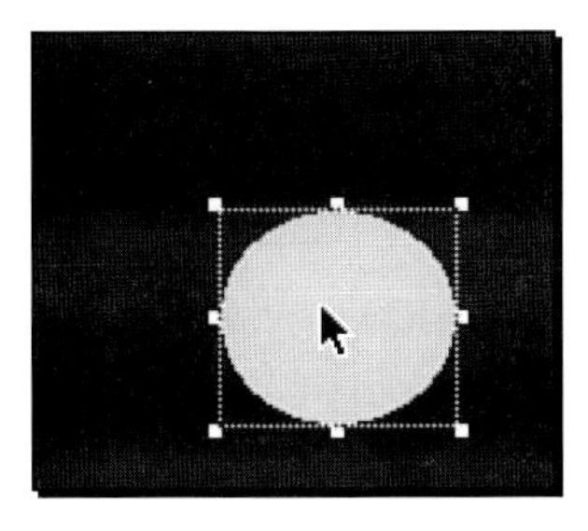

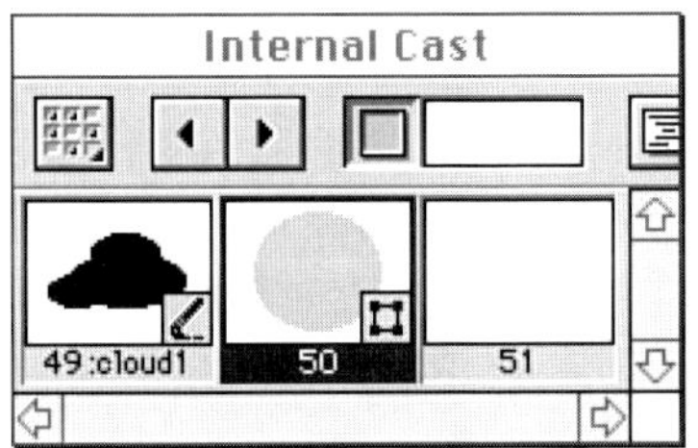

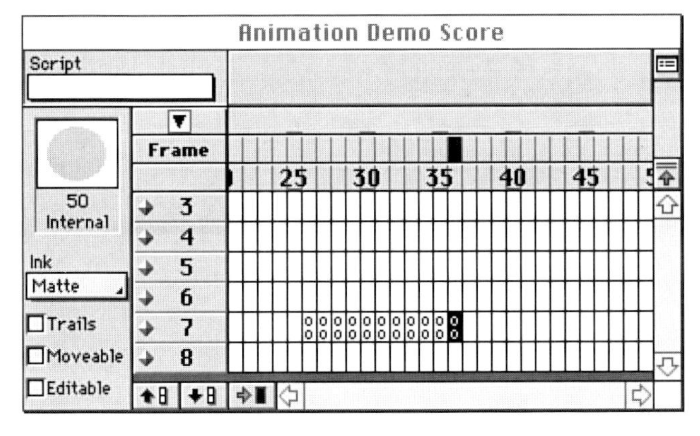

Figure 8.9

Real-time recording in the Score.

Other Animation Techniques

You can also generate in-between bitmap cast members using the Auto Distort command. This command is a kind of poor man's morphing feature.

1. First, distort a bitmap in the Director Paint window.
2. Choose one of the distort commands from the Paint window toolbar, such as Skew, Warp, or Perspective.
3. Before you deselect the bitmap, choose Auto Distort from the Xtras menu. This command will create a sequence of intermediate cast members between the distorted and undistorted versions of the bitmap.

PowerApplets

PowerApplets are utilities for Director for Windows or Java utilities for Macintosh and Windows that automate the process of creating animations. Power Applets for Director for Windows can be used to create Shockwave animations.

Tip

You can also create animated bitmap Filter effects using a similar process with the Auto Filter command.

Currently, there are three Power Applets available:

- Animator, which enables users to animate an image or image sequence across the stage using animation paths
- SlideShow, which creates Shockwave movies that sequence up to 20 images for presentation on a Web page
- Icons, which enable users to create animated bullets and navigation elements

You can find PowerApplets on the accompanying CD or by visiting Macromedia's Web site at:

`http://www.macromedia.com/`

Creating Shockwave Animations for the Web

Tip

Think small when creating Shockwave animations, or for that matter, just about any Web-based multimedia. Create compact files that can be downloaded quickly over slow, sometimes overloaded, network connections. You can do a lot in under 10 KB. This chapter provides some tips on how to create small animations.

You create Shockwave animations the same way you create other animations in Director. Most of the things you can do in Director you can also do in Shockwave.

Here are the basic steps you'll follow to create Shockwave animations:

1. Create the Director movie.
2. Compress the embedded audio, if there is any, with the Shockwave for Audio Xtra (discussed later in the chapter) by choosing Shockwave for Audio Settings... from the Xtras menu.
3. Convert the movie with the Director Afterburner Xtra by choosing Afterburner in the Xtra menu and save it with the .dcr extension.
4. Integrate the movie into an HTML document using the EMBED tag. For example:

```
<EMBED SRC = "myShockingMovie.dcr" WIDTH = 160
➥HEIGHT = 120 PLUGINSPAGE = "http://
➥www.macromedia.com/shockwave/">
```

5. Upload the HTML document and converted movie. Be sure the movie is uploaded as a raw binary file. The Web server must be configured to associate files with the `.dcr` extension to the MIME type `application/x- director`.

Shockwave Text and Graphics

This section provides some tips on using the following content elements in Shockwave:

- Text
- One-bit graphics
- Trails ink effect
- Vector-based graphics

Text

Animated text is an easy way to draw attention to logos, bullet points, and other information. People who use presentation software are used to highlighting their text by using various forms of animation, such as sliding bullet points.

In Director 5, there are two kinds of text-based cast members:

- "Rich text" or simply "text"
- Fields

rich text

Rich text contains many of the same formatting options you have in a word processing program. In addition, Rich text can be anti-aliased against its background so it looks good on screen. (Anti-aliasing uses techniques to blend or blur the jagged edges in computer images so that computer-generated imagery looks like a continuous tone photograph.) Rich text has access to fonts on the authoring machine. It is fully editable in the authoring environment, but cannot be edited in a projector or Shockwave movie.

Warning

When you create a projector or run your movie through Afterburner, Rich text is converted to a bitmap, and thus takes up a lot of space.

To create Rich text, use the Text tool or the Text Window. Figure 8.10 shows a Rich text editor.

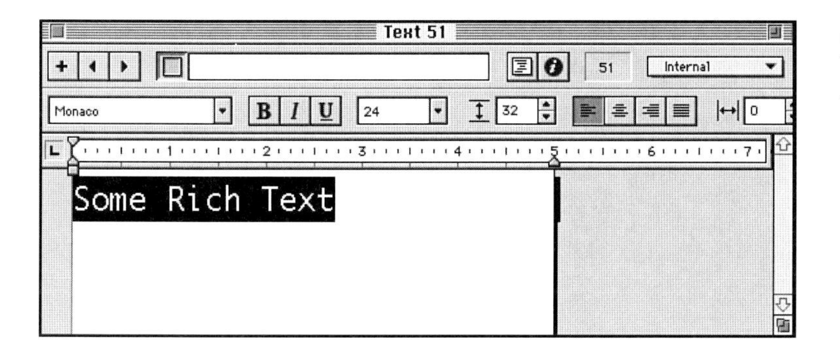

Figure 8.10

Rich text editor.

Field text has more limited formatting options than Rich text does. Field text is also not anti-aliased. Field text can be edited in the authoring environment, but unlike Rich text, it can also be edited by users in a Projector or Shockwave movie. You can make field text editable by selecting the editable check box in the Score, selecting the editable check box in the cast member property dialog box, or with the Lingo "editable of sprite" command.

Tip

Fonts on different Systems have different kerning and leading. Shockwave maps fonts on one system to similar fonts on another, but text kerning and leading is probably different. Be sure to view your Shockwave movie on multiple systems.

Field text uses much less disk space than Rich text or other bitmapped text, so it's especially useful for Shockwave movies. Field text uses the fonts available on the playback machine. It is probably safest to stick with the standard fonts that come with most Macintosh and Windows systems, such as Times, Helvetica, Geneva, and Courier on Macintosh or Arial, Courier New, and Times New Roman on Windows.

To create Field text, use the Field tool on the Tools Palette or choose Field from the Control submenu in the Insert menu. Figure 8.11 shows a Field text editor.

Figure 8.11

Field text editor.

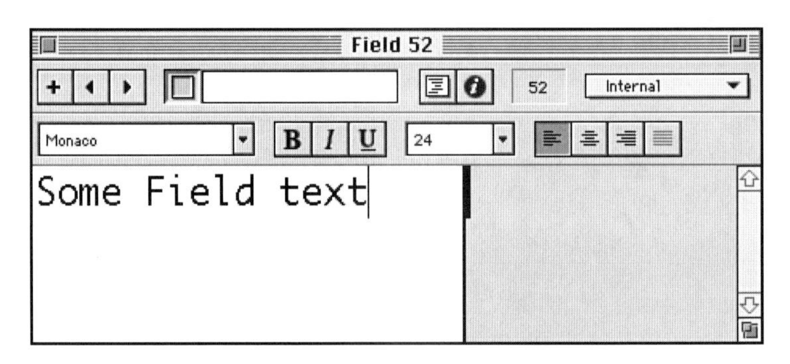

Note

The contents of Fields can be changed while a Shockwave movie is running. Fields are a good way to provide status and help bars for users. Field text can be used for animated text effects. Many Field text properties, such as size and color, can be set by Lingo. For example,

```
set the fontSize of member
"myFieldText" = 18
```

will change the point size of the text in the cast member named "myFieldText" to 18.

You can also create bitmaps of text in the Director Paint window or import bitmaps of text from programs such as Photoshop.

One-Bit Graphics

One way to keep your file size small is to use bitmap graphics that have 1-bit color depth. To convert graphics to 1 bit in Director:

1. Choose the cast member in the Cast Window.
2. Choose Transform Bitmap from the Modify menu.
3. Choose 1 bit from the Color Depth pop-up menu.

You can also use an image-processing program such as Debabelizer or Photoshop to convert graphics to 1 bit.

In Director, 1 bit graphics consist of two colors—a foreground color and background color. You can change the forecolor and backcolor of sprites on the stage by doing the following:

1. Choose the sprite.
2. Click on the color chips in the Tool Palette. This will bring up a 256-color pop-up palette from which you can choose another color for the foreground or background.

Figure 8.12 illustrates choosing a foreground color from the popup palette.

Note

Dithering is a process used by many image processing programs when you reduce the bit depth of a graphic. Dithering uses patterns of pixels to approximate the colors and values of the original graphic. Dithering to 1 bit can produce some interesting effects.

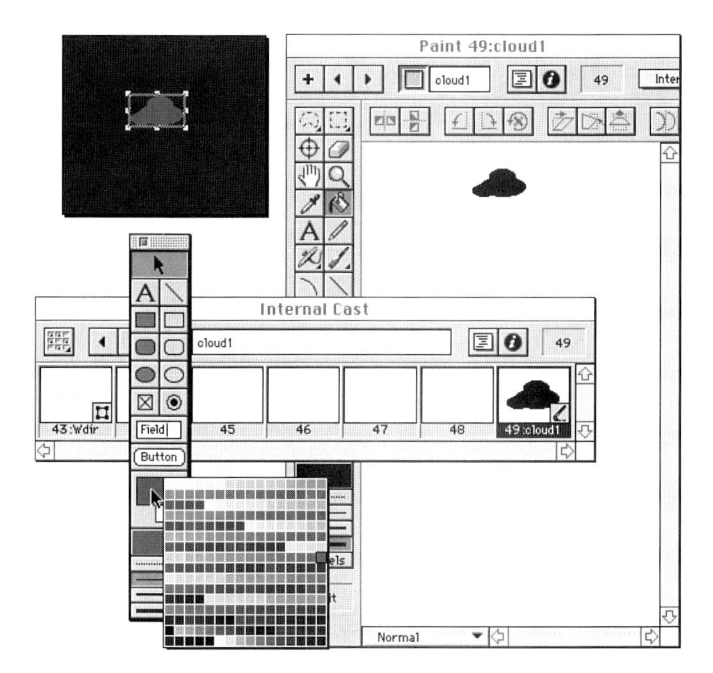

Figure 8.12

Setting the foreground color of a 1-bit graphic.

Vector-Based Graphics

Vector-based graphics are different from bitmap graphics in that the computer stores vector-based graphics as a mathematical formula rather than a collection of pixels. Thus, vector-based graphics are small, and very useful for creating Web-based animations.

Note

You can also change the foreground color and background color of graphics using the Lingo commands *forecolor of sprite* and *backcolor of sprite*. On 8-bit systems, the 256 possible colors are referenced by a number between 0 and 255. For example:

```
set the forecolor of sprite 10
to random(255)
```

will set the forecolor of the sprite in channel 10 to a random color between 1 and 255 in the currently active palette. To change the foreground color and background color of Field text use the Lingo commands forecolor of member and backcolor of member.

shapes

Director 5 comes with a limited set of vector-based graphics tools. In Director 5, vector-based graphics are called **shapes.** Shapes include Lines, Ovals, Rectangles, and Rounded Rectangles. You access shapes from the Tool Palette. Use the Tool Palette buttons to change the type, line size, fill pattern, and color of shapes. Figure 8.13 illustrates using the Tool Palette to create shapes.

Figure 8.13

Vector-based graphics in Director.

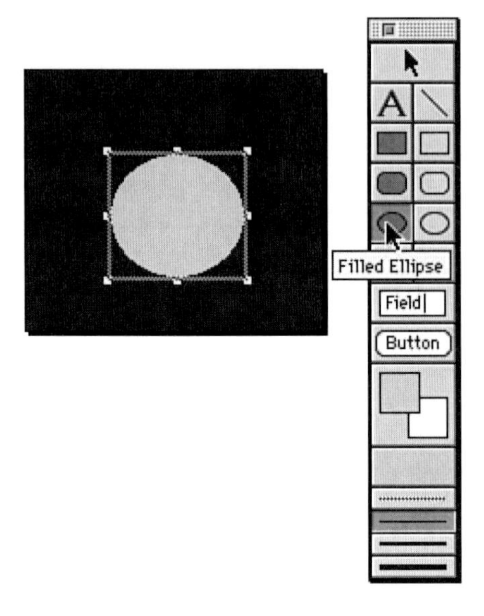

Note

New Lingo commands enable you to change the type of shape, fill, patterns, and line size of Shape cast members from Lingo. For example:

```
set the lineSize of sprite
"myLine" = 4
```

will set the line size of the shape sprite to 4 pixels.

```
set the filled of member
"myCircle" = TRUE
set the pattern of member
"myCircle" = 1
```

will fill the shape cast "myCircle" with a solid color pattern.

Ink Effects

Ink effects are an easy way to create interesting visual effects with 1 bit graphics without creating extra cast members. Ink effects control the way pixels in a 1-bit graphic are composited with underlying pixels. Some ink effects are processor-intensive and can slow screen redraw; see the documentation for details. Generally, ink effects lower down in the Ink effects pop-up menu are more processor-intensive.

Access the Ink effects pop-up from the Score Window or the Paint Window, or press the command key on Macintosh or control key on Windows and select a sprite on the stage. Text cast members only support Copy, Background Transparent, and Blend inks.

The Trails Effect

The Trails effect will leave a copy of a graphic behind as it moves across the stage, as if the graphic was a paint brush.

Trails can be a low-overhead way to add multiple copies of a graphic to the Stage, or to paint large areas of color.

Activate the trails effects by selecting the Trails checkbox in the Score.

A drawback of Trails is that it will not be repainted if the user covers and then uncovers the Shockwave movie with another window.

Tiles

Tiling is an efficient way to build backgrounds and create patterns in Director movies.

Access the Tile Settings from the Pattern Fill button on the Tools Palette (beneath the color chips) or in the Paint Window. Define a Tile pattern by choosing a rectangular region of any bitmap cast member. Figure 8.14 illustrates creating a Tile from a cast member bitmap.

You can define multiple Tiles from the same bitmap. Tiles can be any rectangular size. It's probably best to stick with rectangles with pixel dimensions that are divisible by 16.

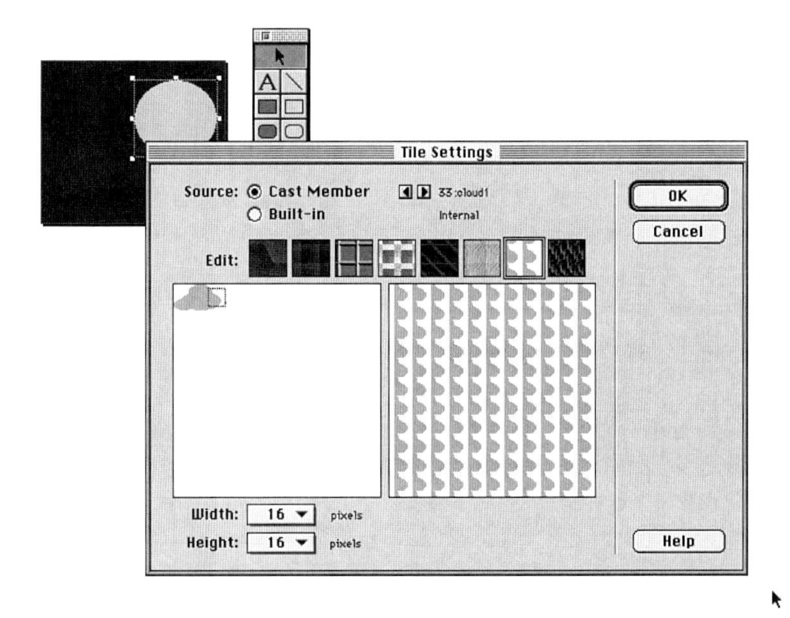

Figure 8.14

Creating a Tile from a bitmap.

Once created, a Tile can be used to fill a bitmap or vector-based shape. Figure 8.15 illustrates selecting Tile Settings to fill a graphic.

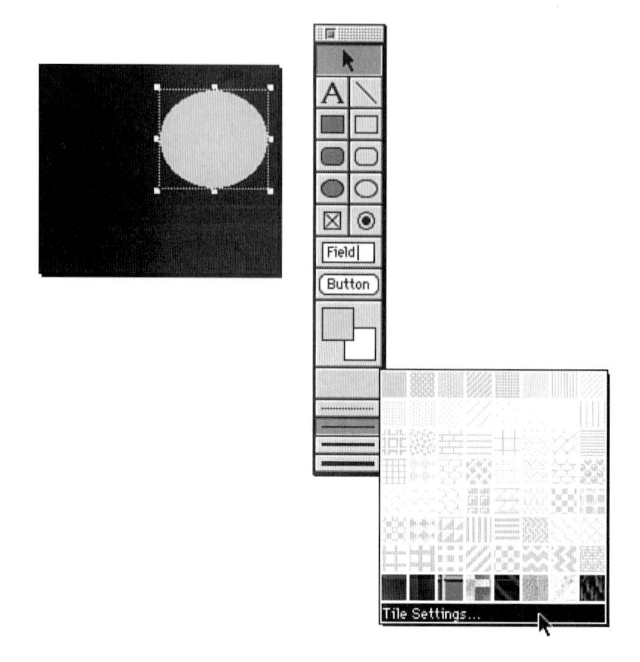

Figure 8.15

Using the Tile Settings option to fill a graphic with a Tile.

Palettes and Colors for Shockwave

Your movie will probably playback on an 8-bit display. For playback on the Web, it's probably best to create 8-bit Shockwave movies. If you author in 16-bit or 24-bit, you can change the color depth of your Director movie by changing your monitor's color depth and then saving the movie.

> **Note**
>
> See Chapter 6, "Using Graphics to Add Dynamic Content," for a discussion of using palettes on the Web.
>
> Lynda Weinman, author of Designing Web Graphics, has placed the browser-safe palette on her web site at:
>
> `http://www.lynda.com/hex.html`

The color in your 8-bit movie will be mapped to the currently active browser palette unless you specify otherwise with the PALETTE parameter in the EMBED tag. This means that colors in your animation that aren't in the browser palette will be dithered to colors that are in the browser palette, which may make some of your graphics look speckled.

If you aren't using custom palettes and want to provide the highest degree of cross-platform palette compatibility, you should probably stick to the 216-color cross-platform web palette (see Chapter 6, "Using Graphics to Add Dynamic Content," for more information). Director 5 includes a special Netscape Web palette within the `Palettes.cst` file in the Xtras folder.

You can embed a custom palette in your Shockwave movie and force the browser to use this palette using the PALETTE attribute within the EMBED tag. Set PALETTE = FOREGROUND to assert a custom Shockwave palette. However, a custom palette will shift all the colors in the rest of the display, which can be disorienting for some users. Also, if the user jumps to a new page, the palette may not get reset.

If you use the Lingo commands, `forecolor of sprite` for bitmaps and `forecolor of member` for Field text, the palette index number used to reference a specific color may be different on different systems. These colors may not display accurately on 16-bit and 24-bit displays.

To set the background color of your Shockwave movie so that it matches the background color of your HTML document, choose Movie/Properties from the Modify menu and select a color for the background on the dialog box.

Shockwave Authoring Tips

This section contains miscellaneous tips for Shockwave authors.

- Use the cast member properties dialog box in Director to see the size of your cast members in kilobytes. Find out the total size of several cast members by selecting them all in the Cast Window and selecting Cast Member/Properties from the Modify menu. You can also access the cast properties by pressing the control key on Macintosh or the right mouse button on Windows and clicking on a sprite on the Stage.
- Use small size-cast members and then use the sprite properties dialog box to resize the sprite on the stage. Access the sprite properties dialog box by selecting Sprite/Properties from the Modify menu or by pressing the control key on the Macintosh or the right mouse button on Windows and clicking on a sprite on the Stage. You can also use this dialog box to set key frame properties to animate sprites over time. Animating sprite sizes can be processor intensive, slowing down screen redraw and tying up the user's machine, so use judiciously and test on your target machine.
- Avoid long repeat loops that tie up the processor. Instead, loop on a frame.
- Use the Lingo `halt` command to stop your movie when it is finished playing. This will ensure that your movie doesn't eat processor cycles after it has finished playing.

- Transitions, such as Dissolve and ink effects, can be processor-intensive, slowing down screen redraw and tying up the user's machine.
- Sprite locations are given relative to the stage. The Lingo commands stageRight, stageLeft, and so on are given in absolute coordinates, relative to the monitor.
- Putting Shockwave movies inside table cells, especially nested table cells, tends to crash browsers.
- To test your Shockwave movie on a Macintosh, drag and drop the `.dcr` file on the Netscape browser window.

Sound with Shockwave

Sound is an important, though often neglected element in multimedia. Shockwave movies are an easy way to add sound to a Web page. The Shockwave for Audio Xtra enables you to compress sounds that are embedded in Director or to create external, streamable audio files using SoundEdit for the Macintosh.

Play sounds in a Director movie by adding them to the sound channels in the Director Score, just as you add other cast members, or use the Lingo `puppetsound` command to play sound cast members. You can also insert an external reference to a streaming Shockwave for Audio file that resides on a Web server and will play back in your Shockwave movie (see the later tutorial on incorporating external, streamable Shockwave files).

Note

Endlessly looping sounds can be annoying, so provide a way for users to stop the the sound. For example:

```
on mouseDown
 if soundBusy(1) then
 sound stop 1
end
```

will stop the sound playing in sound channel 1 when the user clicks the mouse.

Try to keep your sounds to 11 kHz (kilohertz) mono 8 bit or below. For sounds such as button clicks, you may get by with as little as 8 kHz. Test sounds with low sampling rate on different systems to see if the quality is acceptable. To loop sounds, set the Looped property in the sound cast properties dialog box.

Instead of using a sound editor to create fade-ins and fade-outs, use the Lingo commands `sound fadeIn` and `sound fadeOut`. Use the Lingo command to set the volume of a sound relative to the overall sound level of the user's machine.

Using IMA-Compressed Sounds in Shockwave

The Interactive Multimedia Association has defined a compression format for audio called IMA compression. You can use IMA-compressed sounds in Shockwave, but as of this writing, they can only be imported in the Macintosh authoring environment, although they will play back on Windows. To create an IMA-compressed sound on a Mac from a sound-only QuickTime movie in MoviePlayer:

1. Choose "Export" from the File menu.
2. Choose "Sound To AIFF."
3. Click on "Options."
4. Choose "IMA 4:1" for compressor.
5. Choose a sampling rate of 11.025, and Mono.

Using Shockwave for Audio Xtra to Compress Audio in Director

The Shockwave for Audio Xtra for Director enables you to save settings for audio compression of sounds embedded within your Director movie. Compression works best on audio sampled at 16bit, 22kHz, or higher.

To compress embedded audio files for Shockwave movies, first create compression settings:

1. Choose Shockwave for Audio Settings under the Xtras menu.
2. Check the Enabled check box.
3. Select the bit rate in KBits/second from the Bit Rate pop-up menu (see fig. 8.16). A higher bit rate produces larger files of higher quality. A low bit rate produces a small file of lower quality. If your movie will be played back by modem users, choose 32 Kbits/second. This setting is the lowest setting possible within Director.

Note

The Shockwave for Audio Xtra for SoundEdit enables setting a bit rate as low as 8 KBits/second for external streaming audio files.

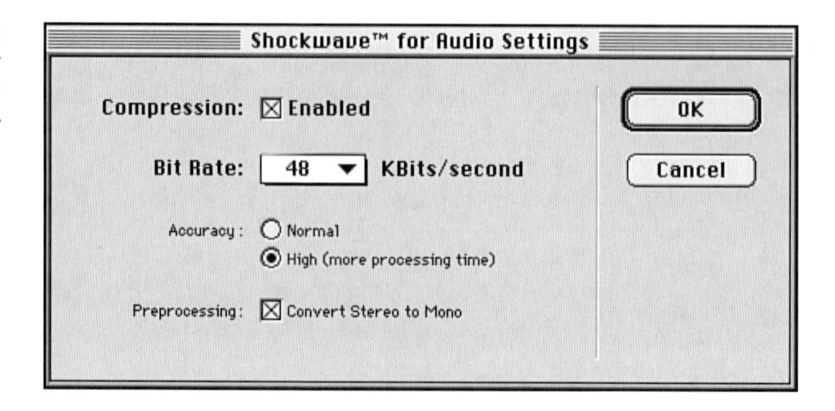

Figure 8.16

Shockwave for Audio Settings in Director

4. If processing time is not an issue, choose the High option.
5. Check the Convert Stereo to Mono checkbox if the bit rate is greater than 32 and you want to convert a stereo file to mono. Most users will probably only have mono playback capability. If you are playing back audio over an intranet in a music lab, for example, where you know that users will have stereo playback, do not check this box.
6. Choose OK.

Using Shockwave for Audio with SoundEdit 16

Shockwave for Audio Xtras for SoundEdit 16 is automatically installed when you install the latest version of Afterburner, if you have SoundEdit installed. See the previous Shockwave for Audio Xtras section for a list of the names and install locations of theses Xtras.

At this time using the Shockwave for Audio Xtras for SoundEdit 16 on the Macintosh is the only way to create Shockwave streamable audio files (SWA, or Shockwave for Audio files). You must have SoundEdit 16 for the Macintosh to create SWA files. Streamable audio files are highly compressed digital audio files that can be played back by a Shockwave movie. SWA files reside on a Web server and are external to the Shockwave movie that plays them. They are referenced from the Shockwave movie via a valid URL.

Before exporting a SWA audio file:

- Use source audio sampled at 16-bit, 22.050kHz or 44.100kHz. Macromedia recommends upsampling 11kHz source to 22.050kHz. 11kHz stereo source files are automatically converted to mono in all cases.
- You may want to experiment with equalization settings. Filtering frequencies in the 4kHz to 8kHz range (high frequencies) may improve quality. To perform filtering of these frequencies in SoundEdit:
    1. Select the area of the sound sample you wish to filter.
    2. Choose Equalizer... from the effects menu.
    3. The rightmost two sliders effect the high frequencies. Move these sliders down to filter out some of the high frequency range (see fig. 8.17).

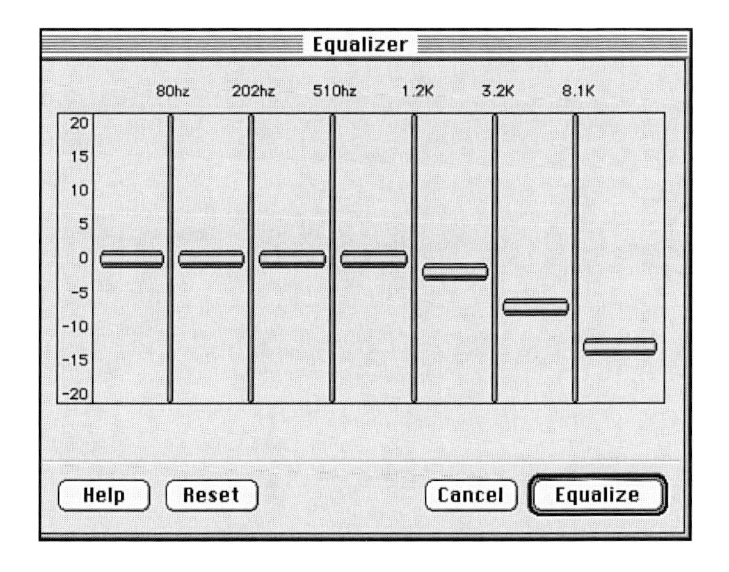

Figure 8.17

Equalizer in SoundEdit

To export a sound file with the SWA Export Xtra:

1. Close SoundEdit 16's Levels palette when exporting SWA files.
2. Choose Shockwave for Audio Settings from the Xtras menu to configure the compression options (see fig. 8.18).

Figure 8.18

Shockwave for Audio settings in SoundEdit

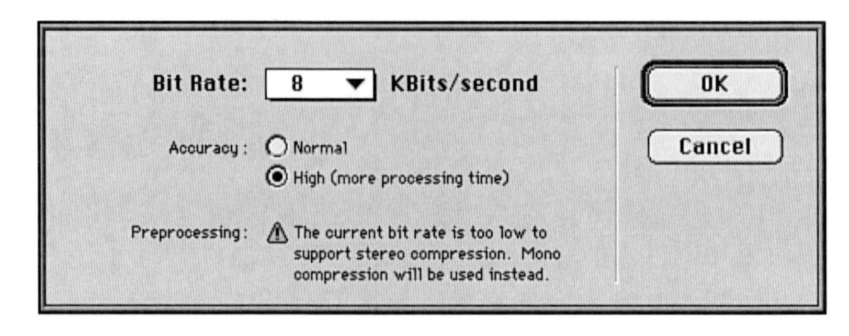

3. Select the bit rate (kbps) you want from the Bit Rate drop-down menu. Lower bit rates will produce lower quality files that will be streamable over modems. Higher bit rates will produce higher quality files that will be streamable over fast connections, such as a corporate or university intranet, but will break up overt slower connections. What bit rate you choose depends on:
   - The connection speed of your users.
   - The characteristics of your sound file. For example, voice and narration audio files can generally be played back at lower bit rates without perceived loss of quality, while music requires higher bit rates.

Table 8.5

Recommended Bit Rates for Representative Connection Speeds

Bit rate	Connection Speed
8 kbps	14.4 modem connections, typical home user
16 kbps	28.8 modem connections
32 kbps-56 kbps	ISDN lines
64 kbps-128 kbps	T1 delivery, corporate or university intranet

4. To convert stereo to mono, check the Convert Stereo to Mono checkbox. This will reduce the file size. Most users probably won't have stereo playback capabilities, so it's probably a good idea to check this option for general Internet play back. The SWA Export Xtra automatically converts a file to mono if you choose a bit rate 32 kbps per second or less.
5. Click on OK.
6. Choose Export from the File menu.

7. Choose .SWA File from the Export Type drop-down menu.
8. Make sure the file name has the `.SWA` file name extension. Give the file a name that follows the file naming conventions of your Web server.

Advanced Shockwave Features

This section discusses some advanced features of Shockwave that go beyond simple animation. These features include:

- Shockwave "Support Folder," Linked Media, Xtras, and External Casts
- Saving User Data Across Sessions in the Shockwave Support Folder
- Lingo Network Extensions in Shockwave
- Targeting Frames
- User-defined Custom Attributes for the EMBED tag

Shockwave Support Folder

The Shockwave support folder is a new feature of Shockwave for Director 5. The support folder is a special folder or cache on the client hard disk that can be used for external files, such as linked QuickTime movies or digital audio, Xtras, XObjects, and external casts.

One drawback of the support folder is that users must download external files separately from the Shockwave movie and also must make sure that these external files are in the correct folder/directory on their hard drive. Possible uses of the support folder include support for on-line services or CD-ROM/Internet hybrids. An installer on the CD-ROM or on-line service software could automatically place external media, such as QuickTime movies that would take a long time to download, in the Shockwave support folder. Then when the user accesses Shockwave movies on the Internet, the external files in the support folder are available to the Shockwave movie.

Table 8.6

Support Folders

Platform	Support Folder	Location
68K Mac	NP-Mac68K-Dir-Shockwave folder	Plug-Ins folder in the Netscape Navigator folder.
PPC Mac	NP-MacPPC-Dir-Shockwave folder	Plug-Ins folder in the Netscape Navigator folder.
Win3.1	NP16DSW	C:\NETSCAPE\PLUGINS directory.
Win95	NP32DSW	C:\ProgramFiles\Netscape\Navigator\Program\Plug-Ins directory.

During authoring, place the external file in the same folder as the Director movie. When you call an external file from your Shockwave movie, Shockwave searches the special support folder on the client hard disk.

Note

Later on in this chapter there is a list of Lingo commands that will not currently work with external files under Shockwave.

Use the following Lingo commands to access files in the support folder:

```
openXLib
closeXLib
open castlib x
```

Use this code to open a Lingo Xtra or XObject in the startMovie handler:

```
on startMovie
     global gXtra
     if objectP(gXtra) then gXtra(mDispose)
     openXlib "NeatoXtra"
     set gXtra = NeatoXtra(mNew)
end startMovie
```

Close the Lingo Xtra or XObject when you are done using it. To be sure you don't forget, and to free up memory, you should include the following code in the stopMovie handler:

```
on stopMovie
     global gXtra
     if objectP(gXtra) then gXtra(mDispose)
     closeXlib "NeatoXtra"
end stopMovie
```

During authoring, place the Xtra in the same folder/directory as your movie file. During play back, the Xtra must be in the appropriate Shockwave support folder on the client machine.

Saving User Data Across Sessions in the Shockwave Support Folder

With Shockwave for Director 5 you can save user data across sessions using a preferences file in the special Shockwave support folder. You can write to and read from this preferences file using the new Lingo commands:

```
setPref prefFileName,prefValue
getPref(prefFileName)
```

The file name of the preferences file (the `prefFileName` parameter in the preceding examples) must be a valid file name. Restrict this name to the 8.3 DOS file naming conventions for compatibility with all systems.

When you first use the `setPref` command within your Shockwave movie, the file is automatically created in the local Shockwave support folder. Thus, for testing purposes, you must be running the Shockwave movie inside a browser.

For example,

```
setPref gamepref.txt,score1:456
```

will create the file `gamepref.txt` in the Shockwave support folder of the local hard disk and append the string `score1:456`.

This function `getPref(prefFileName)` returns the content of the file named prefFileName that is present in the special Shockwave support folder. If the file doesn't exist, getPref returns void. For example:

```
set myPrefText = getPref("gamepref.txt")
```

will load the variable `myPrefText` with the contents of the text file `gamepref.txt` in the special Shockwave support folder.

Lingo Network Extensions in Shockwave

Shockwave comes with extensions to the Lingo scripting language that enable you to make asynchronous network calls.

Your Shockwave movie can use the new network extensions to Lingo to branch to another Shockwave movie anywhere on the Web or to load another Web page. You can also retrieve Internet-based data such as another Shockwave movie or a text file, all within your Shockwave movie. An asynchronous network process doesn't immediately return a result. The process will run in the background while your Shockwave movie continues to play. If you are interested in using the result returned from an asynchronous network call, such as:

```
GetNetText ("http://www.myserver.com/statuslog.txt")
```

you have to repeatedly make Lingo calls (for example in an exitFrame handler) to query the process to see if it has returned a result. For example, initiate an asynchronous network process by putting a call to GetNetText, such as the listing above, in an exitFrame handler. Then, in a subsequent frame, put the following handler in a frame script:

```
on exitFrame
   if netDone(getLatestNetID()) then
        put netTextResult() into field "Status Bar"
        go the frame +1
   else
       go the frame
   end if
end
```

This handler will cause your Shockwave movie to loop continuously on a single frame, waiting for the result of your call to GetNetText. When it gets the result, it places the retrieved text in the field "Status Bar" and then jumps out of the loop to the next frame in the movie.

Providing detailed tutorials on the powerful new network extensions to Lingo is beyond the scope of this chapter. If you'd like to see a simple implementation of an asynchronous network call, the "No-Load Leader" example on the CD uses a single call to gotoNetMovie.

Some tips to keep in mind:

- Currently, you can only open 4 asynchronous network processes at one time using the network extensions to Lingo. Once the network process is done or has returned the data you requested, use the NetDone() command to free up the process.

- Some network Lingo commands don't work in MSIE 2 or later.
- The Lingo command gotoNetPage() clears all Lingo global variables and causes the Shockwave Plug-In to reload.
- Lingo global variables will persist across calls to gotoNetMovie(). This is a way to share data between Shockwave movies.
- Currently, the number of open asynchronous network processes using the network extensions to Lingo is limited by the number of asynchronous processes set in the browser preferences, usually 4 processes. Once the process is done or has returned the data you requested, use the NetDone() command to free up the process.
- Lingo network extensions, such as GetNetText, will not work on local files on your hard disk.

For full documentation of the new network extensions to Lingo, see:

```
http://www.macromedia.com/shockwave/director5/
create.html
```

You can also use Lingo network extensions to retrieve text-based data on the Internet or create richly interactive control bars or navigational panels that load HTML documents into separate frames. Figure 8.19 illustrates a 17KB Shockwave movie that uses a Lingo network extension to collect data on the Internet and present it in a graphical display. With this Shockwave movie, wind surfers can find out about current weather conditions in the San Francisco Bay area.

One of the most annoying things about creating Shockwave animations that use the Lingo network extensions is that whenever you run your movie in the authoring environment you will get script errors for Lingo's network commands. On the CD you will find an external cast containing dummy handlers that will trap network Lingo calls so that you don't get a compiler error.

By uncommenting different lines within each handler, you can have the dummy handlers do nothing, put a message in the Message Windows, display an alert, or return data. You can link this cast to your Director movie during development.

Figure 8.19

Graphical display of real-time Internet-based data using Shockwave.

When you are ready to create your Shockwave movie you can unlink the cast by:

1. Choosing the Movie/Cast command from the Modify menu.
2. Selecting the cast name in the list box.
3. Clicking on Unlink.

Targeting Frames

In Shockwave for Director 5, you can use the network extensions to Lingo to target frames in an HTML document. One application of this would be in a two frame HTML document where one frame contained a Shockwave navigation bar or control panel and the second frame contained content that was accessed from the Shockwave control panel. Shockwave for Director control panels can have features such as button and rollover feedback, and context sensitive help. Figure 8.20 illustrates rich, responsive Shockwave control panels created using the interactivity features in Director and the frames parameter in gotoNetPage.

Figure 8.20

Shockwave control panels illustrating rollover feedback and context-sensitive help. Control panels can change the content of the left frame by using gotoNetPage with the target parameter.

The Net Lingo syntax for targeting frames is:

```
gotoNetPage "chapter1.html","content"
```

where `chapter1.html` is the HTML document that will be loaded into the frame named "content." To integrate this into a navigation bar or control panel, you could place this command in the mouseUp handler of a button.

User-Defined Custom Attributes for the EMBED Tag

Shockwave Plug-In for Netscape Navigator supports user-defined custom attributes in the EMBED tag. Custom attributes are ways to get information from the HTML document into your Shockwave movie. Custom attributes enable you to change aspects of your Shockwave movie without having to recode and recompile a new Shockwave movie. These attributes follow the standard NAME = VALUE syntax of most HTML tag attributes. You place these custom attributes within the EMBED tag in your HTML document. These attributes and their values are accessed from within your

Shockwave Director movie with the Lingo functions:

externalParamValue(ParamNameInQuotesOrNumber)

externalParamName(ParamNameInQuotesOrNumber)

externalParamCount()

The functions externalParamValue() can take either an integer representing the number of an external attribute or a string in quotes representing the NAME in a NAME = VALUE pair.

The function externalParamValue returns the VALUE in the NAME = VALUE pair for the specified attribute. For example, if you EMBED a Shockwave movie with the following HTML:

```
<EMBED SRC="custattr.dcr" WIDTH=160 HEIGHT=64
myCustomAttribute=OFF>
```

the function externalParamValue(1) will return the string "custattr.dcr." The function externalParamValue(WIDTH) will return the string "160."

The function externalParamName returns the attribute NAME for the specified attribute.

The function externalParamCount() takes no parameters and returns the total number of attributes. The total number of attributes includes the SRC, HEIGHT, and WIDTH attributes and any other attributes. For example, if you EMBED a Shockwave movie with the following HTML:

```
<EMBED SRC="custattr.dcr" WIDTH=160 HEIGHT=64
myCustomAttribute=OFF>
```

the function externalParamCount() will return the integer 4.

Director Features Not Supported in Shockwave

Some Director features are disabled in Shockwave. Most of the Lingo commands that provide access to the client hard disk, file system, or operating system have been disabled. This has been done so that downloaded applications do not have access to the local file system.

Here's a list of some of the Director features that are disabled in Shockwave:

- You can't use Director's Movie-in-a-Window feature.
- Most of the Lingo commands that provide access to the client hard disk, file system, or operating system have been disabled. The disabled commands include:

  openResFile

  closeResFile

  open window

  close window

  pasteFromClipboard member x of castLib y,

  importFileInto member x of castLib y

  saveMovie

  printFrom

  open, openDA, closeDA

  quit, restart, and shutdown

  fileName of cast

  fileName of window

  getNthFileNameInFolder

  moviePath

  pathName

  searchCurrentFolder

  searchPaths

  set the filename of castlib
- Mci (media control interface) Lingo commands in Windows are disabled.
- FileIO, SerialIO, OrthPlay XObjects/Xtras are disabled.
- XObjects, XCMDs, XFCNs cannot be embedded as resources in a movie, but can be used in the Shockwave support folder (discussed later in this chapter).
- You can't use "Wait for..." options in the tempo channel. But you can use Lingo to duplicate this feature. See the documentation that accompanies Shockwave for more information.

The following Lingo commands and features have restricted usage under Shockwave. You can use these commands to access external files in the special Shockwave disk cache or support folder. See the previous section on the Shockwave support folder in this chapter for details.

- openXLib
- closeXLib
- open castlib x

Using the Shockwave ActiveX Control

The Shockwave for Director ActiveX Control is an ActiveX control for Internet Explorer 3.0. As of this writing, the Shockwave ActiveX Control only works in MSIE 3 on Windows 95 and NT systems. Support for Macintosh 3.1 and Macintosh may be available by the time you read this.

To embed ActiveX controls in your HTML document, use the OBJECT tag; it can take various attributes or parameters.

Purportedly, the Shockwave ActiveX control will recognize Shockwave movies that are embedded within HTML documents using either the OBJECT tag or the EMBED tag. This feature was not available for testing at the time of this writing.

The Shockwave Plug-In for Netscape Navigator supports user-defined custom attributes in the EMBED tag (see previous discussion). These attributes will not be recognized by the Shockwave ActiveX Control. The Shockwave ActiveX Control will recognize parameters with specific names within the OBJECT tag. You can access these specific named parameters within the OBJECT tag from within your Shockwave Director movie using the same Lingo functions you use to access custom attributes:

```
externalParamValue(ParamNameInQuotesOrNumber)
externalParamName(ParamNameInQuotesOrNumber)
externalParamCount()
```

For example, if you used the OBJECT tag as listed below, the Lingo:

```
put externalParamValue("SRC") into field "paramDisplay"
```

will put the text "myShock.dcr" into field "paramDisplay."

For the complete list of specific named parameters recognized by the Shockwave ActiveX Control see:

http://www.macromedia.com/shockwave/director5/contents.html

CODEBASE Parameter

One advantage of the Shockwave ActiveX control is the ability to provide automatic version control and downloading. This feature is provided with the CODEBASE parameter.

```
Here is a sample of an OBJECT tag for a movie named
myShock.dcr:
<OBJECT CLASSID="clsid:166B1BCA-3F9C-11CF-8075-
➥444553540000"
CODEBASE="//active.macromedia.com/director/
➥sw.cab#version=5,0,1,54"
WIDTH="320" HEIGHT="240" NAME="Shockwave"
➥ID="logoshck">
<PARAM NAME="SRC" VALUE="myShock.dcr">

</OBJECT>
```

The CLASSID parameter specifies the universal class identifier for the Shockwave ActiveX Control. It must be:

```
CLASSID="clsid:166B1BCA-3F9C-11CF-8075-444553540000"
```

The CODEBASE parameter is similar to the PLUGINSPAGE attribute of the EMBED tag. The CODEBASE parameter to the OBJECT tag specifies where the Shockwave for Director ActiveX Control can be obtained if the user doesn't have it already installed in the browser, or has an older version installed. Check Macromedia's Web page for the latest version of the ActiveX control.

The WIDTH and HEIGHT parameters have their usual values. The ID parameter provides a name with which to refer to the Shockwave movie from other parts of the HTML document.

The NAME parameter will enable the Shockwave movie to participate in an HTML FORM submission. See Macromedia's documentation for details.

The PARAM tag enables the setting of various parameters. You must specify a source URL with the NAME parameter. The NAME="SRC" parameter tells the browser where to find the Shockwave movie to display in the Web page. You can also provide additional parameters such as:

```
<PARAM NAME="BGCOLOR" VALUE=#FFFFFF>
```

to set the background color to white

```
<PARAM NAME="PALETTE" VALUE="foreground">
```

to assert a custom palette.

Shockwave Unplugged

Chances are, some browsers that hit your page will not have the Shockwave Plug-In installed. In Netscape Navigator 2.0 or compatible browsers, a broken icon appears if the Shockwave Plug-In is not present. This section shows you how to provide for users who do not have the Shockwave Plug-In installed.

Point Users to the Shockwave Download Page

If you provide Shockwave content on your site, you should provide a link to the Macromedia Shockwave page at:

```
http://www.macromedia.com/shockwave/
```

so users can download the Plug-In for their system.

You can also use the PLUGINSPAGE parameter in the EMBED tag to automatically point user's browsers to the Shockwave download page. For example:

```
<EMBED SRC="myShockWave.dcr" WIDTH= 160 HEIGHT= 120
PLUGINSPAGE= "http://www.macromedia.com/shockwave/ ">
```

Using Shockwave and the <META> Tag

You can also use Shockwave and Lingo network extensions to detect the presence of the Shockwave Plug-In and automatically send the browser to a Shockwave-enabled page, if the Plug-In is present. This method was used by Macromedia on their home page.

1. Create a small Shockwave movie that contains the gotoNetPage command in a frame script. For example:

   ```
   gotoNetPage "myShockwaveEnabledPage.html"
   ```

   The page specified in the gotoNetPage command is your Shockwave-enabled page, in this case, `"myShockwaveEnabledPage.html."`

2. Embed this movie in an HTML document.

3. Place the following HTML between the <HEAD></HEAD> tags of your HTML document:

   ```
   <META HTTP-EQUIV=REFRESH CONTENT="20;
   ➥URL=myNonShockedPage.html">
   ```

When a user loads this HTML document, the little Shockwave movie will load and send the browser to the Shockwave-enabled page if the user has Shockwave installed. If the user doesn't have Shockwave, then the user will see the broken Plug-In icon. If you use the PLUGINSPAGE parameter described earlier, the user will have the choice to go to a page to download the Plug-In. The HTML in the <META> tag will automatically send the user to the non-Shockwave page after 20 seconds.

JavaScript Workaround for Netscape 2.0

The following JavaScript workaround is a variation on sample code from Macromedia's Shockwave Developer's Guide that is designed to provide a solution for the no-Plug-In problem for the most number of browsers. Here's what it does. In Netscape 2.0 compatible browsers, the broken Plug-In icon is displayed when there is no Shockwave Plug-In present and the PLUGINSPAGE parameter automatically points the user to a download site. In browsers that don't support Netscape compatible Plug-Ins, it will usually display the HTML between the NOEMBED tags.

```
<script language="JavaScript">
    <!--hide this script tag's contents from old
➥browsers
    document.write ( '<EMBED SRC="myShockWave.dcr"
➥WIDTH= 160 HEIGHT= 120  ' );
    document.write ( ' PLUGINSPAGE= "http://
➥www.macromedia.com/shockwave/ ">'  );
    <!--done hiding from old browsers -->
</script>
<NOEMBED>
    <IMG SRC="noPlugin.gif">
</NOEMBED>
```

JavaScript Workaround for Netscape 3.0

Another way to detect the presence of the Shockwave Plug-In requires Netscape 3.0 and uses a new feature of JavaScript. This method requires Netscape Navigator 3 or later. See Chapter 14 for a Javascript function you can use to determine if the Shockwave Plug-In is present.

Tutorial: No-Load Leader

When you begin downloading a large Shockwave movie, it doesn't display instantly. Instead, the Shockwave Plug-In displays a default graphic from Macromedia. This graphic is displayed until the movie has been completely downloaded to the user's disk cache. This tutorial uses a technique to replace the default graphic with a small movie that provides the user with feedback during the download time.

No-load leader

If you have a large movie with a long download time, first load a very small movie in its place—a **No-load Leader**. The movie should be small enough (less than 8KB) that it loads in seconds. The No-load Leader loads rapidly and then issues the gotoNetMovie Lingo command with the path name to your large Shockwave movie. When the No-load Leader issues the gotoNetMovie command, Lingo will start the download process of your large movie in the background while still playing your small No-load Leader in the Web page.

When the larger movie has been completely downloaded to the client disk cache it will appear in place of your "No-load Leader" movie. The "No-load Leader" movie should be the same dimensions as your large movie and should provide some low-bandwidth content to entertain your users during a long download. You can create your movie following these steps or use the movie `"noldlder.dir"` on the book's CD.

Here's how to create a No-Load Leader:

1. Open Director with a new blank movie (see figure 8.21).

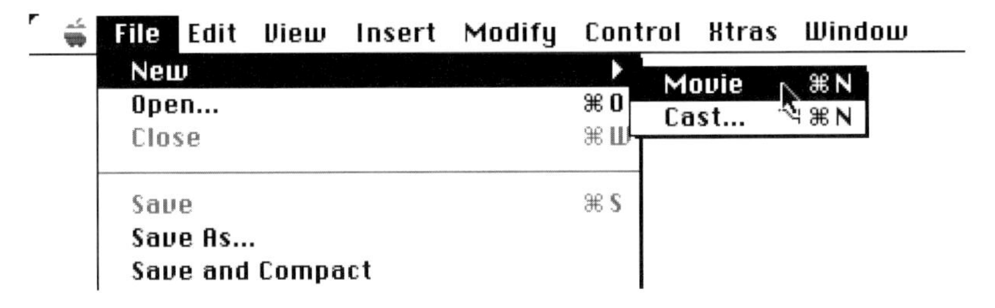

Figure 8.21

Creating a new Director movie

2. Choose Movie/Properties from the Modify menu (see figure 8.22).

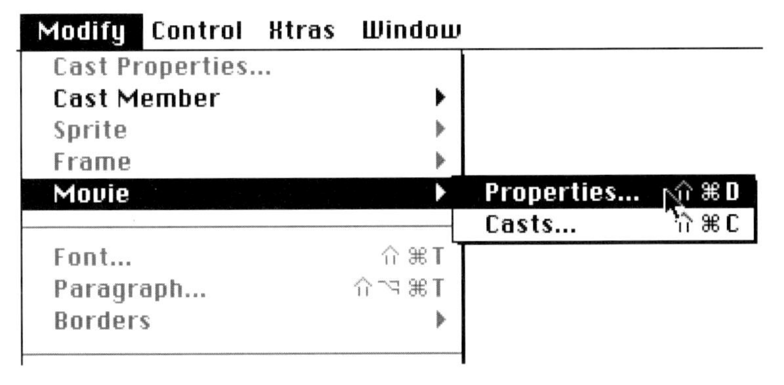

Figure 8.22

Choosing Movie/Properties.

3. Specify a stage size that matches your large Shockwave movie (see figure 8.23).
4. Double-click in the Script channel in the first-frame in the Score.
5. A Script Window (see 8.24) should open with the lines:

```
on exitFrame
end
```

If you are using the `"noldlder.dir"` the script should already be there. Just uncomment the script.

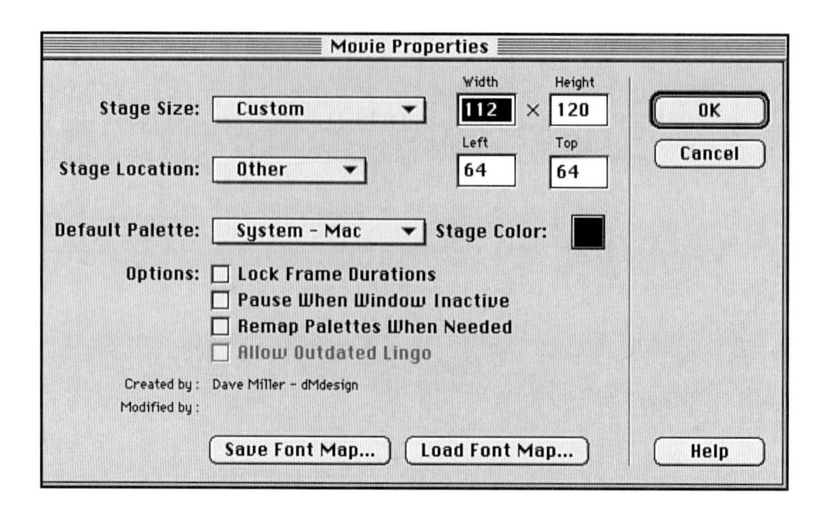

Figure 8.23

Movie Properties dialog box.

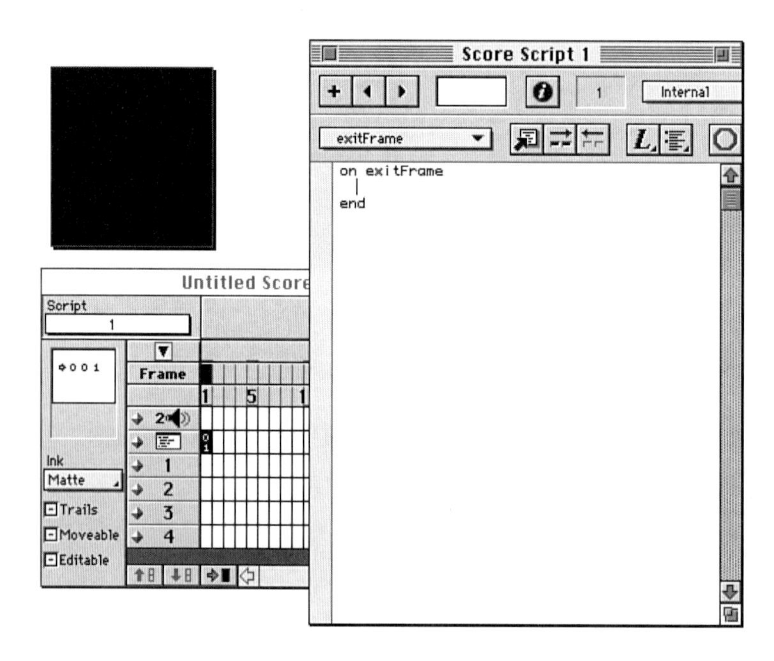

Figure 8.24

Script Window.

6. Between these two lines type:

```
gotoNetmovie "myBigShockwaveMovie.dcr"
```

where `"myBigShockwaveMovie.dcr"` is, is the name of your large Shockwave movie.

If you are using the `"noldlder.dir"` from the CD, replace the name of the movie in the existing handler with the name of your own movie.

7. The Script Window should look like this (see fig. 8.25):

```
on exitFrame
    gotoNetMovie "myBigShockwaveMovie.dcr"
end
```

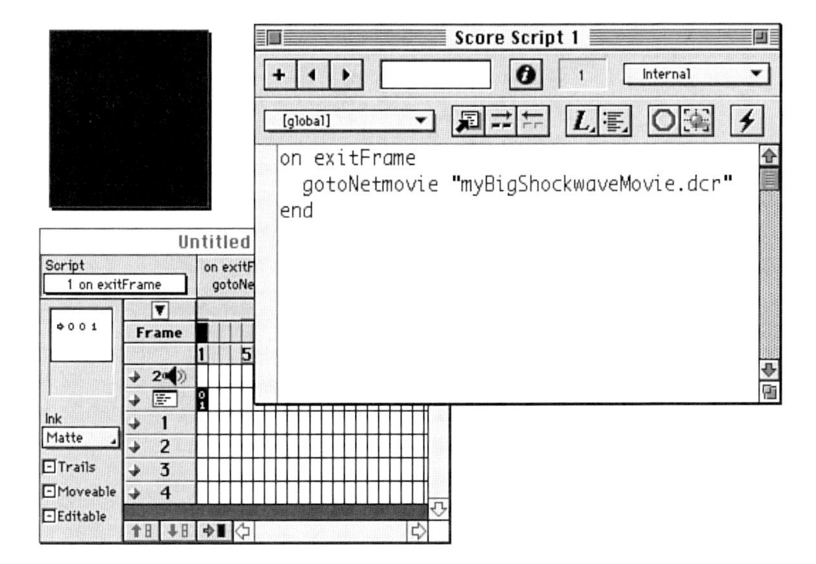

Figure 8.25

Script Window with the gotoNetMovie handler.

8. Create a low bandwidth animation or other indication for the user that downloading is in progress. The example on the CD uses Lingo animation to animate the hand of a clock.
9. Select the Afterburner Xtra from the Xtras menu.
10. Give your movie a name ending with the extension .dcr

Tutorial: Score-Based Animation

This example uses Director to play back a sequence of animation frames created in another animation program. Director is used to add interactivity to the animation. You can use the animation frames and the movie `"heart.dir"` from the book's CD or use your own animation frames. To see the final version of the movie with all the interactivity, see the movie `heartfnl.dir` on the CD. Here's how to do it:

1. First create your animation frames in an animation program. The example on the CD used Extreme 3D, but you can use any animation program that outputs sequences of PICT files. The CD provides a series of graphics you can use for this exercise.
2. Process the graphics for the Web:
   - Reduce the size of the graphics to reduce the total file size and to fit the animation on a Web page. 160 × 120 pixels is a common size.
   - Reduce the bit-depth of the graphics to 8-bit.

   - Give the graphics a Web-compatible palette such as the Macintosh system palette or the 216-color Netscape palette. Use any image-processing program with batch capabilities, such as Equilibrium Debabelizer. The graphics on the CD were processed this way.
3. Put all the graphics in a single folder and make sure they have file names that are numbered sequentially.

4. Open Director with a new blank movie or use the movie `"heart.dir"` on the CD.
5. Choose Movie/Properties from the Modify menu.
6. Specify a stage size that matches the size of your animation (see fig. 8.26).

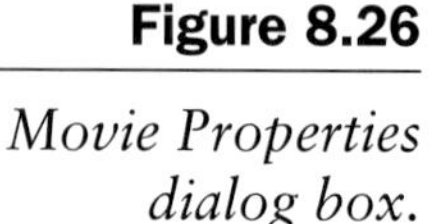

Figure 8.26

Movie Properties dialog box.

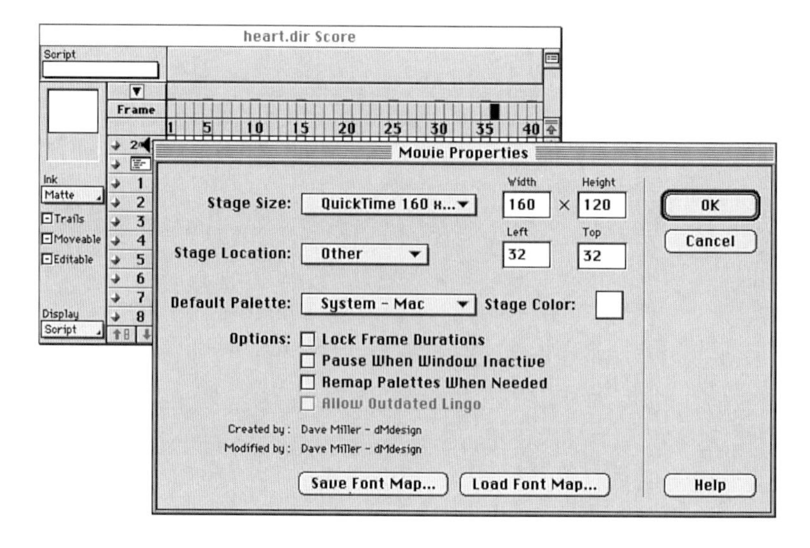

7. Open the Cast Window from the Windows menu.
8. Select an open cast slot. You want to have enough open cast slots in a row so that when you import your sequentially numbered PICT files, they all fit in a contiguous sequence in the Cast Window.
9. Choose Import from the File menu (see fig. 8.27).

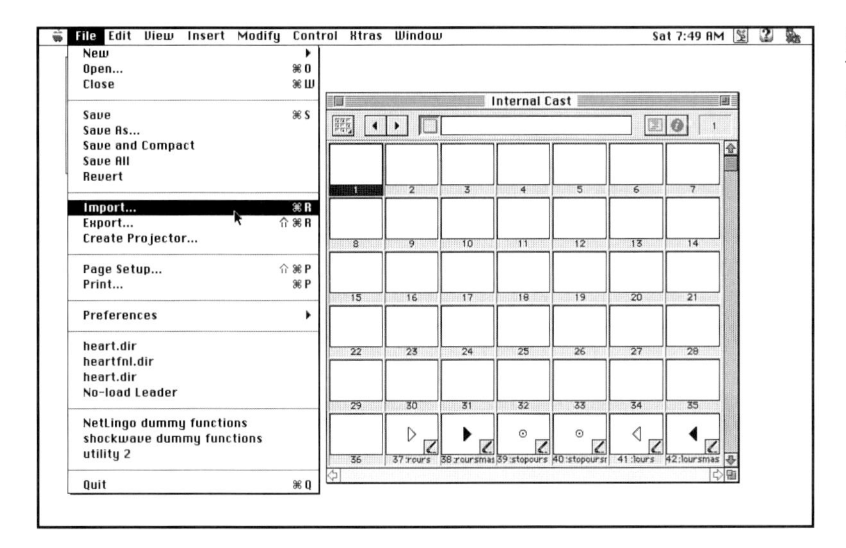

Figure 8.27

Choosing Import from the File menu.

10. Select the first graphic in your animation sequence. If the graphics are all in the same folder, select Import All (see fig. 8.28). The CD provides a series of graphics you can use for this exercise.

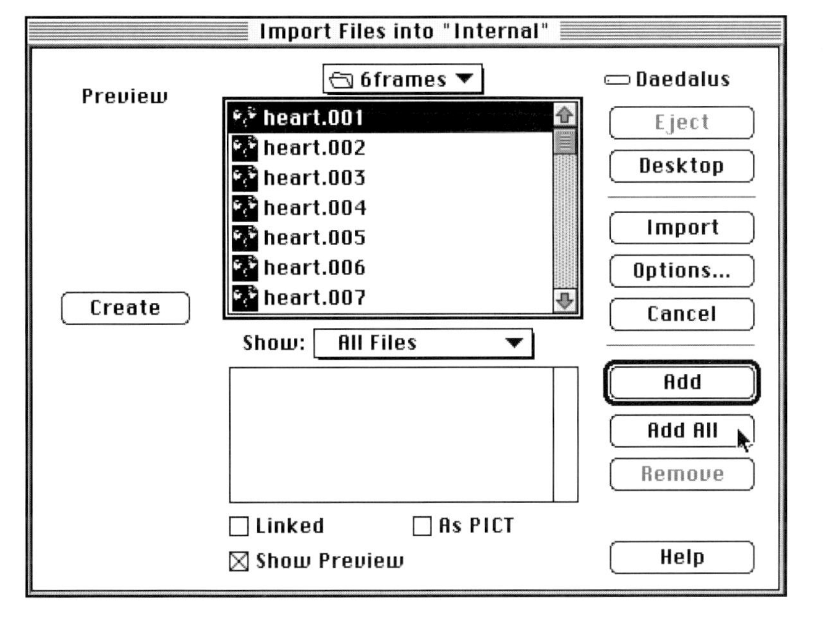

Figure 8.28

Importing animation frames into the Cast.

11. All the graphics will be placed in the Cast Window in sequence, based on file name (see fig. 8.29). That is why it is important to have sequentially numbered files.

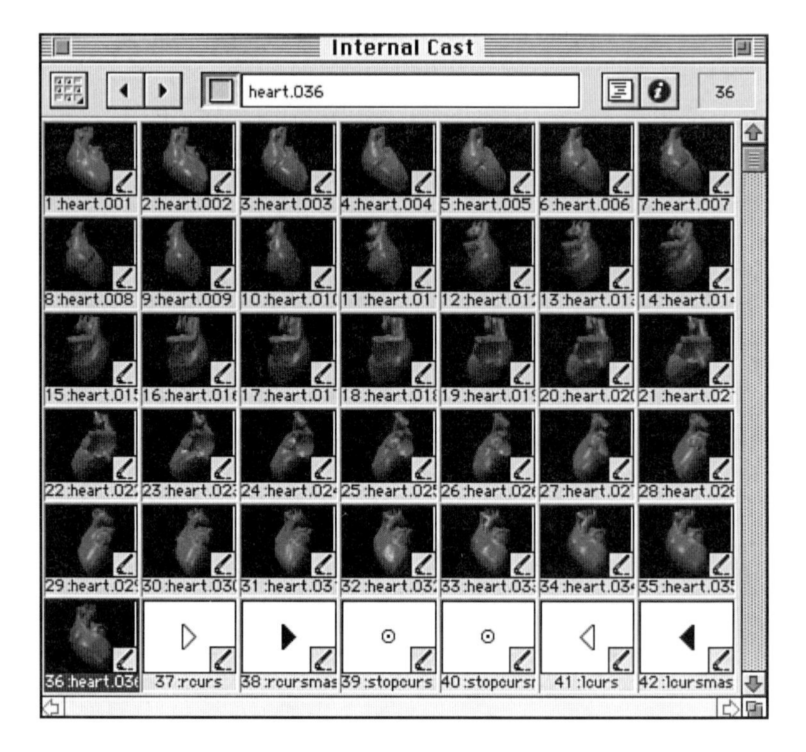

Figure 8.29

Imported animation frames in the Cast Window.

12. If you run out of memory during import, you can import files in smaller batches or quit Director and allocate more memory to the program.

13. In the Score, select frame 1, channel 1.

14. Click on the Cast Window to make it active. Select all the animation frames that you just imported into the Cast Window. Press the shift key to make a multiple, contiguous selection.

15. Choose Cast to Time from the Modify menu (see fig. 8.30).

16. Selected cast members are placed sequentially into separate frames in the Score, beginning at frame 1, channel 1 (see fig. 8.31).

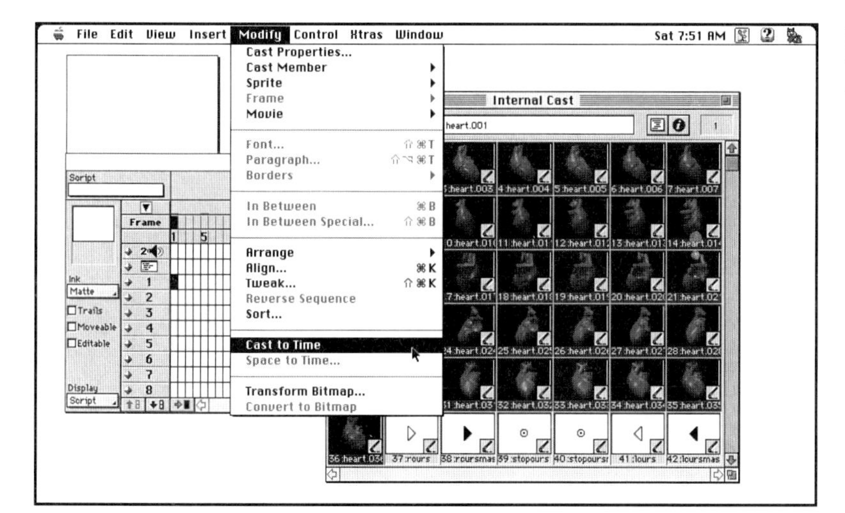

Figure 8.30

Choosing Cast to Time.

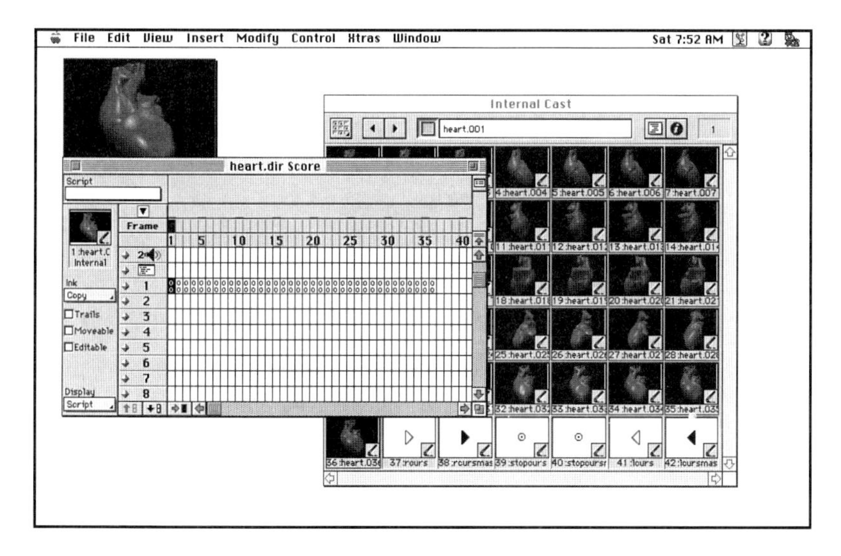

Figure 8.31

Score Window after choosing Cast to Time.

Follow steps 17 and 18 if you are using the movie "`heart.dir`" from the CD.

17. Select frames 1 through 36 in the Script channel.
18. In the Script pop-up menu, select the score script named "`interactivity`" (see fig. 8.32).
19. Select the Afterburner Xtra from the Xtras menu (see fig. 8.33).
20. Give your movie a name ending with the extension `.dcr`.

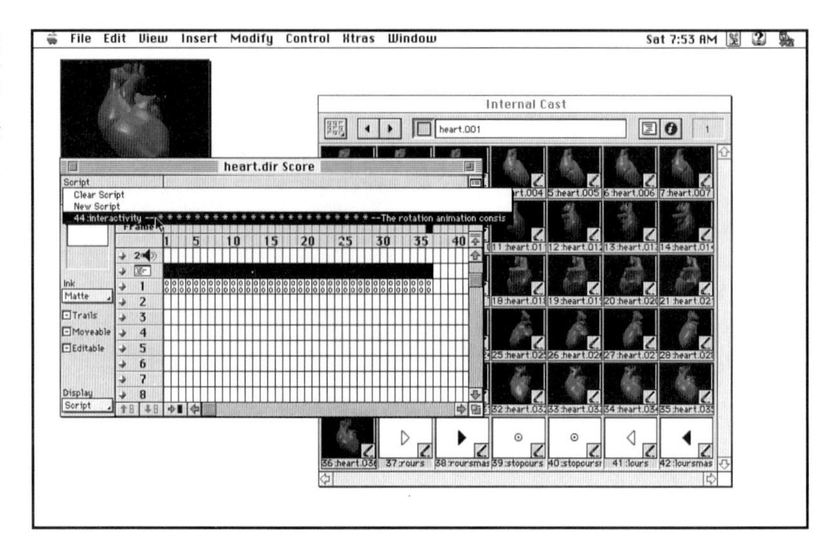

Figure 8.32

Selecting the "interactivity" script from the Script pop-upmenu.

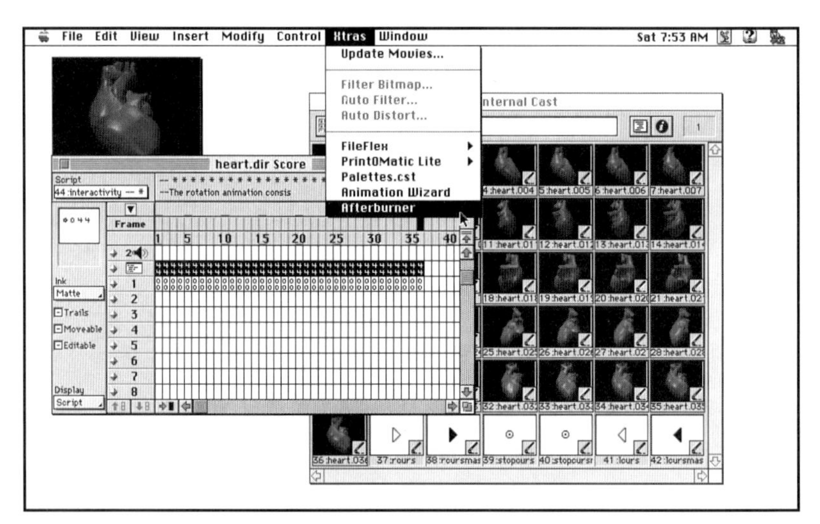

Figure 8.33

Choosing Afterburner from the Xtras menu.

Tutorial: Dynamic Custom, User-Defined Attributes and Shockwave Streaming Audio

In this tutorial you will learn how to:

- Add streaming audio files to your Shockwave movie.
- Access and use custom, user-defined attributes in the EMBED tag inside your Shockwave movie. Custom, user-defined attributes enable you to get information into your Shockwave movie from the HTML document.

- How to use custom attributes to provide dynamic content.

The technique described here requires the following tools:

Tools
Netscape Navigator 2 or later, or a browser that supports JavaScript version 1
Shockwave for Audio Streaming Xtra
files (listed below)

The tutorial requires the Shockwave for Audio Streaming Xtra to be in the special Xtras folder in your Netscape Plug-Ins folder and in your Director 5 Xtras folder. If you performed the standard install of Shockwave, you should be set up. These files are included on the CD-ROM.

This tutorial uses the files:

- `swa.htm`
- `swatutor.dir`
- `citynite.swa`
- `morning.swa`

The file `swa.dir` is the final version of the Director movie used in this tutorial. The HTML document `swa.htm` uses JavaScript and custom user-defined attributes in the EMBED tag to provide different audio content, depending on the time of day that the page is visited. The custom user-defined attribute in this case is `"swaURL."` The value of this attribute is a URL to a valid SWA file for playback by the Shockwave movie.

Here is the JavaScript code:

```
<script language="JavaScript">
<!--hide this script tag's contents from old browsers
var myDate = new Date();
var myHour = myDate.getHours();
if (myHour < 12){
          document.write('<EMBED SRC="swa.dcr"
➥WIDTH=160 HEIGHT=64
swaURL="morning.swa">');
}
```

```
else {
    document.write('<EMBED SRC="swa.dcr" WIDTH=160
➥HEIGHT=64  swaURL="citynite.swa">');
}
<!-- done hiding from old browsers -->
</script>
```

This JavaScript will run in Netscape Navigator 2.0 or later, or a browser that supports JavaScript v1.0. For a detailed description of this and other scripts, see Chapter 14, "Scripting Multimedia Web Pages" on client-side scripting.

To create the Shockwave movie:

Note

You can compress audio files that are embedded in Director, but to create external files that reside as separate files on a Web server you need SoundEdit.

1. You will need to create your Shockwave for Audio streaming audio files or SWA files. The only authoring tool as of this writing is SoundEdit on the Macintosh. To learn how to create SWA files in SoundEdit, see the preceding section "Using Shockwave for Audio with SoundEdit 16."

Two SWA files are provided for you in this tutorial: `citynite.swa` and `morning.swa`. These files were created from sample digital audio files provided on the SoundEdit CD; the files City Night Amb and Birds Desert Morning. Both files are stereo, 16-bit, 44kHz sound files that are several second long and contain various environmental sounds. These files were converted to mono files with data rates of 8kbs (the lowest data rate possible) in SoundEdit, using the Shockwave for Audio Export Xtra. Original file sizes were over 7MB and 4.9MB. These files were converted to 41KB and 29KB size files, respectively, for a compression ratio of over to 170:1.

2. Open the Director file `swatutor.dir`.
3. Insert a cast member reference to an external SWA file.
    a. Open the Cast Window by choosing Cast from the Window menu and pressing command-3 on a Mac or control-3 on Windows.
    b. Click on an empty cast slot to select it.
    c. Choose Other:SWA Streaming Xtra from the insert menu.

d. With the cast member still selected, click in the Cast Member Name text entry box at the top of the movie and enter "swa" without the quotes. You can use any name you want, but "swa" will be used in this tutorial (see fig. 8.34).

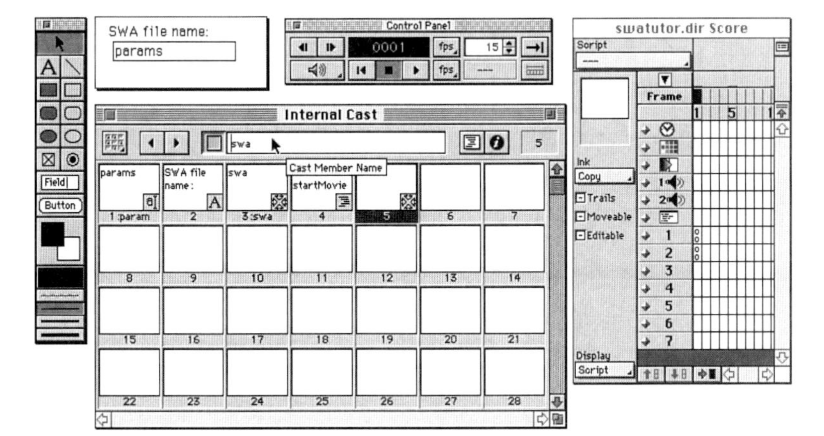

Figure 8.34

Inserting a cast member reference to an external SWA file.

4. Double-click on the startmovie handler in the Cast Window to open the script window.

5. Type in the following handler between the "on startmovie" and "end startmovie" lines:

```
if externalParamName("swaURL") = "swaURL" then
  set myURL =  externalParamValue("swaURL")
  put myURL into field "param"

  set the URL of member "swa" = string (myURL)

  Play (member "swa")
else
  alert "Couldn't load attribute! Doh!"
end if
```

This handler is called when the movie begins. It looks for the custom, user-defined attribute "swaURL" within the EMBED tag of the HTML document in which it is embedded as a Shockwave movie. The EMBED tag looks like this:

```
<EMBED SRC="swa.dcr" WIDTH=160 HEIGHT=64
swaURL="morning.swa">
```

Look at the file swa.htm to see what the HTML looks like.

Then, the handler sets the local variable "myURL" to the value of the swaURL custom attribute, which should be a valid URL to a SWA file; in this case "morning.swa." It sets the URL of the SWA cast member reference you just created (which you named "swa") to the URL stored in the variable myURL, with the line:

```
set the URL of member "swa" = string (myURL)
```

Next, this handler starts playing the SWA sound file with the Play command (see fig. 8.35).

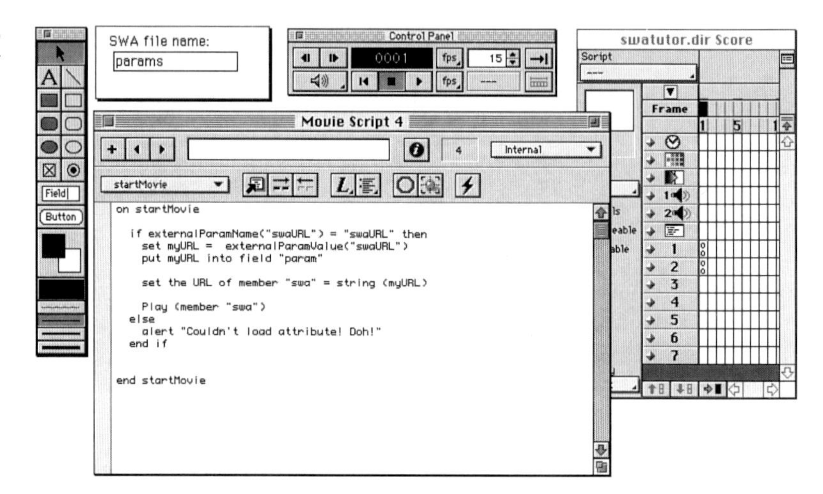

Figure 8.35

Startmovie handler that plays a SWA file based on a custom, user-defined HTML attribute.

6. Now add a button so the user can stop play back. Refer to figure 8.36 as you perform the following steps:

    a. Open the Tools Palette by choosing Tools Palette from the Window menu and pressing command-7 on a Mac or control-7 on Windows.

    b. Click on the Button tool to select it.

    c. Drag across the Director stage to place a button on the stage.

    d. Type the word Stop inside the button.

    e. Open the Cast Window.

    f. Select the button you just created in the cast.

    g. Click on the Script button at the top right of the Cast Window.

h. You should be presented with a Script Window containing an empty mouseUp handler with a blinking insertion point.

i. Type **`Stop(member "swa")`**.

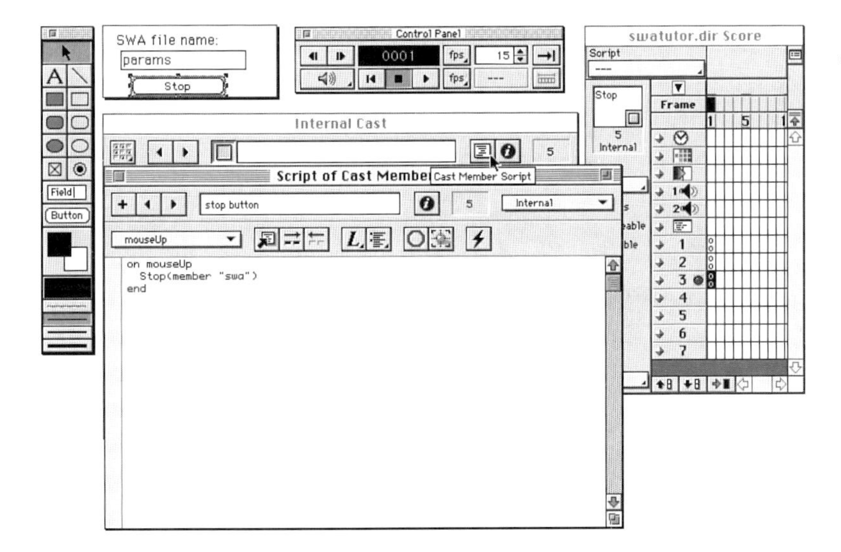

Figure 8.36

Stop button for SWA file.

7. Now you will instruct the movie to loop on frame one (see fig. 8.37). Double-click on the Script channel in frame one.

8. You should be presented with a Script Window containing an empty exitFrame handler with a blinking insertion point.

9. Type **`go the frame`**.

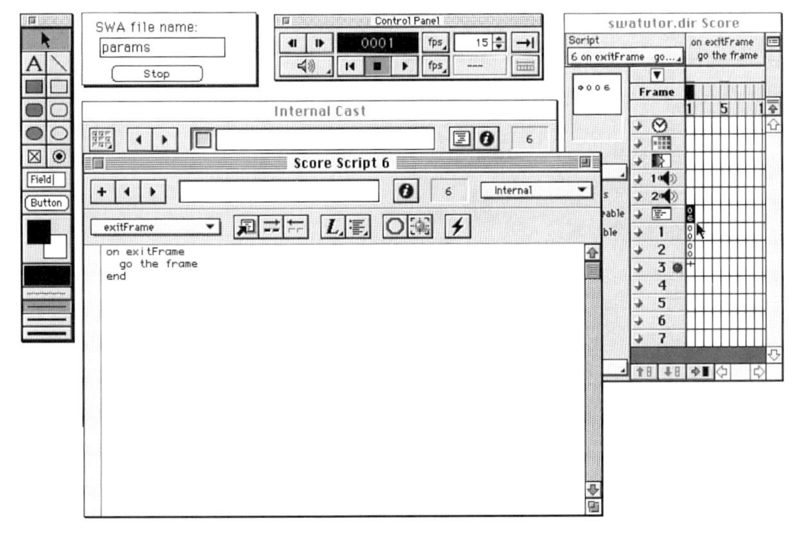

Figure 8.37

Looping on a frame.

10. Choose Save As from the File menu.
11. Save the movie as `"swa.dir."`
12. Select the Afterburner Xtra from the Xtras menu.
13. Name the movie `swa.dcr`.

Conclusion

This chapter doesn't scratch the surface of things you can do with Shockwave and Director. Hopefully, you now know of a place to begin using Shockwave, or if you already use Director, provided you with some tips for creating compact Shockwave movies.

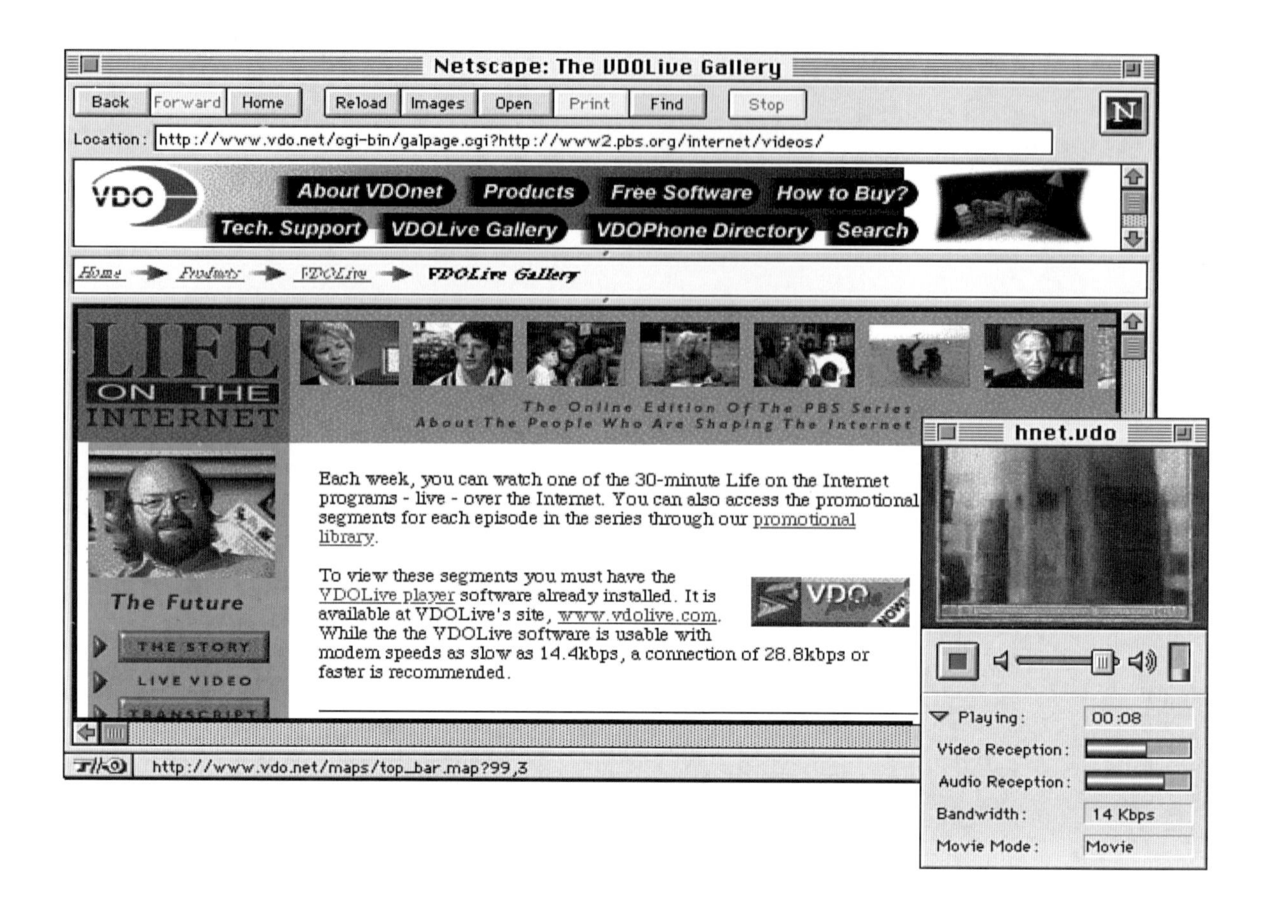

Video content can be the most visually compelling media to add to a Web page. But video is also the most bandwidth-hungry media type.

chapter

9

Video

Providing digital video on the Web pushes the limits of Internet multimedia capabilities. TCP/IP protocol, the language of the Internet, was not designed to provide the continuous, synchronized, data streams that are required for video and audio. Digital video files are huge and can quickly consume the available network bandwidth. Playback of digital video is resource intensive, pushing the limits of older desktop systems.

Video on the Web is more viable in controlled network environments, such as corporate or university intranets. Here, legacy video content, such as training videos and educational CD-ROMs, can be relatively easily repurposed for on-demand Web-based delivery. Under optimal conditions, Web-based video in these kinds of network environments may approach the performance of the slowest CD-ROM drives. See the next section for a discussion of performance and bandwidth issues. If you are willing to put up with lower image quality and lower frame rates (compared to most CD-ROMs), Web-based video provides many of the advantages of Web-based publishing and communications discussed in previous chapters.

Some video-on-the-Internet solutions use proprietary data formats, expensive servers, or expensive encoding and authoring hardware and software that require investments of several thousands to several tens of thousands of dollars. This chapter focuses on more modest solutions that don't require average users to mortgage the ranch to provide video content.

Note

Frame rate is the number of frames per second that are displayed. The frame rate of film is 24 frames per second. The frame rate of broadcast video is 29.97 frames per second.

Until now, digital video formats on the Web have been largely a "wait for it to download and then play it" technology. In these cases, file size is the major limiting factor in providing video content quickly to users. After the digital video is downloaded to the local hard disk, it plays back at hard drive speeds. The new FastStart feature of Web-based QuickTime (described in Chapter 10, "Animating with QuickTime Digital Video"), although not true streaming, has improved the user experience by enabling the start of playback before the entire file is downloaded to the user's hard disk.

Today, video on the Web can be delivered by:

- **Download and Play.** Downloading preexisting video files to local hard disk and playing them back with helper apps or Plug-Ins.
- **Streaming.** Streaming preexisting video files, typically encoded in a proprietary compression format. Users view the video while it is downloading, with the aid of helper apps or Plug-Ins. This option usually requires expensive dedicated servers.
- **Fast-Start QuickTime.** Using Fast-Start QuickTime optimization enables developers to jump-start playback and provides a serviceable approximation of true streaming playback without the need for special servers, authoring tools, or changes to existing QuickTime players and viewers. For Fast-Start movies, data rate is an important factor to consider when rapid and continuous playback is the goal, although Fast-Start optimization improves the user experience for even high data-rate QuickTime media. Data-rate limiting of Fast-Start movies generally requires compromises in image quality, movie size, and movie frame rate.
- **Streaming video with real-time compression/decompression.** An example of streaming live video, "Webcasting" with real-time compression/decompression, is desktop video-conferencing.

Continuously streaming, real-time, high-quality video on the Web is becoming practical over the fastest modems, if you are willing to put up with low-quality images, small viewing windows, and low frame rates. VDOLive and StreamWorks both provide excellent cross-platform streaming video solutions with slightly different features, but they use proprietary data formats, and they require expensive servers or expensive encoding hardware and software.

This chapter provides the background you need to create video for the Web, and discusses:

- Bandwidth and data-rate issues
- Digitizing existing video for your Web site
- Creating your own video for QuickTime
- Embedding AVI content in MSIE for Windows
- Video Conferencing on the Web

Understanding Bandwidth and Data-Rate

Data transfer rate or data-rate for video, as explained earlier in this book, is the amount of information that must be transferred to the user's display for the movie to play smoothly. It is typically measured in kilobytes per second (KB/s). Data-rates are usually limited by the user's hardware. Bandwidth or data-rates for digital video playback from CD-ROM are typically in the range of 100–500 KB/sec. If a digital video movie's data-rate exceeds this amount, the user experiences pauses and break-ups. Table 9.1 shows representative data-rates for various CD-ROM speeds.

Table 9.1

Estimated Data Transfer Rates from CD-ROM Drives

Speed	Data rate in KB/s
1X	90–100
2X	150–200
4X	350–450

On the Internet, data-rates are much lower. Network bandwidth places limits on the delivery of digital video on the Web in two key areas:

- The time spent downloading digital video files. The major limiting factor under the author's control is file size.
- The ability to play continuous, streaming video without break-up and pauses. The major limiting factor under the author's control is data rate.

On networks, playback of digital video can be affected by factors beyond the user's control, such as server load and network traffic, making data rates difficult to estimate.

Fast corporate or university intranets may achieve data-rates of 20–100 KB/s, approaching the slowest CD-ROM. On corporate and university intranets, you can generally get by with digital video file sizes in the 100 KB–1 MB range and data-rates in the 40–50 KB/s range.

Data-rates on the Internet for modem users are around 2.5 KB/sec or less, much slower than CD. For modem users, strive for video with file sizes in the 20 KB to 50 KB range and data-rates in the 1–3 KB/s range.

Here is an estimated range of data-rates to shoot for when providing digital video on the Web. Range represents high-traffic and low-traffic networks. Your mileage may vary.

Connection	Data Rate(KB/s)
14.4 modem	0.5–1.5
28.8 modem	1.5–2.5
ISDN	4–10
T1	5–50
intranet	15–90
CD-ROM	90–450

Content providers need to adjust authoring and compression of digital video for various delivery mechanisms (for example, download and play, Fast-Start QuickTime, streaming, or live "webcasting") in very different network environments. For example, suppose your goal is to deliver the highest quality video to a small LAN or corporate intranet with a dedicated multimedia server and real-time streaming is not required. Reducing data-rate of digital video, the goal of most CD-ROM productions, helps reduce file size, but at the cost of image quality, movie dimensions, and frame rate. Low data-rates improve the performance of the QuickTime's Fast-Start feature, but Fast-Start also works at higher data-rates. You may be able to provide higher quality video than you would for CD-ROM, because video can be distributed over a network during low-traffic periods and cached on a user's hard drive.

Data-rate limiting is important in streaming video solutions. It will become more important in the future, as open, cross-platform compression schemes used in video-conferencing programs, such as QuickTime Conferencing, MBone, and CU-SeeMe are integrated into QuickTime and other video formats.

Given these extreme performance constraints, especially for delivery to modem users, consider alternative media, such as animation or GIFs. Is digital video the most effective way to deliver your content to your target users, or are there better solutions?

Understanding Codecs

codec

A **codec** is a small software module present in system software that compresses and decompresses different digital media types. Codec stands for COmpression-DECompression. Compression and decompression features are essential when working with digital video because of the huge amounts of data involved and the nature of storage and playback on computers.

Codecs contain highly optimized software algorithms that compress digital video when you create it and then decompress it when you play it back. Several different software-based codecs are automatically installed with QuickTime for Macintosh and Windows. Video for Windows also includes codecs. Many of the streaming video solutions for the Web provide encoders and decoders with their own proprietary codecs. Which codec works best for your video depends on the video content. If you compress a movie with a particular codec, the same codec must be installed on the user's machine for the movie to playback.

If your movie must playback on Windows, Macintosh, and Unix systems, one solution is to use QuickTime movies saved with one of the cross-platform codecs. When this book was written, the following decompression codecs shipped with both Macintosh and Windows versions of QuickTime:

- Animation
- Cinepak
- Graphic
- None
- Photo— JPEG
- Video
- Photo CD
- Intel Indeo

QuickTime movies compressed with these codecs playback on Macintosh and Windows systems.

Browser Support of Web Video

Depending on the browser you choose, different video file formats may be supported. QuickTime video has built-in, cross-platform support in Navigator 3.0 and Internet Explorer. AVI has built-in support in Internet Explorer for Windows and Navigator 3.0 for Windows 95 and Windows NT. Netscape Plug-Ins and ActiveX controls support additional formats.

QuickTime

QuickTime playback capabilities are included automatically with Netscape Navigator 3.0 or later on both Macintosh and Windows. QuickTime digital video is supported by third-party Plug-Ins in Netscape Navigator 2.0 or later on both Macintosh and Windows systems. QuickTime is supported by Plug-Ins and natively in MSIE 2.0 on the Macintosh. It is supposed to have cross-platform support in MSIE 3.0. QuickTime digital video is supported by helper apps with most browsers on Macintosh, Windows, and Unix.

AVI

AVI is only supported on Windows systems. AVI playback is included automatically in MSIE 2.0 or later for Windows, Netscape Navigator 3.0 or later for Windows 95, and Windows NT. AVI playback is supported by helper apps on Windows systems.

Other Formats

Native browser support for MPEG, ActiveMovie, and various proprietary video streaming formats will probably be a reality by the time you read this. At this time, the StreamWorks and VDOLive streaming video formats support Windows, Macintosh, and Unix platforms with helper apps, Plug-Ins, or ActiveX controls.

Shooting Original Video

You may want to shoot original video or to digitize from video tape and incorporate the footage in your Web-based digital video. The issues surrounding digital video are themselves worth a book; there are several good books available.

Web video has a long way to go to reach television or even CD-ROM production qualities. Even so, when you compress digital video for the Web or any other medium, it's important to start with the cleanest, highest quality source possible. Video with a lot of visual "noise" and artifacts (blocky patterns of pixels), common on low-quality VHS tapes, does not compress well.

Note

The following are some good books on QuickTime and digital video:

The Official Guide for Macintosh Users
by Judith L. Stern & Robert A. Lettieri
Hayden Books
ISBN 1-56830-129-4

Desktop Video Studio
by Andrew Soderberg & Tom Hudson
Random House
ISBN 0-679-75784-8

How To Digitize Video
by Nels Johnson

Shooting Video for the Web: Quick Tips

Here are some tips if you are shooting video that is to be digitized and compressed for the Web:

1. Start with the highest quality videotape source possible. Ideally, use Betacam SP. If you can't afford Betacam SP, Hi-8 or S-VHS are good choices. VHS video doesn't digitize well. VHS format video contains video noise that digital video codecs waste time trying to compress and decompress.
2. Avoid fast pans and rapid motion.
3. Avoid zooming in and out.
4. Avoid the shakes. Use a tripod at the very least. Shaky video is hard to compress.
5. Lighting is very important for digital video. Many video shoots use a standard three light technique. Use even, low-contrast lighting. Avoid highly reflective objects. High-contrast video increases the work load on your codecs.
    - Key light is the brightest light and should be shining on the subject, typically from the front and off to the side a bit.
    - Fill light is placed on the opposite side of the key light to reduce high contrast shadows on the subject.
    - Back light is typically placed behind and above the subject and is usually the dimmest light. It is used to further reduce high-contrast shadows and separate the subject from the background.
6. Start shooting a few seconds before the action starts and stop shooting a few seconds after the action stops.
7. Keep the action within the center of view. Be aware of the action-safe and title-safe video areas.
8. Avoid visual clutter—make the subject of your shot fill the majority of the view (within the action-safe area).
9. Consider shooting the same scene from different angles. A range of shots gives you more choices in editing and compositing. Two cameras can be handy for this.

10. Shoot a minute or two of background or establishing shots. These shots can be added in post-production to provide visual continuity and bridges between shots.
11. Record a minute or two of background noise. Differences in background or ambient noise levels are very noticeable and distracting. Ambient noise can be useful in post-production to provide audio continuity between disparate shots.
12. Use a microphone that is separate from the camcorder and get it as close to the subject as possible.
13. Turn off noisy appliances and computers when recording audio.

Digitizing Video for the Web

One option for adding video to your Web site is to digitize existing video for the Web. This section discusses the tools you need to ensure that you achieve the highest quality results when digitizing video.

Hardware Considerations for Digitizing and Editing Video

To digitize video, you need a camcorder or VCR to play the video, the appropriate cable to connect it to a computer, video digitizing hardware, such as that built-in to many Macintosh systems or separate video and audio capture cards, a fast hard drive for capturing video, storage for digital video and audio files, (1–20 MB per second of uncompressed video is not uncommon depending on size, frame rate, and color-depth) and video capture software to control the video digitizing process.

non-linear editing

Macintosh systems are used extensively in the broadcast industry for non-linear editing of digital video. **Non-linear editing** refers to the ability to have random access to any point within a video clip, compared to the linear editing of standard videotape. The best solution for "broadcast quality video" is dedicated video boards and editing workstations, such as those from Avid, Data Translation, SciTex, and Radius. For Web-based video, you may not need these types of high-end systems. Many Macintosh systems have built-in system level support for S-Video video capture. For capturing Web video these systems work great. For example, a PowerMac 8500 can digitize 320×240 S-Video at 25 fps (frames per second) out of the box.

On Windows systems you probably need to buy a video capture card. There are several low cost video capture cards in the $200–$500 range. Many cards come with added features such as video acceleration. Try to get a card with S-Video input, motion video capture, a capture ability of 320×240 size video at 25–30 fps, and a card that comes bundled with video capture software.

Digitizing Video: Quick Tips

The following tips work with most AV-capable Macs, some Windows digitizing boards, and video capture software such as Premiere:

1. Use high quality source, such as S-Video. Make sure your video capture board has S-Video inputs.
2. Defragment your hard drive. Digital video takes up a lot of space. File sizes of 1–20 MB per second of video are not uncommon. Defragmenting your hard drive provides all the free space in one contiguous block, making it easier for the drive to write large files.
3. Use an AV-optimized hard drive or disk array on a fast SCSI bus. AV-optimized hard drives are designed to handle large continuous streams of data. Disk arrays enable several drives to work as one drive, improving performance. RAID (Redundant Arrays of Independent Drives) systems are commonly used by video professionals. Fast SCSI-2, Fast and Wide SCSI-2, and new bus architectures such as Fire Wire, improve video capture performance. Having your video capture program and system software on one hard disk while you capture to another disk can help too.
4. If you have a lot of RAM and the video clip you want to capture is short, consider capturing to a RAM disk.
5. Turn off networking, virtual memory, and unnecessary system extensions.
6. Set compression to None or Component Video. Your video capture software won't have to compress video on

the fly, providing precious CPU cycles for video capture, but the sizes of the captured digital video files will be huge. Check your video capture software and see if there is an option for "Post Compression." This option instructs the software program to defer compressing the video until after you stop recording. Choose the Photo-JPEG codec or the Animation codec set to the highest quality setting in these situations. This preserves most of the video data; your video won't become degraded with further compression.

7. Minimize size of capture (for example 320×240 or 240×180). Generally, you want to capture at the largest size possible and then reduce the size later in post-processing.
8. Turn off video playback while recording.
9. Consider digitizing audio separately.

Understanding Video File Formats

There are various file formats to choose from when creating video for the Web. This section discusses:

- QuickTime
- MPEG
- AVI

QuickTime

QuickTime is a multimedia system extension for Macintosh and Windows computers developed by Apple Computer that provides cross-platform, time-synchronized digital video, digital audio, 3D "virtual reality" environments, and other multimedia data types. It is used in numerous multimedia applications, such as CD-ROM and broadcast video production. QuickTime provides standard interface, playback, and compression/decompression features across multiple platforms. QuickTime is a mature technology, supported by most multimedia authoring tools, and it is the closest thing to a standard, cross-platform multimedia file format. QuickTime playback capabilities are included as standard equipment with Netscape Navigator 3.0 and Microsoft Internet Explorer 2.0, so it has become a major vehicle for Web-based multimedia (see fig. 9.1).

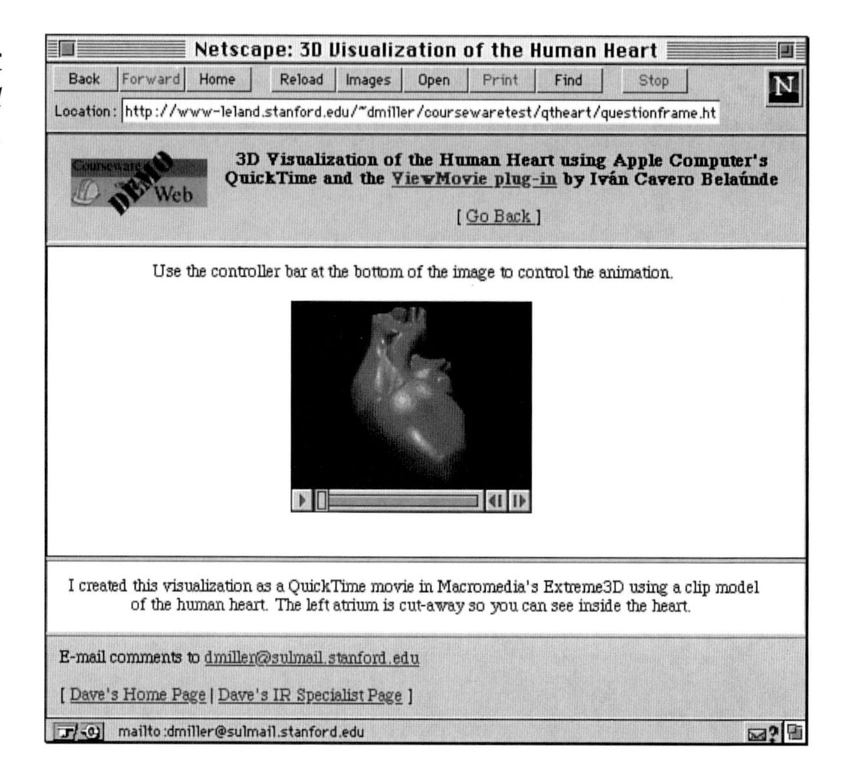

Figure 9.1

QuickTime movie embedded in a Web page.

For many applications, QuickTime is the best cross-platform solution for Web-based video delivery. See Chapter 10 for a more detailed discussion of using QuickTime on the Web.

> **Note**
>
> For the latest versions of the free QuickTime system extensions, QuickTime Virtual Reality tools, and other toys for Macintosh and Windows systems, visit:
>
> **`http://quicktime.apple.com/`**

MPEG

MPEG stands for *Motion Picture Experts Group*. MPEG is a digital video file format specification and compression scheme that was developed by this group. MPEG was one of the first rich media types supported on the Web, and many Web sites have MPEG video and animation.

In the past, MPEG has had limitations, such as the inability to play synchronized video and audio. To create MPEG video usually requires expensive encoding hardware and software. To play back MPEG video smoothly typically requires additional hardware.

MPEG is getting a new lease on life with cheaper encoding and decoding hardware and support in emerging technologies such as DVD (DVD is a new playback technology that is sort of like CD-ROM on steroids; DVD is an acronym in search of a meaning; usually it's taken to mean Digital Video Disc) and the development of MPEG-2 for video-on-demand applications. MPEG playback is supported in many desktop systems with additional, inexpensive hardware.

Support for MPEG

InterVU has developed a cross-platform MPEG player as a Netscape Plug-In. You can find more information at:

`http://www.intervu.com/`

NetTOOB is an inexpensive digital video viewer and helper app for Windows systems that enables viewing of MPEG, QuickTime, and Video for Windows (AVI) files without additional hardware. A version that supports streaming playback is supposedly in the works. For more information visit:

`http://tvnet.com/duplexx/netoob.html`

Sparkle is a Macintosh application that plays back MPEG files without any additional hardware and also converts between QuickTime and MPEG formats. It also enables you to associate an audio file with your MPEG for concurrent audio and video playback (see fig. 9.2). Sparkle is available on the Internet at popular Macintosh software sites, for example:

`http://hyperarchive.lcs.mit.edu/HyperArchive.html`

By the time you read this, MPEG may be installed with QuickTime as just another software-based QuickTime codec. Making MPEG a software-based QuickTime codec ensures MPEG playback on any QuickTime capable system without additional hardware. Another advantage of the new, soon-to-be-released MPEG features in QuickTime is the ability to easily edit MPEG files. This ability has been very rare in the past because of the way the MPEG file format works and has usually required expensive, hardware-based editing suites.

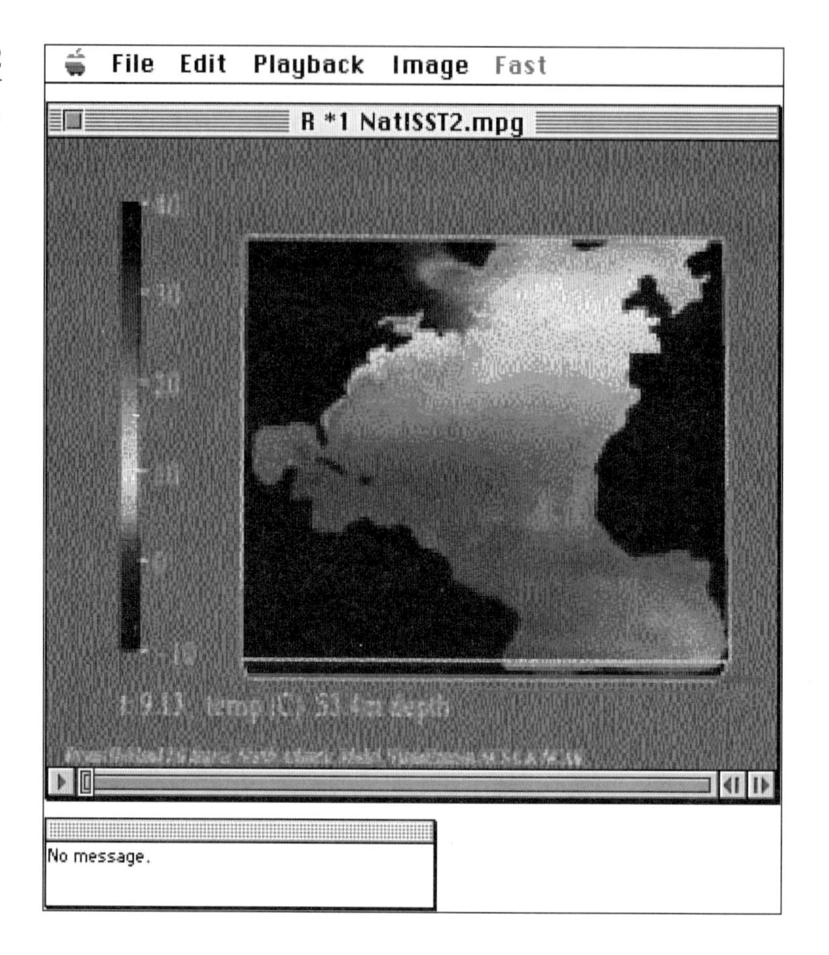

Figure 9.2

Sparkle playing MPEG video.

AVI

AVI stands for *Audio Video Interleave* format. It is the video and animation format used by Video for Windows. Most authoring tools on Windows support the AVI format.

The disadvantage of using AVI files for Web playback is that Mac, SGI, and Sun users have to convert the files to another format for playback. Built-in support for AVI in Netscape Navigator 3.0 is limited to Windows 95 and Windows NT versions.

Also, AVI lacks the sophisticated, track-based, multiple media support and synchronization capabilities of QuickTime. Codecs for QuickTime for Windows are generally more evolved and efficient than their AVI equivalents. There are numerous Macintosh and Windows programs to convert between AVI and QuickTime.

For Macintosh systems, AVI to QuickTime conversion utilities include Video for Windows Utilities 1.1, available at most Macintosh shareware sites. For Windows systems, AVI to QuickTime conversion utilities include Intel's SmartVid, available at:

```
http://www.intel.com/
```

VidEdit is an AVI editing package from Microsoft that was last seen on the Internet at:

```
ftp://ftp.microsoft.com//developr/drg/Multimedia/
➥Jumpstart/VfW11e/ODK/WINVIDEO/
```

Another AVI editor is Personal AVI Editor available from FlickerFree Multimedia at:

```
http://www.flickerfree.com/paesw.html
```

LiveVideo

LiveVideo is a Netscape Plug-In automatically installed with Netscape Navigator 3.0 on Windows 95 and Windows NT systems. The LiveVideo Plug-In plays video files in AVI format on Windows 95 and Windows NT only. The current version also enables control of video playback from JavaScript. For more information on using LiveConnect, see Chapter 14, "Scripting Multimedia Web Pages."

Embed AVI content in HTML documents for Windows 95 and Windows NT versions of Navigator the same way you embed other Plug-In media, with the `EMBED` tag. Here's an example:

```
<EMBED SRC="myAVIMovie.avi AUTOSTART= TRUE LOOP= FALSE
WIDTH=160  HEIGHT= 120>
```

Streaming Video Formats

Streaming, as described earlier, is the continuous delivery of time-based media, such as animation, audio, or video, to a user's machine. The user doesn't have to wait for the file to be completely downloaded before viewing the content. The rest of the file is downloaded from the server—streamed in the background while the animation or other time-based media plays on the client's computer screen.

Streaming can be tricky to implement, because Internet data is packet-based and wasn't designed for the delivery of continuous, synchronized, time-based data. Interruptions in the continuous data stream can cause stutters and gaps during animation playback.

Data-rates for streaming video are typically around 60 KB/s, somewhat practical over fast intranets but barely usable over modem. Even at that rate, video is typically displayed in a small 160×120 window at low frame rates (1–10 fps or less). Web-based, streaming video products include VDOnet Corp.'s VDOLive and Xing Technology's StreamWorks. Viewers are typically free, but both require expensive servers for playback. Streaming video solutions are often scalable; they can adjust playback and data-rates in real-time, based on network traffic and bandwidth. Most solutions try to preserve audio at the expense of video on the assumption that audio break-ups and pauses are more disconcerting to users than video breakup.

VDOLive

VDOLive provides free players for Windows, Macintosh, and Unix systems. VDOLive also provides a free small-scale evaluation server and free authoring utilities. Pricing for server software is based on the number of video streams. Encoding and authoring software is included with the server. The free evaluation server supports up to 2 short video streams, while the commercial server supports up to 100.

VDOLive uses a proprietary, scalable wavelet compression scheme that is termed VDOWave. At low-bandwidth, the compression scheme trys to preserve frame rates and audio at the expense of image quality. Content providers can provide a single high-resolution file that automatically scales its resolution based on bandwidth and network traffic. Figure 9.3 illustrates VDOLive playback with a helper app over a 14.4 modem connection.

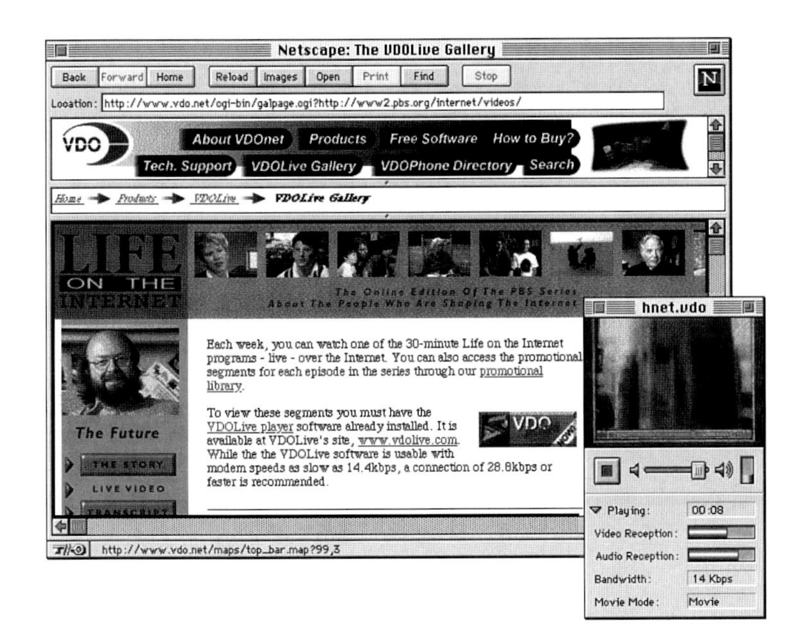

Figure 9.3

Streaming VDOLive video over a 14.4 modem connection.

Hardware Requirements

To create VDOLive content you need:

- Windows 95 or Windows NT.
- Pentium (recommended).
- 8 MB RAM.
- 16-bit sound card.
- Video-capture board that can capture uncompressed video at 160×120 at 15 fps.
- Encoding software. Free encoding utilities are provided by VDOLive. More powerful encoding solutions are provided with the server software. Adobe Premiere for Windows 4.2 can also save files to the VDOWave format.

Visit `http://www.vdo.net/` for more information and downloading of demos, free tools, and viewers.

StreamWorks

StreamWorks provides free players for Windows, Macintosh, and Unix systems. StreamWorks is a little different from VDOLive—it is designed to be a real-time encoding/decoding, multi-point, broadcasting service. Pricing for server software is based on the bandwidth of the connection. Proprietary, expensive encoding, and authoring hardware/software cost extra.

StreamWorks uses a variation of MPEG compression. At low-bandwidths, the compression scheme tries to preserve image quality at the expense of frame rate. At low-bandwidth, such as 28.8 modems, StreamWorks video resembles a high-quality slide show.

Visit: `http://www.streamworks.com/` for more information.

Other Streaming Formats

Here are some other streaming tools you might want to consider using:

MovieStar Maker

MovieStar Maker from Intelligence at Large is an inexpensive, yet powerful QuickTime authoring tool designed to create streaming QuickTime movies. Movies playback with audio and video synchronization and do not require any special server intervention. Users need the MovieStar Plug-In for Macintosh or Windows systems and QuickTime or QuickTime for Windows installed to take advantage of streaming capabilities, otherwise the movies download like normal QuickTime movies.

Vosaic

Vosaic is a new streaming video scheme for the Internet from Vosaic Corp. that doesn't use TCP/IP. Instead, it uses a proprietary protocol called VDP (Video Datagram Protocol) that adapts playback to available bandwidth and network traffic. It delivers streaming video at about 10 frames per second with AM-quality sound over a 28.8-Kbps modem.

For more information go to:

`http://www.vosaic.com`

ActiveMovie

ActiveMovie is Microsoft's OLE/ActiveX technology for playback of digital video and audio on the Web. It is currently in beta and only supported in Internet Explorer 3.0 for Windows 95 and Windows NT. Release versions and other platform support may be available by the time you read this.

ActiveMovie purportedly supports playback of AVI (Video for Windows), QuickTime, MPEG video, WAV, AU, AIFF, and MPEG audio. The ActiveMovie Streaming Format (ASF) is a new media format that supports streaming media content on the Web.

For the latest on ActiveMovie visit:

`http://microsoft.com/imedia/activemovie/activem.htm`

Embedding ActiveMovie Content in HTML Documents

Embedding an MPEG movie with the ActiveMovie ActiveX control looks like this:

```
<OBJECT ID="ActiveMovie" WIDTH=160 HEIGHT=120
➥CLASSID="CLSID:05589FA1-C356-11CE-BF01-00AA0055595A">
<PARAM NAME="FileName" VALUE="myMPEG.mpg">
<PARAM NAME="AutoStart" VALUE="1">
<PARAM NAME="ShowControls" VALUE="1">
<PARAM NAME="ShowDisplay" VALUE="0">
</OBJECT>
```

The CLASSID parameter is required and is usually included in the documentation that comes with the ActiveX control. The CODEBASE attribute, not shown here, enables automatic downloading of the appropriate ActiveX control.

Creating QuickTime Content

Note

http://www.QuickTimeFAQ.org/ is an excellent source of QuickTime information and software and home of the unofficial QuickTime FAQ.

Links to numerous cross-platform QuickTime tools and comparisons of QuickTime and MPEG are maintained by Robert Lentz at:

http://www.astro.nwu.edu/lentz/mac/qt/home-qt.html.

There are numerous tools on Macintosh to create QuickTime movies. On Windows the choices are more limited, but include Adobe Premiere and CorelMOTION 3D. Windows authoring choices will probably increase with the release of QuickTime for Windows 2.5, which supposedly will provide support for Windows authoring.

All of Chapter 10, "Animating With QuickTime Digital Video," is devoted to creating QuickTime movies and animations for Macintosh and Windows systems.

Converting AVI files to QuickTime

If you are creating AVI files on Windows and you want to reach the broadest audience, you will probably want to convert your AVI files to QuickTime format.

Macintosh

On Macintosh, AVI to QuickTime conversion utilities are in the following list (see fig. 9.4).:

Video for Windows (VfW) Utilities 1.1 for Macintosh:

ftp://mirrors-aol.com/pub/info-mac/gst/mov/video-for-➥windows-11p.hqx

http://hyperarchive.lcs.mit.edu/HyperArchive.html

QT to AVI Utility:

http://hyperarchive.lcs.mit.edu/HyperArchive.html

Windows

On Windows, AVI to QuickTime conversion utilities include:

- Intel's SmartVid: http://www.intel.com/
- SF Canyon's TRMOOV.EXE: http://www.sfcanyon.com/

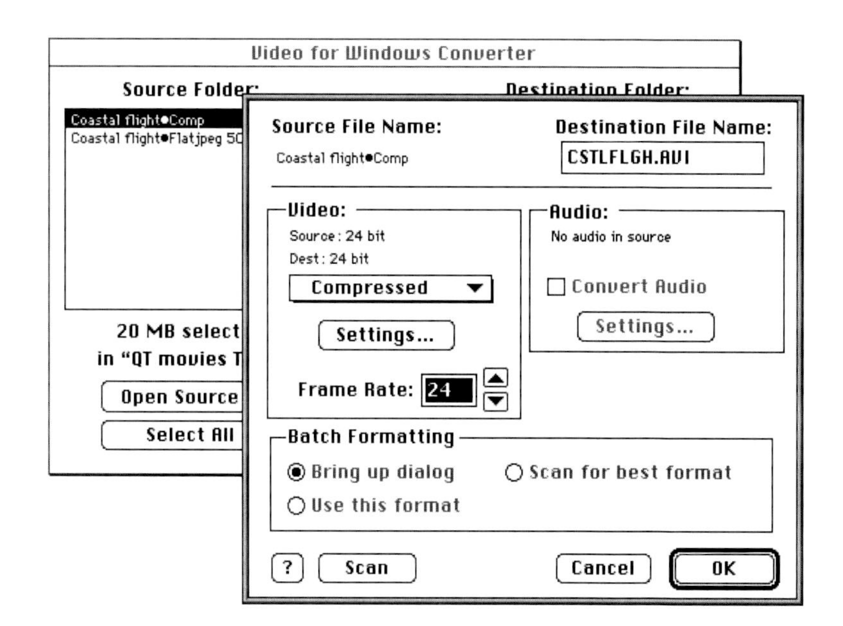

Figure 9.4

Converting AVI to QuickTime with Video for Windows Utilities for the Mac.

SmartVid is available free and is very easy to use. To convert AVI to QuickTime using SmartVid, follow these steps:

1. Choose Open: Source under the File menu.
2. Choose Start under the Convert menu.
3. Type a file name.
4. Choose a destination drive and directory.
5. Select a format (either AVI or QuickTime).

SmartVid also comes in a DOS version for batch processing (see fig. 9.5).

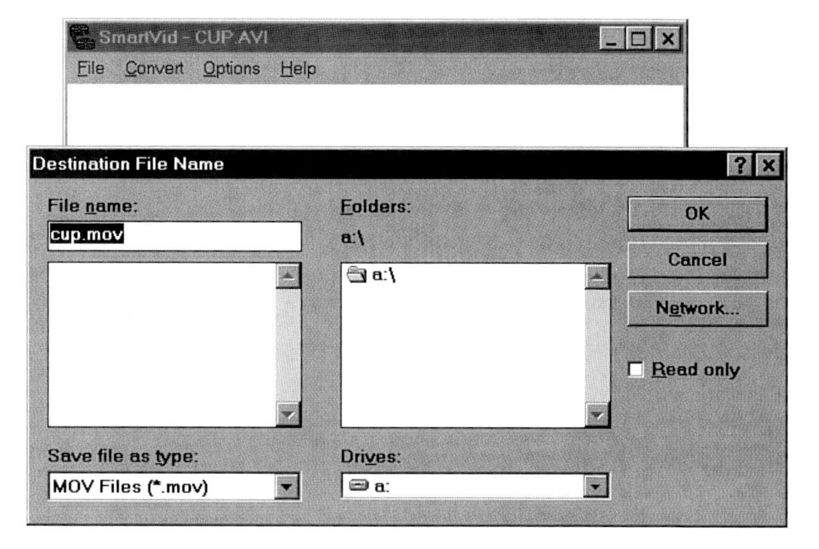

Figure 9.5

SmartVid AVI/QuickTime conversion utility for Windows.

Converting MPEG files to QuickTime

Sparkle, as introduced earlier in this chapter, is a Macintosh program that can convert MPEG to QuickTime and vice versa. Sparkle is available at popular software archive sites such as:

```
http://hyperarchive.lcs.mit.edu/HyperArchive.html
```

Creating Other Digital Video Content

This section takes you through the creation of your own video in AVI format step-by-step, the native format of Windows systems. AVI video will only playback on Windows systems. To be able to view AVI video, users on Macintosh and Unix have to download Web-based AVI video and convert it with a separate conversion utility. Inline AVI video is supported in Windows versions of Navigator and MSIE.

There are a number of editing tools that can be used to create your AVI video content.

Adobe Premiere

Adobe Premiere is a cross-platform video editing tool that enables you to create QuickTime, AVI, and VDOLive format videos. See Chapter 10 for tutorials on how to use Premiere, including how to create transitions effects and composite multiple videos. To create output other than QuickTime in Premiere, choose the output option you would like when you choose the Make Movie... command.

Macromedia Director

Macromedia Director is another cross-platform tool that enables you to create QuickTime video on Macintosh and AVI video on Windows. To create AVI movies in Director for Windows, follow these steps:

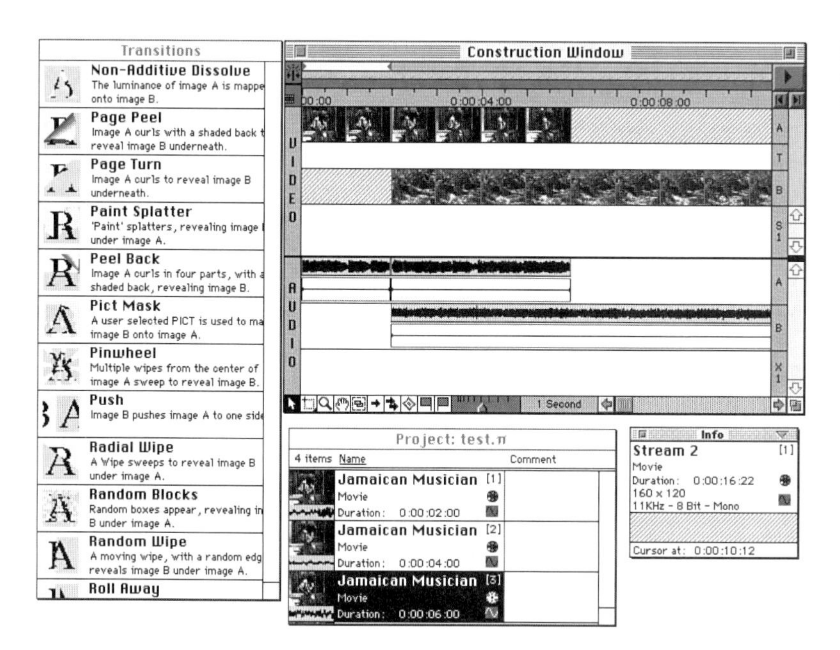

Figure 9.6

Creating movies in Premiere.

1. Choose Export under the File menu.
2. Choose Video for Windows (.AVI) in the Format: pop-up menu.
3. Click the Options button (see fig. 9.7).

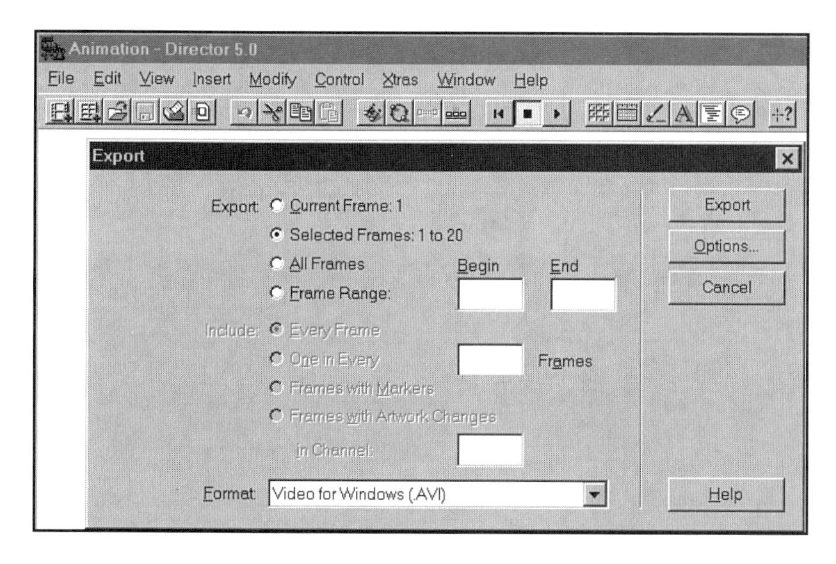

Figure 9.7

AVI Export options in Director.

4. Select the compressor you want to use from the Compressor: pop-up (see fig. 9.8).
5. Adjust other settings if you want.

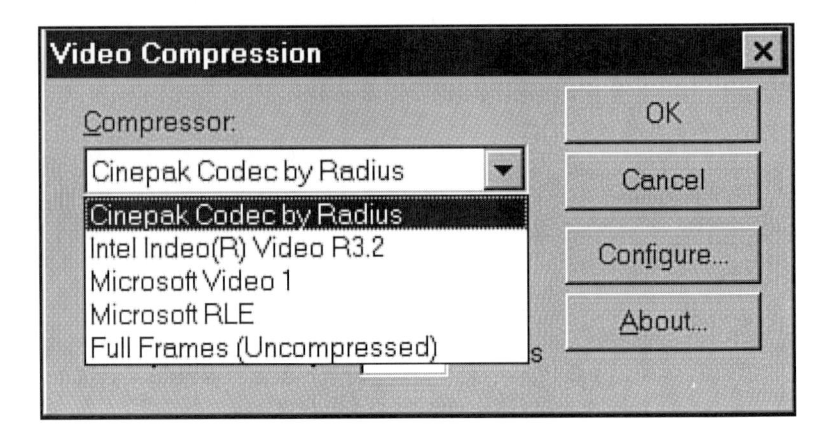

Figure 9.8

AVI compression options.

Warning

The compressor you choose must be present in the user's systems for playback. Microsoft Video 1 is included with the Video for Windows installation and should be present on most users' systems on Windows.

Other AVI Editing Tools

Other AVI editing tools you can choose from include:

- VidEdit, an AVI editing package from Microsoft that can be found on the Internet at:

  `ftp://ftp.microsoft.com//developr/drg/Multimedia/Jumpstart/VfW11e/ODK/WINVIDEO/`

- Personal AVI Editor available from FlickerFree Multimedia at:

  `http://www.flickerfree.com/paesw.html`

Personal AVI Editor has an interface very similar to Premiere. Figure 9.9 illustrates Personal AVI Editor. Personal AVI Editor also provides additional compression settings for AVI video so you can fine tune compression and quality tradeoffs for different delivery environments (see fig. 9.10).

VDONet provides free tools for the creation of short clips for their video streaming products. The VDOLive format is also included as an output file format in Adobe Premiere for Windows 4.2. Visit: `http://www.vdo.net/` for more information and downloading of demos, free tools, and viewers.

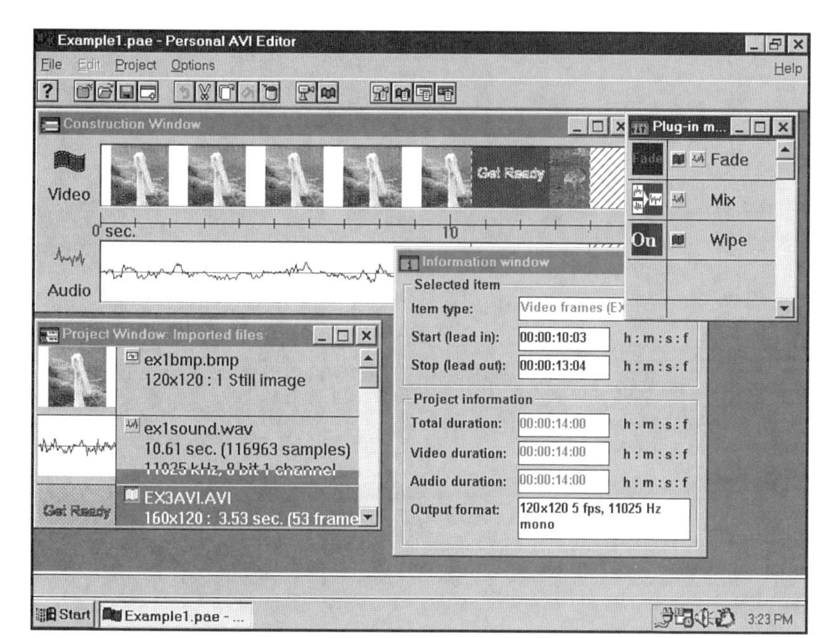

Figure 9.9

Interface of Personal AVI Editor.

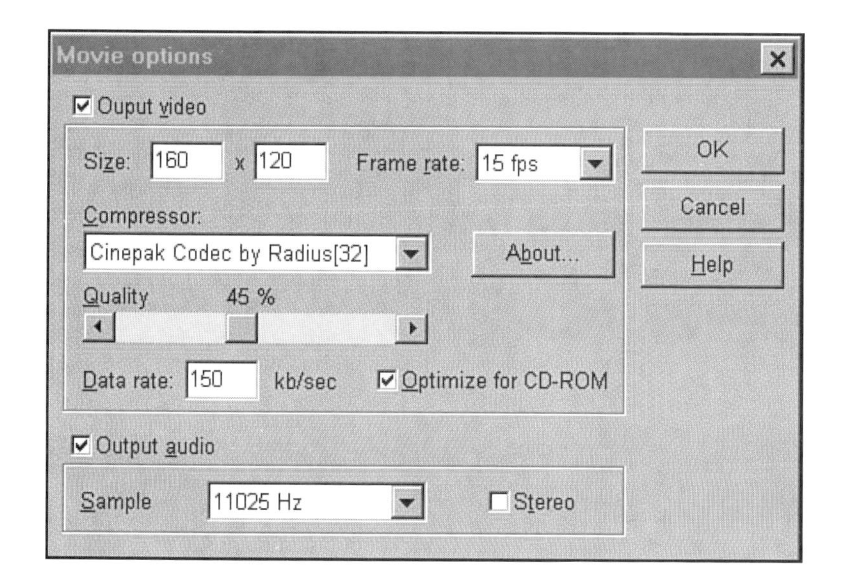

Figure 9.10

Additional compression options Personal AVI Editor.

Embedding AVI Content in MSIE for Windows

To embed Video for Windows (AVI) files (or VRML worlds) in an HTML document for Windows version of the MSIE browsers, use the DYNSRC attribute. The DYNSRC is a custom attribute to the `IMG` tag only supported in MSIE for Windows (see fig. 9.11).

The DYNSRC attribute is used like so:\ `<IMG SRC="MyMovieFrame.gif" DYNSRC = "MyMovie.avi" HEIGHT=120 WIDTH=160>`

Where "`MyMovie.avi`" is the AVI that will be played inline and "`MyMovieFrame.gif`" is the the alternate GIF file that will be displayed in browsers that don't support the DYNSRC attribute, such as Netscape Navigator and MSIE for Macintosh.

The following section provides some HTML code that accommodates some of the variations in browser support.

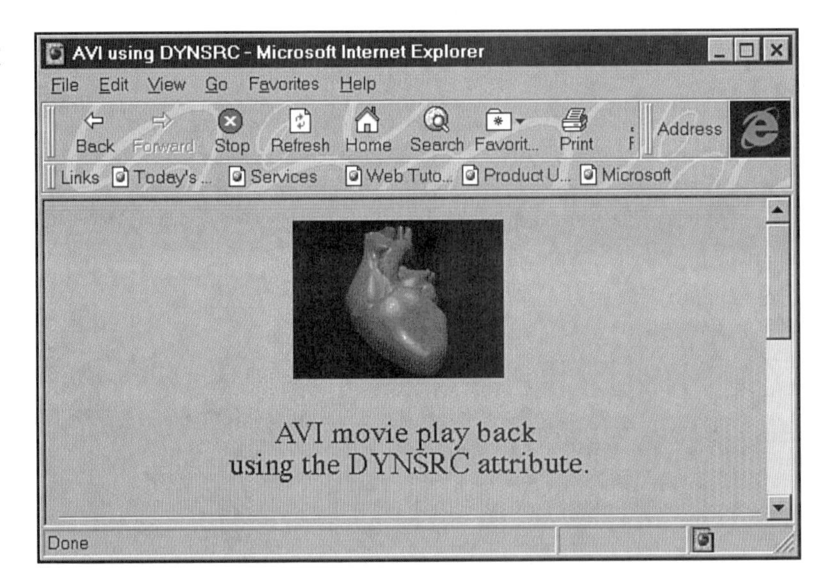

Figure 9.11

Inline AVI in MSIE 3.0.

Providing Alternate Digital Video Content for Multiple Browsers

The following HTML:

- Displays a QuickTime movie in browsers that support the `EMBED` tag and have QuickTime playback.
- In browsers that don't support the `EMBED` tag, it:

1. Displays an alternate GIF
2. Displays an AVI with DYNSRC attribute in Windows versions of Internet Explorer

- Provides a link to the content in browsers that have a helper app set up.

```
<EMBED SRC="MyQT.mov" HEIGHT=144 WIDTH=160
PLUGINSPAGE = "http://quicktime.apple.com/qt/sw/
➥sw.html">
<NOEMBED>
<IMG SRC="MyQTFrame.gif"  DYNSRC = "MyQT.avi"
HEIGHT=120 WIDTH=160>
```

If you don't have the QuickTime Plug-In, but have a QuickTime helper app, click on the link shown below to view the movie.

```
</NOEMBED>
```

You can also view the original `<A HREF="MyQT.mov"> QuickTime movie </A>` if you have your browser set up with the correct helper application.

Using Video-Conferencing on the Web

Desktop video-conferencing applications enable users on the Internet and intranets to share real-time video, real-time audio, and data.

To use the software, you need the tools listed in the Tools box.

Tools
■ Camcorder
■ Computer with motion video-input capabilities
■ TCP/IP Internet connection
■ Fast network, although some applications are just barely practical over fast modems

Shared video is typical in small 160×120 windows, with low frame rates, (1–10 fps) and audio is telephone quality or less.

Users can share data in the the form of text and images, shared whiteboards, and even applications.

multicasting

reflectors

Users can connect point-to-point, for a one-on-one video conference such as a video "phone call." Users can also join multiple participants in a video "conference call." Another option available in some applications is the ability to **multicast** or to send the same video stream to multiple computers. Programs such as CU-SeeMe and Enhanced CU-SeeMe require server software and dedicated computers called **reflectors** to provide multiple participant video-conferences. Users connect to this dedicated machine to participate in a multi-user conference. Other programs, such as QuickTime Conferencing , BeingThere from Intelligence At Large, and VideoPhone from Connectix do not require servers or reflectors for multi-user conferences.

This section looks at some video-conferencing systems that are inexpensive, accessible, and relatively easy to use.

Why Use Video-Conferencing with the Web?

CU-SeeMe, Enhanced CU-SeeMe, and QuickTime Conferencing can be set up as helper apps to launch automatically from a Web page. The Web page could provide additional information and multimedia content that would support and complement a video conference. For example, you could set up a video conference of a lecture at a remote site and then provide supporting text and graphics, such as course notes, in an accompanying Web page. Users could visit your page at the pre-set "webcast" time, and launch the video-conference by clicking on a hyperlink.

Video-Conferencing Standards

Video conferencing applications use different communication standards to send video and audio data back and forth. Interoperability between different applications depends on support for these standards.

UDP is the communications protocol used by CU-SeeMe and Enhanced CU-SeeMe. UDP is similar to TCP, but is more suited to transmitting video and audio streams.

H.320 is a communications standard set by the International Telecommunications Union (ITU) that is supported by QuickTime Conferencing, VideoPhone, BeingThere, and Intel Proshare. The H.320 standard enables interoperability of video-conferencing systems on ISDN or faster networks. The H.323 LAN conferencing standard is an emerging standard for video-conferencing on LANs.

Reducing Network Bandwidth Requirements

Video-conferencing is very bandwidth intensive. Desktop video-conferencing over the Internet via modem is barely possible today. It's important that users and server administrators understand network impacts and ways to reduce bandwidth requirements.

Some video-conferencing packages come with servers or reflectors that provide bandwidth management features. For example, you can limit the transmission rates of individual data streams.

Most video-conferencing applications have bandwidth detection features that enable them to adjust the proportion of the available network bandwidth that they use based on the available bandwidth and network traffic. This feature is especially important over shared, local-area-networks or intranets.

Most video-conferencing applications enable users to adjust audio and video transmission rates. Some applications enable users to set transmission ceilings or maximum transmission rates that help reduce bandwidth requirements. Some applications also enable users to reduce the resolution of the video they are sending to low resolution or standard resolution. Users can help reduce bandwidth requirements further by not transmitting useless video of empty offices or conference rooms or audio of a radio station or background noise. In many applications decreasing the total number of open video windows also decreases bandwidth requirements.

Tip

Consider not using audio at all and communicating via text-based "chat" windows. On modems, simultaneous video and audio is barely usable.

Note

Michael Sattler provides valuable CU-SeeMe information at:

`http://www.indstate.edu/msattler/sci-tech/comp/CU-SeeMe/index.html`

CU-SeeMe

CU-SeeMe is free video conferencing software for Macintosh and Windows systems developed at Cornell University that enables desktop video-conferencing on the Internet. It was originally developed for Macintosh by Cornell University's Information Technology group.

You need a TCP/IP connection to the Internet to use CU-SeeMe. It works very slowly over modems. CU-SeeMe enables you to:

- Send and receive gray-scale video in 160×120 windows.
- Send and receive AM-radio quality audio.
- Have point-to-point, one-on-one video-conferences, such as a video "phone call," with other CU-SeeMe users.
- Participate in multi-user video conferences using CU-SeeMe Unix-based reflector software.
- Communicate with other conference participants with text-based "chat" features with an additional Plug-In.
- Share graphics up to 640×480 in size with other users in a video conference on the Macintosh with an additional Plug-In.

Hardware Requirements-Macintosh

To receive audio and video on most Macintosh systems, you don't need any additional hardware or software.

To send video on a Macintosh you need either:

- A Connectix QuickCam
- A camcorder and an AV-capable Macintosh
- A camcorder and a video capture board

To send audio on a Macintosh, you generally don't need any additional hardware. Just use the audio input features built-in to most Macs.

Hardware Requirements-Windows

To receive audio and video on Windows systems, you need an 8-bit 256-color display, a sound card that conforms to the Windows Multimedia Specification, and speakers.

To send video on a Windows system you need either:

- A Connectix PC QuickCam.
- A camcorder and a video capture board that supports Microsoft Video for Windows.

To send audio you need a sound card that conforms to the Windows Multimedia Specification and a microphone. Support for full-duplex audio is handy.

Multi-user conferences require Unix-based reflector software.

Mac and Windows versions of CU-SeeMe can be obtained from:

```
ftp://cu-seeme.cornell.edu/pub/
```

Note

A list of Windows hardware compatible with CU-SeeMe is available at:

```
http://cu-seeme.cornell.edu
```

Frame Rates

For modem users, video frame rates can be 1 frame per second or less, and video is characterized by blocky artifacts.

Performance over LANs and faster Internet connection, such as ISDN or T1 is much better. Adjusting video and audio transmission rates can improve performance, but it generally takes some experimenting with settings to find optimal settings.

Note

To find out about the inexpensive QuickCam video camera with built-in digitizer visit:

```
http://www.connectix.com/
```

Unfortunately, at this time the free version of CU-SeeMe is only partially compatible with the PCI PowerMacs. Although it is possible to connect to video conferences and receive video and audio, it may not be possible to send video. Visit the CU-SeeMe Web site at Cornell for the latest updates.

Tip

Again, remember that you may get better rates if you turn off audio and communicate via text-based chat. On modems, simultaneous video and audio is barely usable.

Adjusting Audio and Video Digitizing, Transmission, and Reception in CU-SeeMe

When you start CU-SeeMe, the Local Video window, shown in figure 9.12, displays your local video feed. You access many of the controls for CU-SeeMe from this window. Along the bottom of the window is a row of buttons that enables you to access various options. The right-most button is the option button.

Figure 9.12

Local Video window in CU-SeeMe.

If you don't see video in your Local Video window, you may need to tell CU-SeeMe which digitizer to use:

1. Click on the option button.
2. Select Video from the options pop-up menu.
3. Select your digitizer from the digitizer pop-up menu (see fig. 9.13).

Figure 9.13

Selecting a video digitizer in CU-SeeMe.

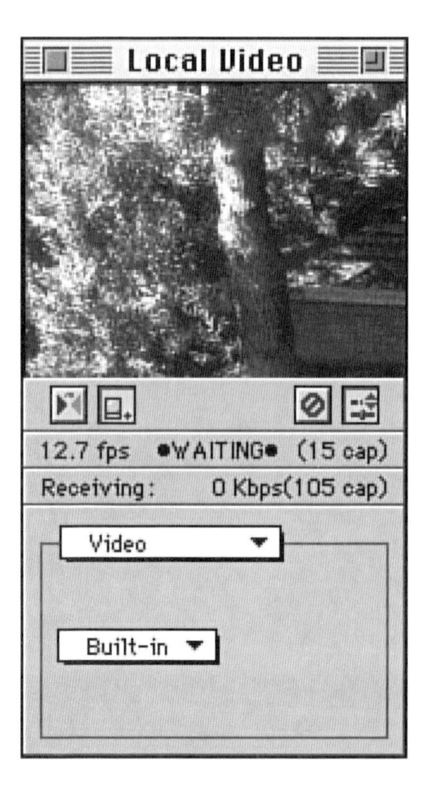

To adjust transmission settings:

1. Click on the option button.
2. Select Transmission from the options pop-up menu.
3. Adjust the rates for various settings using the arrow buttons (see fig. 9.14).

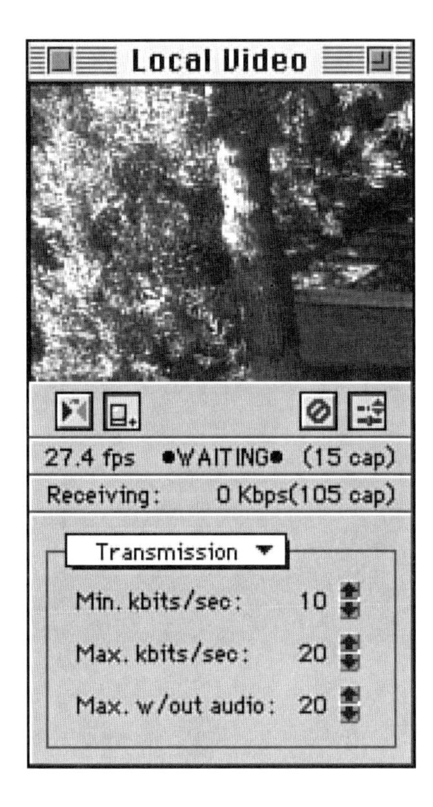

Figure 9.14

Adjusting transmission settings in CU-SeeMe.

Follow a similar procedure for Reception settings adjustments.

Connecting to Other CU-SeeMe Users

To connect to another person using CU-SeeMe, you need to know their IP address. This address is in the form:

```
123.456.789.0
```

and is the number used to identify a machine on the Internet. You can find out your own IP address by looking at the TCP/IP network settings on your machine. These settings vary from machine to machine and with different software, depending on the type of Internet connections you have. Consult the documentation on your Internet connection software or consult your Internet service provider for information on how to find out your IP address.

1. Choose Connect under the Connection menu.
2. Type in the numeric IP address of another person using CU-SeeMe. For a multi-user conference, enter the IP address of a reflector (see fig. 9.15).

Figure 9.15

Connect dialog box in CU-SeeMe.

Tip

Michael Sattler provides a list of reflectors at:

`http://www.indstate.edu/msattler/sci-tech/comp/CU-SeeMe/reflectors/make_nicknames/CUSeeMe_Nicknames`

Enhanced CU-SeeMe

Enhanced CU-SeeMe for Macintosh and Windows is a commercial desktop video-conferencing software from White Pine Software. It is based on Cornell University's free CU-SeeMe. The interface is very similar to the freeware version. To use Enhanced CU-SeeMe you need a TCP/IP connection to the Internet that runs over modems (28.8 kps recommended).

With Enhanced CU-SeeMe for Macintosh and Windows you can:

- Send and receive up to 24-bit color video in 160×120 windows.
- Send and receive audio.

- Utilize text-based chat window.
- Utilize shared white board communications.

Multi-user conferences require a dedicated Unix-based or Windows NT-based server. For information on White Pine's commercial version of CU-SeeMe and instructions on how to get a free demo version, check out their Web page at:

```
http://goliath.wpine.com/cu-seeme.html
```

```
http://goliath.wpine.com/cuprodinfo.htm
```

Adjusting Audio and Video Digitizing, Transmission, and Reception in Enhanced CU-SeeMe

When you start up Enhanced CU-SeeMe, the Local Video window displays your local video (see fig. 9.16). You access many of the controls for Enhanced CU-SeeMe the same way you do for CU-SeeMe— with the right-most button or option button along the bottom of the video window.

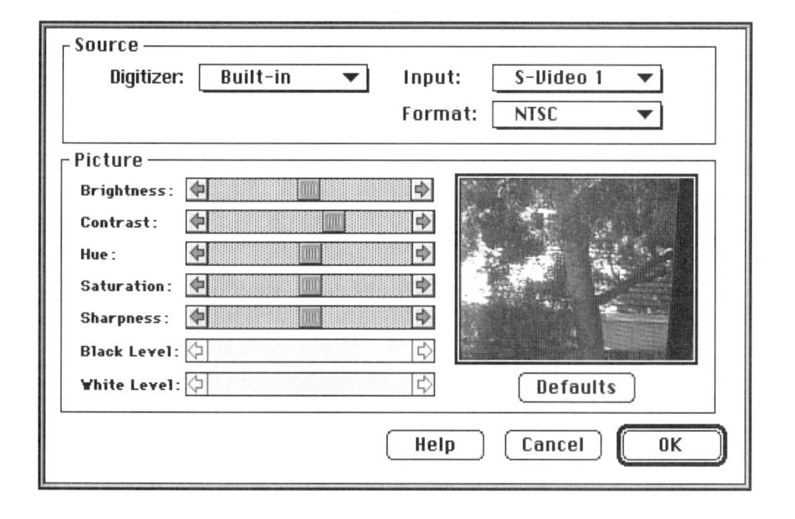

Figure 9.16

Digitizer setup in Enhanced CU-SeeMe.

If you don't see video in your Local Video window, you may need to set up your digitizer (see fig. 9.17):

1. Click on the option button.
2. Select Audio/Video in the Group pop-up in the Preferences dialog box.

3. Click on the Set button next to Digitizer in the Video box.
4. Select the digitizer from the Digitizer pop-up menu.

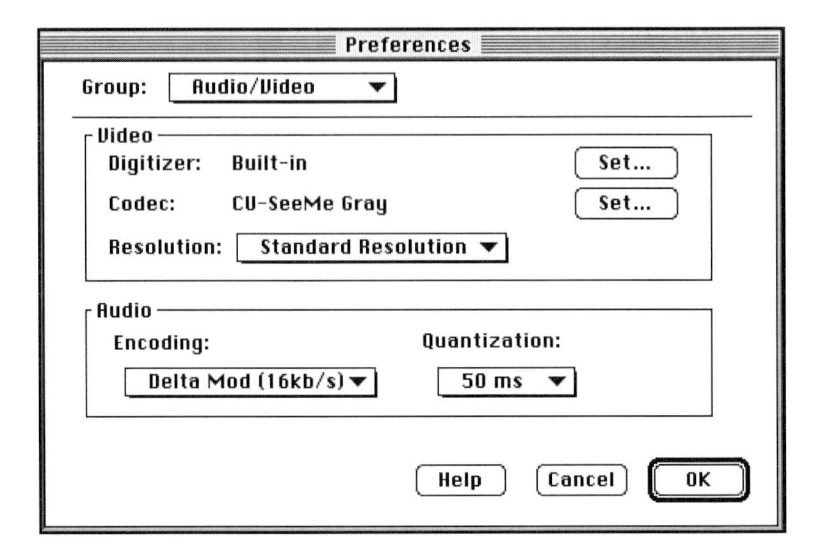

Figure 9.17

Adjusting settings in Enhanced CU-SeeMe.

To adjust transmission and reception settings:

1. Click on the option button.
2. Choose Communications in the Group pop-up menu in the Preferences dialog box.
3. Adjust the rates for various settings using the arrow buttons.

Connecting to Other CU-SeeMe Users With Enhanced CU-SeeMe

The procedure for connecting to other users with Enhanced CU-SeeMe is similar to the procedure for connecting with free CU-SeeMe. Again, you need to know their IP address. Then follow these steps:

1. Choose Call: address under the Connection menu or choose Phone Book under the Connection menu if you have saved the address in your Phone Book (see fig. 9.18).
2. Type in the numeric IP address of another person using CU-SeeMe. For a multi-user conference, enter the IP address of a reflector.
3. Click Call.

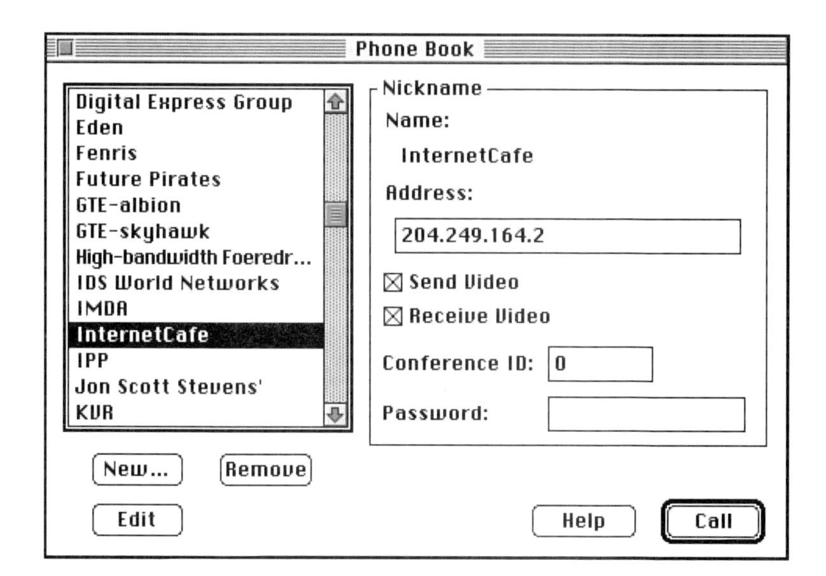

Figure 9.18

Phone book in Enhanced CU-SeeMe.

Launching Enhanced CU-SeeMe from a Web Page

To set up a Web page for use with Enhanced CU-SeeMe you need to:

- Configure your Web server with the correct MIME type (see the next section).
- Create a video conference launcher ASCII text file.
- Configure user's Web browsers to use Enhanced CU-SeeMe as a helper app.

Configuring a Web Server to Recognize Enhanced CU-SeeMe MIME Type

To configure a Web Server to recognize the Enhanced CU-SeeMe MIME type, you must set up your server's configuration file so that it associates the file name extensions "`.cu or .csm`" with type "`application/x-cu-seeme`". Consult your Web server documentation or Web server administrator about configuring the Web server for different MIME types.

Creating the Video Conference Launcher File

The video conference launcher file contains parameters Enhanced CU-SeeMe can use to configure the Web-based video conference. This file must contain the IP address of the video conference or reflector where you would like to connect and the video conference ID number. You can also set various options, such as the maximum transmission rate or the number of visible windows. The file must be a plain ASCII text file that has a file name extension of ".cu" or ".csm".

To launch Enhanced CU-SeeMe from a Web page, create a hypertext link to the video conference launcher file. For example:

```
<A HREF = "myVideoConference.csm">Join the video con-
ference, already in progress! </A>
```

The contents of the file "myVideoConference.csm" might look like:

```
123.444.555.6

0
```

where 123.444.555.6 is the IP address of the conference and 0 is the conference ID. Add additional options following these two lines. Here is a list of the currently supported options:

- **Settings.**

Max Windows=n	n is the number of video windows you want visible on the screen

- **Flow Control.**

MaxCap=n	n is the maximum sending rate
MinCap=n	n is the minimum sending rate
UseFlowControl= Yes	Yes to enable flow control, No to disable

- **Connect Options.**

IWillSendVideo= Yes	Yes to send video, No to send none
IWillRecvVideo= Yes	Yes to receive video, No to receive none
IWillSendAudio= Yes	Yes to send audio, No to send none
IWillRecvAudio= Yes	Yes to receive audio, No to receive none

Setting Up Enhanced CU-SeeMe as a Helper App

The following directions show how to set-up Enhanced CU-SeeMe as a helper application in Navigator 2.0. The process is similar in other browsers.

1. From the Netscape Options menu, choose General Preferences/Helpers.
2. Click the New button.
3. Type in the Mime type **application**.
4. Type in the Mime sub-type **x-cu-seeme**.
5. Type in the extension **cu, csm**.
6. Set the Action to Launch Application.
7. Click on Browse, and select the Enhanced CU-SeeMe application. On Windows, make sure Enhanced CU-SeeMe is in your path, or specify the full pathname for the CU-SeeMe executable.
8. Close the preferences panel of Netscape, and close Netscape. Then, restart Netscape.

QuickTime Conferencing

QuickTime Conferencing is a Macintosh system extension, similar to QuickTime, that enables video-conferencing and collaborations over networks. QuickTime Conferencing is based on open, cross-platform video-conferencing standards. Apple Computer and Intelligence at Large may have a Windows version of QuickTime Conferencing available by the time you read this. Products that use QuickTime Conferencing include: BeingThere for Macintosh and Windows from Intelligence At Large, VideoPhone for Macintosh from Connectix, and the Apple QuickTime Conferencing Kit for Macintosh. Macintosh versions of Netscape Navigator 2.0 and later are configured to use the free QuickTime Conferencing Helper Application as a helper application. The free helper app and other inexpensive software, as well as more information about QuickTime Conferencing, is available at:

```
http://qtc.quicktime.apple.com
```

With QuickTime Conferencing software, a video-conferencing application, an AV Macintosh or a non-AV Mac and extra video board, and a camcorder you can:

- Send and receive up to 24-bit color video in 160×120 windows.
- Send and receive audio.
- Share graphics, text, and sounds via a shared whiteboard.
- Participate in a multi-user video-conference with up to six people at once without the need for special servers or reflectors.

Currently, QuickTime Conferencing works on high-speed networks (ISDN, LANs, or WANs). Modem support may be included with some QuickTime Conferencing-based products by the time you read this. Support for the H.320 international standard for videoconferencing requires extra, inexpensive hardware.

VideoPhone

Connectix VideoPhone for Macintosh is a video-conferencing application for local-area networks and ISDN that includes the QuickCam video camera and digitizer. VideoPhone supports point-to-point and multi-user connections. Full H.320 support requires purchasing an H.320 hardware board. Modem support is planned for a future version.

You'll need a Centris, Quadra (except Quadra 605 or 630) or PowerPC-based Macintosh; a microphone and speaker; System 7.1.1 or later (System 7.5 recommended); and a high-speed connection, typically either ISDN or EtherTalk.

Visit `http://www.connectix.com/` for more information.

BeingThere

BeingThere is an inexpensive conferencing and collaboration software for Internet (ISDN or faster), LAN, and WAN connections. BeingThere supports point-to-point and multi-user conferences without the need for dedicated server connections. As of this writing, the Macintosh version was available and the Windows version was in beta.

You'll need a Centris, Quadra (except Quadra 605 or 630) or a PowerPC based Macintosh, a microphone, System 7.5.1 or later, and a high speed network connection. H.320 support requires purchasing an H.320 hardware board. Modem support is planned for a future version.

Visit `http://www.beingthere.com/` for more information.

Intel ProShare

Intel's ProShare is a Windows-only video-conferencing package designed for use over ISDN or faster networks. It is compatible with the H.320 video-conferencing standards. To find out about the range of products available, pricing, and feature set, visit:

```
http://www.intel.com/
```

Conclusion

Over the next year, there will be many exciting developments in networked digital video that will make it easier to provide digital video content on the Web. Right now, just-in-time, on-demand Web-based digitial video is possible if you are willing to put up lower quality and frame rate compared to most CD-ROM solutions. Over fast intranets, Web-based digital video is currently a viable solution that provides rich content and collaborative services.

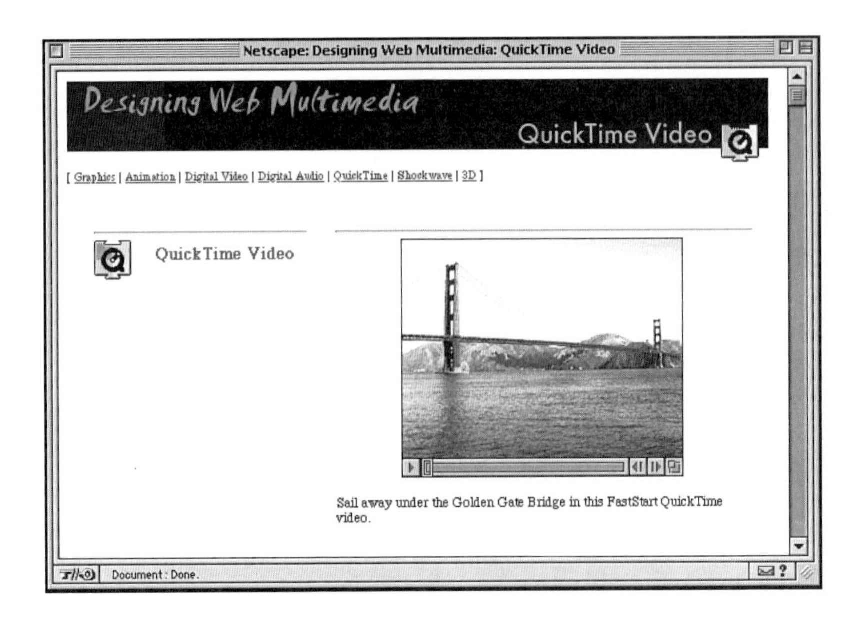

QuickTime has become the closest thing to a standard, cross-platform multimedia container format. QuickTime playback capabilities are built-in to the major Web browsers, but it is more than just digital video. This chapter covers video and animation.

chapter

10

Animating with QuickTime Digital Video

QuickTime is a multimedia system extension for Macintosh and Windows computers developed by Apple Computer. It is used in numerous multimedia applications, such as CD-ROM and broadcast video production, to deliver cross-platform, time-synchronized digital video, digital audio, 3D "virtual reality" environments, and other multimedia data types. QuickTime playback capabilities are included as standard equipment with Netscape Navigator 3.0 and Microsoft Internet Explorer 2.0, so it has become a major vehicle for Web-based multimedia as well.

Why use QuickTime for Web-based multimedia? QuickTime provides standard interface, playback, and compression/ decompression features across multiple platforms (see fig. 10.1). QuickTime is a mature technology supported by most multimedia authoring tools and has become the closest thing to a standard, cross-platform multimedia file format. One of the most compelling reasons to use QuickTime content on the Web is that QuickTime is now integrated with Netscape Navigator and Microsoft Internet Explorer. Developers can be certain that over 90 percent of end users have QuickTime playback capabilities and can develop content accordingly.

Figure 10.1

A QuickTime animation illustrating the standard QuickTime interface.

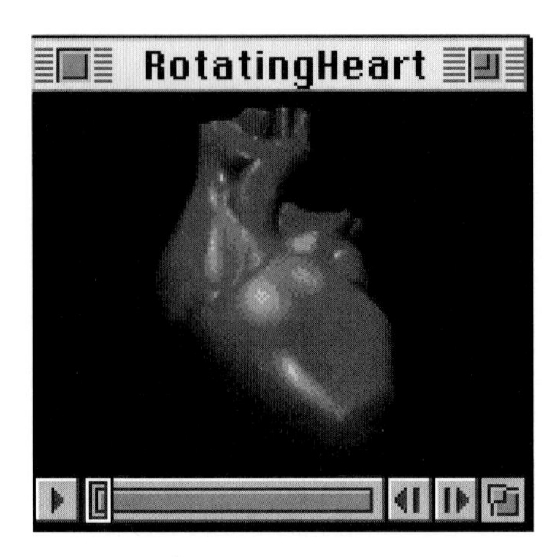

There are numerous freeware, shareware, and commercial applications you can use to create QuickTime content. Most 2D and 3D animation and digital video editing programs output to QuickTime movies. In addition, there are converters that convert most other digital video and animation formats to QuickTime format. New software tools and compression/decompression algorithms (codecs), such as Terran Interactive's Movie Cleaner Pro and the H.263 codec, are emerging to address the special needs of Web-based multimedia.

Many multimedia firms, video production houses, and CD-ROM publishers have legacy QuickTime content that can be repurposed for the Web (see fig. 10.2). Creating Web-based QuickTime content from scratch or repurposing existing CD-ROM or disk-based QuickTime for the Web involves more variables and limitations, compared to creating content solely for CD-ROM, for example.

This chapter discusses some of the issues involved in creating Web-based QuickTime digital video and animation. See Chapter 11, "Audio," for a discussion on using the audio features of QuickTime on the Web, Chapter 12, "3D and Virtual Reality," for a discussion of using QuickTime Virtual Reality on the Web, and Chapter 15, "Java," for a discussion on how to turn existing QuickTime content into Java applets.

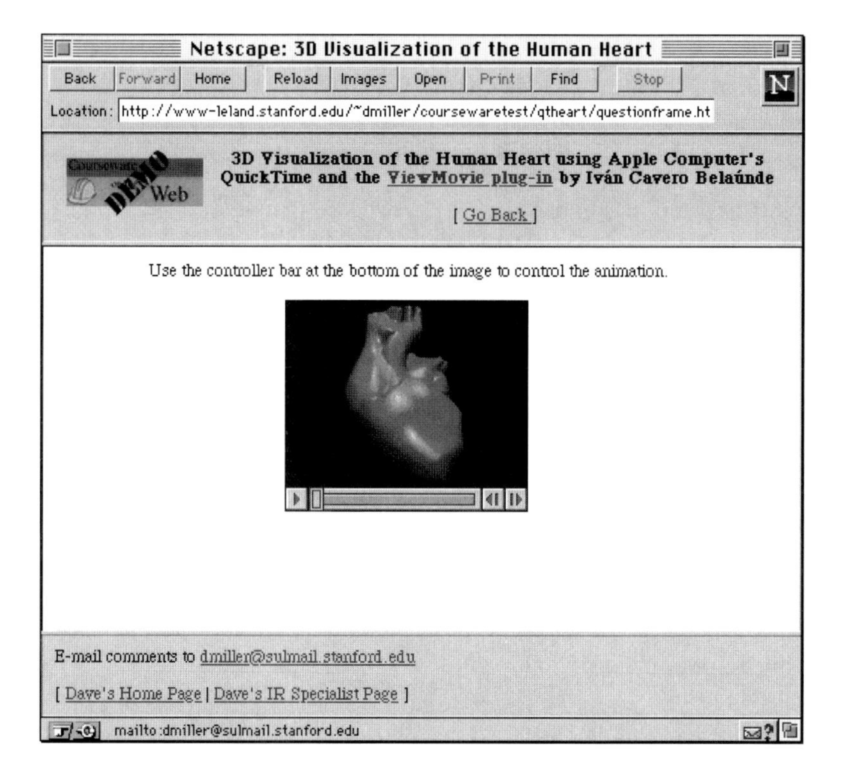

Figure 10.2

A QuickTime animation embedded in a Web page.

This chapter provides:

- A brief overview of QuickTime technology.
- Information on the various ways you can provide QuickTime digital video and animation on the Web, with an emphasis on the new capabilities of Netscape 3.0 and the bundled QuickTime Plug-In.
- Step-by-step examples of using QuickTime authoring tools and QuickTime Virtual Reality authoring tools to create QuickTime multimedia and embed them in your Web page.

See Chapter 9, "Video," for more tips on providing video content on the Web.

QuickTime Technology Overview

QuickTime is a system extension for Macintosh and Windows. It enables applications to display and playback many different kinds of digital media. QuickTime also comes with sophisticated compression/decompression features that are essential for the playback, storage, and editing of digital media.

Media Types

In a QuickTime file, each media type is stored on a separate track. The tracks are automatically synchronized to provide consistent playback across platforms. QuickTime currently supports many different media types as listed in the following paragraphs. You can use QuickTime to create movies and animation, create sound-only movies without pictures, display compressed 24-bit graphics, or enable users to navigate through 3D worlds.

As of this writing, the media types supported on both Macintosh and Windows systems are:

- Digital video
- Digital audio
- QuickTime Virtual Reality
- QuickTime Music (MIDI-compatible synth track)
- Graphics up to 24-bit

As of this writing, additional media types supported on the Macintosh are:

- Text
- Sprites
- 3D Geometry (QuickDraw 3D)
- 3D Animation (Tween tracks)
- Time code

These Macintosh-only media types will supposedly be supported in future versions of QuickTime for Windows and may be available by the time you read this. Software-based MPEG playback for Mac and Windows may also be available in future versions of QuickTime.

As of this writing, the most recent version of QuickTime for the Macintosh is version 2.5. The most recent version for

Windows is version 2.1.2. The Windows version of QuickTime 2.5 should be available by the time you read this. Apple, Truevision, Data Transaltion, and Macromedia are collaborating to port the full QuickTime 2.5 feature set to Windows 95/NT.

The latest versions of the QuickTime system extension for Macintosh and Windows are available for free at:

`http://quicktime.apple.com/sw/sw.html`

For the latest information on QuickTime, check out:

`http://quicktime.apple.com/`

What You'll Need To Use QuickTime

To view QuickTime files you will need a QuickTime-enabled viewer. To create content, you will need an editing application that supports the QuickTime file format. A simple viewer and editor is included in the free QuickTime distribution from Apple.

QuickTime Web Browser Plug-Ins

Plug-Ins are a new feature of Netscape Navigator 2.0 and later that enable developers to extend the functionality of the Netscape Web browser. Microsoft's Internet Explorer 2.0 for Macintosh also supports Netscape Plug-Ins. Most Netscape Plug-Ins generally don't work in Internet Explorer 2.0 for Windows, as of this writing.

QuickTime Plug-Ins for Macintosh and Windows versions of Netscape Navigator 2.0 include the MovieStar Plug-In from Intelligence at Large and numerous others. Apple Computer's cross-platform QuickTime Plug-In for Netscape 3.0 is automatically installed when you install Netscape Navigator 3.0 or later. The QuickTime Plug-In is compatible with Macintosh systems running System 7 or later and with PCs running Windows 3.1, 95, or NT. It will playback all existing QuickTime media types directly within an HTML document in Netscape Navigator 3.0 or later and Macintosh versions of Internet Explorer 2.0 or later. The QuickTime Plug-In from Apple is not compatible with Netscape Navigator version 2.0.

Besides being part of the standard Netscape 3.0 installation, the latest version of the QuickTime Plug-In for Macintosh and Windows systems is available from:

`http://quicktime.apple.com/sw/sw.html`

More information on using the QuickTime Plug-In is provided later in this chapter.

QuickTime Virtual Reality (QTVR)

QuickTime VR (QTVR) is a cross-platform "virtual reality" technology from Apple Computer. QTVR movies are special QuickTime movies that enable users to move through 3D environments, pick up and manipulate 3D objects, and activate hot spots embedded in the 3D scene. The user interacts with the 3D environment with a mouse and keyboard. Users don't need high-end workstations, special headsets, goggles, or other peripherals as they do in other virtual reality environments. QTVR movies are characterized by high-quality photographic images, fast playback, and small file size. QTVR is optimized for photographic images, but it also works with computer-generated images.

To add QuickTime VR capabilities to the Netscape QuickTime Plug-In (so you can view QTVR scenes embedded in a Web page), you will need the QuickTime VR components file. You can download these free components for Macintosh and Windows computers from Apple's QuickTime Web site:

`http://quicktime.apple.com/sw/sw.html`

A free QTVR player and helper application for Macintosh and Windows systems and sample QTVR movies are also available from Apple Computer's web site.

For more information on creating and using QTVR in your Web pages, see Chapter 12, "3D and Virtual Reality".

Features of QuickTime 2.5

QuickTime 2.5 has many playback enhancements enabling smoother playback at larger sizes with higher data rates than previous versions. QuickTime 2.5 provides several optimizations and accelerations for authoring, including substantially increased performance with popular video boards, support for

M-JPEG-A and M-JPEG-B used by these boards, and support for multiple processors. Also included are significant enhancements to the QuickTime MIDI architecture, which should enable very high-quality/ low bandwidth music playback, the ability to natively import many different graphic formats such as GIF and Adobe Photoshop files, and improved audio/video synchronization.

Beginning with QuickTime 2.5, 3D objects are just another media type in QuickTime. You can embed 3D objects saved in the 3DMF file format directly in QuickTime files. The 3DMF or 3D Meta-File format is a file specification from Apple used by QuickDraw 3D and has been adopted as the basis for the file format of VRML 2.0. Users will need to have the QuickDraw 3D system extension installed to interact with 3DMF objects. Animation and geometric data for the 3D object are contained in separate tracks, providing very compact files. The 3D features in QuickTime were in beta testing at the time of this writing. These new 3D features built into QuickTime will provide a powerful new way to deliver 3D animations on the Web.

QuickTime for Windows 2.5 will also supposedly provide significant support for Windows authoring, such as the capability to compress movies with the built-in QuickTime compressors.

Codecs

Codecs contain highly optimized software algorithms that will compress a QuickTime movie when you create it and then decompress it when you play it back. Several different software-based codecs are automatically installed with QuickTime. Which codec works best for your movie depends on the movie's content. If you compress a movie with a particular codec, the same codec must be installed on the user's machine for the movie to playback. For that reason, it's a good idea to stick with the standard codecs that ship with every version of QuickTime. In version 2.1, the following decompression components of codecs ship with both Macintosh and Windows versions of QuickTime:

- Animation
- Cinepak
- Graphic

- None
- Photo—JPEG
- Video
- Photo CD
- Intel Indeo

QuickTime movies compressed with these codecs will playback on both Macintosh and Windows systems.

Lossless Codecs

Lossless codecs preserve all the original movie data when they perform compression. Lossless compression schemes typically use types of run-length encoding, an algorithm that works well with large regions of flat, solid colors. Lossless codecs generally work with computer-generated animations. In QuickTime, the Animation codec set to the most quality setting is a lossless compression scheme.

Lossy Codecs

Lossy codecs will discard some of the original movie data when they compress your movie. Once discarded, the data is gone. This is why it's not a good idea to compress QuickTime movies more than once. If you repeatedly use a lossy codec, more data is lost in each compression pass, degrading the movie's image quality. Cinepak is a lossy compression scheme that is commonly used to create movies for CD-ROM.

Frame Differencing

frame differencing

Frame differencing is a form of temporal compression. It is a way of compressing your movie based on the changes between frames. Frame differencing works best in movies with little movement between frames; for example, a "talking head" against a static background. In frame differencing, redundant data between frames is compressed or discarded. Thus, the movie doesn't have to store data for the entire frame. It only stores the differences between frames. Temporal compression schemes typically enable you to specify key frames (frames against which other frames are compared for differences). Key frames in QuickTime codecs are different from the key frames in animation programs.

Spatial Compression

Spatial compression compresses data in a single frame. Run-length encoding, in which large areas of flat, solid color can be represented by a simple mathematical formula rather than as a bitmap, is a form of spatial compression.

spatial compression

Effectiveness of Different Codecs

One way to measure the effectiveness of a codec is by its compression ratio. The **compression ratio** is the ratio of the original size of the source material to the size of the compressed material. Another measure of the effectiveness of a codec is the time required for compression and decompression. Some codecs, such as Cinepak, are asymmetric, which means it takes a long time to compress source material but very little time during playback.

compression ratio

As of this writing, there are no codecs specifically designed for optimal Web playback, although new codecs specifically for Web playback of QuickTime, such as H.263 for video and G.723 for audio, may be available by the time you read this. QuickTime codecs are generally optimized for use with video source and for digital video playback at 16-bit or 24-bit color-depths. Digital video is characterized by complex color fields, such as skin tones, and live action motion. In contrast, animation is characterized by areas of flat, solid color or narrow color gradients. Playback at 8-bits is sufficient for many animations. You may get better compression ratios from sprite-based or vector-based animation programs for some of your animations.

Because Web-multimedia is usually downloaded to the client hard disk for playback, file size and download time are the main limiting factors. After it is on the client hard disk, playback will be limited only by the speed of the user's hard drive and the processing speed of the user's computer. With new features such as QuickTime Fast-Start and the new H.263 codec, limiting the data rate of your QuickTime movie becomes an important consideration. Which codecs to use for Web playback of digital video and animation are discussed in a following section.

Data Rate

Data rate is an important limiting factor when delivering time-based media such as QuickTime and digital video. For a detailed discussion on data rate, see the previous chapter. On the Web, until recently, QuickTime and other digital video formats have been largely a "wait for it to download and then play it" technology, which means file size is a more important factor than data rate in initiating playback.

The new Fast-Start feature of Web-based QuickTime (described in a subsequent section), although not true streaming, has improved the user experience somewhat, by enabling the start of playback before the entire file is downloaded to the user's hard disk. For Fast-Start movies, lower data rates generally result in faster playback. Most QuickTime content, though, will benefit by being optimized for Fast-Start, whatever the data rate.

Data rate limiting of Fast-Start movies will generally require compromises in image quality, movie size, and movie frame rate. As with most Web-based multimedia, it's a tradeoff. If it's more important that users see video quickly and view the video while it is downloading in real-time, then low data rate movies with the Fast-Start feature will help. If image quality is more important, file sizes and data rates should be higher and users will have to wait longer to see playback of the video.

If you use QuickTime's Fast-Start feature, the first frame will be displayed and a progress bar in the movie controller will indicate the amount of video that can be played back at any one time. High data rate video may pause while it waits for more incoming data, but users will still be able to see the first frame and play the first parts of the video as the rest downloads in the background.

QuickTime and other digital video is more practical on corporate and university intranets, in which data rate and bandwidth limitations approach that of a slow CD-ROM. You can repurpose QuickTime content to provide just-in-time learning and on-demand training videos for students and employees. On corporate and university intranets, you can generally get by with file sizes in the 100KB–1MB range and data rates in the 40–50 KBs range. For modem users, strive for movies with file sizes in the 20 KB–40 KB range and data rates in the 1–3 KBs range.

Data rate limiting will become more important in the future, as open, cross-platform compression schemes used in video-conferencing programs, such as QuickTime Conferencing, MBone, and CU-SeeMe are integrated with QuickTime. Some QuickTime codecs, such as Cinepak, enable you to set a maximum data rate to your movie. Codecs such as Cinepak are called data rate limiting codecs.

QuickTime on the Web

There are basically two ways to view QuickTime content on the Web.

- The first uses helper applications and is compatible with most browsers. QuickTime movies are downloaded to the client hard disk and then displayed in a separate application such as MoviePlayer, SimpleText, or PLAYER.EXE. Until early 1996, this was the standard way to view QuickTime content. This is also the way to view QuickTime Conferencing.
- The second way uses Netscape-compatible Plug-Ins to playback QuickTime content directly in the Web page. To view QuickTime content this way, you will need at least Netscape Navigator 2.0 or Microsoft Internet Explorer 2.0, and one of the supported Plug-Ins. Beginning with Netscape 3.0, a QuickTime Plug-In is bundled with all Netscape browsers and is supported on both Macintosh and Windows platforms.

Helper Applications

One way to provide QuickTime content on the Web that is compatible with most browsers is to use helper applications. A helper application is a separate viewer application on the client machine. When your browser encounters a data type it doesn't understand, it can automatically launch the helper application to handle the data type. Your browser knows what helper application to launch, based on the file name extension of the data. For example, if your browser is asked to display a file with the `.mov` extension, it realizes it is a QuickTime movie, downloads this file to the client hard disk, and then automatically opens the file with SimpleText or PLAYER.EXE.

Note

You can find out more about helper applications at:

`http://home.netscape.com/assist/helper_apps/index.html`

In your HTML document you create links to QuickTime movies using the HREF tag. Clicking a link to a QuickTime movie starts the download of the movie file. When the movie file is completely downloaded to the client hard disk, the helper application is opened to playback the movie. For this to work, your QuickTime movies must have file names ending in the `.mov` or `.qt` extensions and you must configure your Web browser for a QuickTime helper application. Here is an example of some HTML code that creates a link to a QuickTime movie:

You can also view a `<A HREF="MyQTMovie.mov"> QuickTime movie </A>` if you have your browser set up with the right helper application.

`"MyQTMovie.mov"` is the path name to the QuickTime movie file on the Web server. In this case, the QuickTime movie file is in the same directory as the HTML document. Note the `.mov` extension in the file name.

When the user clicks on the link "QuickTime movie" the browser starts downloading the QuickTime movie file called `"MyQTMovie.mov"`. If the user has configured their browser correctly, a helper application is opened to playback the movie after the file has been completely downloaded. If the user has installed a QuickTime Plug-In, clicking on the link will display the movie within a new browser window (see fig. 10.3).

Configuring Browsers for QuickTime Helper Apps

To configure a helper app for QuickTime, tell your browser that files ending in `.mov` and `.qt` have the MIME type video or quicktime and should be launched by an appropriate QuickTime player application such as SimpleText, MoviePlayer or PLAYER.EXE.

If you have Netscape Navigator 2.0, it should come configured for playing QuickTime content with the MoviePlayer, SimpleText, or PLAYER.EXE. Different browsers will have different procedures to configure helper applications. The following directions show how to set up a helper application for QuickTime content in Navigator 2.0. The process is similar in other browsers.

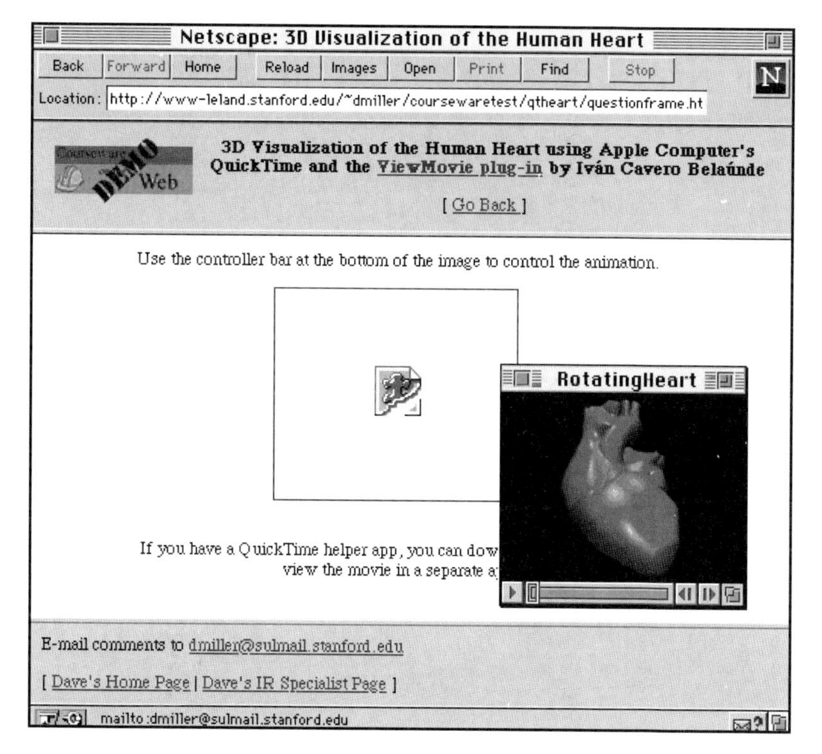

Figure 10.3

A QuickTime animation displayed by a helper app.

1. From the Netscape Options menu, choose General Preferences/Helpers, as shown in figure 10.4.
2. Type the Mime type **`video`**.
3. Type the Mime sub-type **`quicktime`**.
4. Type the extension **`.qt`**,**`mov`**.
5. Set the Action to Launch Application.
6. Click on Browse and select the application you want to use to display and playback QuickTime content, such as MoviePlayer or SimpleText on a Macintosh, PLAYER.EXE on Windows, or PLAY32.EXE on Windows 95.
7. Close the preferences panel of Netscape, and close Netscape. Then restart Netscape.

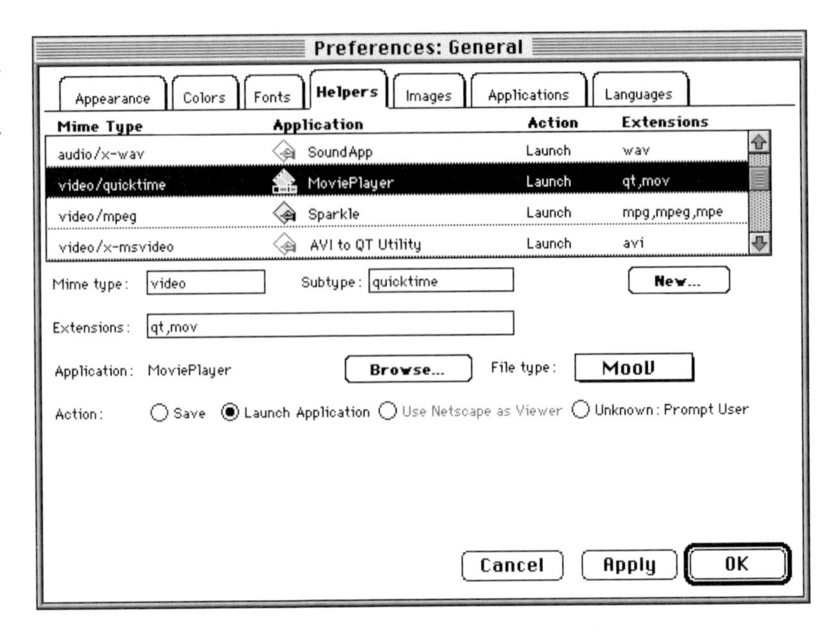

Figure 10.4

The helper application configuration dialog box from Netscape 2.0.

Note

You can also download QuickTime helper apps from Netscape's Web page at:

`http://home.netscape.com/assist/helper_apps/variety.html`

Obtaining QuickTime Helper Applications

On Macintosh, the recent version of the SimpleText application that is shipped with all Macs displays QuickTime movies. MoviePlayer, a more full-featured QuickTime viewer and editor, is available free with the QuickTime for Macintosh distribution.

You can download the free MoviePlayer application for Macintosh systems or the free PLAYER.EXE application for Windows systems and PLAY32.EXE for Windows 95/NT from:

`http://quicktime.apple.com/qt/sw/sw.html`

For both QuickTime and QTVR playback you can download the free, cross-platform QTVR Player at:

`http://qtvr.quicktime.apple.com/`

A QTVR extension to the MoviePlayer application may be available by the time you read this.

QuickTime Support in Internet Explorer

Internet Explorer 2.0 for the Macintosh has a built-in, automatic QuickTime viewer that works much like a helper app.

When you click on a link referencing a QuickTime movie, the movie is automatically opened in a separate viewing window. Internet Explorer doesn't require the user to configure anything or have a separate viewing application.

Internet Explorer 3.0 will implement QuickTime support using ActiveMovie ActiveX controls. As of this writing, the ActiveMovie ActiveX control for QuickTime was not available for Internet Explorer 3.0 for Windows 95 and NT. It will purportedly be available sometime in the fall of 1996. Support for QuickTime in Windows 3.1 and Macintosh versions of Internet Explorer 3.0 will come later, maybe by the time you read this.

You will embed QuickTime content for Internet Explorer 3.0 with the OBJECT tag. See Chapter 9, "Video," for a description of using the OBJECT tag with Microsoft's ActiveX controls for video.

Using QuickTime Browser Plug-Ins

Plug-Ins can be used to provide viewers for different media types. Media types are viewed directly in the Web page without the need to launch a separate viewer application. Plug-In media are placed in an HTML document using the EMBED tag.

There are several Netscape Plug-Ins that enable viewing of QuickTime content in Web pages. Most Plug-Ins are available free for download over the Internet.

Netscape Plug-Ins are also supported by the Macintosh version of Internet Explorer 2.0. The Windows version of Internet Explorer 2.0 generally doesn't support Netscape Plug-Ins. This section discusses the QuickTime Plug-Ins that are compatible with version 2.0 of Netscape Navigator and the Macintosh version of Internet Explorer 2.0.

The QuickTime Plug-In from Apple Computer is bundled with Netscape Navigator 3.0 for all Macintosh and Windows systems. This Plug-In is not compatible with version 2.0 of Netscape Navigator and is discussed in a following section. The following table lists browsers and supported QuickTime Plug-Ins.

Table 10.1

QuickTime Plug-In Browser Support

cell Windows/Navigator 2 = MovieStar

cell Windows/Navigator3 = QuickTimePlug-InBuiltin,MovieStar

cell Windows/IE2 = not available

cell Mac/Navigator 2 = MovieStar,ViewMovie, MacZilla

cell Mac/Navigator3 = QuickTimePlug-InBuiltin,MovieStar,MacZilla

cell Mac/IE2 = native,non-inline QuickTime support,MovieStar

Plug-Ins are placed in Netscape's Plug-Ins folder which is in the same folder as the Navigator application.

Place QuickTime movies into an HTML document using the EMBED tag.

Here is some sample HTML:

```
<EMBED SRC="MyQT.mov" HEIGHT=144 WIDTH=160 PLUGINSPAGE=
"http://quicktime.apple.com/qt/sw/sw.html" AUTOSTART =
➥TRUE  AUTOPLAY = TRUE>
```

The value of the SRC parameter is the path name to your QuickTime movie on the Web server. Be sure to include the HEIGHT and WIDTH parameters, which are the dimensions of your movie in pixels (add 24 to the HEIGHT for display of the default QuickTime controller). A detailed description of the parameters are given in a later section.

QuickTime Plug-Ins for Navigator 2.0 include MovieStar from Intelligence at Large, ViewMovie from Ivan Cavero Belacende, and MacZilla from Knowledge Engineering.

ViewMovie by Ivan Cavero Belacende was one of the first QuickTime Plug-Ins. It has some nice features, including the ability to use movies as link anchors and image maps. As of this writing, it was Macintosh-only, although a Windows 95 version is supposed to be in the works.

MacZilla by Knowledge Engineering is a Navigator 2.0 Plug-In that plays QuickTime, MPEG, AVI video, WAV, AU, and AIFF audio, and comes with a built-in game to keep you company during long downloads. MacZilla's unique compo-nent architecture enables the Plug-In to extend and update itself over the Net with the click of a button. As of this writing, only Macintosh versions were available, although Windows 95 and Windows 3.1 versions had been announced.

MovieStar Plug-In

MovieStar is a QuickTime Plug-In from Intelligence at Large for Mac, Windows 3.1 ,and Windows 95. The MovieStar Plug-In supports Fast-Start QuickTime, a new feature (described in the following section) specially designed for Web playback. Using MovieStar Maker, an inexpensive QuickTime authoring tool, you can perform further Web playback optimization, such as creating streaming movies. Users will need the MovieStar Plug-In to take advantage of these optimizations. If users do not have the MovieStar Plug-In, MovieStar optimized QuickTime movies will playback normally.

The MovieStar Plug-In supports Netscape Navigator 2.0 for Macintosh and Windows, Netscape Navigator 3.0 for Macintosh and Windows, and Internet Explorer 2.0 for Macintosh. It doesn't support QTVR under Windows. It supports additional HTML tags for compatibility with older QuickTime Plug-Ins, but it does not support some of Apple's HTML tags, including those for QuickTime VR.

See Chapter 7, "Animation," for a tutorial on how to use MovieStar to create animations that can be exported as QuickTime movies or GIF animations.

QuickTime Plug-In for Netscape 3.0

The QuickTime Plug-In from Apple Computer is automatically installed with Netscape Navigator 3.0 or later for Macintosh, Windows 3.1, Windows 95, and Windows NT platforms. The QuickTime Plug-In will play QuickTime content, referenced by the EMBED tag within an HTML document, directly in the browser window. You no longer need a "helper application," although helper applications will still work. The Plug-In can play any QuickTime media type supported on the host system, such as digital audio, text, MIDI, and other kinds of media. If you have downloaded and installed the QuickTime VR component, available free from Apple's Web site, you can view QuickTime Virtual Reality movies too.

Note

The QuickTime Plug-in has features developed specifically for Web playback. The new "Fast-Start" feature will display the first frame of a movie almost instantly and enables the movie to start playing before it has been completely downloaded. This feature reduces the amount of time you spend waiting for the movie to download, but is not true streaming video.

Besides being automatically installed with the 3.0 release of Netscape Navigator, the QuickTime Plug-In can also be obtained from Apple's QuickTime site:

```
http://quicktime.apple.com/sw/sw.html
```

In this release, the QuickTime Plug-In only supports Netscape Navigator 3.0 or later. It does not support Navigator 2.0. Support for other browsers may be added in the future.

In Netscape Navigator 3.0, you can assign different Plug-Ins to display different types of content, similar to helper apps. To enable the QuickTime Plug-In, you may need to select the QuickTime Plug-In the "Options/General Preferences/Helpers" dialog box.

Most of the information presented here regarding the QuickTime Plug-In and Netscape 3.0 is based on beta versions of the software, the most recent versions at the time of this writing. Some features will have changed by the time you read this.

System Requirements for the QuickTime Plug-In

The recommended system requirements for the QuickTime Plug-In for Macintosh users are:

- Macintosh or Power Macintosh running System 7 or later.
- Navigator 3.0 or later.
- QuickTime 2.1 or later.
- Macintosh Sound Manager 3.2 or later.
- Apple QuickTime Plug-In for Netscape Navigator (automatically installed with Netscape 3.0).
- QuickTime VR (Virtual Reality) Components.
- Netscape Navigator (Macintosh).
- Sufficient free RAM (9–17 MB).
- For best performance, turn Virtual Memory off.

Macintosh RAM requirements depend on what system and which version of Navigator 3.0 or later you use.

The recommended system requirements for the QuickTime Plug-In for Windows users are:

- A 386, 486, or 586/Pentium PC running Windows 95, NT or 3.1.
- 8 MB RAM.
- Netscape Navigator 3.0 or later.
- QuickTime 2.1.1 for Windows.
- Apple QuickTime Plug-In for Netscape Navigator (automatically installed with Netscape 3.0).
- Version 1.0.3 or later of the QuickTime VR (Virtual Reality) for Windows software (QTVRW.QTC).

As of this writing, the beta versions of Netscape Navigator 3.0 have steep RAM requirements which may delay its adoption.

Obtaining the QuickTime System Extension

As of this writing, the QuickTime system extension is not automatically installed with Navigator 3.0. To view any QuickTime content, users will need the specific QuickTime system extension for their particular system. The QuickTime system extension for Macintosh, Windows 3.1, Windows 95, and Windows NT is available free from Apple's Web site at:

`http://quicktime.apple.com/qt/sw/sw.html`

Note

There are two different Windows versions of QuickTime software: 16-bit (for Windows 3.1 users) and 32-bit (for Windows '95 and NT users). In order for the Plug-In and QTVR extensions to work on Windows systems, all QuickTime components must be the same type and must match your browser. For example, if you are using 32-bit Netscape, you will need 32-bit QuickTime for Windows, and the 32-bit version of the Netscape Plug-in, and the 32-bit version of the QTVR components file.

The 32-bit version of QuickTime for Windows runs on Windows 95 and Windows NT only. It will not run on Windows 3.1 under Win32s.

Creating QuickTime Digital Video and Animations for the Web

This section discusses some of the issues involved in creating QuickTime digital video and animations for playback on the Web, and provides the following:

- Information on the tools you'll need to create Web-based QuickTime.
- General procedures and tips for Web-based QuickTime authoring.

Tutorials on using Premiere and MoviePlayer to create QuickTime digital video and animations are provided in later sections of this chapter.

QuickTime Tools

There are many authoring tools available to support QuickTime. These tools may differ between platforms. This section will begin by looking at some of the Macintosh authoring tools, followed by the less numerous authoring tools for Windows.

Macintosh

Commercial QuickTime authoring tools for the Macintosh are too numerous to mention, but all major 2D and 3D animation programs on the Macintosh support QuickTime output. There are also numerous freeware and shareware tools, so you have a large selection of QuickTime tools to choose from if you use a Macintosh.

MooVer

MooVer is a shareware QuickTime authoring tool for Macintosh by Eduard Schwan that is available on the accompanying CD. To create a QuickTime movie with MooVer, just drag and drop your numbered PICT files onto the MooVer icon and set the compression settings in the ensuing dialog box.

QuickEditor

QuickEditor is an incredible shareware QuickTime authoring tool created by Mathias Tschopp and friends. QuickEditor has unique 3D transitions (dissolves, wipes, and fades, for example) and sophisticated audio processing that is not found in expensive commercial programs such as Premiere. QuickEditor is available at most Macintosh shareware sites, such as:

```
http://hyperarchive.lcs.mit.edu/HyperArchive/Abstracts/
➥Recent-Summary.html
```

Video for Windows Utilities 1.1 for Macintosh

To convert QuickTime movies to AVI (the native Windows format) for Windows users who may not have QuickTime for Windows installed, use the Video for Windows (VfW) Utilities 1.1 for Macintosh (see fig. 10.5). These utilities can be found at:

```
ftp://mirrors.aol.com/pub/info-mac/gst/mov/video-for-
➥windows-11p.hqx
http://hyperarchive.lcs.mit.edu/HyperArchive/Abstracts/
➥Recent-Summary.html
```

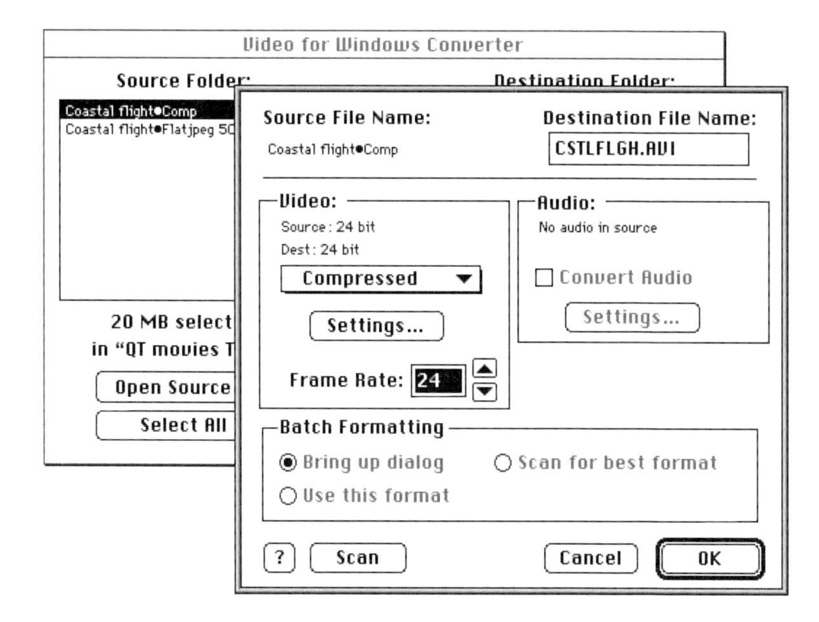

Figure 10.5

VfW utility for converting QuickTime to AVI.

MoviePlayer

MoviePlayer with Authoring Extras from Apple Computer is an excellent movie analysis and simple editing tool that can be found at:

```
http://www.quicktime.apple.com/software/mac/
```

Others

Several programs specifically designed for creating Web-based QuickTime have just been released or announced. The Internet Movie Tool is free from Apple's Web site, MovieStar Maker is an inexpensive QuickTime authoring tool from Intelligence at Large, and the Web Motion Plug-In is an extension to Movie Cleaner Pro from Terran Interactive.

Windows

Options for QuickTime-based Windows authoring are limited. Adobe Premiere for Windows will output QuickTime for Windows files. If your Windows authoring tools output to AVI format you can use one of several conversion tools to convert

AVI to QuickTime format. Windows-based QuickTime/AVI converters include:

- Intel's SmartVid for Windows and DOS.
- TRMOOV.EXE from The San Francisco Canyon Company.
- Adobe's Premiere for Windows will also allow you to convert between AVI and QuickTime formats.

More information on SmartVid, and converting AVI files for QuickTime can be found in Chapter 11.

Shooting and Digitizing Video

The previous chapter provides tips on shooting and digitizing video. As with most content creation, start with the cleanest source material. In video, that means pay attention to lighting, reduce unnecessary motion, panning, and zooming, don't forget audio, and use high-quality equipment. For digitizing, digitize at the highest quality you can, then reduce and downsample for the Web. For more detail, see Chapter 9.

Finding Out Information about Your Movie

When you create QuickTime movies for the Web, you will want to keep track of various characteristics of your movie, such as file size, dimensions, color-depth, and data rate.

In MoviePlayer, you can determine the data rate and other features of your QuickTime movie by following these steps (see fig. 10.6):

1. Open your movie.
2. Choose Get Info from the Movie menu.
3. To determine file size and data rate, select Movie from the Get Info dialog box in the left pop-up menu, and select General in the right pop-up menu. You will need the Authoring Extras for MoviePlayer to view this information. You can obtain MoviePlayer and the Authoring Extras from:

```
http://www.quicktime.apple.com/software/mac/
```

or check at the Apple site:

```
http://www. quicktime.apple.com/
```

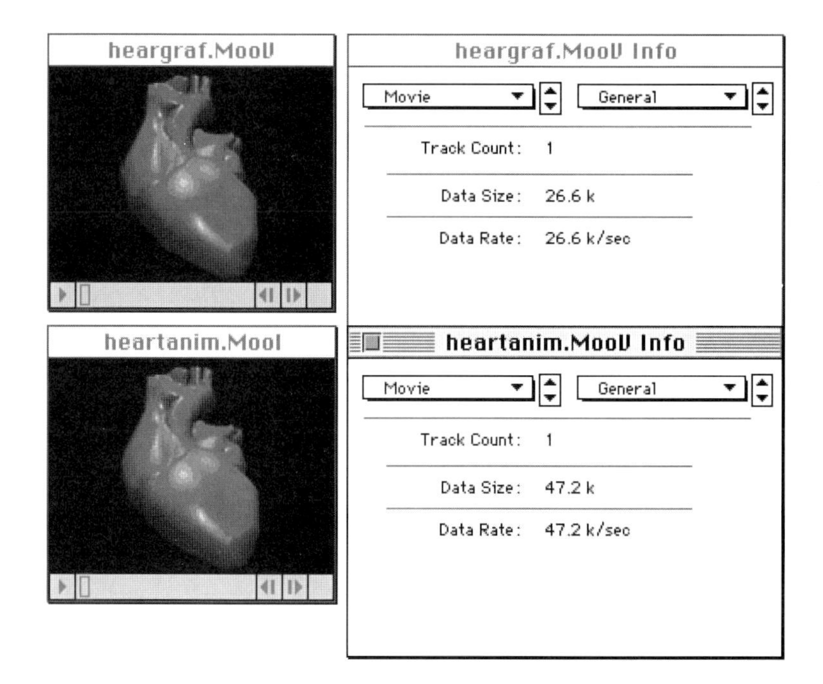

Figure 10.6

Movie information in MoviePlayer.

In Premiere, you can determine the data rate and other characteristics of your QuickTime movie as follows:

1. Choose Tool:Movie Analysis from the File menu.
2. Select the QuickTime movie you want to analyze in the file selection dialog box.

QuickTime on the Web: Quick Tips

At this time, Web-based QuickTime multimedia is a "download and play" technology. Users must download a file to their local hard disk and then play it using the appropriate viewer or Plug-In. Thus, total file size is generally the most important limiting factor. You want to reduce the total file size to as small as possible so users aren't waiting interminably for files to download over slow Internet connections. Fast-Start QuickTime will benefit from low data rates also, giving the impression, in some cases, of streaming video.

With that in mind, Web QuickTime should follow these guidelines:

1. Reduce movie size as much as possible. Stick with one of the standard QuickTime sizes such as 160×120 or 80×60. Dimensions that are divisible by four generally work the best. If you need to resize an existing movie, it is probably a good idea to resize your source material rather than use the built-in scaling features found in most QuickTime authoring programs. Of the QuickTime authoring programs, Adobe After Effects has the best built-in scaling algorithms.
2. Keep frame rates low. The lowest acceptable frame rate depends on your content. You may get by with as little as five frames per second. Try not to have frame rates exceeding 15 fps.
3. You'll also have to compress audio. Consider abandoning audio if you are delivering your movie for modem users. To delete a track such as audio from your movie in MoviePlayer:
   - Open your QuickTime movie in MoviePlayer.
   - Choose Delete Tracks from the Edit menu.
   - Select the track you wish to delete in the Delete Tracks dialog box.
4. Choose an appropriate codec to compress your movie. If the movie has already been compressed once, compressing it again will degrade the image quality. You may need to experiment with different codecs to determine the acceptable quality level. Like everything in multimedia authoring, it's a trade-off. See the section on data rates for a discussion of the trade-offs involved for Web-based QuickTime. The Web Motion Plug-In for Movie Cleaner Pro provides an expert system tailored for creating Web-based QuickTime. A following section contains suggestions for codec settings appropriate for digital video and animations.

Creating Your QuickTime Movie Step-by-Step

The procedure for creating a QuickTime movie and putting it on the Web is pretty simple:

1. Make sure your server is set up properly.
2. Use your favorite QuickTime authoring software to create a movie.
3. Save movies with the `.mov` or `.qt` extension. Follow the 8.3 DOS naming convention if the movie is going to be transferred to Windows 3.1 machine.
4. Save the movie as self-contained and flattened (see fig. 10.7). It is very important that you complete this step. It's probably a good idea to save the file with a new name rather than to overwrite an existing file.

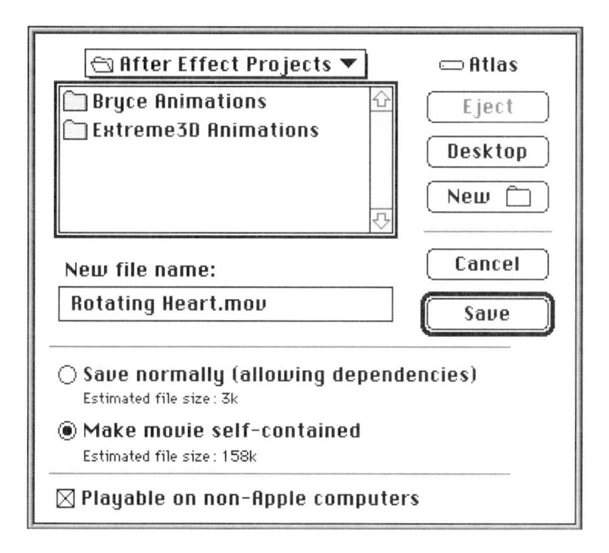

Figure 10.7

Save dialog from MoviePlayer illustrating the save as self contained and playable on non-Apple computers (flattened) options.

5. If you are using original source, such as uncompressed digital video or a sequence of PICT files, compress your movie with an appropriate codec when you save it (see fig. 10.8). You can typically choose a codec in the Save dialog box of most QuickTime authoring programs. Which codec you use depends on the content. If you are compressing animated 8-bit computer graphics for display on 8-bit systems, try the Graphics or Animation codecs. If your source is digital video, try using Cinepak. Picking the correct codec and then picking the correct compression settings is an art. You will probably want to

try several different settings to view quality and playback tradeoffs, or use a compression utility such as Movie Cleaner Pro.

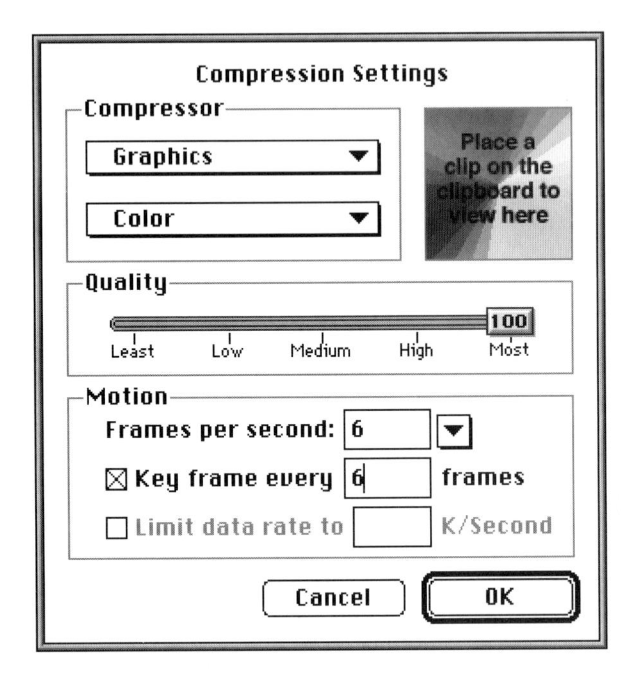

Figure 10.8

Standard QuickTime compression dialog box.

6. You may be able to perform special optimization for Web playback. Many of these optimizations are specific to the authoring tool. Fast-Start playback is a simple optimization performed by many authoring tools and supported by most Plug-Ins.
7. Embed the QuickTime movie in an HTML document using the EMBED tag.
8. Upload the HTML document to the server. Upload the QuickTime movie file as a raw binary file. Make sure the path to the QuickTime movie specified in the HTML document is correct.

The following sections in this chapter provide more detail on these steps.

Self-Contained Movies

Saving a movie as "self-contained" ensures that all the data needed to playback the movie is contained within the movie file. Sometimes during the editing of QuickTime files, the QuickTime editing application inserts references to source material on disc, rather than placing the actual data into the QuickTime file. Saving as "self-contained" ensures that these references are resolved and that the file will be a stand-alone movie. You must save your movies as self-contained for use on the Web.

"Flat" Movies

flat QuickTime movie

To prepare movies for playback on the Web, you also must "flatten" them. A **flat QuickTime movie** is a type of movie that can be played on Macintosh, Windows, and some Unix platforms. A flat movie contains all of the data for the movie in what is called the data fork of the file. All this means is that the movie file can be read on platforms other than a Macintosh. Most QuickTime authoring tools provide a "Save As Flattened Movie" option. You can also convert existing movies to the flat format using MoviePlayer, the Internet Movie Tool, FlattenMoov, and some shareware utilities provided on the CD.

Fast-Start Movies

Fast-Start is a new feature of QuickTime movies developed especially for Web playback. Fast-Start movies are the same as regular QuickTime movies except that some of the movie data that normally is found at the end of the QuickTime movie file is moved up to the beginning of the file. Moving the data to the beginning of the file enables Netscape Plug-Ins such as MovieStar and the QuickTime Plug-In to display the first frame of the movie almost instantly and to begin playing the movie before the file has been completely downloaded to the client hard disk. Downloading progress is indicated by a progress bar in the standard movie controller. Users will typically see the first frame of the movie and then be able to playback the first parts of the movie as the rest of the movie downloads in the background.

The Fast-Start feature is not the same as true streaming, but it does shorten the time that users will have to wait to view a movie over the Web. How much it shortens this time depends upon the particular movie. The Fast-Start feature works best with low data rate and low frame-rate movies. Large movies will still take a long time to download and a long time to begin playing.

Here is how the Fast-Start feature works: Fast-Start movies have information, such as the number of seconds in the movie, at the start of the movie file. The QuickTime Plug-In first reads in this information and will wait until it thinks the remaining download time is 90 percent of the total movie time before it begins playing the movie. For example, if the Plug-In detects it is downloading a 20 second movie, it will start playing the movie when it estimates there is about 18 seconds of download time remaining. Fast-Start is a way to jump start playback over networks.

You can create Fast-Start movies using the Internet Movie Tool from Apple, the MovieMaker software from Intelligence at Large, or new versions of Movie Cleaner Pro from Terran Interactive. As of this writing, there is no way to create Fast-Start movies on a Windows PC. QuickTime developers should be adding a "Save As Fast-Start Movie" feature to their authoring software in the near future.

If you want the movie to start playing as soon as it can, without user intervention, be sure to set the HTML tag `AUTOPLAY = TRUE` and `AUTOSTART = TRUE`. Using both AUTOPLAY and AUTOSTART will ensure compatibility with all QuickTime Plug-Ins. See the following section on HTML tags for more information.

A nice feature of Fast-Start movies is that there is no server intervention. Anyone can add a Fast-Start QuickTime movie to their Web page and anyone can playback a Fast-Start movie using the QuickTime Plug-In or MovieStar Plug-In.

The Internet Movie Tool

The Internet Movie Tool is a simple utility from Apple Computer that enables you to quickly convert QuickTime movies for Web playback. The Internet Movie Tool does two things:

- Flattens the movie for cross-platform compatibility.
- Creates a Fast-Start movie for Web playback.

As of this writing, it will only run on Macintosh computers. You can download the Internet Movie Tool free from:

`http://quicktime.apple.com/.`

Follow these steps to create a Fast-Start movie:

1. Launch the Internet Movie Tool or drag and drop a movie file on the Internet Movie Tool icon. If you use the drag and drop method, Internet Movie Tool will automatically convert the file and then quit.
2. Select the movie you want to convert in the dialog box and click on the Open button.
3. Click on Cancel to quit or convert more movies.

Premiere

The latest version of Adobe Premiere (v 4.1.) comes with a special tool for creating CD-ROM movies. You can use this tool to create movies for the Web.

Choose CD-ROM Movie from the Make menu and you will be presented with a dialog box that enables you to set several options, including attaching a special 8-bit palette to your 16-bit or 24-bit movie to ensure high-quality playback on 8-bit systems (see fig. 10.9). At the present time, Premiere will not create Fast-Start movies.

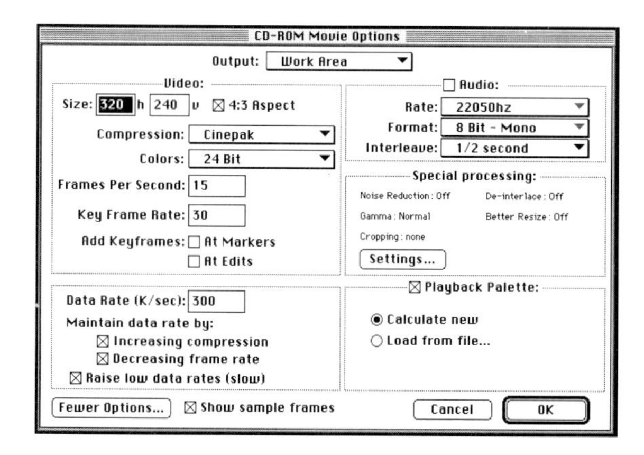

Figure 10.9

A make CD-ROM movie dialog box from Premiere.

MovieStar Maker

MovieStar Maker is an inexpensive QuickTime authoring tool available from Intelligence at Large (`http://www.beingthere.com/`). It is designed to work with the MovieStar Plug-In, but you can use it as a general QuickTime authoring tool. As of this writing, it's Macintosh only.

MovieStar Maker supports the creation of Fast-Start QuickTime movies for Web playback. In addition, MovieStar Maker offers additional Web optimization features through its "Minimize Video" and "Minimize Audio" options. MovieStar Maker also provides authoring features such as scrolling text and fading.

MovieStar Maker and the MovieStar Plug-In support a proprietary data format that enables a kind of "streaming" playback of QuickTime on the Web. Users need the MovieStar Plug-In for playback. If users don't have the MovieStar Plug-In, a "streaming" movie created by MovieStar Maker will playback as a normal QuickTime movie.

To find out the latest about MovieStar Plug-In and MovieStar Maker, visit:

`http://www.beingthere.com/`

See Chapter 7 for a tutorial on using MovieStar Maker.

Movie Cleaner Pro

Movie Cleaner Pro from Terran Interactive is a dedicated QuickTime compression utility for Macintosh. It contains an easy-to-use expert system that helps you choose the right codec for your movie. Plus, it has sophisticated features such as batch processing, adaptive noise reduction, gamma adjustment, de-interlacing, masking, and automated IMA audio compression (see fig. 10.10).

Web Motion Plug-In for Movie Cleaner

Tip

The results provided by Web Motion are probably the best you can get for Web-based QuickTime, and will save you hours of tweaking and testing that you would normally spend searching for optimal compression settings.

The Web Motion Plug-In to Movie Cleaner Pro provides features specifically for optimization of Web-based QuickTime.

Web Motion provides an integrated expert system that has sophisticated analysis and processing designed to optimize digital video for the Web.

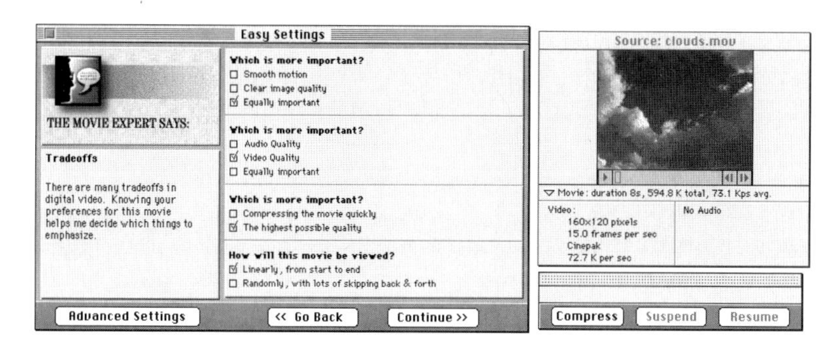

Figure 10.10

Expert system for compressing QuickTime movies from Movie Cleaner Pro.

Codecs for Web-Based QuickTime Digital Video

As of this writing, there are no QuickTime codecs designed specifically for playback on the Web. You'll want to stick with the standard set of codecs that ships with QuickTime to ensure playback on your user's computers. You access codecs and their settings in the Save dialog box in most standard QuickTime authoring tools.

Which codec you use depends a lot on your source material. Motion video contains rapidly shifting color fields that can be hard to compress. Talking head video generally has minimal motion and change over time, helping the compressor but requiring audio synchronization. Logos and animations consist of areas of flat color which may contain blocky artifacts when compressed with some codecs.

The Cinepak codec was developed for CD-ROM, comes standard with QuickTime, and is probably the best general codec for Web-based digital video as of this writing. Cinepak is a data rate limiting codec—you can set a maximum data rate that the compressor will try to stay below. Cinepak data rate limits should generally be set to 10 KBs or above, although you can go lower (for example, for modem delivery) if you can sacrifice movie dimensions and frame rate.

Photo-JPEG might work in some situations where movie dimensions are small; for example, 80×60; and high image quality is more important than frame rate. Photo-JPEG is processor intensive, so playback may bog down on slower computers.

By the time you read this, QuickTime might include special codecs specifically designed for Web playback. These codecs are based on industry standards for video conferencing and are called H.263 for video and G.723 for audio. Check the Apple Website for information as these codecs are released.

The following settings are just suggestions. What works best for you will depend on your source, the quality you want, and the download time you want your users to endure. You will typically have to experiment with settings and see what quality and playback tradeoffs are acceptable. Compression utilities such as Movie Cleaner Pro can save you a lot of time by helping you quickly narrow down your choices.

Table 10.3

Suggested Video Compression Settings

Compressor:	Cinepak
Depth:	Millions (depending on color-depth of source)
Quality:	Medium to Least
Frames per Second:	5–15
Key Frame:	One key frame every 1–3 seconds
Limit Date Rate:	5–10 KB/s or above
Notes:	Attach a custom 8-bit palette if colors are set to millions. Good for "talking head" video; for example, video with limited motion
Compressor:	Photo—JPEG
Depth:	Color
Quality:	Medium
Frames per Second:	5–15
Key Frame:	One key frame per 2 seconds
Notes:	Can be used to provide a high-quality "slide show" effect for motion video

Another factor to consider is whether you want your users to play the video backward and forward or play the video frame-by-frame (like a slideshow) with the standard QuickTime controller. If this kind of user interaction is important, you may want to increase the number of key frames per second (and thus increase file size and data rate).

Codecs for Web-Based QuickTime Animation

Animations typically have different requirements than digital video. Animations generally come from computer-generated or hand-drawn sources and are characterized by areas of flat, clean, and consistent colors. Because of this, creating QuickTime animations involves slightly different issues than creating QuickTime video.

The following are some recommended codec settings to try for your animations. Which codec works best for you depends on your particular animation. Another fact to remember for Web animation is that after the animation is downloaded to the client hard disk, the animation will playback from the local hard drive, so that total file size becomes a more important limiting factor than data rate. For codecs that let you specify the color-depth, such as the Animation codec, be sure to specify a color-depth that is the same or less than your source material. For example, don't choose the 24-bit color setting if your source material is 8-bit.

The following settings are suggestions. Again, what works best for you depends on your source, the quality you want, and the download time you want your users to endure.

Table 10.4

Suggested Video Compression Settings

Compressor:	Graphics
Depth:	Best
Quality:	Most
Frames per Second:	5–10
Key Frame:	One key frame per second
Compressor:	Animation
Depth:	256 Colors or more (depending on color-depth of source)
Quality:	Most
Frames per Second:	5–10

continues

Table 10.4, continued

Suggested Video Compression Settings

Key Frame:	One key frame per second
Compressor:	Cinepak
Depth:	Millions (depending on color-depth of source)
Quality:	Medium
Frames per Second:	5–10
Key Frame:	One key frame per second
Notes:	Attach a custom 8-bit palette if colors are set to millions

Note

If you have 16-bit or 24-bit source graphics, reduce the bit depth to 8-bit in an image processing program such as Debabelizer (see fig. 10.11) before using the Graphics codec. The same advice should be followed when using 16-bit or 24-bit source graphics with the Animation codec set to 256 colors. QuickTime codecs generally don't do a good job of reducing bit depth of source graphics. If you have 16-bit or 24-bit source graphics and want to create an 8-bit movie, you are better off doing the bit depth reduction of the source graphics in another program, rather than doing it in QuickTime.

Of all the available codecs, the Graphics codec generally creates the smallest file sizes for 8-bit movies. The Graphics codec creates the smallest file sizes in general, all other settings, such as color-depth, frame rate, and data rate, being equal. Of the QuickTime authoring tools tested for this book, Equilibrium Technology's Debabelizer, Apple Computer's ConvertToMovie utility (available on the QuickTime Developer's CD from Apple), and Eduard Schwan's Moover utility (available on the CD) created the smallest movies with the Graphics codec. Your mileage may vary.

The Graphics codec produces significantly lower data rates—typically half—than the Animation codec. Cinepak tends to add blotchy artifacts and blur the edges of flat-colored animations at comparable sizes and data rates. Despite this, Cinepak may yield acceptable results, especially using 24-bit source that is compressed with the Millions of Colors color-depth setting. Be sure to attach a custom 8-bit palette if you use Cinepak with the Millions of Colors color-depth setting.

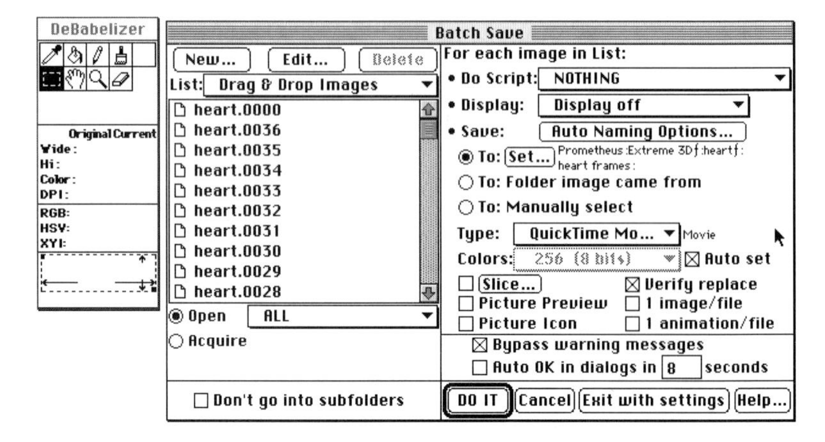

Figure 10.11

Creating QuickTime movies with Debabelizer.

Codecs for Web-Based QuickTime Audio

Currently, IMA (Interactive Multimedia Association) audio compression is probably the best way to compress audio in QuickTime. IMA compression was developed by this group for digital audio. A drawback of IMA compression is that it doesn't support sample sizes less than 16-bit.

Most Windows sound cards only support discrete audio sample rates of 11.025 kHz, 22.050 kHz, and 44.100 kHz. Most Macintosh systems support continuous sample rates. Some compression utilities, such as Movie Cleaner Pro enable you to set audio sample rates below 11.025 kHz, which will significantly decrease file size, but may not playback on some Windows systems. In the compression settings listed in table 10.5, the sample rates given are minimums to be used if you are not worried about going below the 11.025 kHz limit.

Table 10.5

Suggested Audio Compression Settings

Music:

Compressor: IMA 4:1

Sample Rate: 6–11.025 kHz

Sample Size: 16-bit

Use: Mono

Female Voice:

Compressor: IMA 4:1

Sample Rate: 4–6 kHz

Sample Size: 16-bit

Use: Mono

Male Voice:

Compressor: IMA 4:1

Sample Rate: 3–4 kHz

Sample Size: 16-bit

Use: Mono

See Chapter 11, "Audio," for more tips on creating, digitizing, and editing audio for the Web.

Creating IMA-Compressed Audio with MoviePlayer

To create an IMA-compressed sound with MoviePlayer, follow these steps:

1. Start with a sound-only QuickTime movie. You can create a sound-only QuickTime movie by choosing Import from the File menu and selecting an AIFF sound file or System sound file.
2. Choose Export from the File menu.
3. Select Sound To AIFF.
4. Click on Options.
5. Select IMA 4:1 for compressor.
6. Select a sampling rate of 11.025, and Mono.
7. Click on OK.
8. Name the file and click on Save.
9. Choose Import from the File menu and select the IMA audio file you just created.
10. Click on the Convert button.

Palettes

Chapter 6, "Using Graphics to Add Dynamic Content," discusses Web-based palettes in detail. Digital video generally looks best played back at 16-bit or 24-bit color but chances are, on the Web, your movie will playback on 8-bit displays. You can save your movie as an 8-bit movie—with the Graphics codec, for example—which is optimized for 8-bit color. You can also choose 8-bit or 256 colors as a color setting in some codecs, such as the Cinepak and Animation codecs. An 8-bit movie won't look as good on 16-bit and 24-bit displays. All movies, whether 8-bit, 16-bit, or 24-bit will probably be dithered to whatever is the currently active palette when they are played back on 8-bit displays.

If you have 16-bit or 24-bit source graphics and want to create an 8-bit movie, you are generally better off doing the bit depth reduction of the source graphics in another program, such as Debabelizer, rather than doing it with QuickTime.

QuickTime enables you to attach a custom 8-bit palette to a movie. QuickTime will use this palette for playback on 8-bit displays. Movie Cleaner Pro, Debabelizer, and Premiere enable you to create and attach custom 8-bit palettes. Custom palettes will not add noticeably to the movie's file size.

For Web playback of digital video, you might want to provide QuickTime movies compressed with Cinepak set to Millions of Colors and attach a custom 8-bit palette for users on 8-bit systems. For Web playback of animation you might want to use the Graphics codec for your main audience, and then provide a separate link if you would like users to download a larger, higher quality 16-bit or 24-bit version.

Cross-Platform Considerations

- If your movie will be saved to a Windows 3.1 system, the file name of your movie should follow the DOS 8.3 naming conventions.
- PC monitors are generally darker than Macintosh monitors. Some authoring tools have a gamma adjustment that enables you to change the overall darkness of the movie.
- Windows computers can only support one video track and one audio track as of this writing. By the time you read this, this limitation might have been removed from Windows-based QuickTime. Many authoring tools, such as Movie Cleaner Pro, will automatically reduce multiple tracks to a single track when you save the movie for cross-platform playback.
- QuickTime for Windows plays music tracks using the MPC-compliant MIDI driver. QuickTime MIDI files may not playback on many Windows systems. MACE compressed sound is also not supported under Windows.
- On Windows, the standard QuickTime controller is 24 pixels high, while on the Macintosh, it is 16 pixels high. If you add 24 to the HEIGHT parameter of the EMBED tag, you will have eight extra pixels at the bottom of your movie on the Macintosh. If the movie is embedded in a frame or you use a background graphic, this extra space will be painted with a solid color.

Tutorial: Using MoviePlayer for Simple Editing

Tools
MoviePlayer with Authoring Extras
Sample QuickTime Movie

The free MoviePlayer application from Apple Computer is included with the QuickTime distribution for Macintosh. You can cut, copy, and paste sections of your movie in MoviePlayer using the standard commands from the Edit menu. To select a range within your movie, hold down the shift key and drag the slider.

MoviePlayer provides the following QuickTime track editing capabilities:

- To extract a QuickTime track (video, audio, MIDI, text, or any of the other QuickTime media types) into a separate movie, choose Extract Track from the Edit menu.
- To delete a track, choose Delete Tracks from the Edit menu and select the track you want to delete in the Delete Tracks dialog box.
- To enable or disable a track during playback, choose Enable Tracks from the Edit menu and turn the track on or off in the Enable Tracks dialog box.
- To insert a new track such as a text or audio track:
    1. Copy the media you want to add to a new track to the clipboard.
    2. Use the slider to select the place in the movie where you want to insert the new track.
    3. Hold down the option key and choose Add from the Edit menu.
    4. The media on the clipboard, will be added to a new track in your movie.

- To trim a movie to a smaller length:
    1. Hold down the shift key and drag the slider across the range of frames that you want to be contained in your new movie.
    2. Hold down the option key and choose Trim from the Edit menu (see fig. 10.12).
    3. Choose Save As from the File menu.

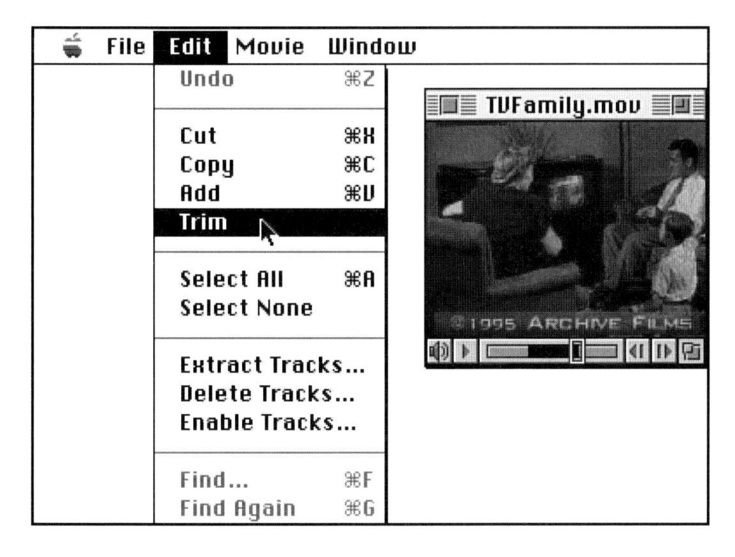

Figure 10.12

Trimming clips in MoviePlayer.

It is generally a good idea to keep the number of tracks and edits to a minimum. When you are ready to save your movie for the Web:

1. Choose Save As from the File menu.
2. Choose the Make Movie Self-contained radio button.
3. Check the Playable on Non-Apple Computers check box.

Tutorial: Creating a QuickTime Animation in Premiere

This tutorial takes you through the necessary steps to create a QuickTime animation with Adobe Premiere, a QuickTime authoring tool for Macintosh and Windows.

Tools
Premiere
Sequence of numbered animation frames as PICT files

The CD contains a folder containing a sequence of numbered PICT files that you can use to create an animation or to batch your own files.

There are many ways to create QuickTime movies. Most 2D and 3D animation programs output directly to QuickTime movies. You might want to perform some post-processing on your movie or animation, such as resizing the movie or animation for the Web. In this case, you might want to output your animation as a sequence of PICT files and then batch process the PICT files in another program.

This tutorial assumes you have used an animation program to create a series of PICT files or animation frames. The PICT files should be numbered sequentially, like so:

myPict.01

myPict.02

myPict.03

By following this file-naming scheme, you make it easier for QuickTime authoring programs to create QuickTime movies from a sequence of PICT files.

Also make sure all of your sequentially numbered PICT files are in the same folder on your hard disk, as shown in figure 10.13.

To create a QuickTime animation in Premiere, follow these steps:

1. Choose New/New Project from the File menu.
2. Choose the appropriate preset for your project, or choose cancel.

   If you're using the PICT files from the CD, choose Presentation 160×120.
3. Choose Import/File from the File menu (see fig. 10.14).

heart frames

Name	Size	Kind	Last Modified
heart.0001	11K	DeBabelizer®1.6.5 d...	Tue, Feb 13,
heart.0002	11K	DeBabelizer®1.6.5 d...	Tue, Feb 13,
heart.0003	11K	DeBabelizer®1.6.5 d...	Tue, Feb 13,
heart.0004	11K	DeBabelizer®1.6.5 d...	Tue, Feb 13,
heart.0005	11K	DeBabelizer®1.6.5 d...	Tue, Feb 13,
heart.0006	11K	DeBabelizer®1.6.5 d...	Tue, Feb 13,
heart.0007	11K	DeBabelizer®1.6.5 d...	Tue, Feb 13,
heart.0008	11K	DeBabelizer®1.6.5 d...	Tue, Feb 13,
heart.0009	11K	DeBabelizer®1.6.5 d...	Tue, Feb 13,
heart.0010	11K	DeBabelizer®1.6.5 d...	Tue, Feb 13,
heart.0011	11K	DeBabelizer®1.6.5 d...	Tue, Feb 13,
heart.0012	11K	DeBabelizer®1.6.5 d...	Tue, Feb 13,
heart.0013	11K	DeBabelizer®1.6.5 d...	Tue, Feb 13,
heart.0014	11K	DeBabelizer®1.6.5 d...	Tue, Feb 13,
heart.0015	11K	DeBabelizer®1.6.5 d...	Tue, Feb 13,
heart.0016	11K	DeBabelizer®1.6.5 d...	Tue, Feb 13,
heart.0017	11K	DeBabelizer®1.6.5 d...	Tue, Feb 13,
heart.0018	11K	DeBabelizer®1.6.5 d...	Tue, Feb 13,
heart.0019	11K	DeBabelizer®1.6.5 d...	Tue, Feb 13,
heart.0020	11K	DeBabelizer®1.6.5 d...	Tue, Feb 13,
heart.0021	11K	DeBabelizer®1.6.5 d...	Tue, Feb 13,

Figure 10.13

Folder of animation frames saved as sequentially numbered PICT files.

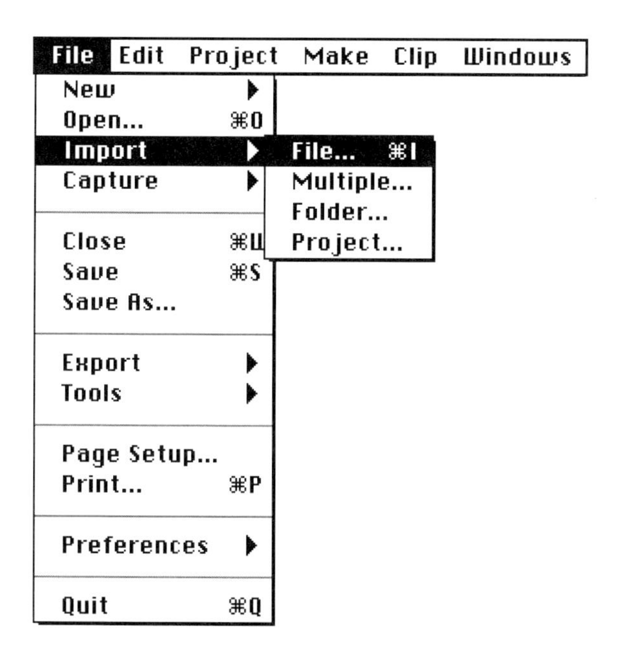

Figure 10.14

The Import/File menu in Premiere.

4. Choose the first PICT file in your sequence of numbered PICT files (see figure 10.15). Premiere automatically creates an animation of the PICT file sequence.

Figure 10.15

Importing files in Premiere.

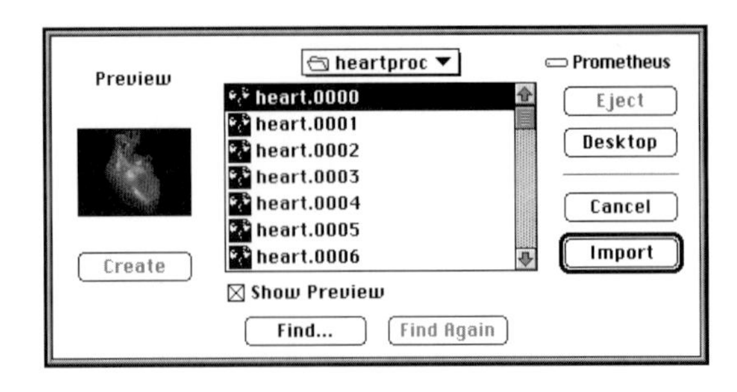

The animation will play at one frame per second. Double-click on the animation in the Project Window to see a preview of the animation in the Clip Window, as shown in figure 10.16.

Figure 10.16

Project and Clip Windows in Premiere.

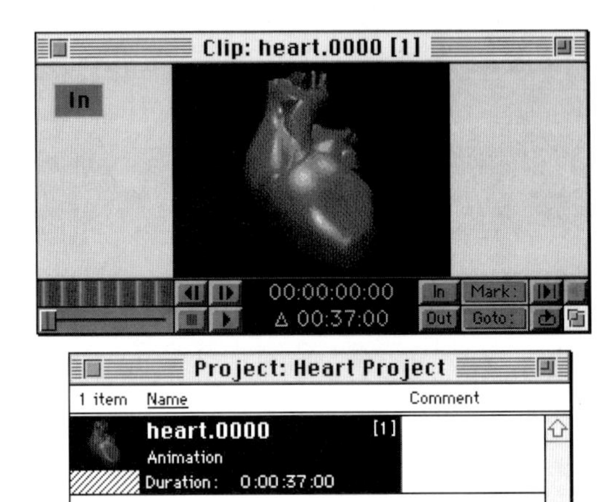

5. Drag the animation from the Project Window to Track A in the Construction Window (see fig. 10.17).

Figure 10.17

Drag the animation from the Project Window to the Construction Window.

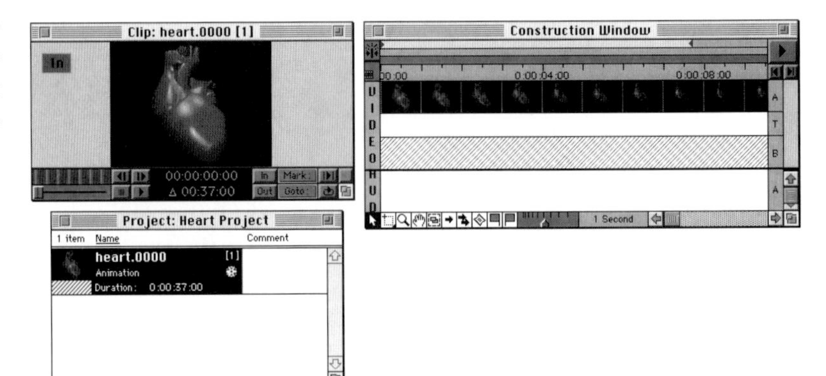

6. Choose Movie from the Make menu (see fig. 10.18).
7. You will be presented with a save dialog box. Choose Output Options.

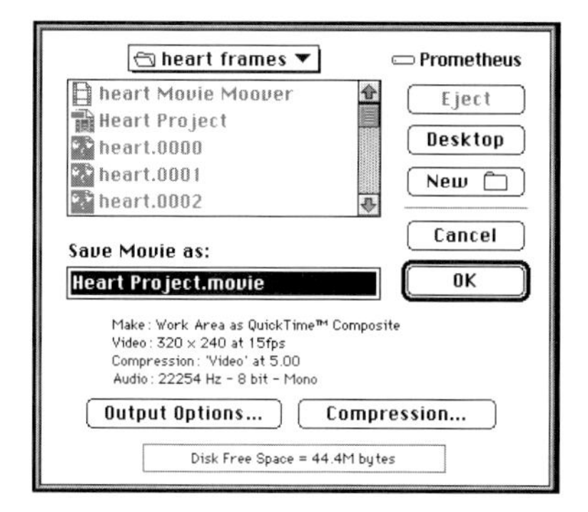

Figure 10.18

Saving a movie in Premiere.

8. Choose the appropriate settings for your movie (see fig. 10.19). Uncheck the Audio option if your movie doesn't contain audio. Be sure and select the Flatten option in the lower part of the dialog box. You must select Flatten for Web-based movies. Choose OK when you are finished.

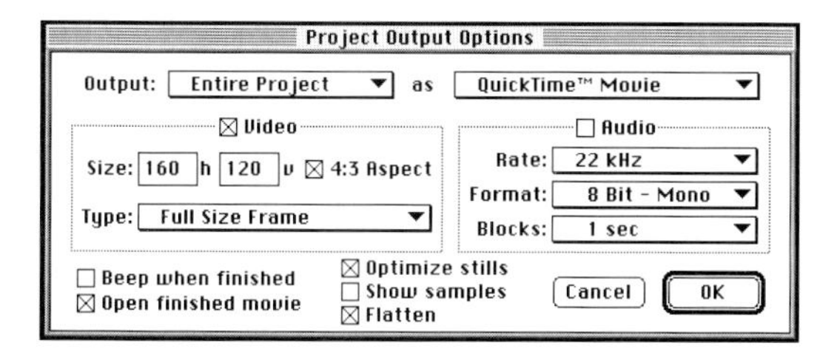

Figure 10.19

Output Options for QuickTime movies in Premiere.

9. Select Compression.
10. You will be presented with a standard QuickTime codec dialog box (see fig. 10.20). The Graphics codec works well for 8-bit animations that will play on the Web. Choose OK when you are finished.
11. Save your movie with a `.mov` or `.qt` extension.

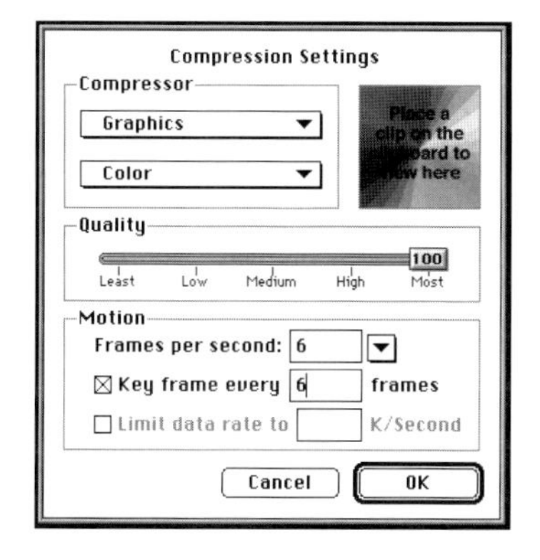

Figure 10.20

Compression Settings dialog box.

Tutorial: Creating QuickTime Digital Video with Premiere

Tools
Premiere
Two QuickTime video clips

This tutorial shows examples of:

- Creating a transition between two video clips
- Compositing two video clips in Premiere

Creating a Transition in Premiere

A transition is a way to flow smoothly between two different video clips. Without a transition, the change from one clip to another is called a jump-cut and can be disorienting for the viewer. Transitions include dissolving from one clip to another, fading from one clip to another, and many others.

Premiere uses a standard A-B track editing system. Figure 10.21 illustrates the A and B tracks in the Construction Window. Between the A and B tracks is the T track or transition track.

First you will need to import a clip or two into the Premiere project. Select Import from the File menu and select at least one movie clip to import. You can create a transition between two different clips or the same clip (see fig. 10.22).

To create a transition:

1. Drag the first clip to track A in the Construction Window.
2. Drag the second clip to track B in the Construction Window.
3. Arrange the two clips so that the end of the clip in track A overlaps the beginning of the clip in track B.
4. To open the Transitions Window, choose Transitions from the Window menu.

5. Scroll through the list and select a transition you like.
6. Drag the transition to the T track at the place where the clip in track A and the clip in track B overlap.
7. Drag the edges of the transition so that it extends across the entire area of overlap.
8. Double-click on the transition in the T track and set the parameters for the transition.

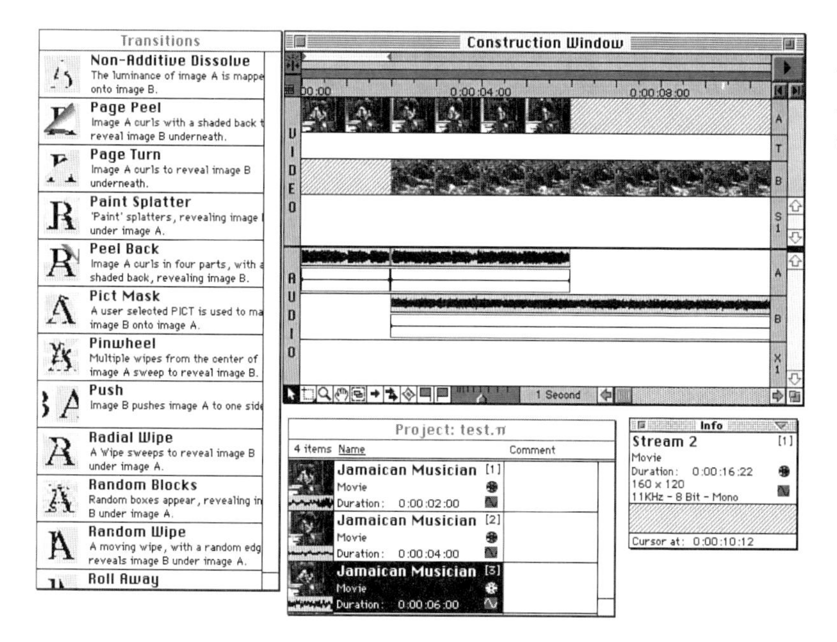

Figure 10.21

Adding a transition in Premiere.

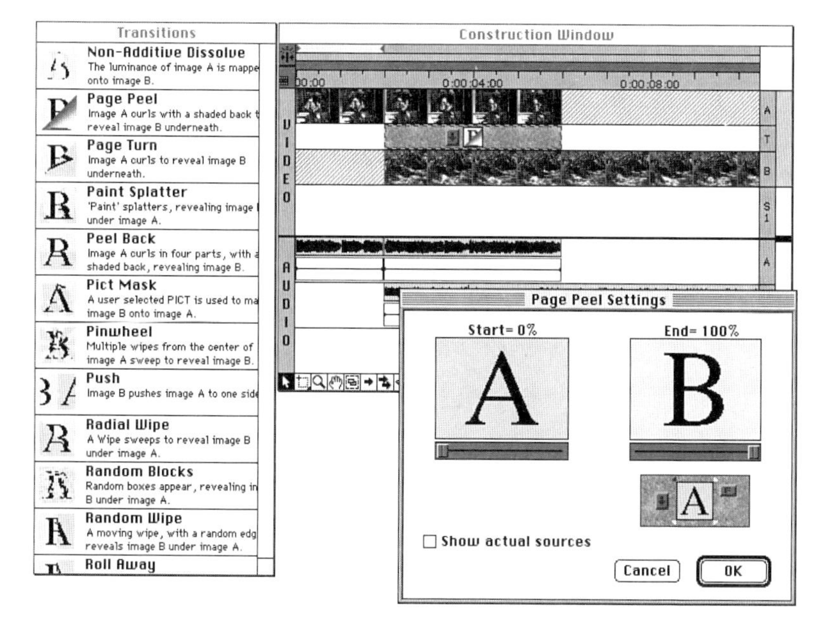

Figure 10.22

A-B tracks set up for adding a transition.

Compositing Clips in Premiere

This section discusses how to composite or superimpose one clip on top of another. To composite two clips, put the background clip in track A and put the superimposed clip in track S1 or the super track. You need to follow these steps:

1. Drag the background clip to track A in the Construction Window.
2. Drag the superimposed clip to track S1 in the Construction Window.
3. Arrange two clips so that the superposition is the way you want it.

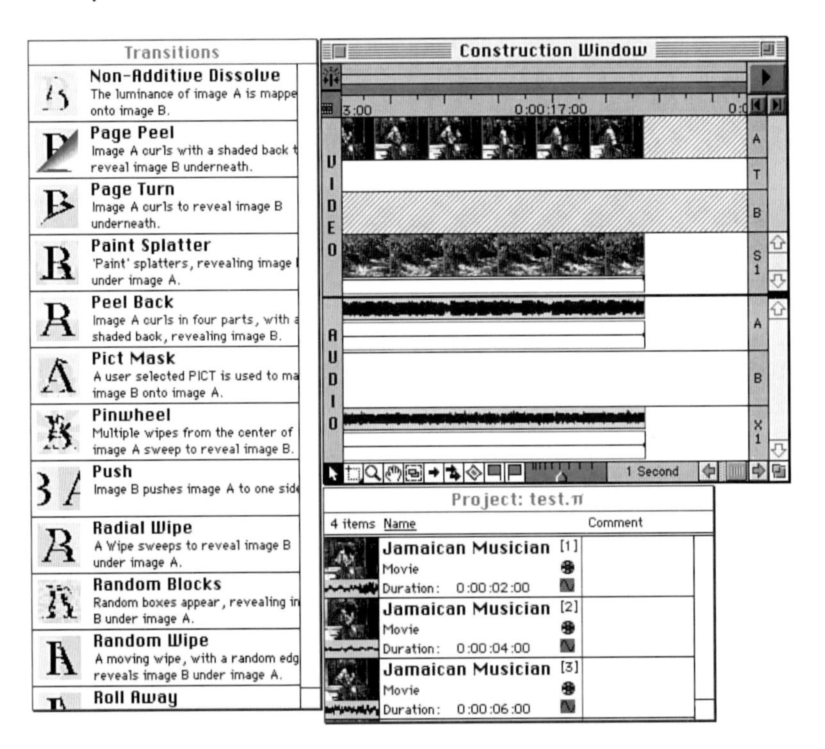

Figure 10.23

Setting up compositing in Premiere.

4. Select the superimposed clip in track S1.
5. Choose Transparency from the Clip menu (see fig. 10.24).
6. Select the key type from the Key Type menu.
7. To composite blue-screen video; for example, a talking head shot against a pure blue background, select Chroma, and select the color you want to be transparent (typically blue because skin tones lack blue colors) with the eye-dropper in the Color box.

8. To preview the superposition, click on the page curl icon in the Sample box.
9. Adjust the sliders to fine tune the transparency effect.

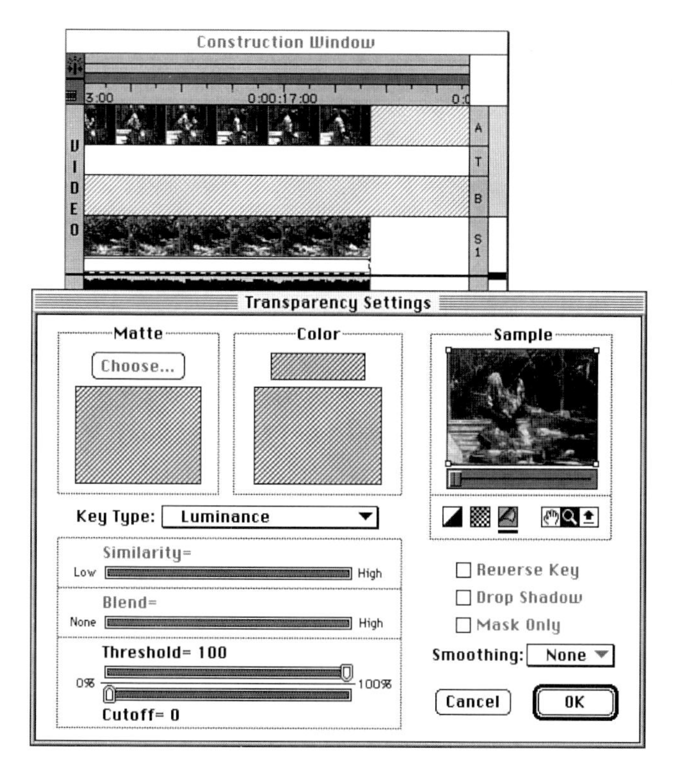

Figure 10.24

Setting Transparency Settings.

To output a small range of your project and not the entire project to a QuickTime movie:

1. Set the Work Area to the area you want to output by dragging the yellow bar at the top of the Construction Window to the section of the project timeline you want to make into a QuickTime movie. Drag the ends of the yellow bar to cover the range of time you are interested in.
2. Choose Output Options from the Make menu.
3. In the Output Options dialog box, select Work Area in the Output Pop-up menu.

Now, when you output your QuickTime movie it will only output the range of time within the Work Area.

Adding QuickTime To Your Web Site

The first step in adding QuickTime to your Web site is to make sure your server is set up to handle QuickTime data. On the server, the suffix mapping preferences should associate the file extensions `.mov` and `.qt` with the MIME type `video/quicktime`. Different server packages handle this differently. If you are unsure how to do this, see your server documentation or contact your server administrator.

Embedding QuickTime in HTML

Add QuickTime movies to your HTML file using the EMBED tag. Here is the minimum HTML code you need to embed QuickTime:

```
<EMBED SRC="MyQT.mov" HEIGHT=144 WIDTH=160>
```

Note

Do not put quotes around the values for HEIGHT and WIDTH, even though it is correct HTML syntax.

The name `MyQT.mov` is the path name to your movie on the Web server (in this case, the movie is in the same directory as the HTML document). The values for HEIGHT and WIDTH are the dimensions of the movie in pixels. Be sure and include the HEIGHT and WIDTH parameters. Add 24 to the height of the movie if you want to display the default QuickTime controller.

Other HTML Parameters

Include the PLUGINSPAGE parameter for users who might not have the QuickTime Plug-In installed.The PLUGINSPAGE parameter directs Web browsers without a QuickTime movie Plug-In to a Web page where they can download the appropriate Plug-In. The value of the PLUGINSPAGE parameter is a fully-qualified URL, in quotes, where the user can download the appropriate Plug-In. Here is some sample HTML code:

```
<EMBED SRC="MyQT.mov" HEIGHT=144 WIDTH=160 PLUGINSPAGE =
"http://quicktime.apple.com/qt/sw/sw.html" AUTOSTART =
➥TRUE  AUTOPLAY = TRUE>
```

Setting the AUTOSTART and AUTOPLAY parameters to TRUE will cause the movie to begin playing as quickly as possible without user intervention. The default value is FALSE; meaning that the user must initiate playback. Use this feature with Fast-Start movies to start playback at the earliest possible time. Although you only need one of these parameters, including both provides compatibility with all QuickTime Plug-Ins. The AUTOSTART and AUTOPLAY parameters only work if the movie is visible within the browser window.

Another parameter you might want to use with your movies is the CONTROLLER parameter. The possible values for the CONTROLLER parameter are TRUE and FALSE. The default value is TRUE; for example, the standard QuickTime movie controller will be displayed with your movie. Add 24 to the height of the movie and give this value to the HEIGHT parameter if you want to display the default QuickTime controller. If you do not want to show the standard QuickTime movie controller, set the value of the CONTROLLER parameter to FALSE. You might still want to give your users the opportunity to stop playback if they want.

There are many more parameters you can use with the QuickTime Plug-In from Apple Computer. For a complete up-to-date list of the currently accepted parameters visit:

```
http://quicktime.apple.com/qt/dev/devweb.html
```

Hidden Movies

You might want to a hide a sound-only QuickTime movie—to provide background music for your Web page.

To provide a sound-only QuickTime movie that automatically starts playback using the AUTOSTART and AUTOPLAY parameters, place the movie at the top of your Web page, and specify a WIDTH = 4 and HEIGHT = 4. As of this writing, WIDTH and HEIGHT values less than 4 tend to crash Netscape Navigator. For example,

```
<EMBED SRC="MyBackgroundSoundTrackQT.mov" HEIGHT=4
➥WIDTH=4 PLUGINSPAGE =
"http://quicktime.apple.com/qt/sw/sw.html" AUTOSTART =
➥TRUE  AUTOPLAY = TRUE>
```

Transferring QuickTime Files to a Web Server

If you use FTP (File Transfer Protocol) to upload your movie to a Web server, be sure you transfer the file as a raw, binary file. The movie file name must have the extension `.mov` or `.qt`.

Be sure the path name and file name match the names you have indicated in the SRC parameter of the EMBED tag.

QuickTime Unplugged

Even though QuickTime is now standard equipment with all Netscape browsers, many users will not have a QuickTime Plug-In installed on their machine or they will be using a browser that is not compatible with Netscape Plug-Ins.

To provide for these users you can follow these guidelines:

- For browsers that don't support the EMBED tag, use the NOEMBED tag to provide alternate content.
- Always use the PLUGINSPAGE parameter of the EMBED tag to point users to a URL where they can download the appropriate Plug-In.
- For users that have helper apps correctly configured provide a link to your movie with the HREF tag. An added benefit of this approach, is that for users with a QuickTime Plug-In, the movie will open in the middle of a new browser window.

Here is some sample HTML that implements all these suggestions:

```
<EMBED SRC="MyQT.mov" HEIGHT=144 WIDTH=160 PLUGINSPAGE =
"http://quicktime.apple.com/qt/sw/sw.html">
<NOEMBED>
<IMG SRC="MyQT.GIF" HEIGHT=120 WIDTH=160>
If you don't have the QuickTime Plug-In, but have a
QuickTime helper app, click on the
link below to view the movie.
</NOEMBED>
```

You can also view the `<A HREF="MyQT.mov">` QuickTime movie `</A>` if you have your browser set up with the right helper application.

User Interface and Page Design Considerations

The following are some general considerations for providing QuickTime content on your Web page:

- Digital video and animation is the latest trendy feature of the Web, but it is easy to overdo it. Be kind to network bandwidth and avoid gratuitous animation. Animations tend to be large files that take a while to download. How many times do your users need to see your spinning logo? Animations can also be distracting on a page with a lot of text you want users to read.
- Give users control of playback or at least provide a way for users to stop playback. Endlessly looping movies can be annoying. This is especially true for movies containing audio. It is easy to create this functionality with QuickTime by providing the standard QuickTime controller with your movies (see fig. 10.25).

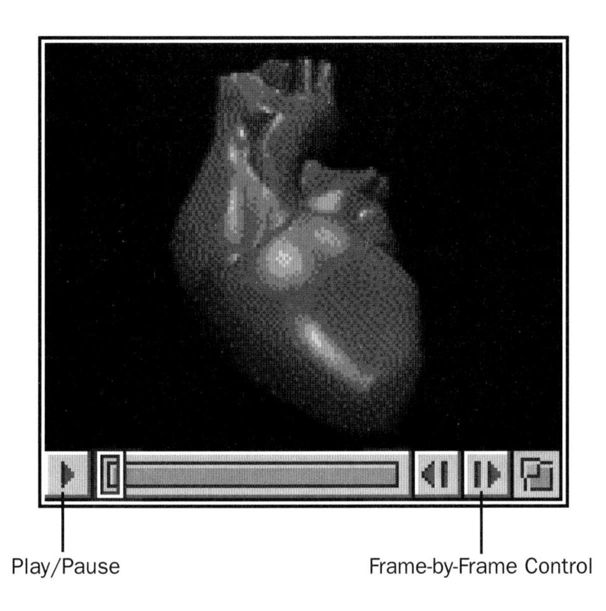

Figure 10.25

Features of the standard QuickTime controller.

- Provide an explanation of the features of the standard QuickTime controller, so users know how to start and stop your QuickTime movie. If you don't provide the standard QuickTime controller, tell your users how to pause playback using the mouse.
- Provide the ability to launch helper apps for users who don't have a QuickTime Plug-In installed.
- Be aware that custom palettes can shift colors on the entire display. Sometimes after leaving a page with a custom palette, the original palette will not be restored.

- Give users short clips or samplers of your full QuickTime movie or display a sample frame as a GIF. Then, give users the choice of downloading the full version after they have seen the sampler.

Fast-Start Movies

If the controller is visible, users might try to click on the start button on Fast-Start movies before the movie has finished downloading. You might want to make sure the movie starts with something interesting. Movie Cleaner Pro provides the ability to create a high-quality first frame, for example. If you don't want the user to be able to click on the Start button, use the CONTROLLER = FALSE parameter and make sure AUTOPLAY = TRUE.

Keyboard Navigation

For navigation of QuickTime and QTVR movies from the keyboard, choose the QuickTime movie or QuickTime VR panorama by clicking on it. For keyboard navigation, the movie cannot have an HREF tag associated with it. After you have selected the movie, use the option and control (shift and control on Windows) to zoom in and zoom out of QTVR movies. Use the arrow keys to step through a QuickTime movie frame by frame on Macintosh. On Windows, the arrow keys do not work.

Saving Movies from the Web

To save an embedded QuickTime movie to your local hard drive, click on the movie and hold the mouse down or use the right-hand mouse button in Windows. A pop-up menu will appear that enables you to save the movie. On the Macintosh, press Command+S to save the movie to disc.

Starting and Stopping Playback

The standard QuickTime controller is a good way to give users control over playback of your movie. If the controller has been hidden using the CONTROLLER = FALSE parameter you can still give users control over playback using the mouse. The movie must be visible (you can't use the HIDDEN tag) and the movie cannot have an HREF tag associated with it.

On a Macintosh, double-clicking on the movie will start the movie and a single-click on the movie will pause it. On a PC, single-clicking on the movie toggles between pause and play. Mouse control over playback also works for movies with a visible controller (for example, with the parameter CONTROLLER = TRUE).

Conclusion

QuickTime is now a standard feature in Macintosh and Windows versions of Netscape Navigator. Web developers can be assured that a large majority of users have QuickTime playback capabilities. Users don't have to bother to download separate Plug-Ins or helper apps to view QuickTime content on the Web. The Netscape Plug-In architecture has been widely adopted and other browsers should be supporting Plug-Ins soon.

Implementation of the QuickTime Media Layer, QuickTime integration with Java, possible QuickTime Conferencing support in Navigator 4.0, and the sharing of 3DMF file formats between QuickTime's 3D tracks and VRML 2.0 promise many new uses of Web-based QuickTime media in the future.

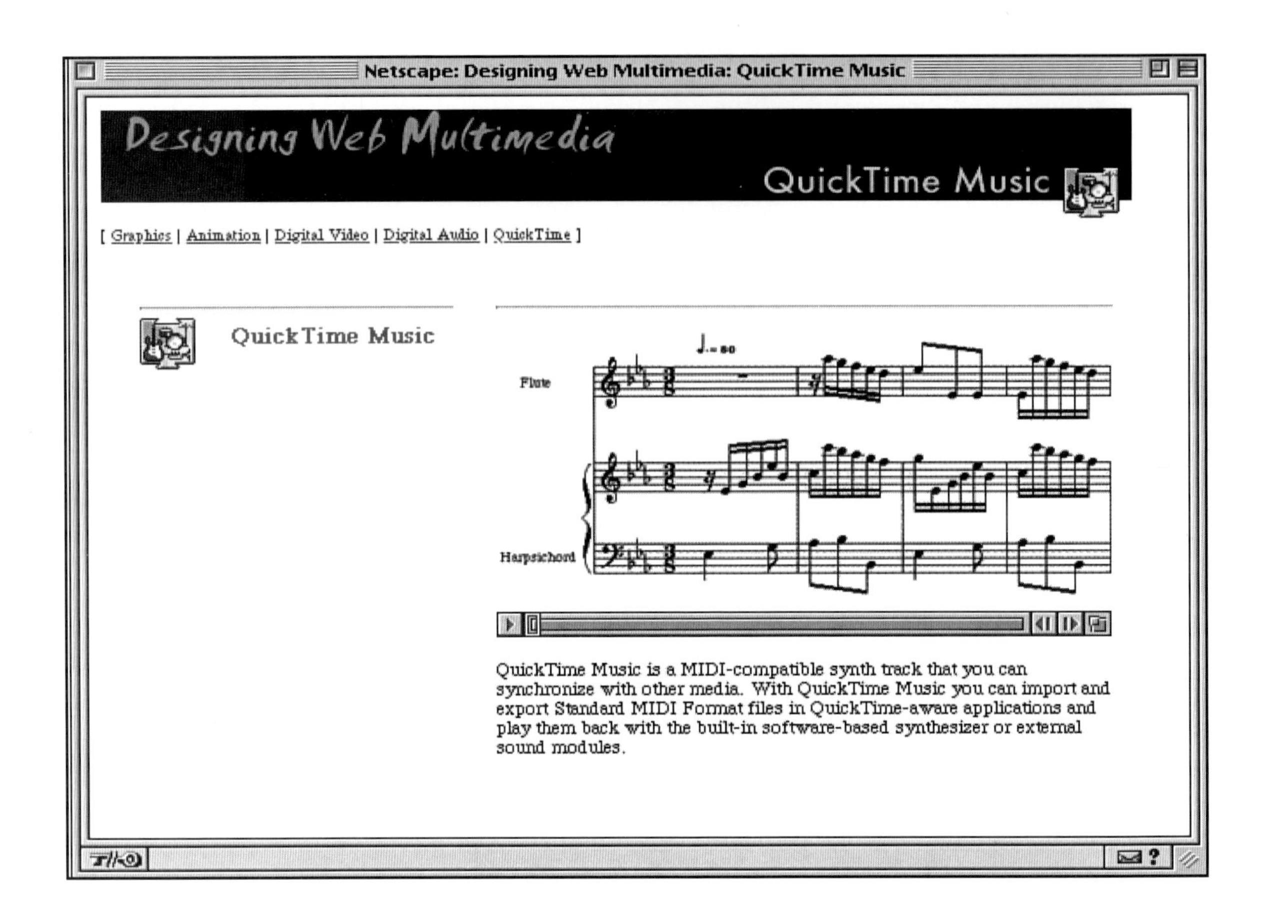
Netscape: Designing Web Multimedia: QuickTime Music
Designing Web Multimedia
QuickTime Music
[Graphics | Animation | Digital Video | Digital Audio | QuickTime]
QuickTime Music
Flute
Harpsichord
QuickTime Music is a MIDI-compatible synth track that you can synchronize with other media. With QuickTime Music you can import and export Standard MIDI Format files in QuickTime-aware applications and play them back with the built-in software-based synthesizer or external sound modules.

Audio is often a neglected and underused part of multimedia, but it can be more powerful than visuals in setting a mood and tone.

chapter

11

Audio

Audio is often treated as the stepchild of Web multimedia. Money and time are commonly spent on the visuals, and animation with audio is thrown in as an afterthought. In some respects, this prioritization is backwards. Psychologically, sound is more effective than visuals in setting tone and mood. Bad audio can be more annoying and turn off users faster than garish graphics. In fact, users typically are more annoyed by audio that breaks up and pauses than video and animation that breaks up and pauses. The reality of digital audio on the Web, generally 8-bit 11 kHz or less, has generated a lot of bad audio because downsampling audio can be trickier than downsampling graphics.

Users may compare Web audio to FM radio or—worse yet—CD-quality audio. It has only been recently that Web digital audio began to approach the quality people are accustomed to on radio, let alone compact disk. MIDI has the potential to provide a low-bandwidth way for delivering high-quality music but is dependent on the setup and sound samples available on the user's machine.

Generally, audio on the Web comes in four flavors:

- Download and play MIDI (Musical Instrument Digital Interface)
- Download and play digital audio
- Streamed MIDI or streamed preexisting compressed digital audio files

- Live streaming audio such as in telephony and audio-conferencing

Note

The Internet Underground Music Archive (IUMA) is a great site to check out for a good use of audio on the Web:

`http://iuma.com/`

The good news about Web-based audio is that the two major browsers, Netscape Navigator and Internet Explorer, have built-in support for the playback of the most popular audio formats, such as AIFF, AU, WAV, and MIDI (see fig. 11.1). QuickTime audio and music tracks are played back with the QuickTime Plug-In. Proprietary streaming formats, such as RealAudio and Shockwave for Audio, require separate Plug-Ins.

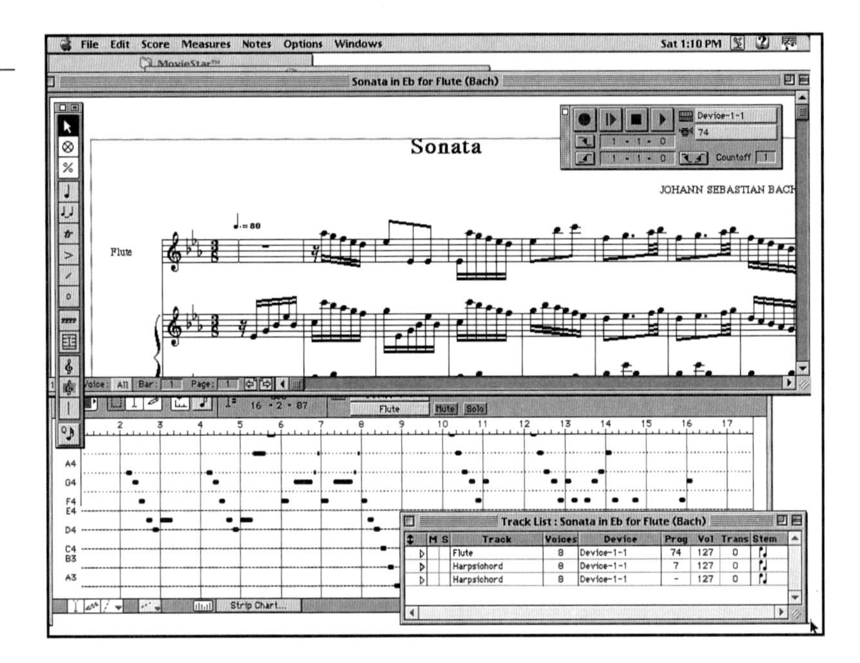

Figure 11.1

MIDI music software at work.

This chapter shows you how to:

- Add MIDI playback to your Web page
- Create and integrate QuickTime Music Tracks (a variation of MIDI) into your Web page
- Capture and edit digital audio
- Add digital audio and QuickTime audio to your Web page
- Edit and downsample digital audio specifically for Web playback
- Integrate RealAudio and Shockwave for Audio into a Web page

MIDI

The Musical Instrument Digital Interface (MIDI) is the standard serial communications protocol used to exchange data between synthesizers, computers, software programs, effects processors, and other devices. MIDI does not require a lot of bandwidth because MIDI data only consists of performance information, some of which is listed here:

- The notes played; for example, B-flat below middle C
- The duration of individual notes; for example, an eighth note
- The particular instrument sound or patch assigned to a note; for example, a conga or a violin
- The key velocity, or how fast a key is pressed

When you edit MIDI data, you can do things such as:

- Change individual notes
- Increase and decrease note durations
- Use different instruments; for example, assign a cello to a snare drum part
- Change tempo without changing pitch
- Quantize or snap notes to time values
- Create envelopes for volume and other effects

What MIDI does not contain is sampled digital audio waveform data. This makes MIDI data very compact.

MIDI Playback Requirements

To play back MIDI data requires a synthesizer. A synthesizer can be an external device with a keyboard, a computer chip, or a software program. A synthesizer takes the MIDI data and re-creates or synthesizes the performance using whatever sound synthesis is available on that particular playback device—for example, *FM synthesis*, which uses combinations of mathematically generated waveforms, and *wavetable synthesis*, which uses digital samples of waveforms to produce sounds.

MIDI is a great way to provide music data on the Web and is supported by most browsers and platforms. But playback of the music is dependent on the MIDI setup and available sounds on the user's machine. Thus, the hard-edged guitar sounds you programmed may play back as a harp on another system. The quality of the music is also dependent on the user's audio playback capabilities.

MIDI Formats

Note

To find out the details about the General MIDI specs, visit:

`http://www.earthlink.net/~mma/gminfo.htm`

General MIDI is a standard set of MIDI patch assignments and features that enable MIDI authors to be assured of certain minimum configurations. MIDI playback will still sound different on $150 sound cards and $1,500 synthesizers, but by authoring to the General MIDI standard, composers can be assured that their compositions will sound similar on General MIDI-compliant systems.

Composing to the General MIDI specs ensures relatively consistent playback on General MIDI-compliant systems. General MIDI organizes patches, sounds, voices, or instruments into 16 groups containing eight sounds each.

General MIDI supports 16 MIDI channels. Each channel can play a different instrument, voice, or patch. Channel 10, for example, is reserved for percussion. Each key of an instrument in channel 10 is assigned a different percussion patch. Tables 11.1 and 11.2 show the patch list for instruments and percussion respectively.

Table 11.1

General MIDI Patch List

Patch Number/Instrument	Patch Number/Instrument
PIANO	*CHROMATIC PERCUSSION*
1. Acoustic Grand	9. Celesta
2. Bright Acoustic	10. Glockenspiel
3. Electric Grand	11. Music Box
4. Honky-Tonk	12. Vibraphone
5. Electric Piano 1	13. Marimba
6. Electric Piano 2	14. Xylophone
7. Harpsichord	15. Tubular Bells
8. Clav	16. Dulcimer

Patch Number/Instrument	Patch Number/Instrument
ORGAN	*GUITAR*
17. Drawbar Organ	25. Acoustic Guitar (nylon)
18. Percussive Organ	26. Acoustic Guitar (steel)
19. Rock Organ	27. Electric Guitar (jazz)
20. Church Organ	28. Electric Guitar (clean)
21. Reed Organ	29. Electric Guitar (muted)
22. Accordion	30. Overdriven Guitar
23. Harmonica	31. Distortion Guitar
24. Tango Accordion	32. Guitar Harmonics
BASS	*STRINGS*
33. Acoustic Bass	41. Violin
34. Electric Bass (finger)	42. Viola
35. Electric Bass (pick)	43. Cello
36. Fretless Bass	44. Contrabass
37. Slap Bass 1	45. Tremolo Strings
38. Slap Bass 2	46. Pizzicato Strings
39. Synth Bass 1	47. Orchestral Strings
40. Synth Bass 2	48. Timpani
ENSEMBLE	*BRASS*
49. String Ensemble 1	57. Trumpet
50. String Ensemble 2	58. Trombone
51. SynthStrings 1	59. Tuba
52. SynthStrings 2	60. Muted Trumpet
53. Choir Aahs	61. French Horn
54. Voice Oohs	62. Brass Section
55. Synth Voice	63. SynthBrass 1
56. Orchestra Hit	64. SynthBrass 2
REED	*PIPE*
65. Soprano Sax	73. Piccolo
66. Alto Sax	74. Flute
67. Tenor Sax	75. Recorder
68. Baritone Sax	76. Pan Flute
69. Oboe	77. Blown Bottle

continues

Table 11.1, continued

General MIDI Patch List

Patch Number/Instrument	Patch Number/Instrument
70. English Horn	78. Skakuhachi
71. Bassoon	79. Whistle
72. Clarinet	80. Ocarina
SYNTH LEAD	*SYNTH PAD*
81. Lead 1 (square)	89. Pad 1 (new age)
82. Lead 2 (sawtooth)	90. Pad 2 (warm)
83. Lead 3 (calliope)	91. Pad 3 (polysynth)
84. Lead 4 (chiff)	92. Pad 4 (choir)
85. Lead 5 (charang)	93. Pad 5 (bowed)
86. Lead 6 (voice)	94. Pad 6 (metallic)
87. Lead 7 (fifths)	95. Pad 7 (halo)
88. Lead 8 (bass+lead)	96. Pad 8 (sweep)
SYNTH EFFECTS	*ETHNIC*
97. FX 1 (ice rain)	105. Sitar
98. FX 2 (soundtrack)	106. Banjo
99. FX 3 (crystal)	107. Shamisen
100. FX 4 (atmosphere)	108. Koto
101. FX 5 (brightness)	109. Kalimba
102. FX 6 (goblins)	110. Bagpipe
103. FX 7 (echoes)	111. Fiddle
104. FX 8 (sci-fi)	112. Shanai
PERCUSSIVE	*SOUND EFFECTS*
113. Tinkle Bell	121. Guitar Fret Noise
114. Agogo	122. Breath Noise
115. Steel Drums	123. Seashore
116. Woodblock	124. Bird Tweet
117. Taiko Drum	125. Telephone Ring
118. Melodic Tom	126. Helicopter
119. Synth Drum	127. Applause
120. Reverse Cymbal	128. Gunshot

Table 11.2

General MIDI Drum Sound Assignments for Channel 10

MIDIKey/Drum Sound	MIDIKey/Drum Sound
35. Acoustic Bass Drum	59. Ride Cymbal 2
36. (C1) Bass Drum 1	60. (C3) Hi Bongo
37. Side Stick	61. Low Bongo
38. Acoustic Snare	62. Mute Hi Conga
39. Hand Clap	63. Open Hi Conga
40. Electric Snare	64. Low Conga
41. Low Floor Tom	65. High Timbale
42. Closed Hi-Hat	66. Low Timbale
43. High Floor Tom	67. High Agogo
44. Pedal Hi-Hat	68. Low Agogo
45. Low Tom	69. Cabasa
46. Open Hi-Hat	70. Maracas
47. Low-Mid Tom	71. Short Whistle
48. (C2) Hi-Mid Tom	72. (C4) Long Whistle
49. Crash Cymbal 1	73. Short Guiro
50. High Tom	74. Long Guiro
51. Ride Cymbal 1	75. Claves
52. Chinese Cymbal	76. Hi Wood Block
53. Ride Bell	77. Low Wood Block
54. Tambourine	78. Mute Cuica
55. Splash Cymbal	79. Open Cuica
56. Cowbell	80. Mute Triangle
57. Crash Cymbal 2	81. Open Triangle
58. Vibraslap	

Standard MIDI File Format

The Standard MIDI File (SMF) format is a standard format that MIDI sequencers and editors can use to share files. It is analogous to RTF files in word processing or DXF in 3D applications. There are two types of SMF files:

- Type zero combines all the data into a single track.

Note

Some excellent MIDI resources include:

`http://www.midifarm.com/`

`http://www.harmony-central.com/MIDI/`

`http://www.eeb.ele.tue.nl/midi/index.html`

`http://www.aitech.ac.jp/~ckelly/SMF.html`

Tip

If you try to download files with the MIDI extension in a Web browser with a MIDI Plug-In installed, such as LiveAudio or Crescendo, you invoke the MIDI Plug-In instead of downloading the file. If this is the case, press the Option key on a Macintosh or, in Windows, press the right button on the mouse and choose Save Link As to save the file to disk, instead of invoking a Plug-In to play it.

- Type one assign each MIDI channel to a separate track. This is often useful if you want to edit the file later or assign different instruments to a track.

Creating SMF files that conform to the General MIDI specs will ensure maximum compatibility when creating MIDI files for the Web.

There are many standard MIDI files on the Internet that you can download to use in your Web pages. MIDITyper on a Mac is a useful utility to change type and creators of downloaded MIDI files on the Mac.

MOD Files

MOD files are sound files typically created on Amiga computers. Playback from the Web is possible via helper applications. There are a lot of MOD files floating around the Internet. MOD files are interesting in that sound sample data is stored with MIDI-like performance data. When MOD files are played, the audio samples are loaded into RAM, and the performance data uses these samples to play back sounds.

MIDI Hardware and Software

Creating MIDI music usually requires the following hardware and software:

- A MIDI-capable keyboard controller and synthesizer.
- MIDI editing and playback software or sequencer (see fig. 11.2).
- A MIDI interface device between the computer and external synthesizer. These can be inexpensive or more elaborate. Some devices, such as sound cards and external sound modules, have interfaces built-in.
- The appropriate cables (5-pin DIN connectors). Here is how it all fits together: To create MIDI music files, you typically play a keyboard controller and capture the performance in a MIDI sequencing application. You can then edit the MIDI data in the program. Most sequencers have easy-to-use graphical user interfaces that enable you to drag visually represented notes around a score and create envelopes for volume and other effects.

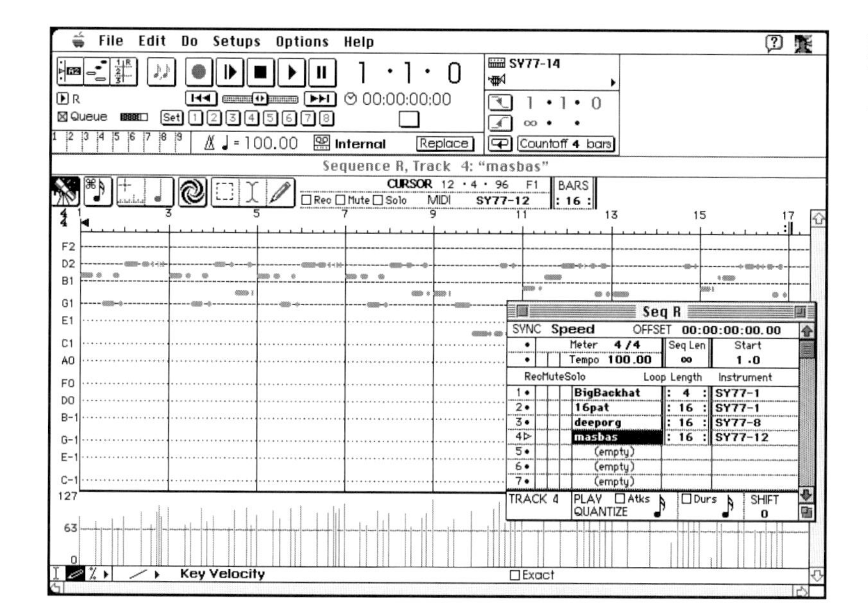

Figure 11.2

An opcode MIDI sequencer.

MIDI Support on Macs

On Macs, system-level MIDI support is provided by the Apple MIDI Manager, Opcode Music System (discussed in the section "MIDI Support on PCs"), Mark of the Unicorn's FreeMIDI, or by QuickTime through the QuickTime Music Architecture. MIDI devices are connected to printer or modem ports.

For MIDI playback on a Mac, you can use the QuickTime Musical Instruments, a RAM-based software synthesizer and system extension that contains General MIDI samples licensed from Roland Corporation. For composing, you probably want to use an external synthesizer or sound module. By the time you read this, you should be able to install custom sound samples for QuickTime Musical Instruments and also include sound samples with QuickTime Music Tracks, similar to the earlier-mentioned MOD files.

MIDI Support on PCs

Many PC sound cards come with a MIDI synthesizer on the card. Many of these synthesizers support General MIDI. Some cards claim General MIDI support but only partially implement the specs or provide low-quality sound samples. Some sound cards have MIDI ports that enable you to send and receive MIDI data from external devices.

Opcode Music System (OMS) is a system-level driver software, licensed by Microsoft for Windows 95 and by Apple Computer for QuickTime, which provides communications between MIDI devices and software programs. You can use OMS to set up MIDI pathways in a multi-device studio, for example, along with other useful features.

Note

On Windows, the MIDI setup is controlled via the MIDIMapper Control Panel.

Popular Sequencers and Utilities

Some popular commercial sequencers include the following. URLs have been provided when available:

- Opcode System's Studio Vision Pro, Vision, and EZVision
- Steinberg Cubase Audio
- Twelve Tone Systems Cakewalk Pro
- Mark of the Unicorn's Digital Performer

  `http://www.motu.com/`
- Passport MasterTracks Pro

  `http://www.mw3.com/passport/`
- MIDIGraphy

  `http://ux01.so-net.or.jp/~mmaeda/`

  MIDIGraphy is an amazing $20 shareware MIDI sequencer for the Mac that has many of the features of commercial programs costing hundreds of dollars (see fig. 11.3). You can use MIDIGraphy to create and edit standard MIDI files and QuickTime Music Tracks.

Note

Opcode Systems maintains an excellent Web site and FTP site for their MIDI and digital audio products and OMS, including inexpensive MIDI sequencers and digital audio editors at

`http://www.opcode.com/`

Some useful commercial utilities for MIDI composers include the following. URLs have been provided when available:

- Ear Level Engineering HyperMIDI XCMD (Mac only)
- InVision Interactive CyberSound VS (Mac only)

  `http://www.cybersound.com/`

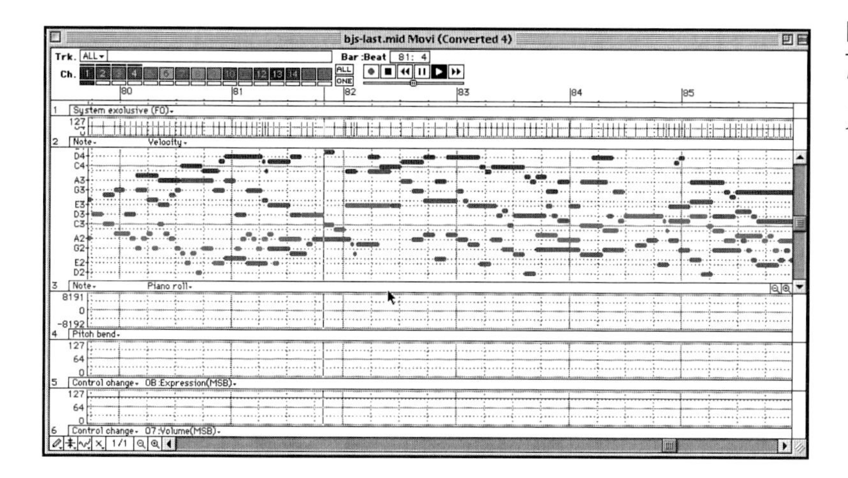

Figure 11.3

The MIDIGraphy shareware MIDI sequencer.

- Yamaha MIDI Xtra for Director 5

  `http://www.yamaha.co.jp/english/xg/html/midhm.html`

Shareware MIDI utilities for Windows include:

- MIDIGate

  `http://www.prs.net/midigate.html`

- WPlany

  `http://www.ncsa.uiuc.edu/SDG/Software/WinMosaic/Viewers/wplany.htm`

Shareware MIDI utilities for Mac include:

- MIDITyper

  `http://hyperarchive.lcs.mit.edu/HyperArchive/Archive/gst/midi/midi-typer-104.hqx`

- MidiIt!

  `http://hyperarchive.lcs.mit.edu/HyperArchive/Archive/gst/midi/midi-it-125.hqx`

- Arnold's MIDIPlayer

  `http://hyperarchive.lcs.mit.edu/HyperArchive/Archive/gst/midi/arnolds-midi-player-271b.hqx`

Putting MIDI on the Web

MIDI files are typically small. A whole symphony can fit on a disk with plenty of room to spare. Compact file size makes MIDI an ideal delivery vehicle for Web-based audio.

Provide MIDI files on the Web the same way you provide other multimedia content by following these instructions.

1. Make sure your server is set up to handle MIDI files. See the following table for MIME type (see chapter 1 for information on MIME) and file name extension associations.
2. Save your MIDI file in SMF format.
3. Place your SMF file on a Web server.

MIME Information for MIDI Files

File Type	MIME Type	MIME Subtype	File Name Extensions
Standard MIDI Format	audio	midi	mid, midi
Standard MIDI Format	audio	x-midi	mid, midi
QuickTime Music Tracks	video	quicktime	mov, qt

MIDI File Options with HTML

Serve MIDI files from Web pages via hyperlinks or EMBED tags. Internet Explorer only recognizes the BGSOUND tag. Options for serving, embedding, and playing MIDI files with HTML are presented in the following list:

- To serve MIDI file as hyperlinks, use HTML code such as:

  ```
  <A HREF SRC = "mySong.mid"> Play my song!</A>
  ```

  When a user clicks on this link, they initiate the download of the MIDI file. In Navigator 3, the LiveAudio Plug-In launches. Playback can be controlled from the LiveAudio standard controller.

- To embed MIDI files in Web pages for Netscape Navigator 2 or later and compatible browsers use the EMBED tag. Attributes you can use with the EMBED tag depend on the Plug-In.

- To play a MIDI file as background sound with the LiveAudio Plug-In, use the AUTOSTART and HIDDEN attributes, in this form:

```
<EMBED SRC = "mySong.mid" AUTOSTART = TRUE HIDDEN
➥= TRUE>
```

- To provide a MIDI file that can be controlled by the user with the standard LiveAudio controller (see fig. 11.4), use the CONSOLE or SMALLCONSOLE attributes, as in the following example:

```
<EMBED SRC="mySong.mid" HEIGHT=15 WIDTH=144
➥CONTROLS = SMALLCONSOLE>
```

Figure 11.4

The LiveAudio MIDI controller.

- To embed MIDI files in Web pages for Internet Explorer use the BGSOUND tag, such as:

```
<BGSOUND SRC="mySong.mid">
```

- To embed background MIDI files that are compatible with both Navigator and Explorer, include both of the following tags:

```
<EMBED SRC = "mySong.mid" AUTOSTART = TRUE HIDDEN
➥= TRUE>
<BGSOUND SRC="mySong.mid">
```

Tags not recognized by a browser are ignored.

Plug-Ins that Support MIDI

The LiveAudio Plug-In that is bundled with Netscape Navigator 3 supports M-law, AIFF, WAVE, and MIDI files. Internet Explorer version 2 or later has built-in MIDI support.

The Crescendo and Crescendo Plug-In and ActiveX control from Live Update provides additional MIDI playback features and is compatible with versions 2 or later of Netscape Navigator and Internet Explorer. For more information, go to the following site:

```
http://www.liveupdate.com/
```

Other Plug-Ins that provide enhanced MIDI playback on the Web include:

- MIDIPlugin from Arnaud Masson is a great MIDI Plug-In for Macs.

  ```
  http://www.planete.net/~amasson/midiplugin.html
  ```

- YamahaXG Midi Plug-In has recently released a MIDI Plug-In with some great features, including a built-in software synth.

  ```
  http://www.yamaha.co.jp/english/xg/html/midhm.html
  ```

QuickTime Music Tracks

Starting with QuickTime 2.0, you can add Music Tracks to QuickTime movies. QuickTime Music Tracks are MIDI-based performance data tracks. Playback uses the software-based synthesizer built into QuickTime with the QuickTime Musical Instruments system extension that shipped with QuickTime, or you can assign another external synthesizer for playback. OMS integration is also featured in the QuickTime 2.5 release. Although not technically MIDI, you can easily import and export SMF files from QuickTime Music Tracks with programs such as MoviePlayer. You can also convert QuickTime Music Tracks to AIFF files with MoviePlayer. Apple's name for these new features of QuickTime is the QuickTime Music Architecture (QTMA).

QT Musical Instruments is a system extension that implements a software synthesizer in RAM. QT Musical Instruments contain samples licensed from Roland Corporation that are a subset of the Roland Sound Canvas General MIDI Sound Set. Users will soon be able to add their own sound samples to this set and to embed samples in QuickTime movies for consistent cross-platform playback. You can play back multiple simultaneous instruments in stereo, constrained by the user's CPU and RAM. For example, a QuickTime Music Track with a single instrument can use up about 1–5 percent of the available CPU cycles depending on the instrument.

On a Windows machine, the QuickTime Music Tracks play through MIDI hardware on the sound card, using the MIDIMAPPER driver, with minimal CPU load. Although QuickTime Music Tracks will play back from any PC sound card that supports MIDI playback under Windows, the sounds of the instruments will vary depending on the particular sound card installed.

QuickTime distinguishes between Sound Tracks, which are digital audio tracks, and Music Tracks, which are the QTMA tracks. QuickTime movies can contain a Video Track, a Sound Track, and a Music Track, for example, or you can create a sound-only QuickTime movie with a single Music Track or single Sound Track.

Enabling QuickTime Music Synthesizer

To enable the software-based, QuickTime synthesizer on a Mac:

1. Choose the Control Panels, QuickTime Settings under the Apple menu.
2. Choose Music in the upper pop-up menu.
3. Check the QuickTime Music Synthesizer check box in the QuickTime Settings dialog box (see fig. 11.5).

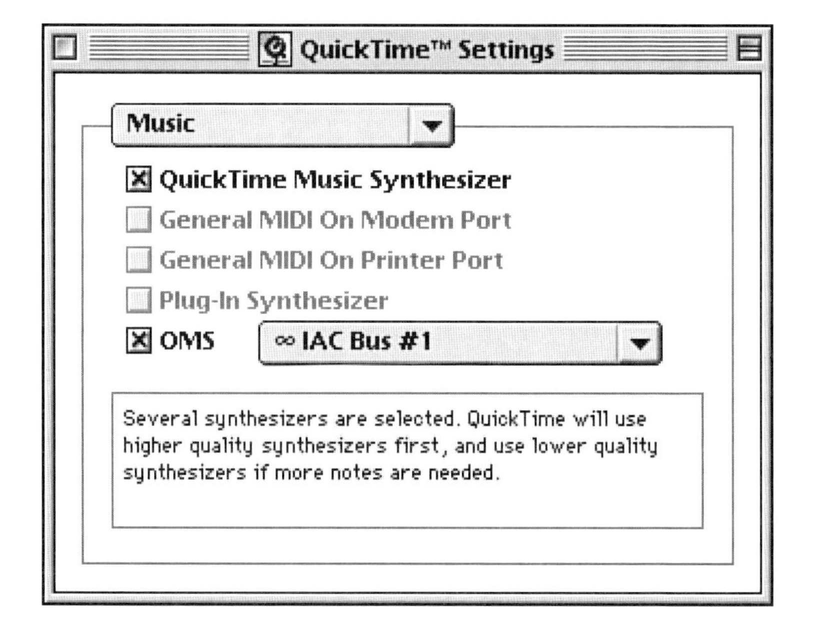

Figure 11.5

Enabling the QuickTime Music Synthesizer in its QuickTime Settings dialog box.

You can use this dialog box to assign playback through external synthesizers, sound modules, and OMS, if they are available.

> **Note**
>
> Be sure to use the version of MoviePlayer that contains the Goodies and Authoring Extras Plug-Ins. Visit the following for more information about these Plug-Ins:
>
> `http://www.quicktime.apple.com/software/mac/`
>
> `http://www.QuickTimeFAQ.org/`

Converting a Standard MIDI File to a QuickTime Movie with MoviePlayer

Although this technique is for MoviePlayer, it can apply to any program that uses the standard QuickTime import function.

1. Choose Import under the File menu. If MoviePlayer or another application does not recognize the MIDI file, you might need to use a drag-and-drop utility, such as MIDITyper or AllMIDI, to change file type and creator information.
2. Choose the SMF file you want to convert (see figs. 11.6 and 11.7).
3. Click on the Convert button.

Figure 11.6

Importing standard MIDI format files.

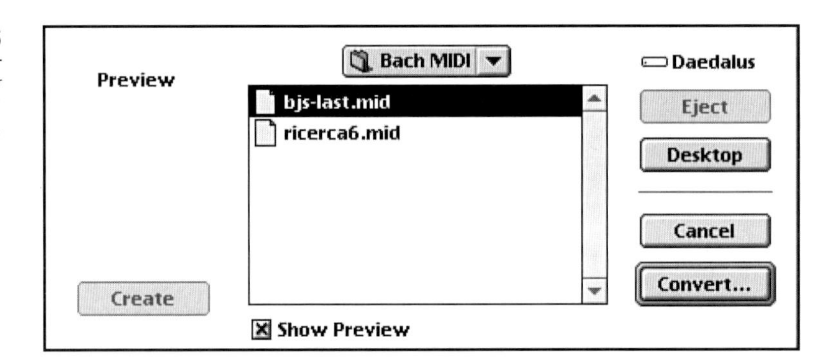

Figure 11.7

Converting a standard MIDI format file to QuickTime Music Tracks.

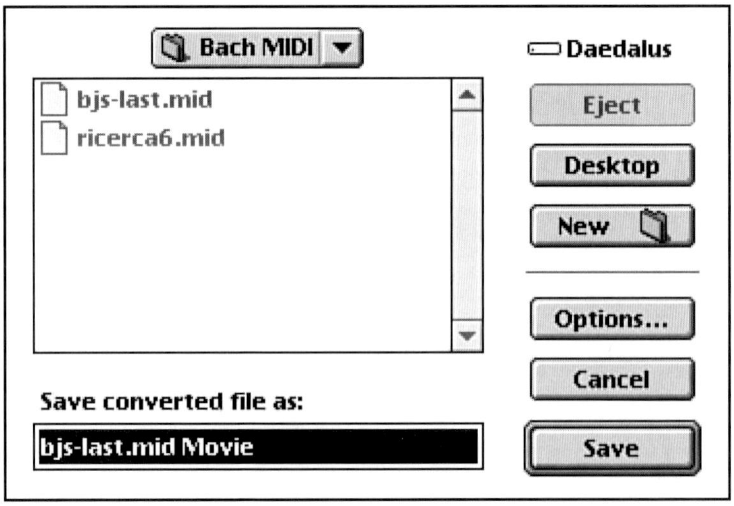

4. Click on the Options button if you would like to Add silence to the beginning or end of the file (see fig. 11.8).

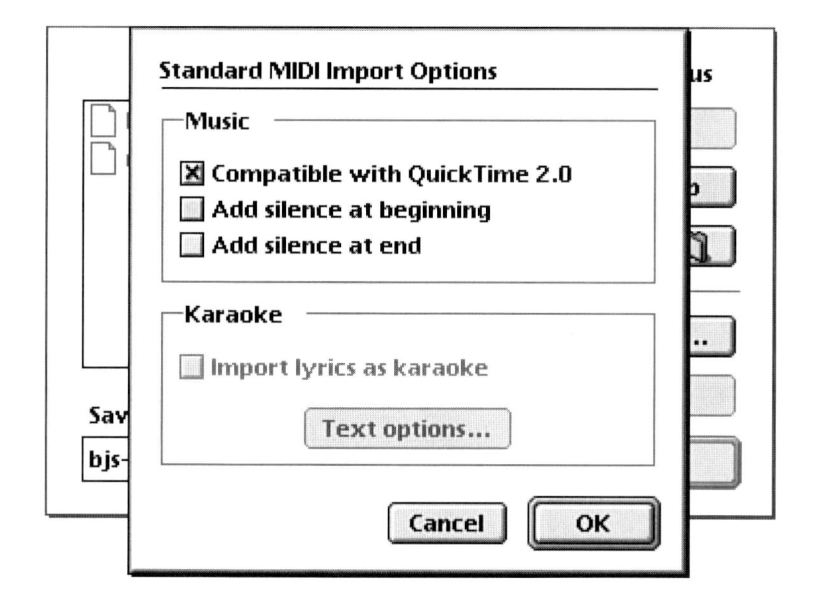

Figure 11.8

The Standard MIDI Import Options.

5. Click OK.

Editing Instruments in MoviePlayer

1. Choose Get Info under the Movie menu.
2. In the Movie Info dialog box, choose Music Track in the upper-left pop-up menu and choose Instruments in the upper-right pop-up menu.
3. You should see a list of instruments contained in the MIDI piece. Double-click on an instrument you want to change.
4. You are presented with the QuickTime Instrument dialog box. In the upper pop-up menu, choose QuickTime Music Synthesizer or another synthesizer if you have attached an external device to your computer.
5. Select the instrument type and instrument. You can audition the music sample for that instrument by clicking on the keyboard in the dialog box (see fig. 11.9). Instrument names in italics are not present in the currently selected synthesizer.

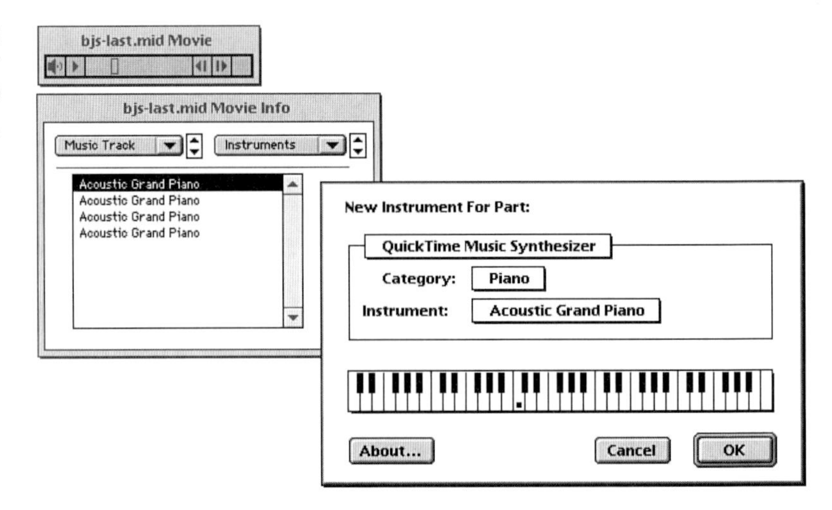

Figure 11.9

Changing instruments in QuickTime Music Tracks.

6. When you hear a sound you like, click OK and Save your movie with the new settings.

Embedding QTMA files in a Web page

To playback QTMA files from a Web page, users need the following tools:

Tools
QuickTime for the Mac or Windows
QuickTime Musical Instruments on a Macintosh (or have set MIDI mapping in Windows)

You embed a QuickTime Music Track in your Web page the same way you embed all other QuickTime media types. Chapter 10, "Animating with QuickTime Digital Video," discusses QuickTime in detail:

1. Save the QT Music Track as a sound-only QuickTime movie.
2. Use the MOV file extension.
3. Select the Make Movie Self-Contained and Playable On Non-Apple Computers options to make the movie cross-platform compatible.
4. To embed the music, use the following code:

```
<EMBED SRC = "bjs-last.mov" CONTROLLER = TRUE
➥HEIGHT = 32 WIDTH = 160>
```

To embed a QuickTime Music Track on a Web page for Internet Explorer, use MoviePlayer to export the track as a Standard MIDI Format file. Give the file name the MID extension and use the Internet Explorer tag BGSOUND to embed it in the Web page. This is discussed in detail later in this chapter.

Tip

To embed an invisible QuickTime Music Track on your Web page, you would, for example, use the following to play back the track as a background sound:

```
<EMBED SRC = "bjs-last.mov"
➥WIDTH=4 HEIGHT=4
➥AUTOSTART=TRUE AUTOPLAY=TRUE >
```

Hitting the spacebar toggles between pause and play if the movie is invisible. Provide users with this information on your QTMA-enabled Web page so that they can stop playback if they want.

Digital Audio

Digital audio playback has been available since the earliest days of the Web. Digital audio gives the Web page author the ability to provide high-quality spoken voice narration and music. Drawbacks of digital audio on the Web include the huge file sizes needed to provide high-quality audio and playback on cheap computer sound systems; however, proprietary audio compression schemes—RealAudio and Shockwave for Audio, for example—are beginning to address the file size issue.

Digital audio is a sampled audio waveform. A **sample** is the numeric value of the amplitude of an analog audio waveform at a specific point in time. The **sample rate** is the number of discrete samples taken along the waveform per unit time. The **sample resolution** is the number of bits used to represent the numeric value of the amplitude, usually 8 or 16 bits. Digital audio files come in different sample resolutions and sample rates, analogous to color-depth and dpi for graphics. Digital audio files can be mono or stereo.

sample

sample rate

sample resolution

Table 11.3 illustrates file sizes for uncompressed digital audio at different rates and resolutions.

Table 11.3

File Sizes for Uncompressed Digital Audio at Different Rates and Resolutions

Sample Rate	Sample Resolution	Channels	KB/Minute of Audio
44.1 kHz	16-bits	Stereo	10584
44.1 kHz	16-bits	Mono	5292
22.05 kHz	16-bits	Stereo	5292
22.05 kHz	16-bits	Mono	2646
22.05 kHz	8-bits	Stereo	2646

continues

Table 11.3, continued

File Sizes for Uncompressed Digital Audio at Different Rates and Resolutions

Sample Rate	Sample Resolution	Channels	KB/Minute of Audio
22.05 kHz	8-bits	Mono	1323
11.025 kHz	8-bits	Stereo	1323
11.025 kHz	8-bits	Stereo	662
7.418 kHz	8-bits	Mono	445

Tip

Sample resolution comes in two flavors: 16-bit and 8-bit. Sixteen-bit samples have much higher quality. For editing and processing, use 16-bit files, then downsample to 8-bit for the Web.

For maximum cross-platform compatibility of your digital audio files, stick to these standard sample rates, also shown in figure 11.10:

- 44.100 kHz
- 22.050 kHz
- 11.025 kHz

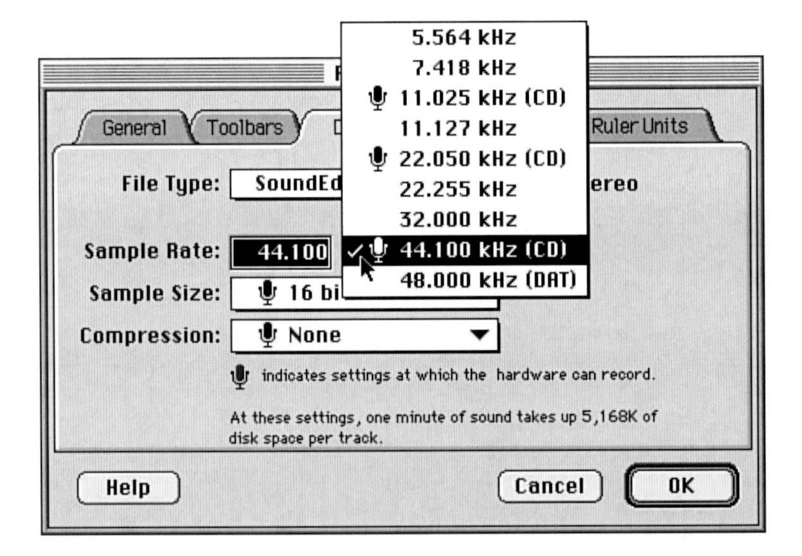

Figure 11.10

Available sample rates for digital audio editing in SoundEdit.

The range of human hearing extends to about 20 kHz. The higher frequencies often contain the overtones and audio information that add richness to sound. Digital audio can represent sounds up to half the sample rate. Audio sampled at 11.025 kHz can only represent sound frequencies up to about 5.5 kHz, which is why these samples sound flat. Table 11.4 lists some common sample rates and the highest frequencies that can be represented at that rate.

Table 11.4

Representative Sample Rates and the Highest Frequencies Present in Sound Sampled at Those Rates

Sample Rate	Highest Frequency*	Notes
48.000	24 kHz	Digital Audio Tape (DAT)
41.100	20 kHz	Audio CD
32.000	16 kHz	Broadcast Standard
22.255	11 kHz	Multimedia, IMA-compressed sound
11.025	5.5 kHz	Common on Windows
7.418	3.7 kHz	Lowest recommended for speech—telephone quality

* The upper range of human hearing is about 20 kHz.

You might use a rate lower than 11.025 kHz for some voice narration, but you will run into playback problems with some sound cards on Windows. Also, sound cards on Windows may not play back sound at the advertised rate.

File Formats

The most popular digital audio file formats on the Web are the following (table 11.5 lists MIME information for digital audio files):

- **AU files** are the standard audio format on Sun computers. They are generally 8-bit and typically have lower quality than other sound formats, but are very common on the Internet.
- **AIFF (Audio Interchange File Format)** is common on Macs and SGI computers. AIFF files can be 8-bit or 16-bit, support multiple channels, sample rates up to 44.1 kHz, and generally have good sound quality. AIFF-C is an AIFF file format with compressed samples, usually IMA, M-law, or MACE (compression schemes are discussed later in this chapter).
- **QuickTime** is Apple Computer's cross-platform multimedia container format that you can use to create audio-only movies. These movies provide all the standard

QuickTime features, such as synchronization to other media, and FastStart playback, along with features such as the standard QuickTime controller and interface.

- **WAV (waveform)** audio is the native format on Windows. WAV files can be 8-bit or 16-bit, with 11.025, 22.050, or 44.1 sample rates, and generally have good sound quality.

Table 11.5

MIME Information for Digital Audio Files

File Type	MIME Type	MIME Subtype	Filename Extensions
μ-law	audio	basic	au
AIFF	audio	aiff or x-aiff	aif, aiff
QuickTime Soundtrack	video	quicktime	mov, qt
WAVE	audio	wave	wav

Netscape 3 provides built-in support for these audio media types. IE 3 provides support through the addition of the ActiveMovie component. Probably the best cross-platform formats are AU, AIFF, and QuickTime audio on QuickTime-capable machines.

Digital Audio Hardware on a Mac

Since 1991, Macs have had built-in audio digitizing features integrated at the system level. Built-in digitizing features range from simple microphone input to full 16-bit 48-kHz digital audio subsystems. These features may be all you need to record audio for the Web. In addition, there are several flavors of digitizing cards—such as Digidesign's AudioMedia and Spectral Innovation's Numedia—for more demanding professional-level digitizing tasks that require digital I/O. Also, most video digitizers—such as Radius, Targa, Avid, and Data Translations—incorporate audio digitizing features.

Note

MPEG audio is the audio version of the MPEG video format. MPEG audio usually requires expensive encoding hardware and decoding hardware for playback. Software-based players include Sparkle, SoundApp,MPEG/CD, Xing's MPEG Sound Player, InterVU's PreVU.

The PowerPC processor has enabled applications, such as Deck II, to turn a PowerMac into a multi-track digital, direct-to-disk recording studio without the need for additional hardware (see fig. 11.11). Audio playback on all PowerMacs is stereo, CD-quality (16-bit, 44 kHz), with some models featuring multimedia optimized speaker systems.

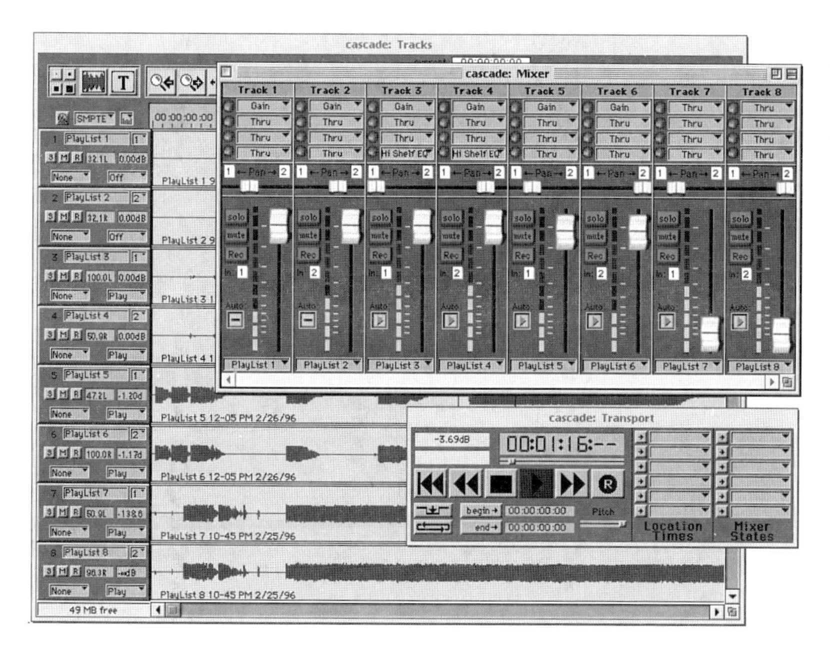

Figure 11.11

Deck, a multi-track, direct-to-disk, digital recording studio on a PowerMac.

At the system level, the Sound Manager handles most audio tasks, including decompressing IMA-compressed and M-law compressed audio (discussed later in this chapter), automatic sample rate conversion, multi-channel mixing, and asynchronous playback.

Digital Audio Hardware on a PC

On Intel-based PCs you generally need a separate card and separate speakers. SoundBlasters are ubiquitous and come in various flavors, with sound input and output, built-in wavetable MIDI, and other features. For audio production work, you may consider cards from DigiDesign and Digital Audio Labs. Playback on Intel PCs is highly variable. Microsoft has created a new Multimedia PC (MPC) standard, MPC III, that has considerable enhancements for audio playback, such as stereo 16-bit audio.

Microsoft's ADPCM Audio Compression Manager (ACM) provides similar quality as the IMA 4:1 compressor on a Mac. It is included with Windows 95, but some installs may require special setups. IMA-compressed audio is not as well-supported in Windows 3.1. DirectSound is the new sound architecture introduced by Microsoft and should become a factor for PC audio in the coming year.

Digital Audio ToolKit

Digital audio editing programs, include the following:

- Macromedia SoundEdit (Mac only)
- Macromedia Deck II (Mac only)
- Opcode's AudioShop (Mac only)
- Opcode's DigiTrax (Mac only)
- DigiDesign's ProTools products (Mac only)
- Sonic Foundry's SoundForge for Windows
- Bias Systems Peak (Mac only)

Digital audio utilities include:

- Several great utilities from Waves:

  Steinberg's Time Bandit

  Passport Design's Alchemy 3.0

  Waves WaveConvert

  Arboretum HyperPrism

Shareware Mac tools include:

- SoundApp

  `http://www-cs-students.stanford.edu/~franke/SoundApp/`

  `http://hyperarchive.lcs.mit.edu/HyperArchive/Archive/gst/snd/sound-app-211.hqx`

- SoundMachine Player

  `http://hyperarchive.lcs.mit.edu/HyperArchive/Archive/gst/snd/sound-machine-262.hqx`

- SoundEffects (see fig. 11.12)

  `http://hyperarchive.lcs.mit.edu/HyperArchive/Archive/gst/snd/sound-effects-092.hqx`

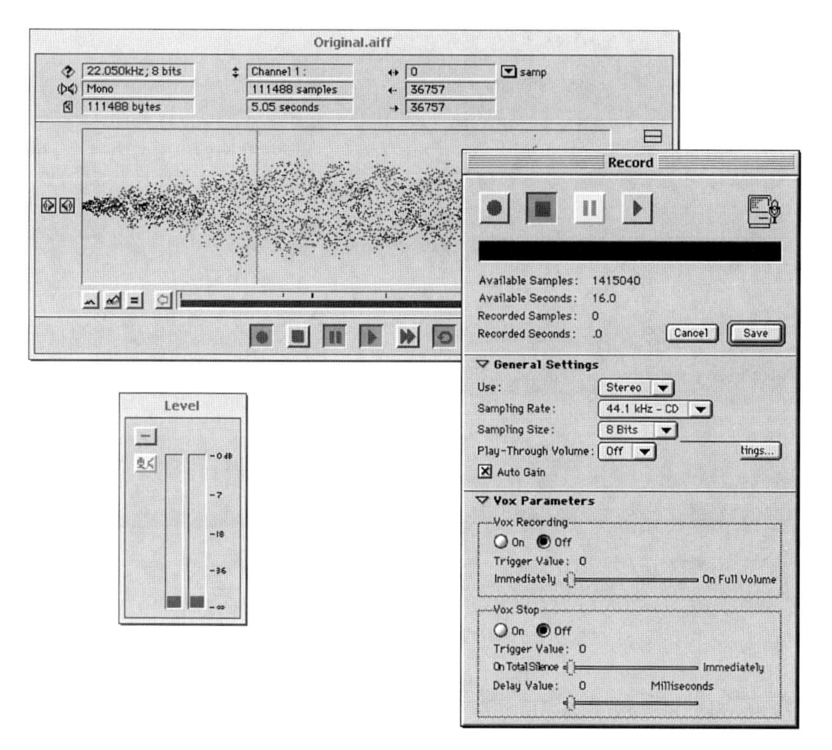

Figure 11.12

Digitizing audio with Sound Effects.

- SoundSculptor

  `http://hyperarchive.lcs.mit.edu/HyperArchive/Archive/gst/snd/sound-sculptor-ii-20.hqx`

- D-SoundPRO 2.3

  `http://hyperarchive.lcs.mit.edu/HyperArchive/Archive/gst/midi/d-sound-pro-23.hqx`

Shareware Windows tools include:

- GoldWave
- CoolEdit

  `http://www.netzone.com/syntrillium/`

- SoundGadget Pro

  `http://www.cs.man.ac.uk/~magnayn/SGPro.html`

Non-destructive editors, such as Deck II, are more expensive and consume more disk space and system resources, but provide additional flexibility and power. During non-destructive editing, audio data is never destroyed or deleted. Instead, edited data is saved with the original audio data.

EQ

Non-destructive editing makes it incredibly easy to try different takes, use different **EQ** settings (EQ, or **equalization**, is discussed later in this chapter), and create entirely new mixes without worrying about destroying or degrading the original data.

Capturing and Digitizing Audio

Most Macs since 1991 and PCs, with the appropriate sound cards, have audio inputs. You can digitize audio on these systems using programs such as SimpleSound on Mac and SoundRecorder on PC. This may be okay for recording a Happy Birthday greeting for Grandma to put on your Web page, but you probably want to look at some other programs.

Digitizing Audio with GoldWave

GoldWave is a Windows shareware sound editor and digitizer. It's available on the Web and has an intuitive interface that is easy to use. GoldWave is typical of many shareware sound editors.

1. Use the software that came with your sound card to make sure the card is set up for audio input and that the settings are what you want.
2. Launch GoldWave.
3. Select New under the File menu.
4. In the dialog box, choose the settings you want.
5. Play a short piece of the audio you want to record, or talk into the microphone to test the audio input levels.
6. To start recording, click on the red button in the Device Controls window.
7. To stop recording, click on the purple Stop button.

Digitizing Audio with SoundEdit

SoundEdit is a popular Mac-only commercial digital audio editor from Macromedia. It's been around a while and is part of Macromedia's Studio bundle. Many people have it in their toolkit. It's PowerMac native and takes advantage of the PowerPC.

1. To choose the input device, select Recording Options under the Modify menu.
2. To open the Controls window, choose Controls under the Windows menu.
3. Check audio levels in the level meter.
4. To start recording, click the Record button.
5. To stop recording, click the Stop button.

Digitizing Audio with Premiere

Many developers already have Adobe Systems' Premiere in their toolkit. Besides video capture and editing, you can capture audio and perform very simple digital audio editing. Premiere is cross-platform.

To digitize audio in Premiere, first set your preferences for audio processing (see fig. 11.13).

1. Choose Audio Preferences in the File menu.
2. Check the Process audio at check box.
3. Select the resolution and rate of the audio files you will be processing.

There are two ways to capture audio in Premiere: you can capture audio into an AIFF file or onto a sound-only QuickTime movie. To capture audio to an AIFF file, follow these steps (see fig. 11.14):

1. Choose Capture, Audio Capture in the File menu.
2. Choose Sound Input in the Audio Capture menu.
3. Click on Options.
4. Select the sound input source and click on OK.

Figure 11.13

Setting audio preferences in Premiere.

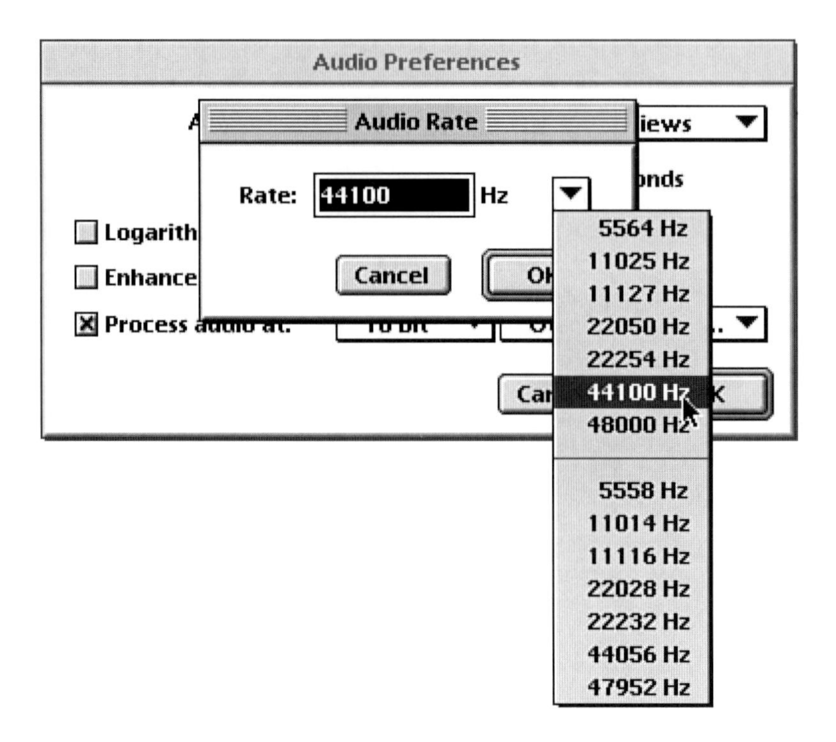

Note

Be sure to set your rate at 44.100, 22.050, or 11.025.

5. Choose the sample settings for capture.
6. Play some sound and check levels.
7. Click on OK.
8. Click on Record to begin recording.

Tip

Premiere has an annoying habit of resetting your sample settings when you select input sources, so double-check your capture settings before you record.

To capture audio into a sound-only QuickTime movie:

1. Choose Capture, Movie Capture under the File menu.
2. Under Movie Capture, make sure Video Off is checked and Sound Off is unchecked.
3. Choose Sound Input under the Movie Capture menu. You will see the Sound dialog box, as shown in figure 11.15.
4. On the left side of the dialog box is a pop-up menu that enables you to set various options. For compression choose None. If you have to compress while digitizing, choose IMA4:1 for the best quality.
5. Choose Sample from the pop-up menu. If you can, choose 44.100 kHz, 16-bit, and stereo if you have the disk space and need the highest quality capture for music, for example. It may be adequate to choose 22.050 kHz, 16-bit, mono for voice recordings.

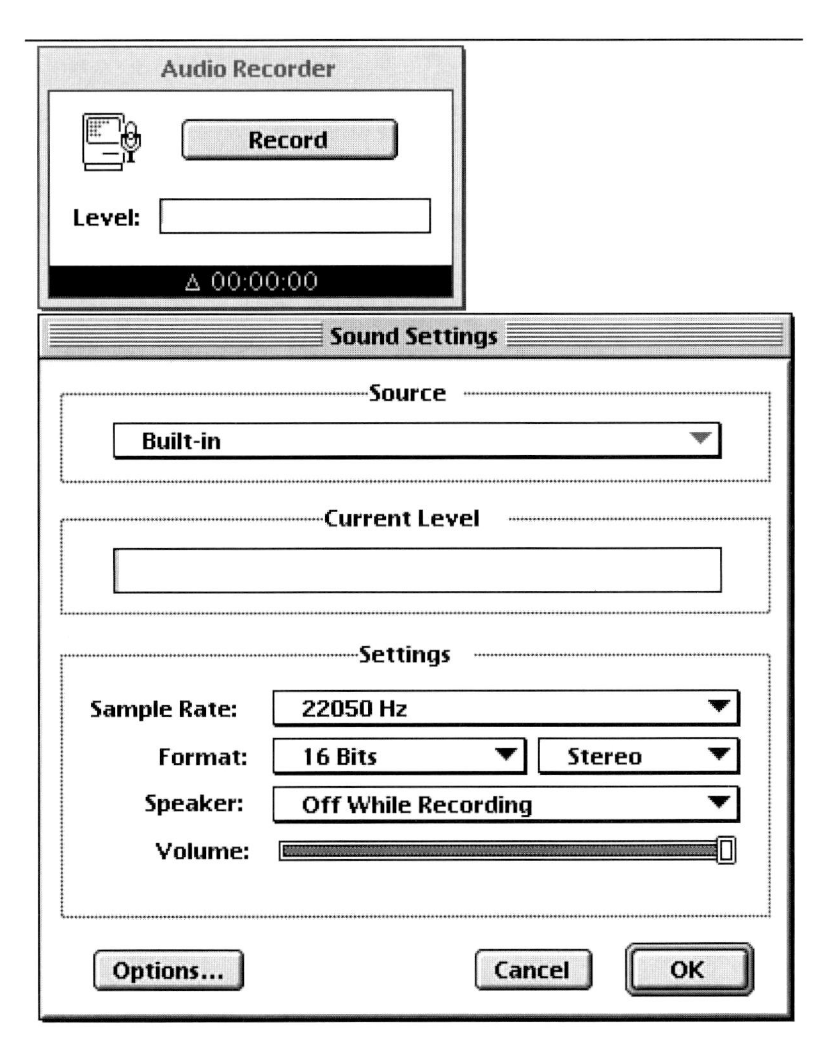

Figure 11.14

Settings for Audio Capture.

6. Choose Source and select the digitizing device and the input source.
7. In the right side of the dialog box is a level meter and a slider you can use to adjust the gain, or amplitude. Begin playing the sound you want to record and see whether you are recording at maximum volume without clipping. Adjust the gain slider if appropriate. Take into account transients in the source that will cause spikes and clipping.

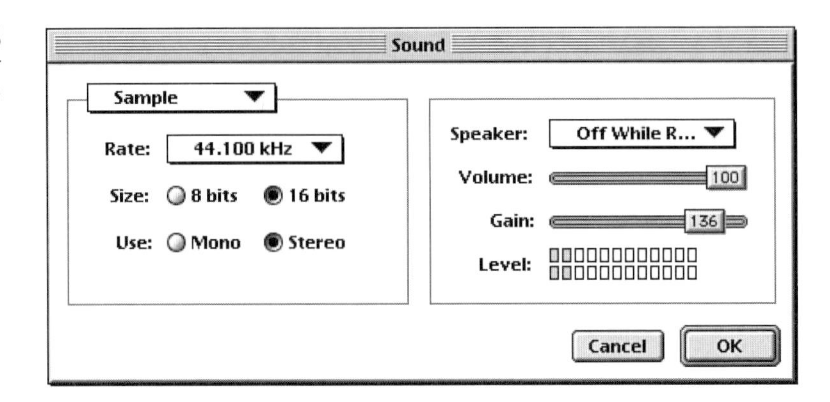

Figure 11.15

Setting for QuickTime Audio Capture.

General Tips for Digitizing Audio

When you are concerned with the quality of your Web audio, there are certain rules of thumb you should follow:

- **Input Levels.** Record hot—that is, use the highest volume input level you can that does not clip or distort so that you optimize dynamic range. Most digitizing software has a level indicator you can use to determine whether clipping is occurring. Typically, clipping is indicated by a red indicator light. Some software enables you to adjust input levels. You can also use a mixer or tape deck to adjust levels. Typically set the levels around 70 to 80 percent of the maximum. If you are using a consumer tape deck, you might be able to adjust levels by adjusting the record level in the record/pause mode. If you are using a microphone without a mixer, move the microphone farther or closer to the sound source to adjust levels.
- **Capture at high resolution and rate.** As with most digitizing, it's generally good to capture the most information that you can given time, disk space, and processing speed limitations, and then downsample in the last step. The same is true for audio. Generally, digitize audio at 16-bit, 44.1 kHz, if you can. If you can't digitize at that setting or can't fit the resulting sound file on your hard disk, try 16-bit, 22.05 kHz and digitize in mono.

  As always, it depends on your content and design goals. If all you want to do is record your cat meowing so you can pop it on your home page, you can probably capture at the resolution and rate you deliver, for example 8-bit 11 kHz. But if you are recording voice narration that you are going to want people to listen to, or music, capture at the highest resolution and rate that you can.

- **Use clean source.** If your source material is low-fidelity, the digital file will sound even worse. Digitize from CDs, DAT tape, the best tape deck you can find (use high-quality tape), or a professional quality microphone.
- **Use good equipment and shielded or balanced cables.** To minimize interference from electric motors, computers, and power chords, don't run audio cables next to these devices. Be sure you connect line level sources, such as an audio CD or mixer, to the live level input on your audio digitizer and be sure you connect the microphone level source to the microphone input on your digitizer.
- **Turn-off extra extensions, virtual memory, and networking.**
- **Use an AV optimized hard drive.**
- **Defragment your hard drive.**
- **Consider using a compressor and noise gate, especially when recording voices.** A compressor smooths out variations in the volume of audio and a **noise gate** can filter out background noise. Some digital audio software enables you to apply these effects in software.

noise gate function

- **Use your system software's playthrough option to monitor the sound on computer speakers.** To monitor sound on external amplifiers and speakers, run a cable from the computer's sound output to your mixer's stereo return input.

Editing Digital Audio for the Web

In a digital audio file, silence takes up the same amount of space as sound. So one of the first tasks is to trim the silence from your audio, unless there is a good reason not to, such as synchronization with other media. Be sure to leave at least 50–100 milliseconds of silence at the start of your clip, though, to give time for some sound cards to kick in.

If you are going to deliver mono sound files, don't use stereo effects such as panning (which shifts the sound in the stereo soundspace) or stereo chorus.

Other common editing functions include normalization, the creation of looping sounds, cross-fades, and the application of sound effects, such as a noise gate, compressor, or equalization (EQ, discussed later in this chapter).

Normalization

Normalization is a feature of many sound editing programs. *Normalization* looks at the maximum amplitude in an audio waveform and adjusts the amplitude of the rest of the waveform based on it's peak value, without clipping or distortion. Normalization can add a lot of presence to a sound. When you normalize a sound, you will also be increasing the amplitude of noise and any distortion. Always use the cleanest source possible. If you hear crackling or other distortion in the sound after normalizing, try normalizing at a value less than 100 percent.

Be careful of spikes in amplitude or transients that might skew normalization functions. If an amplitude spike is embedded in your sound file, use your sound editor to zoom in as close as you can and use the adjust amplitude or gain command to bring the volume of the spike down. Be careful not to alter adjacent audio data.

Tip

If you add a lot of EQ to a normalized sound, you might introduce distortion. When you normalize audio, use a value less than 100 percent, say 50–90 percent, to give yourself some headroom.

Whether you normalize (see fig. 11.16) and when you normalize in the editing process depends on the quality of the source, the editing you plan on doing, and the output you want. Generally, it's better to normalize at the outset of the editing process so you are working with audio data at the optimal amplitude. If you have a noisy voice recording, you may first want to apply a noise gate function, or if you are creating looping music, you may want to normalize first, before you edit the loop points.

Looping

Creating audio loops is one of the most common tasks in creating Web-based audio. Audio loops are small—the goal of all Web content development—and play in the background endlessly. But loops can grate on listeners' ears after awhile. Composing and creating a loop that loops seamlessly and doesn't become boring and repetitive takes a lot of skill.

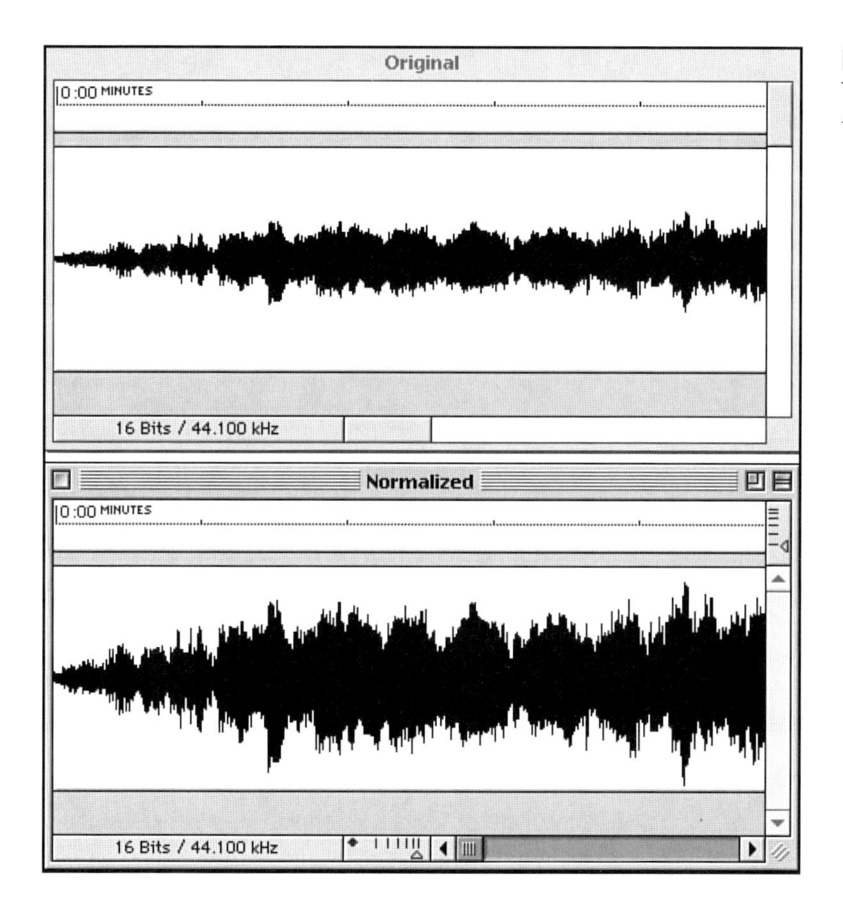

Figure 11.16

A normalized audio waveform.

Musical Tips for Composing Loops

Use the following rules of thumb when composing loops:

- Start with an unresolved chord, a seventh chord, leading phrase, or turnaround, such as V in a I-IV-V progression, so that the tonic falls on an offbeat.
- Use an unusual time signature such as 5/4 or mix up different time signatures.
- High notes can get crunched during future downsampling, especially high ringing sounds.
- To hide downsampling artifacts, use instruments such as fuzzy synth pads, vocal ahs, or brushed cymbals.

Digital Audio Editing for Loops

Use the following standards when editing loops:

- Set the start of the loop and the end of a loop at zero crossing points. Programs such as SoundEffects and

SoundEdit have tools to help you do this. (See the following section in this chapter to see how to do this with SoundEdit.)

- Cross-fade the beginning and end of a loop clip. (See a later section to see how to cross-fade with SoundEdit.)
- If you are recording from a MIDI loop, use the second or third iteration of the loop so that sustained notes and other long sounds are captured.
- If you are splicing a bar or two from a digital audio file to use as a loop, consider starting the loop on an offbeat to add rhythmic interest.

Using Loop Tuner in SoundEdit

To create a loop from a piece of a digital audio file in SoundEdit, follow these steps:

1. Select the piece of the file you want to loop.
2. Choose Loop Tuner from the Xtras menu. You will see the Loop Tuner dialog box, as shown in figure 11.17.
3. Adjust the start and end point of the loop with the arrow buttons, until there is no gap in the waveform.
4. Click on the Set Loop button.

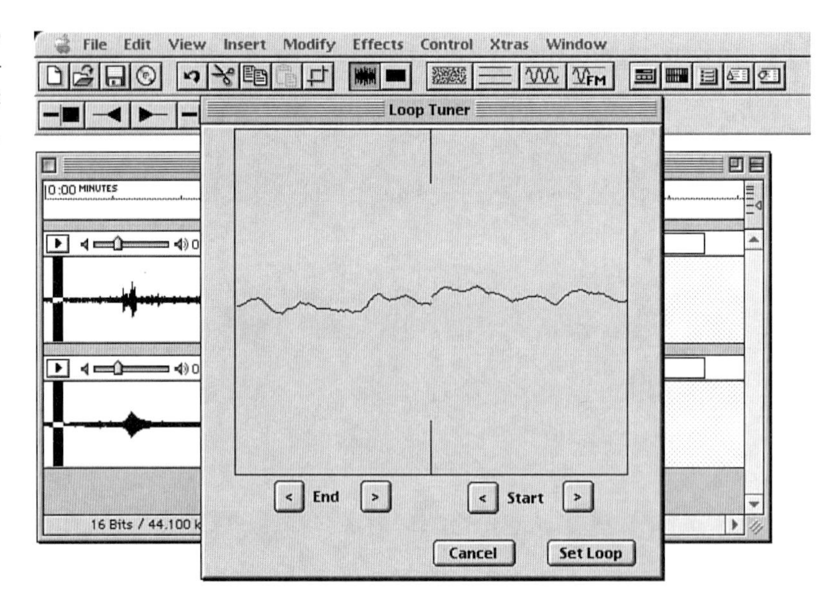

Figure 11.17

The Loop Tuner in SoundEdit.

Creating Cross-Fades for Loops with SoundEdit

cross-fade

Another technique for creating loops is to **cross-fade** the beginning and end of the music segment you want to loop. It is probably easier to do this in non-destructuve editors, such as Deck II, but the following steps show how to do cross-fades for loops in SoundEdit:

1. Save the music clip you want to loop in a separate SoundEdit file.
2. Open this file in SoundEdit.
3. To insert a new track, choose Track under the Insert menu.
4. Select approximately the first second of audio at the start of the clip (see fig. 11.18).

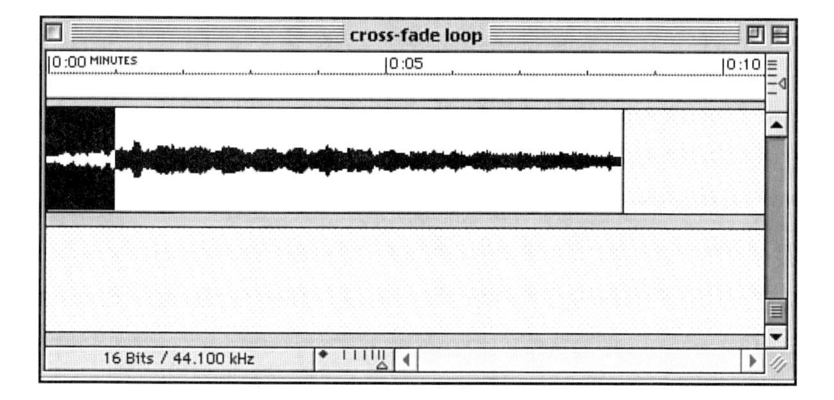

Figure 11.18

Selecting the beginning of a loop for a cross-fade.

5. Choose Selection under the Window menu to open the Selection dialog box (see fig. 11.19). Note the length of the selected segment.

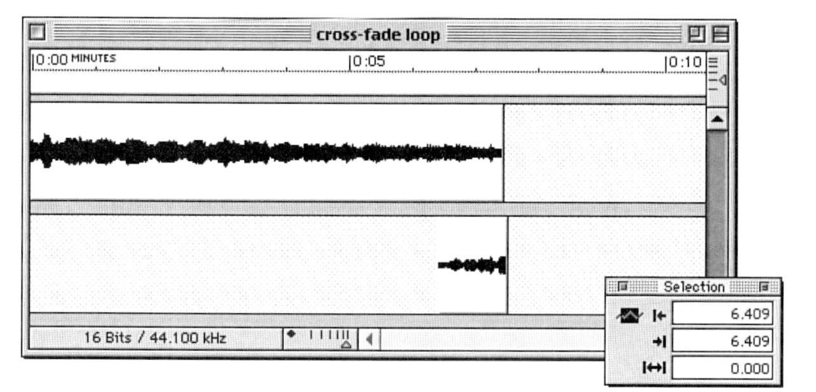

Figure 11.19

Lining up the beginning and end of a loop.

6. Choose Cut from the Edit menu or press Command+X.
7. Paste this clip at the end of the new track you just created.
8. Choose Track Offset under the Modify menu and enter an offset value that will line up the end of this clip with the end of the main clip.
9. Select the overlap of both clips.
10. Choose Envelope from the Effects menu.
11. Create a cross-fade envelope for the two clips (see fig. 11.20).

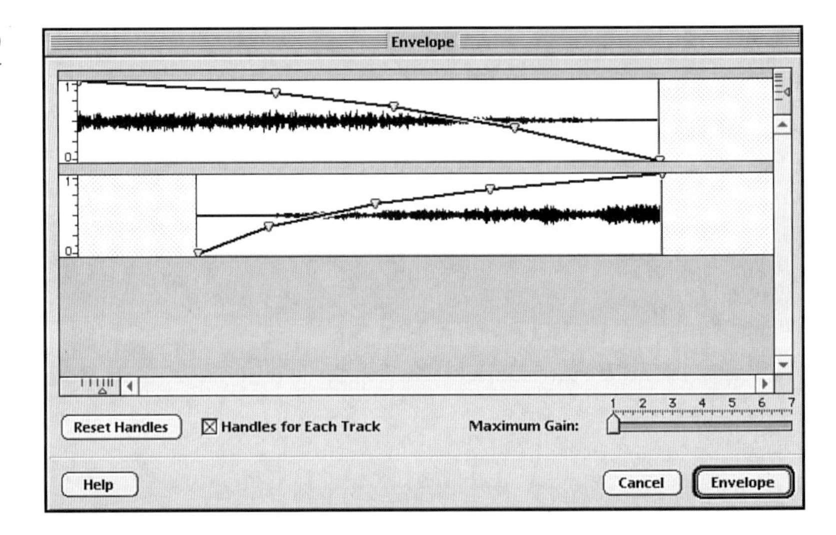

Figure 11.20

Cross-fade envelope.

12. Choose Mix under the Effects menu and mix to a mono file.

Downsampling Digital Audio for the Web

You've laid down the perfect track. Now you want to put it on the Web. Be prepared to turn it into a muddy crackling mess!

Seriously, by now you realize that downsampling, whether graphics, video, or audio, is one of the most common tasks you will perform when you create Web content. Downsampling audio is especially tricky because of the complex source data and the annoying and grating aliasing artifacts in audio.

You will probably want to downsample digital audio to 8-bit 11 kHz; you can go even lower for audio, such as a male voice. Another option is to use IMA-compressed audio, discussed later in this chapter. IMA-compression requires 16-bit 22-kHz source files.

Although some audio tools enable you to perform downsampling in one step, it is often best to perform a two-step downsample:

1. First downsample the sample rate, from 44.1 kHz to 22.050 kHz, for example.
2. Listen to the sound on target systems. Adjust EQ or perform other sound shaping.
3. Downsample sample resolution from 16-bit to 8-bit.

Some programs, such as Deck and SoundEdit, enable you to set options for downsampling, such as rounding and dithering, that may improve downsampling to 8-bit sounds. Arguably the best downsampling and post-processing tool for professional-quality results is LI Ultramaximizer from Waves, which is a Plug-In for SoundForge, SoundEdit, Deck, Premiere, and Sound Designer.

Downsampling in GoldWave

To reduce the sample rate, choose Resample under the Effects menu and set the rate to the desired rate.

To reduce the sample resolution, choose Save As from the File menu and select one of the 8-bit options.

Downsampling in Sound Effects

SoundEffects is a $15 shareware digital audio editing application for the Mac from Alberto Ricci. It provides a wide range of powerful editing, digitizing, conversion, and effects capabilities.

To reduce the sample rate in SoundEffects, choose Resampling, Resample Rate from the Effects menu.

To reduce the sample resolution in SoundEffects, choose Resampling, DownSample Bits rate from the Effects menu (see fig. 11.21).

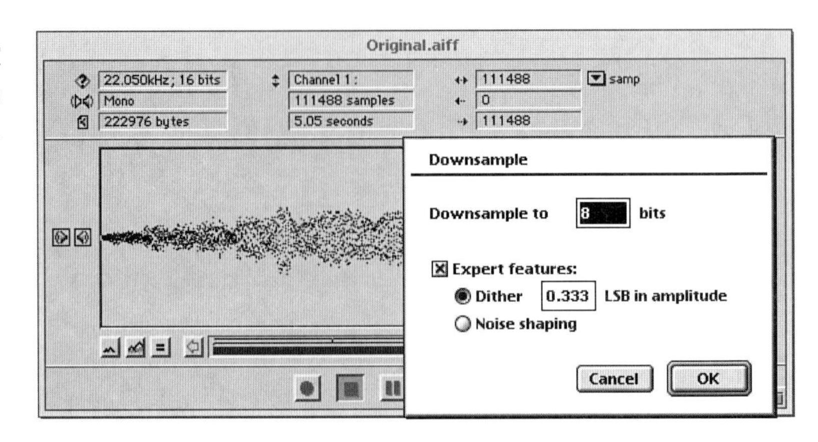

Figure 11.21

Saving an 8-bit file in SoundEffects.

Downsampling Audio in Premiere

Premiere ships with a Downsample Plug-In for audio. If you don't see the Plug-In installed in Premiere, look in the Extra Goodies folder in your Premiere Goodies folder. To downsample audio in Premiere, use these steps:

1. The audio clip must be in an audio track in the Construction Window. Select the clip you want to downsample.
2. Choose Filters from the Clip menu.
3. Select Downsample from the Available list.
4. Click the Add button.
5. Select the Quality setting. The lowest quality will probably introduce noticeable sizzling and crackling (see fig. 11.22). Try a higher quality setting.
6. Click OK.

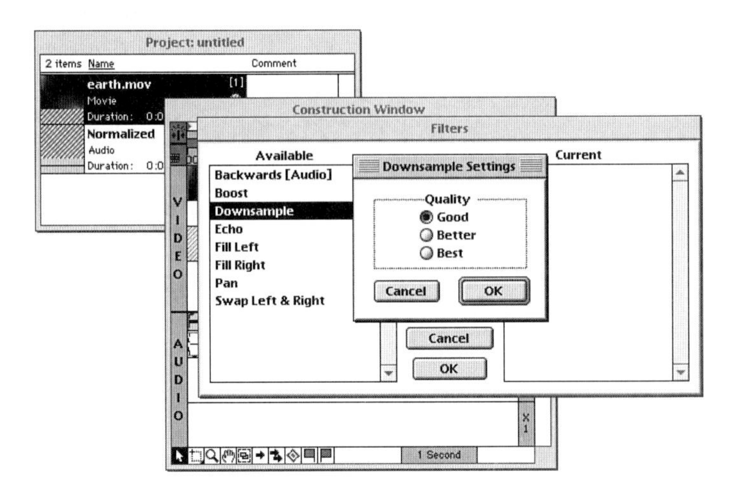

Figure 11.22

Setting the downsampling quality in Premiere.

Downsampling Audio in SoundEdit

Work on a copy of your original when you downsample so you always have a high-quality, high-resolution original. To downsample an audio file in SoundEdit, use these steps:

1. Choose Sound Format from the Modify menu. You will see the Sound Format dialog box, as shown in figure 11.23.
2. To change Sample Rate, choose values from the pop-up menu or enter values in the Sample Rate dialog box if, for example, you want to crunch the recording of a male voice even smaller than the smallest available rate. Be aware that playback of these sounds may be a problem on some Windows systems.
3. If you plan on performing further EQ or other editing, leave the resolution at 16-bit and perform this downsampling in a second pass.
4. If you will be using IMA compression you must use 16-bit, 22-kHz audio; otherwise, choose None from the Compression pull down menu.
5. Select Boost Highs and Use Dither to see if that will help preserve audio quality.
6. Click on OK.

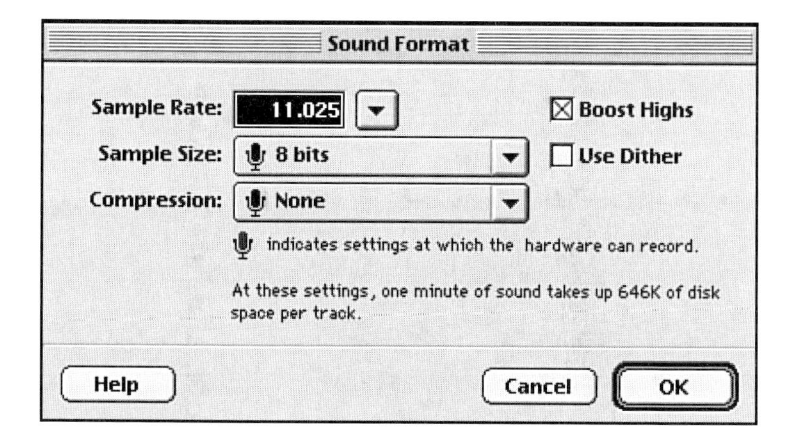

Figure 11.23

SoundEdit's Sound Format dialog box.

Pitch Shift Downsampling

Pitch shift downsampling is a technique you can use to downsample sounds, that sometimes works better than the built-in downsampling algorithms in software programs.

Again, it depends on your sound and your sound-editing program. You might want to perform multiple downsampling techniques to see which one works the best with your sound.

Here's how to perform pitch shift downsampling with SoundEdit. Other digital audio editors should follow a similar process.

1. Open an 8-bit 22-kHz file in SoundEdit.
2. Choose Select All under the Edit menu.
3. Choose Pitch Shift under the Effects menu.
4. Lower the pitch one octave or enter .5 in the times pitch text box, as shown in figure 11.24.

Figure 11.24

Pitch-shift downsampling.

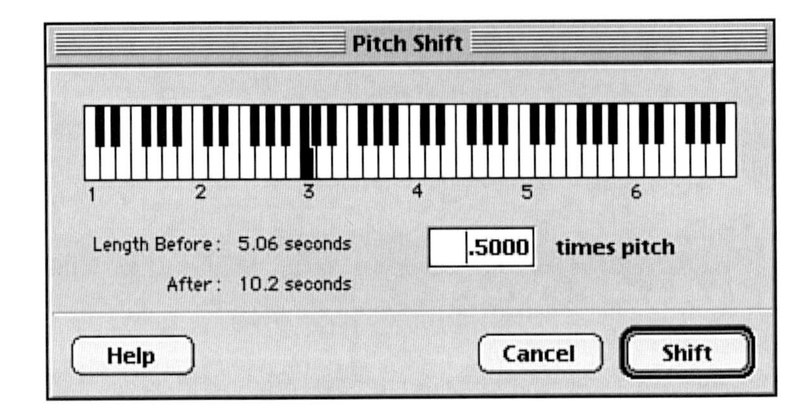

5. Select Copy under the File menu.
6. Select New under the File menu.
7. Select Paste under the File menu.
8. Choose Sound Format from the Modify menu.
9. Set Sample Rate to **11** kHz.
10. Choose Pitch Shift under the Effects menu.
11. Raise the pitch one octave or enter 2 in the times pitch option box.
12. Select Save under the File menu.

EQ for the Web

Perform a test downsampling on your sounds and listen to them on your target speakers, not your headphones or studio speakers. Most computer speakers have no bass response.

Downsampling will remove high frequencies, making the sound flat, and add artifacts, which adds noticeable hissing or crackling.

EQ, or equalization, can be a way to mitigate the bad effects of downsampling, poor source, and poor playback systems. It can also quickly turn your sounds into a muddy mess. Be judicious in the use of EQ and test the sound on target systems.

EQ can be performed several different ways depending on your software. You are probably most familiar with the graphic equalizer on a stereo, where sliders enable you to adjust amplitude of selected frequencies, like those shown in the electronic equivalent in figure 11.25.

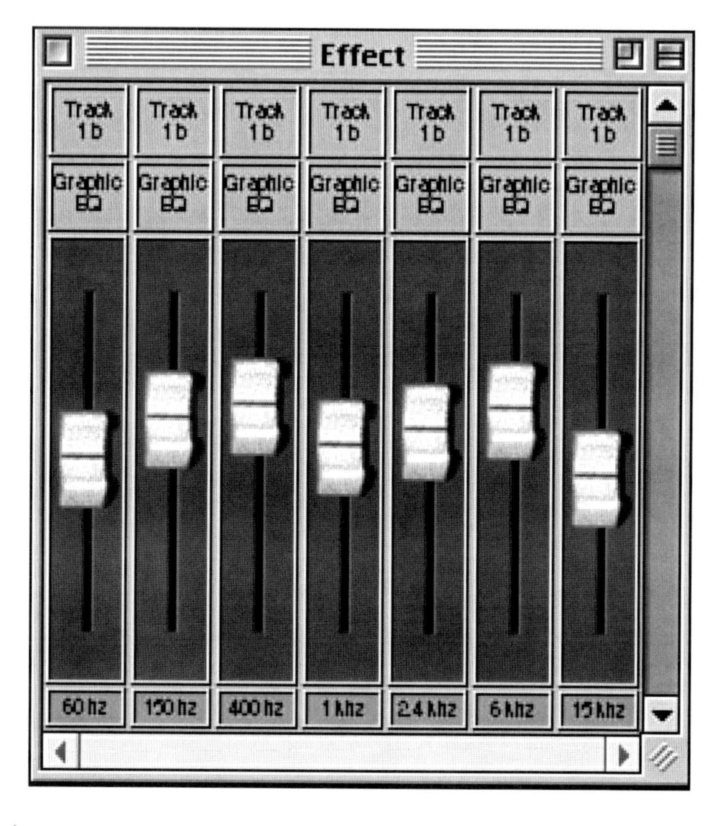

Figure 11.25

A graphic EQ in software.

Most computer speakers have poor bass response. To get more low-end sounds on computer speakers, don't boost the bass frequencies, but instead boost the low-mid range to around 250 Hz. If you desire to boost a certain frequency range, it's often better to reduce the adjacent frequencies range.

Boosting the mid-range to around 1–2.5 kHz can add a lot of presence to sounds that have been rendered flat by downsampling. It can also help to make voices more intelligible.

Downsampling to 11 kHz destroys high frequencies in your sound. You may be able to make the sound a little livelier by boosting the 4–5.5 kHz range a bit.

Finally, try not to use a lot of EQ. Experiment. Trust your ears and listen to the sounds on target speakers.

Using QuickTime Digital Audio

You can use QuickTime as a container format for digital audio on the Web and take advantage of features such as Fast-Start, the standard Quicktime controller, IMA-compression, synchronization with other tracks, and built-in QuickTime support in most browsers. When you save QuickTime audio-only movies, be sure to save them as self-contained, flattened movies that are playable on non-Apple computers. See Chapter 10, "Animating with Quicktime Digital Video," for details.

To use MoviePlayer for QuickTime authoring, be sure to use the version of MoviePlayer that contains the Goodies and Authoring Extras Plug-Ins. Visit the following sites for these authoring tools.

```
http://www.quicktime.apple.com/software/mac/

http://www.QuickTimeFAQ.org/
```

IMA-Compression and other Audio Compression Schemes

When editing and creating Web content, work at high resolution and then downsample and compress as the last step. This is one of the basic rules of creating Web multimedia, and it also applies to audio.

Most compression schemes are *lossy*—they discard some audio data when they perform compression. For this reason, it is a good idea to compress only copies of high-quality source material and to perform compression only after on a file. Each compression pass degrades the file's fidelity because more data is discarded with each pass. Another consideration when using compression is that users must have the ability to decompress the file. This usually means having the appropriate player or system-level codec.

IMA/APDCM stands for Interactive Music Association/Adaptive Differential Pulse Code Modulation. What a mouthful! IMA-compression provides high-quality compression of 16-bit, 22-kHz or 44-kHz audio samples with a 4:1 compression ratio. It is supported at the system level in Mac and Windows 95 systems and can be applied to WAVE, AIFF, and QuickTime Sound format audio. IMA-compression of audio is a great option for compressing standard audio files for the Web.

MPEG, MACE, M-law, a-law, G.723, and G.721 are other audio compression schemes. Other Web and network-optimized audio formats include proprietary formats used by products such as RealAudio, Shockwave for Audio, and numerous Internet telephony products and some video-conferencing applications. On the horizon, audio compression algorithms developed for audio-conferencing applications may be incorporated at the system level in QuickTime for Mac and Windows and in Windows 95.

Creating IMA-Compressed Audio

IMA-compression requires at least 16-bit, 22-kHz source files. To create an IMA-compressed sound with MoviePlayer, follow these steps:

1. Start with a sound-only QuickTime movie. You can create a sound-only QuickTime movie by choosing Import under the File menu and selecting an AIFF sound file or System sound file.
2. Choose Export from the File menu.
3. Select Sound To AIFF.
4. Click Options.
5. Select IMA 4:1 for compressor.
6. Select a sampling rate of 11.025 and Mono.
7. Click on OK.
8. Name the file and click Save.

To import an IMA-compressed file into a QuickTime Sound Track:

1. Choose Import under the File menu and select the IMA audio file you just created.
2. Click the Convert button.
3. Save as a QuickTime movie.

Serve sound-only QuickTime movies containing IMA-compressed audio the same way you serve other QuickTime content on the Web.

To create IMA-compressed audio on Windows choose, the IMA ADPCM or MSADPCM Compression option when you save your file in your favorite sound editor.

Synching Sound with Other Media

There are several ways to synch audio playback with other media on the Web page.

- LiveConnect and ActiveX Scripting provides ways for Java applets, Plug-Ins, ActiveX controls, and Web pages to coordinate and share data. These features are just starting to be integrated into browsers (see the section, "Embedding Digital Files for LiveAudio"). LiveAudio also enables a single controller to control playback of multiple audio.
- Use JavaScript event handlers to trigger audio playback. See Chapter 15, "Java," for a description of JavaScript event handlers.
- QuickTime excels at providing synchronization of diverse media types. If you can integrate all the media that you want to be synchronized into a QuickTime movie, that is probably the best way to go.
- Shockwave is another excellent tool for media integration and synchronization. See Chapter 8, "Animating with Shockwave for Director," for examples of providing Shockwave audio content. Shockwave also has limited capabilities to communicate with the Web browser environment, which open up opportunities for

synchronization and integration with other multimedia elements on a Web page.

- It's also possible to perform actions such as updating a Netscape Navigator frame at specific times within a pre-recorded RealAudio stream. Thus, you could provide a self-running recorded narrative that would be synchronized to graphic display in a Web page frame. Creating synchronized media with RealAudio requires access to command-line utilities on a RealAudio server. These utilities create a special binary file based on a text file you create that contains synchronization instructions. Find out more at:

  `http://www.realaudio.com/help/ccguide/synchmm.html`

Embedding Digital Audio in a Web Page

You embed audio in your Web page the same way you embed other media—by doing the following:

- Providing a hyperlink to the file for users with helper apps set up
- Using the EMBED tag with LiveAudio or other Netscape-compatible Plug-Ins
- For Internet Explorer 2 or later, using the BGSOUND tag for background audio—for example, `<BGSOUND SRC = "mySound.wav">`
- For Internet Explorer 3 for Windows 95 and Windows NT, using the OBJECT tag with ActiveX controls

Table 11.6 shows audio support for different browsers.

Table 11.6

Browser Audio Support

File Type	Netscape 2.0	MSIE 2	Netscape 3.0	MSIE 3
AIFF	Yes	No	Yes	Yes
WAV	Need Plug-In	Yes	Yes	Yes
AU	Yes	No	Yes	Yes
MIDI	Need Plug-In	Yes	Yes	Yes
QuickTime	Need Plug-In	Yes	Yes	Yes

Embedding Digital Files for LiveAudio

The latest versions of browsers provide integrated support for most audio file formats. LiveConnect is Netscape's name for the technology providing integration of JavaScript, Java applets, and Plug-Ins in the Netscape Web browser environment. LiveAudio, LiveConnect's audio Plug-In for Netscape Navigator, provides many sophisticated functions for presentation and playback control. To embed a digital audio file for LiveAudio that automatically begins playback, use this form:

```
<EMBED SRC = "mySound.aif" AUTOSTART = TRUE>
```

Tip

For the latest information on the new LiveAudio commands and HTML attributes, see

http://home.netscape.com/comprod/products/navigator/version 3.0/developer/newplug.html

To provide an audio file that can be controlled by the user with the standard LiveAudio controller, use the CONSOLE or SMALLCONSOLE attributes. For example, the following code provides both EMBED and BGSOUND tags for compatibility with both Navigator and Explorer.

```
<EMBED SRC="mySound.aif" HEIGHT=15 WIDTH=144 CONTROLS
➥SMALLCONSOLE>
```

One feature of LiveConnect-enabled Plug-Ins such as LiveAudio is its capability to be controlled from JavaScript. A snippet of code follows that fades out a LiveAudio background sound after a specific length of time, using the JavaScript setTimeOut function:

```
<HTML>
<HEAD>

<TITLE>Fading Out LiveAudio Background Sounds</TITLE>

</HEAD>
<BODY>

<EMBED SRC="hum.aif" NAME=greetings AUTOSTART = TRUE
HIDDEN=TRUE>

<SCRIPTLANGUAGE="JavaScript">window.setTimeout('document.embeds
["greetings"].fade_from_to(100,0)',1000)

</SCRIPT>


</BODY>
</HTML>
```

See Chapter 14, "Scripting Multimedia Web Pages," for more on client-side scripting.

Embedding QuickTime Audio

To use QuickTime audio-only movies on the Web, be sure they are saved as flattened and self-contained movies that are playable on non-Apple computers. You can also save them as Fast-Start movies for quick playback. See Chapter 10 for details and tools you can use.

To embed a QuickTime audio-only movie in a Web page, use the same HTML tags you use for other QuickTime media types, as in the following example:

```
<EMBED SRC = "mySound.mov" CONTROLLER = TRUE HEIGHT =
➥32 WIDTH = 160>
```

To embed an invisible QuickTime audio-only movie on your Web page—to playback as a background sound for example—use this form:

```
<EMBED SRC = "mySound.mov" WIDTH=4 HEIGHT=4 AUTOSTART=
➥TRUE AUTOPLAY=TRUE >
```

Hitting the spacebar toggles between pause and play if the movie is invisible. Provide users with this information on your QuickTime-enabled Web page so that they can stop sound playback if they want.

Shockwave for Audio

Shockwave for Audio is a recent addition to the Shockwave suite of Web multimedia tools from Macromedia. Shockwave for Audio provides high compression ratios, streaming playback, and very high-quality audio.

Note

To find out more about the components necessary for SWA file playback see Chapter 8, "Animating with Shockwave for Director." See figure 11.26 for a look at the SWA player.

To play back Shockwave for Audio files requires the most recent Shockwave for Director 5 Plug-Ins. These free Plug-Ins are available at `http://www.macromedia.com`.

The standard install should set you up to play back Shockwave for Audio (SWA) files.

To create your own Shockwave for Audio files, however, requires SoundEdit on the Mac. To create custom applications that use SWA files requires Director, but you don't need Director to embed SWA files in your Web pages. A free player application is included with the Shockwave distribution that you can use in your own pages to play back SWA files.

Figure 11.26

Macromedia's Shockwave for Audio controller.

Embedding SWA Files

This section discusses how to embed SWA files in Web pages if you don't have Director. A folder of SWA Examples should be included in the Shockwave for Director 5 distribution. This folder contains two DCR files (compressed Shockwave for Director movies) that you can use to play back SWA files on your Web page:

- The file player.dcr is a Shockwave for Director movie that enables you to set up a SWA playback controller (see fig. 11.27). This controller enables users to control playback of the SWA audio. You can set up the controller to have various functions using custom attributes to the EMBED tag.

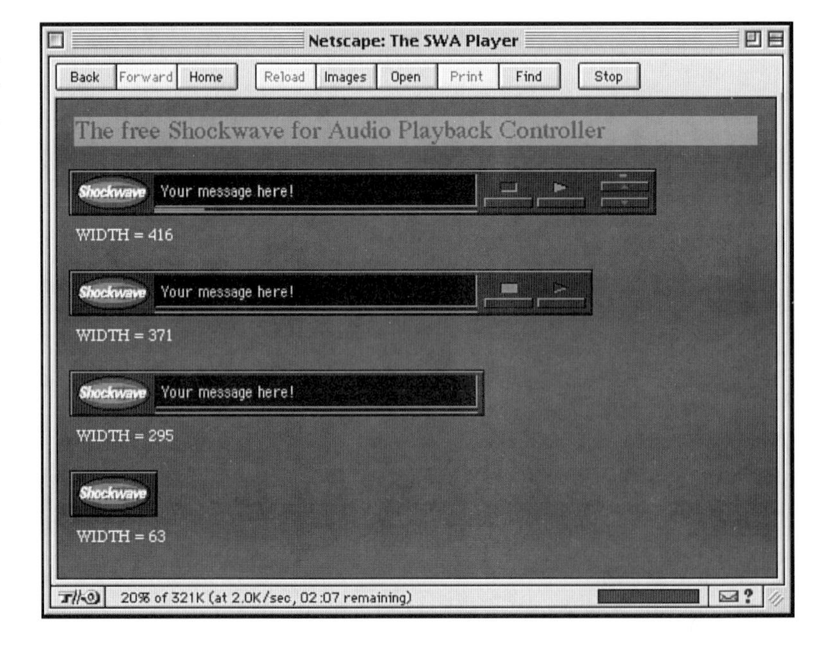

Figure 11.27

Visible options for Macromedia's Shockwave for Audio controller.

- The file 1by1.dcr is a Shockwave for Director movie that enables you to set up SWA playback without a controller. Audio plays back automatically in the background.

  You can configure the controller to have different features. To use Shockwave for Audio with a configurable controller on your own pages, use the EMBED tag like so:

  ```
  <EMBED  WIDTH=416 HEIGHT=32 SRC="http://
  MYSERVER.NET/player.dcr"  swURL="http://
  MYSERVER.NET/mySWA.swa" swTEXT="Your message
  here!" swPreLoadTime=3 sw1=off sw2=0 >
  ```

  where: `WIDTH` and `HEIGHT` are the usual `EMBED` attributes. By changing the `WIDTH` attribute you can change what part of the controller is displayed:

  A. To display the full controller use values of `WIDTH=416`

  B. To display the full controller without volume controls use values of `WIDTH=371`

  C. To display the full controller without volume controls, play, or stop buttons of `WIDTH=295`

  D. To display the full controller without volume controls, play, stop buttons, or text message box, use `WIDTH=63`

- `SRC` is a fully qualified URL to the location of the player.dcr file.
- `SWURL` is a fully qualified URL to the location of the `SWA` file.
- `SwTEXT` is a text string to display in the controller's message window, such as the file name.
- `swPreLoadTime` is the number of seconds of preloading that will be performed before the file begins playing.
- `SW1` is a special debugging attribute. Be sure to set this to **off** when you create your Web pages.
- `SW2` is the auto-start attribute. Set this attribute to one to automatically start playback—for a background sound, for example.

To embed an invisible SWA file in a Web page that won't show any controller, use the file 1by1.dcr. The following is an example of using the EMBED tag with this file:

```
<EMBED WIDTH=2 HEIGHT=1 SRC="http://MYSERVER.NET/
1by1.dcr" sw1=off swURL="http://MYSERVER.NET/
mySWA.swa" swTEXT="" swPreLoadTime=3 sw2=1>
```

Talking Web Pages and Speech Recognition

Macintosh systems come with system level support for speech synthesis and speech recognition. Several Plug-Ins enable you to create talking Web pages that use the computer to generate speech and to control Web pages with spoken commands.

Macintosh Text-to-Speech synthesis is a very low-bandwidth way to provide spoken audio on the Web. But computer speech synthesis can be annoying after a while. Speech synthesis may have uses for people with disabilities, to teach pronunciation, or in other situations where short snippets of computer speech won't be grating on user's ears.

The Macintosh Text-to-Speech Plug-In from MVP Solutions requires version 2.0 of the Netscape Navigator and can be found at:

```
http://www.mvpsolutions.com/PlugInSite/Talker.html
```

This Plug-In will speak the text of Web pages to you, using Apple Computer's PlainTalk speech synthesis. You'll also need, at the least, the Speech Manager system extension installed in the System Extensions folder on your Mac.

> **Note**
>
> Another plug-in that uses Apple's Text-to-Speech technology is Speech Plug-In, by William H. Tudor. More info can be found at
>
> **http://www.albany.net/~wtudor/**

In addition to speaking text in a regular text file, Talker enables you to specify which computer voice to use and to create singing Web pages.

Speech recognition is an enabling technology with many applications for users. ListenUp, by Bill Noon, is a Netscape Plug-In for PowerMacs that enables you to create Web pages that respond to spoken commands by associating an URL to a spoken phrase. It is very easy to use and set up. Users will need the PlainTalk speech recognition systems extension installed on their local machines. Information and a demonstration of ListenUp can be found at:

```
http://snow.cit.cornell.edu/noon/ListenUp.html
```

ShockTalk, by Digital Dreams, enables Macromedia Director Shockwave developers to add speech recognition to Shockwave movies. A speech recognition Plug-In is in the works. For more info, go to:

```
http://www.surftalk.com/shocktalk
```

TrueSpeech

Another option for providing digital speech on the Web for Mac and Windows systems is the DSP Group's TrueSpeech. Authoring requires a Windows 95 system. The TrueSpeech codec is part of the SoundRecorder audio digitizing application that ships with all Windows 95 systems. The TrueSpeech helper app is available for Mac and Windows systems. A Netscape Plug-In is in the works. Serving TrueSpeech does not require a dedicated server.

TrueSpeech audio is referenced in a Web page using the HREF tag, like so:

```
<A HREF = "myTrueSpeechMetaFile.tsp">
```

The file myTrueSpeechMetaFile.tsp is the URL to a text file containing a single line that is an URL to a TrueSpeech-encoded WAV file.

Although TrueSpeech is not the greatest in terms of streaming quality or bandwidth optimization, nor is it up to the task of providing simultaneous multiple streams, TrueSpeech is free and may be applicable to small-scale uses.

Audio Webcasting

Progressive Networks RealAudio, Xing Technology's StreamWorks, and CU-SeeMe can be used to broadcast, streamed, simultaneous, one-to-many audio over TCP/IP-based networks. Consider the following when looking at one-to-many audio over networks:

- Server requirements.
- Encoding and authoring tools.
- Playback requirements on the client machine.
- Live broadcast capabilities versus serving prerecorded compressed audio.
- Support for low-bandwidth transmission, such as modems.
- Platform support.
- Whether or not it can use adaptive streaming—that is, scale compression and bandwidth utilization based on connection speed and network traffic.
- Whether or not it can use multiple servers to spread the load over a network.
- Whether or not it will work through firewalls.

RealAudio

RealAudio from Progressive Networks is probably the most common of the proprietary, server-based streaming audio solutions for the Web. RealAudio data can be streamed as pre-exisiting files that are compressed with a free encoding utility or can be broadcast live over the Web.

The RealAudio system consists of the following:

- A free player or Plug-In, or an inexpensive, enhanced player/Plug-In
- A free encoder
- Server:
    A. Personal Servers (currently free and in beta testing) enable delivery of two audio streams across the Web and one local stream.

    B. Scalable, industrial-strength servers can deliver from 5 to 100 simultaneous audio streams.

You need the servers to provide streaming audio, but the free players will play back encoded RealAudio files in the familiar download and play mode if you don't have a dedicated server. The RealAudio system is very easy to install and is cross-platform (Mac, Windows, Unix, and OS/2). Audio streams adjust automatically to connection speed. With the RealAudio Player (see fig. 11.28), playback is asynchronous—that is, you can start playing a file and keep listening after you unload the Web page.

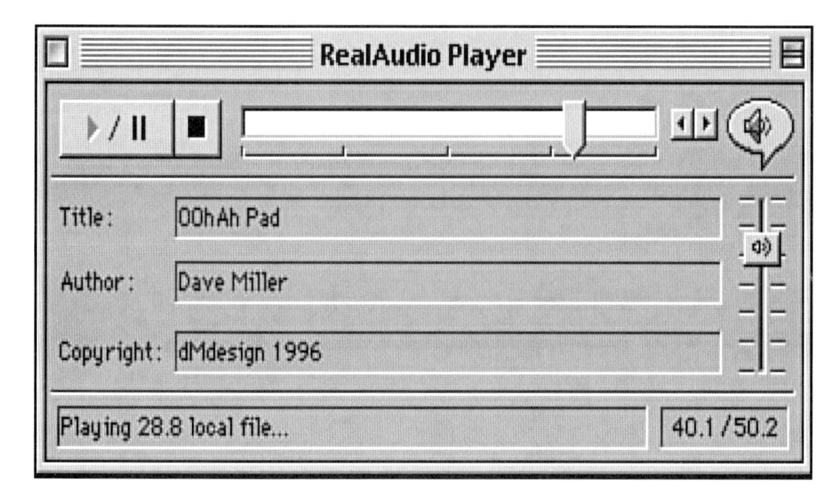

Figure 11.28

The RealAudio Player dialog box.

Progressive Networks has recently released RealAudio Player Plus, an inexpensive enhancement to their free player. Features of this new release include:

- Pre-set buttons—a RealAudio hot list feature
- More efficient connections to Web sites with RealAudio content
- Capability to save audio files to the local PC
- Better audio quality for 14.4 modem users

RealAudio MIME Information

Mime Type	Mime Subtype	File name Extensions
audio	x-pn-realaudio	ra, ram, rpm

Encoding RealAudio Files

You can encode RealAudio files using the free RealAudio Encoder. Encoding makes the files smaller and streamable by the RealAudio Player. A RealAudio Xtra for SoundEdit is also available. The free encoder only encodes mono sound files, 16-bit preferred, and it includes batch processing features. There are two encoding options, which are chosen in the RealAudio Encode, shown in figure 11.29:

Note

RealAudio has provided excellent documentation for their product at this URL:

`http://www.realaudio.com/`

- RealAudio 14.4 is optimized for speech delivery.
- RealAudio 28.8 has better dynamic range and frequency response and is better for music.

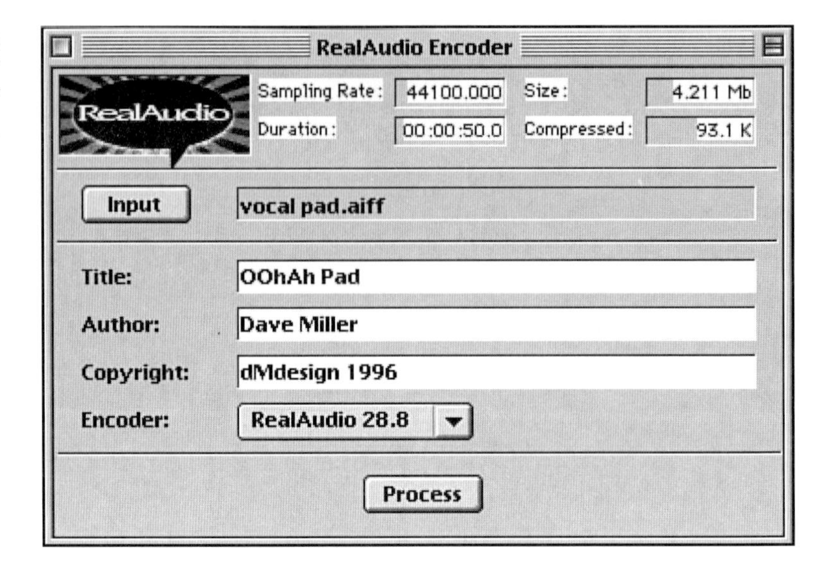

Figure 11.29

The RealAudio Encoder dialog box.

Embedding RealAudio Files

To embed RealAudio files in your Web page for the RealAudio Plug-In, use HTML code like so:

```
<EMBED SRC="myRealAudio.rpm" WIDTH=300 HEIGHT=134>
<NOEMBED> <A SRC="myRealAudio.ram">Play the audio
using the stand alone player</A></NOEMBED>
```

> **Note**
>
> Find great tips for optimizing audio for RealAudio encoding at
>
> `http://www.realaudio.com/help/ccguide/index.html`

The `myRealAudio.rpm` and `myRealAudio.ram` are URLs to text files that contain a line of text that is the URL to the RealAudio file on the RealAudio server. These URLs have the special address type of pnm://. In the following example:

```
pnm://myRealAudioServer.com/myRealAudioFile.ra
```

the `RPM` extension tells the browser to launch the Netscape Plug-In. The `RAM` extension tells the browser to launch the RealAudio Player helper app.

For details on setting up RealAudio content visit:

```
http://www.realaudio.com/help/ccguide/config.html
```

Telephony and Audio-Conferencing

In recent months the number of Internet phones applications has increased greatly. These applications enable the transfer of real-time, live, often full-duplex, audio data over the Internet. Internet telephony products include the following:

- WebTalk

  `http://www.quarterdeck.com/`

- CineTalk

  `http://www.cinecom.com/`

- CoolTalk

  `http://home.netscape.com/comprod/products/navigator/version_3.0/cooltalk/`

- DigiPhone

  `http://www.planeteers.com/`

- Internet Phone

  `http://www.vocaltec.com/`

- Internet PartyLine

  `http://www.intel.com/iaweb/aplets/iplpage.htm`

- CyberPhone

  `http://magenta.com/cyberphone`

- WebPhone

  `http://www.itelco.com`

- NetMeeting

  `http://www.microsoft.com/ie/ie3/netmtg.htm`

You can also use many video-conferencing applications such as CU-SeeMe and QuickTime Conferencing to share audio data.

There currently is little integration of Internet phones with Web browsers. This lack of integration is likely to change as Netscape's CoolTalk and Microsofts NetMeeting are added to their respective browsers. Possible uses on the Web include the ability to share voice communications between two people as they view the same Web page, which might be a slide from a presentation or output of research results.

Some features to consider when you look at Internet phones:

- Does it work over modems?
- Is it cross-platform?
- It is interoperable with other telephony applications?
- Is it full-duplex (that is, does it enable users to talk at the same time) or half duplex (like a CB-radio or walkie-talkie)? PC users will need a sound card that supports full-duplex audio.
- Does it support multiuser conferences or just point-to-point calls?
- Does it support multiple codecs?
- Does it scale compression and bandwidth utilization based on connection speed and network traffic?
- Will it work through firewalls?

CoolTalk is a helper application for Netscape Navigator 3 that provides real-time, full-duplex (on sound cards that support it), audio and data collaboration that includes text-based chat, and a whiteboard for sharing text and graphics. It is currently available for Windows 95/NT and various Unix flavors. A Mac version should be available by the time you read this.

Conclusion

Sound is an important addition to a multimedia Web site, but can also be bandwidth intensive. There are numerous ways to include sound on a Web page, including MIDI, digital audio, QuickTime, Shockwave, RealAudio, and other streaming audio formats. Most browsers have built-in support for the common file types, so adding sound is easy.

On the horizon, new audio codecs specifically designed for the Web and audio-conferencing, and telephony integration with browsers, will change the sound landscape yet again in the coming year.

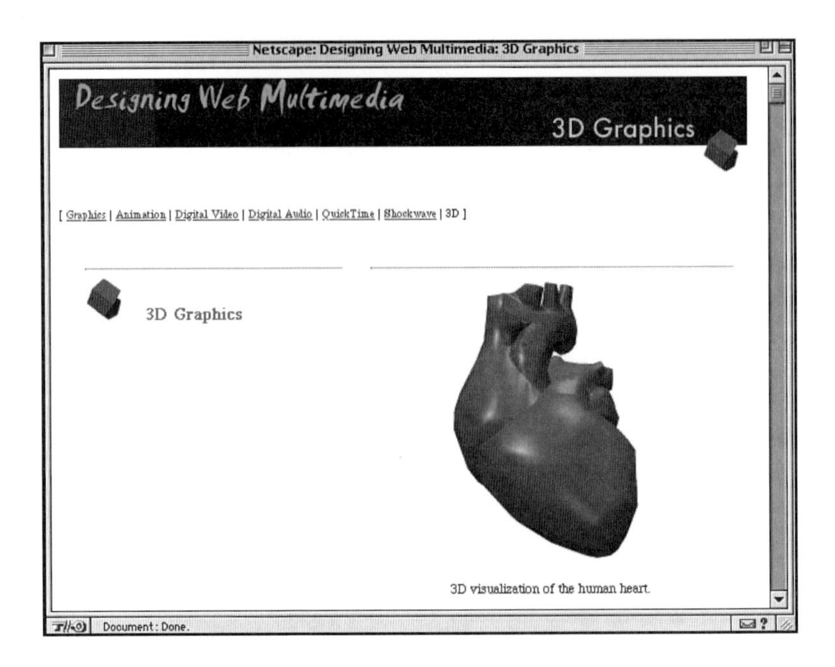

3D graphics can add "punch" to a flat Web page and can be as easy to add to a Web page as adding an in-line GIF or JPEG.

chapter

12

3D and Virtual Reality

Adding 3D graphics to a Web page can be as simple as adding any other kind of graphic. If you stick to the standard Web graphics formats, users won't need any special Plug-Ins or viewers. You can create 3D graphics and 3D effects in a 2D program such as Photoshop, FreeHand, Illustrator, CorelDRAW, or PaintShop Pro. You can also use a 3D graphics program to create 3D graphics. One of the advantages of using 3D graphics programs is that after a 3D model is created it is the ultimate reusable graphic asset. A 3D model can also be rendered from different views and perspectives, and with different lighting and surface materials.

Another way of adding 3D graphics to Web pages is by incorporating 3D graphics into Shockwave animations and QuickTime movies, as many of the examples in this book do. QuickTime Virtual Reality extensions enable you to embed navigable interactive scenes of photographic quality in a Web page that can be viewed with the QuickTime Plug-In or MovieStar Plug-In.

You can also use Netscape Plug-Ins, ActiveX controls, and Java applets that enable interactive viewing of 3D graphics formats. You can use free Plug-Ins such as Whurlplug from Apple Computer or Topper from Kinetix, to embed animated, interactive 3D objects. Support for 3D graphics at the system level, such as QuickDraw 3D and QuickTime Virtual Reality, in QuickTime for Macintosh and Windows, and Direct3D support in Windows systems, is bringing more sophisticated 3D effects to desktop systems.

Adding 3D graphics to Web pages has several advantages. 3D graphics add visual punch to an otherwise flat page. Animation and 3D can make a user interface easier to understand and use. A 3D animation can provide alternate views of a complex structure, such as a sculpture, a human heart, or a flower. A 3D simulation can illustrate a process better than static images in a text book. As with all Web multimedia, be kind to your users and keep downloads small—don't put distracting animations and garish 3D graphics on a page that you want people to read.

This chapter discusses how to integrate 3D graphics into your Web page using 2D and 3D graphics programs. Although the graphics programs used in the examples in this chapter include Photoshop, Extreme 3D, and MetaTools' Bryce, the basic principles apply to any 2D or 3D graphics programs. This chapter looks at the 3D extensions to QuickTime and how to add QuickTime Virtual Reality to your Web pages using free QuickTime VR authoring tools.

This chapter teaches you how to:

- Create 3D graphics in 2D programs such as Photoshop.
- Use a 3D graphics program to create fully-realized 3D objects and VRML worlds.
- Create QuickTime Virtual Reality movies and add them to your Web pages.

Using 2D Programs to Create 3D Graphics for the Web

You can use programs such as Premiere, AfterEffects, Photoshop, Fractal Design Painter, FreeHand, Illustrator, CorelDRAW, and PaintShop Pro to add dimensionality to 2D images. Most of these programs come with built-in features for adding drop shadows, textures, lighting effects, and embossed surfaces.

Now you will be introduced to some features of these programs and their functions. Later in this section you learn how to use tools to create the dimensionality effects mentioned above.

Premiere and AfterEffects are QuickTime-based, digital video editing programs you can use to add simple 3D effects to animations and digital video. FinalEffects is a series of Plug-Ins for AfterEffects that includes a particle animation system for special effects such as rain, fire, smoke, and explosions.

In Photoshop and Painter, you can paint in shadows and highlights using the dodge, burn, or airbrush tools. You can also use several different techniques to add drop shadows to objects. If you add drop shadows, create them on a separate layer in Photoshop or Painter so that you can composite and animate them separately. If the shadow is on a separate layer you can give the shadow perspective by choosing the Effects: Skew command under the Image menu in Photoshop.

Painter and Photoshop enable you to use gray-scale images as bump maps to define surface texture. Furthermore, Painter has a rich set of lighting effects that add dimensionality to graphics. You can use its Apply Surface Texture command to texture your graphics and add dimension to type. Additional Plug-Ins for Photoshop and Painter can add more sophisticated 3D effects.

Note

See Chapter 7, "Animation," for an example of a technique that you can use to add drop shadows to a graphic image in Photoshop.

PaintShop Pro has several options that enable you to quickly give dimensionality to 2D graphics. For example, to create text with drop shadows:

1. Choose the text tool in PaintShop Pro.
2. Click in the image where you want to add text.
3. Choose the Shadow Option.

Using the Emboss Filter with Text in Photoshop

This example shows you how to create embossed text against a background. The text and background should be high contrast. This example works best with light-colored text against a dark-colored background.

1. Create a New Photoshop document with the dimensions you want and set the Mode to RGB Color.
2. Add the background graphic or color that you want by painting, copying, pasting, and so on.
3. Invert the color chips so that white is the foreground color and black is the background color. Press the D key, then press the X key.
4. Choose the Type tool or press the Y key.
5. Click in the image where you want to add text.
6. In the Text dialog box, add the text you want, choose the options for the text such as bold or anti-aliased, then click OK.
7. While the text is still a floating selection, make it a separate layer (see fig. 12.1).
    - Choose Palettes: Show Layers under the Window menu.
    - Double-click on the floating selection in the Layer palette.
    - Name the layer and click OK.

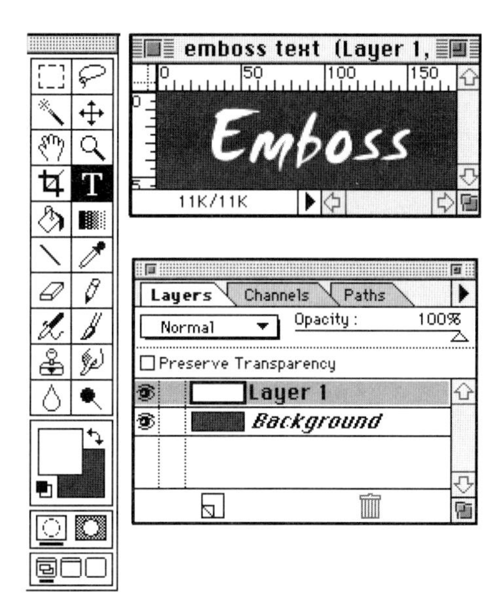

Figure 12.1

Setting up a text layer in Photoshop.

8. Deselect by choosing None under the Select menu or pressing Command+D in Macintosh or Ctrl+D in Windows.
9. Choose the text layer in the Layers palette to make it the active layer.
10. Choose Stylize: Emboss under the Filter menu. Figure 12.2 shows the Emboss filter.

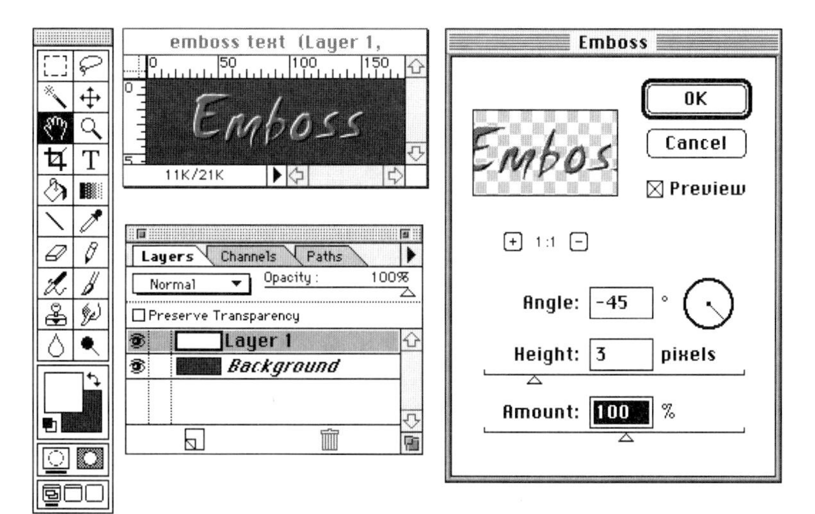

Figure 12.2

Using the Emboss filter in Photoshop.

Using Lighting Effects in Photoshop to Create Embossed Text

In this example, you use Photoshop's lighting effects to create embossed text.

1. First, create an image that contains the background color, texture, or graphic that you want for your embossed text and set the Mode to RGB color (see fig. 12.3).

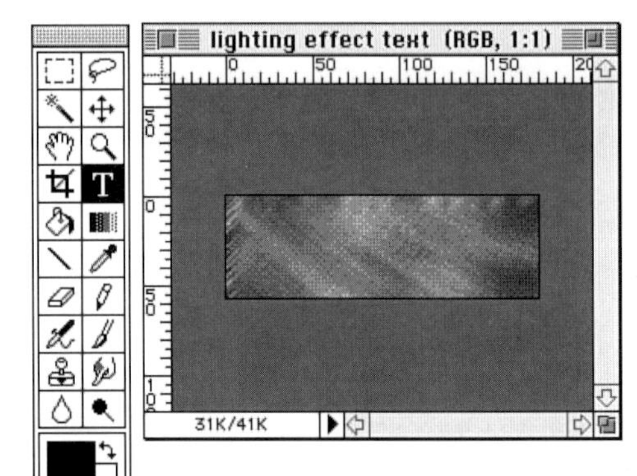

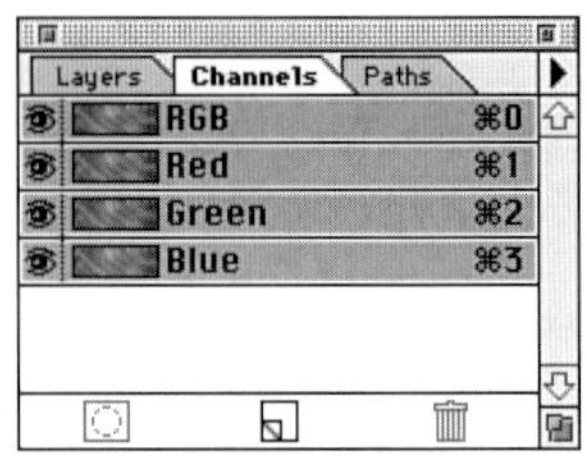

Figure 12.3

Textured graphic for background.

2. Choose Palettes: Show Channels under the Window menu.
3. Choose New Channel from the channel pop-up menu on the Channels palette.
4. Invert the color chips so that white is the foreground color and black is the background color. Press the D key, then press the X key.
5. Choose the Type tool or press the Y key.
6. Making sure the channel you just created is selected in the Channels palette, click in the image where you want to add text.
7. In the Text dialog box, add the text you want, choose the options for the text such as bold or anti-aliased, then click OK (see fig. 12.4).

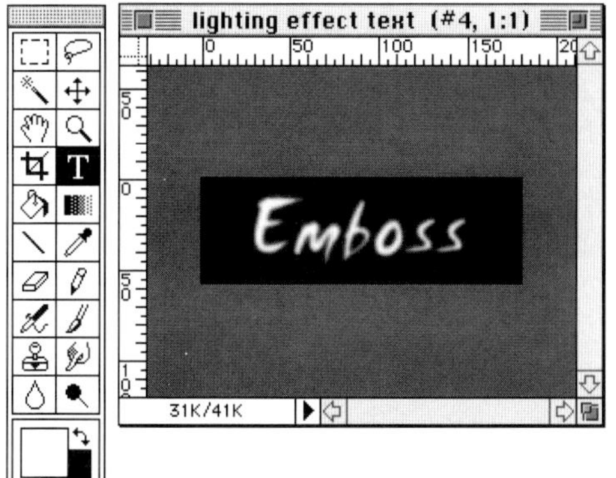

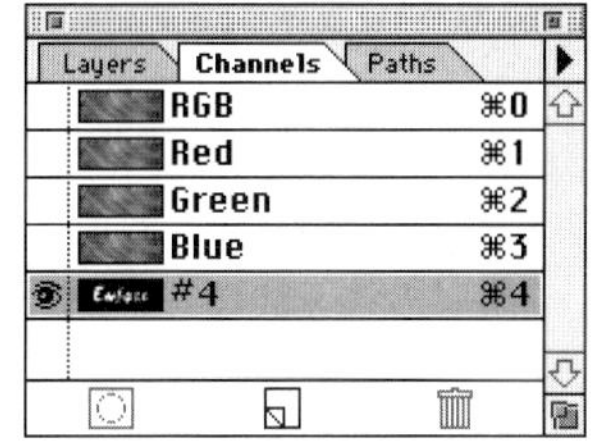

Figure 12.4

Text channel.

8. Now blur the edges of the text you added to the Channel. Choose Blur: Gaussian Blur from the Filter menu, as shown in figure 12.5.

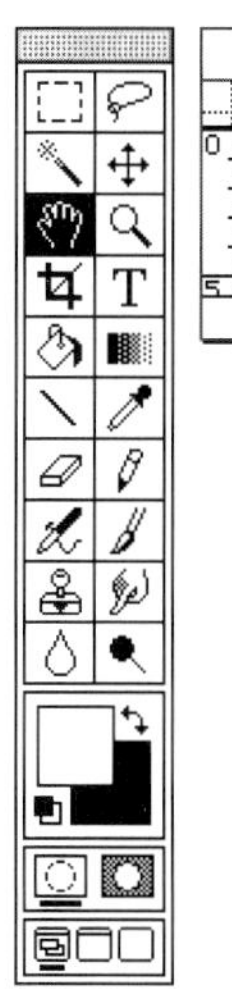

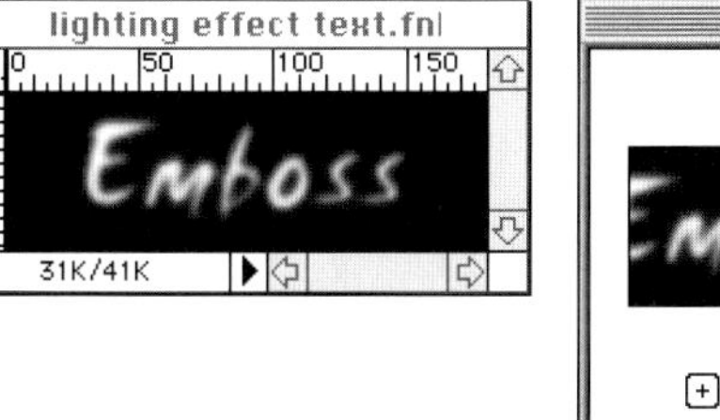

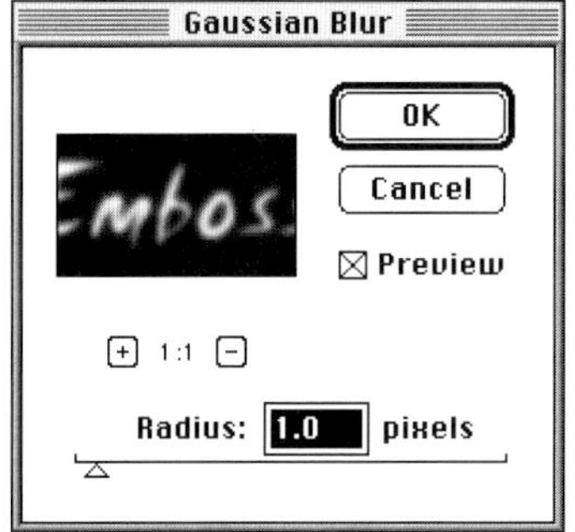

Figure 12.5

Blurring the text channel.

9. Choose 1.0 pixel or whatever makes the edges of the text appear fuzzy without losing readability.
10. Choose Render: Lighting Effects from the Filter menu.
11. In the pop-up menu at the bottom right labeled Texture Channel, choose channel #4, or the number of the channel in which you just created the radial gradient. Make sure the White is high check box is checked (see fig. 12.6).

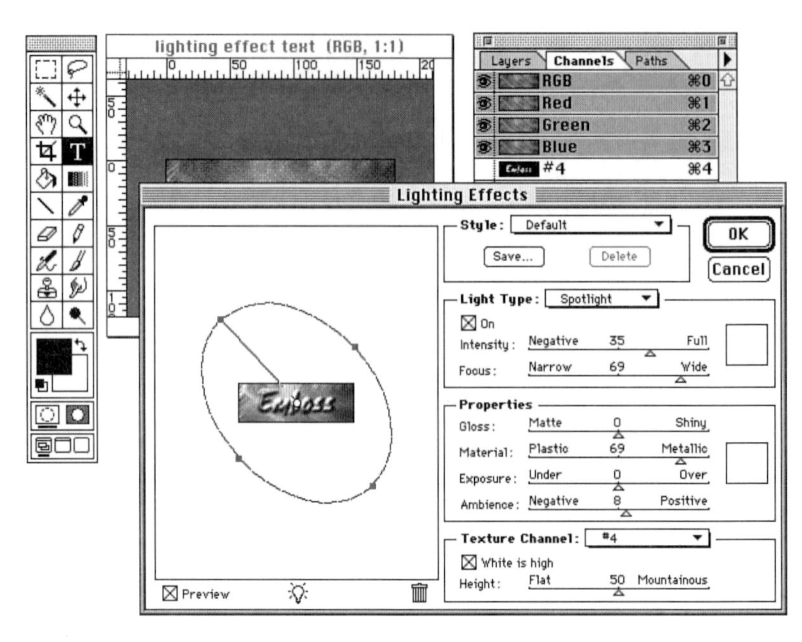

Figure 12.6

Using Lighting Effects.

12. Now experiment with the lighting settings and directions. If you have a fast computer the preview updates in real-time (see fig. 12.7).

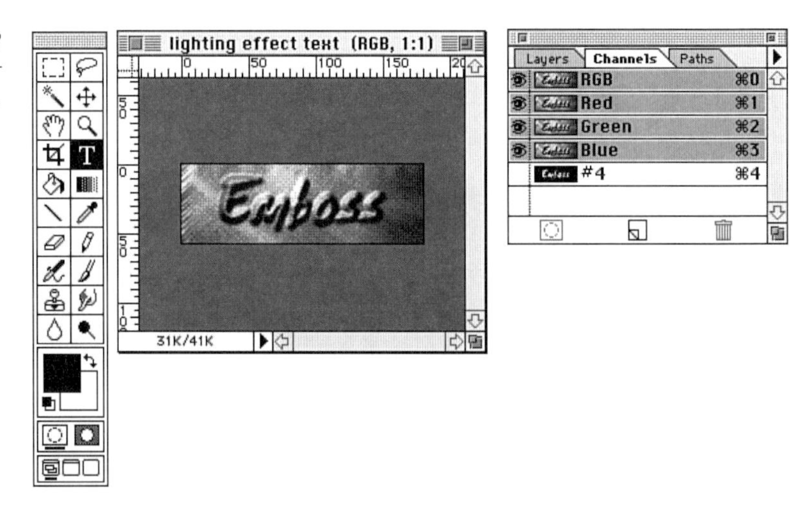

Figure 12.7

The results.

13. Save the graphic for the Web. See Chapter 7 for tips on how to optimize Web graphics.

Gray-Scale Bump Maps

height fields

Photoshop and Painter use gray-scale images to create 3D surface textures and lighting effects. The idea is to create a textured 3D surface. These programs interpret the white areas of a gray-scale image to be the bumps, or raised areas of the surface. The black areas of the gray-scale image correspond to the pits or the lowest points of the surface. Gray areas have intermediate heights depending on the gray level. Gray-scale images used in this way are sometimes called gray-scale bump maps or **height fields.**

Adding lighting effects to an image with a gray-scale bump map shades the image based on the bumps in the gray-scale bump map. This effect is similar in some respects to the emboss filter, but is more powerful. You can use this feature to create intricate, detailed surface textures. You can also use this technique to create 3D interface objects, such as buttons.

In Photoshop, use the Filter: Render: Lighting Effects command and any gray-scale image to create quick 3D textures and surfaces. Texturize and emboss any image by using a gray-scale version of the image in conjunction with the Filter: Render: Lighting Effects command.

Note

In Photoshop, create a gray-scale image from another image or channel with the Calculations command under the Image menu. If the transitions between gray values are too sharp, add blur to smooth out the gray-scale image.

Using the Lighting Effects in Photoshop to Create 3D Buttons

In this example, you use Photoshop's Lighting Effects to create 3D buttons.

1. Choose New under the File menu, give the image the dimensions you want and set the Mode to RGB color.
2. Now, create the gray-scale bump map for the button Channels palette.
3. Choose Palettes: Show Channels under the Window menu.
4. Choose New Channel from the pull-down menu on the upper right of the Channels palette.
5. Invert the color chips so that white is the foreground color and black is the background color. Press the D key, then press the X key.

6. Double-click on the Gradient Tool in the Tool palette to open the Gradient Tool Options dialog box (see fig. 12.8). At the bottom of the Gradient Tool Options dialog box, choose Type: Radial and make sure the Dither check box is not checked.
7. Now, create the radial gradient. With the Gradient Tool selected, start at center of the image and drag to the lower right corner. You should create a radial gradient with a round white area in the center.

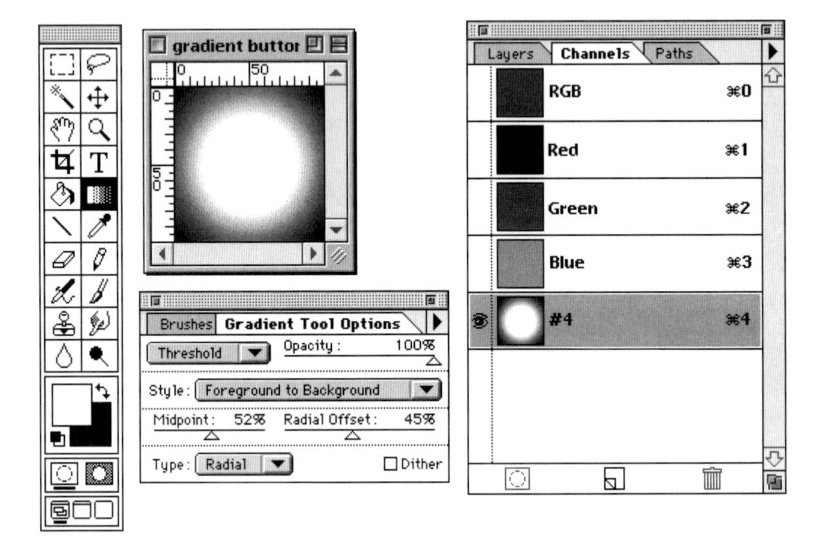

Figure 12.8

Radial gradient.

8. Now, create the surface texture for the button. First, choose the RGB channel by pressing Command+0 on the Macintosh, Ctrl+0 on Windows, or the RGB channel in the Channels palette.
9. Use the Paint Bucket tool to fill the document with a color or to paste in a graphic or texture.
10. Now, give the graphic a 3D look. Choose Render: Lighting Effects from the Filter menu.
11. In the pop-up menu at the bottom right labeled Texture Channel, choose channel #4, or the number of the channel where you just created the radial gradient. Make sure the White is high check box is checked, as shown in figure 12. 9.

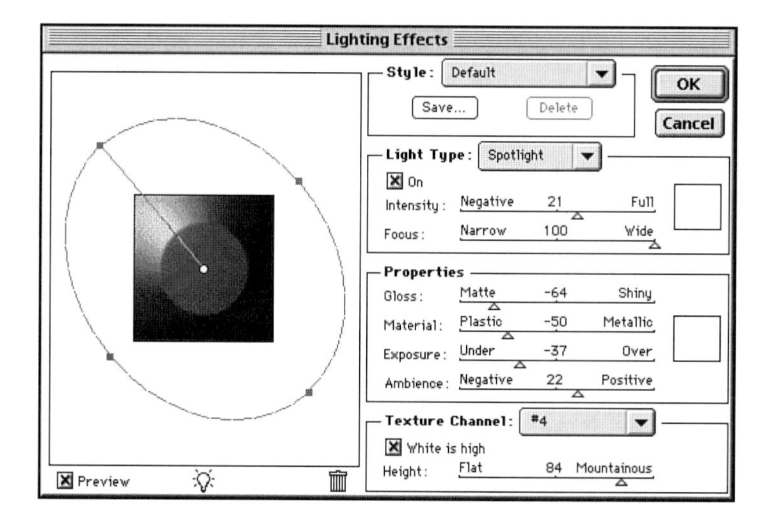

Figure 12.9

Lighting Effects with a gray-scale bump map.

12. Now experiment with the lighting settings and directions. If you have a fast computer the preview updates in real-time.

13. Save the graphic image for the Web. See Chapter 6, "Using Graphics to Add Dynamic Content," for tips on how to optimize Web graphics.

Using 3D Programs to Create 3D Graphics for the Web

Going from computer-based 2D illustration to 3D graphics and animation can be daunting because it involves a different way of creating computer graphics. Creating 3D graphics is an iterative process that involves several different tasks.

- In the modeling task, you create the basic structure of your objects and place them in a 3D world.
- In animating, you typically assign different keyframe positions to objects along a timeline. The computer generates intermediate frames between keyframes (**tweening**) to simulate motion in your 3D world and does all the work of creating perspective, lighting, shadows,

tweening

and environmental effects. This task is similar to key-frame animating in 2D animation programs, but more powerful.

- In rendering, the computer paints your 3D world based on the lighting, material properties, and camera views that you've created. Material properties define an object's color, texture, and surface properties. Lights and atmospheric effects define the environment of your world.
- The final task is often to merge or composite 3D graphics with other graphic elements using programs such as Photoshop, Debabelizer, Director, AfterEffects, or Premiere.

Designing a 3D world isn't a simple, linear, step-by-step process. It usually involves alternating between modeling and animation, performing test renders at different stages to see whether the various aspects of your world look right, and then performing a final, high-quality render that may take many minutes, hours, or even days. The processes of modeling, animating, rendering, and compositing are discussed in greater detail later in this chapter.

After the 3D graphics and animations are created, they can be added to Web pages in numerous ways; by converting them to Web-friendly formats such as GIF and JPEG, using dedicated 3D viewers and Plug-Ins, or by incorporating the 3D graphics and animation in Shockwave for Director, QuickTime, GIF animations, or another Web-ready format.

The following sections provide more detail about what you need in terms of system requirements and software to create 3D graphics.

System Requirements for 3D

Three-dimensional graphics programs require a lot of RAM. The more complex your models and animations are and the more texture maps you use, the more RAM you need. You may want to have other programs, such as Photoshop, open while you work in your 3D program—another need for more RAM. Plus, you want to leave room for your system RAM to expand to accommodate for changing memory requirements.

In short, get as much RAM as you can afford. Most 3D programs perform best with at least 16–20 MB of RAM for the program, although you can get by with less. A machine with 32 MB of total RAM would make a serviceable 3D graphics workstation. Workstations with 100 or 200 MB of RAM are not unusual.

Your CPU should be the fastest possible, a Pentium, Pentium Pro if you use 32-bit programs, or a PowerPC. The PowerPC is a good chip for 3D work because of its superior floating-point math performance. Three-dimensional programs for the Macintosh are PowerPC-native and are typically optimized for the PowerPC chip.

Tip

If you have an older Macintosh, make sure it has an FPU (floating-point unit).

Consider purchasing a 3D accelerator board. As of this writing, several companies have announced low-cost 3D accelerator boards for desktop systems. Also consider the video-out capabilities of your system if you plan on outputting 3D animations to videotape.

You need a lot of disk space. As a rule of thumb, a 1 MB 3D animation can easily generate 10 MB of intermediate and scratch files.

3D Software

The 3D design process involves several different tasks. These tasks, as mentioned earlier, are modeling, animating, rendering, and compositing. Three-dimensional software programs handle one or more of these tasks. You'll probably use more than one program to create your 3D graphics.

Macromedia Extreme 3D, Strata StudioPro, Specular Infini-D, VIDI Presenter Pro, NewTek Lightwave 3D, Hash's Animation Master, Ray Dream (now part of Fractal Design), Designer Studio, Caligari TrueSpace, and Crystal Topas are integrated programs that provide a mix of modeling, animating, and rendering to a varying extent. auto-des-sys formZ is primarily a modeler. Virtus Walkthrough Pro, Gryphon Morph, the Valis Group PixelPutty, and Metaflo provide specialized modeling, animating, or rendering features.

MetaTools Bryce is a unique naturalistic terrain modeler with detailed control of procedural textures and ray-traced rendering. If you have a lot of money, you can use high-end tools

Note

Extreme 3D is an integrated, cross-platform modeling, animation, and rendering program. It's a very capable and relatively inexpensive package good for desktop multi-media. The demos and tips in this chapter use Extreme 3D but the same concepts should be applicable to other 3D programs. Figure 12.10 is an example of an Extreme 3D interface.

such as ElectricImage Animation System for the Macintosh, 3D Studio Max on Windows NT, or Alias/Wavefront products on Silicon Graphics workstations.

Specular Logomotion, CorelMotion3D, Crystal Flying Fonts, and Strata StrataType are inexpensive programs for creating and animating 3D type. Fractal Design Poser is a tool for modeling and rendering the human form.

POV-Ray is a free, cross-platform ray-tracer with a built-in scene description language and many powerful features. It can be downloaded from:

`http://www.povray.org/`

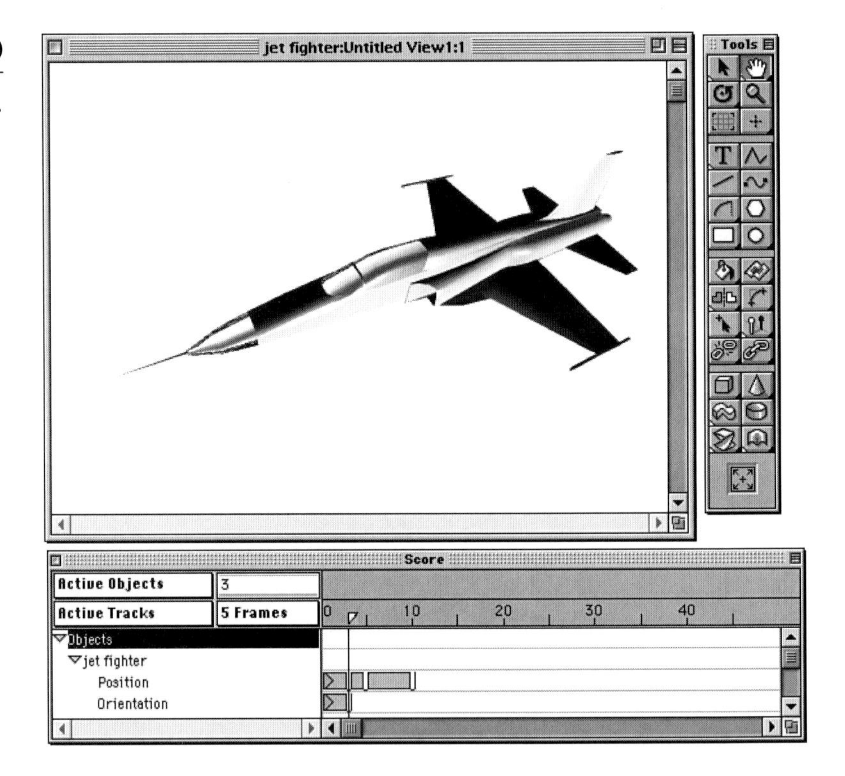

Figure 12.10

Extreme 3D interface.

Even if you're using an integrated 3D program such as Extreme 3D or StudioPro, you probably want to exchange files between different 3D and 2D programs during the production process. The 3D program you choose should be able to export animations such as QuickTime movies, a sequence of numbered PICT files, BMP files, or TARGA files. PICs is a common animation export format. DXF import/export should also be supported. DXF is a common, though limited, format used to exchange 3D models between different programs. EPS or EPSF import enables you to import 2D Bézier curves and graphics from such programs as FreeHand and Illustrator.

Many 3D programs now export to VRML (Virtual Reality Modeling Language) format. VRML files can be viewed on the Web using VRML viewers such as Live3D in Netscape Navigator, Liquid Reality's DimensionX viewer for Internet Explorer, or stand-alone viewers such as Virtus' Voyager or Silicon Graphic's Cosmo Player. You learn more about VRML in Chapter 13, "VRML."

Note

The VRML Repository at **http://sdsc.edu/vrml/** is a comprehensive VRML resource on the Web.

Apple Computer's QuickDraw 3D (QD3D) is a cross-platform, software-based, 3D graphics architecture. It provides real-time, workstation-quality rendering, interactivity, and animation of 3D graphics on PowerPC and Pentium-class PCs. For all the latest developments and free downloads of the software and development kits, see:

`http://product.info.apple.com/qd3d/QD3D.HTML`

3DMF (3D Metafile or QuickDraw 3D format) import/export is starting to turn up in some programs. 3DMF is the basis of the binary file format for version 2 of the VRML standard. You can embed richly, interactive 3DMF objects in Web pages using the free Whurlplug Plug-In.

Whurlplug, created by John Louch, is currently a technology demonstration of a Netscape Plug-In for viewing 3DMF models. Whurlplug enables users to interact with 3D objects, spin them around, zoom-in and out, and otherwise manipulate 3D objects with the mouse, keyboard, and a built-in toolbar.

Note

You can obtain a Macintosh version of the free Whurlplug Plug-In at:

http://quickdraw3d.apple.com/Whurlplug.HTML

A Windows version may be available by the time this book is published.

Direct3D is Microsoft's desktop 3D graphics architecture that is specifically designed for games on Windows platforms. By the time you read this, several programs should be supporting Direct3D features on Windows. Visit:

`http://www.microsoft.com/`

for the latest information.

How the 3D World Works

> **Note**
>
> The same programs that you use for 2D graphics and digital video editing can be used to create the building blocks for 3D graphics and texture maps, to post-process and composite 3D graphics for final output, and to add effects to 3D animations. Macromedia FreeHand, Adobe Illustrator, Adobe Photoshop, Fractal Design Painter, Adobe Premiere, Adobe AfterEffects, Avid Videoshop, and Equilibrium Technologies' Debabelizer can all provide supporting functions in 3D graphics production work.

In 2D programs such as FreeHand and Illustrator the screen is divided into an X and Y, 2D coordinate system. You may be familiar with FreeHand, which enables you to set precise X and Y values for the positioning and alignment of objects. In 3D programs, a third dimension is added to this coordinate system. The third axis or Z axis extends into the computer screen. Many programs, such as Extreme 3D, enable CAD-accurate positioning and alignment within this 3D coordinate system.

> **Note**
>
> The camera is a special object. The view you use to edit your 3D world can be the same view as the camera view, but it doesn't have to be. Camera position and look-at points can be animated to provide panning, dollying, tracking, zooming, and fly-throughs.

You view your 3D world through a window on the computer screen. This view has editable parameters such as perspective and orientation. At first, it's easy to become disoriented as you construct your 3D world. Become familiar with the way you change and edit view parameters in your 3D program. In the beginning, it may be easier to stick with a set of default views (Front, Back, Top, Right) if your program provides them.

This section discusses the processes of modeling, animating, rendering, and compositing, and provides some tips on creating 3D graphics and animations for the Web.

Modeling

model

Modeling is the process that you use to construct your 3D objects or models and create the basic structure of your 3D world (also called a **model**). Many 3D programs provide a set of primitive shapes, such as cube, sphere, and cone, that you can use to create more complex models. Most 3D programs provide a rich set of tools to construct 3D models from 2D profiles. The tool set usually includes extrusion, lathe, sweep, and skin (loft) tools. Extreme 3D models are built up from true Bézier curves. You can edit and animate models at the vertex or point level to create complex organic shapes. Figure 12.11 is an example of an Exteme 3D model.

You position objects in your 3D world by using the mouse or by entering 3D coordinates. Many programs, such as Extreme 3D, enable you to place an object at precise points in your 3D world. Sometimes, it can be hard to tell exactly where your object is within the 3D coordinate system. Therefore, when you first create an object, it's often handy to align it to the 0, 0, 0 point in your world and then move it at right angles along the X, Y, and Z axes, just to get a feel for how the object is oriented in the 3D space.

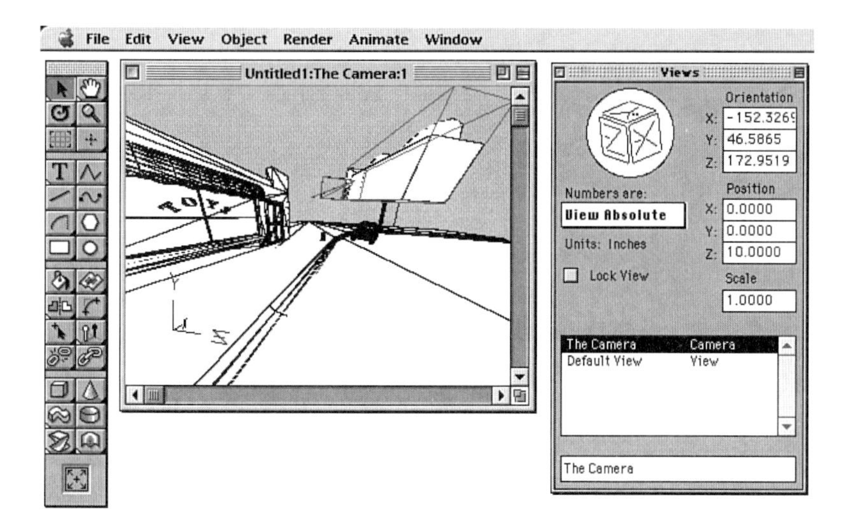

Figure 12.11

3D modeling in Extreme 3D.

Animating

Animation is created from a sequence of still images or frames that are played rapidly in succession so that the eye is fooled into perceiving continuous motion.

Three-dimensional programs with animation capabilities typically use a keyframe-based timeline. The computer calculates all the intermediate frames between keyframes. In Extreme 3D, you can animate almost every editable property, including texture maps and individual vertices or control points. Motion paths are fully editable curves.

If you output your 3D animations as a sequence of bitmaps or as a QuickTime movie, it is relatively easy to put the animations on the Web. Several of the examples in this book use the output from 3D programs in Shockwave animations, QuickTime animations, and GIF animations.

The Material World

To make your 3D world look realistic, assign different material properties to objects, and create lights and atmospheric effects.

Shadows and Light

Lighting a 3D world is similar to lighting a stage or movie set, except that you can place lights anywhere in 3D space and you can easily change the properties of each light, such as color or dustiness. Light sources in 3D programs include distant lights, spotlights, and ambient light.

Distant lights simulate the sun and throw parallel light rays.

Spotlights are typically cone-shaped lights that can focus on specific points.

Ambient light is the global, environmental light that suffuses a scene from all directions.

Lights in the 3D world don't have to follow the laws of physics! You can have lights that don't cast shadows. Anyone who has done photographic, stage, or film lighting can appreciate this feature. Lights can even have negative intensity.

Procedural Textures and Texture Maps

The surface properties of your 3D objects reflect the materials that they are made of and the lighting and environment of your 3D world. Texture mapping and procedural textures are two commonly used ways to simulate materials for your objects.

texture mapping

Texture mapping is the process of applying a bitmap image, such as a PICT file, to a 3D surface. At the simplest level, texture mapping is similar to stretching a decal or placing a label on the surface of an object. But you can also animate and tile textures, and project and place textures with different orientations. You can simulate surface roughness, lighting effects, and transparency settings with texture maps. You can overlay several texture maps on the same surface. Some programs even support QuickTime movies as texture maps.

procedural textures

Procedural textures use mathematical equations to generate surface properties. Because procedural textures are mathematical calculations, they don't require as much disk space or memory as texture maps. They are also resolution independent. You can get very close to an object with a procedural texture and the texture won't become pixellated.

Because procedural textures extend through an object, you can also carve into objects and still see the texture. Procedural textures can take a lot of time to render and sometimes require a lot of tweaking to look realistic. Bryce is a 3D program that uses procedural textures extensively to recreate natural forms and textures.

Note

On the Web, texture maps typically are JPEG or GIF files that reside on a Web server. Texture maps can add significantly to download times and rendering overhead.

Creating Textures

Painter, Photoshop, and most 3D programs come with libraries of textures. You can use dedicated texture creation programs or Painter and Photoshop to create original texture maps for your 3D models. Any bitmap can become a texture map.

Instead of creating intricate detail in a 3D model, draw the detailed look you want in a 2D program, then import it as a texture map into your 3D program. Sometimes adding a little noise to texture maps in Photoshop gives them a less sharp-edged, computer-generated look. Scanning and video capture are other ways to create real-world textures.

You can easily create a seamless, tiling texture in Painter. See Chapter 7 for some tips on how to create a seamless texture graphic.

Note

If you are creating your 2D profiles in FreeHand, here are some tips for using FreeHand with Extreme 3D.

1. Before you save your FreeHand file for import into Extreme 3D, choose the Document Inspector and drag your page to the lower left corner of the pasteboard.
2. After you import your FreeHand file into Extreme 3D, you may need to select the View: Fit to Window command to see the profiles in the Extreme 3D workspace.
3. It's also a good idea to align the profiles in the workspace using the Object: Align command. If the sharp corners of your 2D profiles look rounded in Extreme 3D, press the B key as you manipulate the handles of the corner points. Pressing the B key breaks the point handles and enables you to create sharp corners in your profiles.

Creating 2D Bézier Curve Profiles

Extreme 3D provides spline-based drawing tools, similar to tools in FreeHand and Illustrator, that you can use to create 2D curves or profiles. Various 3D object tools turn your 2D profiles into 3D objects. Sometimes, it may be easier to create 2D profiles directly in FreeHand or Illustrator and then import them into Extreme 3D.

Extreme 3D imports FreeHand 4.0 or 5.x files directly. It also imports 2D files saved in EPSF format. Extreme 3D creates profiles from the Bézier curves in your 2D files. It ignores such elements as the fill patterns and bitmaps in your 2D drawing.

3D Interface Design

Chiseled gray buttons and dialog boxes have become commonplace in user interfaces. Three-dimensional graphics and textures appeal to the tactile sense and enhance the feeling that you are directly manipulating objects on the computer screen.

A well-designed 3D user interface can look better organized and give a clearer visual impression of interface functions.

Three-dimensional user interface design uses the same principles as 2D user interface design. Three-dimensional interfaces have a tendency to accentuate bad interface design, so design carefully. Here are some tips:

- When you create 3D interfaces, don't overpower the content with sumptuous textures.
- Don't compete with the dimensionality of other 3D elements on the screen.
- Restrict the height of 3D interface objects to two or three levels.
- Avoid closely-packed, chiseled buttons that create distracting grids.
- Subdue the tonal range of shadows and highlights in the interface. Just a few tenths of a percent difference in the gray values of shadows and highlights is enough to give the impression of a third dimension. Depending on the kind of interface you are designing, keep the shadows and light sources consistent across your interface.
- Use parallel lighting (distant lights in Extreme 3D) to reduce banding, especially if you need to restrict your interface to a few colors.
- Use numeric positioning of objects to ensure consistent placement.

You can use 2D programs such as Photoshop to create your interface elements, or you can use a 3D program. For example, draw your interface as 2D Bézier curves in FreeHand, leaving holes for the content. Then, import the curves into Extreme 3D and extrude them slightly. Another way to create intricate, molded interfaces is to use a gray-scale bump map with the Filter: Render: Lighting Effects command in Photoshop.

Rendering

rendering

Rendering is the process that the computer uses to generate an image based on all the material properties, positions, lights, and models that you have in your 3D world. There are several different rendering methods. The highest quality methods take the longest time to render.

- **Bounding box rendering.** Represents 3D objects as boxes that enclose each object. This method is the fastest and is used to show the basic positions of objects.
- **Wireframe rendering.** Represents the underlying structure of 3D objects as a grid of interconnected lines and is commonly used for interactive rendering of animations.
- **Flat-shading.** Method that renders objects with faceted polygons.
- **Gourand shading.** Provides realistic shading and smoothness.
- **Ray-tracing and Phong shading.** These methods take the longest time, because each pixel is calculated based on the simulated light rays from every light source, including reflections.

Note

Phong shading and ray-tracing are the highest quality render methods, take the longest time, and are generally used for final output.

Interactive rendering is the rendering used to display your 3D world on the screen while you are working on it. You want the screen display to be fast but you also want enough information to be able to create your model and see what you're doing. Many programs use the wireframe rendering method for interactive rendering.

interactive rendering

This chapter uses Extreme 3D for some examples. Extreme 3D provides very fast interactive rendering. In Extreme 3D you can assign different render modes to different objects. This feature can save a lot of time during interactive rendering. QD3D also provides system-level support for fast interactive rendering.

At several stages in your project you want to run high-quality test renders using final output settings. Most programs can render high-quality test renders to the screen instead of to disk. You may want to render selected keyframes at the highest possible setting to make sure your 3D world is shaping up the way you want. Or you could render short, but critical parts of animations to see what they look like at the final output settings.

Note

Final rendering at high-quality settings can take a long time. Many programs enable you to distribute renderings across multiple machines on a network. Extreme 3D has a built-in distributed renderer.

You may want to render images at larger sizes and higher color-depth than you need for a particular project and reduce size and color-depth during post-processing using programs such as Photoshop, Debabelizer, or AfterEffects. Also consider rendering against a solid color background to make compositing easier.

Compositing

compositing

Compositing is the process of merging or layering separate graphic elements into a single image or animation. Sometimes it is better to render 3D objects and animations separately. For example, for a Shockwave animation in Director, several simultaneous small animations generally have better playback performance than one large animation that takes up the whole stage. Or you could use AfterEffects, Photoshop, Premiere, or Director to composite separate 2D and 3D graphic elements against different 2D backgrounds, so that you can re-use the graphic elements in different projects.

Compositing enables you to add different backgrounds, change motion paths, or add and delete individual elements without having to re-render the entire scene. Also, you might want to render one object at a higher level of detail and quality (and a corresponding longer render time) compared to other objects in a scene. Then you could composite the high detail and low detail objects together to save rendering time.

Alpha Channels

alpha channels

If you plan on compositing your 3D graphics with other graphics, render them with an alpha channel. An **alpha channel** is an invisible, 8-bit, gray-scale image that is automatically created in most 3D programs when you render for final output. An alpha channel is useful for compositing in such programs as AfterEffects and Photoshop, because you can use it for masking, transparency, and selection. You can also use it with the GIF89a Export Plug-In in Photoshop to set the transparency for transparent GIFs. A file has an alpha channel if it has a color-depth of millions+ or 32-bits (24-bits plus an 8-bit alpha channel).

Note

To load the alpha channel as a selection in Photoshop, choose the alpha channel (typically Channel #4) with the Select: Load Selection command.

Premiere has an A-B roll editing system and multiple superposition layers with alpha channel support. AfterEffects supports layering and alpha channels. It has powerful masking, transparency, compositing, and animation controls. Premiere and AfterEffects export animations as QuickTime movies for integration with Web pages or as a sequence of PICT files to be processed into GIF Animations, Shockwave, WebPainter, WebAnimator, FutureSplash Animator, or Java Applets.

Compositing and Post-Processing 3D Animation

All the compositing and post-processing issues for static 3D graphics apply to 3D animation; they are multiplied by the number of animation frames. Here are a number of things to remember as you composite and post-process.

You can use the symmetry of your 3D object to reduce the render time and the number of separate frames and cast members in your animation. For example, if you want to rotate the letter A 360 degrees about its vertical axis, you only have to rotate it 180 degrees because of the mirror-plane symmetry along the vertical axis.

Animated 3D graphics look more realistic if they throw shadows across the background, so determine the layering order of your 3D graphics before you start rendering, and plan your compositing accordingly. The shadows change shape as the element animates and they fall on different surfaces and objects. Plan from the start how you will composite animated shadows.

As you post-process separate animation frames, you might want to preserve the original size of each frame to preserve its registration points. Outline each frame with a solid line or paint small, solid-color squares in the upper left and lower right corners of the image. When you import these graphics into an animation program, the original size and registration points are preserved. Remove these marks after you set up the animation.

Most 3D programs render images at a color-depth of 24 bits. You have to reduce the color-depth if you want to use images in an 8-bit Web project.

A common problem with reducing color-depth in 3D graphics is that a smooth gradient, such as a smooth, shadowed surface, becomes banded when it's reduced from 24 bits to 8 bits. Before you reduce the color-depth, use Photoshop to add a small amount of noise to smooth gradients and see if this helps reduce banding. You can also render the image at a color-depth of 8 bits in your 3D program.

super palette

Large areas of flat, solid color in animations can have annoying pixel drift when dithered to 8-bit color. Avoid dithering solid color areas when you reduce color-depth. It's a good idea to output a short test animation at your final render settings and to run a test color-depth reduction to see what the 24-bit animation looks like at 8-bit. Consider creating an 8-bit super palette in Equilibrium Technology's Debabelizer. A **super palette** is an optimal palette based on the colors found in a range of different images, such as frames in an animation.

Note

Debabelizer is an essential tool for batch processing animation files and creating optimal palettes. You can automate repetitive processes using a macro utility such as QuicKeys. Daystar Digital's free Photomatic utility automates many Photoshop processes and can be downloaded from:

`http://www.daystar.com/`

3D Backgrounds

An easy way to add dimensionality to your Web page is to use a 3D background. A 3D background can be as simple as a picture frame for a QuickTime movie or as complex as a fully-realized stage set for a character animation. By creating your background as a model in a 3D program it's easy to change perspective, lighting, and atmospheric effects, or to render different parts of the scene separately.

Set up an interesting perspective for your background by using the camera and view parameters in the 3D program. Avoid flat surfaces parallel to the computer screen. Dramatic, low-angle lighting and shadows can also add a sense of depth. Consider rendering your background model in foreground, middle-ground, and background layers. Then composite them in Photoshop. A simple technique such as adding a slight Gaussian blur to the background layer creates a sense of depth in a scene. Make sure your background doesn't visually compete with the content or the interface and ensure that the background has a similar graphic style as the rest of the project.

When designing a 3D background or image map for your Web page, follow the design guidelines presented in Chapter 6, "Using Graphics to Add Dynamic Content." Don't overpower the content that will be layered over the background graphic. Remember, you want people to read your Web page.

3D Objects

When compositing 3D elements that have been rendered separately, it's important that they have stylistic consistency so that elements don't look out of place. Therefore, follow these guidelines:

- All elements should be lighted from the same direction so that shadows fall consistently.
- The lights should be of similar intensity and color.
- Global environment settings such as ambient light and fog should be the same in your rendered 3D graphics, unless you are designing for a particular effect.
- Use similar colors and surface properties to give your graphics stylistic unity.

Before you start rendering, determine the layering order of your 3D graphics and plan your compositing accordingly.

At the outset, decide how you want to composite shadows. Do you want to render the shadows with the 3D object, add them later as a separate layer in Photoshop, or paint them directly on the background with the Photoshop airbrush tool? Shadows aren't sharp-edged. They are blurry, and it can be a challenge to merge shadows realistically with the background.

It's a good idea to render your 3D images with larger dimensions than you need. Resize the image to the dimensions you want for your project. The quality of resized graphics is better if you start with a large graphic and reduce the size, rather than starting with a small graphic and increasing the size.

Tutorial: Rotating a 3D Object in Extreme 3D

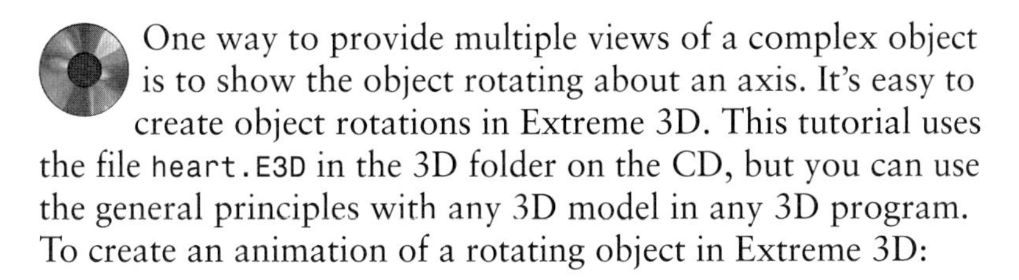

One way to provide multiple views of a complex object is to show the object rotating about an axis. It's easy to create object rotations in Extreme 3D. This tutorial uses the file `heart.E3D` in the 3D folder on the CD, but you can use the general principles with any 3D model in any 3D program. To create an animation of a rotating object in Extreme 3D:

1. First, select the object.
2. Choose a keyframe for the end of the animation. The number of frames for a full-circle rotation depends on the requirements of your project. Thirty-six frames for a full circle rotation generally provides a smooth rotation, but you might be able to get by with fewer frames (see fig. 12.12).

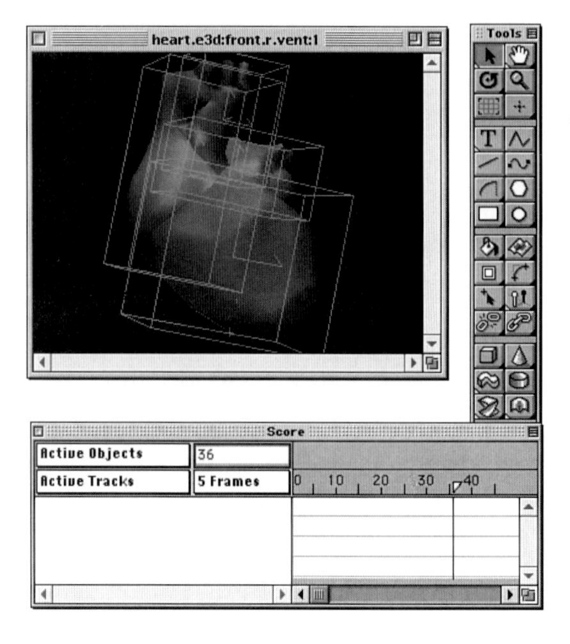

Figure 12.12

Set keyframe at frame 36.

3. Choose Auto Rotate under the Animate menu.
4. Specify a rotation angle of 360 degrees for a full circle rotation in the Auto Rotate dialog box, shown in figure 12. 13.
5. You probably want to rotate about the Object's Y axis (vertical axis) but whether you do so or not depends on how you set up your 3D world and what you want to do.
6. Click OK.

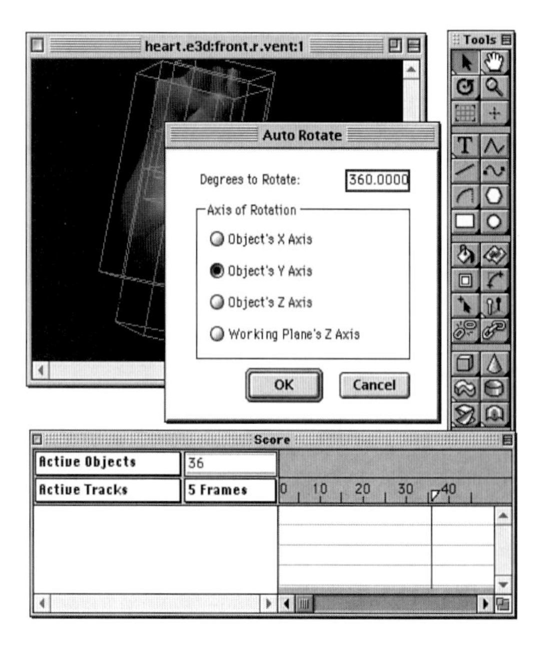

Figure 12.13

Auto Rotate dialog box.

Extreme 3D automatically creates an animation of the object rotating 360 degrees about its center point along the axis you specify (see fig. 12.14).

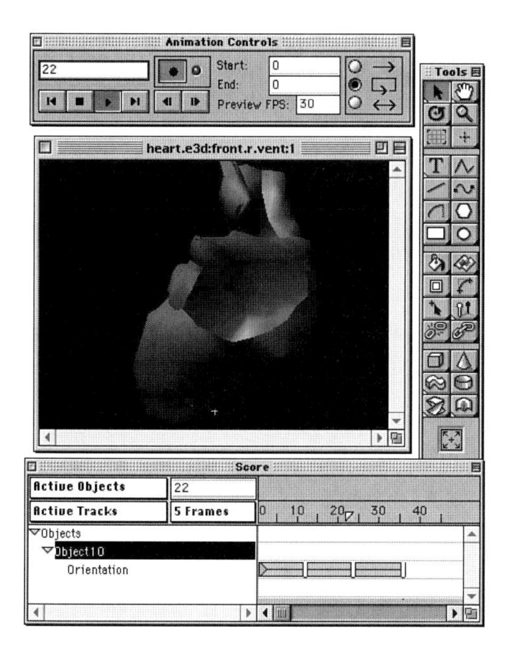

Figure 12.14

Playing the animation.

If the object swings out of view or doesn't rotate the way you want, you might need to move the object's center point. The axis of rotation you specify in the Auto Rotate dialog box passes through the object's center point. Most 3D programs have a tool to do this, in Extreme 3D it is called the Object Center Tool.

construction points

Another trick is to link the object to a construction point that has been placed on the axis of rotation. A **construction point** is a virtual object that doesn't show up when you render. You use construction points, lines, and planes similar to guides in 2D programs, as convenient guides for object placement and alignment. Link the object that you want to rotate to a construction point, and then use Auto Rotate to rotate the construction point. The object appears to rotate or orbit around the construction point.

Output your animation as a QuickTime movie or a sequence of PICT images. To place your animation in a Web page you can convert it to a GIF animation, QuickTime movie, VRML, Shockwave, Sizzler, WebPainter, or other Plug-In based animation. See the chapters on QuickTime, Shockwave, and animation for suggestions on how to do this. In the next chapter you learn how to convert Extreme 3D models to VRML format for the Web.

Creating Animations in POV-Ray

ray-tracing

POV-Ray is an incredible 3D ray-tracer. **Ray-tracing** is a computationally intensive (slow) but high-quality type of rendering. Ray-tracing excels at creating photo-realistic lighting effects, such as reflections and refractions. POV-Ray is based on David Buck's original ray-tracer, DKB-Trace, and has been developed and maintained over the years by a group of hard-working, volunteer programmers. It is available free on the Internet at `http://www.povray.org/`.

Currently, version 3 of POV-Ray is available for DOS, Windows 3.1, Linux, SunOS, Unix, PowerMac, and Macintosh 68K systems.

There is quite a large collection of software related to POV-Ray, including modelers, viewers, utility programs, scene files, and rendered images. Many of these are available at the POV-Ray Web site and on the Raytrace! CD-ROM from Walnut Creek. You can check out some of the contents of the CD at:

`http://www.povray.org/pov-cdrom/`

An updated version of the POV-Ray CD-ROM for version 3 might be available by the time you read this.

How POV Rendering Works

POV is a rendering engine only. Figure 12.15 shows an example image included in the POV-Ray distribution. You create 3D objects and worlds using a text-based scene description language. You can also use one of several shareware modelers and conversion utilities to convert or create models for rendering in POV-Ray. `Wcvt2pov.exe` on this book's CD converts files created in some modelers to POV-Ray format and POV-Ray format files to other formats.

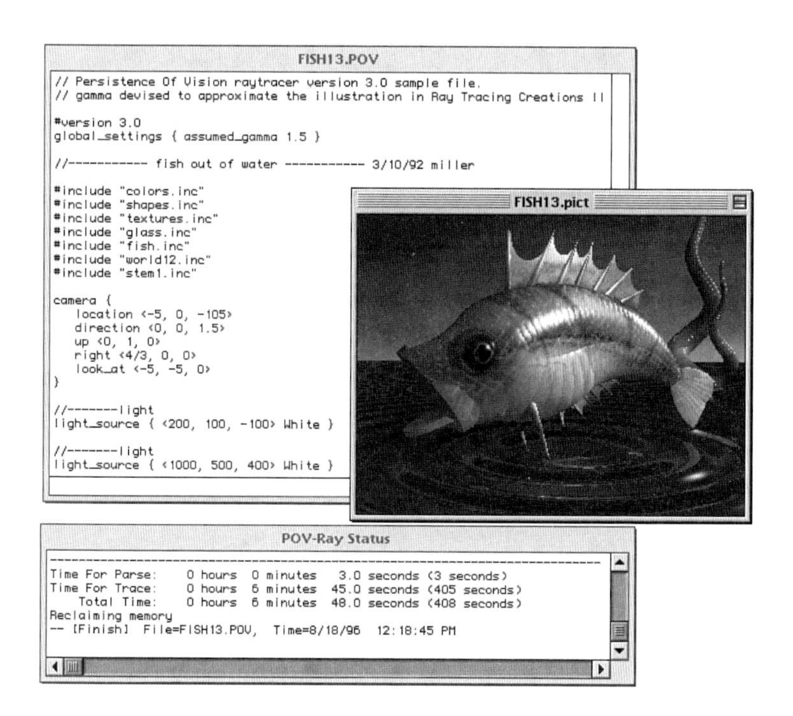

Figure 12.15

POV-Ray image and scene description file.

The instructions that describe a POV-Ray image are stored in a text file. The file contains commands and parameters in the POV-Ray scene description language that tell the POV-Ray renderer how to render your scene. These commands tell the renderer about the geometry of objects, surface properties, lighting, and many other things. Instructions and parameters are usually grouped within curly braces. For example,

```
object {
   Cube
   scale <10000, 1, 500>
   translate -25*y
}
```

tells the POV-Ray to render a box-shaped object that is scaled along the X, Y, and Z axes and moved or translated 25 units along the Y axis. All objects are initially created at the 0, 0, 0 point of the 3D world.

The commands:

```
object {
   Cube
   scale <10000, 1, 500>
   translate -25*y
```

Tip

An excellent FAQ for POV-Ray beginners can be found at **http://www.whoville.com/pov-ray/faq/**

```
    texture {
        pigment { color red 0.0 green 0.07 blue 0.0 }
}
```

tell the renderer to give the box a greenish color.

The command:

```
light_source { <200, 100, -100> White }
```

adds a white light source to the scene at the indicated coordinates. You see similar commands when you look at VRML worlds.

Tutorial: Using POV-Ray's Clock Variable

The POV-Ray scene description language contains many useful features to help you create beautiful imagery and animations. It is beyond the scope of this chapter to describe in detail the features of this language; however, to give you an idea of the capabilities of POV-Ray, this section looks at one of the most useful features for animations: the clock variable. Using the clock variable you can animate a property over time.

The clock variable is a number that is incremented by a set amount in each animation frame. You can specify the initial and final values of the clock variable in the Rendering Preferences dialog box. The clock variable can be added, multiplied, subtracted, or otherwise used to modify any numeric property in your scene.

First, you must set up your POV-Ray scene to render a sequence of animation frames.

1. Choose Preferences: File Rendering from the Edit menu.
2. Choose Animation from the Settings for pop-up menu (see fig. 12.16).
3. Check the Turn on "clock" animation check box.
4. You can also specify a restricted range of frames to animate in the Start At: and End At: settings if you want to render only a part of the total animation.

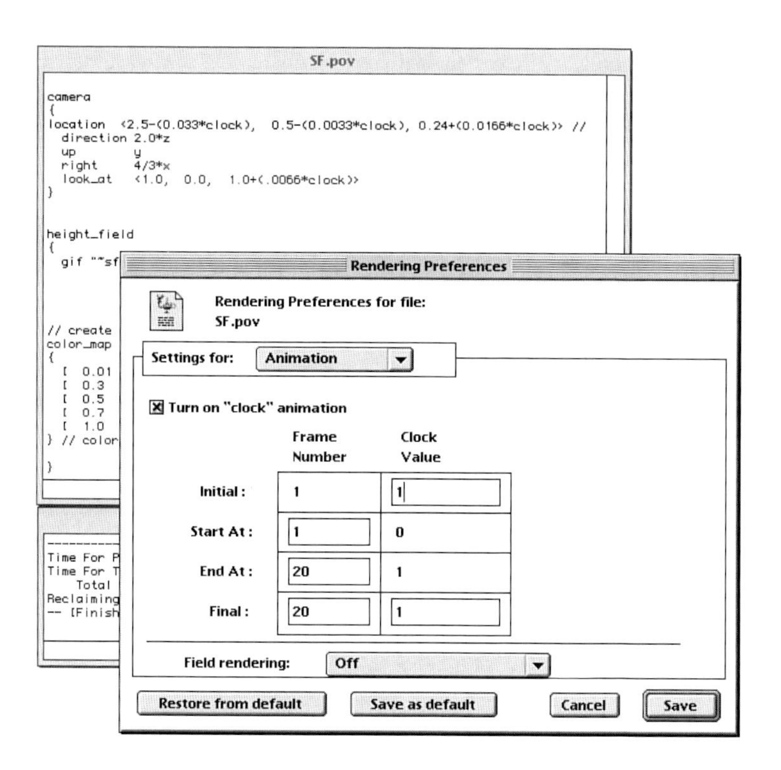

Figure 12.16

Animation settings in POV-Ray.

5. Enter an initial value for the Clock Value. This value is the initial value of the clock variable in the first frame.
6. Enter a final value for the Clock Value. This value is the final value of the clock variable in the last frame.
7. In each frame, the clock variable is incremented by the number of frames.
8. Click Save.

Now you can use the clock value to animate properties over time. The clock variable is incremented in each frame. For example, to create a fly-through animation, you could add the clock value to the values for camera location and camera look-at point in the scene description file. For example:

```
camera
{
location  <2.5-(0.33*clock),  0.5-(0.0033*clock),
0.24+(0.0166*clock)>
  direction 2.0*z
  up        y
  right     4/3*x
  look_at   <1.0,  0.0,  1.0+(.0066*clock)>
}
```

would create a camera that would fly-through your scene. The factors `(0.33*clock)`, `(0.0033*clock)`, `(0.0166*clock)`, and `(.0066*clock)` are added to the camera's location parameters and look at point. The values of these factors change in each frame with the changing clock variable and move the camera through the scene.

When creating animations this way, it's often useful to define key frames and perform test renders at the key frames. Then, divide up the animation into smaller pieces with starting and ending points defined by key frames. Use the key frame values of the parameters that you want to animate and calculate the clock values. See figure 12.17 for an example of fly-through animation.

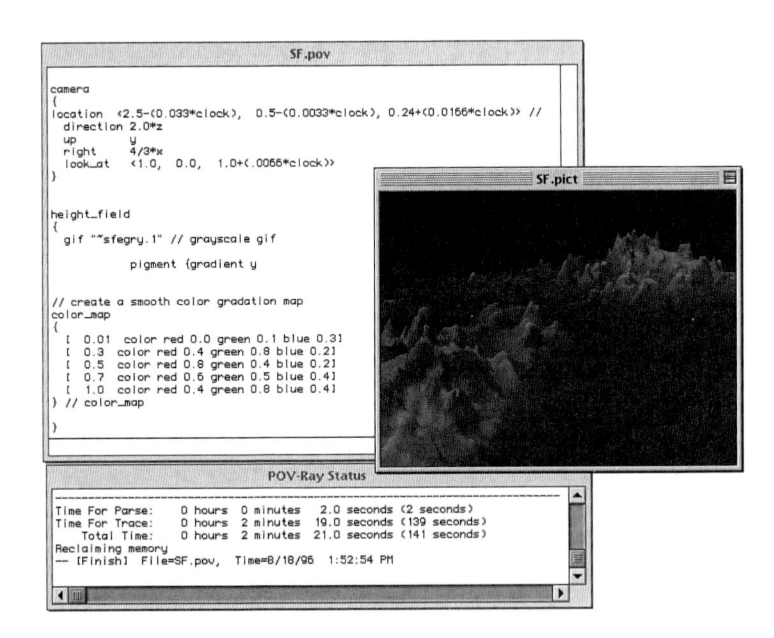

Figure 12.17

Fly-through animation in POV-Ray.

QuickTime Virtual Reality (QTVR)

QuickTime VR (QTVR) is a cross-platform virtual reality technology from Apple Computer. QTVR movies are special QuickTime movies that enable users to move through 3D environments, pick up and manipulate 3D objects, and activate hot spots embedded in the 3D scene. The user interacts with the 3D environment by using a mouse and keyboard. Users don't need high-end workstations, special headsets, goggles, or other peripherals. QTVR movies are characterized by high-quality, photographic images, fast playback, and small file size. QTVR is optimized for photographic images, but it works with computer-generated images.

To view QTVR movies you need a QuickTime-capable Macintosh or Windows computer. On the Mac, the minimum system requirements are:

- 68030, 25 MHz processor
- 8 MB RAM
- QuickTime 2.0 or later
- System 7.1
- 8-bit video

On Windows, the minimum system requirements are:

- 386SX
- 33 MHz processor
- 8 MB RAM
- QuickTime 2.0 (or later) for Windows
- Windows 3.1, Windows 95, or Windows NT
- 8-bit video

To add QuickTime VR capabilities to the Netscape QuickTime Plug-In, so you can view QTVR scenes embedded in a Web page, you need the QuickTime VR components file. You can download the free QuickTime VR components for Macintosh and Windows computers from Apple's QuickTime Web site:

`http://quicktime.apple.com/sw/sw.html`

A free QTVR player and helper application for Macintosh and Windows systems and sample QTVR movies are available from Apple Computer's Web site:

`http:// qtvr.quicktime.apple.com/`

Note

At this time, to view QuickTime VR files on 16-bit Windows systems, such as Windows 3.1, you need to be running the 16-bit version of Netscape, the 16-bit version of QuickTime, and have the QTVRW.QTC file in your WINDOWS or WINDOWS\SYSTEM directory. To view QTVR files on Windows 95 and Windows NT, you need the 32-bit version of Netscape Navigator, the 32-bit version of QuickTime, and the 32-bit version of QTVRW.QTC in your WINDOWS or WINDOWS\SYSTEM directory.

QuickTime Virtual Reality on the Web

The (QuickTime Virtual Reality) QTVR extensions to QuickTime enable you to view QTVR scenes embedded in a Web page. To add QuickTime VR capabilities to the Netscape Plug-In you need to have the QuickTime VR components file. The QuickTime VR components file contains software used by the QuickTime Plug-In to play QuickTime VR Panoramas and Objects. On Macintosh systems the QuickTime VR components must be in the same folder as the QuickTime Plug-In. On Windows systems it must be in your WINDOWS or WINDOWS\SYSTEM directory.

You can download the free QuickTime VR components for Macintosh and Windows computers from Apple's QuickTime Web site:

```
http://quicktime.apple.com/qt/sw/sw.html
```

QuickTime VR Tools

As of this writing, there are two ways to create QTVR movies, both available from Apple Computer.

1. The full-featured QTVR Authoring Kit
2. The free Make QuickTime VR Object and Make QuickTime VR Panorama Tools

You can obtain free authoring tools from:

```
http:// qtvr.quicktime.apple.com/
```

At this time, authoring tools are available for Macintosh systems only.

Optimizing QTVR Movies for the Web

Like all Web multimedia, optimizations involve trade-offs in quality and file size. You have to balance these competing demands based on your content and your goals. Here are some tips to optimize QTVR movies for the Web.

- Because color-bit depth has little effect on the size of a QTVR movie, do not reduce the color-bit depth of your source files.

- Consider cropping the source panorama or object movie to the smallest size possible.
- Use areas of flat color, such as a flat color background if you can. You can post-process video frames in an application such as Photoshop or Debabelizer to reduce noisy backgrounds.
- For Object movies, reduce the number of frames, for example, to a single row of 12 frames.
- When you make the QTVR movie, reduce output dimensions to the smallest possible size such as 240×180 or 160×120. Output dimensions probably have the greatest effect on file size for the Web.
- Currently, the Cinepak codec at 50 percent or 75 percent quality settings probably produces the best results for both Macintosh and Windows computers. New Web-optimized codecs for QuickTime and QuickTime VR may be available by the time you read this.

Note

Do not use Internet Movie Tool on QuickTime VR movies. Use MoviePlayer if you need to flatten a QTVR movie.

Tutorial: Creating a QuickTime VR Panorama

This section discusses creating a QTVR Panorama movie for playback on the Web. To create a QTVR panorama you need:

Tools

The Free Make QTVR Panorama tool from Apple Computer available at `http://qtvr.quicktime.apple.com/newdown.html`.

A panoramic PICT file.

A Macintosh running System 7 or later, QuickTime 2.0 or later, and enough memory to load the source PICT, plus 2 MB.

You can create a panoramic PICT file in a 3D graphics program such as MetaTools' Bryce, Strata Studio Pro, or POV-Ray, or you can use a special panoramic camera. To ensure cross-platform playback, the width of the panoramic PICT file in pixels should be evenly divisible by four and the height should be evenly divisible by 96. The file `gldngate.pic` on the

CD is a panoramic PICT file created in MetaTools' Bryce that you can use to create a QTVR panorama movie (see fig. 12.18).

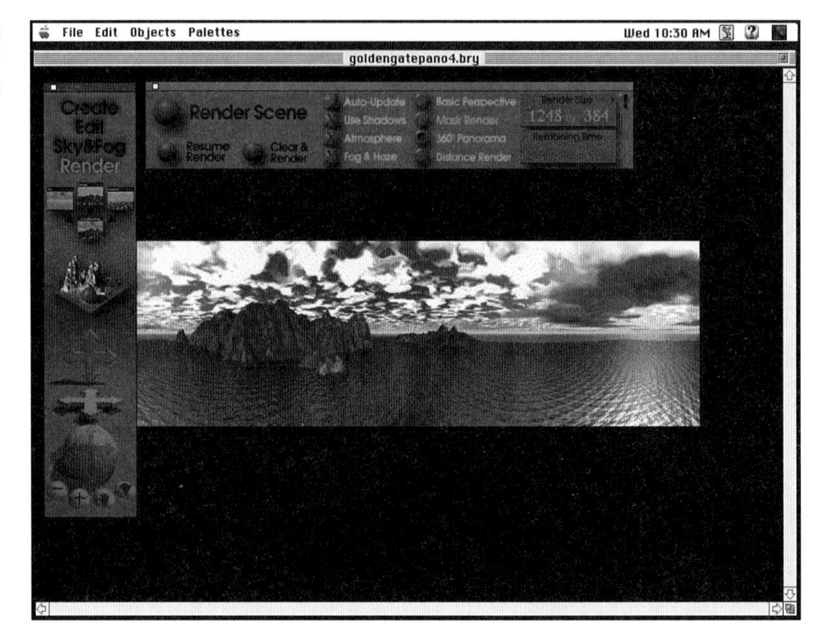

Figure 12.18

Rendered panorama in Bryce.

Creating a Panoramic Image in Bryce

Here's how to set up a panoramic render in Bryce:

1. Choose Render under the Palettes menu.
2. Select the 360° Panorama option in the Render Palette.
3. Choose User Custom from the Render Size pop-up menu.
4. Enter dimensions for the rendered image. As mentioned previously, the width of the panoramic image in pixels should be evenly divisible by four and the height should be evenly divisible by 96, such as 576×384, 1248×384, or 2016×756.
5. Now set up the camera. In Bryce 1.0. double-click on the ball with the cross on it in the lower part of the Master palette.
6. In the Camera dialog box, under the Angle settings, enter 0 for x° settings and 0 for z° settings (see fig. 12.19).

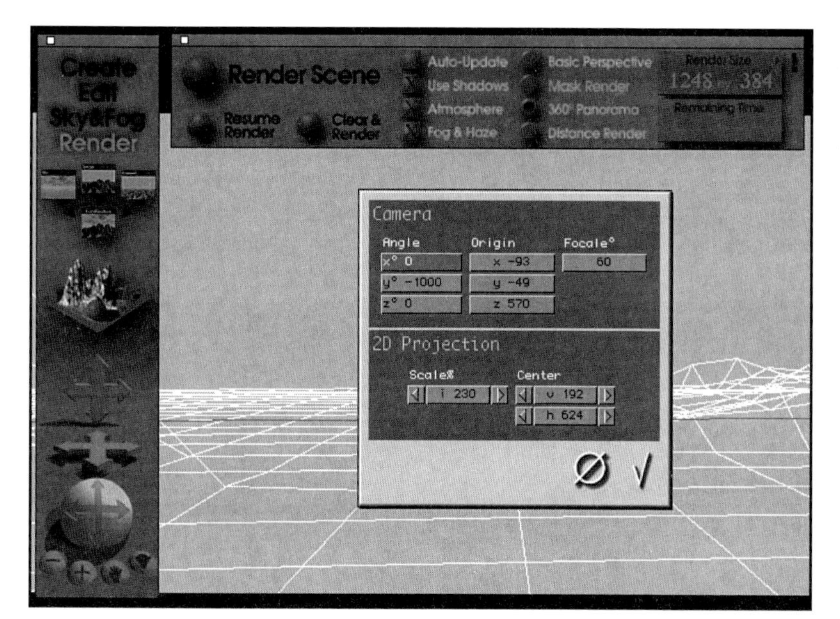

Figure 12.19

Setting up the camera for a panoramic render in Bryce.

7. Click on the check mark in the lower right corner of the Camera dialog box.
8. Click on Render Scene.

Creating a Panoramic Image in POV-Ray

Here's how to set up a panoramic render in POV-Ray:

1. Set up the camera in your scene description file. The following is a fragment of the POV-Ray scene description language that sets up a camera to render a panoramic image from QuickTime VR:

```
camera
{
  // Creates a 360 degree camera view for QTVR
panorama

  cylinder 1

  right  1*x
  up     4*y  // increasing the up vector com-
presses the scene vertically
  angle 360

 location  <0.0, 0.0, 0.0>
  look_at   <0.0, 0.0, 1.0>
}
```

2. Choose Preferences: File Rendering from the Edit menu.
3. Choose Output Size from the Settings for pop-up menu.
4. Enter the dimensions for the rendered image (see fig. 12.20). As mentioned previously, the width of the panoramic image in pixels should be evenly divisible by four and the height should be evenly divisible by 96. Try 576×384 for low-resolution renders or 2016×756 for high-resolution renders.

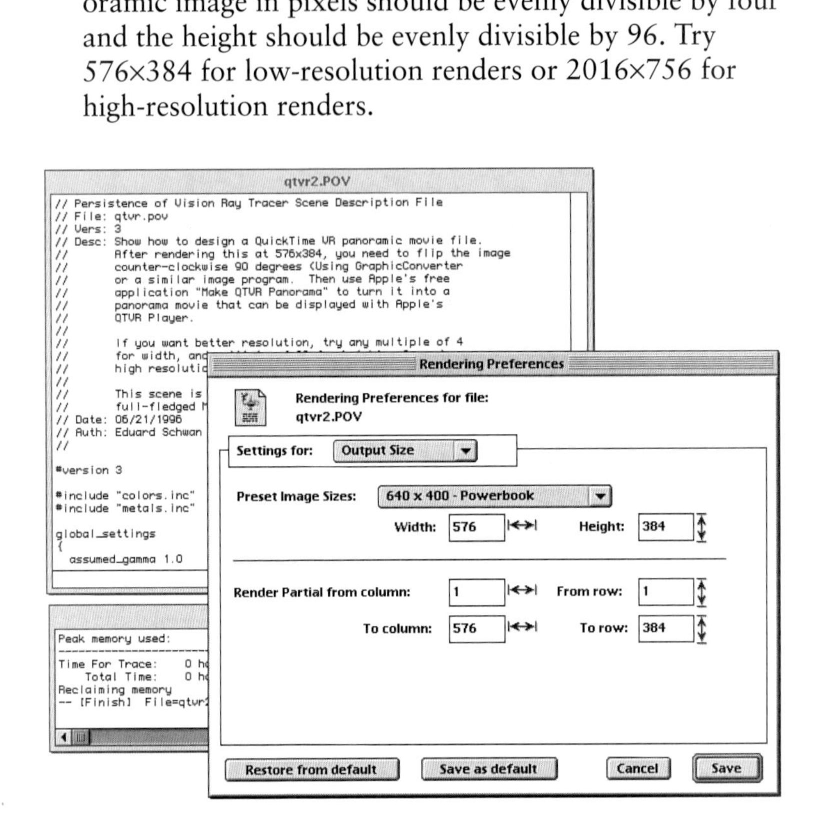

Figure 12.20

Setting up a panoramic render in POV-Ray.

5. Choose Start Rendering from the Render menu.
6. After you complete these steps, you have a panoramic graphic suitable for use in QTVR (see fig. 12.21).

   Eduard Schwan has provided a sample POV-Ray scene description file for QuickTime VR in the Scenes: QuickTime VR! folder contained within the POV-Ray 3 distribution.

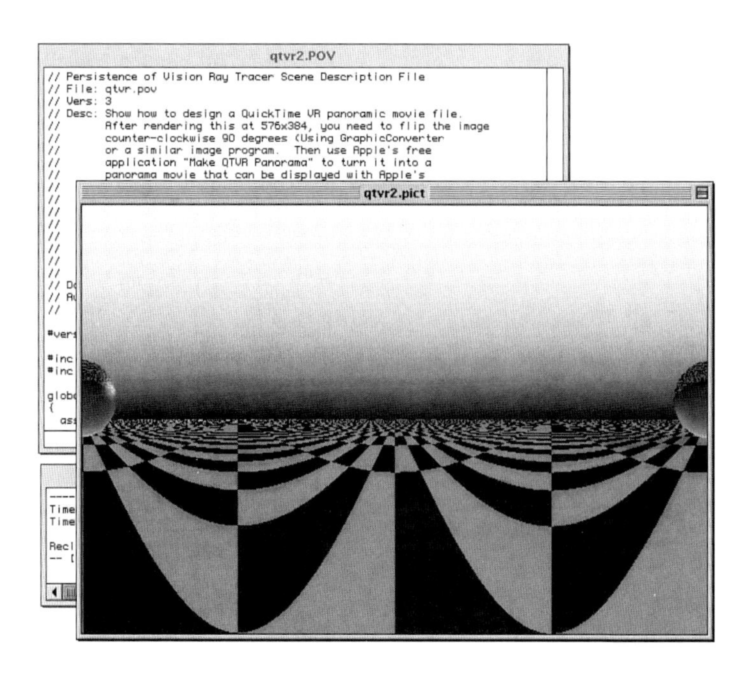

Figure 12.21

Panoramic image rendered in POV-Ray.

Using the Make QTVR Panorama Tool

Converting a panoramic PICT to a QuickTime VR panorama involves the following steps:

1. Rotate the PICT 90 degrees counter-clockwise (so that the bottom of the image is to the right), in an image processing program such as Photoshop (see fig. 12.22).

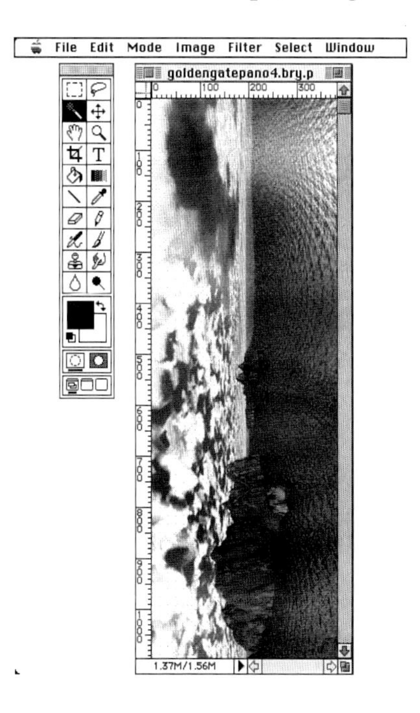

Figure 12.22

Rotated panorama in Photoshop.

2. Start the Make QTVR Panorama tool and open the PICT you want to convert or drag-and-drop the PICT file on to the Make QTVR Panorama icon.
3. The default compression settings work pretty good for Web-based QTVR (see fig. 12.23). You probably want to change the dimensions of the movie to something more appropriate for Web playback such as 240×180 or 160×120.

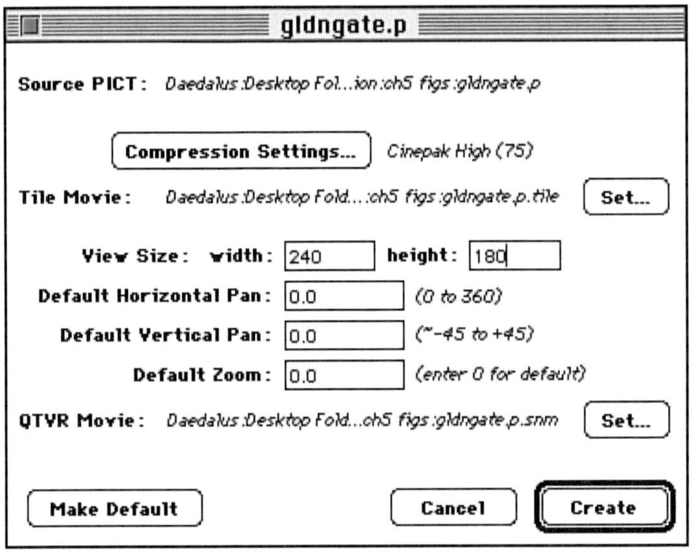

Figure 12.23

Settings dialog box in the Make QTVR Panorama tool.

gldngate.p

Source PICT: Daedalus:Desktop Fol...ion:ch5 figs:gldngate.p

Compression Settings... Cinepak High (75)

Tile Movie: Daedalus:Desktop Fold...:ch5 figs:gldngate.p.tile Set...

View Size: width: 240 height: 180

Default Horizontal Pan: 0.0 (0 to 360)

Default Vertical Pan: 0.0 (~-45 to +45)

Default Zoom: 0.0 (enter 0 for default)

QTVR Movie: Daedalus:Desktop Fold...ch5 figs:gldngate.p.snm Set...

Make Default Cancel Create

4. Choose Create. The PICT is saved as a QuickTime VR panorama.

HTML for QTVR

> **Note**
>
> For a complete list of the latest HTML tags, visit **http://qtvr.quicktime.apple.com/**.

You embed a QTVR movie in a Web page the same way you embed a QuickTime movie. The QuickTime Plug-In that ships with Netscape Navigator 3.0 supports special attributes to the EMBED tag specifically designed for QTVR movies. You can use these attributes to control the appearance of your QTVR file on the Web page. The following attributes are all optional:

- **PAN attribute.** Enables you to specify the initial horizontal pan angle for a QuickTime VR movie as an integer between zero and 360.
- **TILT attribute.** Enables you to specify the initial tilt angle in the range-43 to 43 degrees.

- **FOV attribute.** Enables you to specify the initial field of view in the range of five to 85 degrees.

The following attributes are extensions to the EMBED tag recognized by the QuickTime Plug-In for Netscape, but should NOT be used with QTVR movies. In most cases they are ignored, in some cases you get a blank frame. Therefore, to ensure consistent display, do not use these tags for QTVR:

- HIDDEN
- AUTOPLAY
- CONTROLLER
- LOOP
- PLAYEVERYFRAME
- HREF,TARGET

See Chapter 10, "Animating with QuickTime Digital Video," for general hints about embedding QuickTime files in Web pages.

Embedding a 3DMF File in a Web Page

3DMF stands for 3D MetaFile. As mentioned earlier in this chapter, it is the format supported by QuickDraw 3D, Apple Computer's system-level 3D architecture, and forms the basis for the binary file format of VRML 2.0.

Users need the following to view embedded 3DMF files in Web pages.

Tools
PowerMac
QuickDraw 3D
Whurlplug Plug-In

A Windows version of QuickDraw 3D should be available by the time you read this, along with a Windows version of the Whurlplug Netscape Plug-In.

Note

Find out the latest about QuickDraw 3D and download the free systems extensions at:

`http://quickdraw3d.apple.com/`

Find out the latest about the Whurlplug Plug-In and download the free Plug-In at:

`http://quickdraw3d.apple.com/Whurlplug.HTML`

Embedding 3DMF files in Web pages is pretty easy.

1. First, create your 3DMF file in a program such as Strata Studio Pro, Vision 3D, or Specular's Infini-D.
2. Save it with the `.3dmf`, `.3dm`, `.qd3d`, or `.qd3` file name extension for the Web.
3. Be sure that you have the Whurlplug Plug-In in your Netscape Navigator Plug-Ins folder and that your browser is set up to associate the MIME type of 3DMF files, `x-world/x-3dmf.`, with `3dmf`, `.3dm`, `.qd3d`, `.qd3` file name extensions.
4. Then, embed 3DMF files in a Web page like any other Plug-In content. For example:

   ```
   <EMBED SRC="3DObject.3dmf" WIDTH=200 HEIGHT=200
   ROTATE="2 10 3" TOOLBAR=true>
   ```

   embeds the file `3DObject.3dmf`. The object rotates about X, Y, and Z axes with the specified values, which are integers between –180 and 180. The built-in navigation and view toolbar is enabled in this example. Figure 12.24 illustrates several display options for 3DMF files on the Web.

Visit the Whurlplug Web site referenced previously for a description of many other useful attributes.

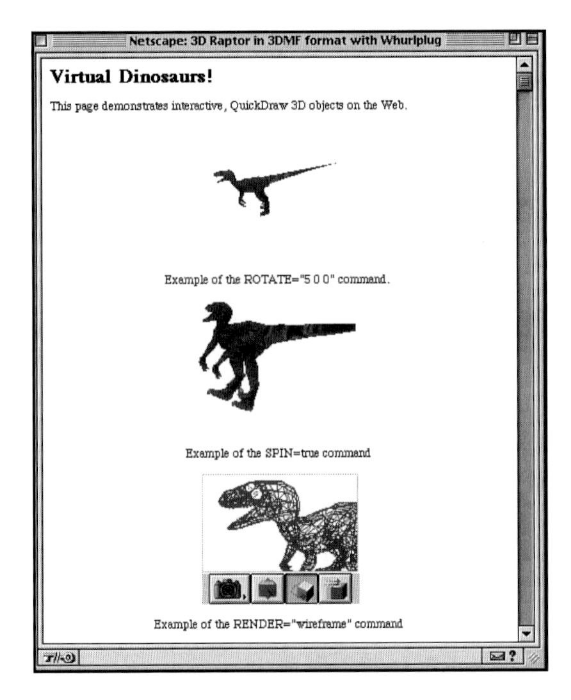

Figure 12.24

Interactive 3DMF files on the Web.

Virtual Reality Modeling Language enables you to create interactive, navigable 3D worlds in your Web page, bringing a new dimension to cyberspace.

chapter

13

VRML

Virtual Reality Modeling Language (VRML, pronounced "vermil") is an ASCII text-based language that describes 3D scenes—to create interactive, navigable 3D worlds. To a certain extent, VRML is similar to HTML, which is an ASCII text-based language that describes a Web page.

VRML viewers are included or provided free with Netscape Navigator and Microsoft Internet Explorer. On the Web, VRML worlds are accessed like other Web content, by clicking on a link. VRML worlds are viewed through a window, either embedded in a browser or via helper apps. Users typically navigate and interact with the world using mouse and keyboard commands. Hyperlinks can be embedded in objects so users can jump to different worlds, Web pages, or other sites.

VRML is a rich language with many options that are beyond the scope of this book. This chapter will give you a quick start and the incentive to explore VRML further.

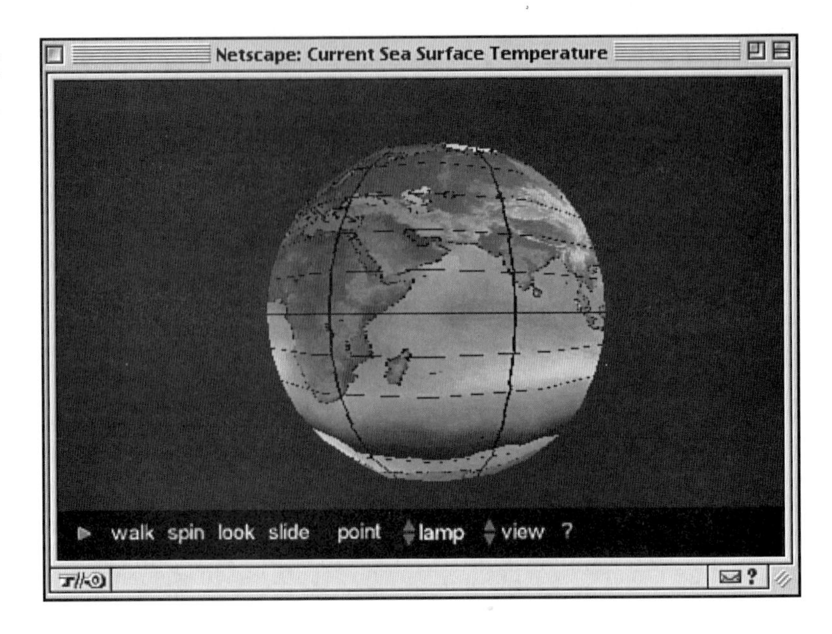

Figure 13.1

VRML Earth.

VRML Benefits and Obstacles

VRML worlds provide many benefits to users. Humans naturally organize information spatially and have a lifetime of experience moving through three dimensions. An interface that clusters data into information landscapes can be easier to model conceptually. For example, VRML can provide the following three-dimensional elements:

- Site maps
- Libraries
- Information visualizations
- Scientific visualizations
- Database visualizations
- Simulations
- Geographical information systems
- Interactive advertisements
- Online presentations

Interactive 3D collaborative environments are the next step in VRML. Enhancements to the original VRML specifications enable two or more users to navigate and interact in an information landscape in real-time. Uses of collaborative environments include multi-user 3D games and chat environments.

> **Tip**
>
> Netscape provides a good introduction to VRML at: **`http://home.netscape.com/eng/live3d/`**

Similar to what happened with HTML, different companies are adding extensions to VRML faster than VAG (VRML Advisory Group) can develop consistent and uniform implementations. Some aspects of a VRML world might, therefore, not be rendered in some viewers.

Also, because each VRML tool creates VRML code differently from other tools, some code variations won't be rendered in individual viewers. It's a good idea to know the basics of the VRML language so you can go in and edit the ASCII text file generated by VRML world builders.

At present, each VRML viewer or browser implements its own navigational controls, commands, and 3D interface, forcing users to relearn interfaces with different viewers. VRML navigation can be tricky at first, and users can become disoriented. It is a good idea to provide an easily accessible help page or explanation of navigational controls for your site.

> **Note**
>
> Two good books about VRML, written by Mark Pesce, one of VRML's creators, are *VRML: Browsing and Building Cyberspace* and *VRML: Flying Through the Web.* Both are available through New Riders Publishing.

VRML 2.0

VRML 2.0 is the next generation of the VRML specification that provides support for animation, interactivity, integration with JavaScript and Java, audio, and multi-user environments. It is currently still in draft form. For details on VRML specs see `http://www.sdsc.edu/vrml/spec.html`.

As of this writing, the following browsers or toolkits support the draft version of VRML 2.0:

- DimensionX's Liquid Reality toolkit

  `http://www.dimensionx.com/products/lr/`

- Real Space's RealVR Traveller

  `http://rlspace.com/`

- Silicon Graphics' Cosmo Player for Windows 95

  `http://vrml.sgi.com/`

- Sony's CyberPassage

  `http://vs.sony.co.jp`

Note

Find out the latest about the VRML 2 spec at:

`http://webspace.sgi.com/moving-worlds/`

Variations on VRML

Some interesting virtual worlds that use proprietary variations to VRML are provided by:

- Black Sun Interactive, `http://www.blacksun.com/`
- Worlds Inc, `http://www.worlds.net`
- The Palace, `http://www.thepalace.com`
- Superscape, `http://www.superscape.com`

RealVR Traveler is a Netscape Plug-In and Director Xtra from RealSpace, Inc. (`http://www.rlspace.com`) that provides photographic panoramas with sprites (animated objects) VRML objects, and a free editing tool for converting QuickTime VR movies to the RealVR format.

OLiVR is a multi-resolution, streaming VR file format from OLiVR Inc. that provides excellent quality VR objects. For more info on the OLiVR viewer, authoring tools, and server, visit: `http://www.olivr.com/`.

Another exciting and potentially very useful variation on VRML is the integration of VRML worlds with JavaScript and Java applets, and with other multimedia data types such as Shockwave and RealAudio. Netscape maintains a Web site listing examples of some of these cutting-edge applications of VRML at the following URLs:

`http://home.netscape.com/eng/live3d/`

`http://home.netscape.com/comprod/products/navigator/`
`➥version_3.0/index.html`

Browsers and Tools Support

At this time Netscape is providing its Live3D VRML viewer Plug-In with Netscape Navigator 3.0 for PowerMac, Windows 95/NT, and Windows 3.1. Several VRML Plug-Ins exist for Navigator 2.0 or later. Microsoft Internet Explorer 3.0 for Windows 95 and Windows NT support VRML viewing with an additional ActiveX control from DimensionX available with the MSIE 3.0 download.

A free cross-platform VRML browser and helper app, Voyager, is provided by Virtus Corporation, illustrated in Figure 13.2. This helper app works on most platforms and with most browsers back to version 1 of Netscape Navigator. As of this writing Voyager supports the VRML 1.0 spec, but not extensions such as the AsciiText and LevelOfDetail instructions.

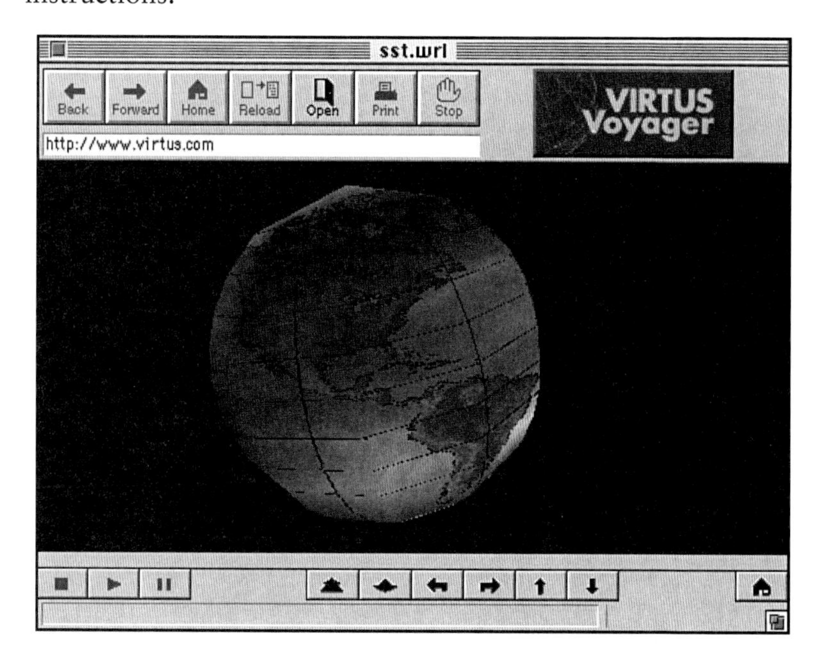

Figure 13.2

The VIRTUS Voyager VRML helper app.

To set up VIRTUS Voyager as a helper app in Netscape Navigator 2.0 (see fig. 13.3), do the following:

1. Choose General Preferences/Helpers under the Options menu.
2. Click New.

Note

You can download the free Voyager browser from:

`http://www.virtus.com/`

3. Type in the Description box: **VRML Worlds.**
4. Type in the Type box: **x-world/x-vrml.**
5. Type in the extensions: **wrl,vpy,vvr,wtp,wlk,vmd,wsb.**
6. Select the Application option in the Handled by box.
7. Click on the Browse button.
8. Select VIRTUS Voyager or another VRML helper app.
9. Close the preferences panel of Netscape Navigator, and close Navigator. Then, restart Netscape.

Figure 13.3

Setting up the VIRTUS Voyager VRML helper app.

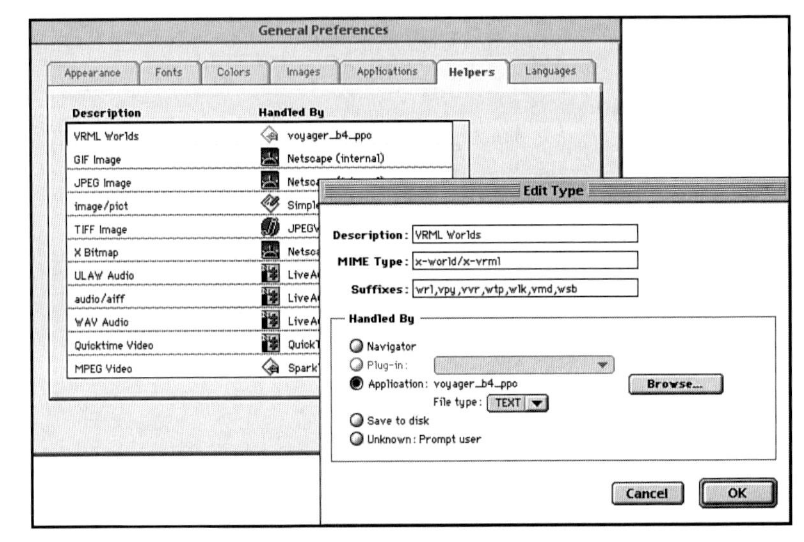

Note

The VRML format is supported by several desktop 3D graphics programs such as 3D Studio Max, Strata Studio Pro, and Extreme 3D. Paragraph's Home Space Builder and Virtus' 3D Web Site Builder are dedicated VRML authoring tools.

A comprehensive list of VRML browsers, Plug-Ins and authoring tools is maintained at `http://sdsc.edu/vrml/browsers.html`.

VRML authoring tools and converters are listed at `http://sdsc.edu/vrml/dvcontent.html`.

Optimizing VRML

VRML files tend to be small. VRML worlds containing high-resolution graphics—such as texture maps, sounds, and video, can take a long time to download. Evaluate the necessity of adding these enhancements. You might be able to get by with a simpler, plain VRML rendering.

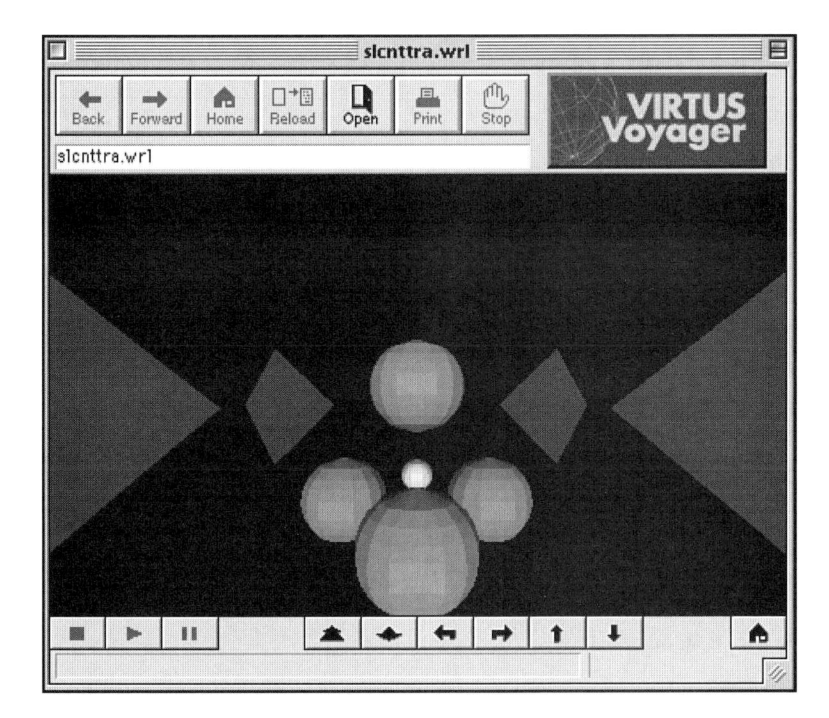

Figure 13.4

A simple VRML world without texture maps.

Check your VRML authoring tools to see if they provide ways to optimize VRML files. Possible optimizations include:

- Using ShapeHints. ShapeHints are VRML instructions that help VRML viewers parse geometry.
- Using LOD. LOD or Level of Detail instructions provide progressively more detailed renderings of models as the viewer moves closer.
- ASCII file optimizations. An example is removal of white space.
- VRML optimizations. Examples of this are removing unnecessary VRML geometry normals, streamlining node hierarchies, reducing floating-point precision, and using VRML primitives.

Gzip compression is a common way to compress VRML files. Use gzip compression with the Unix gzip command, MacGzip on the Mac, or WinZip (`http://www.winzip.com/`) on Windows. Gzipped VRML files have the file name extension "`.wrl.gz`". Your VRML viewer must support gzip compression. Many viewers, such as Live3D, automatically decompress gzipped VRML files. Otherwise users have to decompress gzipped files manually.

Creating a Simple VRML World

VRML is a scene description language, similar to the scene description language you saw for POV-Ray. The instructions that describe a VRML scene are stored in a text file. The instructions are interpreted by a VRML viewer, which then renders the VRML world on your computer screen.

In this tutorial you will create a simple VRML world with a simple text file. All you need is a text editor and a VRML-capable viewer.

You will probably use 3D authoring tools such as the VRML tools described in this book to create VRML worlds rather than create VRML world files in an ASCII text editor. There are advantages of writing VRML worlds in ASCII however, because that way you can create a simple VRML world with any text editor. Also, you might have to edit VRML files created by different 3D programs because they do not support features you want, the VRML files contain errors, or the files contain elements not supported by your browser.

You can use your knowledge of 3D graphics to create VRML world. For example, if you use 3D graphics programs, you are already familiar with the x-y-z 3D coordinate system for VRML, with the center of the world at the 0,0,0 coordinates and the z-axis indicating depth.

VRML files

Note

Another good VRML book by New Riders Publishing is:

VRML 2.0—The Next Step in Cyberspace by Mark Pesce.

VRML files typically have the `.wrl` (for world) extension. Some files have the `.wrl.gz` extension. These are files compressed with gzip compression. To view these files in a VRML browser you must download them and uncompress them yourself or the browser must support decompressing `.gz` files.

The `.wrl` file must contain a single line at the top of the file that tells the browser what kind of VRML to expect in the `.wrl` file. Most VRML files you see on the Web begin with:

```
#VRML V1.0 ASCII
```

which tells the browser to expect an ASCII text file containing VRML version 1 instructions. As of this writing, VRML 2.0 browsers are just beginning to appear. This initial line will be different for VRML 2.0 worlds, for example:

```
#VRML V2.0 ASCII
```

Note

See the previous section, "VRML 2.0" of this chapter for a list of VRML 2.0 browsers and the status of the VRML 2.0 specs—as of this writing.

The rest of the `.wrl` file contains a description of the scene in VRML. This description is called the **scene graph**. The scene graph contains VRML instructions that tell the browser how to render your scene and include information about the geometry of objects, their position in the VRML world, surface properties, lighting, and many other things.

scene graph

Groups, Shapes, and Properties

VRML instructions and their parameters are usually grouped within curly braces. Related instructions are grouped with the Separator keyword. For example, if you specify a cube with a certain color, location, and dimensions, these instructions would be grouped within curly braces that followed a Separator keyword. The Separator keyword is used to bundle together related geometry instructions, surface properties, and other data. For example, a VRML file that describes a sphere would look like:

```
#VRML V1.0 ASCII
Separator {
Sphere { radius 1.0 }
}
```

The sphere would be rendered in the VRML browser in the default gray color (see fig. 13.5), and would be given a radius of one meter in the VRML world. To give the sphere a blue color, add a material property:

```
#VRML V1.0 ASCII
Separator {
Material { diffuseColor 0 0 1 }
Sphere { radius 1.0 }
}
```

Figure 13.5

A VRML sphere.

group node

property node

shape node

Nodes are the individual elements of your 3D world. In the preceding example, the Separator element is a **group node** that groups together related properties of a VRML object. The Material element is a **property node**. It defines the color of the Sphere object and any other object within that Separator group. All objects you embed within this Separator will inherit this Material property. The sphere is defined by a **shape node**.

fields

Fields are the parameters of each node. For example, radius 1.0 is a field of the Sphere node. The diffuseColor field contains the r,g,b values of a color in decimal fractions of 1.

All objects are initially created at the 0,0,0 point of the 3D world. You move an object to a different position in the VRML world using the Transform node. For example, the following code:

```
#VRML V1.0 ASCII
Separator {
Transform {translation 0 0 -1 }
Material { diffuseColor 0 0 1 }
Sphere { radius 1.0 }
}
```

moves the sphere one meter away from the viewer along the Z axis or into the computer screen.

VRML distance units are measured in meters, and angles are measured in radians. Most other units are expressed as decimal fractions of 1. The following code:

```
Material { diffuseColor 0 1 0.5 }
```

describes a color that is 0 percent red, 100 percent green, and 50 percent blue.

Adding Textures to a VRML World's Object

Now that you have a basic idea of how VRML works, let's create an interesting application with some real value. This VRML world is very simple, but demonstrates the potential of VRML worlds to provide unique visualization capabilities to complex data sets.

1. First, start with a version of the VRML world you created in the previous section:

   ```
   #VRML V1.0 ASCII

   Separator {
   Material { diffuseColor 0 0 1 }
      Sphere { radius 2 }
   }
   ```

   As you recall, this created a boring blue sphere floating in space.

2. Now, add a custom texture. Custom textures can be GIF or JPEG files that reside in the same folder as the VRML file or anywhere on the Internet. For your texture, use a JPEG file of recent global sea surface temperatures provided by the Space Science and Engineering Center (SSEC), of the University of Wisconsin-Madison's Graduate School. The URL for this file is:

   ```
   http://www.ssec.wisc.edu/data/sst/latest_sst.gif
   ```

3. Use the Texture2 node to add this texture to the sphere. Here's what the VRML file looks like:

   ```
   #VRML V1.0 ascii
   Separator { #BEGIN Node
   Material { diffuseColor 0 0 1 }
   Texture2 { filename "http://www.ssec.wisc.edu/
   ➥data/sst/latest_sst.gif" }
   Sphere { radius 2 }
   }#END Node
   ```

Figure 13.1 illustrated a VRML world as viewed with a Mac, and figure 13.6 illustrates the same world on a Windows machine. You just created an interactive 3D view of a complex data set, in this case the recent global sea temperatures provided by the SSEC are automatically updated in near real-time.

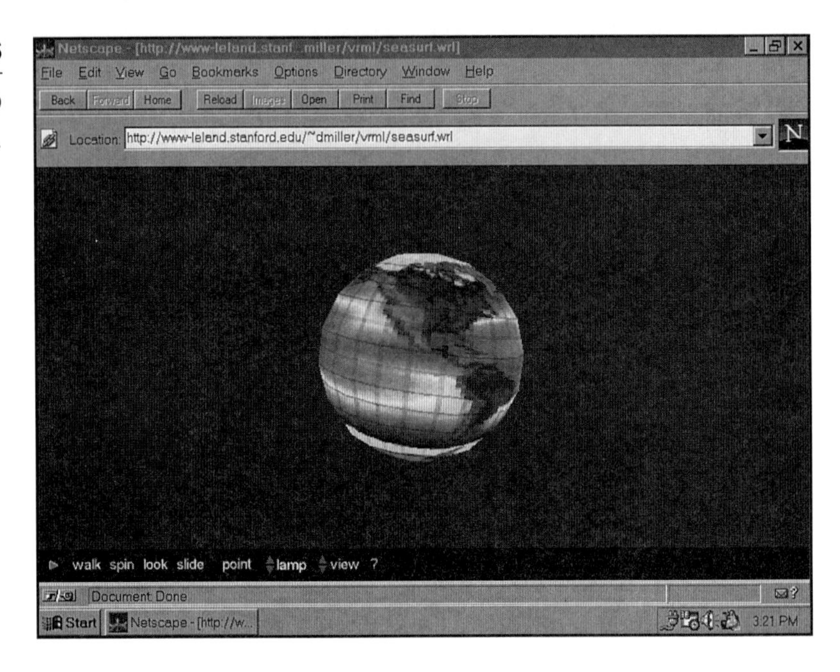

Figure 13.6

A VRML Earth in Live3D on Windows.

Adding Animation to a VRML Object

SpinGroup is a VRML instruction supported by Live3D. It is a simple way to add animation to VRML 1.0 files. To spin the texture-mapped sphere created in the previous section, place the sphere inside a SpinGroup node. Here's the VRML file:

```
#VRML V1.0 ascii
Separator {
     Material { diffuseColor 0 0 1 }
     Texture2 { filename "http://www.ssec.wisc.edu/
➥data/sst/latest_sst.gif" }
     SpinGroup {
         rotation 0 0.5 0 -0.1
         local TRUE
         Sphere { radius 1.5 }
           }#END SpinGroup
}#END Separator Node
```

The first three values of the rotation field of the SpinGroup node specify the speed of rotation around the X, Y, Z, axes with zero being no rotation and one being maximum rotation speed. The final value specifies that the direction of the rotation is clockwise.

Adding Animated Textures to a VRML Object

Another simple technique that adds a lot of pizzazz to a simple VRML world is to use an animated GIF as a texture for an object. Adding animated GIFs as texture maps to a VRML object is as simple as specifying a GIF animation file in the file name field of a Texture2 node. For example:

```
#VRML V1.0 ascii
Separator {
     Material { diffuseColor 0 0 1 }
     Texture2 { filename "animated.gif" }
     SpinGroup {
         rotation 0 0.5 0 -0.1
         local TRUE
         Sphere { radius 1.5 }
           }#END SpinGroup
}#END Separator Node
```

For best results, create a square animated GIF that is 128×128 pixels in dimension. See Chapter 7, "Animation," for instructions on how to create animated GIF files.

Creating VRML Worlds with 3D Web Site Builder

This tutorial describes creating a simple VRML world using Virtus' 3D Web Site Builder. You can use the file `silitut.wsb` on the CD, or create your own world from scratch.

Tools
3D Web Site Builder
`silitut.wsb` file

The 3D Web Site Builder interface consists of three main windows, illustrated in figure 13.7. On the left is the Gallery window that displays libraries of 3D objects you can add to your VRML world. In the upper-right is the Design View window. Here you create VRML worlds using tools from the tool palette. In the lower-right is the Walk View window, where you see and walk around the VRML world.

1. Open the file `silitut.wsb` from the CD or create a new file.
2. To add a sphere shape to your VRML world:
    a. Choose Advanced Shapes from the pop-up menu at the top of the Gallery Window.
    b. Scroll down until you find the 16-sided sphere.
    c. Click on the the 16-sided sphere and drag it into the Design View window.
3. At the top of the Design View tools palette, notice three buttons labeled T, F, R, corresponding to Top, Front, and Rear views respectively. Make sure you are in Top view by clicking on the T button.
4. Click the Plus Magnifying Glass button to zoom in if you need to.
5. Select the Resize tool from the Design View tools palette.
6. Press the shift key and hold it down to preserve proportions as you resize; then select the sphere you just added to your world, and drag the mouse to resize the sphere (see fig. 13.8).

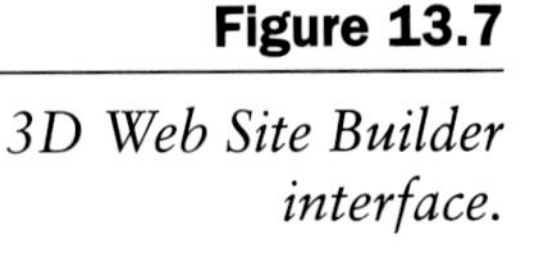

Figure 13.7

3D Web Site Builder interface.

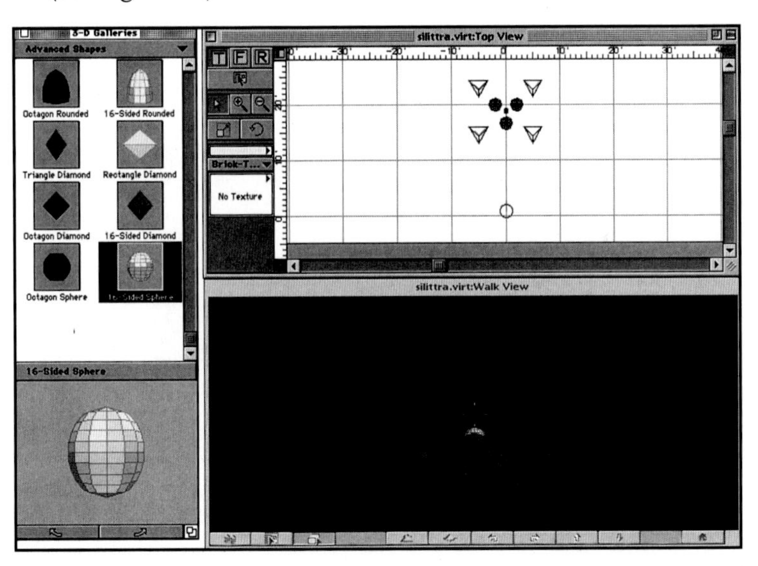

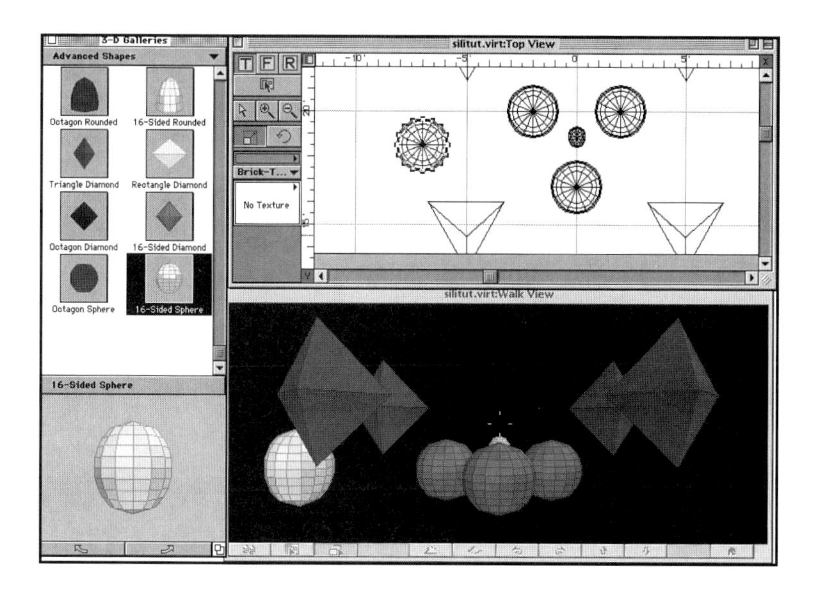

Figure 13.8

Resizing a sphere object in the Design View.

7. Select the Pointer tool from the Design View tools palette.
8. Click on the sphere and drag it into the center of the group of three large spheres.
9. Click the F button to change to Front view. Zoom in if you have to.
10. Being careful not to grab the gray handles, which resize the sphere, move the sphere up so it is floating above the group of three spheres (see fig. 13.9).
11. While the object is selected, give it a new color from the color palette pop-up, or a new texture from the Texture pop-up menu (see fig. 13.10).

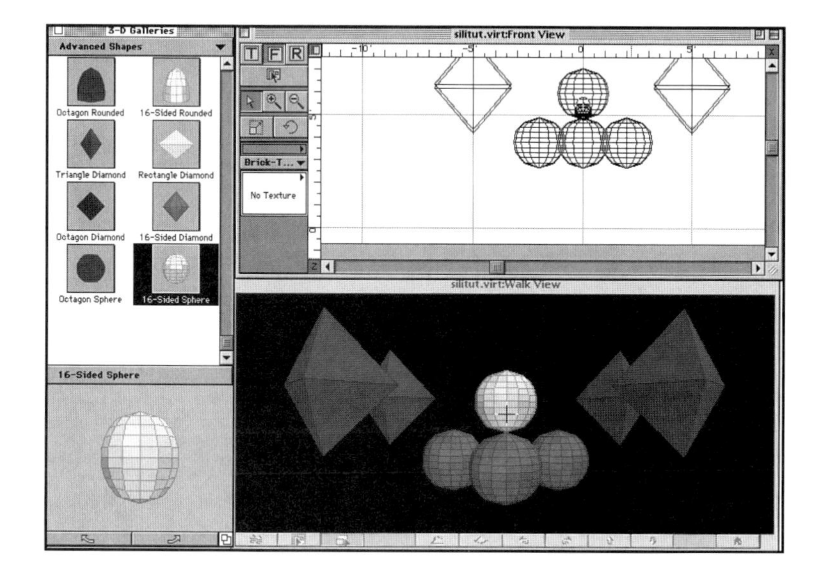

Figure 13.9

Moving an object in 3D space.

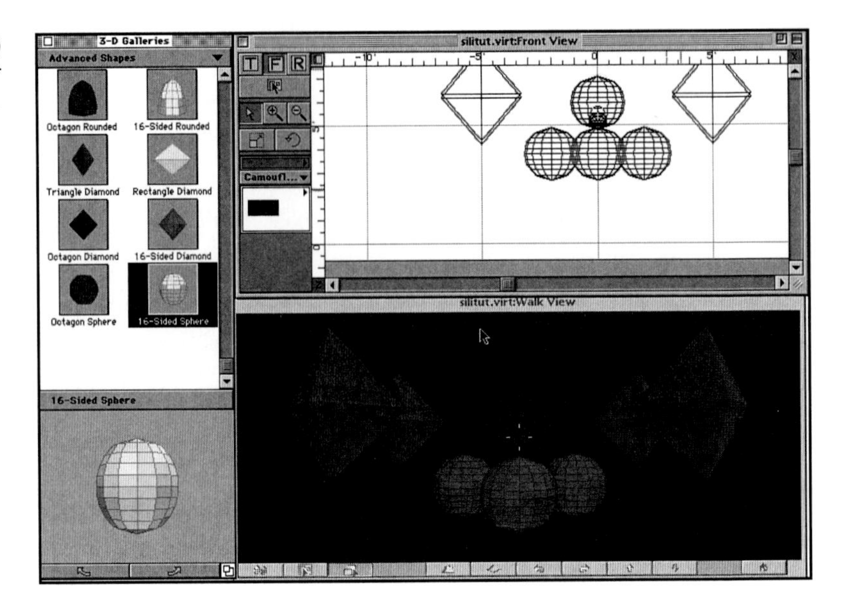

Figure 13.10

Adding a texture.

12. While the object is still selected, choose Add VRML Anchor under the Edit menu.
13. Enter a URL. Click OK (see fig. 13.11).

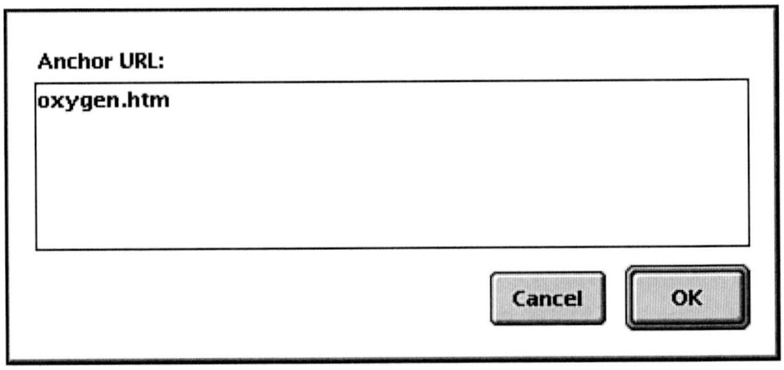

Anchor URL:

oxygen.htm

Cancel OK

Figure 13.11

Adding a URL to a VRML object.

14. Choose Export: VRML under the File menu.
15. Select the Export Texture Links option (see fig. 13.12).
16. Choose a file format in the pop-up menu.
17. Give your file a name ending with the `.wrl` file name extension.

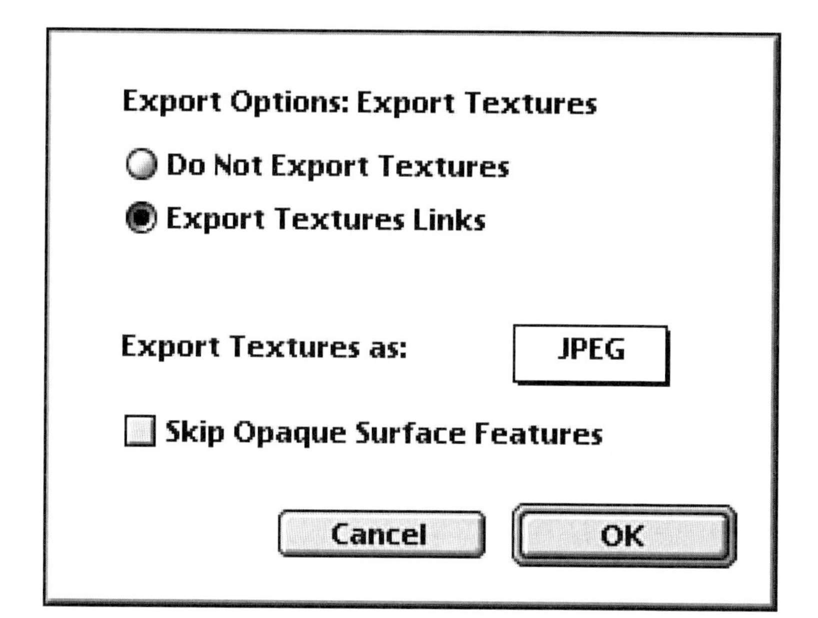

Figure 13.12

Exporting a VRML world.

Creating VRML Worlds with Extreme 3D

Macromedia provides a free conversion tool for Extreme 3D, which is one of the first authoring tools to support the VRML 2.0 spec. The E3D2VRML converter supports conversion of both VRML 1.0 and VRML 2.0 worlds. As of this writing, the converter supports the VRML 2.0 Draft #2 spec. The VRML 1.0 output is based on the official VRML 1.0 specs that can be found at `http://vag.vrml.org`.

The E3D to VRML converter is available at:

```
http://www.macromedia.com/software/extreme3d/vrml/
➥index.html
```

The converter runs under Windows NT 3.51, Windows 95, and PowerMacs running System 7.5.1 or later.

Features of the E3D2VRML Converter

In addition to converting polygons, meshes, lights, and cameras, the E3D2VRML Converter enables you to:

- Save in VRML 1.0 or VRML 2.0 format.
- Selectively turn off conversion for individual elements of the scene.
- Attach a URL to an object.
- Attach a texture file to an object.
- Substitute a geometric primitive or an inline node for an object as an optimization.
- Add **World Info** to the scene.

The following Extreme 3D features are not supported by the converter:

- Animation
- Lines, polylines, circles, ellipses, and splines
- Fog color, ambient color, and background color
- Taper and Skew deformations
- Render styles
- Conversion of layers to VRML Groups

Also, trimmed objects must be simplified twice.

Converting Extreme 3D Files to VRML

To convert an Extreme 3D file to VRML, you need the following tools:

Tools
Extreme 3D file
E3D2VRML Converter

Follow these steps:

1. Launch the E3D2VRML Converter.
2. Choose Open Extreme 3D file under the File menu.
3. Select an Extreme 3D file to convert.
4. Turn off the conversion of selected elements in the file by selecting the element from the list of elements and clicking on the Toggle Convert Status button. Deselect every camera element except for one (see fig. 13.13).

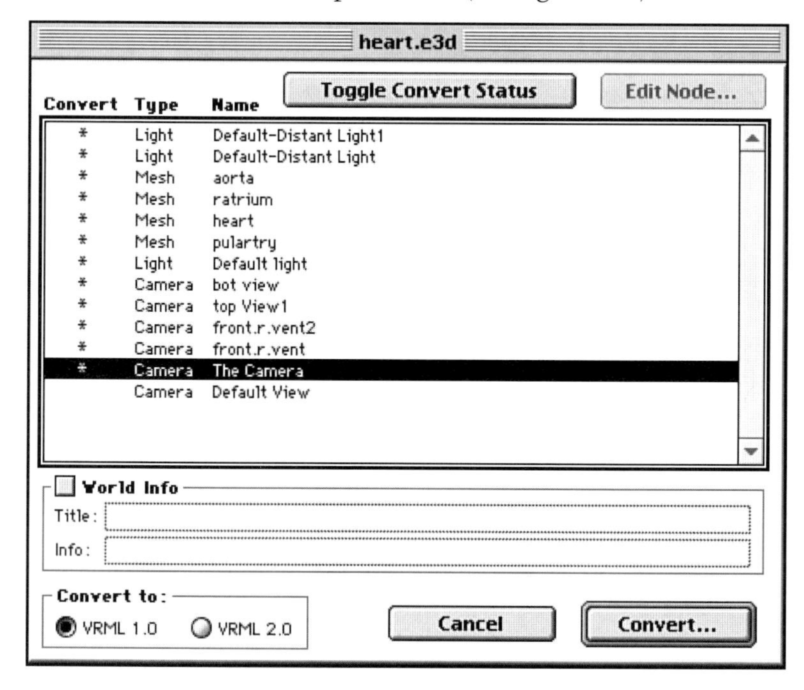

Figure 13.13

Conversion dialog box in E3D2VRML Converter.

5. In the lower-left corner, select the VRML 1.0 option if you want to maintain compatibility with the largest number of VRML viewers.
6. If you want to attach a URL or Texture to an object or simplify its geometry to reduce file size, select the object in the list view and click the Edit Node button (see fig. 13.14).

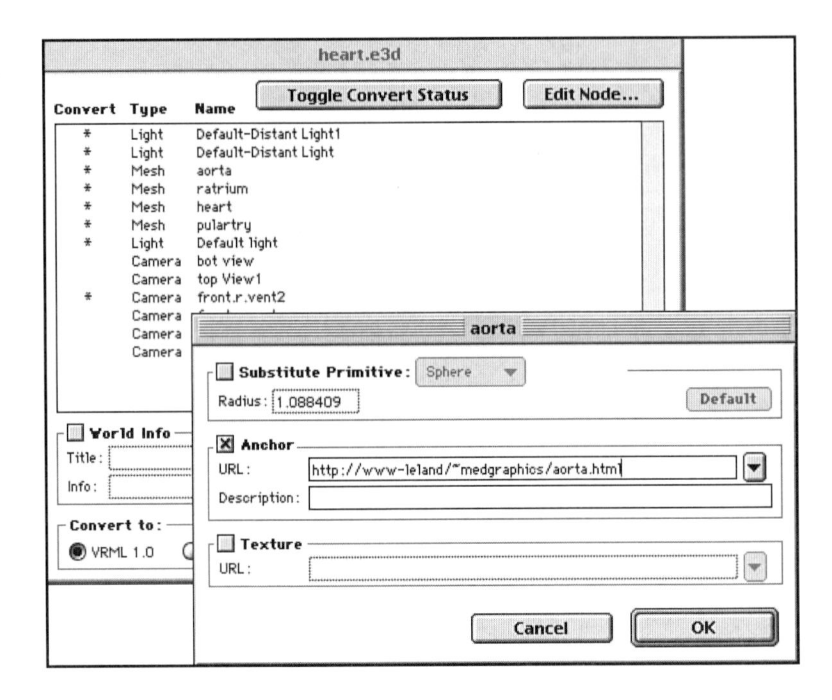

Figure 13.14

Edit node dialog box in E3D2VRML Converter.

7. Check the check box of the option you want to activate for that object and enter information in the appropriate fields.
8. Click OK.
9. Click Convert (see fig. 13.15 and fig. 13.16).
10. Perform other conversions on the file or click the Cancel button.

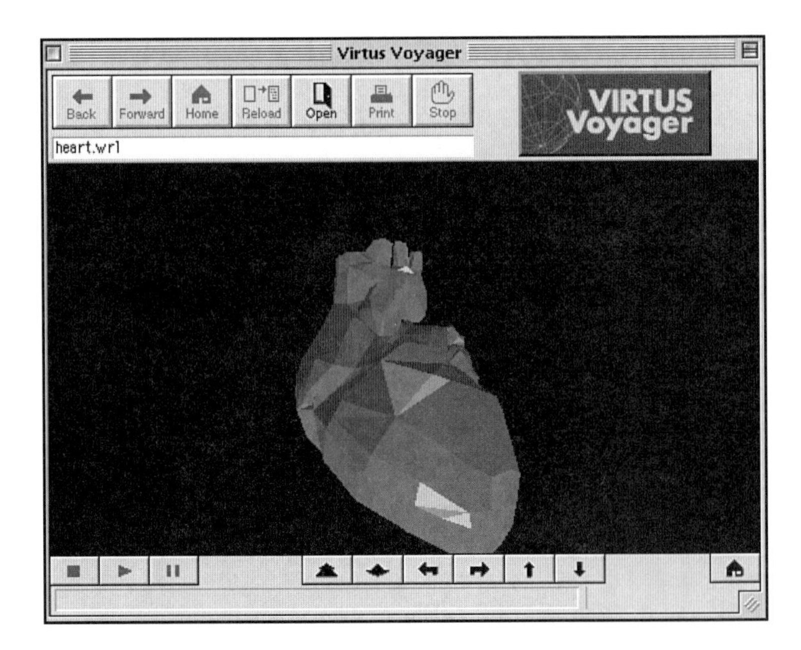

Figure 13.15

The VRML heart converted from an E3D model in the VIRTUS Voyager browser.

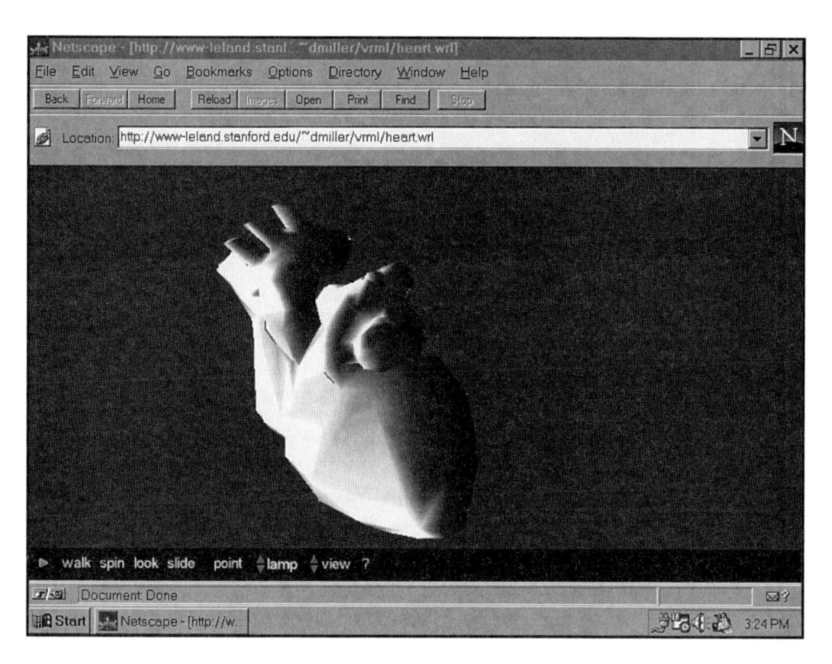

Figure 13.16

The VRML heart converted from an E3D model in Live3D on a Windows machine.

Extreme 3D texture maps that are stored in the Scripts: Material folder of the Extreme 3D folder are automatically converted to GIF or JPEG. To apply these texture maps to your VRML objects, convert them by hand and then perform the following steps:

1. Select the object with the texture map in the list view of Extreme 3D elements.
2. Click Edit Node.
3. Check the Texture option and provide a URL to the converted GIF or JPEG file. If the GIF or JPEG is in the same folder as the "`.wrl`" file, you can just specify the file name.

Because the Extreme 3D texture map file is read by many graphics programs, keep an original version of the graphic file that you imported into Extreme 3D to use as a texture map, so you can convert it to GIF or JPEG in a graphics conversion program.

Also, because of the various ways different VRML viewers handle camera position, you might need to edit the VRML file generated by the converter so that the inital camera view is properly positioned when users open the VRML world in their browsers. To edit the camera position, open the `.wrl` file in any text editor and search for the PerspectiveCamera node. Within the PerspectiveCamera node, add a position field with the X, Y, Z coordinates of the camera in 3D space.

```
Separator{
   PerspectiveCamera{
      position 0 0 10  #Add this line to change the
initial camera view
      focalDistance 10
      heightAngle 0.4
}
}
```

Figure 13.17 shows a rendering of a E3D model.

Figure 13.17

E3D model rendered in Extreme 3D.

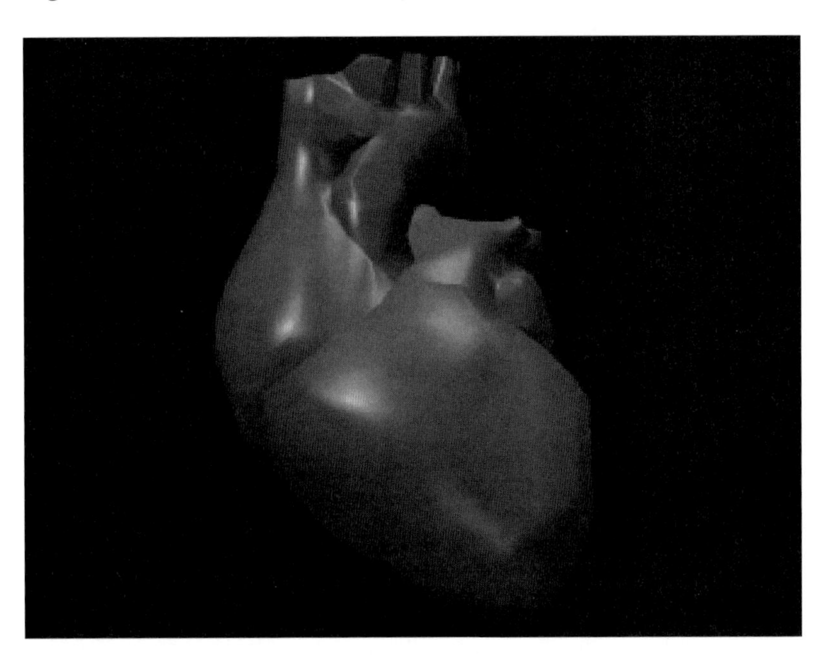

Using WCVT2POV to Convert 3D Files to VRML

Keith Rule created a great program for Windows systems that converts many 3D file formats (including converting from the DXF format) to VRML and POV-Ray formats. As of this writing, WCVT2POV opens the following 3D file formats:

File format	File extension
AOFF	.geo
DXF	.dxf
3D Studio	.3ds
Neutral File Format	.nff
RAW	.raw
TPOLY	.tpo
TrueType font	.ttf
Wavefront	.obj

WCVT2POV converts files to the following formats:

File format	File extension
DXF	.dxf
3D Studio	.3ds
Neutral File Format	.nff
OpenGL	.c
POV-Ray 2.2	.pov
POV-Ray 2.2 include files	.inc
POVSB	.psb
RAW	.raw
TPOLY	.tpo
VRML 1.0	.wrl
Wavefront	.obj

For converting files to VRML 1.0, you get the best results by changing some of the File Preferences:

1. Choose Preferences: View under the File menu.
2. Check the Draw Vertex Normal option.
3. Check the Normal Calc Direction option.

4. Check the Cull Backfaces option.
5. Choose Preferences: Output under the File menu.
6. Uncheck the Groups Supported in Raw Format option.
7. If converting DXF files, do the following:
    a. Choose Preferences: DXF under the File menu.
    b. Check the Extrude 2D item.
    c. Set the Extrude Amount to a 1.

Now you should be setup to perform VRML conversions.

WCVT2POV enables you to perform limited editing of your 3D model, such as rotating, flipping, and changing surface colors. A problem for VRML conversions is that sometimes models have inverted normals. In the WCVT2POV view window, the facets of the model have perpendicular green lines pointing inward. These are surface normals. For VRML, make these normals point outward. To reverse the direction of surface normals, click on the x|x, y|x, and z|z buttons on the toolbar.

3D graphics and VRML are a new frontier in cyberspace. Integration with major Web browsers is just beginning. 3D and VRML have steep system requirements, which may be a barrier for some users, but this will lessen as more powerful desktop systems become commonplace.

In the coming year there will be many exciting developments, including finalization of the VRML 2.0 spec, as well as the appearance of sophisticated VRML authoring tools and integration of 3D graphics capabilities in desktop system software. Integration of 3D graphics libraries with Java will make possible custom, distributed 3D applications. Even today, however, you can use simple, inexpensive tools to create Web-based 3D worlds that add unique value to your multimedia Web site.

Client-side scripting is an exciting new tool that Web authors can use to create sophisticated, interactive multimedia applications on the Web.

chapter

14

Scripting Multimedia Web Pages

One of the recent enhancements for Web authoring is the integration of client-side scripting capabilities into Web browsers. Client-side scripting means that a script, or mini-program, executes, or runs, on the local client machine or Web browser rather than on a Web server. Client-side scripting enables Web authors to provide features such as image maps, form processing, and dynamic content. Previously these functions required CGI programming in PERL or C and special access to Web servers. Client-side scripting gives more authoring power to Web page authors and reduces loads on Web servers.

This chapter discusses how JavaScript scripts can be used in Web pages to provide dynamic content. JavaScript is a client-side scripting language, a computer language like HyperTalk, C, or Lingo that enables Web authors to run mini-programs from within Web pages. A Web browser must support JavaScript for JavaScripts to run. Both Navigator and Internet Explorer support JavaScript. Figure 14.1 shows what can be done using JavaScript.

Figure 14.1

An interactive slide show application created with client-side scripting in JavaScript.

Defining JavaScript 1.0

JavaScript began at Netscape as LiveScript. It was originally intended to help manage LiveWire Web servers and enable Web authors to validate forms and communicate with Java applets, without having to interact with a Web server or perform CGI scripting. You will still see references to LiveScript around the Web. In December of 1995, Sun Microsystems, the company responsible for the Java programming language, joined Netscape in development of the LiveScript scripting language and it was renamed JavaScript.

> **Note**
>
> JavaScript really has nothing to do with the Java programming language, although it can be used to communicate with Java applets and it does share some common syntax.

JavaScript enables Web authors to embed scripts in HTML documents for execution on the user's machine. JavaScript scripts and client-side scripts can do many things, such as:

- Validate form entries before submitting them to a server
- Create custom HTML documents on-the-fly
- Respond to user interaction

- Determine the kind of environment in which a Web page is being displayed
- Update and create dynamic content based on user interaction
- Communicate and share data between HTML, Netscape Plug-Ins, and Java applets

JavaScript syntax is similar to the C programming language and might look a little strange at first if you are unfamiliar with C. If you have used other scripting languages such as Lingo, AppleScript, or HyperTalk, JavaScript won't be hard to learn. Even if you have never programmed or scripted before, you should be able to pick up the basic functionality of JavaScript and use the scripts presented here in your own pages.

First, this chapter gives a whirlwind tour of basic elements of JavaScript scripting and then looks at some simple JavaScripts that you might find handy for your multimedia Web pages.

Warning

Although most of the features of JavaScript version 1.0 have been incorporated in Internet Explorer 3.0, to be on the safe side you should test your scripts to ensure that they work in Explorer.

Browser Support

JavaScript was introduced in Netscape Navigator 2.0. That version of JavaScript is called JavaScript 1.0.

In Navigator 3.0, Netscape introduced more functionality to JavaScript. This version of JavaScript is called version 1.1. New features include the capability to have JavaScript communicate with Netscape Plug-Ins and Java applets. This functionality is called LiveConnect by Netscape. Many of these features might be specific to Netscape Navigator 3.0 and might not be fully implemented in MSIE 3.0 at this time.

Security

JavaScript was designed to make execution of JavaScripts secure for users; hence, JavaScript cannot access user's local files. In the first JavaScript implementation, clever programmers were able to create tiny external windows, one pixel in size, which ran JavaScript scripts that tracked a user's path around the Web. Netscape has fixed these and other potential security holes and has given users the opportunity to turn off JavaScript execution in Navigator's Network Preferences settings.

Tip

You can turn off JavaScript in Navigator 3.0 by selecting Network Preferences: Languages under the Options menu, and unchecking the Enable JavaScript check box (see fig. 14.2).

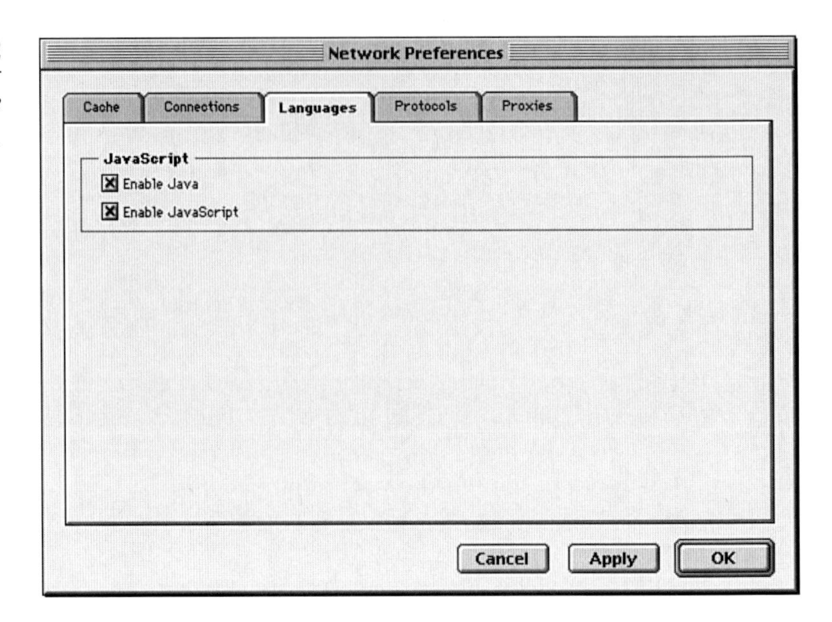

Figure 14.2

Enabling JavaScript in the Preferences settings.

Embedding JavaScripts in HTML Documents

You embed JavaScripts in your HTML document by using the SCRIPT tag. The SCRIPT tag requires a LANGUAGE attribute. Embedding a JavaScript in an HTML document looks like the following:

```
<SCRIPT LANGUAGE="JavaScript">

//some JavaScript stuff here

</SCRIPT>
```

The double slash mark, //, indicates a comment in JavaScript. Comments are ignored by the browser. Comments are a good way to annotate your scripts so you can remember later how they work.

JavaScript functions are typically embedded within the HEAD tag of an HTML document. Embedding JavaScripts in the HEAD tag ensures that functions are loaded into memory and can respond to user-initiated events before the body of the HTML document is loaded. You can also embed JavaScripts within the body of an HTML document.

Navigator 3.0 Extensions to the SCRIPT Tag

In Navigator 3.0, the <SCRIPT> tag has an optional attribute, SRC. The SRC attribute enables you to specify an external file that contains JavaScript code. This code is then executed as if it were embedded in the HTML document.

For example:

```
<SCRIPT LANGUAGE = "JavaScript"
SRC="myJavaScriptFunctionLibrary.js"> </SCRIPT>
```

uses the JavaScript statements in the file `"myJavaScriptFunctionLibrary.js"`, as if the file were embedded in the HTML document. In this example, the external file is located in the same directory as the HTML document, but it could be anywhere on the Internet. Any JavaScript code within the SCRIPT tag that has a SRC attribute is ignored.

JavaScript files specified in the SRC attribute must be plain-text files that only contain JavaScript code. These files can be in a local directory or anywhere on the Web. If the file specified in the SRC attribute is not served locally, you have to configure the Web server to associate files with the `".js"` suffix to the MIME type `"application/x-javascript"`.

Providing Alternate Content for Non-JavaScript Browsers

If a user visits your site with a browser that doesn't support JavaScript, that browser might display the contents of the SCRIPT tag as text within the HTML document. To prevent this from happening, you can surround the JavaScript statements with an HTML comment statement, as depicted in the following example:

```
<SCRIPT LANGUAGE="JavaScript">

<!-- Hide this script from non-Navigator 2.0 browsers.

 //some JavaScript stuff here that will be hidden from
non-JavaScript browsers

<!-- Done hiding from non-Navigator 2.0 browsers. -->

</SCRIPT>
```

Providing Alternate Content for Non-JavaScript Browsers in Navigator 3.0

Beginning with Navigator 3.0, you can use the NOSCRIPT tag to provide alternate content if users don't have a JavaScript-enabled browser or have turned off JavaScript in the browser's preferences.

Between the NOSCRIPT tags, you should place an explanatory comment such as the one provided below:

```
<NOSCRIPT>
This page requires a JavaScript-enabled browser, such
as Netscape Navigator 2.0 or later. If you are using
Navigator 2.0 or later, and you see this message, you
need to enable JavaScript by checking the Enable
JavaScript check box after choosing Network Prefer-
ences: Languages under the Options menu.
</NOSCRIPT>
```

Elements of JavaScript

JavaScript consists of several different elements, including:

- **Functions.** These are similar to subroutines or procedures in other computer languages. Functions are small code modules that perform specific tasks. A function can also return a value, such as true or false.
- **Events and event handlers.** Events are user actions, such as clicking on a button or loading a Web page. Event handlers are JavaScript functions that are executed when an event occurs.
- **Objects.** Objects are data structures that store a collection of properties and methods related to some "thing" in the Web browser environment, such as the current HTML document or browser window.

JavaScript Functions

functions

JavaScript **functions** are small chunks of code that perform a small task or action. You invoke a function by calling it from your HTML documents. Define your own custom-made functions using the “function” keyword in JavaScript. A function definition looks like:

```
<SCRIPT LANGUAGE="JavaScript">

function myJavaScriptFunction()
{

     //JavaScript code goes here

}

</SCRIPT>
```

Following the function keyword is the name of the function; in this case, `"myJavaScriptFunction()"`. You use this name to execute the function.

```
<BODY onLoad = "myJavaScriptFunction()">
```

The statement in the above example runs the function `"myJavaScriptFunction()"` when the body of the HTML document is initially loaded.

It is a good idea to put your function definitions within the HEAD tag of the document so that the functions are loaded into memory and are ready to go when the body of the document loads.

The JavaScript statements that make up the function are defined within a pair of curly braces “{}”. An opening curly brace must appear at the start of the function statements and a closing curly brace must appear at the end of the function statements.

You can also give your function custom parameters. For example, if you define this function in the head of your HTML document:

```
<HEAD>
<SCRIPT LANGUAGE="JavaScript">

function CheckPassword(myString)
{//Begin Function CheckPassword

if (myString == "thePassword")

{ return true}

else
```

```
{return false}

}//End Function CheckPassword

</SCRIPT>
</HEAD>
```

and then included this statement in the body of your HTML document:

```
<BODY>

<SCRIPT LANGUAGE="JavaScript">

document.write(CheckPassword('thePassword'))


</SCRIPT>
</BODY>
```

you call the CheckPassword() function with the parameter `"thePassword"`, (the quotes indicate the parameter is a text string) and the word "true" is written into the HTML document using the `document.write` JavaScript method.

A lot is going on with this little bit of code, including using return values from functions and using the built-in JavaScript method `"document.write()"` to generate HTML documents on-the-fly. You look at these features in more detail in a following section.

Scripting Event Handlers

events

You can write JavaScript functions that respond to events. **Events** include mouse movements and form submittal. Events typically occur as the result of user interaction, such as clicking on a button, entering data in a form, or loading a Web page. When the event occurs, the JavaScript function defined for that event is run.

You create a JavaScript event handler by assigning a JavaScript function to a special JavaScript event handler name. The event handler name is an attribute of an HTML tag.

```
<BODY onLoad="alert('Doh!')">
```

The above example causes a JavaScript alert with the word `"Doh!"` to appear when the document is loaded; meaning it assigns the JavaScript statement `"alert('Doh!')"` to the onLoad event handler of the HTML document.

Figure 14.3

A JavaScript Alert.

Notice the double quotes around the JavaScript statement and the single quotes around the parameter `'Doh!'`. Because JavaScript event handlers embedded in HTML must be enclosed in quotes, you must use single quotes to delimit arguments within the JavaScript statements. Single quotes (') enable JavaScript to distinguish the string literals that are parameters within attribute values enclosed in double quotes.

JavaScript comes with many places where you can assign a custom event handler; for example, when a user clicks on a form button, enters text in a field, or clicks on a hyperlink.

Table 14.1 lists the event handlers recognized by Netscape Navigator 2.0 and later, and compatible browsers. Table 14.2 lists the new event handlers introduced with Netscape Navigator 3.0.

Table 14.1

Event Handlers Defined for Netscape Navigator 2 or Later and Compatible Browsers

Event handler	When it occurs	HTML tag
onBlur	User removes input focus from form element	FORM,INPUT TYPE = text,textarea,select
onClick	User clicks on form element or link	FORM,INPUT TYPE = button,checkbox,radio,A HREF
onChange	User changes value of text, textarea, or select element	FORM,INPUT TYPE = text,textarea,select
onFocus	User gives form element input focus	FORM,INPUT TYPE = text,textarea,select
onLoad	New HTML document loads in browser window	BODY,FRAME,FRAMESET
onMouseOver	User moves mouse pointer over a link or anchor	A

continues

Table 14.1, continued

Event Handlers Defined for Netscape Navigator 2.0 or Later and Compatible Browsers

Event handler	When it occurs	HTML tag
onSelect	User selects from element's input field	FORM,INPUT TYPE = text,textarea
onSubmit	User submits a form	FORM
onUnload	Current HTML document unloads	BODY,FRAME,FRAMESET

Table 14.2

New Event Handlers in Netscape Navigator 3.0

Event handler	When it occurs	HTML tag
onAbort	User aborts loading of an image	IMG
onFocus	Now applies to windows and framesets when user clicks inside them	BODY,FRAME, FRAMESET (Mac and Unix only)
onBlur	Now applies to windows and framesets	BODY,FRAME, FRAMESET (Mac and Unix only)
onError,window. onerror	Executes when the loading of an image or document causes an error	IMG
onLoad	Now applies to the loading of an image	IMG
onMouseOut	Executes when the mouse pointer leaves an area (client-side image map) or link	AREA,A HREF
onMouseOver	Executes when the mouse pointer is over an area (client-side image map) or link	AREA,A HREF
onReset	User clicks reset button	FORM

JavaScript Objects

You've seen the "document.write()" method, which is a built-in method of JavaScript, that enables you to create HTML code on-the-fly at runtime. This section looks at this method and other built-in JavaScript features.

JavaScript includes several predefined, built-in objects that you can use in your scripts. A JavaScript **object** is a data structure that stores a collection of properties and methods related to some "thing" in the Web browser environment. These "things" can be the characteristics of the current HTML document, the date on the local machine, the version of the browser, and so forth.

object

For example, JavaScript includes a useful built-in object called the **document object** that contains references to all the characteristics of the current HTML document, such as the background color, links, and the date it was last modified. The document object contains a collection of useful methods you can use with the object, such as the document.write() method encountered previously. The document object is automatically created by the Web browser when a new document is loaded. Another built-in JavaScript object is the date object, which contains the day, month, year, and time on the local computer and provides several built-in methods you can use to access this information.

document object

The dot syntax is used to access the properties and methods of a JavaScript object. For example, document.write() refers to the write method of the current document object. Document.write can take some parameters, such as the text string to write out. You access other methods and properties of the document object using the same syntax. For example, document.title contains the content of the TITLE tag for the current document.

```
<HTML>
<HEAD>

<TITLE>An HTML document created by JavaScript</TITLE>
</HEAD>
<BODY >
<SCRIPT LANGUAGE="JavaScript">
     document.write(document.title)
</SCRIPT>
</BODY>
</HTML>
```

The previous HTML document, for instance, consists of a single line that is the same as the title of the document in the browser window menu bar.

> **Note**
>
> Some useful resources on learning JavaScript and a language reference can be found at:
>
> `http://home.netscape.com/eng/mozilla/3.0/handbook/javascript/index.html`

JavaScript contains numerous built-in objects, methods, and properties you can use in your scripts. You'll barely scratch the surface here.

Dynamic Frames Using JavaScript

Frames were introduced in Navigator 2.0. Implementing frames is discussed in Chapter 4 "Designing the Layout of Your Web Pages." You either love frames or hate them. This section shows how to change the content of one frame based on user input in another frame. JavaScript 1.1 is compatible with Netscape Navigator 2.0 or later and browsers that support JavaScript 1.0.

This example sets up a two-frame window (see fig. 14.4). One frame (called the questionframe) contains a simple form consisting of a group of radio buttons. The onClick event handler for each radio button is a single JavaScript statement. This JavaScript statement changes the URL of the HTML document contained in the second frame (called the feedback frame) to another URL.

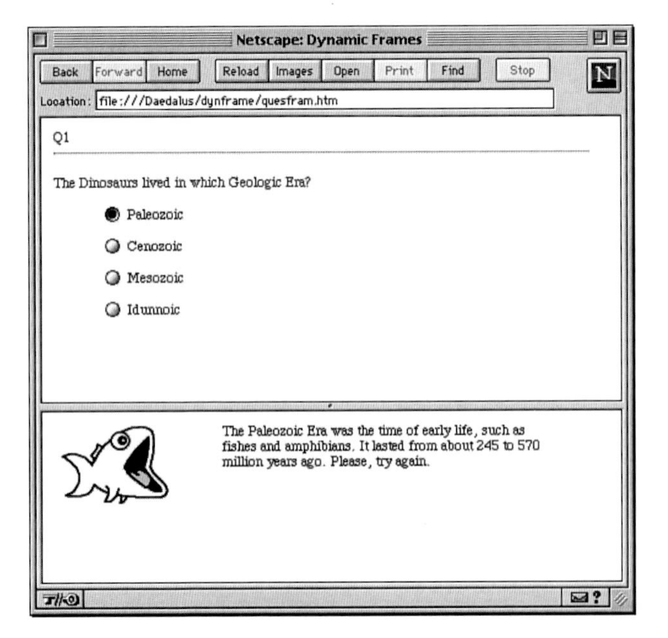

Figure 14.4

Updating frames based on user input.

```
<HTML>
<TITLE>Dynamic Frames</TITLE>

<FRAMESET ROWS="50%,*">

<FRAME SRC="question.htm" NAME="questionframe"
MARGINWIDTH="10" MARGINHEIGHT="10"  RESIZE>

<FRAME SRC="feedback.htm" NAME="feedbackframe"
MARGINWIDTH=10 MARGINHEIGHT="10" RESIZE>

</FRAMESET>

<NOFRAME>
This demo requires a browser that supports frames, such
as Netscape 2.0 or later.
Please <A HREF="ftp://ftp.netscape.com">download</A>
➥Netscape to view this demo.
</NOFRAME>

</HTML>
```

When the user clicks on the radio button in the first frame, a separate HTML document is loaded into the second frame. Now, look at the HTML code that implements the frame update when the user clicks on a radio button. Here is the listing for `"question.htm"`:

```
<HTML>
<HEAD>
<TITLE>Question 1</TITLE>

</HEAD>

<BODY BGCOLOR="#ffffe0">
<P>
Q1
<HR><BR>
The Dinosaurs lived in which Geologic Era?<P>

<FORM>

<BLOCKQUOTE>

<INPUT TYPE="radio" NAME="geologicera"
➥VALUE="Paleozoic"
   onClick="parent.feedbackframe.location =
➥'paleoans.htm' ">
Paleozoic<P>
```

```
<INPUT TYPE="radio" NAME="geologicera" VALUE="Cenozoic"
   onClick="parent.feedbackframe.location =
➥'cenoans.htm' "> Cenozoic
<P>

<INPUT TYPE="radio" NAME="geologicera" VALUE="Mesozoic"
   onClick="parent.feedbackframe.location =
➥'mesoans.htm' "> Mesozoic<P>

<INPUT TYPE="radio" NAME="geologicera" VALUE="Idunnoic"
   onClick="parent.feedbackframe.location =
➥'dunnoans.htm' "> Idunnoic
</BLOCKQUOTE>

</FORM>

</BODY>
</HTML>
```

The line of code that contains the event handler that is executed when the radio button is selected is:

```
<INPUT TYPE="radio" NAME="geologicera"
➥VALUE="Paleozoic"
   onClick="parent.feedbackframe.location =
➥'paleoans.htm' ">
Paleozoic<P>
```

The JavaScript statement:

```
parent.feedbackframe.location = 'paleoans.htm'
```

sets the location object of the frame called `"feedbackframe"` to the location `'paleoans.htm'`, an HTML document in the current directory. The **location object** is a built-in JavaScript object that contains information about the URL of a frame or window.

location object

Parent refers to the window object that contains the frameset window for "`feedbackframe"`. Parent is one of the magic window names you can use in JavaScript to reference browser windows and JavaScript-created windows. Table 14.3 shows the names that refer to browser windows.

parent

The name `"feedbackframe"` is the name of the frame that is updated when the radio button is clicked.

Table 14.3

Special JavaScript Names that Refer to Browser Windows

Name	Refers to:
parent	The frameset window of the document or the top-most browser window if there is no frameset
top	The top-most browser window

When users click a radio button, the contents of "`feedbackframe`" are changed to reflect their choice.

Generating HTML Documents On-the-Fly with JavaScript

One of the most useful built-in JavaScript methods is "`document.write`". You saw this method in action in previous sections. You can use this method to create custom HTML documents at runtime. The "`document.write`" method takes as a parameter some text that is written into the currently open document. This text can be plain text or HTML code, which is then interpreted by the Web browser. Beginning with Navigator 3.0 and JavaScript 1.1, JavaScript-generated documents created using `document.write` can be printed, saved as files, and viewed with View Document/Frame Source.

This section contains two examples of creating dynamic documents using `document.write`. The first example involves the creation of floating windows; the second helps create custom HTML code based on user environment.

Creating Floating Windows with Dynamic Content

This section shows how to use JavaScript to create floating windows and how to fill those windows with custom content generated at runtime.

The html documents and GIF files referenced in this section are on the CD in the folder "jswindow". This example creates a custom browser window that contains a GIF animation based on user input in a form. When the user selects one of the options in the form, a custom window displays the requested GIF animation (see fig. 14.5). The heart of this implementation is contained in the file "question.htm".

Figure 14.5

A Multimedia Viewer in JavaScript.

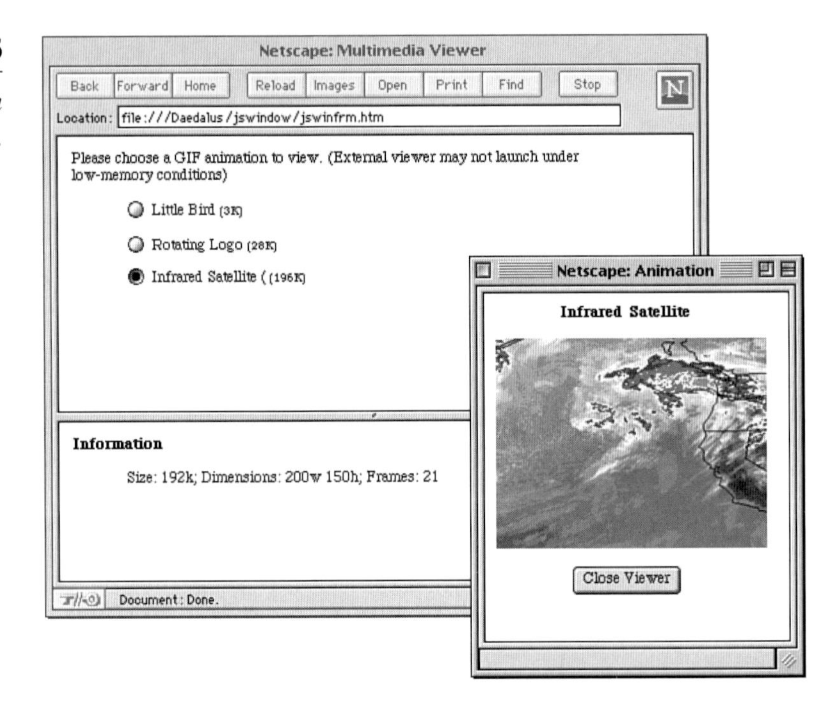

The code for the form looks like this:

```
<FORM>

<INPUT TYPE="radio" NAME="anim" VALUE="lwanim.gif"
   onClick="animation_viewer('Little
Bird','lwanim.gif',81,44,'lwfeed.htm')">
   Little Bird <FONT SIZE = -2> (3K) </FONT> <P>

<INPUT TYPE="radio" NAME="anim" VALUE="blob.gif"
   onClick="animation_viewer('Rotating
Logo','logo.gif',90,90,'lofeed.htm')">
   Rotating Logo <FONT SIZE = -2> (28K)</FONT><P>

<INPUT TYPE="radio" NAME="anim" VALUE="ir.gif"
   onClick="animation_viewer('Infrared
Satellite','ir.gif',200,150,'irfeed.htm')">
   Infrared Satellite (<FONT SIZE = -2> (196K)</
➥FONT><P>

</FORM>
```

Each button contains an onClick event handler. This handler calls the "animation_viewer" JavaScript function with five parameters. These five parameters are:

- A text string to be displayed in the custom HTML document.
- The file name of the GIF animation.
- The width of the GIF animation.
- The height of the GIF animation.
- The URL for an HTML document containing information about the GIF animation that will be displayed in a separate frame.

When the user clicks a radio button, the "animation_viewer" function is called. The function opens a separate floating window and assembles a custom HTML document based on the parameters that are passed to the function.

```
myWindow = window.open("", "viewer",

"toolbar=0,location=0,directories=0,status=0,menubar=0,

➥scrollbars=0,resizable=0,copyhistory=0,width=224,
➥height="+winH);
```

The previous code opens a window with the `window.open` function that has the indicated features. It assigns that window to the variable "myWindow" for easy reference in subsequent JavaScript statements.

The following line

```
if (myWindow != null)
```

tests to see if the window was actually created; otherwise, it displays an alert. If the window is created, then a series of `document.write` statements fill the window with content. Of special note is the line:

```
var myImgSrc = "http://www-
leland.stanford.edu/dept/SUL/irs/edu/projects/gifanim/
➥"+myGif
```

The variable `myGif` at the end of this line contains the file name of the GIF animation that was passed in as a parameter. This line creates a fully qualified URL to the location of the GIF animation on the Internet and assigns it to the variable `myImgSrc`. A fully qualified URL is required when using `document.write` to embed images in a JavaScript-generated document. To customize this handler you want to change the base URL "http://www-leland.stanford.edu/dept/SUL/irs/edu/projects/gifanim/" to a URL appropriate for your content. Another option is to generate the URL on-the-fly with JavaScript, which is beyond the scope of this discussion.

Here's a complete listing of JavaScript and HTML code for a floating window. You can check out the HTML documents and GIF files on the CD in the folder "jswindow".

```
<HTML>
<HEAD>
<SCRIPT LANGUAGE="JavaScript">

function animation_viewer(myName,myGif,myW,myH,myFb)

{

top.feedbackframe.location = myFb;
var winH = myH + 98;
myWindow = window.open("", "viewer",
"toolbar=0,location=0,directories=0,status=0,
menubar=0,scrollbars=0,resizable=0,copyhistory=0,
➥width=224,height="+winH);

if (myWindow != null)
{
        myWindow.document.open();

        myWindow.document.write("<HTML><HEAD>");

      myWindow.document.write("<TITLE>"+"Animation"+"</
➥TITLE>");

        myWindow.document.write("</HEAD><BODY
➥BGCOLOR=FFFFFF
TEXT=000000>");

        myWindow.document.write("<CENTER><B>" +

            myName + "</B><P>");

var myImgSrc = "http://www-
leland.stanford.edu/dept/SUL/irs/edu/projects/gifanim/
➥"+myGif

           myWindow.document.write("<IMG SRC =
➥"+myImgSrc+" WIDTH="+myW+"  HEIGHT=" + myH+">");

        myWindow.document.write("<P><FORM><INPUT
➥TYPE='button' VALUE='Close Viewer' " +
```

```
"onClick='window.close()'></FORM>");

        myWindow.document.write("</CENTER>");

        myWindow.document.write("</BODY></HTML>");

        myWindow.document.close();

    }else {alert ("Could not create external viewer!
➥Doh!")}

    } //end function

</SCRIPT>
</HEAD>

<BODY BGCOLOR="#ffffe0">
<P>

Please choose a GIF animation to view. (External viewer
➥may not launch
under low-memory conditions)<P>

<FORM>
<BLOCKQUOTE>

<INPUT TYPE="radio" NAME="anim" VALUE="lwanim.gif"
   onClick="animation_viewer('Little
Bird','lwanim.gif',81,44,'lwfeed.htm')">
   Little Bird <FONT SIZE = -2> (3K) </FONT> <P>

<INPUT TYPE="radio" NAME="anim" VALUE="blob.gif"
   onClick="animation_viewer('Rotating
Logo','logo.gif',90,90,'lofeed.htm')">
   Rotating Logo <FONT SIZE = -2> (28K)</FONT><P>

<INPUT TYPE="radio" NAME="anim" VALUE="ir.gif"
   onClick="animation_viewer('Infrared
Satellite','ir.gif',200,150,'irfeed.htm')">
   Infrared Satellite (<FONT SIZE = -2> (196K)</
➥FONT><P>

</BLOCKQUOTE>


</FORM>
</BODY>
</HTML>
```

Creating Custom HTML Documents Based on User Environment

You can use JavaScript to find out information about the user's operating environment and to create custom HTML documents based on that information. This example uses the built-in date object to find out the local time. Then, it uses the `document.write` method to create a different HTML document depending on whether the time is before 12 noon or after 12 noon.

This JavaScript script runs in Netscape Navigator 2.0 or later, or in a browser that supports JavaScript 1.0.

The content for this example uses content created in the Shockwave chapter and can be found on the CD.

Here's the code:

```
<SCRIPT LANGUAGE ="JavaScript">
<!-- hide this script tag's contents from old browsers
var myDate = new Date();
var myHour = myDate.getHours();

if (myHour < 12){

            // place your  code here that should be
➥executed in the morning

       document.write('<EMBED SRC="swa.dcr" WIDTH=160
➥HEIGHT=64
swaURL="morning.swa">');
}

else {

            // place your  code here that should be
➥executed after 12 noon

    document.write('<EMBED SRC="swa.dcr" WIDTH=160
➥HEIGHT=64
swaURL="citynite.swa">');
}
<!-- done hiding from old browsers -->
</SCRIPT>
```

This script should be placed within the BODY tag of a document. Here's what it does:

1. The line `var myDate = new Date();` creates a new date object (a built-in JavaScript object) called `myDate`. This object contains the local date set on the user's machine.
2. The line `var myHour = myDate.getHours();` extracts the hour (between 0 and 23) from `myDate`.
3. If the value of `myHour` is less than 12, then the script writes out one HTML document that contains a Shockwave for Audio file customized for morning listening. If the value of `myHour` is greater than 12, then it writes out a different HTML document that contains a Shockwave for Audio file customized for evening listening.

JavaScript 1.1 in Navigator 3.0

With Navigator 3.0, Netscape added new features to JavaScript. The new version of JavaScript integrated in Navigator 3.0 is called JavaScript version 1.1. Among the enhancements Netscape added are new objects that do the following:

- Enable you to find out if a certain Plug-In is installed
- Dynamically change images within a document
- Enable you to call Plug-Ins and Java applets from JavaScript

The following sections show how to use these new features.

Using JavaScript 1.1 To Determine What Plug-Ins Are Present

This example shows how to use some of the new features of JavaScript 1.1 to determine if a user has installed a particular Plug-In. This example only works in Netscape Navigator 3.0 or later.

Note

In Navigator 3, Javascript-generated documents can now be printed, saved as files, and viewed with View Document/Frame Source.

The function described here uses the mimeTypes property of the built-in navigator object. When passed a valid MIME type and sub-type, this function:

- Returns 1 if Navigator recognizes the MIME type and has an enabled Plug-In to handle it.
- Returns 0 if Navigator recognizes the MIME type, but does NOT have an enabled Plug-In to handle it, for example, if the MIME type is handled by a helper app.
- Returns –1 if Navigator does NOT recognize the MIME type.

Here's the function:

```
<SCRIPT LANGUAGE="JavaScript">
function CheckForPlugin (myMime)

{
hasMimeType = navigator.mimeTypes[myMime]

if (hasMimeType)
{
   // The MimeType is recognized by Navigator, now
➥determine if there is a Plug-In present

   hasPlugin = hasMimeType.enabledPlugin

   if (hasPlugin)

      // Plug-In is present

      return 1

   else

      // No Plug-In, but the MIME type is recognized
➥so, maybe a helper app is set up

      return 0
}
else
{
   // MIME type not recognized
   return-1
}

} //end function
</SCRIPT>
```

The function has one parameter, `"myMIME"`. This parameter is a quoted text string that is the MIME type and sub-type of the media type you are interested in, for example `"application/x-director"`. for the Shockwave Plug-In or `"video/quicktime"` for QuickTime.

The line:

```
hasMimeType = navigator.mimeTypes[myMime]
```

checks to see if the MIME type is registered with the navigator object and stores the results in the hasMimeType variable.

If the MIME type is recognized, then the line:

```
hasPlugin = hasMimeType.enabledPlugin
```

checks if this MIME type has an enabled Plug-In associated with it. If it does, then the function returns 1. If the MIME type is recognized but does NOT have an associated enabled Plug-In, then the function returns 0. If the MIME type is NOT recognized, then the function returns –1.

Use this function with the `document.write` method to create an HTML document at runtime based on the user's browser environment. For example, if the CheckForPlugin function is present within the HEAD tag of an HTML document, the following code within the BODY tag would create custom content based on the return value of the CheckForPlugin function:

```
<SCRIPT LANGUAGE="JavaScript">


if (CheckForPlugin ("application/x-director")==1)
➥document.write("You have the Plug-In!")

if (CheckForPlugin ("application/x-director")==0)
➥document.write("You have the Helper App!")

if (CheckForPlugin ("application/x-director")==-1)
➥document.write("Get Plugged!")
</SCRIPT>
```

In practice, you would put appropriate HTML code with the `document.write` method for each possibility. Here's the complete listing for determining if a user has installed a particular Plug-In. You can also check out the file `"checplug.htm"` on the CD.

```
<HTML>
<HEAD>

<TITLE>Checking for Plug-Ins with JavaScript</TITLE>

<SCRIPT LANGUAGE="JavaScript">
function CheckForPlugin (myMime)
```

```
{
hasMimeType = navigator.mimeTypes[myMime]

if (hasMimeType)
{
   // The MimeType is recognized by Navigator, now
➥determine if there is a Plug-In present

   hasPlugin = hasMimeType.enabledPlugin

   if (hasPlugin)

      // Plug-In is present

      return 1

   else

      // No Plug-In, but the MIME type is recognized
➥so, maybe a helper app is set up

      return 0
}
else
{
   // MIME type not recognized
   return -1
}

} //end function
</SCRIPT>



</HEAD>
<BODY>

<SCRIPT LANGUAGE="JavaScript">

if (CheckForPlugin ("application/x-director")==1)
➥document.write("You have the Plug-In!")

if (CheckForPlugin ("application/x-director")==0)
➥document.write("You have the Helper App!")

if (CheckForPlugin ("application/x-director")==-1)
➥document.write("Get Plugged!")

</SCRIPT>


</BODY>
</HTML>
```

Dynamic Graphics Using JavaScript 1.1

A new object added to JavaScript 1.1 is the **image object**. Image objects contain the characteristics of graphics referenced by the IMG tag in an HTML document. Image objects are properties of the document object. You can refer to them using the dot syntax, for example "`document.myImage`". This section, devoted to how to create dynamically changing images within a document, uses as its example the creation of a "dynamic billboard" (see fig. 14.6) that utilizes the new image object.

image object

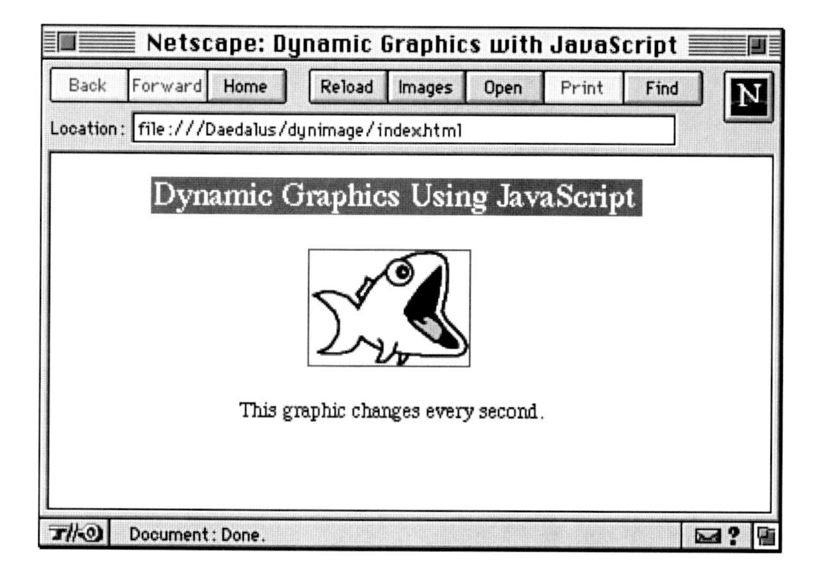

Figure 14.6

A "dynamic billboard" created with JavaScript.

Images have several properties. Some properties are attributes to the IMG tag, such as SRC, HEIGHT, and WIDTH. You access these properties with the dot syntax, for example, "`document.myImage.src`". New properties have also been defined for image objects. New properties are specified in custom attributes of the IMG tag.

This sample HTML code features a new custom attribute:

```
<IMG NAME="dynamicImage" SRC="image0.gif" WIDTH = 119
➥HEIGHT = 68 ALT="Dynamic Gif"
onLoad="setTimeout('changeGif()', secondsToWait)">
```

The custom attribute NAME is the name of the image. You can use this name to refer to images from other JavaScript statements, for example "`document.dynamicImage`". Images can have event handlers. This example shows an onLoad event handler, which executes when the image loads in the browser window.

To create dynamic billboards that change graphic content automatically, put this script within the HEAD tag of your document:

```
<SCRIPT LANGUAGE = "JavaScript">

var secondsToWait = 1000*1  //number of milliseconds
➥between changes
var imageNum = 1    //index number of first image
var imageMax = 3    //number of images

// Create an array and load it with images

myImages = new Array()
for(i = 1; i < (imageMax + 1); i++) {
   myImages[i] = new Image()
   myImages[i].src = "image" + i + ".gif"
   }

// Function that changes images

function changeGif() {
   document.dynamicImage.src = myImages[imageNum].src

   imageNum++

   if(imageNum > imageMax) {
   imageNum = 1


   }
}


</SCRIPT>
```

The previous code is very simple. The function `"changeGif"` changes the graphic named `"dynamicImage"` after the time specified in `"secondsToWait"` has passed. Here's a more thorough explanation of the code that shows you how to customize the function `"changeGif"`:

1. In this example, images are displayed for one second, then changed. To change the number of seconds that each image is displayed, change the `"secondsToWait"` variable. For instance, to have each graphic display for 30 seconds, you write:

```
var secondsToWait = 1000*30  //number of
➥milliseconds between changes
```

2. To add your own graphics, create a series of graphic files. The graphic files must be named like this:

   `image1.gif`

   `image2.gif`

   up to the number specified in imageMax. The graphics must be in the same directory as the HTML document that contains this script.

3. To change the number of graphics that display, change the imageMax variable to the total number of images.

4. To create a dynamic image in the HTML document, you set the onLoad event handler of that image to `"setTimeout('changeGif()', secondsToWait)"`, shown in the complete HTML listing that follows. The function `"setTimeout"` is a built-in JavaScript function. It calls the `"changeGif"` function after `"secondsToWait"` seconds have passed. This function resets every time you load a new image.

Here's the complete HTML listing. You can also check out the folder `"dynimage"` on the CD:

```
<HTML>
<HEAD>

<TITLE>Dynamic Graphics with JavaScript</TITLE>

<SCRIPT LANGUAGE = "JavaScript">

var secondsToWait = 1000*1  //number of seconds between
➥changes
var imageNum = 1    //index number of first image
var imageMax = 3    //number of images

// Create an array and load it with images

myImages = new Array()
for(i = 1; i < (imageMax + 1); i++) {
   myImages[i] = new Image()
   myImages[i].src = "image" + i + ".gif"
   }

// Function that changes images
```

```
function changeGif() {
   document.dynamicImage.src = myImages[imageNum].src

   imageNum++

   if(imageNum > imageMax) {
   imageNum = 1


   }
}


</SCRIPT>
</HEAD>


<BODY BGCOLOR="ffffe0">

<CENTER>
<TABLE>
<TR>

      <TD BGCOLOR = "3399ff">
      <FONT COLOR = "ffffe0" SIZE = +2> Dynamic
➥Graphics Using JavaScript</Font>
      </TD>
</TR>
</TABLE>
<P>

<IMG NAME="dynamicImage" SRC="image0.gif" WIDTH = 119
➥HEIGHT = 68
ALT="Dynamic Gif" ➥onLoad="setTimeout('changeGif()',
secondsToWait)">
   <P>
   This graphic changes every second.

</CENTER>
</BODY>
</BODY>
</HTML>
```

LiveConnect

Netscape's LiveConnect enables you to integrate and communicate with Java applets, JavaScript, and Navigator Plug-Ins. You can use it to control Plug-Ins and applets from JavaScript, for example. Or you can use it to enable Java applets to access data in a Plug-In.

As of this writing, much of the LiveConnect functionality had just been incorporated in the Navigator 3.0 browser. Therefore, most Plug-Ins and Java applets need to be recompiled to take advantage of LiveConnect, discussed in the following section "LiveConnect and JavaScript." For the latest info on this subject, see:

`http://home.netscape.com/comprod/products/navigator/version_3.0/connect/`

`http://home.netscape.com/eng/mozilla/3.0/handbook/plugins/index.html`

`http://home.netscape.com/eng/mozilla/3.0/handbook/javascript/index.html?moja`

To view a showcase of LiveConnect-enabled applcations:

`http://home.netscape.com/comprod/products/navigator/version_3.0/connect/lc-showcase.html`

To find out the latest about the LiveConnect implementation in Netscape Navigator's bundled Plug-Ins, go to these sites:

`http://home.netscape.com/comprod/products/navigator/version_3.0/developer/mojava.html`

`http://home.netscape.com/comprod/products/navigator/version_3.0/developer/newplug.html`

This section lists some resources for currently available LiveConnect-enabled Plug-Ins and then demonstrates how to use LiveConnect with the LiveAudio Plug-In that ships with Navigator.

LiveConnect and JavaScript

To make a Plug-In accessible to JavaScript, two things must be done. First, the Plug-In must be programmed using the LiveConnect application programming interfaces. As of this writing, only a handful of Plug-Ins had been recompiled for LiveConnect. These Plug-Ins are:

- Tumbleweed Envoy Plug-In—digital document viewer
  `http://www.tumbleweed.com`
- FutureSplash 1.1—interactive animation viewer
  `http://www.futurewave.com/`
- Jamba—Java development
  `http://www.aimtech.com/`

- Koan—audio player
  http://www.sseyo.com/
- mBed—multimedia viewer
  http://www.mbed.com/
- PointPlus—PowerPoint presentation viewer
  http://www.net-scene.com/

Netscape's bundled Plug-Ins—LiveAudio, LiveVideo, and Live3D must also be recompiled.

Second, in order for LiveConnect to work with JavaScript, Java and JavaScript must both be enabled in the Options: Network Preferences: Languages preferences settings.

LiveConnect-enabled Plug-Ins have a custom NAME attribute specified in the EMBED tag, such as:

```
<EMBED SRC="hello.aif" NAME="greetings" AUTOSTART =
➥TRUE>
```

You can then reference or address this embedded media type from JavaScript by its NAME attribute, for example:

```
document.greetings.play()
```

You can also reference Plug-Ins from JavaScript using the new "embeds" array object. The Plug-In for the first EMBED tag in a document is referenced as `"document.embeds[0]"`, the second as `"document.embeds[1]"`, and so on.

callbacks

Some Plug-Ins enable you to create special functions called **callbacks** which are similar to event handlers. See the documentation for each Plug-In for details on how to use callbacks.

As of this writing, many LiveConnect features are not available. Visit the previously mentioned Netscape Web sites for the latest information.

Using LiveConnect to Fade-out Background Audio

Here is a snippet of code that uses LiveConnect commands to fade out a LiveAudio background sound after a specific length of time. This code uses the JavaScript `"setTimeOut"` function:

```
<HTML>
<HEAD>
```

```
<TITLE>Fading Out LiveAudio Background Sounds</TITLE>


</HEAD>
<BODY>


 <EMBED SRC="hum.aif" NAME=greetings AUTOSTART = TRUE
➥HIDDEN=TRUE>
 <SCRIPT LANGUAGE = "JavaScript">
window.setTimeout('document.embeds["greetings"].
➥fade_from_to(100,0)',1000)

</SCRIPT>


</BODY>
</HTML>
```

Here's what is going on in this code: The HTML code within the EMBED tag embeds an AIFF audio file in a Web page. Following are LiveAudio attributes to the EMBED tag:

- The NAME attribute assigns a name to the Plug-In media so that it can be referred to in LiveConnect JavaScript statements.
- The AUTOSTART attribute is set to TRUE so that the sound file starts playing automatically.
- The HIDDEN attribute hides the standard LiveAudio controller.

In the following example:

```
window.setTimeout('document.embeds["greetings"].
➥fade_from_to(100,0)',1000)
```

the JavaScript statement uses the built-in JavaScript function `"setTimeOut"` to fade-out the LiveAudio sound after a specified length of time. Earlier in this chapter, you saw the `"setTimeOut"` function used to create a dynamic billboard of changing graphics. In this example the `"setTimeOut"` function takes these two parameters:

- The first parameter to `"setTimeOut"` is a function that automaticallys runs after a specified length of time. The function:

  ```
  document.embeds["greetings"].fade_from_to(100,0)
  ```

uses the new `embeds` object in JavaScript 1.1 to reference the LiveAudio media. The method `"fade_from_to(100,0)"` is a new feature of LiveConnect-enabled LiveAudio Plug-Ins. This method fades out or fades in the LiveAudio sound. The method takes two parameters. These parameters are integer values in percent of the sound volume of the starting point of the fade and the ending point of the fade. In this example, the fade starts at 100 percent volume and fades out to zero percent volume.

- The second parameter to the `"setTimeOut"` function specifies the time in milliseconds that pass before the function specified in the first parameter is called. In this example, one second passes and then the `"fade_from_to"` method is called.

VBScript and OLE/ActiveX Scripting

VBScript is a client-side scripting language developed for Internet Explorer by Microsoft. It is a subset of Visual Basic. At this time VBScript is in beta and is only available in Microsoft Internet Explorer 3.0 for Windows 95 and NT. More platforms should be supported by the time you read this.

Note

Visit:

`http://www.microsoft.com/`

for all the latest info on VBScript.

VBScript performs similar functions to JavaScript and LiveConnect. VBScript enables you to create HTML documents on-the-fly and communicate between the HTML document, OLE/ActiveX controls, and Java applets.

VBScript syntax is similar to JavaScript. It may become an important part of a Web author's tool kit because of the numerous existing Visual Basic applications that can be repurposed for the Web. At this time, it is still a nascent technology and is not supported in any browsers other than Internet Explorer 3.0 for Windows 95 and NT.

VBScript Functions

subroutines

VBScript enables you to create custom functions similar to JavaScript functions. VBScript functions are called **subroutines**. To create subroutines, use the VBScript keyword

"SUB" in much the same way use the JavaScript keyword "function," for example:

```
SUB showAlert
    alert "A VBScript alert"
END SUB
```

defines a VBScript subroutine `"showAlert"` that you can call from other VBScripts in your HTML document.

VBScript Event Handlers

VBScript also supports event handlers, similar to JavaScript event handlers. The main difference is that instead of calling a JavaScript function, the event calls a VBScript subroutine. For example, if you have previously defined the showAlert subroutine, the HTML code

```
<A HREF="http://myserver.net/somedoc.html"
➥onClick="showAlert"> A hyperlink.</A>
```

calls the event handler subroutine `"showAlert"` when the user clicks on the hyperlink.

Creating Custom HTML Documents Based on User Environment with VBScript

VBScript enables you to create custom HTML documents on-the-fly based on a user's environment. You can also use the familiar `"document.write"` command with VBScript. This example creates an HTML document depending on the time of day:

```
<HTML>
<HEAD>

<TITLE>Dynamic Documents with VBScript</TITLE>

<SCRIPT LANGUAGE="VBScript">

<!--

If Hour(time) < 12 then
 document.write('A morning document');
```

```
Else
document.write('An afternoon document'');

End If

-->

</SCRIPT>
</HEAD>
<BODY>
</BODY>
</HTML>
```

The comment tags hide the VBScript statements enclosed within the SCRIPT tag from browsers that don't support VBScript, such as Netscape Navigator and Internet Explorer 2.0.

Client-side scripting provides Web authors with new power to create dynamic interactive multimedia Web documents. As integration features such as LiveConnect and ActiveX scripting develop it will be possible to create Web-based multimedia applications that integrate Java applets, Plug-Ins, OpenDoc parts, and ActiveX controls.

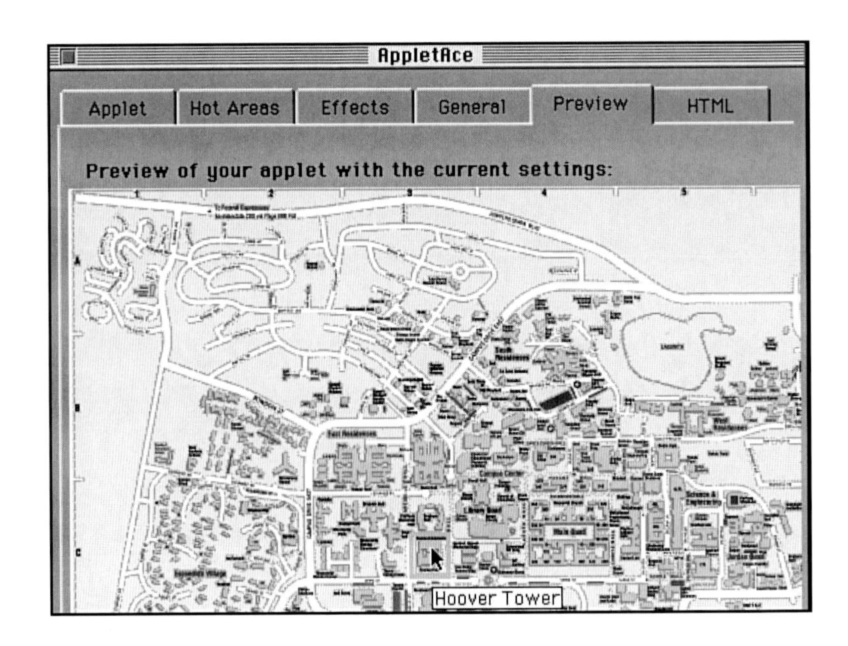

You've heard the hype. Now, learn how to use cutting edge Java tools to create compelling, cross-platform content.

chapter

15

Java

Java is a programming language developed by people working at Sun Microsystems. It was originally designed for TV set-top boxes for video-on-demand applications that never materialized. It was repackaged later as a language in which to program distributed, cross-platform software for TCP/IP-based networks such as the Web and the Internet.

A *Java applet* is a program written in the Java programming language that runs within a Web browser. A Java applet can be embedded in a Web page, much like a GIF graphic, Plug-In, or ActiveX control. You can write desktop applications in Java, but applets are more restricted than desktop applications in what they can do, because applets must be contained within the Web browser.

Java and Web multimedia are often mentioned in the same sentence. Java is frequently touted as a means of enabling multimedia and animation on the Web, because it promises distributed, cross-platform multimedia that will play back on any Java-enabled system. The reality at this time, however, is that compared to mature technologies such as QuickTime or Director, Java multimedia is primitive and lacks sophisticated authoring tools for development. For Web multimedia, you can often accomplish more, faster, with higher quality and less effort, through such technologies as QuickTime, Shockwave, RealAudio, and VDOLive, using Plug-Ins and ActiveX controls (see fig. 15.1).

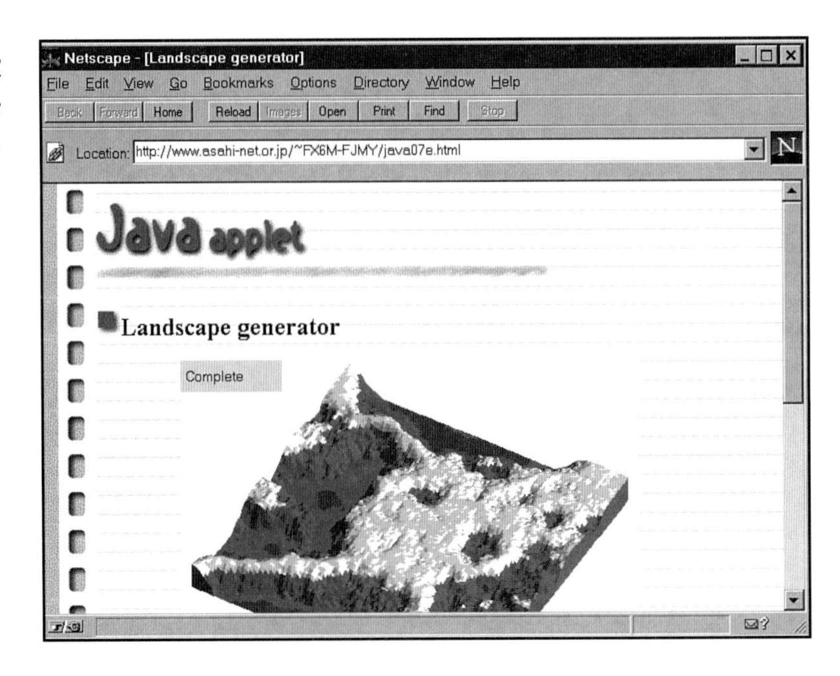

Figure 15.1

A 3D landscape generator in Java.

The limitations of Java compared to other multimedia development environments is rapidly changing, however. This chapter shows you some of the new free or inexpensive Java authoring tools you can use to provide Java-based multimedia.

> **Note**
>
> For more information on Java programming, see New Riders Publishing's *Inside Java* by Colin Fraizer and Tim Ritchey.

This chapter won't show you how to program in Java, because there are many books on that subject. It will show you how to use some free authoring tools that create Java applets without having to write a single line of Java code. These tools enable you to repurpose existing media into Java applets and create new applets that you can embed in Web pages.

Java Basics

Java is a programming language similar to C++. You write Java programs in the same way you write other programs. A simple Java program might look like this:

```
class DisplayText {
    public static void main (String args[]){
        System.out.println("The simplest Java applet:);
}
}
```

Java code can be written in any text editor. This Java program is contained in a **source file** that typically has the file name extension `.java`.

source file

After you write your Java program, the next step is to compile it with a Java compiler. There are several compilers available from Sun, Metrowerks, Natural Intelligence, and other companies. The compiler takes your source file and turns it into a Java class file. The **class file** is the file that you will put on your Web server and reference from the APPLET tag, so that Java applets can run on your Web page. Class files have the `.class` file name extension.

class file

Java class files contain platform-independent Java **byte code**. To run the Java code contained in the class file you will need a **byte code interpreter**. The byte code interpreter takes the Java byte code and translates it into code that can run on the local machine. Netscape Navigator 3 is Java-enabled, which means it has a built-in Java interpreter that interprets and runs Java byte code. Interpreters can also be integrated with the local system, such as the MacOS Java Runtime from Apple Computer.

byte code

byte code interpreter

Java class files make up the Java applet that you embed in your Web page with the APPLET tag. A Java applet usually requires several class files. You reference the main class file with the CODE attribute of the APPLET tag. Other supporting Java class files that the applet needs to run are typically contained in the same directory as the main class file.

Just-In-Time (JIT) compilers translate Java byte codes into machine code for the local machine. They run faster than byte code interpreters. JIT compilers can improve the performance of Java applets, especially those that are computationally intensive. JIT compilers can be integrated at the system level or browser level.

Java's Advantages and Disadvantages

Because of Java's features there are advantages to using Java for multimedia.

- **Cross-platform**. Java applets will run on any system with a Java byte code interpreter.
- **Object-oriented**. Java programs can be written with modular, reusable class libraries, which generally make programming easier and faster.
- **Distributed**. Java applets are very happy living on a network. They can find and use chunks of code that reside on client machines, on the local Web server, or on another machine on the Internet. Another benefit of this feature is that updating code is easier, because it is easier to update a single piece of code that resides in a single place than to try to update all the versions of the code that exist on multiple machines.
- **Multithreaded**. A single Java applet can run multiple processes at once, for example, downloading graphics, displaying text, and acting on user input. This feature is very handy for multimedia applications.

Other advantages include the fact that:

- Java is similar to C++, which makes it easy to program if you are a C++ or C programmer.
- Java provides built-in memory management.
- Java contains built-in support for streamed graphics.

There are, however, disadvantages to using Java for your Web multimedia:

- Not all browsers have Java byte code interpreters, for example, browsers for Windows 3.1 systems.
- Java applets can run slow because they are interpreted on the local machine.
- Java applets can take a long time to download, the big obstacle for all Web multimedia. This problem is compounded with some Java applets, because if an applet is gathering pieces of class libraries scattered around the Internet, connections may time out if traffic is high, and the applet won't be able to get the pieces it needs to run.
- Poorly written Java applets can consume processor cycles and freeze out other interactivity.

- Java has primitive multimedia support. Sound support is particularly lacking, being limited to 8-bit, 8kHz .au format at this time.
- Java applets are the last element to load in a Web page; therefore, even if an applet implements streaming playback, it can take a while for the playback to start.

Browser Support

As of this writing, Netscape Navigator 3 supports Java on Mac 68K, PowerMac, Unix, and Windows 95/NT platforms

Internet Explorer 3 supports Java on Windows 95/NT.

Netscape Navigator 3 for Windows 95/NT includes a JIT (Just-In-Time) Java compiler that speeds execution of Java byte code. A JIT compiler may be integrated with the MacOS by the time you read this. Other companies have announced integration of JIT compilers at the system level or browser level.

Java Tools

visual development environments

In the last year, numerous tools have appeared that enable non-programmers to create Java applets. Tools that support GUI-based (graphical user interface) development of Java applets are often called **visual development environments** to distinguish them from programming environments such as Metrowerks CodeWarrior or Natural Intelligence's Roaster (see fig. 15.2).

Commercial visual development tools include:

- Cosmo Code, by Silicon Graphics
  `http://www.sgi.com/Products/cosmo/code/`
- Hyperwire, by Kinetix
  `http://www.ktx.com/products/hyperwire/`
- Jamba, by AimTech
  `http://www.aimtech.com/prodjahome.html`
- JFactory, by Rogue Wave
  `http://www.roguewave.com/rwpav/products/jfactory/jfactory.htm`

Note

Find out the latest about Java at:

`http://www.javasoft.com/`

- Mojo, by Penumbra
  `http://www.penumbrasoftware.com/`
- WebBurst, by PowerProduction
  `http://www.powerproduction.com/`
- WebPainter, by TotallyHip
  `http://www.totally.hip.com/`

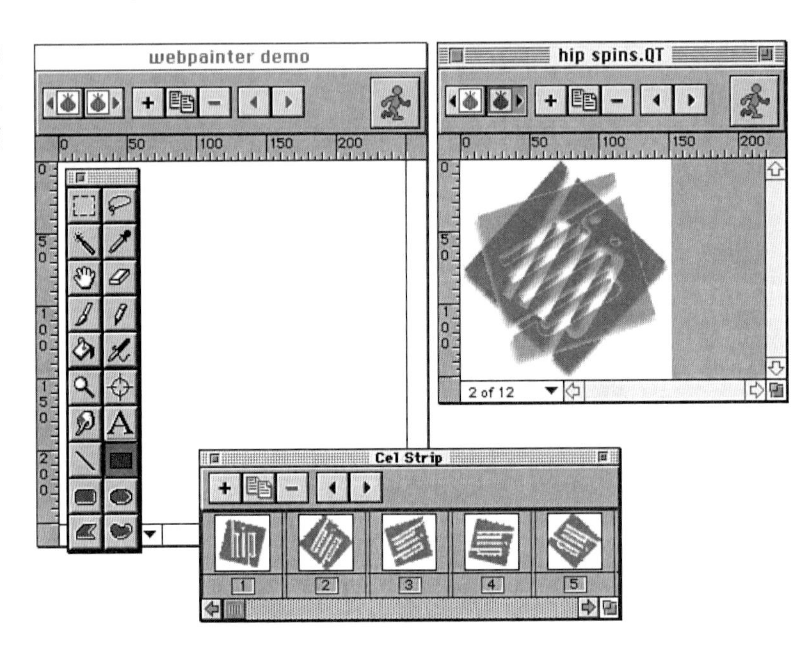

Figure 15.2

WebPainter—a Java animation applet that is a visual development environment.

> **Note**
>
> The following Web sites contain extensive lists of Java applets and other Java-related resources:
>
> `http://www.gamelan.com/`
>
> `http://www.jars.com/`
>
> `http://www.yahoo.com/Computers_and_Internet/Languages/Java/Applets/`

There are numerous free and shareware tools and ready-made applets you can use to create custom Java applets without programming. Some of these free or shareware applets are:

- AppletAce, by Macromedia
  `http://www.macromedia.com/`
- Sizzler converter, by Totally Hip
  `http://www.totally.hip.com/`
- Sun's Animator applet
  `http://java.sun.com:80/applets/applets/Animator/index.html`

Later sections of this chapter look at AppletAce, Egor Animator, and Sizzler, which are available on the Web.

Embedding Java Applets in Web Pages

You embed Java applets in an HTML page using the <APPLET></APPLET> tag. The APPLET tag takes several attributes, some of which are required and some of which are optional. The following attributes are required:

- CODE is generally the file name of the class file of the applet.
- WIDTH and HEIGHT are the dimensions of the applet in pixels.

Here is sample HTML code for Java applets that contains these required attributes:

```
<APPLET CODE  = myJavaApplet.class WIDTH = 160
➥HEIGHT=120></APPLET>
```

These attributes are optional:

- CODEBASE is the path name to the applet that is specified in the CODE attribute. If the class file and supporting files are in the same directory as the HTML document, you don't need this tag. Also, if the class file is in a directory relative to the HTML document, you can specify the relative path name in the CODE attribute. Generally, Java applets are served from a standard directory on the Web server. Specify the URL to this directory in the CODEBASE attribute; for example, `"http://myServer.com/myJavaApplets/"` in the following HTML code:

  ```
  <APPLET CODE  = myJavaApplet.class CODEBASE =
  ➥"http://myServer.com/myJavaApplets/"WIDTH = 160
  ➥HEIGHT=120></APPLET>
  ```

- ALIGN takes values of TOP, MIDDLE, and BOTTOM, and aligns text similar to the IMG tag.
- ALT enables you to provide alternate text if the user doesn't have a Java-enabled browser or has disabled Java.

- The <PARAM> tag is used to pass applet-specific parameters to the Java applet. It is used like this:

```
<APPLET CODE  = myJavaAnimationApplet.class WIDTH
➥= 160 HEIGHT=120>
<PARAM NAME=frame VALUE = "animationFrame1.gif">
</APPLET>
```

- Each parameter consists of a name value pair. In this example, the parameter named `"frame"` has the value `"animationFrame1.gif"`.

Providing Alternate Content for Non-Java Browsers

You can use the ALT attribute to provide alternate content for users who do not have a Java-enabled browser or have disabled Java in the browser's preferences.

```
<APPLET CODE  = myJavaAnimationApplet.class
ALT = "Java Applet"
WIDTH = 160 HEIGHT=120>
</APPLET>
```

If Java is not available, the above code makes the text "Java Applet" appear in the rectangular space reserved for the Java applet.

You can also put alternate HTML code within the APPLET tag, as in the following example:

```
<APPLET CODE  = myJavaAnimationApplet.class  WIDTH =
➥160 HEIGHT=120>
<PARAM NAME=frame VALUE = "animationFrame1.gif">

<H3>This page contains a Java-based animation.</H3>
You will need a <A HREF http://www.javasoft.com>Java</
➥A>-enabled browser to view this animation.
</APPLET>
```

The HTML code within the APPLET tag will appear in the browser if Java is not available.

Turning QuickTime Movies into Java Applets with Sizzler

This section shows you how to take an existing QuickTime movie and turn it into a Java animation that you can embed in your Web page. You won't have to code a single line of Java. All the Java code you need to do this is provided with the Sizzler suite of tools.

Tools
Sizzler Conversion tool
Sizzler Java classes
QuickTime movie

Introducing Sizzler

Sizzler is a suite of free viewers, simple conversion tools, and Java class libraries for Mac and Windows 95/NT. These tools enable you to view and create Web-based animations with short sounds, called **sprite files**. Animations are viewed with the Sizzler Netscape Plug-In, ActiveX control, Cyberdog part, or the SizzlerViewer Java applet.

sprite files

Sizzler animations are streamed without special servers. A low-resolution version of the animation downloads rapidly and then becomes progressively more detailed as more data is downloaded. The effect is somewhat like an interlaced GIF.

With the Sizzler free stand-alone conversion utility, you can create Java applets from:

- QuickTime movies and PIC files on Macintosh
- AVI and DIB files on Windows 95/NT

QuickTime movies, AVI movies, PIC animations, and DIB file lists are converted to Sizzler's sprite-format graphics file so that they can be displayed using the SizzlerViewer Java applet. Sizzler takes a QuickTime movie and:

Note

To view Java applets created with Sizzler, users need a Java-enabled browser.

- Converts the QuickTime Video Track to a streamable Sizzler sprite file playable by the SizzlerViewer Java applet.
- Converts the QuickTime Sound Track to an ".au" audio file that is played back by the SizzlerViewer Java applet.

Figure 15.3

Streamed graphics in a SizzlerViewer Java applet.

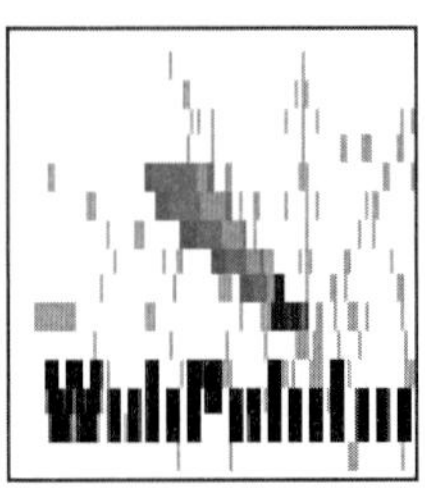

Low resolution

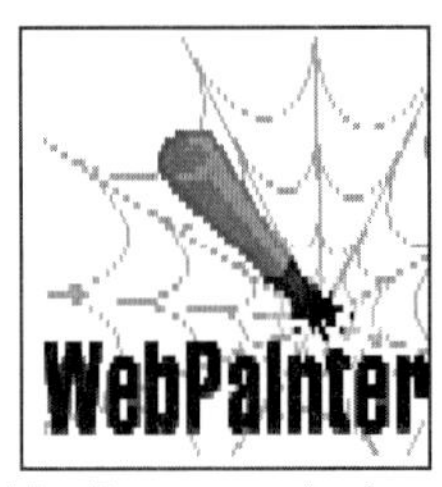

Medium resolution

Unfortunately, ".au" audio files are generally of lower quality than QuickTime Sound Tracks. Also, there is no interactivity that is comparable to the standard QuickTime controller. The benefits of converting QuickTime movies to Java applets, therefore, are confined to the streamed, progressive display of the movie and the fact that playback is assured in any Java-capable browser.

WebPainter

Note

WebPainter is currently available in beta for Macintosh. A Windows version may be available by the time your read this. Check out **http://www.totallyhip.com/** for more information.

WebPainter is a full-featured animation program that will import QuickTime movies, animation files, and graphics, and create Sizzler sprite files for use with Sizzler-Viewer Java applet, Netscape Plug-Ins, ActiveX controls, OpenDoc, GIF animations, and QuickTime.

WebPainter can import GIFs, PICTs, PICs, and QuickTime movies. WebPainter projects can be exported as:

- Animated GIFs
- Separate GIF animation frames
- PIC files
- Separate PICT animation frames
- QuickTime movies
- QuickTime Sprite Track movies
- Sizzler for ActiveX
- Sizzler for OpenDoc parts (Cyberdog)
- Sizzler for Netscape Plug-Ins
- Sizzler Java applets

Converting QuickTime Movies to Java Applets with Sizzler Converter

For best results, you may want to save your QuickTime movie as flattened and playable on non-Apple computers (see Chapter 10, "Animating with QuickTime Digital Video").

On a Macintosh:

1. Drag-and-drop a QuickTime movie or PIC file onto the Sizzler icon, or launch Sizzler and choose Open from the File menu.
2. In the dialog box, select the options you'd like—such as Frames/Second—and a hyperlink for the animation file (see fig. 15.4).
3. Choose the Java Applet output option.

The Sizzler converter creates a file with the same name as your movie with the addition of the sprite extension.

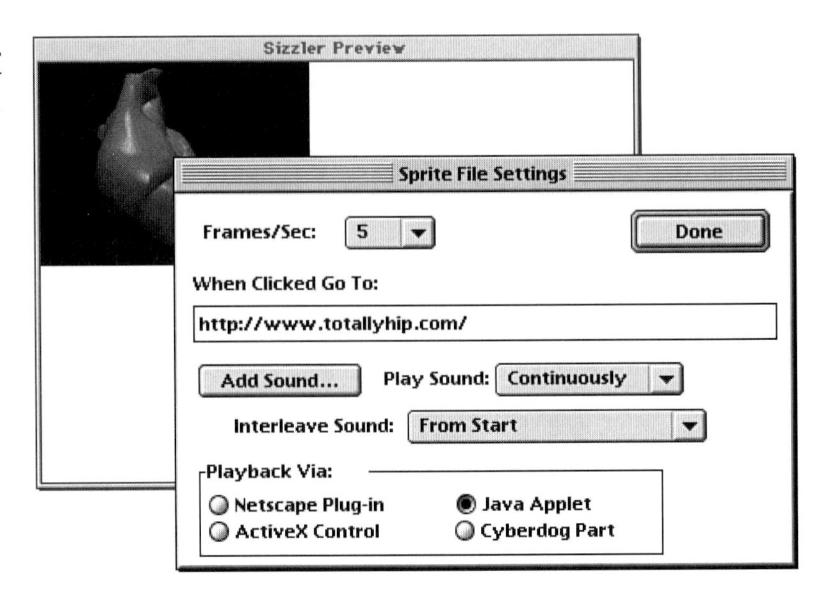

Figure 15.4

The Sizzler converter.

Embedding Applets in HTML

The Sizzler converter generates the HTML code that you use to display your applet in a Web page. Just cut and paste the code into your HTML document.

Your HTML code might look like:

```
<HTML>
<TITLE>Sizzled QuickTime and Java</TITLE>


</HEAD>
<BODY>

<APPLET CODE="SizzlerViewer.class" CODEBASE="http://
➥www.myServer.com/COM/totallyhip/sizzler/"
WIDTH=166 HEIGHT=121>

<PARAM NAME=sizzlerFile VALUE="heartmov.sprite">

</APPLET>

</BODY>
</HTML>
```

The CODE attribute must specify the name "SizzlerViewer.class". This name is the file name of the SizzlerViewer Java applet.

The CODEBASE attribute must specify the path name to the directory on your Web server that contains the "SizzlerViewer.class" and all the supporting class files. See the following section on setting up Web server directories.

The value of the "sizzlerFile" parameter is the file name of the converted QuickTime movie. This file must be in the same directory as the HTML document.

If the movie has sound, Sizzler creates an ".au" format file. On your Web server, this file must be in the same directory as the converted QuickTime movie file, "heartmov.sprite," in this example.

Setting Up Directories on the Server

For playback, the converted QuickTime movie requires the SizzlerViewer Java class library. This library is contained in the COM/totallyhip/sizzler directory in the Sizzler installation. This directory contains a bunch of files with the ".class" extension (see fig. 15.5). These are the Java class files that are used to play back Sizzler animations and converted QuickTime movies as Java applets. There are basically two options for putting these files on your Web server:

1. Copy these files to the directory where you will serve your HTML files.
2. Copy these files to another directory beneath the root level of your server, which you should reference with the CODEBASE attribute of the APPLET tag.

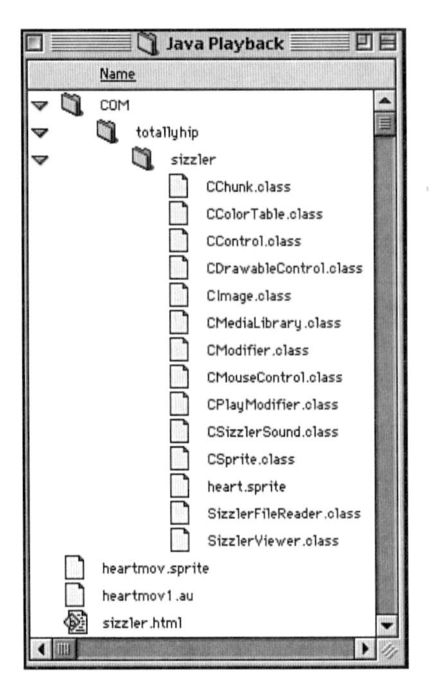

Figure 15.5

Directory structure for Sizzler Java applet on a Web server.

Creating Java Applets with AppletAce

AppletAce is an authoring tool and free set of Java applets from Macromedia. With AppletAce you can easily create Java applets that provide the following benefits:

- Dynamic, animated text that can be updated at runtime
- Animated bullets
- Dynamic charts that can be updated at runtime, based on changing data that resides in a text file on the Internet or Web server (see fig. 15.6)
- Richly interactive image maps and control panels

AppletAce is available free at Macromedia's Web site:

```
http://www.macromedia.com/
```

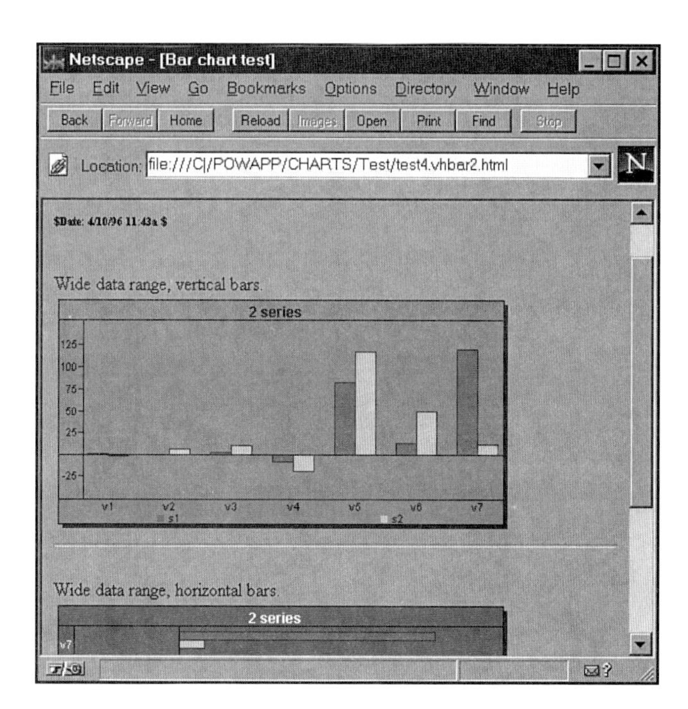

Figure 15.6

Dynamic charting in Java.

To use Java applets created with AppletAce, you have to copy the class files in the PowerApplets directory of the AppletAce distribution to your Web server. This directory contains all the Java class files you need to run your applets from your Web server.

Creating Interactive Image Maps with AppletAce

Imagemap is a Java applet you create through AppletAce that enables the rapid creation of interactive Java-based image maps. Imagemap provides rich interactivity and user feedback by means of the following features:

- Custom highlighting for hot areas when the user rolls over them with the mouse.
- Pop-up text that describes the hotlink when the user rolls over the hotlink with the mouse.
- Feedback when the user clicks on a hot area.

To create an Imagemap Java applet with AppletAce, follow these steps:

1. Create the graphic you want to use as a map.
2. Copy the image to the same directory as your HTML file.
3. Launch AppletAce.
4. To start creating your image map, choose ImageMap from the Applet Name: pop-up menu. The AppletAce window should look like Figure 15.7.
5. The section labeled Options to ensure correct relative path names enables you to specify the following:
   - The directory path to the HTML file on the Web server
   - The directory path to the directory on the Web server that contains the Imagemap Java class files

   If you leave these fields blank, AppletAce assumes that the class file for the Imagemap Java applet can be found at the `"./PowerApplets/Imagemap/ImageMap.class"` relative to the directory containing the HTML file. These values for the directory paths are used in the HTML code that is automatically generated by AppletAce. You can change the values by editing the CODE and CODEBASE attributes within the APPLET tag.
6. Click on the Hot Areas tab (see fig. 15.8).

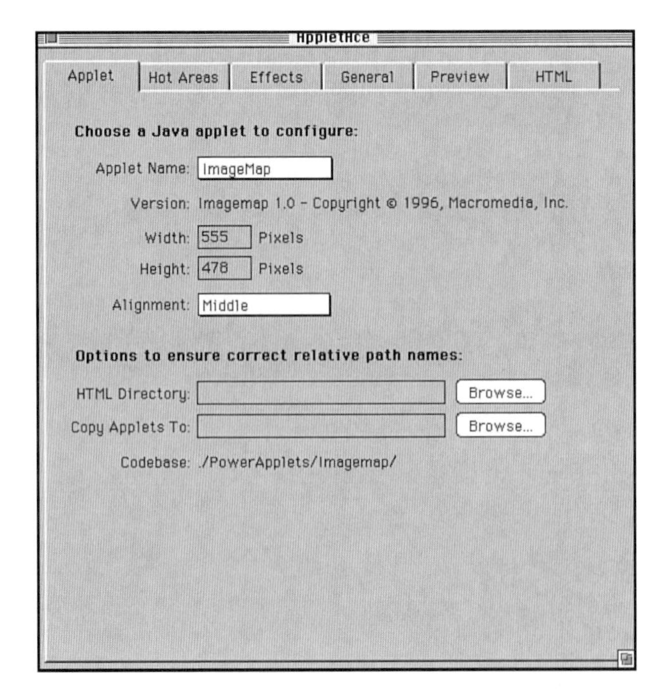

Figure 15.7

Using AppletAce to set up a Java-based image map.

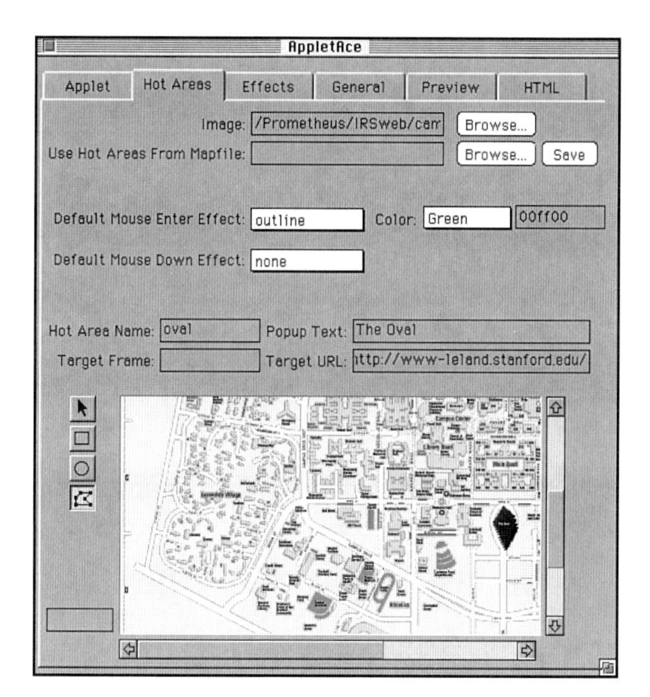

Figure 15.8

Setting up Hot Areas in a Java-based image map.

7. Enter the name of the image map graphic in the Image text box or click on Browse. If you click on Browse, the path name to the image map graphic is the path name on your local system. If you upload the image map to a Web server, you will have to change the value of the `"image"` parameter in the generated HTML code to reflect the path to the image map graphic, as shown below:

```
<PARAM NAME="image"          VALUE="/Prometheus/
➥campus-map-small.gif">
```

8. Specify the Default Mouse Enter effect and Default Mouse Down effect for hot areas.
9. Create hot areas with the tools at the bottom of the panel.
10. Specify a name and URL for each Hot Area, Popup Text, and Target Frame if you want.
11. To customize mouse feedback for a hot area or to provide a replacement image for a hot area, click on the Effects Tab (see fig. 15.9).
12. To specify background color, replacement image options, and popup text options, click on the General tab.
13. To preview your image map, click the Preview tab (see fig. 15.10).

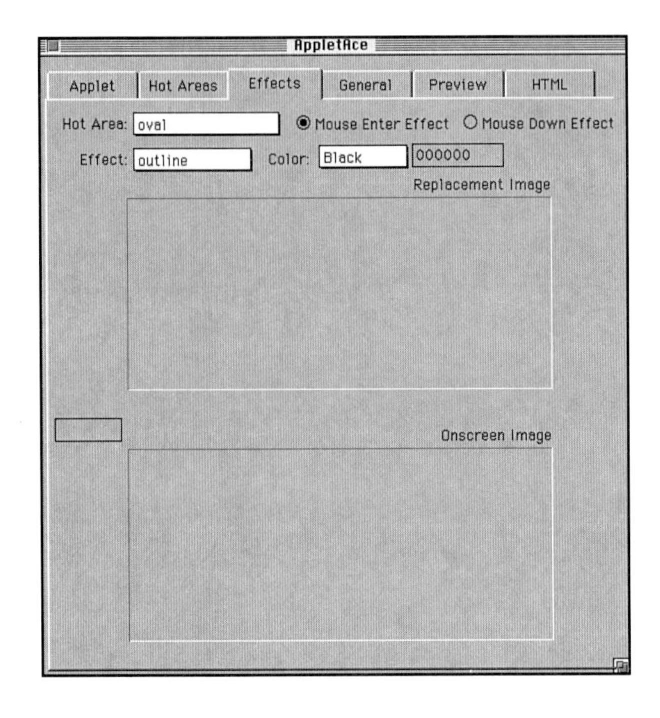

Figure 15.9

Customizing mouse feedback for a hot area.

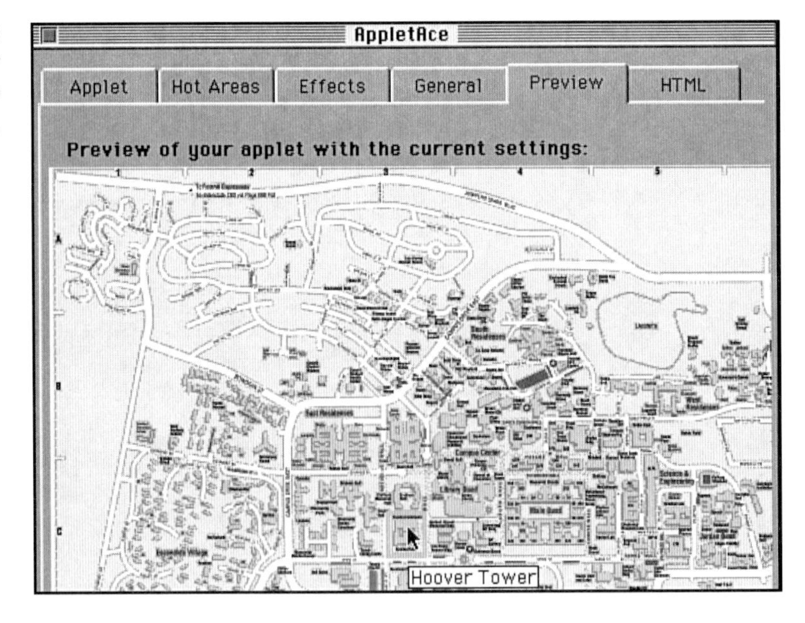

Figure 15.10

Using AppletAce to Preview the image map.

14. To generate HTML code for your Java applet, click the HTML tab (see fig. 15.11). To save the HTML code to disk as a text file so you can cut and paste it into an HTML document, click on the Save button.
15. Upload the HTML document containing the APPLET tag and the image map graphic to your Web server.

16. Copy the PowerApplets class files to a directory on your Web server, if you haven't already done so.

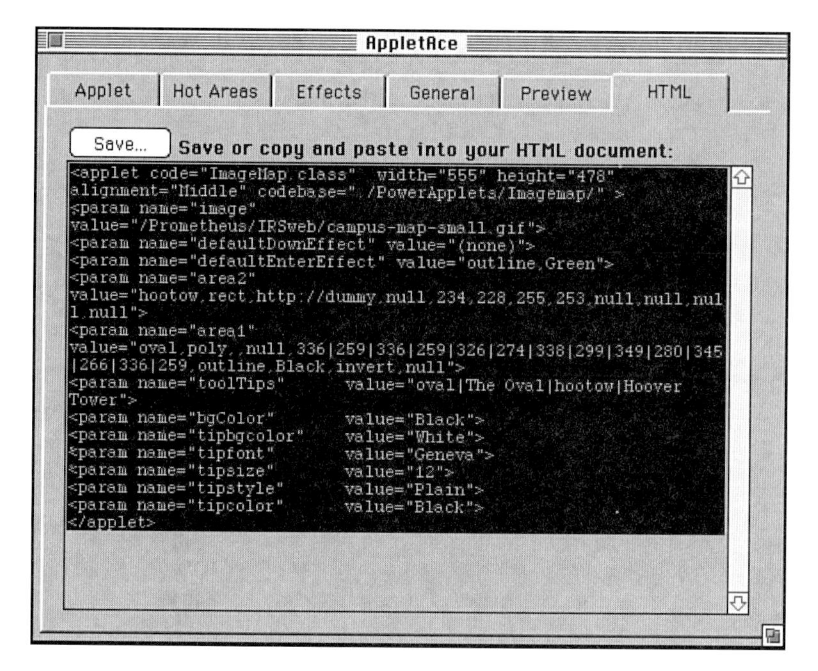

Figure 15.11

Generated HTML code.

17. Review the following attributes and parameters of the APPLET tag, to make sure the path names are correct:

   - `CODE="ImageMap.class"` should specify the name of the Java applet class file, in this case `"ImageMap.class"`.
   - CODEBASE = "pathname to the directory containing the `ImageMap.class` file and supporting class files".
   - This path name will depend on how you have set up your Web server. If you have copied the `PowerApplet/Imagemap/` directory to the directory containing your HTML file, you won't need this attribute.
   - `<PARAM NAME="image" VALUE="campus-map-➥small.gif">`

   If the image map graphic is in the same directory as the HTML document, VALUE should just specify the file name. Otherwise, it should specify the relative path name or URL to the image map graphic.

Creating Animations with Egor Animator

Egor Animator is a great application for Windows systems from Sausage Software that you can use to create Java animations. Egor imports a sequence of GIF graphics, enables you to set various properties such as looping, frame rate, and simple motion paths, then creates an animation file that can be used with an included Java applet for playback. This section shows you how to create animations with Egor Animator. Egor Animator can be downloaded from:

```
http://www.sausage.com/
```

Here are the steps necessary to create animations with Egor:

1. Launch Egor.
2. Click on the Add button (see fig. 15.12).
3. In the Egor File Manager dialog box, select the animation frames you want to use for your animation (see fig. 15.13).
4. When you are done, click Close.

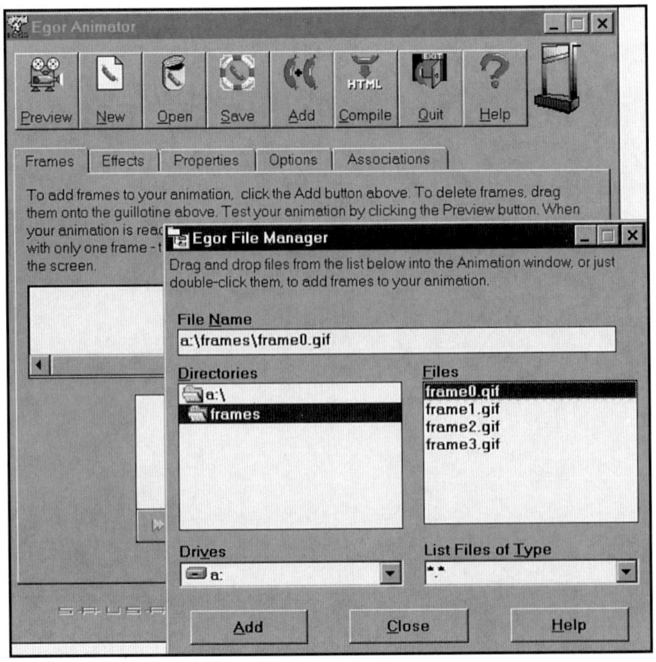

Figure 15.12

Adding animation frames to Java animation.

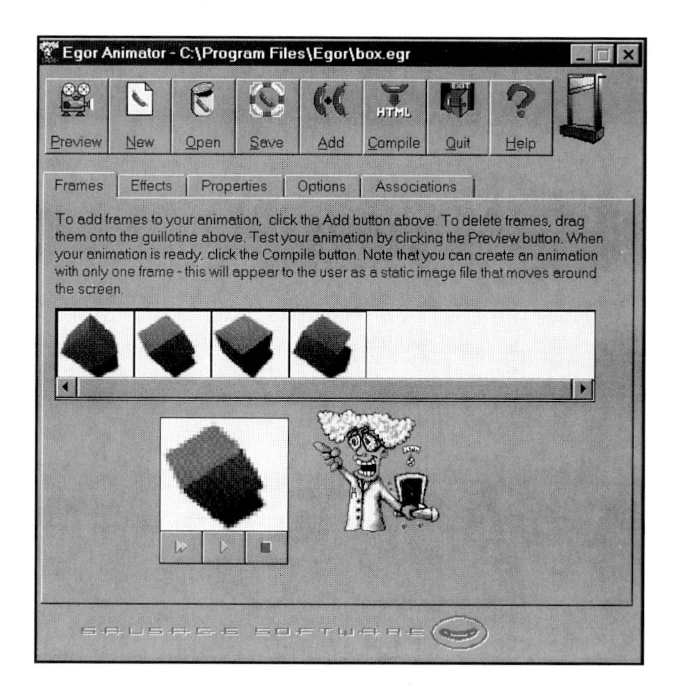

Figure 15.13

Animation frames in Egor.

5. To set the frame rate, looping, the length of time the animation plays, and simple motion paths, click the Effects tab (see fig. 15.14).
6. To set up display characteristics within the Web page, such as width and height (required), and background color, click the Properties tab.

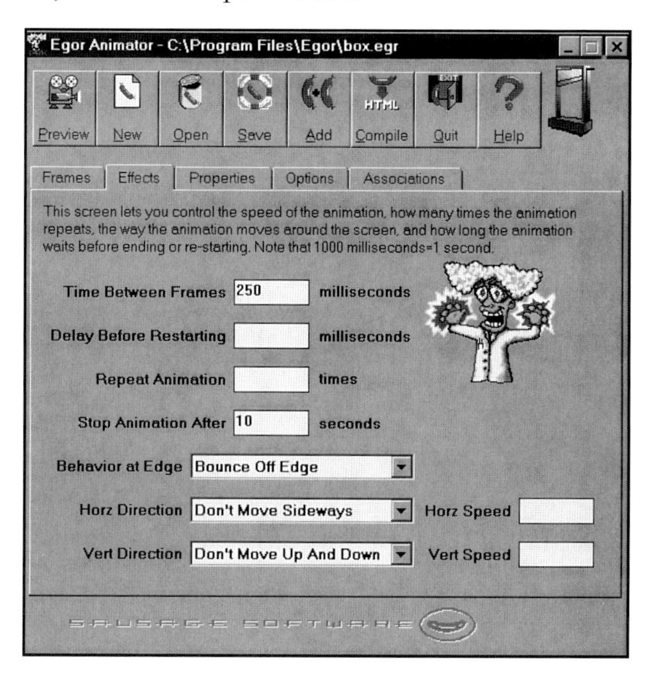

Figure 15.14

Setting the frame rate in Egor.

7. To add an `".au"` format sound to your animation, click on the Associations tab (see fig. 15.15).

Figure 15.15

Adding sound in Egor.

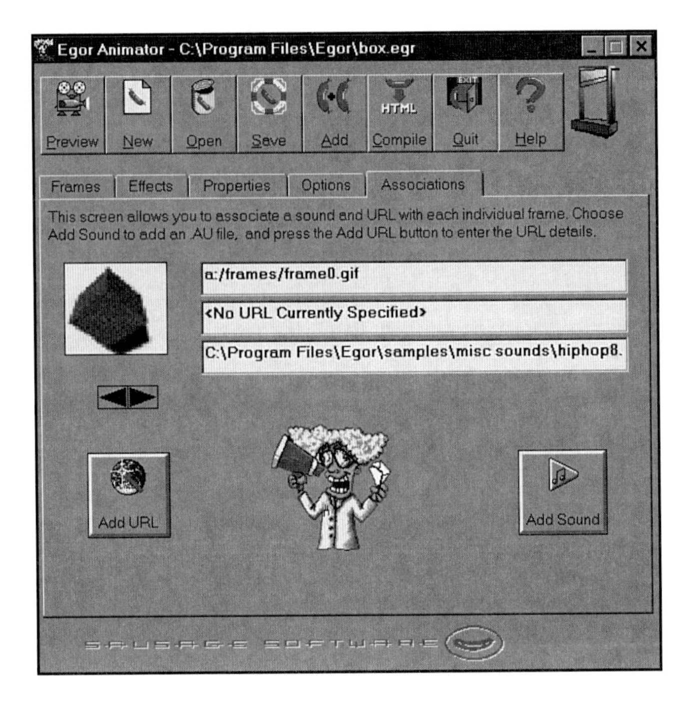

8. When you are done, click the Compile button.
9. The HTML code you can use to embed the applet in a Web page is copied to the Windows clipboard.
10. Upload the HTML document, the Egor animation file, the GIF animation frames, the sound file (if present), and the `anim.class` Java class file to the directory on the Web server where you will be serving your animated Web page.

Conclusion

This chapter showed you how to incorporate Java multimedia in your Web pages and how to use readily available authoring tools to create Java multimedia without writing a line of Java code.

Although Java multimedia is primitive by most standards, this is likely to change in the near future with companies such as Silicon Graphics, Apple Computer, Macromedia, Adobe, Sun, and Netscape working to integrate more sophisticated multimedia features in the Java language. Watch the Web sites of these companies for the most recent Java developments.

chapter

16

Keeping an Eye on the Horizon

It's been a busy year for Web multimedia. The cross-platform, Netscape Plug-In architecture is about a year old as of this writing, and ActiveX for Windows 95/NT has just appeared. Integration of multimedia playback and viewer technologies with the major browsers is underway. Multimedia tool vendors are rapidly producing Web-optimized extensions to the most popular authoring tools and multimedia formats such as QuickTime, Director, SoundEdit, Painter, and FreeHand. New tools specifically designed for the many unique aspects of Web-based multimedia—such as RealAudio, VDOLive, MovieCleaner Pro, MovieMaker, WebPainter, FutureSplash Animator, and WebAnimator—are making the job of repurposing and creating Web multimedia content easier. Streaming audio and video are becoming a reality for many users; moreover, tools are beginning to appear that make it easy to create cross-platform Java-based multimedia.

This book has shown you how to create high-quality graphics, animation, digital video, audio, music, 3D graphics, and VRML within the technical constraints of the Web. But the pace of change on the Web is phenomenal, especially in the multimedia realm. During the writing of this book, new technologies were introduced or adapted to the Web. You have to continually add to your multimedia toolkit based on what you have to deliver to users. Some things to look out for in the coming year include:

- More deployment of Web-based multimedia on intranets
- Enhancements to existing multimedia formats and authoring tools
- Advances in streaming and compression technologies
- Java integration with operating systems and improved visual development tools
- More Java multimedia, 3D, and VRML classes
- Multimedia collaboration and communication tools
- Version 4.0 of the Navigator and Internet Explorer browsers
- Integration of Navigator with MacOS and Internet Explorer with Windows
- New Web clients that use TV sets and PDA-style displays

A major obstacle for multimedia on the Web is the limited bandwidth available for most users. Another limiting factor for the Internet in general, is the capacity to handle increased traffic and move large multimedia files on the Web. Already, Internet "brown-outs" are fairly common in North America during workday business hours, adding noticeably to download times and making some sites nearly inaccessible.

Some emerging technologies are appearing to address this problem. Unfortunately, all have drawbacks and high infrastructure costs and probably won't be a factor on the Web for a couple of years. For instance, cable modems promise increased downloading bandwidth to the user's machine and less uploading bandwidth, which will limit their usefulness for serving multimedia files. These modems require substantial investments in equipment by cable companies. Asymmetric Digital Subscriber Line and related technologies promise similar performance over existing phone lines but were just entering field tests as of this writing. Wireless satellite, such as DirecPC, has potential, but has high costs for users. One thing is certain, the Web will probably look different in a year and Web multimedia will only get easier to create and deliver to your users.

To keep tabs on the latest developments in Web multimedia, including revisions of the products presented in this book, you might want to frequently visit the following Web sites.

3D Animation

Direct3D
http://www.microsoft.com/

Extreme3D
http://www.macromedia.com/

POV-Ray
http://www.povray.org/
http://www.whoville.com/pov-ray/faq/
http://www.povray.org/pov-cdrom/

QuickDraw 3D
http://product.info.apple.com/qd3d/QD3D.HTML
http://quickdraw3d.apple.com/Whurlplug.HTML

QuickTimeVR
http:// qtvr.quicktime.apple.com/
http://quicktime.apple.com/sw/sw.html

Strata—Studio
http:/www.strata3d.com/

GIF Animation

GIFBuilder
http://iawww.epfl.ch/Staff/Yves.Piguet/clip2gif-home/GifBuilder.html

GIFMation BoxTop Software
http://www.aris.com/boxtop/GIFmation/

GIF Construction Set
http://www.mindworkshop.com/alchemy/alchemy.html

GifMerge
http://www.iis.ee.ethz.ch/~kiwi/gifmerge.html

GIFLOOP Perl script
http://www.homecom.com/gifanim.html

Smart Dubbing 1.0v6 by Alco Blom and Vincent Verweij
http://www.xs4all.nl/~polder/

Animation

Astound Web Player

http://www.golddisk.com/awp.html

Emblaze

http://Geo.inter.net/Geo/technology/emblaze/downloads.html

FutureSplash

http://www.futurewave.com

mBED

http://www.mbed.com/

Director

http://www.macromedia.com/

mFactory—mTropolis

http://www.mfactory.com/

MovieStar

http://www.beingthere.com/

SCREAM

http://www.savedbytech.com/sbt/Plug_In.html

Server-push

http://worldwidemart.com/scripts/animation.shtml

Shockwave for Director

http://www.macromedia.com/shockwave/

http://www.macromedia.com/shockwave/director5/contents.html

http://www.macromedia.com/shockwave/director5/moviedocs/download.html

Sizzler/WebPainter

http://www.totallyhip.com/

WebAnimator

http://www.deltapoint.com/

CGI Scripts

http://worldwidemart.com/scripts/

Desktop Video-Conferencing

BeingThere

http://www.beingthere.com/

CU-SeeMe

http://cu-seeme.cornell.edu

http://www.indstate.edu/msattler/sci-tech/comp/CU-SeeMe/index.html

Enhanced CU-SeeMe

http://goliath.wpine.com/cu-seeme.html

http://goliath.wpine.com/cuprodinfo.htm

QuickTime Conferencing

http://qtc.quicktime.apple.com

ProShare

http://www.intel.com/

VideoPhone

http://www.connectix.com/

Graphics

Browser palettes

http://www.netscape.com/assist/support/client/tn/windows/10117.html

http://www.connect.hawaii.com/hc/webmasters/Netscape.colors.html

http://www.lynda.com/hex.html

Debabelizer

http://www.equil.com/

http://www.equil.com/SoftwareScripts.html

Dynamic Image—CGI

http://worldwidemart.com/scripts/image.shtml

Dynamic Image—Java

http://www.db.erau.edu/java/billboard/

Lightning Strike Plug-In

http://www.infinop.com/html/infinop.html

PNG Format
http://www.boutell.com/boutell/png/

Shockwave for FreeHand
http://www.macromedia.com/
http://www.macromedia.com/shockwave/freehand/index2.html

Photoshop
http://www.adobe.com/prodindex/photoshop/main.html

ProJPEG Plug-In for Photoshop
http://www.aris.com/boxtop/ProJPEG/

Helper Apps

This is a list of various helper apps for different platforms.

http://home.netscape.com/assist/helper_apps/index.html

http://home.netscape.com/assist/helper_apps/mac_helpers.html

http://home.netscape.com/assist/helper_apps/unix_helpers.html

http://home.netscape.com/assist/helper_apps/windows_helpers.html

ftp://ftp.ncsa.uiuc.edu/Mosaic/Unix/viewers/

HTML

These URLs provide information on various HTML topics.

Specs
http://www.w3.org/

OBJECT tag
http://www.w3.org/pub/WWW/TR/WD-object#object

Tables
http://www.ncsa.uiuc.edu/General/Internet/WWW/HTMLPrimer.html#TA

Frames
http://home.netscape.com/comprod/products/navigator/version_2.0/frames/index.html
http://home.netscape.com/assist/net_sites/frame_syntax.html
http://home.netscape.com/assist/net_sites/frame_implement.html
http://home.netscape.com/comprod/products/navigator/version_3.0/new_features.html

Extensions
http://home.netscape.com/comprod/products/navigator/version_3.0/
http://help.netscape.com/docs.html
http://microsoft.com/ie/ie3/
http://home.netscape.com/assist/net_sites/html_extensions_3.html

Java

Java
http://www.javasoft.com/

Commercial Visual Development Tools

Cosmo Code—SiliconGraphics
http://www.sgi.com/Products/cosmo/code/

Hyperwire—Kinetix
http://www.ktx.com/products/hyperwire/

Jamba—AimTech
http://www.aimtech.com/prodjahome.html

JFactory—Rogue Wave
http://www.roguewave.com/rwpav/products/jfactory/jfactory.htm

Mojo—Penumbra
http://www.penumbrasoftware.com/

WebBurst—PowerProduction
http://www.powerproduction.com/

WebPainter—TotallyHip
http://www.totally.hip.com/

AppletAce—Macromedia
http://www.macromedia.com/

Egor Animator—Sausage Software
http://www.sausage.com

Sizzler converter—Totally Hip
http://www.totally.hip.com/

Sun's Animator applet
http://java.sun.com:80/applets/applets/Animator/index.html

Java Applets
http://www.gamelan.com/
http://www.jars.com/
http://www.yahoo.com/Computers_and_Internet/Languages/Java/Applets/

JavaScript

http://home.netscape.com/eng/mozilla/2.0/handbook/javascript/index.html

http://home.netscape.com/eng/mozilla/3.0/handbook/javascript/index.html

http://home.netscape.com/comprod/products/navigator/version_2.0/script/script_info/index.html

http://www.gamelan.com/

OLE/ActiveX

http://www.ncompasslabs.com/

http://www.busweb.com/

http://www.microsoft.com/workshop/

Shareware

Windows:

Stroud's Consummate Winsock List
http://www.frontiernet.net/cwsapps/inx2.html

Mac:

Info-Mac HyperArchive
http://hyperarchive.lcs.mit.edu/HyperArchive.html

University of Michigan Archives
http://www-personal.umich.edu/~sdamask/umich-mirrors/

University of Texas Mac Archive
http://wwwhost.ots.utexas.edu/mac/

Sound

Arnold's MIDIPlayer
http://hyperarchive.lcs.mit.edu/HyperArchive/Archive/gst/midi/arnolds-midi-player-271b.hqx

CoolEdit
http://www.netzone.com/syntrillium/

D-SoundPRO 2.3
http://hyperarchive.lcs.mit.edu/HyperArchive/Archive/gst/midi/d-sound-pro-23.hqx

GoldWave
http://web.cs.mun.ca/~chris3/goldwave/goldwave.html

Internet Underground Music Archive
http://iuma.com/

InVision Interactive CyberSound VS
http://www.cybersound.com/

LiveAudio
http://home.netscape.com/comprod/products/navigator/version_3.0/developer/newplug.html

LiveUpdate/Crescendo
http://www.liveupdate.com/

Mark of the Unicorn's Digital Performer
http://www.motu.com/

MIDI

MIDI information
http://www.midifarm.com/
http://www.harmony-central.com/MIDI/

http://www.eeb.ele.tue.nl/midi/index.html
http://www.aitech.ac.jp/~ckelly/SMF.html
http://www.earthlink.net/~mma/gminfo.htm

MIDIGraphy
http://ux01.so-net.or.jp/~mmaeda/

MIDI Xtra for Director 5
http://www.yamaha.co.jp/english/xg/html/midhm.html

MIDIGate
http://www.prs.net/midigate.html

Midi Plug-In
http://www.yamaha.co.jp/english/xg/html/midhm.html

MIDITyper
http://hyperarchive.lcs.mit.edu/HyperArchive/Archive/gst/midi/midi-typer-104.hqx

MidiIt!
http://hyperarchive.lcs.mit.edu/HyperArchive/Archive/gst/midi/midi-it-125.hqx

MIDIPlugin
http://www.planete.net/~amasson/midiplugin.html

Opcode Systems
http://www.opcode.com/

Passport MasterTracks Pro
http://www.mw3.com/passport/

QuickTime Music Tracks
http://www.quicktime.apple.com/software/mac/
http://www.QuickTimeFAQ.org/

RealAudio
http://www.realaudio.com /
http://www.realaudio.com/help/ccguide/index.html
http://www.realaudio.com/help/ccguide/config.html
http://www.realaudio.com/help/ccguide/synchmm.html

Shockwave for Audio

SoundEdit
Deck
http://www.macromedia.com

SoundApp
http://www-cs-students.stanford.edu/~franke/SoundApp/
http://hyperarchive.lcs.mit.edu/HyperArchive/Archive/gst/snd/sound-app-211.hqx

SoundEffects
http://hyperarchive.lcs.mit.edu/HyperArchive/Archive/gst/snd/sound-effects-092.hqx

SoundGadget Pro
http://www.cs.man.ac.uk/~magnayn/SGPro.htm

SoundMachine Player
http://hyperarchive.lcs.mit.edu/HyperArchive/Archive/gst/snd/sound-machine-262.hqx

SoundSculptor
http://hyperarchive.lcs.mit.edu/HyperArchive/Archive/gst/snd/sound-sculptor-ii-20.hqx

QuickTime and Digital Video

ActiveMovie
http://microsoft.com/imedia/activemovie/activem.htm

Apple Computer
http://quicktime.apple.com/
http://quicktime.apple.com/qt/sw/sw.html
http://quicktime.apple.com/qt/dev/devweb.html
http://www.quicktime.apple.com/software/mac/

MovieCleaner Pro
http://www.terran-int.com/

MovieStar
http://www.beingthere.com/

NetTOOB
http://tvnet.com/duplexx/netoob.html

Personal AVI Editor
http://www.flickerfree.com/paesw.html

QuickEditor
http://hyperarchive.lcs.mit.edu/HyperArchive.html

SmartVid
http://www.intel.com/

Sparkle
http://hyperarchive.lcs.mit.edu/HyperArchive.html

StreamWorks
http://www.streamworks.com/

Unofficial QuickTime FAQ
http://www.QuickTimeFAQ.org/

VDOLive
http://www.vdo.net/

VidEdit
ftp://ftp.microsoft.com//developr/drg/Multimedia/Jumpstart/VfW11e/ODK/WINVIDEO/

Speech Recognition

ListenUp
http://snow.cit.cornell.edu/noon/ListenUp.html

ShockTalk, SurfTalk
http://www.surftalk.com/shocktalk

Text-to-Speech

Talker Plug-In
http://www.mvpsolutions.com/PlugInSite/Talker.html

Speech Plug-In
http://www.albany.net/~wtudor/

WPlany
http://www.ncsa.uiuc.edu/SDG/Software/WinMosaic/Viewers/wplany.htm

Telephony

CineTalk
http://www.cinecom.com/

CoolTalk
http://home.netscape.com/comprod/products/navigator/version_3.0/cooltalk/

CyberPhone
http://magenta.com/cyberphone

DigiPhone
http://www.planeteers.com/

Internet Phone
http://www.vocaltec.com/

Internet PartyLine
http://www.intel.com/iaweb/aplets/iplpage.htm

NetMeeting
http://www.microsoft.com/ie/ie3/netmtg.htm

WebPhone
http://www.itelco.com

WebTalk
http://www.quarterdeck.com/

VBScript

http://www.microsoft.com/workshop/

Video for Windows Utilities

ftp://mirrors.aol.com/pub/info-mac/gst/mov/
video-for-windows-11p.hqx

Vosaic

http://www.vosaic.com

XAnim

http://www.portal.com/~podlipec/home.html

VRML

3D Website Builder (Free cross-platform VRML browser and helper app, Voyager)
http://www.virtus.com/

Black Sun Interactive
http://www.blacksun.com/

Cosmo Player
http://vrml.sgi.com/

CyberPassage:
`http://vs.sony.co.jp`

E3D to VRML converter
`http://www.macromedia.com/`

Live3D
`http://home.netscape.com/eng/live3d/`
`http://home.netscape.com/comprod/products/navigator/version_3.0/index.html`
`http://home.netscape.com/eng/live3d/`

Liquid Reality:
`http://www.dimensionx.com/products/lr/`

RealVR Traveler
`http://www.rlspace.com/`

Superscape
`http://www.superscape.com`

The Palace
`http://www.thepalace.com`

Virtual Home Space Builder.
`http://www.paragraph.com`

VRML Repository
(Comprehensive list of browsers, converters and authoring tools)
`http://sdsc.edu/vrml/browsers.html`
`http://sdsc.edu/vrml/dvcontent.html`

VRML 1.0 spec
`http://vag.vrml.org`

VRML 2 spec
`http://webspace.sgi.com/moving-worlds/`

Worlds Inc
`http://www.worlds.net`

appendix

A

Other Multimedia Formats

This appendix provides a list of tools that help you:

- Put multimedia presentations on the Web
- Use digital documents to present multimedia and rich content
- Convert existing documents to Web formats
- Repurpose existing multimedia applications for the Web

A common problem for publishing groups within organizations as they migrate departmental services to an internal intranet or publish existing documentation on the global Internet, is converting vast amounts of desktop publishing files to indexed and hyperlinked HTML. Issues to consider are:

- Maintaining a consistent look and feel
- Maintaining links
- Version control and updating

The following list of resources might help you in converting or publishing existing documents and multimedia files on the Web.

Applications

E-mail

Eudora2HTML
http://arpp1.carleton.ca/machttp/doc/util/html/eudora2html.html

Hypermail
http://www.eit.com/software/hypermail/hypermail.html

Excel

Excel Internet Assistant
http://www.microsoft.com/msdownload/

Excel to HTML
http://rhodes.edu/software/readme.html

Microsoft Excel Viewer
http://www.microsoft.com/msdownload/

FrameMaker

WebMaker
http://www.cern.ch/WebMaker/whywebmaker/AboutWebMaker.html

WebWorks
http://www.quadralay.com/Products/WWPub/wwpub.html

Latex

Hyperlatex
http://www.cs.ruu.nl/people/otfried/html/hyperlatex.html

latex2html
http://cbl.leeds.ac.uk/nikos/tex2html/doc/latex2html/latex2html.html

Myrmidon (Amazing general purpose HTML converter for Mac)
http://www.terrymorse.com/readme.html

tex2rtf
http://www.aiai.ed.ac.uk/~jacs/tex2rtf.html

News

Hyperactive
http://www.york.ac.uk/ftparchive/WWW/utils/hyperactive/

Hypernews
http://union.ncsa.uiuc.edu/~liberte/hypernews/moody.hypernews.shar

HyperNews
ftp://edgar.stern.nyu.edu/pub/perl/hypernews/

Newslist
http://pelican.cl.cam.ac.uk/people/qs101/newslist/

Nisus

NisusHTML
http://www.unimelb.edu.au/~ssilcot/docs/SilcotsHTMLMacrosReadMe.html#aa2

OLE/ActiveX

NCompass
http://www.ncompasslabs.com

OpenScape
http://www.onewave.com

Pagemaker

Dave
http://www.bucknell.edu/bucknellian/dave/

Persuasion

WebPresenter
http://www.adobe.com/

PostScript

ps2html
http://stasi.bradley.edu/ftp/pub/ps2html/home.html

PowerPoint

Microsoft PowerPoint Viewer
http://www.microsoft.com/msdownload/

PointPlus
`http://www.net-scene.com`

PowerPoint Animation Player for ActiveX
`http://www.microsoft.com/msdownload/`

PowerPoint Internet Assistant
`http://www.microsoft.com/msdownload/`

Webify
`http://cag-www.lcs.mit.edu:80/~ward/webify/webifydoc/`

QuarkXpress

BeyondPress
`ftp://ftp.uwtc.washington.edu/pub/Mac/Network/WWW/BeyondPressEval1.0.sit.bin`

CollectHTML
`http://www.logic.be/ftpserver/X0001_Collect_HTML_read_me.html`

E-gate
`http://www.rosebud.fr/rosebud/e-gate.html`

HTMLXport
`ftp://ftp.uwtc.washington.edu/pub/Mac/Network/WWW/HTMLXPort1.22.sit.bin`

qt2www
`http://the-tech.mit.edu/~jeremy/qt2www.html`

RTF

rtftohtml
`http://www.sunpack.com/RTF/rtftohtml_overview.html`

rtf2html
`ftp://oac.hsc.uth.tmc.edu/public/unix/WWW/`

Text

RosettaMan
`ftp://ftp.cs.berkeley.edu/ucb/people/phelps/tcltk/rman.tar.z`

troff2html
`http://www.cmpharm.ucsf.edu/~troyer/troff2html/`

txt2html
http://www.cs.wustl.edu/~seth/txt2html/

Windows Help

HTMheLp
http://www.hyperact.com

Word

Microsoft Word Viewer
http://www.microsoft.com/msdownload/

Word Internet Assistant
http://www.microsoft.com/msdownload/

WordViewer
http://home.netscape.com/comprod/products/navigator/version_2.0/plugins/

WordPerfect

WordPerfect Internet Publisher
http://wp.novell.com/elecpub/intpub.htm

wp2x
http://www.milkyway.com/People/Michael_Richardson/wp2x.html

Digital Documents

Acrobat
http://www.adobe.com/acrobat/main.html

Envoy
http://www.twcorp.com/

Multimedia Applications

Astound
http://www.golddisk.com/

HyperCard

LiveCard
http://www.interedu.com/LiveCard.cgi

IconAuthor

IconAuthor Plug-In
`http://www.aimtech.com`

Marionet (Supercard, Hypercard, Director)
`http://www.allegiant.com/marionet/`

Quark Immedia
`http://www.quark.com/immedia.htm.`

Shockwave

Shockwave for Director
Shockwave for Authorware
Shockwave for FreeHand
`http://www.macromedia.com/`

SuperCard

Roadster
`http://www.allegiant.com/`

Toolbook

Neuron Plug-In
`http://www.asymetrix.com/`

Index

Symbols

A

B

C

J

K-L

M

P

Q

R

S

U

V

W-Z

REGISTRATION CARD

Web Multimedia Development

Name ______________________ Title ______________________

Company ______________________ Type of business ______________________

Address ______________________

City/State/ZIP ______________________

Have you used these types of books before? ☐ yes ☐ no

If yes, which ones? ______________________

____

How many computer books do you purchase each year? ☐ 1–5 ☐ 6 or more

How did you learn about this book? ______________________

Where did you purchase this book? ______________________

Which applications do you currently use? ______________________

____

Which computer magazines do you subscribe to? ______________________

____

What trade shows do you attend? ______________________

____

Comments: ______________________

____

____

Would you like to be placed on our preferred mailing list? ☐ yes ☐ no

☐ **I would like to see my name in print!** You may use my name and quote me in future New Riders products and promotions. My daytime phone number is: ______________________

New Riders Publishing 201 West 103rd Street ◆ Indianapolis, Indiana 46290 USA

Fax to **317-581-4670**

Fold Here

NO POSTAGE
NECESSARY
IF MAILED
IN THE
UNITED STATES

BUSINESS REPLY MAIL

FIRST-CLASS MAIL PERMIT NO. 9918 INDIANAPOLIS IN

POSTAGE WILL BE PAID BY THE ADDRESSEE

NEW RIDERS PUBLISHING
201 W 103RD ST
INDIANAPOLIS IN 46290-9058

Check Us Out Online!

New Riders has emerged as a premier publisher of computer books for the professional computer user. Focusing on CAD/graphics/multimedia, communications/internetworking, and networking/operating systems, New Riders continues to provide expert advice on high-end topics and software.

Check out the online version of *New Riders' Official World Wide Web Yellow Pages, 1996 Edition* for the most engaging, entertaining, and informative sites on the Web! You can even add your own site!

Brave our site for the finest collection of CAD and 3D imagery produced today. Professionals from all over the world contribute to our gallery, which features new designs every month.

From Novell to Microsoft, New Riders publishes the training guides you need to attain your certification. Visit our site and try your hand at the CNE Endeavor, a test engine created by VFX Technologies, Inc. that enables you to measure what you know—and what you don't!

http://www.mcp.com/newriders